GARBO

Garbo

BARRY PARIS

University of Minnesota Press
Minneapolis

First University of Minnesota Press edition, 2002

Published by the University of Minnesota Press
111 Third Avenue South, Suite 290
Minneapolis, MN 55401-2520
http://www.upress.umn.edu

Library of Congress Cataloging-in-Publication Data

Paris, Barry.
    Garbo / Barry Paris.— 1st University Press ed.
        p. cm.
    Originally published: New York : Knopf, 1995.
    Includes bibliographical references and index.
    ISBN 978-0-8166-4182-6 (pbk. : alk. paper)
        1. Garbo, Greta, 1905-1990 2. Motion picture actors and actresses—Sweden—
    Biography. I.Title.

PN2778.G3 P35 2002
791.43'028'092—dc21
    [B]   2002072604

Printed in the United States of America on acid-free paper

The University of Minnesota is an equal-opportunity educator and employer.

17 16 15 14 13 12 11 10   10 9 8 7 6 5 4 3 2

FOR THE BIG GUY AND MISS K—

WHO WERE ALWAYS THERE

How could any portrait be complete of her, in whom the play of swiftly-changing color made discord only to produce a poetic confusion? For in her shined a divine luminosity, a radiance of youth blending all her bewildering qualities in a certain completeness. From gracefulness came unity. Nothing was feigned. Passions and semi-passions, the fitful yearnings contrasting with pettiness, the coolness of mood and warmth of impulse, were spontaneous and unaffected. . . . She was a creature apart; she put herself proudly above the world and beneath the shelter of her name. There was something of the egoism of Medea in her life.

—BALZAC, *La Duchesse de Langeais* (1834)

CONTENTS

A photo insert follows page 464.

The greatest phenomenon in film—if not all twentieth-century art—
was, by her own design, the least known. The first actress to touch
the erotic consciousness of men and women across all boundaries remains
the most misunderstood. But was that due to her "mystery" or to our
ignorance? And speaking of ignorance, what did Garbo do with and during
the last fifty years of her life?

The purpose of this book is to answer those questions, and the purpose
of this preface is to preempt one that haunted me throughout the research
and writing. It came in multiple forms, from the polite "Found anything
new yet?" to the rude "Hasn't she been done to death?" Since 1931, there
have been two dozen books on Garbo, plus thousands of magazine and news
stories. Why more?

I had a defensive litany: The only serious Garbo biography was written
thirty-nine years ago, by John Bainbridge; twenty-five years later, Alexander
Walker crafted a solid, MGM-approved portrait. Norman Zierold took an
honest stab at it in between. Aside from those and some recent memoirs,
the rest is either photographic or just the error-ridden rehash of previous
material; her last half-century is virtually unplumbed. But that still skirted
the question: Was there a *need* for more?

My own doubts were only gradually erased by the revelations of those
who contributed to this book: Peter Viertel and Deborah Kerr, for example,
gave me the crucial fifty-year correspondence between Garbo and her closest
friend, Salka Viertel—sixty-seven affectionate, revealing letters. Sam Green
provided me with an astounding one hundred hours of Garbo conversations

on tape—the single most important record of her last decades, never previously released.

I owe a special debt of gratitude to Gray Reisfield, Garbo's niece and executor; her husband, Dr. Donald Reisfield; their children, Scott, Derek, Craig, and Gray; and Theodore Kurz of Debevoise & Plimpton, who cooperated with me in a circumscribed but invaluable way. Their trust—in view of Garbo's lifelong torments and betrayals in print—was beyond the call of duty and is gratefully acknowledged. It is important to note, however, that this biography has not been "authorized" or approved by the Garbo Estate in any way; that it does not represent the views of Mrs. Reisfield or the Estate; and that they are not responsible for, nor do they necessarily agree with, its conclusions.

Hundreds of others contributed to this project, a full list of whom is in the Acknowledgments. But I extend special thanks to David Diamond, Roddy McDowall, Kevin Brownlow, Steven Bach, Scott Eyman, and Lawrence Quirk—who were with me from the start—and to Chris and Martha Horak, Richard Lamparski, Leonard and Alice Maltin, Hugo Vickers, Judd Klinger, David Stenn, Raymond Daum, Shelley von Strunckel, Annika Goldfarb, and my superb and long-suffering research assistant, Maria Ciaccia.

For first-hand Garbo reminiscences, I am especially indebted to Lew Ayres, Billy Wilder, Liv Ullmann, Jack Larson, and the late Eleanor Boardman and Irene Mayer Selznick. My most valuable sounding boards were Bob Gottlieb, Martha Kaplan, Dan Strone, my friend and editor Victoria Wilson at Knopf, Susan Hill at Sidgwick & Jackson, Wayne Lawson at *Vanity Fair*, John Simon at *New York*, and Kevin Thomas of the *Los Angeles Times*. Equally essential were Bernard Schwartz (aka Tony Curtis), Lina Basquette, John and Margie Barba, Albert French, Sean Connolly, Rick and Deborah Geary, Charles Busch, Eric Myers, and such Parises as Claire, Wyoming, Merica, and Ben. Most of all, I thank the devoted Myrna Paris—my domestic and conversation partner over five obsessive Garbo years, who critiqued every draft and nuance with a sharp, loving, common-sensical eye.

I began this project in beautiful neutrality due to utter ignorance of Garbo. Assured that I would come to hate the woman, I ended up with a yearning fondness for her instead. The reasons are in these pages (and in the picture on the back of the dust jacket). But before getting on with it—a brief biographer's manifesto:

Prior to this, I spent years interviewing octogenarians about another early film actress, Louise Brooks. The Garbo project was a kind of continuation of that work, and meeting Garbo herself was to be its apotheosis. When she died on April 15, 1990, I was in Pebble Beach with novelist Marcia Davenport, who responded to my laments with a reproach: Why mourn the release of a magical creature from an ailing body? Didn't I know that the important thing—her work—lived on as vibrantly and accessibly as always? Mrs. Davenport was right, as ever. But I was disturbed, then and since, by the nature of biography itself.

Garbo and Brooks have only two things in common. The first is historical: Both were enthralling for their complex sexuality, which threatened the men and studios for whom they worked. The second is philosophical: Their claim to serious biographical attention is suspect because their lives were ambiguous and their profession "inferior." No Pulitzer Prize, for instance, has ever been awarded to the biography of a film (or any other performing) artist. Writers and other creative types may enter the pantheon, but beautiful movie stars need not apply. They are intrinsically "un-literary" subjects, despite (or because of) the fact that film is the one great mass art form of our century. Popular appeal precludes intellectual cachet. The belief that a brain and a great erotic presence are mutually exclusive still obtains.

The working title of this book, when commissioned two years before her death, was "In Search of Garbo." I set out to find a connection between the woman Garbo was and the actress-goddess she'd briefly been; to find out if she conducted some fascinating journey through her private self, or just watched *Hollywood Squares* and fussed about her health.

The answer is both—and more. Along the way, with the help of Carolyn Heilbrun's *Writing a Woman's Life*, I discovered that triumph and tragedy aren't the only criteria. Louise Brooks—whose views on Garbo are heavily quoted in these pages—once called biography "the greatest fiction." Roland Barthes dubbed it "a novel that dare not speak its name," reprehensible for a "counterfeit integration of the subject." The only solution was to resist fake "conclusiveness," however annoying that might be to those who require neat pigeon-holing of biographical subjects.

For the reader's sake and my own, I have tried to streamline certain well-known aspects of Garbo's life, if no corrections or illuminations were called for. But discrepancies are the rule rather than the exception in Garbo literature and required a thousand decisions on authenticity. This is a narrative and not an academic biography, but the bibliographic source of every major fact and quotation is listed in the Notes and qualified when warranted. A pedant at heart, I agonized long and hard before deciding not to clutter the text with citation numbers. This puts the burden on scholarly (or just suspicious) readers, while removing it from casual ones who find such notes distracting.

Garbo is often considered a Janus who presented one face to the public and the other—to whom? A few friends and family members? Even *they* weren't sure. "Except physically," wrote Kenneth Tynan, "we know little more about Garbo than we know about Shakespeare"—and, as if to prove his own point, went on to state incorrectly that she had two sisters instead of one.

Why more about Garbo? My great friend James Card, the legendary curator of George Eastman House, finally supplied the answer: "Only that, on screen, she's the greatest who ever was or ever will be."

Barry Paris
Pittsburgh, August 1993

GARBO

A 1906 postcard captures Garbo's birthplace and Söder neighborhood in Stockholm: the Gustafsons' walk-up apartment (center building on left) on Blekingegatan.

CHAPTER 1

GRETA GUSTAFSON
1905–1922

I was born. I had a mother and father. I lived in a house. I went to school. What does it matter?

—GARBO

On their first visit to New York, the young European couple had already taken in the standard tourist highlights—Broadway, the Statue of Liberty, the United Nations—all quite nice, if not terribly exciting. But on their last day in town, they were in a state of high anticipation en route to the East Side for an appointment requested far in advance but unconfirmed until the last minute. The woman they were coming to visit, for her part, was just as nervous: The King and Queen of Sweden were coming to pay their respects. Normally, it would be the other way around, but where Greta Garbo was concerned, all rules were suspended.

The door was opened. Carl XVI Gustaf, his royal consort, Silvia, and the eighty-two-year-old former actress exchanged a proper protocol of handshakes and bows, then sat down to tea and chatted in Swedish about the weather and other simple things, excluding movies. In Swedish history, no private citizen had ever declined a king's invitation and then been rewarded by his visit. But this was Garbo. The royal couple left after forty-five minutes, dazzled. By mutual agreement, the meeting was kept secret. The news media, for once, were eluded.

A king and two queens wanted to be let alone.

"She was magical" is all Queen Silvia will say about the meeting. Garbo, of course, said nothing. Two years later, as she lay dying in New York Hospital on East Sixty-eighth Street, her friend Jane Gunther also used "magic" to describe the spell she still cast: The perfect features of the perfect face were heavily lined, but the complexion remained flawless, even in the ugly fluorescent flicker of a hospital room. The world's most private woman, forced to endure the presence of strange people and medical machines, did so without complaint, oblivious to the padding of the nurses and the buzzing in the hallways.

    . . . Whose turn is it to give her her medication? . . . My God, that face! . . .

    "There is so much to say to someone who is dying," wrote Selma Lagerlöf in *The Saga of Gösta Berling*. "The words come in great numbers when one knows that someone is lying in the next room whose ears will soon be closed forever. 'My friend, my friend,' one wants to say, 'can you forgive? . . . Oh, thank you for all the happiness you have given me!' One wants to say at least that much, and more."

She became the greatest of all screen actresses in just twenty-seven films. Her impact was like no one's before or since. Amid a wealth of feminine beauty on screen, hers alone metamorphosed into an eroticism that transfixed audiences around the world—and then suddenly she disappeared. After her abdication, the cult and cultural phenomenon around her did not subside. It mushroomed, and it complicated her "bachelorhood," as well as her baffling relationships with some of the most celebrated men and women of her time. She occupied a unique place in the American and European social fabric—the toast of its epicenters, from the Hollywood salons of the twenties to the jet sets of midcentury. In fame and oblivion alike, she was ridden with angst and hunted into a kind of paralysis. But she had humor and humanity, too—this Woman of the Century, who spent half of it trying to hide.

In the end, even her "mystery" was a myth. There was nothing really so mysterious about Garbo, but people wouldn't believe it. The incredulity itself is illuminating: Actress and icon, person and persona, Garbo kept everyone spellbound more for what she held back than for what she gave forth. In eighty-four years on earth, nothing was more important to her than her dignity, and not once did she lose it. For her, even the final indignities of dying were mercifully short. Four days after being hospitalized, on Easter Sunday, April 15, 1990, Garbo died. Five days later, she was ashes, and even the whereabouts of the ashes were a secret.

But no flame could consume the image. At the flick of a projection switch, her exquisite phoenix in shadows rises up to enchant and confound, heedless of time.

Her opening antibiographical declaration says it all—or at least Garbo kept insisting it should. Among its variations was this: "Some people were born in red brick houses, others in plain white board ones. We were all born in houses. I do not want it printed that I was born in this house or that—that my mother is this or my father was that. They were my mother and father. That is enough. Why should the world talk about them?" It was uttered not by a cranky veteran but by a Hollywood newcomer of *nineteen*, and, if nothing else, debunks the belief that her aversion to publicity was studio-cultivated. But to Garbo's chagrin, and to the end of her life, such reticence only fueled the obsessive probings into her childhood.

The traumas of that childhood explain much of the "mystery." Greta Lovisa Gustafson was born in Stockholm into a family of recently urbanized peasants who had tilled Swedish soil from the year 1700. Genealogical records in Sweden are well kept, and though surnames are only a thing of the nineteenth century, some sources hold that the Gustafson family line is traceable a thousand years back to the Viking kings. If so, the millennium brought a steady decline in their fortunes, and by the late 1800s the Gustafsons were working the land in the poor, southern part of Sweden, and none too profitably. One account calls them "plain, rugged, law-abiding country folk whose lives were as dull as their common occupation," but that pejorative description merely reflects the urbanite's ignorance of the farmer: Garbo's parents' lives were simply agrarian, characterized by hard work and a fatalistic worldview based on the earth.

Karl Alfred Gustafson's family had farmed the same ground in Småland ("little country") for many generations. He was born and reared there and had no real desire to leave, but times were hard and farming unprofitable in that wooded terrain, where the few inland villages were hidden amid swamps, heaths, and juniper hills. In 1898, he and Anna Lovisa Karlsson, at the ages of twenty-seven and twenty-six, respectively, left the land for the city. It was an eventful year for the young couple, to say the least: They moved to Stockholm in April, they married in May, and Anna delivered their first child, Sven, ten weeks later in July. Under the gun of Anna's premarital pregnancy, they perhaps forsook rural for urban life in search of respectability as well as employment.*

Industrialization arrived in Sweden under King Oskar II in the 1880s and 1890s—late but intense—and produced a large, working-class ghetto in the

---

* But illegitimacy and common-law marriage in Scandinavia were never so stigmatized as elsewhere. In most of the Northern countries, it is above 30 percent. In Iceland, it is 50 percent.

Left to right: *Uncle David, grandfather Johan, and her father, Karl Gustafson (age ten) in Småland, c. 1880*

Parents Anna Lovisa and Karl Alfred Gustafson, c. 1905, around the time of her birth

Södermalm ("Southside") section of Stockholm, where the Gustafsons settled. Five years after Sven's birth, their daughter Alva was born and, soon after, the last child, Greta. At the time of her birth on September 18, 1905, in the Söder Maternity Hospital, the Gustafsons were so poor that Karl's employer reportedly offered to adopt her. The offer was declined, but Karl Gustafson's economic straits were evidently grim enough for it to be considered.

Garbo guarded her family privacy so well that, during her lifetime, even her father's occupation remained a subject of debate. One chronicler says he was "an impoverished sailor." Others say he worked in the city sanitation department as a street sweeper, janitor, or "unskilled laborer." In fact, according to the family story, his work history was not unlike that of other Smålanders who came to the capital with some modest trade: He had been a butcher's assistant, but the only job he could find in Stockholm, after briefly apprenticing with a master gardener, was as a landscaper taking care of trees and streets for the city.

Karl, at the time of Greta's birth, was thus but a few years removed from the powerful atavistic ways of farm life. He kept a vegetable and potato and flower garden on the outskirts of Stockholm by Lake Årsta—a piece of land jutting out into the sea, to which the family commuted by trolley each week for the tilling and weeding. Many other Stockholmers did the same, both for practical reasons and because all Scandinavians love the earth. Nearby was a summerhouse where the children could change clothes for swimming.

The Gustafson family's little garden outside the city provided a fine example of Greta's industry and determination, her friend Kaj Gynt recalled. There, she decided to raise strawberries for market—rising early to hoe and water and tend them. But the neighborhood boys would steal them. Undaunted, she sized up a tiny wooden toolshed on the family plot and many a night slept there to guard her fruit. She then picked the berries herself, took them to market, "and came home with the money, proud as a peacock of what she had done."

By some accounts, Karl longed to return to "real" farming, but he was a reserved and uncomplaining man in general. We know only for certain that he had a fine singing voice and that, aside from spending time with his children, whom he adored, his happiest moments were spent with the local choir. "Kalle" Gustafsson was over six feet tall and unusually handsome, with high cheekbones, fair skin, and large, sad eyes—features remarkably like those of his second daughter. His photographs suggest a sensitive nature weighed down by economic woes. What they do not reveal is that he suffered from severe kidney trouble. For relaxation—he was in the habit of taking long, solitary walks.

On the job, he often had to lift heavy loads, which further weakened his fragile constitution. He was easily exhausted and often depressed. "Local custom was not to tip laborers with money but to invite them in for a drink," says one Swedish account. "For Karl, this meant a fair amount of drinking, and he would often return home from work visibly tipsy. To Anna's frequent reproaches he made the excuse that he needed the drinks to endure the monotony of a job he hated. When Karl could not find a better job, Anna called him a weakling. As time went on, she treated him with growing contempt."

The most lurid claim holds that Garbo's mother was a cruel woman who beat her children; that she taunted her father for his failures as a wage earner and as a lover; that the parents had knockdown fights in which Anna was the aggressor, and that Garbo hated her mother for humiliating her father and was scarred psychologically thereby. That characterization of Anna contains fine melodrama but no basis in fact or evidence.*

"[Anna] was a warm, loving, caring human being—everything you think of as 'the perfect grandmother,'" says Garbo's niece. "I never remember her raising her voice. She never hit me or anyone else, and my aunt adored her. As for beating up my grandfather, she was a *tiny* woman, maybe five foot three or five foot four, and my grandfather was well over six feet tall!"

Anna Lovisa Karlsson was no abuser. She was just a robust woman of peasant stock who had more energy and better health than her husband, and many frustrations. She lacked much formal education but had an endless supply of folktales and songs to entertain her children, of whom Sven was her favorite. In view of Karl's problems and personality, the running of the family fell to her. The difficulties were severe, and so was Anna. Her children's sympathies in general, Greta's in particular, were with the father.

Mild, unambitious Karl Gustafson was aware of his failings and his existential dilemma, in spite of which his younger daughter loved him all the more. The partiality was reciprocal. All three of his children were tall, well built, and outgoing: Sven and Greta were the most playful, Alva the most extroverted; everyone in the family was musical. But Karl encouraged Greta's desire to sing and perform more than her siblings'. His sister, Maria Petersson, one day found her five-year-old niece deep in thought and asked what was on her mind. "I am thinking of being grown up and becoming a great actress," Greta replied. Around this time, Karl gave her a paintbox, with which she painted her own face, because that was her view of what actresses did. Her mother often worried about her.

"I was always inclined to melancholy," she said. "Even when I was a tiny

---

* For the source of these and other fabrications concerning Garbo's mother and childhood, see Appendix A, "Garbo and Oranges: The Fantasies of Antoni Gronowicz," page 555.

girl I preferred being alone. 'Go and play now,' mother would say. But I did not want to, and I still firmly believe that it is wise and essential to leave small children alone now and then—to find peace, and to dream and wonder about the strange ways of this world in which they find themselves. I think this is even more important than play. Apart from skating and other winter sports, my best games were played by myself. I could give my imagination free rein, and live in a world of lovely dreams."

She hated housework and left all things domestic to her mother and sister—a preference that was catered to and, surprisingly, had no negative effect on her relationship with Alva. They were nearly twins in age. Everyone remarked on the sisters' closeness—including Garbo, years later, reflecting on their oddly reversed childhood roles:

> My sister! My little sister—I called her that, in spite of the fact that she was two years older than me. . . . I don't think anyone ever regarded me as a child. . . . Though I am the youngest of three, my brother and sister always looked on me as the oldest. In fact, I can hardly remember ever having felt young, in the ordinary sense. I always had opinions, and the others looked to me for decisions, and for the solutions to their childish problems. But my moods were changeable. Happy one moment, the next plunged in despair. Yet they came to me for help and comfort.*

"Were they poor?" asks Garbo's niece, rhetorically. "Yes. They were a working-class family; she came from a very modest background. But they didn't live in slum conditions. Being poor in Stockholm was not like being poor in the slums of New York City in the early years of this century."

From Garbo's birth until she left Sweden in 1925, she never lived anywhere but the four-room, cold-water flat on the fourth floor of 32 Blekingegatan, a five-story walk-up tenement in the Söder district. Located on the south bank of the River Mälar and surrounded on all sides by water, it was a city within the city, with its own slang, humor, and morality. Söder boys and girls had a certain proud, lower-class toughness about them. Söder's main artery is Göta Street, which contained the big stores and movie houses and dance halls and such neon lights as their proprietors could afford. Off Göta was Blekingegatan, a side street with dingy shops and apartments built up to the sidewalks, and clotheslines stretched overhead. The original building was razed in 1967. Nowadays, No. 32 houses "Greta's Krog & Bistro," with

---

* The verbatim accuracy of those words, made years later to Swedish journalist Åke Sundborg, is a matter of speculation. Garbo's family believes she would never have said such things to a stranger, and, assuming that the conversation was in Swedish, the English is suspect. But if some of the words are doubtful, the sentiment seems correct.

Portrait of a schoolgirl (age nine), c. 1914

Garbo's caricature on a shingle, among the bingo gambling spots and bars. In the early teens, the little towheaded girl who lived there was called "Katha" ("Ka-ta"), from the way she pronounced her own name.

More often than not, she could be found alone, hugging her knees under the kitchen table, where a sympathetic adult might draw her out. She was fond of her father's brother David, a taxi driver and the most affluent of the Gustafsons, who had a fine house and car and, when he came to visit, indulged his brother's children with sweets or coins. To Uncle David, she once confided: "I'm going to become a prima donna or a princess, and when I'm rich I'll give all I can to poor children." Later, she said: "When I was a little girl and knew nothing of the theater, I used to make up, as I imagined actresses did, and play theater with my brother and sister."

Her stolid mother was not the type to reinforce theatrical dreams, but one who did was Anna's friend Agnes Lind, a widow who ran a nearby stationery-tobacco shop, on the walls of which she pinned up postcard pictures of Swedish performers. Greta ran errands for her and was sometimes rewarded with a photo. Her favorites were Naima Wifstrand, a light-opera star, and Carl Brisson, the heartthrob matinee idol of his day.

The Katarina grammar school, where she was enrolled at age seven, was a rude intrusion into her fantasies. She did poorly at gymnastics and drawing but came to life for the reading of Selma Lagerlöf's children's classic, *The Wonderful Adventures of Nils*, a folkloric geography lesson in which naughty

Nils Holgersson is miniaturized and carried on the back of a wild goose over the length and breadth of Sweden. To children, Nils's great journey represented freedom from the oppressive grown-up world. When finally deposited back home, he once again "felt that shyness which always came over him when he was near human beings."

The young Garbo could identify with that, and with the longing to explore other Swedish times and places. There was no wild goose to transport her, but there was an earthbound equivalent that was almost as good: her class trips to the enchanting recreational-historical park called Skansen.

Skansen was the world's first open-air museum, built in 1891 by the wealthy ethnographer Arthur Hazelius, who was disturbed that Sweden's traditional ways were fast disappearing in the wake of the country's belated industrial revolution. Located in Djurgården just outside Stockholm, the multiacre site had first been developed around 1815 by Crown Prince Carl Johan as a lavish playground-fort for his son. Hazelius obtained it and spent years "collecting" shops, homes, and barns from all over Sweden—some dating to the sixteenth century—and reconstructing them to preserve a sample of Swedish rural life and culture. Skansen was Sweden in miniature. Visiting it was the perennial favorite outing of local schoolchildren and many of their parents, too.

Skansen's Market Street, for example, is lined on both sides by old structures from Småland, notably a *snickerifabriken* (the uniquely Swedish word for furniture factory), where heavy oak tables and chairs were crafted. Karl and Anna Gustafson especially liked such reminders of Småland, but the whole family loved the *stadskvarteren* (town quarters), whose buildings came from their own neighborhood in Stockholm: Its hilly plan was modeled on Södermalm, the shops dating from the 1760s, including a *gubbhyllan* ("old men's retreat" or tobacconist's), a *glasbyttan* (glassblower's), an 1804-vintage tannery, printshop, bakery, and goldsmith's, plus a charming little wooden summerhouse from the very Katarina parish where the Gustafsons lived. Nearby was a skittle alley where that popular ninepins game of nineteenth-century Swedish inns could be played.

Elsewhere at Skansen, Greta explored a humble farm laborer's cottage from the south, half-dug into a hillside and made of stones because they were free. On certain days, her class could drop in on a service or wedding at the tiny Lutheran church dating from 1729, in which men sat on the right, women on the left, wealthy people in front, poor people in the rear. On their way through the churchyard, they passed an original whipping post and *straffstocken*—the intimidating stocks, also from Småland, which parish elders erected for the maximum humiliation of wrongdoers as all the good churchgoers filed past.

Skansen's farms were supplied with native breeds typical of Swedish agriculture: black-and-white lowland cattle, red poll cattle, northern Swedish horses, and hardy Jämtland goats famous for producing first-class milk on sparse grazing. Bird life included the Skåne goose, the Swedish blue duck, and the much-loved herons. A lamb shelter from Farö held—and still holds—a small flock of *gutefar* (Gotland sheep), whose ewes have horns. Habitats were provided for wild animals ranging from southern deer and northern wolves to Scandinavian reindeer (*ren*). The Lapp camp featured old-fashioned reindeerkeeping—a trade long since modernized, unromantically, by snow scooters.

Garbo spent many magical childhood hours there, pausing to puzzle over the mystical eleventh-century rune stones scattered about the park, and riding the funicular that curves dramatically up through the woods, affording a fabulous view of the baroque Nordiska Museet—the Nordic Museum, also founded by the beneficent Hazelius.

The other school excursions she loved were to the ancient mounds of Uppsala, where the Viking kings were buried. Sweden's Viking spirit was and is still strong, especially in the language. The Old Norse word *vindauga* ("wind-eye")—the ceiling hole for smoke to escape, and the sole light source in ancient cottages—became "window" in Swedish, and English as well. If one shrinks from going out in the rain, Swedes say, "You're not a Viking!" And no child could resist the romance of Swedish history, whose bellicose heyday ran from the Thirty Years' War (1618–48) through Charles XII's fierce campaigns against Denmark, Poland, and Russia. One amazing fact suffices to convey the powerful abilities of the Swedes: In 1628, when Sweden controlled as much as half of Europe, the population of Stockholm was fifteen thousand. When Sweden lost Finland in 1809, the king was promptly and simply fired, but by the twentieth century an enlightened liberalism characterized the country. The year Garbo was born, Norway voted for independence and the Swedish government quietly acquiesced.

Said Garbo of her school days—and other ancient history:

> I lived in a constant state of fear, disliking every moment of it . . . especially mathematics. I could never understand how anyone could be interested . . . in trying to solve such ridiculous problems as how many liters of water could pass through a tap of such and such width in one hour and 15 minutes. . . .
>
> The only subject I really liked was history, which filled me with all kinds of dreams. I read my schoolbooks on history just as if they were

novels and often let my fantasy wander. According to my fancies I might shorten the life of a cruel king and replace him by a romantic knight, or reawaken an unhappy queen centuries after her death.

I went to public school and hated it. I hated its confinement, its repression. I dare say all children feel this way, even if they do not dare to be frank about it. . . . Geography I detested. I could never understand maps. They frightened me. Unlike most children, I actually dreaded recess! I could not bear the thought of playing by order, by the clock, in the schoolyard! My only comfort was that recess brought nearer the end of classes for the day, when I could escape, go home, be free!

From Stockholm proper, Söder is just an unspectacular silhouette of cliffs across the Mälar. On a side street up the hill from Göta were two playhouses, the Söder and the Mosebacke, in Mosebacke Square, "Stockholm's Montmartre," which Greta now began to haunt. The Söder, which still stands, is a long, yellow, dignified old theater with faux pillars, high atop the hill. Across from its courtyard is a bridge on which she often stood, gazing at the panorama of Stockholm and its great, sprawling world below. A few steps away, at the gateway to the stage entrance, she would wait for hours for a quick glimpse of the performers as they hurried in or out.

The Gustafson children had no money for such luxuries as theatergoing; Garbo never sat inside a playhouse until she was twelve years old. But the actors at the Söder gradually began to recognize and occasionally even talk to her, and one night a kindly doorman let her go inside for her first glimpse of the wonderland:

> When I was seven or eight came my first experience with . . . the stage. Each evening, at about seven, I used to go to the courtyard of the Southside Theater and watch the actors and actresses pass to and from their work. Then I would steal home, fearful of a scolding. . . . My sole wish [was] to creep inside the magic stage door. . . .
>
> At last [inside], I caught wonderful glimpses of the players at their entrances, and first smelled that most wonderful of all odors to a devotee of the theater—that backstage smell, compounded of grease-paint, powder and musty scenery. No odor in the world will ever mean as much to me—none!

For a child at night, the Söder Theater was a long way from home, and it is surprising that she roamed so freely, with or without her parents' knowledge. "Well do I remember how worried her father and mother were," Kaj Gynt recalled, "and how the neighborhood used to talk, and

Snapshot of an adolescent (age twelve), c. 1917

how we knew that often at night her brother Sven or her father would go out to seek her." In fact, she was transporting herself much further than the distance from Blekingegatan, and was soon drawing others into the new universe: At girlfriends' houses, her favorite role was that of harem girl, though the sheiks rarely satisfied her. "Noo-oo! A sheik wouldn't bow," she would say; "he'd just come in, don't you see?" If the friend protested her inability to play a man, Greta would reply, "There's nothing to it," and then demonstrate—switching from seductive maiden to dashing swain and back again.

Schoolmate Elizabeth Malcolm recalled that she and Greta first became friends because they were taller than the others and were seated together in the back of the classroom. When playing London Bridge Is Falling Down at recess, they were the logical choices to hold hands and form the bridge for the others. After school, said the friend, they visited each other's homes almost daily:

> When we were walking home . . . , her parting words usually were, "Now, you hurry up, Elizabeth, and come over as soon as

you have had dinner. Then we can go coasting on Helgalund Hill."
And hurry up I did, for coasting on Helgalund Hill was the grandest
fun we knew. Greta had a big sled, blue as the sky, that she had
inherited from her older brother and sister . . . , and on that
sled we risked life and limb many a wintry day. I can still see her
going down Helgalund Hill like a streak, her braids standing straight
out behind her. There was nothing languid or weary about that
Greta!

On bad days we played indoors. We never played with dolls. . . .
But my brother's tin soldiers—*there* was something the future Miss
Garbo could appreciate. For hours at a time we waged war on the
kitchen floor. . . .

[Greta's home] was modest but immaculately clean. . . . Her father
loved children dearly and always had some jolly greeting for Greta and
me when he came in. Mrs. Gustafson was forever seeing to it that we
weren't hungry. She knew we were fond of ginger snaps. . . .

In the courtyard of the house where Greta lived there was a shed
with a gently sloping tin roof. Of course, we were forbidden to climb
up on that roof, but many a summer's day we lay there sun-bathing
for hours, until the janitor chased us down. . . . "We are on a sandy
white beach," Greta would say. "Can't you see the waves breaking
against the shore? How clear the sky is, Elizabeth! And do you hear
how sweetly that orchestra at the Casino is playing? Look at that girl
in the funny green bathing suit! It's fun to lie here and look at the
bathers, isn't it?" . . .

One day when I came to see her she was very much excited. She
had seen her first show and could talk of nothing else. "Elizabeth, we
are going to become actresses," she announced. [They made up with
the waterpaints.] Now, we were ready to act!

"You must come in like this and pretend you are very much surprised
to see me and look like this," Greta instructed me. Again and again I
tried to follow her directions, but she was not satisfied.

"This will never do," she broke out at last. "You see, Elizabeth,
you've got to act. Now take that chair and sit down. You can be the
audience and I'll show you how one really *acts*." And Greta acted. She
was a show in herself. She danced and she kicked, she recited and
sang. . . .

Greta and I played theater whenever we had a chance. When we
weren't actually imitating actors and actresses we would dress up as
boys, making good use of her brother Sven's belongings. Once we even

went to the shoemaker's down the street rigged up this way. I felt a little embarrassed at showing myself in public in boy's clothes, but not Greta.

"I'm Gustafson's youngest boy, you know," she said to the shoemaker, "and this is a pal of mine." She then proceeded to whistle and act the part of a boy as best she could until the shoemaker and his assistants roared with laughter.

The real world of school put a serious crimp in her fantasies and she tended to deal with it through escape, actual or metaphorical. On one occasion, she and a similarly disaffected friend named Olivia simply took off. Two days later, the police found them eight miles away at a place called Barkeby. The punishment for such a major infraction was caning. Olivia wept at the thought; Greta was stone silent. Sister Alva went to the principal and begged for clemency, and, in the end, they were let off with a severe reprimand. But Greta was pale and shaken when she came out of the principal's office. The threat of physical violence agitated her deeply.

She was a big and nervy girl for her age, and this was the first of three times she ran away. "At that time my size embarrassed me horribly," she said. "Everywhere people seemed to be whispering about my awkwardness." On the other hand, her size contributed to a successful rescue mission one day when she and Elizabeth came across a crowd surrounding two drunks in an argument on the street. When the smaller of the two men was knocked down, Greta—to everyone's surprise—intervened. "Why do you beat him so?" she demanded. "You mustn't do that!" The larger man stopped and said to his victim, "So your kid sticks up for you, eh? All right, you can go." It was not her way—at twelve or any age—to correct a wrong impression, and her victory was tarnished by the fact that many thought the drunk on the pavement was actually her father.

The following year, she ran off again, this time to Skåne in the south of Sweden, where a conductor discovered her hiding in the toilet of a train and arranged for her return. Her third flight—in the other direction—occurred in 1919, during the summer of her last year at school. The children of poor families were sent to a holiday camp at Björkö, a small island in Lake Mälaren. Greta loathed it, feigned illness, and disappeared after being told to help in the kitchen. She turned up at home the next day.

Home was safer, if no more exciting, judging by a Garbo rumination (ghostwritten and probably embellished by her editor-publisher friend Lars Saxon after many conversations) in the Swedish magazine *Lektyr*:

It was eternally gray—those long winter's nights. My father would be sitting in a corner, scribbling figures on a newspaper. On the other side of the room my mother is repairing ragged old clothes, sighing. We children would be talking in very low voices, or just sitting silently. We are filled with anxiety, as if there is danger in the air. Such evenings are unforgettable for a sensitive girl.

Where we lived, all the houses and apartments looked alike, their ugliness matched by everything around us. Even the grass gave up trying. Usually in May some greenery tried to grow amid the ugly wilderness. I watched it with tenderness and watered the few blades of grass each morning and night. But in spite of my care they languished and died. They died just as did the children in our forlorn neighborhood. . . . I was always sad as a child, for as long as I can think back. I hated crowds of people, and used to sit in a corner by myself, just thinking. I did not want to play very much. I did some skating or played with snowballs, but most of all I wanted to be alone with myself.

When would the school—and the world—get that message?

Garbo was at the Katarina school for seven unremarkable years until forced to drop out in 1919 because of her father's serious illness. As a semi-invalid during World War I, he received an extra ration of bread and butter. Typical of Karl's pathetic kindliness, he pretended to be healthy and encouraged the children to eat his portion of the bonus ration, but the kids knew better. His inability to work meant that they and his wife now had to find jobs— Anna doing cleaning and sewing, Sven in a candy store, Alva as an office clerk. "Our lives were always ruled by extreme poverty," Garbo would later say. Their domestic problems were complicated in 1918, when a neighborhood dairy maid gave birth out of wedlock to Sven's son. One source claims the Gustafsons housed and supported the mother and child for a time, during which Greta and Alva had to sleep on a settee made into a bed at nights. Sven's son said, "I have been told that Greta, who was then fourteen, took great care of me and liked to walk around with me in her arms." But that was just a pleasant myth: Garbo later said she never laid eyes on the boy until a chance encounter at a train station when he was ten years old.

The influenza epidemic hit Sweden during that terrible winter of 1919. Many died, and many more were out of work. The Gustafsons reportedly took advantage of the Salvation Army soup kitchens in Söder, where the SA also sponsored games, temperance activities, and neighborhood shows in which children took part. Greta was one of them; she sang and acted—her first public appearance, of sorts—and was praised by John Philipsson, the SA treasurer, who encouraged her ambition "to become an actress." During the Christmas holidays, she would join in the hymn singing. One of her favorites, which she learned by heart and could still sing sixty years later, was "Roll, Jordan, Roll." She found something thrilling about the flags, the songs, the horn music, and the drums.

Greta had a part-time job at a fruit store but was so secretive, even at fourteen, that she would only tell her friends it was "in Sveavägen." Her real job was to stay home—or be on call—to care for her father. Decades later, she told writer S. N. Behrman that one day when she was due at work, her father called her in and said he was sick: "She found that he was burning with fever and took him to the public clinic. They had to stand in line. . . . He was terribly sick but still they had a long wait to get into this free clinic. When they finally got to the window, the man told her father to take off his hat and proceeded to ask a million questions all seeming to indicate that the hospital was interested mostly in their income. All this time Greta felt that her father was dying." The humiliation of that experience was a deep source of "fury against life in that girl," Behrman believed. She took her father there more than once and privately vowed it would never happen to her.

On June 1, 1920, after a lingering agony, Karl Gustafson died of nephritis. He was just forty-eight. Greta, who was only fourteen, later recalled:

> From that time there was only sobbing and moaning to be heard in our home. My brother and sister would not even try to control their grief, and I often had to ask them to be quiet. To my mind a great tragedy should be borne silently. It seemed disgraceful to me to show it in front of all the neighbors by constant crying. My own sorrow was as deep as theirs, and for more than a year I cried myself to sleep every night. For a time after his death I was fighting an absurd urge to get up in the night and run to his grave to see that he had not been buried alive.

He died just two weeks before Greta and her friend Eva Blomgren were confirmed in the Swedish State Church, but she hid the trauma well in her official confirmation photograph. Garbo was born in the Katarina parish, where even her name had to be approved and registered. Though only 2 or 3 percent of Swedes are active in the church, they automatically belong to it at birth and, as the state religion, it is formally studied in school.* Swedish

---

* The conversion of Sweden—from Catholic to Lutheran—was a political decision by King Gustav Vasa in 1541. The state thenceforth owned all churches and their revenues, and the king could expropriate Catholic gold and silver to hire mercenaries and conduct his wars. From then on, services were to be held in Swedish. (The old magician's incantation "hocus-pocus" is said by Swedes to derive from how the Latin "Hoc est corpus" sounded to Swedish ears.) There were a few Jews in Sweden and there was one Catholic church for diplomats and foreigners in Stockholm, but—especially after the Papist defection of Queen Christina in 1654—it was technically illegal to be anything but Lutheran in Sweden until the middle of this century.

society is rigid: You are christened in your parish; if you move, your papers move with you, and good track is kept of the documents. In the summer before confirmation, children attend daily lessons for about six weeks, and then—once confirmed—are not further obliged. Swedes tend to appear in church only at their baptism, confirmation, marriage, and death; regular Sunday attendance is exceptional. "I never remember my grandmother going to church," says Garbo's niece.

Even so, Greta and Alva had been given religious instruction—severely, it seems—by Pastor Hjalmar Ahlfeldt, who stressed the Lutheran dogma of human sinfulness for which rigid self-denial was the remedy. Parallels in the films of Ingmar Bergman are inescapable. "We shall live in an atmosphere of purity and austerity," says the frighteningly strict bishop to his new wife and stepchildren in *Fanny and Alexander* (1982). When their father dies, the terrified children hear the primal screams of their mother. That night, they find their dead father tinkling sadly at the piano. For Bergman—for all Swedes?—encounters with the deceased are frequent. Everyone in the Gustafson family was lonely and touchy at this point, as suggested by Greta's letter of July 7, 1920, to Eva Blomgren just a month after her father's death—with no mention of it:

> If you and I are to continue friends, you must keep away from my girl friends, as I did from yours. I'm sure you wouldn't like it if you met me with your most intimate friends and I completely ignored you. I did not mind your going out with Alva but I realized that you intended to do the same with all my acquaintances. Eva, I am arrogant and impatient by nature, and I don't like girls who do what you have done. If you hadn't written, I should never have made the first move toward reconciliation. And then your writing to Alva. Frankly, I think you're making yourself ridiculous. If you hadn't done that, perhaps my letter would have been more friendly. But now I can't be. If this letter offends you, then you don't need to write to me again, but if it doesn't and you will promise to behave as a friend, then I shall be glad to hear from you again soon.
>
> Yours truly, Greta.

Eva's reply is not extant, but she evidently begged Greta's pardon, in response to which Greta was not exactly magnanimous: "Well, so you promise to mend your ways. Then all can be as before, provided I have no cause to complain again. As for your thinking that I treat you like a child, I only do that when you behave like a child or make yourself ridiculous. . . ."

The loud and clear message was: Don't try to steal Alva's affections. Jealous and fiercely possessive, she had just lost her father and would not be deprived

Greta Gustafson's 1920 confirmation picture taken two weeks after the death of her father

of her sister. Trust and betrayal were real issues. She was tremendously hypersensitive. It was not only the loss and the poverty but the *humiliation* that she could not bear, and that was so indelible.

Garbo's father, it seemed, was the only person who never mocked her size, her silence, her ungainliness, or her dreams. When he died at her most vulnerable age, she lost the one in whom she could always seek and find comfort. His death marked the end of her childhood. She decided—or her mother decided for her—that she would leave school permanently. Accordingly, at fourteen, she now set forth into the working world.

Garbo's first "real" job was as *tvålflicka*—a soap-lather girl—in a neighborhood barbershop on Horn Street in Söder. After a few weeks there, she took a similar job at a bigger shop on Göta, where the pay was four kronar a week (about one dollar) plus a like amount in tips. Her duties included mixing the lather, laying out the razors, cleaning up after the barber—the usual unappetizing men's-hygiene chores of such establishments. That experience perhaps affected her general attitude toward the male sex, but by all accounts, she held her own: Like most Söder girls she had a quick tongue and wielded a mean shaving brush when she had to.

A young woman in a working-class barbershop tended to mature fast, and this one was fairly mature to begin with. A taxi driver who knew Greta and Alva then described both sisters as "very 'free.'" Mrs. Arthur Ekengren, the owner's wife and cashier at the second shop, recalled fifteen-year-old Greta as "almost buxom" and quite cheerful rather than melancholy: "We were all very fond of her. She was a sunbeam. . . . She was wild about Carl Brisson. She used to sing his songs—she knew them all—and her locker, where she kept her smock and wraps, was covered with pictures of him."

Brisson was a Danish boxer-turned-variety-artist.* At the time of Mrs. Ekengren's cheery characterization, he was a popular headliner at the Mosebacke Theater, drawing crowds to a revue called *The Count of Söder*—an ironic title akin to "The Count of Brooklyn." According to one of Brisson's colleagues, Miss Gustafson had to be chased away from the stage door every

---

* Carl Brisson (1895–1958), born Carl Pederson, won the Central Europe amateur middleweight boxing championship in 1915 and began to appear in Copenhagen nightclubs and Swedish stage productions soon after. Following great success in Stockholm, he went to London in 1923, sang the role of Prince Danilo in hundreds of performances of *The Merry Widow*, and starred in two of Alfred Hitchcock's last silents, *The Ring* (1927) and *The Manxman* (1928). In the thirties, Paramount imported him to Hollywood with his son Frederick Brisson (1912–1984), who became a Broadway producer (*Damn Yankees, Pajama Game*) and developed screen vehicles for his wife, Rosalind Russell.

Carl Brisson, Swedish matinee idol of 1920

evening, "but she kept coming back and in the end got so bold that she scratched a heart on the cement wall with 'I love you, Kalle' inside it."

One winter night outside the theater, she handed Brisson a bunch of violets—a costly item in January in Stockholm. He was touched and offered to get her into the auditorium if she would agree to start the applause for him when he came on. She did so, returning several times, and because she knew his songs by heart, Brisson pretended to single her out "at random" to lead the chorus in his audience-participation number—but not for long: The spotlight and the attention made her horribly self-conscious.

Garbo later made a general but not specific denial of that legend. Asked in 1928 if she had any favorite stage performers, she replied, "*Never!* I never had what American girls call 'crushes.' Individual actors never interested me. It was the roles they played that . . . fascinated me." In any case, her Brisson encounters were the exceptions, not the rule. "Very little" of her time was spent at plays, she said, and "sometimes going to the theater caused me real pain." The audience and its bad-mannered chattering shattered her illusions, and the plays never seemed to measure up to the dramas of her imagination.

Whether Garbo had a precocious interest in movies is unclear. So, for that matter, is whether she saw more than a handful of films. Various sources say her movie idols then, in the post–World War I period, ranged from William S. Hart to Thomas Meighan, Norma Talmadge to Mary Pickford. But, if so, she never referred to them in adulthood.

Nevertheless, despite the hypercritical perfectionism that marred her enjoyment of it, acting became a growing obsession. According to Elizabeth Malcolm, she organized something called the Attic Theater in a local garret—whose, we don't know. She had given up on Elizabeth as a performer, but some of her other friends were more promising members of the troupe. Props and costumes consisted of whatever furniture and clothing could be filched from their homes. The show itself, said Malcolm, was "a sort of revue" starring Greta as everything from the Goddess of Peace (solemnly singing "Why do we fight, why must blood be shed?") to a three-year-old crooning lullabies to her baby doll.

One night during her vigil at the Söder, actor Josef Fischer noticed and startled her by asking, "Are you thinking of going on the stage?" She hesitated before saying, "I don't know if I dare." That was the extent of the exchange, but, walking home, she was deeply agitated. A real actor had asked if she wanted to perform. Why? Did he think her talented? Good looking? *Might* she actually do it?

This or a similar incident around that time was The Moment that cinched her transition from stage-door Jane to potential actress, and her whole character began to change as a result. She screwed up her courage to call Fischer (on Eva Blomgren's phone), but when he didn't seem to take her seriously, she quickly hung up. Discouraged by this as by any setback, before and after, she temporarily gave up. Of more pressing concern was the family's dire financial straits and her need to make more money than a barbershop job could provide.

Alva, now an insurance company stenographer, had two friends who were clerks at the Paul U. Bergström department store emporium (PUB) on Hötorget Plaza opposite Stockholm's beautiful Konserthuset, where the Nobel Prizes are annually given out. PUB is a huge brown-and-white-stone building with "1916" carved on its peak and a clock above the entrance to tell customers and employees when they are late for work. With an entrée from her sister's friends, Greta was engaged there as a trainee on July 26, 1920, and hired soon after as a clerk in the fourth-floor millinery department at 125 kronor ($25) a month.

After a fortnight on the job, she wrote Eva: "I have got a job at Paul Bergström's. . . . Can you imagine it, me a shopgirl! But don't worry, I haven't given up thought of the stage because of this. Not a bit; I'm just as keen as ever."

In the meantime, clerking at PUB was pleasant enough, and so was the

*PUB, Stockholm's stylish verison of Macy's, where Greta Gustafson
sold hats for more than a year*

kindly Mr. Bergström. His store was Stockholm's finest and most fashionable,
and still is. Nowadays, PUB customers shop to the soothing strains of Mozart,
and hats await buyers in the same place and on the same type of elegant
antler racks on which they rested in 1920.

Millinery, she discovered, had theatrical elements of its own: "I was really
interested in selling hats. It seemed like play. I never seemed to have to
think how to treat the individual whims of each customer. . . . How I
admired and envied the actresses among my customers!" She also discovered
the social value of her position when Max Gumpel, the wealthy construction
baron and man-about-Stockholm, showed up at her counter one day, was
immediately attracted to her, and invited her home to dinner. Rather boldly,
she accepted. Gumpel served artichokes to the dismayed girl, who had never
seen such a complex vegetable before. When they became better friends, he
gave her a gold ring set with a small stone which she told him was "as
beautiful as a diamond in the English Royal Crown." Swedish discretion
has erased any evidence, but Gumpel was very likely Garbo's first lover. A

year or so later, he married and they parted amicably, but their paths would cross again.

These days, she was quite lively and outgoing, with a ready laugh. Like most Swedes, she was also an excellent swimmer. "None of us could excel Greta Gustafson, not even the boys," according to her friend Kaj Gynt. "Her speed and strength in the water were remarkable. How she glided, like a real mermaid! But here, as in everything, she was different. Always she swam alone, with that lightning speed of hers, with those true powerful strokes, until she came to the rocks, gray and brown, and there she would perch in the sun and watch the others from a distance, and if anyone came near her she would dive away and swim to another rock."

She also loved walking, and as her embryonic beauty now blossomed, she began to notice other people noticing *her*. That, and the resurgence of her longing for the stage, were the themes of several fabulously self-absorbed adolescent letters to Eva, such as the following one on August 15, 1920:

> They all look at me with such interest [at PUB], because I'm only 15. If you were to come, I'll bet they'll all ask you if it's true. In the autumn, Eva, you and I must go out and have fun together, otherwise I'll die. I long so tremendously for someone that I can really like. Whenever I'm left to myself, I long so dreadfully for the theater, for after all, Eva, everything I want is there. I feel as though I had been alive for a whole eternity and not at all like a high-spirited 15-year-old. Just imagine, I shall be 16 next month.

But as she became more deeply wrapped up in dreams of the theater, her nerves started to suffer. An extraordinary need for solitude began to take hold of her—documented for the first time in an August 27, 1921, letter written on holiday in the west Swedish town of Nykroppa. Then, as always, her friends had to have thick skins—especially poor Eva:

> Eva child, . . . To be honest, I haven't thought of you, for the simple reason that I don't think of anything. I have become pretty indifferent to everything. . . . I am quite satisfied to be here and don't long to be back. The fact is that I wanted to get to a place where there weren't so many people, so that I could just rest. I have had my wish very well fulfilled in that most of my company I provide myself. . . .
>
> —Katha (alias Greta)

Garbo's youthful letters to Eva reveal the melancholy self-obsession and paradoxical need to perform and withdraw that remained with her for life. Although her stage interest was intense at this point, she was unwilling to do amateur theatricals—or perhaps just too shy and passive to explore the possibility. Asked later why she never joined PUB's dramatic club, she replied, "That was not the real theater—it was play."

But fashion was something else, and when asked to help pick out and model the hats to be featured in PUB's upcoming promotion, she eagerly agreed. According to Magdalena Hellberg, manager of ready-made women's clothing, Mr. Bergström asked Hellberg to recommend a model and "without hesitation" she replied, "Miss Gustafson should be perfect for that. She always looks clean and well-groomed and has such a good face." Informed of this, Greta was ecstatic: "Aunt Hellberg can arrange anything for me. Oh, how happy I am!" Hellberg called it "probably the longest sentence I ever heard her say at one time."

Thus came about the photographic debut of Greta Garbo, wearing a not terribly flattering array of headgear in PUB's 1921 spring mail-order catalogue, fifty thousand of which were distributed throughout Sweden. Though still just fifteen, she looked nineteen or twenty. In spite of her shyness, she wanted to be a model. For some odd and prophetic reason, her inhibitions seemed to vanish before a camera's lens.

They would certainly have to vanish for her first motion-picture appearance. *How Not to Dress* (1921) was directed by "Captain" Ragnar Ring, a former cavalry officer and adventure writer hired by PUB to make short commercial films promoting its line of women's apparel. Ring's concept—fully contained in the title—was comical and slightly daring for the day. He had no difficulty finding his main complement of pretty girls but realized, near the last minute, that he hadn't yet found any funny ones. Having once seen Greta Gustafson at PUB (or in its catalogue), he now remembered "the tall, awkward, yet strangely attractive girl in the millinery department who photographed so well" and invited her to make a screen test.

The film's principal actor was among the skeptics. When he first saw her, he told Ring, "You're not going to have that fat girl in the picture, are you? She won't fit the screen!"* Ring not only cast her but added more comic touches to her part. He put her in a man's ugly checkered riding habit, the pants two sizes too large. With her hands in her pockets and her shoulders hunched up, she modeled that getup as blithely as if wearing the finest new high-fashion design. In a second, slightly less bizarre outfit, she looked more like the tall, gawky teenager she was. Thus did the great tragedienne begin as a comedienne in film.

---

*Many years later, Garbo ran into the actor in Sweden. To his enthusiastic greeting she replied, "The last time we met, you weren't nearly so polite."

℗ PAUL U. BERGSTRÖMS AKTIEBOLAG. STOCKHOLM

DAM-HATTAR

från de enklaste till de mest eleganta

Mod. ›CLARY›
Damhatt av filt i
beige, marin, svart,
brunt, fraise el. röd=
brunt   Kr. 28.—

Mod. ›ETHEL›
Damhatt av sammet
i cerise, ljusblått,
mörkblått,   brunt,
mullvad, lilas eller
beige   Kr. 25.—

Mod. ›JANE›
Damhatt   av
sammet i grönt,
marin, brunt el.
mörk lilas
Kr. 48.—

Mod. ›HELNY›
Damhatt av filt i beige, mullvad, brunt,
neger, jade, vinrött el. marin Kr. 28.—

Mod. ›SOLVEIG›
Damhatt av filt i brunt, svart, grönt,
marin el. mullvad   Kr. 35.—

Miss Gustafson advances from selling to modeling PUB's millinery.

*The potential comedienne, in one of her
first moments on celluloid, as "pastry-
eating woman" (1922)*

How or why this helped sell PUB's clothes is a mystery, but the
Swedish sense of humor is a peculiar one, and within the film's crude
framework, Garbo managed to be both humorous and noticeable.* Ring
felt vindicated in his hunch that she was a potential comic in the style
of Lili Ziedner, a fat and popular variety actress of the day, and engaged
her a few months later for *Our Daily Bread* (1922), a film promoting the
bakery products of the Consumers' Cooperative Association of Stockholm. In that bagatelle, a barely recognizable Garbo with thick eyebrows
plays "the pastry-eating woman," cavorting with three other girls around a
tea table on the roof of the Grand Hotel. The young man with whom she
flirts is Lars Hanson—her future friend and co-star in Hollywood—who
suavely blows cigarette smoke through his nose while Garbo stuffs herself in burlesque fashion, as a "pastry-eating woman" might be expected
to do.

---

* Ring reportedly cast her again the following year in a film illustrating Swedish culture and
industry, to be shown in Japan, and in PUB's fortieth-anniversary film, *From Top to Toe*
(1922), as one of the daughters in the story of a family whose home burns down and who
then visit PUB to replace their lost clothing. But neither film is extant.

All things considered, the humble Ring films constituted a major career advance, and everyone knew it. Yet when Eva wanted to attend the premiere of *Our Daily Bread*, Greta wouldn't allow it. Even then, she was gun-shy of openings. Eva was hurt by her friend's evident "superiority." She could not understand the complexities of a girl who had profound self-doubts yet called her older sister "Little One" and bossed around a brother who had already done military service. Sven had recently taken an interest in a girl at the corner tobacco shop on Göta Street, and Greta not only disapproved but plotted to use poor Eva to lure Sven away (to no avail).

"She had a sense of purpose that carried everything in front of it," recalls Sven's daughter. "She was very forceful."

Indeed, she was becoming more imperious in general and more insistent on having her way. She fumed and brooded when forced, during the next few months, to turn down more work from Captain Ring, who wanted her to play a Valkyrie in his new industrial film—"a northern romance to be made on a grand scale." By then, she was too valuable both as saleswoman and mannequin, and PUB would give her no more time off for non-PUB moviemaking.

"I felt that I MUST go on stage," she said. "I had to!"

The store was thwarting her will and her Great Escape, and Garbo's adolescent disappointment verged on despair: Was she doomed forever to a life of drudgery? The fear of that plunged her brooding Nordic soul more deeply into melancholia.

Sweden's long nights and endless winters lend themselves to depressing thoughts and a shockingly high national suicide rate. But conversely, a certain joyous, homogeneous simplicity also shapes Swedish society: politeness, tolerance, and a firm determination to *survive* characterize the vast majority of Swedes. However angst ridden, they wrestle with their demons in private, and the young Greta Garbo—no less than the old one—was a classic mixture of all such paradoxical traits.

Garbo by midteens was well along in a process of emotional estrangement that defined her life. "Abandoned" by her father (and, soon, her sister), she was developing a kind of orphan complex and a range of insecurities to match. Her alienation would later be intensified by a dichotomy between the strict Swedish culture from which she sprang and the freewheeling American one into which she was propelled.

The great Jewish film moguls in Hollywood had been poor, too, but their roots were in volatile, extroverted Central Europe; Garbo's were sunk in the sullen, silent North. The way Scandinavians processed their experiences was radically different. And beyond ethnicity, there was Garbo's intrinsic nature:

Greta (age seventeen) at Skansen, an open-air park in Stockholm, 1922

Anna Gustafson with her older daughter, Alva, who was born two years before Greta

"I am the same now [as in childhood]," she said in 1931, "—finding it difficult to adjust to other people."

The events of Garbo's childhood illuminate what made her and her later film acting so *internal:* a strong vocation was mirrored by an equally strong sense of deprivation. For now, Greta Gustafson could never become an actress—much less a goddess—on her own.

From The Saga of Gösta Berling *(1924): Greta Garbo in her first major film. She was eighteen.*

CHAPTER 2

BEAUTY AND THE BEAST
1922–1924

Garbo's process of Acting and Becoming was amazingly rapid. She was never trained in a thorough way, nor doted upon as a talented or aspiring juvenile. Lacking self-confidence and with no early sense of herself either as a prodigy or a beauty, she had to work from the inside out. The real actress did not take shape until she came under the tutelage of a powerful figure, Mauritz Stiller, whose "discovery" of her—and whose brutal methods of mesmerizing and manipulating her—have been often but erroneously reported.

For the moment, in the summer of 1922, it seemed to her that she had no real need of a mentor and that her career was coming along just fine, even if its existence was largely in her head. The afterglow of her two advertising films was still fresh when one day, as she was manning her millinery post at PUB, in walked comedy producer-director Erik Petschler —the "Mack Sennett of Sweden"—accompanied by two popular actresses, Tyra Ryman and Gucken Cederborg, whom Garbo recognized immediately. They were in search of dresses for a film, and she contrived to wait on them. Since Ryman seemed friendly, Garbo asked her how to approach Petschler about getting a part. "Just go over and talk to him," the actress advised, but the salesgirl lacked the nerve. She did, however, obtain his phone number and later worked up her courage to call him for an appointment.

Petschler's account is a little more dramatic: He stopped to look at some shoes in PUB's display window just as Garbo, on her way to work, was doing the same. He was discreet enough not to stare at her directly but at her reflection, yet she caught him at it and quickly flounced inside, unaware of his identity until he and the actresses appeared in her department soon after. In any case, Garbo later phoned Petschler to set up an appointment. "To this day," she said later, "I think this is the boldest thing I have ever done."

When she arrived, Petschler recalled, "I asked her to speak something and without hesitation she recited a school piece or two. She did well." He was not a man who agonized over casting, and his films reflected it. Impressed by her "good looks and bouncy figure," he offered her a part on the spot. "I tried to get her summer vacation changed to the time I intended beginning my picture," he said, but her boss said firmly that no changes could be made. Petschler said he wouldn't think of jeopardizing her position, but Garbo was determined. "I don't care about my holiday—or my wages, either," she told him. "I am going to act in your film!" Confronted with the biggest decision of her life, she made it boldly: She quit. "Reason for leaving?" asked the line on her employment card. "To enter the films," she wrote in a firm hand. She told her mother of her decision and, "as always, she stood by me. Her only answer was—'I think you know what is best for you.' "

Luffar-Petter (*Peter the Tramp*) was Petschler's epic at hand and, as usual, he was producing, directing, writing, and starring. Pratfalls, chase scenes, and itching powder characterized this broad farce in which Petschler played both a bum and a dude, à la Chaplin, and displayed his frolicsome girls in bathing suits, à la Sennett. Miss Gustafson would be one of those frisky if slightly overweight bathing belles, a daughter of the mayor in whose town Peter's army regiment is stationed.

At 15,000 kronor (about $4,750), it was low budget indeed. Aside from Petschler and Gustafson, only four other performers got screen credit, and the all-outdoor filming took just a few days. The first shots were made at suburban Djurgården, but when it came time to film the swimsuit action, Petschler discovered that a local ordinance forbade bathing—even by movie actors—so close to the city. Always resourceful, he transported his little troupe to the island of Dalarö, an hour's boatride from Stockholm. For Garbo, who had never been there (or virtually anywhere else), it was a major adventure.

"Greta was quite shy in front of the camera, especially when she felt people were looking at her," said the cameraman. "She was critical both of herself and of others and repeatedly could be heard saying, 'Ugh, how silly it looks!' " But she had no aversion to swimming.

"I particularly remember how difficult it was to keep little Greta from flinging herself into the inviting water," Petschler recalled. When a sudden rainsquall burst over their heads, everyone except Garbo and Tyra Ryman ran for cover. "As we others crouched unhappily under our chance shelter,

Tyra Ryman, a well-known actress in Stockholm who appeared with Garbo, in 1922

From Peter the Tramp *(1922), directed by Erik Petschler*

Greta and Tyra in their bathing suits improvised a wild Indian dance in the pouring rain. It was a sight for the gods."

The final product was somewhat less divine. It opens with a lady martinet gym instructor drilling the girls in their tight leather pants. Garbo laughs insolently and is next seen in a boat, revving the throttle and then speeding off to their island destination, where she helps set up tent, chop wood, cook fish, and peel potatoes before delicately venturing out onto the rocks in the marshy lake. An iris close-up reveals her bad teeth. She wades around a bit, Petschler leering and spitting all the while. A fat man in a striped bathing suit is mocked. Garbo stretches to show off her chest. The other girls push her down. Then they play ring-around-a-rosy, and the film ends.

Luffar-Petter premiered at Stockholm's Odeon Theater on December 26, 1922, to reviews that were neither good, bad, nor important. A comment on her performance appeared in the Swedish magazine *Swing* beneath a photo of the new Petschler discovery: "[The film] cannot perhaps compete with foreign models . . . where comic situations and technical finesse are concerned; but, though American bathing beauties may be lovelier and more subtle, our Swedish ones have more freshness and charm. . . . Greta Gustafson . . . may perhaps become a Swedish film star. Reason—her Anglo-Saxon appearance."

This was a high, if ironic, compliment. Garbo's first and last comedy until *Ninotchka*, seventeen years later, was also her first and last time in a bathing suit until *Two-Faced Woman* (1941). The consensus was expressed in another newspaper review:

"Miss Gustafson had the doubtful pleasure of playing a bathing beauty for Mr. Erik A. Petschler, so we have had no idea of her capabilities." Politely and prophetically, the critic added, "We hope that we shall have occasion to mention [her] again."

Instinctively and without the aid of newspaper critics, Garbo knew that she needed more training—or, rather, *some* training—if she hoped to become a professional actress. But she lacked a job as well as acting experience, and the prospects of honing her skills, let alone making a living, in low-budget comedies were not encouraging. At sixteen, when she quit PUB to make *Luffar-Petter*, she had still never set foot on a stage, and her obsession to do so increased during the lag time between the filming of Petschler's comedy and its public exhibition late in the year. The girl's stage fixation was well grounded in the society at large, for the playhouse was to Swedes as the movie house to Americans: Stockholm, with just 400,000 residents in those days, supported twelve legitimate theaters.

Petschler had no more work for her at the moment but felt a pang of responsibility for her unemployment, and one day over lunch he had some advice: Why not apply for a scholarship to Kungliga Dramatiska Teatern —the Royal Dramatic Theater Academy, a hallowed institution founded in 1788 by King Gustav III?* It had produced Sweden's greatest actors and all young thespians aspired to it. The Academy was state supported and its training free, but competition for the handful of openings was fierce.

Garbo's first reaction was typically fatalist bordering on defeatist: She wouldn't stand a chance. Not necessarily, the old comedian replied. His friend Frans Enwall, the Academy's former director, was now a private acting coach. Petschler said he could arrange an introduction and was as good as his word.

At their meeting, Garbo told Enwall, "as young people always do to older people of the theater, that I MUST become an actress and asked how to go about it." Enwall was impressed by her sincerity and her lovely, deep voice and agreed to take her on for coaching. When, soon after, he fell ill, his daughter Signe, a prominent stage actress, inherited her.

Academy applicants had to perform three scenes for their audition. Signe Enwall later said she had many acting pupils before and after the young Garbo, but never one as inhibited. At every lesson, the girl sat long and silently, gathering her thoughts and her courage. "May I just wait a bit?" she would ask, and then, after a false start or two, "Sorry . . . can I begin again?" She seemed to need a degree of nervous self-irritation to get going, after which "the lines [flowed] calmly and without hesitation; she took her eyes off the ground and became more and more animated and her voice rang out freely. She was most receptive and never needed to have a mistake pointed out twice."

Signe Enwall recalled an extraordinary episode: Garbo once handed her a letter she had written to a "socially superior" friend and asked Signe to address the envelope because "my handwriting is so horribly uncultured."† She was ashamed of her minimal education, but if her schooling had been lackadaisical, her determination to learn acting was not. The Enwalls gave

---

* King Gustav III, himself an avid performer, was obsessed with the theater and lavished millions of kronor on the staging of battle spectacles with papier-mâché dragons and casts of thousands for the court's amusement. This make-believe bloodshed kept him busy and nourished the arts in Sweden but also provided the perfect opportunity for a group of disgruntled nobles to assassinate him at a costume ball in 1792. Artistically, the king might almost have been pleased: His murder inspired not one but two important operas, Esprit Auber's *Gustave III, ou Le bal masqué* (1833) and the more famous Verdi rendering, *Un ballo in maschera* (*A Masked Ball*), of 1859.

† To the end of her life, Garbo hated her own penmanship, which was one of the secret reasons behind her pathological refusal to give autographs.

her a monologue from the third act of Selma Lagerlöf's *Dunungen* (*The Fledgling*), the first-act scene from Victorien Sardou's *Madame Sans-Gêne*, and a speech from Ibsen's *The Lady from the Sea* (Ellida's "I'm haunted by this irresistible longing for the sea . . ."). In a crash course of less than a month, Garbo memorized and rehearsed her three scenes with a vengeance, in preparation for the test that would determine the shape of her whole life.

"I approached the ordeal with mixed feelings—of heavenly bliss and extreme panic," Garbo recalled. "On the fatal day, my knees almost caved in. I hardly remember my entrance." It came in late August 1922, and she was so jittery she asked her brother Sven to go AWOL from his bakery job to accompany her up to the gilded baroque portals of the theater. Her nervousness was justified by the ten-to-one odds: More than seventy applicants showed up at the Academy hall to vie for seven positions in front of a tough audience. Taken in alphabetical order, some were dismissed after just a few lines. Years later, the experience was still sharp in Garbo's mind:

> There were about 20 people in the jury—newspapermen, critics, people from the theater, and dramatic teachers. They sat before us, in orchestra seats. [But] all I could see was that black pit—that black open space. While I waited my turn, I heard whispers in the darkness out front, I felt doomed to failure. . . . I was so shy! I had never tried to act. . . . I thought I was going to faint. Then I thought of my mother, sitting at home, tense with anxiety and love for me. . . .
>
> At last my moment came. I stepped to the stage and recited my piece like one in a trance. . . . The one-year pupils read the lines of the parts which were not mine. I said my speech, all right. . . . Afterward, I collapsed in the wings, and then I just ran off. I forgot to say good-bye. . . . On the way home I was in an agony of remorse. Perhaps I had ruined all by leaving without making polite farewells!

That first day, she did the Lagerlöf monologue ("There's no blood in my veins; there is only tears!") and made the first cut. The second day, she gained confidence. But the night before she was to perform her third piece, she suffered a terrible bout of stage fright and couldn't sleep. *Sans gêne* means "without constraint," which was how Signe Enwall told her to play it—especially a wild laugh at the scene's climax with Napoleon's sisters. Her own low, restrained laugh was all wrong. She rehearsed ad nauseam but couldn't get it to her satisfaction and, by the time she got to the theater, had worked herself into a raging headache—but *Garbo laughed*, and the phone call of acceptance came a few days later.

"Oh, God, I was happy!" she remembered. "I thought I should die of joy! Oh, now, even now [1931] I can hardly breathe when I remember."

The other new students of the Royal Dramatic Theater Academy in September 1922 were Lena Cederström, Karl-Magnus Thulstrup, and Curt Andersson—all to become important Swedish stage actors—and Alf Sjöberg, who, like Garbo, was destined for films.* Garbo's closest friend, however, would be a second-year student named Mimi Pollack, later a popular member of the Royal Dramatic repertory company and one of its directors.

To Mimi, something about young Greta's aloof insecurity was both appealing and inviting of protection. "When she did join in, she was gay, fun, and full of mischief," said Pollack, "but never spoke of her family." She went out frequently in a black velvet evening cape, either for dramatic effect or because it was one of the few garments she possessed, maybe both. She dressed badly in general, and her peers felt sorry for her because they knew she was hard up. She walked the two and a half miles from home to the Academy to save carfare, and at lunch she and Mimi often shared a twenty-cent dish. Alva gave her money for clothes and other necessities during her first year at RDTA, thus strengthening the already close bond between the sisters. Even at this stage, a certain mystery surrounded Garbo, largely because she kept her thoughts to herself. "We never knew whether she knew it all or knew nothing," said one of her classmates.

She went to the theater a great deal. "It was a necessary part of my training, and we students were given passes," she said. "My comrades and I got on well. After morning classes we drank coffee at a nearby café and I talked unendingly." On the other hand, in this new environment, she was more painfully aware than ever of her scanty education; by some accounts, she was inhibited to the point of paralysis. But, paradoxically, she seemed to be the center of her circle—high spirited and often maliciously funny, with her distinctive little guttural laugh. Her "charismatic inhibitions" would stay with her for life, along with her petulant self-indulgence:

> I was a very bad child. I upset the whole school. I liked to go out at night. We lived right in Stockholm and distances are not as far there. . . . You can take a taxi and be almost anywhere in five minutes. Any theater in the city. I liked to go to the theater in the evening.
>
> So I was late almost every morning! Exercises came first—and I almost always missed them. The other pupils were charming, lovely

---

* Sjöberg (1903–1980), after Sjöström and Stiller, would become the most important Swedish director before Ingmar Bergman, who began his career as one of Sjöberg's screenwriters. Among his influential films—harbingers of Bergman—were *The Road to Heaven* (1942), *Torment* (1944), *Only a Mother* (1949) with Mimi Pollack, and his great *Miss Julie* (1951). He was also chief director of the Royal Dramatic Theater for exactly half a century, from 1930 until his death.

Student members of the Royal Dramatic Theater Academy, 1922. Standing, from left:
*Arnold Sjöstrand, Tore Lindwall, Alf Sjöberg, Karl-Magnus Thulstrup, Johannes
Laurin, Mimi Pollack, Greta Gustafson;* middle: *Mona Mårtenson, Vera Schmiterlöw,
Lena Cederström;* seated front: *Barbro Djurberg, Georg Funkqvist*

girls who were always on time. Then, in would come Garbo, late as
usual. I'd come in the door and say, "There's a rumor about that this
school is still here. But I'm so tired; Garbo's so tired—" And nobody
would say a word to me!

Then it became serious. I started being late [all the time]. They didn't
scold me. If I had been scolded, I'd have been there. I cannot stand to
be scolded.... They taught us dancing. But I can't dance. I was ashamed
to dance. I was so big. Oh, yes, I was big. I was just the same size I
am now when I was 12 years old. I haven't grown a bit since then.
Everywhere I went as a child, I was pointed at because I was so big—
so very big.*

The Academy's curriculum included voice training, deportment, and eurythmics (fencing and dancing, neither of which she liked, due to her physical

---

* Garbo's height and weight have been given as 5′6″, 125 pounds (*Photoplay*, 1936); 5′6″ as
a teen, 5′7″ in adulthood (Bainbridge); 5′7″, 127 pounds (*Current Biography*, 1955); and 5′7½″
(Gray Reisfield, July 15, 1991).

awkwardness). But she enjoyed elocution and those aspects of movement involving the projection of emotion. A few surviving pages from Garbo's dramatic-academy notebook afford a precious glimpse into what she was taught and how she adapted it later to film acting. Her eurythmics teacher adhered to the Delsarte/Dalcroze stage-movement system whose theory was that all gesticulation stems from inner instincts and can be broken down, quite scientifically, by body parts and angles—the head, for example:

"Any forward movement," Garbo copied down from one lecture, "symbolizes submission or expression of spiritual fatigue. The movement of the head backwards expresses the opposite—a person who is proud, tall, and grave. The head bent forward equals a mild concession [or] condescending attitude. The head kept straight [signifies] calmness in the self. The throwing back of the head—a violent feeling such as love."

Garbo, in silent films, would employ that system of gestural meaning to a high degree. Vocally, too, she took her lessons to heart—including the theory that laughter conveys different meanings, depending on the primary vowel of the laugh. An *A* ("ha-ha-ha") indicates "an open, honest person," according to her notes. *E* ("heh-heh-heh") implies a "phlegmatic, melancholic" type. *I* ("hee-hee-hee") suggests childishness, and so on. Karl Nygren, her vocal teacher, said her voice showed great promise.

All in all, the training was brief but rigorous. Typically, she and a second pupil would be given selected scenes to study and prepare under an instructor's guidance. "The school was wonderful," she later enthused. "We had the very best teachers. What a wonderful time this was in my life! It had its worries, for my family was poor, and though instruction was free I needed many things. However, my mother was sympathetic and hopeful, and my brother's and sister's financial situation gradually grew better. We managed."

Actor Nils Asther, also a student at the Academy, said she was "always shy" and it was true—even in the provinces. She spent Christmas at Mimi Pollack's home in Karlstad and was terrified about having to perform a little recital Mimi had arranged at the high school there. It "spoiled the holidays" for her, she said, despite the fact that the Karlstad newspaper critic praised her voice and delivery.

Maria Schildknecht, who taught at the Academy, remembered how repressed Garbo was in front of others. Once when asked to read a passage from Schiller's *Maria Stuart*, Garbo whispered in horror to Mimi, "Who was Maria Stuart? Did she ever live?" Yet when Eugene O'Neill's *Anna Christie* was playing at the Royal Dramatic, Garbo was looking on from the wings every evening. In the corridors, on the stairs—everywhere she acted the sailor's girl, with hoarse voice and cigarettes, bewitched by the part. "I should like to play that," she said.

But unless intrigued, she was indifferent to the point of apathy. When her literature professor once asked when Strindberg was born, she thought for a bit and said, "In the winter." "In the winter?" echoed the astonished teacher. "Yes, I think it actually was in the winter," she replied. After that, "actually in the winter" became a stock gag line at the school.*

The first line Garbo ever spoke on a stage consisted of six words—"Excuse me, Count, for being late"—in *La Belle aventure*, by Gaston Caillavet and R. de Flers. Her affection for everything theatrical was obvious. People at the school particularly noticed her walk—twisting herself forward, it seemed—which was not pretty, and earned her bad marks in deportment, but which was unique. Everyone agreed that her face was beautiful and that she was particularly charming as Hermione in Shakespeare's *The Winter's Tale*. She also performed a few minor character roles in such main-stage productions as Arthur Schnitzler's comedy *A Farewell Supper* and in a Finnish play called *Daniel Hjort*.

Greta Gustafson was finally entering the theater.

Mauritz Stiller, on the other hand, had left it a decade earlier, in favor of the new arena of Swedish films.

He was born Moses Stiller—"Mowscha" or "Moshe" in his youth—on July 17, 1883, in Helsingfors (some sources say Ruthenia), when both were part of the Russian Empire. The fourth of six children, he lived in the relatively unmolested Slavic-Jewish shtetl where his father, Hirsch, an army musician, died when the son was three. Soon after that, his mother, a Polish-Jewish doctor's daughter, committed suicide. Then boarded out to a hat-maker, he attended Hebrew school and remained a Russian citizen until 1921. In Helsinki, from 1899, he worked as a bit player in various repertory groups.

Political turmoil at that time was compounded when the Russian governor-general was shot by a Finnish student, after which several of Stiller's brothers and sisters left for America. During Finland's nationalist uprisings of 1904, all young men were called up for military service, and when Stiller failed to report, the tsarist police went looking and nabbed him during a performance of *Romeo and Juliet* (he was playing Tybalt). He was sent to St. Petersburg and sentenced to six years for desertion. Now he deserted for real and, with a fake passport, found his way to Stockholm. There, Stiller scrounged a few stage parts, honed his Swedish, and eventually, in 1910, became manager and actor-director of Stockholm's avant-garde Lilla Teatern, relocating to Sweden permanently. He had a flamboyant tendency to

* Knowledgeably or accidentally, Garbo was right: Strindberg was born on January 22, 1849.

overact, but his affair with the theater was anyway coming to an end: He had fallen in love, instead, with movies.

The grand old man of early Swedish film was Charles Magnusson (1878–1948), whose Svenska Bio film company boasted the country's greatest cameraman, Julius Jaenzon (1885–1961). In 1911, Magnusson added the theatrical actor-directors Victor Sjöström (1879–1960) and Stiller to his staff, but Stiller soon decided he hated the sight of himself on screen and turned exclusively to directing. Everything about film-making fascinated him. He loved "discovering" people in the streets and cafés of Stockholm. His enthusiasm was as boundless as it was risqué: One of his first films, *The Broken Spring Rose*, was banned by the fairly liberal Swedish censors for its hero's excessive kissing and fondling of the heroine's breasts.

In 1919, during this golden age of Swedish film, Magnusson's outfit merged with the rival Skandia company to form Svensk Filmindustri (SF), which was controlled by "Match King" Ivar Kreuger, its chief investor.* SF has been the dominant force in Swedish cinema from that day to this, and in forging its intimate relationship with nature. Nature, especially in the movies of Stiller and Sjöström, was a dramatic element in itself, menacing human existence and serving as a perfect backdrop to man's psychic collisions with the supernatural.

For story material, in its 1916–24 heyday, SF's policy was to tap Sweden's rich treasury of national literature. Strindberg, for one, could not have been more obliging: Shortly before his death in 1912, the great playwright told one producer, "You may film as many of my works as you wish." But the chief *oeuvre* for filming belonged to the Nobel Prize winner of 1909, Selma Lagerlöf (1858–1940). Her works now seem dated but, in her lifetime, she was the bard of Sweden—a kind of Nathaniel Hawthorne or Sir Walter Scott—in a country where women were the chief storytellers and preservers of tradition. She was provincial and universal, naïve and sophisticated at the same time. Her books were translated into forty languages.

Unlike Strindberg, however, Lagerlöf closely scrutinized all film scripts based on her books. SF had an agreement to make five of them, putting its ace directors on such projects as her two-volume epic, *Jerusalem* (which Sjöström turned into *three* films). Sjöström's adaptations were faithful to the originals. Stiller's took liberties, reflecting his own artistic agenda. Lagerlöf, not surprisingly, preferred Sjöström's approach.

While Sjöström leaned toward drama and the mystical depths, Stiller was

---

* Director John Brunius (1884–1937) was the pillar of Skandia. Various sources list Greta and Alva Gustafson as extras in his *En Lyckoriddare* (1921, *A Soldier of Fortune*), but no confirmation or print of the film can be found.

*Mauritz Stiller, a young director on the rise for
Svenska Bio, c. 1915, by which time he had
directed more than two dozen pictures*

more interested in textures and comedy. Sjöström was a poet, Stiller a painter,
of the screen. Both thought of film as high art, and their advances were
widely admired, but Stiller was a conceptual step ahead of his friend.

Between 1911 and 1923, Stiller churned out forty-three pictures, but of
the three dozen before 1917, a catastrophic fire in the SF archives wiped out
all but one—his playful *Love and Journalism* (1916, *Kärlek och journalistik*).
It stars Karin Molander (divorced wife of Gustaf, future wife of Lars Hanson)
as a reporter who poses as a domestic to gain access to an explorer-hero just
returned from the South Pole.* A harbinger of comic style and streamlined
narration, it employs just twenty-five intertitles to advance its racy plot.

Most amazing of Stiller's early pictures were two comedies based on Gustaf
Molander scripts, *Thomas Graal's Best Film* (1917) and its sequel, *Thomas
Graal's First Child* (1918), both with Victor Sjöström in the title role. The
first is a sophisticated spoof (and rare behind-the-scenes glimpse) of the

---

* The plot of *Love and Journalism* was recycled by Hollywood in 1937 for Tay Garnett's *Love
Is News*, with Tyrone Power and Loretta Young.

Swedish movie business. A director fusses over the hanging of a recalcitrant stuntman: "Take him away and find somebody else we can hang with more sense," he decrees. Sjöström plays an absentminded screenwriter. Karin Molander, his sexy secretary, "rescues" a girl from being beaten, thus ruining the shot but letting us see the state-of-art, hand-cranked cameras. It is a surreal, film-within-a-film send-up—brilliant but esoteric.

Stiller's more popular breakthrough came two years later with *Sir Arne's Treasure* (1919), whose script simplified Selma Lagerlöf's meandering tale of Scottish mercenary guards who rob and murder an innocent family. Its funereal finale—a line of dark figures on a white plane of snow and ice— is one of the most powerful images of silent film, later borrowed by Eisenstein for *Ivan the Terrible* and by Bergman for *The Seventh Seal*.

The following year, Stiller's *Erotikon* (1920) dazzled Sweden and all of Europe with its wit and technical sophistication. It was an intimate comedy of manners with lavish production values, including aerial photography and a performance by the Stockholm Opera ballet. The plot concerns an entomologist's bored wife (Tora Teje), whose husband drones on in the lecture hall, oblivious to his own double entendres:

"The communal life of the striver beetle is extremely illuminating. We find that the red spotted ones freely choose polygamy, whereas the blue ones are monogamous. . . . The truth compels me to tell you that *Ips typographus* sometimes keeps as many as three females. As a rule it is satisfied with two—but never, gentlemen, *never* with one."

Teje falls in love first with flying ace Vilhelm Bryde and then with sculptor Lars Hanson, while the professor is chased by Karin Molander. A happy, amoral ending awaits them all.

Erotikon's spicy cynicism shocked and entertained Sweden and made for an even bigger hit in Germany, where Max Reinhardt and Ernst Lubitsch, among others, found it inspirational. The "Stiller Touch" would later influence Jean Renoir and Billy Wilder, too.

Sjöström, meanwhile, made *Terje Vigen* (1916), a beautiful adaptation of the Ibsen poem, and *The Outlaw and His Wife* (1917), filmed with stunning realism in Lapland, where human conflict meshed with the Protestant need for trial and redemption by nature. But Sjöström's true masterpiece was *The Phantom Carriage* (1920), a tour de force for which he wrote the script, played the lead, and devised a host of new technical effects.

Sjöström and Stiller, in different ways, consciously sought to express new subtleties in film. It is easy to imagine them working together, plunged in heavy cinematic discussions—easy but incorrect. In private, said Sjöström, "What we talked of least was film. Maybe we read each other's scripts and of course we went to each other's premieres and were pleased about each other's successes—we were, and remained, friends—but that was all. There was never any kind of artistic partnership."

They were not, in fact, bosom buddies. In Sjöström's four hundred letters to his wife, Stiller is mentioned rarely, most notably in April 1920, after a dinner party at the home of Danish set designer Axel Esbensen: "I have never had such a nice time with Stiller," Sjöström wrote. "I found him quite different yesterday. He didn't shout, and we could talk well together."

Esbensen's collaboration with both men, on costumes as well as sets, continued through all of Sjöström's major films and most of Stiller's but ended in tragedy. On New Year's Day 1923, following a quarrel with Stiller, he killed himself. Sjöström and others privately held Stiller's bullying responsible. Emil Jannings, Germany's great silent actor, called Stiller "the Stanislavski of the cinema" whose own volatile "Method" with actors often broke them down. A harsher view was that he cared little for human beings at all, except as they served his professional ends and those of his secret homosexual life.

Stiller's public and private life were both characterized by a love of opulence and a restless blend of artistic sensitivity and commercial savvy. His visual mastery and vigorous storytelling made him one of the pioneer geniuses of the screen, but his heyday was short. The masses, faced with a choice between Hollywood fun and Scandinavian "art," soon showed a preference for the former. Before long, Sweden would lose both of her star directors to America, and the decline of Swedish cinema would coincide with their departure. But at the moment, Stiller was riding high toward the zenith of his career.

Greta Garbo was just mounting the horse of hers. In late spring of 1923, Academy director Gustaf Molander summoned her with some exciting news: the great Stiller was casting his new film and had asked for two student actresses to be tested—the prettiest, not necessarily the best. She and Mona Mårtenson, a second-year student, should report at ten the next morning to Svensk Filmindustri studios.* Stiller had previously seen Mårtenson but not

---

* Gustaf Molander (1888–1973) studied at the Royal Academy from 1907 to 1909 and was a director there from 1921 to 1926. If Molander chose the girls, then it was he, not Stiller, who was truly responsible for Garbo's "discovery." He and Stiller were old colleagues from *Sir Arne's Treasure* (1919), for which Molander co-wrote the script. Molander was later a leading film director in his own right. His original Swedish *Intermezzo* (1936) catapulted Ingrid Bergman to fame.

Another version of the story is that Stiller first heard of Garbo from Carl Brisson while she was still laying siege to his dressing room at the Mosebacke Theater. Hoping to get rid of her, Brisson suggested Stiller give her a movie part. In later years Brisson often took credit for introducing them.

*Mona Mårtenson, with her close friend Greta
Gustafson, at the Royal Dramatic Theater
Academy*

Gustafson, and he wanted a look at her first. A meeting was arranged for
later that day.

"I was overawed at meeting such a great man," said Garbo. "He was not
at home when I called, and I waited full of fear. At last he came in—he
and his big French bulldog, Charlie. Without a word, he looked at me a
long time. Much later, he told me exactly how I was dressed that day, down
to details of shoes and stockings. After a long silence, he talked of inconsequential things, like the weather—and I sensed that he was watching me
all the time.

"Suddenly he asked, 'Why don't you take off your hat and coat?' I did
so. 'Let me have your telephone number.' That was all he said. It was clear
to me that I had failed to interest him. I put on my hat and coat, said goodbye
and left."

But to her astonishment, Stiller called and asked her to come to Råsunda
Film City for a test, and the next day, she and Mona rode out together on

Greta and fellow student-actress Vera Schmiterlöw on a joyride, 1923

the streetcar. That fateful, tension-filled ride formed the basis of their close friendship—by some accounts, a romantic relationship.* But for the moment, "I wasn't happy—I was nervous and frightened," Garbo remembered, and the two girls gave each other much-needed support.

Upon arrival, they were made up and taken to a set. Stiller's immortal first words to Garbo were: "If you want the part, you'll have to lose at least twenty pounds." And yet he exclaimed to all present, "Look, isn't she beautiful? Did you ever see such eyelashes?" returning now and then to, "But, miss, you are much too fat. . . ."

Eventually, he showed her a bed and told her to lie down on it and be ill. "I thought the whole business was silly," she said. "Stiller looked at me a long time. Then he asked—'Good heavens, don't you know what it is to be terribly ill?'" She couldn't do it to his satisfaction and was alternately chastised for that and praised for her looks. A historic pattern had begun: He would knock her down and build her up simultaneously.

"It was hard for me to understand just what he wanted," she said, "but I tried my hardest. That was the whole test. I went home puzzled and with a lost feeling." So did the attending studio personnel, none of whom thought she had made much of an impression. To their doubts, Stiller replied, "That's

* See Chapter 8, page 250.

because she's so shy. When you look at her, she goes quite rigid. She doesn't dare show what she feels."

Greta Gustafson, then seventeen, was thunderstruck a few days later to learn she had been cast as Countess Elisabeth Dohna in *The Saga of Gösta Berling*. "I was deliriously happy," she said. "Much had been written about this film, expectations of success were high and my role was wonderful." In Sweden, the part was the rough equivalent of Melanie in *Gone With the Wind*. From that moment on, Stiller's concentration on everything about her was intense: He even personally supervised her make-up and once pointed out that two hairs in one of her eyebrows were out of alignment.

Mauritz Stiller was then forty—a giant of a man, with huge head, hands, and feet. His friends (there weren't a lot of them) called him Moje ("*mo*-yeh"). He had strong opinions about everything and attacked everyone who disagreed with him. He was loud, egotistical, and imperious. "Give me a cigarette!" was his trademark demand, and people complied. He could be tender and generous, or positively vicious. From poverty, he had invented himself first as a theatrical and then as a film virtuoso. He wore fancy embroidered waistcoats and had a passion for jewelry. He sped around Stockholm in his custom-made canary yellow Kissel Kar. They called it "The Yellow Peril"; a sudden stop once propelled his dog Charlie out the window, and Stiller had to go back and pick him up. Always mercurial, he often lost his temper but was quick to forgive. His friend Sjöström observed that Stiller was a born director: He loved to tell people what to do.

Garbo's and Stiller's opposite personalities were attracted from the start, and she was willing to submit to the "Dream Woman" process he had in store for her, including a change of identity. There are at least five versions of how Greta Gustafson became "Garbo," the most absurd of which is that it derived from the Polish word *wygarbowac*—"to tan leather"—an alleged twist on Stiller's desire to shape her psychic hide. The claim that her name had to be changed in order to fit on a marquee is likewise mythical: Surname length didn't hinder such actors as Sixten Malmerfeldt or Jenny Öhrström-Ebbesen. Sweden had few Hollywood-style marquees anyway.

More plausible is the account by which Stiller wanted to follow up *Erotikon* with a similar vehicle for Tora Teje in which the heroine's name was "modern and elegant and international [and] says just as clearly who she is in London and Paris as in Budapest and New York." His manuscript assistant Arthur Nordén suggested "Mona Gabor," derived from Gábor Bethlen, the seventeenth-century Hungarian king. Stiller rather liked it but kept trying out different variations: Gábor, GabOR, Gabro . . . Garbo! Tora Teje was soon abandoned, but when Greta Gustafson later fired his imagination, she

At a costume ball in Stockholm: Greta as harem girl, and Mimi Pollack
a South Seas beauty

had just the right Christian name to go with the surname he already had in mind.

The most romantic etymology holds that *garbo* was an old Norwegian word for wood nymph or forest sprite, and that Stiller chose it to signify "a mysterious being that comes out in the night to dance in the moonlight." There is, in fact, an ancient Nordic word *gardbo*, for "farm guardian," but *garbo* has no meaning in Swedish.

It does have meaning in the Romance languages—with which Stiller and Garbo were largely unfamiliar. Some claim Stiller knew the Italian musical term *con garbo*, "with grace," or the similar definition of the word in Spanish: "gracefulness, elegant carriage," often applied to bullfighters.

And not to be dismissed out of hand is the claim of Mimi Pollack, who insists it was she and Greta—not Stiller—who came up with "Garbo." In Pollack's account, Greta herself felt Gustafson was too long and ordinary for a stage name. She consulted Mimi, who knew a registrar at the Ministry of Justice, where one day they looked through thousands of names. They liked "Gar-" as a beginning, she said, and their fancy was caught by the ending "-bo" on another name.

The pseudonym is said to be a mark of power—a second chance for destiny, as well as anonymity; Coleridge said pseudonyms had to accommodate all meanings and connotations attached to them. Even if Garbo didn't actually choose hers, she at least had to approve it. Whatever its genesis and its owner's feeling about it, Stiller had a name.

But did he have an actress? What talent did he see that nobody else could? It was largely intuitive, of course—a sixth sense for raw material; as noted, he often offered parts to amateurs because they were more flexible and more economical than professionals. They had only to look right.* On a higher plane, Stiller's fanatical belief in Garbo was like Sternberg's in Dietrich: a creative instinct that could only be executed within the film medium's ability to turn a malleable woman into an image that would feed the creator's emotional needs—and those of the audience.

Stiller and Ragnar Hyltén-Cavallius adapted their script for *The Saga of Gösta Berling* from the novel by Selma Lagerlöf, who had not been pleased with Stiller's deviations from her originals in *Sir Arne's Treasure* (1919) and *Gunnar Hede's Saga* (1923). It took some skillful diplomacy on Stiller's part before she finally gave the project her approval.

It was a kind of Swedish *Elmer Gantry*, set amid Värmland aristocratic life in the 1820s. Its Faustian element is the Devil himself, who induces the Byronic title character to sign a pact in blood. Its episodes are peppered with grotesque characters, superstition, and the Swedish notions of retribution and penance: Gösta is bold but shiftless, with every human strength and weakness—a hard-drinking, womanizing minister who falls low, indeed, until redeemed by the pure and beautiful Countess Elisabeth.

"You worship alcohol!" Gösta tells the enraged bishops and parishioners who assemble to judge him at the outset. "You deserve to have a drunken priest." When they defrock him, he moves in with a group of ne'er-do-well Napoleonic war veterans at Ekeby Hall, the estate of wealthy Major Samzelius and his wife, where the idle warriors live up to their solemn pact never to do anything "sensible, useful or effeminate."

In the title role was Lars Hanson, now the leading Swedish film actor. Beloved stage actress Gerda Lundequist—the Helen Hayes of Sweden—played the critical part of the Major's wife, to whom the spongers at Ekeby all have a love-hate attachment. They owe her everything yet stand by quietly when her husband casts her out. They themselves then become masters of the estate—guarding it "as wolves guard sheep or as the spring sun guards the snow."

* But he often changed his mind. When he wanted an amateur for the title-role hero of *Gösta Berling*, his first choice was the Swedish poet Sten Selander—who had no inclination to be an actor. Stiller convinced him to come to the studio, but when he arrived, the director just stared at him in silence for several minutes, then waved his hand in dismissal and said, "No, a person would go crazy if he had to watch that face for five minutes."

Gerda Lundequist, the great Swedish star, and the
newly "rechristened" Greta Garbo, out of Gösta
costume, in Stockholm, 1924

Mona Mårtenson had been successful in her audition, too: She was Countess Ebba, Elisabeth's ill-fated sister-in-law, whose love and life Gösta destroys.
The two Academy girls shared a hotel room during the exterior location
shooting at Öresund, and grew much closer. For six months' work, they
were paid 3,000 kronor (about $600). Stiller scrimped on salaries but spared
no expense on production values: Art director Vilhelm Bryde presided over
the construction of forty-eight sets. Stockholm's leading couturier was engaged to design gowns, and Stiller personally accompanied Garbo to her
fittings. Photography was by Julius Jaenzon, and he and Stiller took
extreme care with Garbo's scenes, constantly retaking for better angles and
light.

Playing opposite Lars Hanson was educational for Garbo, who listened
raptly when he held forth about acting. But Stiller let no one else hold her
attention for long and kept jealous watch over her. He felt she should be
more grateful than she was, and said so, openly criticizing that and all of
her faults. As always on the set, his directorial style involved tormenting his
actors to break down their resistance, mentally and sometimes physically.
"You move your legs as though they were gateposts!" he would shout, adding:

Stiller, second from left, directing Lars Hanson and Garbo on the set of Gösta
Berling. *Julius Jaenzon is at the camera.*

"And this is supposed to be an actress!" to any bystanders who cared to
listen.

"I'm doing as well as I can," replied Garbo to one such explosion, and
then burst into tears. Once, goaded beyond endurance, she shouted back,
"Damn it, Stiller, I hate you!"—a rare display of anger that was probably
just what he sought to provoke. Next he would tactically relent: "No, but,
Garbo, I only want your best, you know that," followed by an embrace and
tender drying of tears. First he savaged, then he soothed.

"On the first day of shooting I was so frightened I could not work," she
recalled. "I was really ill this time! Finally they left me alone in the studio—
everyone from Stiller to the lowliest stagehand. But I felt that the director
was in a corner, watching. When I recovered my poise, the filming went
on. It was slow work. Snow scenes had to wait till winter and the whole
summer passed in filming interiors. To this day I am anxious and nervous
while playing. I want to sit by myself. If I am spoken to, or interrupted, I
am jolted clear out of my character."

Making *Gösta Berling* "was torture for her," said one of Stiller's assistants.
"She cried a great deal"—not just because Stiller was mean, but also in the

process of getting into character. Friends and colleagues were certain that she was undergoing the emotional strain of the Countess. Before several important scenes, she went to cameraman Jaenzon and asked for champagne to bolster her courage—and evidently she got it.

Stiller's methods left a lasting mark on her, personally and professionally. He gave her "dissatisfaction with herself," said S. N. Behrman years later. "Stiller told her she was gauche. He was a sadist in an artistic way, but he was devoted to her, like Henry Higgins."

There could be no arguing with the screen results. From her first scenes, the inner thought in Garbo's eyes speaks volumes. In close-up, she is gorgeously understated when her husband humiliates her in front of Gösta (see opening photo of this chapter, p. 32) and during her climactic reunion scene with Lundequist. She has a strange, enchanting, believable restraint in her first dramatic moments on film. (Never mind the noticeably bad teeth.)

The apotheosis of Stiller's technical virtuosity was the fire scene in which the Major's wife burns Ekeby to the ground—the most expensive scene ever shot in Sweden, filmed with pyromaniacal glee. Seventy years later, its impact is still spectacular and explains why it became the model for all film conflagrations thereafter. But it is Garbo's performance that most captivates, especially in the frantic sleigh chase over an icebound lake, with wolf pack in pursuit.* Her dawning awareness of being kidnapped is revealed gradually and subtly, in counterpoint to Gösta's wild lashing of their horse.

But for that matter, Stiller made the most of her extraordinary presence in every scene. It had been a great risk on his part to give such a role to someone who had never done a serious film before—a risk brilliantly rewarded.

At nearly four hours, *The Saga of Gösta Berling*† was premiered in Stockholm in two installments on March 10 and 17, 1924—Sweden's first two-part film. Purists, including the author, protested the ersatz happy ending: "Mr. Stiller has seen too many poor serials." But the public loved its action and spectacle. At first, not much was said one way or the other about Garbo. Selma Lagerlöf, after meeting her, described her as withdrawn and "beautiful with sorrowful eyes." That was also Hyltén-Cavallius's prophetic theme in a booklet he wrote for the opening:

"Stiller has [cast] two young pupils from our Royal Dramatic Theater— Mona Mårtenson and Greta Garbo. What are these young and charming girls but clay in the hands of the master-modeler? Does then the clay not

---

* Only the sharpest eyes can tell that the "wolves" are Alsatian shepherd dogs with added hair and weighted tails, to prevent their usual friendly wagging.
† Sometimes titled *The Story, The Legend,* or *The Atonement of Gösta Berling.*

Garbo as Countess Elisabeth in The Saga of Gösta Berling

have the same value as the hands that form it? Infinitely more! In a few years Greta Garbo will be known and admired all over the world. For hers is the gift of beauty—a rare personal and characteristic beauty!"

Stiller himself spoke expansively at the premiere: "I venture the paradox that films, as well as stage productions, ought to be played by amateurs. . . . When an actor is really 'great' he is always trying to simplify his means of expression. He is always trying to get back to the natural simplicity that was his when he knew nothing about the technique of acting. This is the most difficult thing of all."

With her 3,000 kronor, Garbo felt sufficiently prosperous to buy a ring for her mother and a coconut mat and sofa bed for herself. She invited Eva to celebrate over coffee and liqueur and to admire her modest new acquisitions, and Eva brought with her a clipping that said, "Greta Garbo's way to stardom seems clear." Wasn't she happy? Eva asked cheerfully. Garbo's diffident reply: "I didn't think I was quite that good. I hope I'll be better in my next part."

During and after *Gösta Berling*, she kept up her studies at the Academy. Now, with increased prestige from the film, she was offered a contract as "leading pupil," with a thirty-dollar-a-month raise in her stipend. She signed herself "Greta Gustafson Garbo" this time and was soon playing small roles in such main-stage shows as *The Tortoise Comb*, a German comedy that ran forty-three performances, and Barrie's *The Admirable Crichton* (she was Fisher, a lady's maid).

Nowadays, she and Stiller dined together often, and during their intense conversations, she told him more than once that he criticized her too much. "I must criticize you, since you're so inexperienced," he would reply. His justification was always the same: He had to catch and shape her before she had time to acquire silly mannerisms. Furthermore, he said, she was so good, she ought to quit the Academy and let him take charge of her career—in film—and, soon enough, she decided to let him.

The late winter and early spring of 1924 held an eventful few weeks for Garbo: She signed her Royal theatrical contract in February, then resigned in March upon deciding to take up her mentor's offer. Her painful education under Stiller was better than any classroom could provide. She was aware of something witnessed by Stellan Claussen, a production executive at Svensk Filmindustri who had watched the *Gösta* shooting:

"To us she appeared to be just a shy, mediocre novice. . . . We tried to make Greta one of our little family but we didn't get very far because Stiller scarcely permitted anyone else even to speak to her—he hardly let her out of his sight for a moment. . . . We nicknamed them 'Beauty and the Beast.' . . . I can still see Stiller and that young girl—forever walking up and down, up and down, in the shade of a little grove just outside the studio. Stiller was always teaching and preaching, Greta solemnly listening and learning. I never saw anyone more earnest and eager to learn. With that hypnotic power he seemed to have over her, he could make her do extraordinary things. But we had little idea then that he was making over her very soul."

He was also making over her approach to her art and to everything surrounding it, including the press. Garbo began as a rather open and forthcoming person. During the filming of *Gösta Berling*, she spoke with journalist Inga Gaate, who asked if she found movie-making difficult.

"Terrible," Garbo replied. "I have had a Gethsemane, but Stiller is the best human being I know. . . . He creates people and shapes them according to his will. As for myself, I am a nice girl who gets very sad if people are unkind to her, although that may not be very feminine. Being feminine is a lovely quality which I may not have very much of."

It was, among other things, a sweet and curious example of her sexual ambivalence. Why was it unfeminine to be sad in the face of unkindness? And then at the close of the interview, she suddenly sensed danger: "You must not write up everything I say. I am one of those people who do not think, you see, who talk first and think afterwards."

When Gaate printed the remarks anyway, Garbo felt betrayed and embarrassed. Stiller was irate. He didn't like reporters or interviews in general, and this was a good example why: Whether deliberately or not—it didn't matter which—they made you look silly. Gaate and Stiller's reaction were the source of Garbo's lifelong antipathy to press. Henceforth, he decreed, avoid reporters like the plague, and stick close to Moje for further instructions.

Garbo obeyed. She not only took the name he picked for her, and all the acting tips he chose to give, but his tutorials in personal development and social conduct, as well. Stiller took her to shows and films (if their cab driver was David Gustafson, the uncle and niece pretended not to know each other) and introduced her into his circle of artists and writers. He told her what to wear and what to say, and even got her to sing some of Lili Zeidner's burlesque songs, on command, at his own parties. Left to her own devices, she would usually sit silently in a corner, giving the impression not of mystery but a mere *absence* of personality. She seemed to have shed her youthful buoyancy without yet having found a replacement. It was an identity void that to some extent would remain with her in America, where silence and simplicity looked a lot like "deep mystery."

The grooming continued. On Stiller's advice, she attended a ball in Saltsjöbaden for Douglas Fairbanks and Mary Pickford. One of her dancing partners was Ivar Kreuger, the film financier, who took a shine to her.

Stockholm drama critic Hjalmar Lenning did not. He found her "dull, uninteresting and very taciturn." But Stiller never wavered: "She is like wax in my hands. Greta will be all right. I believe in her."

She, meanwhile, was adopting many of his characteristics and phobias, and not just concerning the press. In negotiations, for example, Stiller always began with a show of disinterest—an effective tactic that lent itself to Garbo's own temperament. Carl Brisson maintained that a famous Garbo remark of later years was borrowed from Stiller: "When he was very displeased with anything, he often would say in his deep voice, 'Ah, that is very, very bad. I think I will go now.'"

A neurotic perfectionist himself, Stiller turned Garbo into one, too. Throughout her career, she always arrived on the set dialogue-perfect; her refusal to let outsiders watch her perform was also traceable to Stiller.

Their private relationship was more shrouded, but there, too, Garbo took Stiller's cues in terms of secrecy—or at least discretion. If the public required *some* image of its film darlings and their love lives, better to construct and control it oneself. Stiller, a lifelong bachelor, "liked to have beautiful women around him," said his friend Bryde. Even though not sexually attracted to women, he had a powerful mental image of his feminine ideal—"supersensual, spiritual and mystic"—and his search for her was obsessive. Young Mary Johnson, the star of *Sir Arne's Treasure*, had been the first candidate. She had the soulfulness and mysticism but not the malleability. His next choice was *Erotikon*'s Tora Teje, who had sophistication and warmth, but lacked mystery. The Gustafson girl had it all.

The theory and practice of Stiller's sexuality sheds light on Garbo's own sexual orientation, and on their relationship, as we will later see. But for now, the mode was concealment, not exploration. Despite countless claims, there is no proof or even circumstantial evidence that Garbo and Stiller were ever lovers. Though Swedish society was liberal in its attitudes about sex, most of the rest of Europe was not; the Roaring Twenties had not yet crossed the Atlantic. It was still an era in which nothing sexually, aside from marriage, was condoned. Stiller was also aware, and would soon be more so, that she was a teenager whose moral protection he had a clear legal obligation to ensure.

It was mental, not physical, sex Stiller was having with Garbo. For years, he'd been developing the Ultimate Screen Woman in his mind and viewfinder, with a kind of pent-up cerebral lust, while she was developing in Södermalm. Stiller was not a man to abuse any woman sexually. But he was a chauvinist, a megalomaniac, and a psychological tyrant who liked to give orders, and he was currently in charge of a beautiful girl who liked to take them.

The opportunity that awaited her was extraordinary, but Garbo had certain regrets. She later told actress Valeska Gert "she was always sorry she had to go out and work too soon." It was curious and fascinating that, except for the brief stint at RDTA, all her early acting breaks came in film rather than theater. After *Gösta Berling*'s Stockholm opening she went to the country to rest but wasn't there long before Stiller wrote to ask her to attend the film's German premiere in Berlin—a city he loved and knew his way around. As Garbo always needed rest, Stiller was always restless. Now, more than ever, he felt Sweden was too small for him. When the German dirigible *Bodensee* came to Stockholm, he arranged to be on it for the return flight to Berlin. There, he sold *Gösta Berlings* German exhibition rights to the Trianon company for the huge sum of 100,000 marks, plus an all-expense-paid trip (and clothes-buying expedition).

"I had never been away from Sweden," Garbo said. "I was nervous. I asked Stiller if I was to go alone. He laughed at my fears and told me that he and Gerda Lundequist were going too." Upon their arrival a few days before the screening, Garbo went sightseeing with Lundequist, while Stiller began Machiavellian negotiations for their future. All the while, he never neglected his coaching of Garbo. "Put your feet on that stool," he told her one day before the hotel manicurist's arrival. "You're tired. A film star is always tired. It impresses people." It was the one condition she never had to feign.

On August 21, 1924, Garbo and Stiller entered their box at the theater. Everyone turned to look, and when she pushed back her chair from the edge of the box, Stiller pulled it forward again. "Berlin received us charmingly," she recalled. "The premiere was a grand affair. . . . We appeared on the stage, and were bombarded with flowers. I like the Germans. They don't try to get too near one." At the postpremiere dinner, as they were about to take their places, Garbo asked, "How do you say 'I'm going home' in German?"

"Don't you try to slip away," Stiller warned.

Gösta Berling was a great critical and commercial success in Germany, far more than in Sweden. Trianon took in 750,000 marks in Berlin alone, instantly making back its investment and misleading itself into granting Stiller's extravagant demands for films-to-be. Garbo returned to Sweden to fulfill her final commitments with the Royal in a Russian drama, *Violins of Autumn*, and in Per Lagerkvist's *The Invisible Man*, in which she played a

*Garbo (age eighteen), Stiller, and Gerda Lundequist in Berlin for the
German premiere of* The Saga of Gösta Berling, *August 1924*

prostitute. The tiny part of Mariette, a receptionist, in the new Jules Romains
farce *Knock*, would be the last stage appearance of her life.

Stiller, meanwhile, agreed to a Trianon contract providing 150,000 marks
per film for himself and a multiyear deal for Garbo at 500 marks per month.
The German firm thought it was commissioning a sentimental German love
story, but Stiller had a brighter idea: He had recently read a melodramatic
Stockholm newspaper serial by Russian refugee Vladimir Semitjov, bought
the screen rights, and had already reworked it into a script: In *The Odalisque
from Smolna*, a girl caught up in the Russian civil war flees Sevastopol and
crosses the Black Sea to Constantinople in search of her fiancé. She is drugged
and sold into a Turkish harem, her escape from which is but one of many
breathless adventures.

Stiller had convinced Trianon that by producing the film in Turkey,
fabulous backgrounds, crowds, and perpetual sunshine could be obtained for
free. By the time he finished his sales pitch, they were begging him to do
it. On September 10, 1924, Trianon executive David Schratter gave Stiller
a fatal guarantee in writing, telling him "not to worry" about anything, that
the company intended to let him make his film "the way you want."

Garbo at a railway station in Bulgaria, December 1924, en route to Turkey
for Stiller's (abortive) production, Odalisque from Smolna

Stiller assumed Garbo would acquiesce to everything, and she did. She
had, after all, been practicing the role of harem girl since she was ten. In
mid-December 1924, Stiller, Garbo, actor Einar Hanson, and writer Hyltén-
Cavallius left Stockholm, stopping first in Berlin to pick up their German
camera crew, then going on to Turkey by way of Bulgaria. At this stage,
Stiller had cash and spent it. He installed his little troupe in the Péra-Palace
Hotel, Constantinople's grandest, where Garbo's beauty caused a sensation.*

---

* Mercedes de Acosta, who figured prominently in Garbo's later life and was prone to foresight
in hindsight, claimed to have had her first close encounter with Garbo at this time: "One
day in the lobby of the Péra-Palace Hotel I saw one of the most hauntingly beautiful women
I had ever beheld. Her features and movements were so distinguished and aristocratic-looking
that I decided she must be a refugee Russian princess. The porter said he did not know her
name but he thought she was a Swedish actress who had come to Constantinople with the
great Swedish film director [Stiller].

  "Several times after this I saw her in the street. I was terribly troubled by her eyes and I
longed to speak to her, but I did not have the courage. Also I did not even know what
language to use. She gave me the impression of great loneliness. . . . As the train pulled out
of the station which carried me away from Constantinople I had a strong premonition that
I might again see that beautiful and haunting face on some other shore."

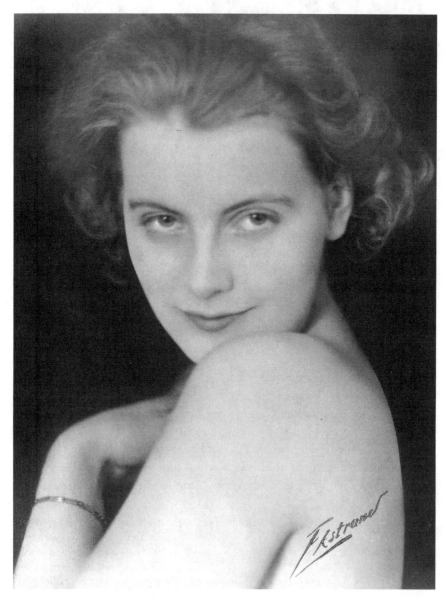

Garbo by Ekstrand, Stockholm, 1924

She spent her first Christmas away from Sweden looking out her window at the Bosporus. The extravagant Stiller threw a big Christmas Eve party for the city's Swedish and German residents and presented Garbo with a fur coat. He purchased two fine cars and two trucks and went looking for picturesque backgrounds. Wending through the stalls of the Grand Bazaar, he haggled for Persian carpets and bought elaborate Oriental costumes for Garbo, including a brick-red silk Chinese outfit with yellow flowers. She wore it to a Swedish legation party, where everyone was in high spirits; she danced the *hambo*—a boisterous Swedish folk dance—with Cavallius, and she seemed to be overcoming her fear of Stiller. At one point, she sat on his knee, taking cigarettes out of his mouth and playfully admonishing him not to smoke.

Filming was to start within ten days of their arrival and to be completed in about two months. But the camera equipment was held up for eighteen days in a customs snarl at the frontier, and the money was running out fast. When Stiller wired Trianon for more—a cool million marks—there was no reply. Stiller has always been accused of squandering Trianon's movie budget in Istanbul, but that was not really true. The money he squandered was for travel expenses; production funds were to be forthcoming. He had other problems, too. He began rehearsing a scene in which the lovers meet outside a mosque, but it met with violent Muslim protests. Moreover, he didn't and couldn't know that Trianon was going broke for investment reasons unrelated to him. Years later, with the Trianon disaster still in litigation, Garbo was required to make a court deposition.

"All I know is that the whole thing busted, and naturally I did not understand anything about those things," she said.

From whom did she receive her salary?

"I didn't receive any money, as far as I can recollect."

After a second unanswered cable, Stiller went to Berlin personally to learn that Trianon was bankrupt, at which point he wired Einar Hanson to bring Garbo and the rest of the company back to Germany. But there wasn't even enough money to do that, and it was left to the charity of the Swedish legation to bail them out with a batch of train tickets.

Hanson was upset, but Garbo was not: "Don't worry," she told him. "Everything will be all right when we get to Berlin. Stiller will take care of everything."

G. W. Pabst in Berlin, around the time of filming The Joyless Street *(1925)*

CHAPTER 3

PABST AND BERLIN
1925

Garbo was right that Stiller would take care of things. In fact, he was playing all the angles and prepared to doublecross everybody, thanks to two and possibly three backup deals he'd been exploring behind Trianon's back. Dearest to his heart and his ego was the formation of a giant pan-European film combine that would internationalize the production and distribution of films by such major companies as Germany's UFA, France's Pathé, and Sweden's Svensk Filmindustri, with Stiller at the top and Ivar Kreuger as chief investor. It was no mere pipe dream: UFA and SF had already tentatively agreed.

Simultaneously, and unbeknownst to Trianon or UFA or SF, Stiller was invited by Louis B. Mayer to come to Hollywood. An MGM agreement was drawn up and sent to him in November 1924—before he even left for Constantinople!* The contracts were flying thick and fast, and Stiller evidently signed *all* of them, figuring he would have plenty of time to choose the best deal—preferably the Euro-combine—once his Turkish film was finished. But Trianon's unexpected collapse brought him and his cash flow up short. Something had to be improvised in the hiatus.

For the moment, in January 1925, the dilemma was whether Garbo, Stiller, and Einar Hanson should return to Stockholm or stay in Berlin. It was resolved, as usual, by Stiller's unilateral decision: They would all remain in Germany. He owed everybody money, but Stiller knew a loan shark or two in Berlin and, to keep up appearances, engaged first-class quarters at the Esplanade Hotel.

* For the full details of Stiller's MGM dealings, see Chapter 4.

Garbo wandered about there, silently watching people, more or less at home anywhere and nowhere. While Stiller wheeled and dealed, she and Hanson timidly sampled Berlin's dazzling nightlife to the extent their Scandinavian reserve and poverty allowed: homosexual clubs, male and female prostitutes of every variety, the Negro revue with Josephine Baker, Stanislavsky's Chekhov productions, and cosmopolitan kino fare from American Westerns to Eisenstein's *Battleship Potemkin*. Five months after its premiere, *Gösta Berling* was still playing and gasps still rising from the audience when the face of the young Garbo first appeared on screen. But that was small consolation when one was broke. In film history, the universal homage to Stiller's shaping of Garbo glosses over the fact that they made a total of one picture together. Virtually ignored is her seminal experience—only her second "real" film role—in Germany, under a great director who was the most unsung influence of her career.

The man who finally rescued the Swedes from dire financial straits was G. W. Pabst (1865–1967), then casting the picture that would bring him international fame. Pabst's film career was at this point as embryonic as Garbo's. This, his second film, was based on Hugo Bettauer's novel *Die freudlose Gasse* (*The Joyless Street*), a tale of Vienna during the post–World War I inflation period, contrasting the corruption of the rich with the impoverishment of the middle class. Pabst's independent Sofar-Film company was unconnected with the big German UFA concern. His friend and assistant director Marc Sorkin had helped him find the money to finance the film in Paris. They had already cast Werner Krauss and Asta Nielsen, two of Europe's leading film actors, but were still seeking the perfect actress for the key role of a dutiful daughter who tries to keep up her family's honor.

"We saw Garbo in *Gösta Berling*," said Sorkin. "But Garbo was nothing; she was just a good-looking girl. . . . We put her up as a pin-up girl, you know—a beauty. She was very photogenic. In real life she didn't look so wonderful, but in movies. . . . Pabst said, 'This is the right girl; we have to use her in our picture.' [People said], 'Are you crazy? For a big picture?'

"[But] we had decided to try to get Garbo. We knew they were in Istanbul, and we knew that Trianon was not well off, so Pabst went directly to Trianon in Berlin and told them, 'We want to use Garbo. Give us your contract with her.' But Trianon said, 'You cannot get Garbo; look for another girl.' "

Stiller and Garbo, in the meantime, had returned to Berlin, and Sorkin tracked them down for Pabst and arranged a meeting. Stiller, always the superb bargainer, said he doubted Garbo would be interested unless she were paid $4,000 in U.S. dollars—a huge sum. He also declared that his colleague Julius Jaenzon was the only one who could film Garbo properly. Pabst said he had already hired Guido Seeber, one of the best photographers, but gave in on the money. "We had to pay Garbo the same amount we paid Asta Nielsen," said Sorkin. "[Stiller] knew, evidently, that he was dealing with suckers, and he made us take Einar Hanson, too, and we paid *him* the same salary as Garbo. . . . And all the expenses."

The Garbo flower was about to blossom in the miraculously creative soil of 1925 German film. Its dominant stylistic rage was Expressionism, which portrayed the inner life through a wild exaggeration of the outer. That movement first appeared in art and spread to literature, theater, and inevitably film—from *The Cabinet of Dr. Caligari* (1919) through the masterworks of F. W. Murnau, Paul Leni, Fritz Lang, and others.

But G. W. Pabst was no Expressionist at heart. At twenty-five, he'd gone to New York with the Deutsche Volkstheater, acting in and directing plays for the German immigrant population. When he returned to Europe four years later, it was to recruit a new troupe of German actors for America, but he was caught in the outbreak of World War I and interned in a French camp at Brest as an enemy alien. Released at the end of the war, he became director of the Neuen Wiener Buhne (New Vienna Stage).

Pabst was a latecomer and late bloomer in film. In 1921, he finally left the theater and went to Berlin to join director Carl Froelich as an actor, assistant, and scenarist. He didn't direct his first film, *Der Schatz* (*The Treasure*), until 1923, at the advanced age of thirty-eight. His encounter with Garbo came two years later, and he would soon be ranked with Murnau and Lang among "the big three" of German cinema.

But at this point, Pabst was still a neophyte and, unlike Lang and Murnau, an independent producer in charge of his own scenarios, and with a different agenda. He was a passionate scrutinizer of the human soul; he used his camera to make psychological X rays—detached and amoral. For him, the film challenge of psychology, as opposed to sociology, could not be met through the hysterical frenzy of Expressionism. Something less self-conscious was in order, Pabst felt—something more "real."

Die Neue Sachlichkeit—the New Objectivity—was a term coined in 1924 to define the new painting style of George Grosz (1893–1959) and Otto Dix (1891–1969), related to the realist schools of America ("Ashcan"), England ("Kitchen Sink"), and the USSR ("Socialist Realism"). But the German brand had no political ideology; instead, it marked a state of paralysis and reluctance to take sides. Its catalytic figure was Sigmund Freud, whose influence on Pabst (and whose wider impact on all the arts) was enormous. The sloppy belief persists that both Freud and Pabst were "German." They were, of course, Austrian—a minor difference in America but a crucial one in Europe. The German film was all pillars, but Pabst was Viennese nuances.

Pabst epitomized the emotional disillusionment of European intellectuals between the wars. That attitude could only be communicated in film through the players' performances, and thus the key to Pabst's style lay in his handling of actors. Years later, Louise Brooks, whom Pabst directed in *Pandora's Box* (1928), put her finger on it—and on the challenge to all directors:

> In order to see things from the director's viewpoint, one might think of how difficult it is to get a true smile in a single snapshot of a person we know. Then think of a director who faces a group of strangers, all of them certain about how they want to play their parts, some of them antagonistic, all of them full of a thousand secrets of pain and humiliation which, accidentally touched upon, may defeat the director in an utterly baffling way. No director will ever admit his fear of failing to get a performance out of an actor. Some, like Erich von Stroheim, try to arouse by viciousness any violent emotion and photograph it; some fortify themselves by the use of mugging actors; some use trick photography or symbolism. But a truly great director such as G. W. Pabst holds the camera on the actors' eyes in every vital scene. He said, 'The audience must see it in the actors' eyes.' . . . Pabst's genius lay in getting to the heart of a person, banishing fear, and releasing the clean impact of personality which jolts an audience to life.

It was Pabst's most important insight: Especially in close-up, the actor must understand what his eyes are expressing, or the audience cannot. "Pabst never demonstrated," said Sorkin. "He explained." He wasn't the first to cultivate realistic acting. Paul Wegener, back in 1916, seemed to skip Expressionism and move directly to the New Realism when he insisted that "the only effective acting [is] discreet acting: restrained movements, calm and expressive faces, eloquent eyes, and a dignified naturalness of bearing. Anything in the nature of affectation or gratuitousness would be exposed at once on the vast surface of the screen, where the actor is seen as if under a microscope."

Wegener went unheeded at the time, but Charles Chaplin was on to the same principle in his direction of *A Woman of Paris* (1923), telling an interviewer: "As I have noticed life in its dramatic climaxes, men and women try to hide their emotions rather than seek to express them. And that is the method I have pursued in an endeavor to become as realistic as possible."

Psychology—especially feminine psychology—was Pabst's specialty, and though his most spectacular results were with women, the integrity of his approach inspired all: "Everybody, down to the last property man, could come to him on the set and say, 'You know, Mr. Pabst, I think so-and-so is wrong,'" recalled Sorkin. "And if it was a very good idea, he'd give the man a mark (a dollar at the time). Pabst said that he wanted everybody to be involved in the picture he was working on. You could never do that with other directors. They were afraid of advice. Not Pabst. He would listen to everybody."

But the essence was choice of actors. "If you find the right actor for the part, you have the picture," he said. In Stiller's Swedish girl, he'd seen a certain "vulnerable despair" that was precisely what he wanted for *The Joyless Street*. Paul Falkenberg, his editor, quoted Pabst's belief "that movies were THE coming art form and the medium of expression of our time, and that cinema would supercede in [intensity and possibilities] all present art forms like the theater; that it would help make the world a better place for human understanding. I fell under Pabst's spell right away."

So did Greta Garbo.

The German realist "street tragedy" films of the midtwenties were a subgenre unto themselves, and *The Joyless Street* was one of the best of them.* Its tale of moral and social chaos lays out the separate but intersecting stories of Grete (Garbo) and Maria (Asta Nielsen), who never meet but form a dramatic counterpoint to one another. Garbo is the virtuous girl compromised by rogues: At work, they think she's tired out from carousing when, in truth, she was waiting in line all night at the butcher's. She is oblivious to the money her boss stuffs in her pocket, but her co-workers see the bills as incriminating. Her father makes her buy a costly coat on credit, and when she wears it to the office, she is fired and pushed toward prostitution. By contrast, the Nielsen character *willingly* prostitutes herself and commits a murder.

After Stiller read the script, he summoned Pabst and told him "that with this film he had a chance of becoming very big," said Sorkin. "But he was worried that Pabst [had] miscast Garbo. He said, 'I gave you Greta Garbo only to make money; but I cannot let you ruin it.' He wanted to give us back the contract. Pabst answered him, 'I am not afraid. . . . I shall manage it. It is none of your business.'†

---

* Among the others: Karl Grune's *The Street*, Lupu Pick's *Scherben* and *Sylvester*, Pabst's *The Loves of Jeanne Ney*, Murnau's *The Last Laugh*, and Dupont's *Varieté*.

† There was no affection between Pabst and Stiller, but neither was there animosity. The claim that Trianon asked Pabst to take over *The Odalisque from Smolna* in Constantinople is unlikely. So is the colorful report that Stiller believed Pabst was having an affair with Garbo during the making of *The Joyless Street* and arranged for a Berlin hooker to give him a social disease.

"Stiller then gave Pabst the most important idea for the film: the fur coat. Before, it was a regular coat. Stiller suggested, 'Give her an expensive fur coat. . . . She can never have the money to pay for a fur coat. A regular coat is just a coat; how can you explain in the movie that it is expensive? It is not photogenic. But a good fur coat, that you can see.' "

Shooting began in March 1925. On the first day, Garbo was nervous and so was Pabst when he saw the results: Due to her fair complexion and the fact that the Germans used much stronger lights than the Swedes, she did not photograph well. "When we got our first rushes, we saw nothing special," said Sorkin. "Pabst wanted the same photography that she had in *Gösta Berling*, so we asked Stiller to come to the studio and he tried to explain the light for her."

Stiller explained, none too patiently, that Garbo's face required only the best Kodak film, not the German Agfa stock they were using. Though much more expensive and nowhere to be found in Berlin, some Kodak-Pathé film was located in Paris and, thenceforth, sent in daily. That left the problem with Seeber, the dean of German cinematographers, whose landmark film credits included *Student of Prague* (1913), *The Golem* (1920), and *Fridericus Rex* (1923). During Stiller's visit to the set, he lectured Seeber "as if I'd never been behind a camera in my life. He seemed even more wrought up than the frightened young woman he was so worried about."

Seeber was a fine technician who knew all the optical tricks that, in those days before the "special effects" laboratory, had to be executed by the cameraman during shooting. But his lighting was not exceptional, and Pabst knew it. He understood the symbiosis of light and camera, and now—for one of the first times—he separated those functions, hiring a specialist named Oertl, who soon discovered Garbo's optimum light mix.

Pabst and his crew rose to every Garbo challenge. In addition to the lighting difficulties, they were chagrined to discover that when filmed in close-up, she developed a visible nervous tic in her cheek; their first shots were unusable. Stiller had had the same trouble, and advised Pabst to crank faster, thus eliminating the twitch by trickery until she could overcome the nervousness that caused it.*

No one in the cast but Asta Nielsen thought Garbo was worth all the trouble. When she remarked on the girl's beauty, Pabst agreed and replied, "Such a face you see once in a century." With his new, improved camera results, he coaxed her into the projection room to watch rushes, complimenting her and bolstering her confidence while embellishing her part. They

---

* Some sources say it was Seeber, not Stiller, who hit upon the speed-up idea, by which—when projected—the close-ups were imperceptibly in slow motion.

Asta Nielsen, a stunning vision of vice and cor-
ruption in Joyless Street

worked sixteen-hour days, and though Garbo was invariably up late being coached by Stiller the night before, she was always the first to arrive on the set each morning. *The Joyless Street* was completed in just thirty-four days.

From her first scene to her last, Garbo is a wan, wistful, proto-Camille. When she faints in the butcher-shop line, Werner Krauss leers hideously; his currency is meat, indeed. Pabst cuts for contrast to a Viennese nightclub, where Asta Nielsen asks her beau, "How can I convince you I love you?"

"Get rich," he replies.

"I'll make you so happy," she rejoins.

"Happy?" he snorts. "Only money can give me my kind of happiness."

After Garbo's foolish father tells her she looks shabby, she makes her way to the shop of Valeska Gert, who greets her with lewd stares and sensual caressings of that fur coat. Cylindrical Gert hovers and hops about, a puckish procuress with fuzzy little moustache, crazed eyes, and huge nose.*

---

* Valeska Gert (1896–1978), frequent member of Pabst's unofficial "company," was also a Berlin cabaret operator. A few months later, she turned in a superb performance as the touch-of-evil maid in Jean Renoir's 1925 rendering of Zola's *Nana*. She did two more brilliant roles

Garbo, the opposite vision of long-suffering virtue

Garbo admires herself shyly in the mirror, as Gert admires Garbo in the act of admiring herself: Don't worry about money, she says—just come back Thursday to meet an influential visitor. He turns out to be the same repulsive butcher with whom her troubles (and the film) began. In that tea-table scene, Pabst gives us a masterful play of the eyes—crosscutting from Krauss's crude stare to Gert's unctuous anticipation to Garbo's frightened-animal look.

Later, into the same room—and the same eerie mirrors—come the male "customers" who find her and her triple image in a revealing gown before the looking glass. Finally, an American relief officer (Einar Hanson) shows up to take her away from it all, and perhaps he does. But revolution suddenly turns the denouement into Eisenstein: The butcher is murdered. The hungry

---

for Pabst, as the reformatory mistress in *Diary of a Lost Girl* (1929) and as Mrs. Peachum in *The Threepenny Opera* (1931). After fleeing the Nazis, she came to New York and operated a club there, reestablishing contact with Garbo, in the late forties and fifties. Her swan song was as the living mummy in Federico Fellini's *Juliet of the Spirits* (1965).

Garbo, as a fallen woman, and a customer in
Joyless Street

crowd rebels. The elegant nightclub guests are pelted with stones as they run out in panic . . . *Apocalypse Then!*

Pabst's social realism—the misery, the prostitution, the bread lines—was relentlessly downbeat and struck everyone as shocking and gloomy. But the May 18, 1925, simultaneous premiere of *The Joyless Street* in Berlin and Paris was a big success: Its investors made money, and Pabst made his reputation.

In Paris, it played at Les Ursulines art house and ran there for two years. "This was a time of inflation in France too, and people were frightened," Sorkin recalled. "In Parliament one day, one of the deputies [said], 'Go to the Ursulines and see *La rue sans joie*, and there you will see what misery inflation brings!' That appeared in the press, so people had to go and look. It pushed the picture. After that, Pabst was considered one of the big directors. He was bigger in France than in Germany."

The success of *The Joyless Street* came both in spite and because of the controversy it engendered. The original was 10,000 feet, almost the "spectacle length" of *Ben-Hur* or *The Big Parade*. But even in France, where its reception was best, 2,000 feet had to be deleted. In England, public showings were banned altogether and it was screened only once, privately, at the Film Society. In Vienna, all sequences with Krauss, the butcher, were excised; in Russia, the American lieutenant was turned into a doctor and Krauss into the murderer. In America, it wasn't exhibited until two years later in a truncated version that caused Garbo to be dismissed as "completely unsophisticated." The best *The New York Times* could say of it, on July 6, 1927, was, "There are moments when this picture doesn't seem so bad, but then these are killed by some preposterous exhibitions of agony." One enterprising medicine man in the Midwest leased it for use with his lectures on the perils of social disease.*

In Weimar Germany, *The Joyless Street* reflected a variety of crises—political, economic, sexual—and was intensely scrutinized by the all-male German Film Censorship Board, which, on March 29, 1926, demanded revisions in view of the film's potential detriment to *women*:

> The film [shows] how Viennese girls are forced to sell their moral honor and to earn their bread in brothels as a result of need and the misery of inflation. . . . In the whole film, only one girl [Garbo] resists the temptation to sell her honor for money or meat. But even this girl ends up in the brothel. . . . Through this forced situation, in which the girls are brought without exception into depravity, the impression must emerge that the girls' action is the necessary consequence of misery and need. This must have a demoralizing effect on the female viewer.

Afraid that women might emulate those screen characters, the censors ordered radical changes but evidently lacked the teeth for enforcement: Pabst did not comply. In any case, no amount of censorship short of complete withdrawal could have totally defused *The Joyless Street*. Film historian Lotte Eisner called it the epitome of the Germanic visions of the street, "wavering between images of tyranny and chaos," that would soon enough lead to Hitler.

---

* In 1935, a sixty-five-minute edition was re-released in the United States on the assumption that audiences would pay to see what Garbo looked like a decade earlier. In that version, Asta Nielsen's whole role and subplot—nearly 40 percent of the film—were cut. That mutilated 1935 version is still being rented as "Pabst's *Joyless Street*" to unsuspecting college film classes and TV stations in America. The original *Joyless Street* is not extant, but in the 1950s, Marc Sorkin supervised an eight-reel reconstruction at the Museum of Modern Art from two incomplete French and Italian prints. In 1991, the Munich Film Archives further restored it to near-original condition.

Valeska Gert, the sinister procuress, fondles Garbo in Joyless Street.

Coincidentally, just before *The Joyless Street*'s release, an American film on the same subject appeared: D. W. Griffith's *Isn't Life Wonderful?* (1924). Shot in Germany, it was a romantic drama in which postwar hardships were overcome through the power of love—a typically sentimental Griffith "statement," said the critics. Pabst's film was similarly criticized for the fact that, just when Garbo seems lost, a Yankee deus ex machina shows up to save the day.

But by contrast to Griffith, in the classic European versus American film dialectic of the day, Pabst's goal was not to suggest remedies. His realism was a moral protest, not a social prescription. "No film or novel," wrote film historian Paul Rotha, "has so truthfully recorded the despair of defeat, and the false values after war, as *The Joyless Street*."

If so, much of the credit went to the Swedish girl who now, to many, was *Pabst's* discovery as much as Stiller's, especially in France and elsewhere where *Gösta Berling* was little known. Garbo's acting had a restraint that was startling at the time, as fragile as her personality—even if it was largely the result of stage fright. That ripening style would become familiar in her later Hollywood films, and her director here was an important factor in nurturing it. Garbo, the "European actress," matured substantially in her short time with Pabst, whose brilliant direction of women depended on the nature of the women themselves.

"No director can take out of an actress what is not already her essence," said Louise Brooks—Asta Nielsen's "submissive sorrow," Brooks's own "corruption," Garbo's "purity." It was Pabst's deep and sympathetic understanding that brought Garbo's performance to fruition in *The Joyless Street*.

Pabst, for his part, never got over his awe of her.

"When I met him in '28," Brooks recalled, "he said, 'Do you know Garbo very well?' I said, 'Pretty well.' One's always very careful. And he raved about her. And one day we had tea in his apartment [with] Heinrich Mann and other people. Very intellectual tea and very boring. But he took me to a big cupboard, and he had just hundreds of stills of Garbo. Oh, he thought she was so marvelous! And he showed me all these stills, and talked about her, and talked about her, and talked about her."

Garbo was reciprocally fond of Pabst, and grateful, but there were few people she could tell about it—least of all, Stiller. Things were now seriously strained between them for the first time. After Garbo's lighting problem had been solved, Pabst banned Stiller from the set, which wounded Stiller's vanity and aroused powerful jealousy. Both his business affairs and his nerves were in bad shape, more so because he was dependent on Garbo's salary.

She, on the other hand, felt rather fine. She had liked working with Pabst, had picked up enough German to understand direction, and thought perhaps she might be happy living and making pictures in Berlin. In an uncharacteristically bold move, without consulting Stiller, she had spoken informally with Pabst about the possibility of signing a long-term contract with him, but when Stiller learned of it, he was enraged by the effrontery—and by the time it was taking for his own grander plans to materialize. At the Esplanade, in front of Einar Hanson, he accused her of monumental ingratitude and deceit. Tearfully, she promised to take no more initiatives without his approval, whereupon, switching to the patient father and taking her hands in his, he said, 'Stay with me, Greta. Moje knows what is best for you.' "

Pabst and Stiller had only one thing in common: Neither cared a bit about reviews, only about what they saw on screen. What they both saw—and competed for—was the coalescing of an extraordinary and unique film presence. Her German experience—the unexpectedly final stage of Garbo's European development—had an incalculable effect on the shaping of an artiste-in-the-making. If Stiller was her "outer" director, Pabst was the "inner" one who cultivated her psychological naturalism. During the first days of shooting *The Joyless Street*, said Louise Brooks, "everyone was screaming at Pabst to get rid of Garbo. 'She stinks, she is costing us money!' He heard them not. . . . He gained her confidence and she gave him the purest performance of her career."

Pabst, clearly, was more Garbo's kind of director—gentle, suggestive, unbullying. He rarely spoke above a whisper and always took her aside, very privately, for criticism. He was a revelation (and a relief) compared to Stiller, and he opened up a whole new perspective for her: the director as *non-tyrant*—a father figure without intimidation. Reevaluated in terms of her subsequent evolution, Pabst's influence on Garbo's acting was far more profound and lasting than Stiller's.

But just as she was reaching this threshold of "serious European film actress," the quintessential American movie mogul arrived in Berlin and set into motion the tearing away of her career from Europe forever.

Garbo blithely occupies the star's chair for a touch-up and script consultation with interpreter Sven-Hugo Borg, on the set of Torrent *(1926).*

CHAPTER 4

THE GREAT TRANSITION
1925–1926

The legend of Garbo's transition to America and her metamorphosis into a worldwide sensation are well known. And largely wrong. The myths of how Hollywood snared her can now be dispelled but are less intriguing than what happened once she got there: In the fierce competition among MGM actresses to reach stardom, all came up through the ranks except Garbo. She alone *began* as a star—clearly due to her own special qualities but also, less clearly, to a well-kept financial secret.

The hatching of MGM's "Garbo" from the Gustafson egg begins in Berlin with the fateful meeting of Stiller, Garbo, and Louis Mayer in November 1924—several weeks before the abortive Constantinople film and several months before *The Joyless Street*. Mayer was in Europe, wife and two daughters in tow, attending to a serious crisis having nothing to do with Swedes.

"The whole Berlin trip was very low-key because my father wanted discretion—there might be nothing accomplished," recalled Irene Mayer Selznick in her drawing room at the Hotel Pierre in New York, shortly before her death. "I don't think we stayed more than a day or two. He had to get back because the situation in Culver City was fraught with problems and he couldn't be fooling around."

Mayer (1885–1957) would become the most powerful film magnate in Hollywood during his quarter century at MGM's helm. But at that point, he was just vice president and general manager of a new company forged by Marcus Loew a few months earlier in the merger of Loew's Metro Pictures, the Samuel Goldwyn company, and Mayer's own film outfit. The huge headache of MGM's first year in operation was *Ben-Hur* (1926), inherited from Goldwyn, who had obtained screen rights to the Lew Wallace novel for the astounding price of 50 percent of the film's future income. Production problems were as massive as the picture's sets in Rome, where the snail-paced shooting was costing a fortune.

"The whole regime was new," said Irene Selznick, "and my father had never run such a big studio before. *Ben-Hur* had brought the company into Europe prematurely, and *Ben-Hur* was the whole point of that trip. There were kingdoms within kingdoms on that film. They'd created a world of their own, and unless stopped it was going to go on forever. The tail was wagging the dog. Rex Ingram, Alice Terry—they were all having a wonderful time at the Excelsior Hotel. He had to wind it up, decide whether to scrap it. June Mathis [*Ben-Hur*'s "writer-supervisor"] had to be eased out, and lots of other people had to be gotten rid of—heads were going to roll! The whole thing had to be dismantled, and it had to be done immediately.

"But even so, he was always interested in new talent, and he was very keen on Scandinavians. The one who had him really whipped up was Seastrom.* My father was mad about Seastrom—simplicity, dignity, charming European gentleman, big reputation and unspoiled, no show biz about him. He had talent and poise and my father believed every word he said. He was the one that put it in his head to go to Berlin and meet Mauritz Stiller, who happened to be in Germany with Garbo. Time was short, but it was arranged that we go to a projection room to see *Gösta Berling*."

The Sunday-afternoon screening was attended by Irene Mayer and her sister Edie, their parents, and Mayer's friend Basil Wrangell, who translated the titles so Mayer could follow the story. "My father was saying, 'This director's wonderful, but what we really ought to look at is the girl,'" the daughter recalled. "This we learned on our way to the projection room."

How did he know to look for her? Mayer had as many secrets as Stiller and then some. His rival B. P. Schulberg at Paramount called him "Czar of all the rushes." Nothing escaped Mayer, who had, in fact, already seen *Gösta Berling* in Hollywood before leaving for Europe. Lillian Gish had asked him to look at it because she wanted Lars Hanson to play opposite her in *The Scarlet Letter*. No one present knew that this dramatic moment in Berlin was actually Mayer's *second* viewing of the film.

Irene Selznick recalled the film as not very fascinating, but Mayer's reaction to Garbo as very much so:

> The first look my father got, he spoke up—"Look at that girl! There's no physical resemblance, but she reminds me of Norma Talmadge—

---

* The Americanized version of Victor Sjöström's name.

her eyes. The thing that makes Talmadge a star is the look in her eyes." He didn't stop talking. I never heard him talk so much, comparing Garbo to Norma Talmadge—the feeling they both gave you as a womanly heart, a kind of gentleness you rarely saw in an actress. He said, "Stiller's fine, but the girl, look at the girl!" Then he said he'd have to be careful, that tact was required—and my father was not too tactful. He kept saying if he had to choose, the director could stay, he was taking the girl. He said, "I'll take her without him, or I'll take them both. Number one is the girl."

So it was not true that Mayer primarily wanted Stiller and took Garbo only in order to get him?

"Absolute nonsense," Selznick declared. "It was settled within ten minutes. He was hell-bent.* He said it had not to do with beauty, 'It's what she conveys and the expression emanating from her eyes.' He wanted to meet her that day, and a meeting was arranged for our hotel."

Mayer preceded his family back to the Adlon, where Irene and Edie returned later in the afternoon for dinner. "We got in the elevator and this girl got on with us and got out on our floor," Irene recalled. "Her black taffeta hat was not flattering, nor chic nor youthful. Everything she wore was dark—the clothes didn't enhance her. She had on no make-up. She certainly didn't look like an actress. You wouldn't turn your head. While we were waiting for someone to open the door, we smiled. Inside, my father and Stiller had been conferring for quite a while. We were all introduced, and then the Mayer girls politely withdrew."

Mayer's daughters were never to be present when business was discussed.† But they were soon informed that the Swedish guests had been invited to dinner. Be ready in ten minutes. Downstairs to the Maiden Room of the Adlon trooped the Mayers, Stiller, Wrangell, and Garbo, whom Irene described as "shy but not bashful at the table. She was contained—charming, reasonably poised. You didn't think, 'Oh, the poor thing.' She didn't try to do a rise-and-shine number. No performing, perfectly normal." Irene's attention was riveted not on Garbo but on Stiller:

---

* This account contradicts and postdates the one in Selznick's memoirs: "The only advance reservation my father had about [Stiller] was the stipulation that he wouldn't come to Hollywood without his new leading lady, an obstacle my father thought he could overcome. Instead, Miss Garbo overcame him in the first reel."

† Stiller and Mayer, contrary to many accounts, did not converse in Yiddish. "I never heard my father speak Yiddish in any business situation," said Irene. "He spoke Yiddish only with some of the poor relatives or very rarely to my mother so the children wouldn't understand." The talks with Stiller were conducted in a mix of English and German, with the assistance of the polyglot Wrangell.

He was such a frightening-looking man. Enormously tall. Since when is tall bad? In this case, it was bad. His fingers and hands and feet were so long—it was a kind of disease [acromegaly], this extra growth. It was hard to look at him because he had something wrong with one eye—it wandered and watered off and on, you've seen it on a dog—unattractive. He wasn't revolting, but it was hard to shake hands with him, with those abnormally big hands and the fingers misshapen. He was gentle, but very unnerving with that eye—a kind face, but the features were out of proportion. If I'd been younger, I'd have been scared to death. He looked like Jack the Giant Killer on the bookjacket when I was a kid. He and the girl were an odd combination, indeed.

Four years later, Garbo told a Swedish journalist:

"Not much was said about me. Mr. Mayer hardly looked at me the first time I met him. He put a contract before me. I asked Stiller if I should sign. I always obeyed Stiller instinctively. Often I did not even know what my salary was to be. He arranged everything and gave me the money. . . . Stiller told me to sign it, and I did. I was to get $100 a week for forty weeks the first year, $600 the second year and $750 the third."*

She was intrigued but unenthusiastic about the prospect of coming to America. Always conservative, she was inclined to stay in Berlin, or at least Europe, with its known quantities. But Stiller's pressure, as always, outweighed her ambivalence.

"All this transpired instantly," said Irene. "My father's enthusiasm was enormous, and Stiller was delighted with the reception and the fact that the girl met with approval."

Over the years, many would lay claim to the discovery of Greta Garbo, including Josef von Sternberg, who had arrived in Hollywood earlier that year and declared that Mayer "consulted me often, and had even accepted my advice to import Mauritz Stiller and asked him to include Greta Garbo in his luggage." Maybe or maybe not. In any case, Irene recalled that her father spoke no more of them until many months later: "It was a to-be-continued thing. This was just the first chapter. It was a long time before she showed up. This was not, 'Hollywood, here I come!' "

Certainly not on Garbo's part. Stiller, too, was in no hurry. He had the Constantinople film to make for Trianon, and his grand European film combine deal with UFA and Ivar Kreuger was still in the works. But Mayer knew nothing of Stiller's other schemes and options. On November 27, 1924,

* Mayer also offered contracts to Lars Hanson and Mona Mårtenson, the other *Gösta Berling* co-stars. Hanson came immediately and had great success. Mårtenson didn't show up for five years and was a disaster when she did.

just twenty-four hours after their meeting, he dictated a letter of agreement
to Stiller on MGM-Berlin stationery:

> This is to confirm our oral contract of November 26, 1924. . . . We
> have the exclusive right to use of your name which is to be known as
> Maurice Stiller. . . . You agree to sail from Europe not later than May
> 1st 1925. . . . Your salary is to be $1,000 per week. . . . You are to
> receive the same kind of advertising and publicity as Victor Seastrom
> and others of our first class directors. . . . It is also understood and
> agreed that you will conduct yourself in America in a manner that
> your name and standing shall not become [disreputable] with the
> public. . . .

The most fascinating thing about that document is its omission: no mention
whatsoever of Greta Garbo. If Mayer truly wanted Garbo more than Stiller,
he was doing his best to make sure neither of them knew it. When weeks
went by without a response, Mayer's lobbying escalated to the shameless use
of Victor Sjöström. On February 7, 1925, Sjöström from San Diego wired
Stiller in Berlin: "Splendid treatment. Got no percentage yet [for his hit film
He Who Gets Slapped] but received bonus."

The Trianon film had fallen through by then. Stiller—as if unaware of
his MGM commitment—negotiated a two-year UFA contract on April 20,
1925, for "Greta Gabor" ($450 per week for the first year, $650 the second).
But his maneuvers were now catching up with him. In a May 18, 1925,
telegram to Mayer from Stockholm, he tried to stall: His complex financial
ties to Svensk Filmindustri prevented his coming to Hollywood until a
distribution arrangement for his future films was worked out between SF
and MGM. "All this," he said, "together with what I before have wired you
of my artistical state of mind is the reason [for] my hesitation."

Mayer was unmoved by Stiller's artistical state of mind. On May 27, 1925,
he fired back a telegram informing Stiller: "We have contract with you and
expect you [to] live up to it. . . . Cannot complicate contract with matters
connected with [SF]. If you have obligations with [SF] you must adjust them;
you were not afraid [to] come [to] America when you talked with me; and
Seastrom doing very well in America. All these matters are your personal
affairs. We cannot change from original proposition. Advise me when you
sail."

With no firmer deal in hand, Stiller gave in. His and Garbo's transition
to the New World had been delayed for six months. It began, finally, on
the last day of June 1925, with a short train ride from Stockholm to the
Swedish port of Göteborg.

"Both Mother and I were sad about my going," Garbo said. "But we never let on. Mother and my brother and sister saw me off at the station. Mother's eyes were swollen. 'Don't cry,' I said, 'I'll be back in a year—12 short months that will hurry by!' 'Yes,' said Mother. 'Just a year. . . .' "

Had mother and daughter known it would be three years before they saw each other again, Stiller might not have coaxed the nervous, nineteen-year-old girl up the gangplank of the *Drottningholm* for the first and most important ocean voyage of her life. But once on board, she was enchanted.

"The sea is wonderful," Garbo said later. "Nowhere does one feel so free! At the same time one is caught—there is no escape. Then, in port, one is free to go, and the sense of freedom is gone. . . . Never before or since have I enjoyed the bliss of perfect solitude as I did on that journey."

Bliss reverted to angst upon arrival in New York, July 6, 1925, where her reception was less than tumultuous. A few days before, MGM publicity man Hubert Voight had received a telegram in his Manhattan office: STILLER ARRIVING GRIPSHOLM ACCOMPANIED BY GRETA GUSTAFSSON. MEET THEM AND EXTEND COURTESY. No more, no less. "I hate that name, 'Garbo,' " MGM publicity chief Howard Dietz told Voight that day. "It reminds me of 'garbage.' See if you can come up with something better for her." It was an indication of her unimportance that the publicity department never got around to it and was never reminded to do so. Dietz asked Voight to arrange accommodations and entertainment for Garbo and Stiller in New York but added, "For God's sake, Voight, don't spend any money on them!" Voight tried to lure some newsmen to meet them at the bay, but the advance photos of a plump, frizzy-haired Swedish girl failed to tempt them. For ten dollars, paid in advance, he induced free-lance photographer James Sileo to show up, with Kaj Gynt—her childhood friend, relocated to New York—as interpreter. As the boat docked, they saw Garbo in a checked suit gazing in rapture at the skyline. Sileo had exactly three plates in his camera, but when he saw her childish delight at being asked to pose, he went through the motions of shooting her for another half-hour. Said Voight later: "She would have climbed the smokestack if the idea had been suggested to her."

Voight had dutifully arranged for the Swedes to stay at the Commodore Hotel, a modest Forty-second Street establishment (now the Grand Hyatt) that was part of Grand Central Station and within walking distance of MGM's office on Broadway. He was told to get them two rooms with an adjoining door, and he did so. As soon as the photo session was over, he hailed a cab. "On the way there," he said, "she wanted to see the Woolworth Building. She had terror in her eyes over the big buildings, but Stiller was placid and hunched down in his seat in the corner. . . . She thought I was a lot of fun . . . probably because I was the first American boy she had ever met [and] she was such a kid herself."

Voight and Garbo were together virtually every day of her first six weeks in America. "I took them out to dinner every evening and took them to the shows and the speakeasies," he said. "They danced together and enjoyed themselves immensely night after night. Yet Stiller always made sure that I kept my distance so that nothing developed between Garbo and me. He was always in the middle, with Garbo on one side of him and me on the other. I never danced with her. I wanted to, but when I asked her she deferred to him, and [he] just wouldn't allow it."

During the day, Voight and Garbo went sightseeing while Stiller haunted the MGM office with unsolicited script ideas, handwritten in Swedish. Voight persuaded reporter Gladys Hall of *Movie Weekly* to interview Garbo, but all she could get her to say was, "Mr. Stiller, he is a great director."

After she begged him for two days, Voight took Garbo to Coney Island, where she stayed on the roller coaster for almost an hour. "I was nearly broke," he said. "She ate all sorts of hot dogs and popcorn and taffy and shouted like a little boy over the different amusing things." But in the excitement and windy weather that day, Garbo caught cold and was in bed, sniffling, the next morning when Voight brought columnist W. Adolphe Roberts of *Motion Picture Magazine* to the Commodore, with interpreter Gynt, for an interview.

"I had got down on my knees and begged him to do it," recalled Voight. "We knocked on the door but she did not answer. My heart was in my mouth. Finally, I shoved the door and it opened just so far where a chain held it. 'Greta!' I called. Then I looked in. She was sitting in bed reading calmly. I told her why I had come, and . . . she finally glanced up at me over the top of her magazine. Her eyes looked very blue and clear. 'Hoobert,' she said, 'Hoobert, go avay and stay avay!'"

Roberts got in a question or two through the door: "It would not be the right thing for the photographer and myself actually to enter the room, we were told. It was a lesson in Swedish etiquette. [She said] she adores America but is it always as hot as this in summer? She looks forward to her work in Hollywood—if she survives the heat—marvelous skyscrapers here—the world's best movies—but heat, *heat*, HEAT!"

Once over her cold, she wanted to go to the theater, and Voight took her to *Valencia*. "Garbo started to hum the tune when we left the theater," he said, and "was singing it furiously by the time we got home. She loved that song. She doesn't sing very well, either. . . . She loves jazz. . . . I introduced her to my boss, [Howard] Dietz, but he was unimpressed. I phoned Nicholas Schenck and asked if he wouldn't like to meet Garbo, but Mr. Schenck said, 'No-thank-you-he-was-much-too-busy.'"

Undaunted, the diligent Voight persuaded photographer Russell Ball to take pictures of her at the hotel. At one point, Ball said he'd like her in something colorful, but Garbo was uncomprehending. Voight did a kind of Spanish-dance pantomime, pointing to some bright colors. She nodded sagely, left, and returned "wearing a veil of gossamer-like material—very alluring, and but for that had nothing on but her skirt."

One day, Garbo dropped by the MGM office in New York, where an executive asked her, "Well, Miss Garbo, are you satisfied with your fine contract?" According to Kaj Gynt, who accompanied her to translate, Garbo was wandering about his office, looking at the framed pictures of the stars, and replied over her shoulder, "No. I am not. Is not enough."

The wait in New York dragged on for a month and took its toll on everyone's nerves, Stiller's most of all. To pass the time, they took in more Broadway shows, including the *Ziegfeld Follies of 1925*, with W. C. Fields, Will Rogers, and Fanny Brice. According to legend, the delay was premeditated by Mayer—to let Stiller cool his heels and learn who was boss. In fact, the Swedes were just low on the priority list in Culver City, where a couple of legal problems had developed: Garbo was a minor when she signed her Berlin contract, which would not stand up in an American court and had to be redrafted. Moreover, Mayer was now demanding that she sign up for two additional years. "I tried to explain, in my bad English, that . . . I wanted no changes until I had at least played a part for him," said Garbo later. "But he insisted, saying that he could not risk his money on me unless I was under a five-year contract."

The summer heat and the number of Garbo's cold baths to escape it increased, while the battle of wills—or simple procrastination—went on. Stiller was so disaffected by the delays that he tried to negotiate out of his whole deal, but the studio refused to release him. Failing that, he introduced a new stumbling block, insisting on a 400 percent increase in Garbo's salary as part of her revised contract.

He was emboldened to do so, in part, by a stroke of luck. One of his few friends in New York was Swedish actress Martha Hedman, who introduced him and Garbo to Arnold Genthe—a philologist who longed to be a painter but became a photographer instead. At Genthe's studio on the top floor of a house on Forty-ninth Street, Garbo was impressed with his portraits and said she would like him to photograph her someday, to which he replied, "Why not now?"

"No, not now," she demurred. "Look at my dress—and I don't like my hair."

"Never mind that," said Genthe. "I am more interested in your eyes and in what is behind that extraordinary forehead."

Genthe's subjects had included Anna Pavlova, Isadora Duncan, and Fyodor Chaliapin. Chaliapin had sat down, thrown back his head, sung a Russian ballad, and then informed Genthe that he was ready to "make pose"—by which time Genthe had already made photos. Genthe hated the fact that all film-star portraits looked alike. If he were in Hollywood, he once said, he would never take a single smile. At the moment, he was fascinated—among other things—by his subject's hands. "Unconsciously," he said, "Garbo's hands express the feeling of her soul."

The Garbo-Genthe photo session yielded spectacular results. In Genthe's portraits, she is extraordinarily expressive, vulnerable, and brooding.* Excited by their quality, he took his pictures to Frank Crowninshield, editor of *Vanity Fair*. Who was the girl? he wanted to know. When told, he replied, "Never heard of her," but allowed as how he might be able to use one of the shots. "Only if you give it a full page," Genthe insisted, and Crowninshield okayed one for the November issue.

But that was five months away and of little use now. In August, Garbo stopped by Genthe's studio to thank him—and to say goodbye. "They don't seem to want me," she told him. "They say I'm [not] a type. I'm going back to Berlin." She and Stiller were, in fact, perilously close to doing so, but Genthe insisted they show his portraits to MGM before giving up. Stiller followed through and sent a packet of them by messenger to MGM, where Genthe's images aroused keen interest.

The essence of Garbo could only be seen through a camera lens, and when the front office saw Genthe's evidence of her haunting sensuality, things suddenly changed: MGM sent money and told Stiller to head west immediately, agreeing to the revised salary of four hundred dollars a week for Garbo, in exchange for her signature on a new contract saying she had her mother's permission to work as a minor.

Not everyone was convinced of her worth. After Garbo signed her new contract in New York, MGM vice president Edward Bowes held Voight back and whispered, "What an awkward girl . . . a peasant type! She'll never live out that contract. The studio will have her back here in six months and on her way back to Sweden."

Famous last words. In effect, it was the first in Garbo's unbroken string of victories over her studio. Genthe's photos were compelling, but no more than the needs of the MGM legal department, which was inclined to bail out of a costly deal with two risky foreigners. A four-hundred-dollar starting salary for an unproven actress was unusual proof of how much MGM really wanted her. Stiller's gamble had paid off—for Garbo. Mayer, after all, wanted

* See photo insert for Genthe "Portrait Portfolio" shot.

"the girl." But Moje's heavy-handed bargaining tactics earned him the ominous rage of his new boss.

In the first week of September, after two months of waiting and sweltering, the *Twentieth Century* looked like a chariot to heaven when Garbo and Stiller boarded it at Grand Central. They were accompanied on the five-day journey west by a mysteriously acquired "secretary" to Stiller, Olaf Rolf, who was never heard from again once they arrived in California.

That was perhaps a relief: Stiller's previous "private secretary" in Sweden, a man named Carlo Keil-Moller, was currently causing him a lot of problems. A few days earlier, on August 31, Keil-Moller had sent Stiller a telegram reminding him that he had been engaged for a full year at one thousand kronor per month and was filing suit for the unpaid balance of his salary. Two days later, on September 2, he again cabled Stiller in New York, this time with an ugly threat: "Non-acceptance [of this demand] entailing sequestration Swedish property, your renown irrevocably ruined." Stiller had a history of engaging handsome young men for duties that sometimes went beyond the secretarial and into the sexual realm. In this case, his lawyers on both sides of the Atlantic advised him to pay off, and Stiller did.

He and Garbo and presumably Olaf had a relaxing trip. Their train route was to Chicago, then south through the heart of the Midwest—Illinois, Kansas—and southwest through Colorado, New Mexico, and Arizona. The incredible expanse of the Great Plains and grandeur of the deserts had a strong impact on the Swedes, neither of whom would ever see much more of the United States than this.

The goal of the odyssey was what Dorothy Parker called "72 suburbs in search of a city"; a place with "all the personality of a paper cup," in Raymond Chandler's view; but in Moss Hart's, "the most beautiful slave quarters in the world": Los Angeles. On September 10, Garbo, Stiller, and Olaf were met there by a score of Scandinavians, including Victor Sjöström, Karl Dane, Anna Q. Nilsson, Gertrude Olmstead, and Stiller's brother Wilhelm, "real estate and investments" consultant in Los Angeles, whom he had not seen in thirty-five years. By contrast with New York, it was a truly warm reception. A number of bona fide reporters and photographers were on hand to record it, and before MGM publicity man Pete Smith could take control, a newsman got to Garbo and asked where she was going to live. Her charmingly naïve response was, "I would like to find a room with a nice private family." The scribes traded "uh-oh" glances, and Smith would soon be having a little talk with her—the message of which was "Be careful, not honest." Right off the bat, she had committed a faux pas that, when explained to her, made her even warier of the press thereafter.

The Swedish colony in Hollywood welcomes Garbo and Stiller on their arrival,
September 10, 1925.

Garbo was installed in Santa Monica, not with a nice private family but
at the Miramar Hotel (now the Miramar-Sheraton) on Wilshire Boulevard.
She had a bedroom–living room, a kitchenette, a bathroom, and window
that looked out onto the Pacific Ocean. The Miramar, at that time, consisted
of the 1889 mansion built by Nevada silver tycoon John P. Jones, plus a new
six-story brick addition erected the year before, where Garbo's rooms were
located. She lived there longer than at any subsequent address in Los
Angeles—nearly three years. Stiller was settled not far away in a small Santa
Monica beach house rented for him by the studio. Of all the émigré film
figures to invade Hollywood, Stiller and Garbo struck everyone as among
the most out of place. Even at the beach, they could be observed in their
odd domestic ways, Stiller with his pipe and Garbo peeling potatoes.

"They were a melancholy pair," said an anonymous Miramar resident at
the time. "She was really quite unattractive. Her hair was kinky, and her
teeth were not good. Nobody paid any attention to her, and she was very
unhappy. So was Stiller. They used to sit on the terrace, staring out at the
ocean and looking gloomy. We used to call them 'grandma and grampa.'"
In those first lonely weeks, she was largely snubbed. Once, she overheard

someone say, "I don't see why Stiller brought that Garbo girl to Hollywood with him. It's like bringing a sandwich to a banquet."

Without much else to do, she spent hours wandering along the beach and through the windswept grass overlooking the bay—a solitary and scenic form of waiting that suited her melancholy. September, October, and most of November went by, and still no film project. She and Stiller went out rarely, but in early December, Erich Pommer invited them to a Shrine Auditorium concert by Chaliapin, the great basso, and to dinner later at Pommer's home. Among the guests was director Rowland V. Lee, who tried to make conversation with Garbo but found her withdrawn and laconic to the point of appearing half-asleep:

> She spoke very little English. Sometimes she pretended to know even less. But when Jack Gilbert's name came up—he was the hottest thing in pictures just then—her eyes lit up. When I told her I knew him, she roused herself to a pitch of excitement. Her English became better. . . . She asked me question after question about him. Jack Gilbert was all she wanted to talk about, how marvelous, how wonderful, how charming he was. . . . She stayed glued to my side for the rest of the evening and never once allowed me to change the subject.

In 1925, after Calvin Coolidge, John Gilbert was probably the most famous man in America. His previous popularity was magnified by his starring roles in MGM's two great films that year, von Stroheim's *The Merry Widow* and King Vidor's *The Big Parade*, the powerful World War I spectacle that proved Gilbert a serious dramatic actor as well as a lover. The preeminence of Louis Mayer's new company was speedily established: If *Ben-Hur* first put MGM on the map, *The Merry Widow* was its coming-of-age. With *The Big Parade*, MGM not only caught up with Paramount but pulled ahead of its rival and lent new stature to the whole industry.

"During the shooting my father caught the excitement of Irving [Thalberg] and King Vidor," wrote Irene Selznick. "It was the beginning of the Thalberg legend and also of Irving's habit of retakes"—the extravagant practice behind Thalberg's theory, "Movies aren't made, they're remade." In *The Big Parade*, that approach resulted not only in a superb film but in turning a simple matinee idol, John Gilbert, into a great star.

No one but Stiller was much interested in a great star-to-be from Sweden. He badgered Thalberg daily to come up with her first vehicle and his own as a Hollywood director—in the same film, it was assumed. Meanwhile, he had to park her somewhere, and the perfect place was right on the MGM lot in something close to an "all-Scandinavian production."

———

Victor Sjöström, Garbo, and Mauritz Stiller on the MGM lot in Culver City, 1925

When Louis B. Mayer first told Lillian Gish that *The Scarlet Letter* was morally off-limits for the screen, she replied, "Mr. Mayer, this cannot be. It's an American classic, taught in all our schools." She was a persuasive woman of unassailable virtue, and permission to make the film was finally granted on the condition that Gish—and no one else—play the lead. Asked which director she wanted, Gish chose Victor Sjöström.

"I felt that the Swedes were closer to the feeling of the New England puritans than modern Americans," she said and, as usual, her instinct was correct. MGM was eager to duplicate the success of Sjöström's recent *He Who Gets Slapped* (1924)—so popular that two parodies (*He Who Gets Kicked* and *He Who Gets Belted*) were quickly slapped together to capitalize on it—and to develop Sjöström seriously as one of its flagship directors. In *The Scarlet Letter*, he would not only be working with the great Gish but also, for the first time in America, with a Swedish actor he knew well, Lars Hanson, who turned in a moving performance as Dimmesdale. Other Nordic types abounded: Gangly Karl Dane had a small comic role. Costumes were by the Swedish-Danish designer Max Rée. Behind the camera was Dutch-born Henrik Sartov, one of the industry's finest cinematographers and lighting experts.

Being around fellow Scandinavians might cheer Garbo up, Stiller thought, and with Sjöström's approval, he deposited her almost daily on the *Letter* set, while he laid siege to the executive offices in search of a directing assignment. He thought she might learn from watching Gish perform, and maybe even from watching Sjöström. Garbo did learn a lot—and so did Lillian Gish.

"His direction was a great education for me," said Gish. "In a sense I went through the Swedish school of acting. I had got rather close to the Italian school [which] is one of elaboration; the Swedish is one of repression." In *The Scarlet Letter*, Sjöström fused tragic lyricism and landscape.*

Gish, in turn, was an education for Garbo. There could have been no more professional role model than Gish, carefully studying and rehearsing her Hester, always attentive to how the camera angles and lighting would most enhance each scene. Equally revealing to Garbo was the way Gish dealt with MGM, declining bad projects and eschewing publicity nonsense.

The studio's promotional concept for Garbo was crude: Swedish girls were

---

* Two years later, in 1928, Sjöström achieved an even greater fusion of those elements with Gish in *The Wind*, his neglected American masterpiece. The poor reception for *The Wind* is usually attributed to its lame-duck status as a silent in the transition to sound film. But ironically, it was due more to MGM's waning interest in Gish and full concentration on Garbo at that time.

athletic and outdoorsy, right? When Garbo complained of having to pose with the USC track team and with lions, Gish advised her simply to refuse. She got similar advice from Lon Chaney, a favorite of the Swedish colony ever since working with Sjöström in *He Who Gets Slapped*. "If you let them know too much about you," Chaney told her, "they will lose interest." Retaining a sense of mystery had worked for him, and would for her.*

As Garbo studied and spoke with Gish at work, a personal friendship was developing as well. Gish seemed to understand the girl. "Garbo's temperament," she wrote later, "reflected the rain and gloom of the long, dark Swedish winters. . . . They were humiliating her, putting her in a one-piece bathing suit and taking pictures of her, and you know her personality—how embarrassed she would be."

Stiller, too, was protesting the undignified nature of the photo sessions—to Mayer personally—and soon the word came down to Pete Smith, who passed it along with a fine snarl to his staff: "No more pictures of this Swedish dame." She wasn't so great to look at anyway, in his opinion. Indeed, one reason for the delay in Garbo's Hollywood film debut was her appearance, which as yet did not bowl over her studio chiefs. She was still in training: A strict diet had been ordered by Thalberg, who further decreed that her teeth be straightened. After those cosmetic enhancements came another valuable service from Lillian Gish.

Before Henrik Sartov entered motion pictures, he had taken some of Gish's best portrait photos in New York. She had provided his entrée to D. W. Griffith and was rewarded with Sartov's genius at soft-focus effects that showed her to fine advantage in *Hearts of the World* (1918) and many other Griffith films. Sartov had devised a method of reducing a dozen lenses to one combination that could fit into other lenses without f-stops. Stiller, to his fury, had been excluded from the making of Garbo's original MGM screen test, which failed to impress anybody. Gish now suggested that Sartov shoot a new one. Stiller excitedly—Thalberg, grudgingly—agreed.

Garbo's first test, Sartov told film historian Kevin Brownlow, had been badly lit, failing to bring out her depth. "I had the reputation, on account of this lens, that I could make anybody beautiful—or seem to bring out their beauty." Sartov's lens and magical ability to "clean out" the face through spot lighting did exactly that for Garbo. When the studio executives viewed

---

* A year later, Chaney declared, "Garbo is the Bernhardt of the screen. She is the greatest feminine personality I ever have ever seen in the theater or in films."

*Garbo, here with
USC athletic trainer
and masseur Jannes
Andersson, will soon
flex her star power
and refuse to pose for
this kind of
photograph.*

*Another of the early
MGM publicity shots
Garbo loathed, 1925*

ABOVE: *In* Joyless Street, *Garbo's right front tooth is decidedly protruberant over the left one.*
BELOW: *Thalberg had the problem corrected, and two years later in 1927 her teeth were perfectly aligned.*

Sartov's results—along with some newsreel flood footage for an upcoming film, *Torrent*—director Monta Bell immediately pegged Garbo to play opposite "the MGM Valentino," Ricardo Cortez.

Her improbable role—turned down by Norma Shearer—was Leonora in a melodrama based on *Entre Naranjos* (*Among Orange Trees*) by Vicente Blasco Ibáñez. But the joy of getting to work was dampened by a huge letdown: Had Garbo and Stiller known that Bell—not Stiller—would direct her first American movie, neither Swede would have come to America. They were both deeply disturbed. It was galling to Stiller that he would not be allowed to shepherd his own "creation" through her initial Hollywood challenge. Yet his devastation has been exaggerated. He was still in control of Garbo's every move; had he told her to refuse the assignment, she would have done so. But instead of recommending rebellion, he advised her to accept. Stiller knew that playing opposite Cortez would be a prestigious launching of her American career. Ever calculating, he was also willing to distance his own career from hers, to some extent, in case she should fail. Garbo was his greatest treasure, but not his only option; as a matter of pragmatism and ego, he did not regard his own aspirations as tied exclusively to her.

Besides that, Stiller saw no danger of losing control of his protégée: He would surreptitiously "direct" her by night, coaching her every move for the next day's shooting. Leonora starts out as an innocent village girl who falls in love with a mother-dominated weakling. It was not a complex role, but the more difficult for its cardboard nature. Garbo needed all the help she could get from Stiller, especially in view of the language barrier. Director Bell's assistance was minimal, and she got none at all from her haughty co-star.

The "Latin" Ricardo Cortez was really Jack Krantz of Vienna, married to actress Alma Rubens, whose fatal heroin addiction contributed to his bad disposition. "He was rude, nasty, pompous and everybody hated him," says Lina Basquette, who later co-starred with Cortez in Frank Capra's *The Younger Generation* (1929), in which he played a Jew who changes his surname to gain social acceptance. "He was one of the first 'temperamental' male stars because he thought he was going to be the next Valentino. In the Capra picture, even Jean Hersholt couldn't stand him, and Jean loved everybody!"

Cortez took pride, afterward, in claiming (erroneously) to be the only person ever billed above Garbo. "No one had any idea she was going to bust into a topflight star," he told Kevin Brownlow forty years later. "She was unknown—kind of a gawky individual. Not what we'd consider an attraction. The structure of the face and eyes, I think, is what people were attracted to. Strange quality—introverted, electric."

Photographed for Torrent *(1926)*

On the set, Cortez was highly disdainful of a newcomer with whom he felt "stuck." Faced with his contempt and separated from Stiller, Garbo withdrew even further. Her state of mind was revealed one day to cameraman William Daniels, who heard her say, "I'm important." Someone replied, "Why, you're the most important person around." And she said, "Important Garbo—important sardines—just the same." Still struggling with English, she meant "imported." Indeed, her first real language classroom was the *Torrent* set.

"I didn't learn English quickly," she said later. At first, she had an interpreter named Sven-Hugo Borg, who translated Monta Bell's directions to her. "I used to ask him to let me puzzle out things by myself before he'd help me. . . . The first English I learned was slang. I remember how proud I was when I learned to say, 'Applesauce!' with just the right accent. . . .

"One night I got quite eloquent in my broken English when we were filming *Torrent* and had to do a rain-storm scene. Monta Bell told me I ought to be used to cold, coming as I did from Sweden where there is nothing but ice and snow. I became quite insulted and insisted upon telling him all about our beautiful lakes, our orchards and the wonderful climate."

Brevity was the soul of her English, for the most part. One day during *Torrent* production, she was standing beneath a fig tree on the MGM lot, eating a piece of the fruit in ignorance of a sign that said not to touch it. A studio cop approached and barked, "Don't pull them figs! Whatsa matter, can'cha read?" Garbo eyed him coldly and, as she strolled away, said by way of reply, "Beat it!"

There were xenophobic chips on many shoulders. *Photoplay* had recently published a tirade against the "menace" of invaders from abroad: "Foreigners are going through the studios with the speed of mumps through a day nursery." Fred Niblo, with whom Garbo would soon come in closer contact, expressed an opinion common among American directors of the period:

"An all-American cast is an unknown quantity in movietown. The English tongue is becoming a lost art in Hollywood. Russian, Swedish, and German interpreters are regularly employed in the studios. I have yet to direct one picture in which other nationalities are not dominant."

Monta Bell had his own communication difficulties with Garbo and once yelled, "Get that big woman back here on the set!" But all things considered, production went rather smoothly. In retrospect, everything about *Torrent* seemed of historical note, including the fourteen-year-old double hired to ride for her—Joel McCrea: "My job was to ride a horse onto the scene and pull him up so sharply that he would slide through the mud on his hind legs. I did it twice for the cameras. [But Garbo] protested it was too dangerous

Garbo confers with Monta Bell, the director of Torrent, *in a publicity rather than a candid photograph: Little could have been communicated between them without an interpreter.*

Garbo with studio musicians, the mood-makers on the Torrent *set*

Left to right: *Monta Bell, Garbo, unidentified, Ricardo Cortez. Garbo is now transformed with sleek butch hairdo.*

for a youngster and insisted on trying it herself. She did—but it was my stuff that was used. She had plenty of nerve."

In the first reels, Garbo appears much as Cortez described her: tall, gawky and not especially beautiful. She resembles many another actress of the period, a bit frumpy and with a distinctly unflattering coiffure. But after she goes to Paris and becomes "La Brunna," the great opera singer, Garbo is suddenly a different woman—sexy, sleek, and sophisticated in her new "butch" hairdo. She keeps her diva status a secret when she returns home, hugging her mother in the slightly stooped posture that would become her trademark —a self-conscious effort to compensate for the fact she was often taller than her co-stars. During her rejection by Cortez, she overacts badly, to match the intertitle ("Oh God, why can't I hate him?"). But on the lighter side, Garbo laughs! She does so frequently, thirteen years before *Ninotchka*—a wild, rueful rather than joyous laugh.

Except for a few such striking moments, there is nothing spectacular about the film or the photography, save for the flood scenes that Daniels did not shoot and some lovely close-ups—particularly the final one—of Garbo's face. Nor was there anything noteworthy about Bell's direction or MGM's backlot Spain.

When *Torrent* previewed in a little theater in Beverly Hills, no one noticed Garbo and Stiller as they slipped quietly into seats in the rear and then stole out as the picture ended; she set her own precedent by not appearing at the premiere.

She had played just a hussy with some redeeming qualities, opposite a wimp with none, but the film's redemption was in her eyes and her restraint, and MGM was thrilled with the steamy results. Studio executives had been watching the daily rushes with amazement—watching Garbo create something soulful and enchanting out of something quite stale and thin.

The critics, too, were pleased, noting her "surprising propensity for looking like Carol Dempster, Norma Talmadge, ZaSu Pitts and Gloria Swanson in turn." Some of her gestures and attitudes—thrown-back head, imploring eyes—seemed to come straight out of Talmadge's *Camille*. Mayer had been right! Richard Watts, Jr., in the New York *Herald Tribune* stressed the Swanson resemblance; in one "Gloria Garbo" pose, she had puffed languidly on a cigarette and declared, "I will not come between a man and his mother."

A few sharp eyes even noticed a "cloak of tender irony" with which she transcended such material.

Six decades later, ninety-three-year-old silent star Aileen Pringle was still furious with Louis B. Mayer: "He gave Garbo two of my films—they were supposed to be *my* pictures!" It was bad enough to lose *Torrent* and watch it launch Garbo. Insult to injury was *The Temptress*—the Swede's second MGM outing, which likewise came at Pringle's expense.

Having "defined" her as a vamp, the studio rushed to package Garbo again in an even more exotic Blasco Ibáñez melodrama, *La Tierra de Todos* (*Everyone's Land*). Its film version, *The Temptress*, was a series of clichés, but Garbo's consolation was that Stiller would direct. He had aggravated the studio on several counts, but he still might have survived at MGM—had he not now run afoul of Garbo's new co-star, Antonio Moreno.

"Tony Moreno was everything Ricardo Cortez would like to have been —not least of all, an authentic Latin," says Lina Basquette. A veteran star with powerful studio influence, Moreno had definite ideas about how his public wished to see him. Among the weighty issues over which he and Stiller instantly locked horns was his moustache (the director wanted him to shave it). Then came a row over Stiller's order, and Moreno's refusal, to wear larger shoes in order to make Garbo's feet look smaller. Everyone was

Historic production photos shot moments apart.
ABOVE: *Mauritz Stiller coaxes the willing Garbo and the hostile Antonio Moreno.*
William Daniels holds the camera for The Temptress, *April 17, 1926.*
BELOW: *Stiller and stars with unlikely visitors Lon Chaney, in grotesque makeup on a*
break from shooting The Road to Mandalay, *and director Fred Niblo—aware or*
unaware that he would replace Stiller within forty-eight hours?

irate, most of all Stiller: "They get me over here to make pictures because they like my methods. Then they will not let me use my methods. Instead they try to tell me how to make the picture."

In Sweden, Stiller's word had been law on the set, and in Hollywood he would tolerate no interference—least of all from the performers. But he was frustrated by his poor command of English and often got mixed up when excited, shouting "Stop!" instead of "Go!" for camera action, and then howling in exasperation at the result. Behind his back, people were laughing at him. Moreno's bitter complaints to Thalberg, plus mounting concern about Stiller's slow, expensive "European" production methods, sealed the director's removal from the project after just ten days on the job. Some expected Garbo to quit in a solidarity move—and criticized her for not doing so. Had Stiller wished it, she undoubtedly would have resigned with him in protest. But he would not drag her down with him. He told her to stay.

A sign of how important Mayer viewed the picture and his new hot property was that he sent Fred Niblo into the breach. Niblo was fresh from troubleshooting *Ben-Hur* under similar crisis conditions. *The Temptress*'s opening credit would proclaim it "Personally directed by Fred Niblo"— with no mention of Mauritz Stiller at all. "Personally" seems superfluous in view of Niblo's faded reputation now; but at the time, his name was big, and his function was to restore calm to the stars and efficiency to the shooting process.

"I was frantic when Mr. Stiller was taken from the picture," said Garbo after his dismissal. "It is difficult for me to understand direction through an interpreter. Everything over here is so strange and different. And this studio is so large it confuses me. . . . I would get lost if someone did not take me to the many different stages where we work. You all hurry so much. Everyone goes on the run. We do not rush so in Sweden. It took months and months to make *Gösta Berling's Saga*. . . . We had to wait for [the right winter and summer weather]. Here you make any climate you want right in the studio. You finish a picture in a few weeks. I don't know whether I like it or not. . . . I was heartbroken—and so was Stiller. . . . But I worked on. For six months, from morning till night."

Garbo was exaggerating, but not by much: *Temptress* was in production more than four months—extraordinarily long for Hollywood in 1926, when the average shoot (on *Torrent*, for example) was four or five weeks. No other Garbo film ever took longer, and most of her subsequent movies less than half that time.

The Temptress opens with Garbo married to dilettante Marc MacDermott, who has "given" her to banker Armand Kaliz in exchange for something like bounce-free checking. Stiller's opening masked-ball sequence—the kind of scenic orgy on which he loved to lavish time and money—was retained. An Eiffel Tower backdrop pops up, and the ersatz moonlight illuminates Garbo's first torrid encounter with Moreno. After they pass the night together, he is shocked to learn that she is married. To his reproach, she makes an odd defense: "If I lied, it's because I love you."

Next comes a wonderful reverse dolly shot down the long length of a banquet table, past all the splendidly attired guests. At the head of the table, her host announces that Garbo has driven him to ruin and then promptly commits suicide in front of his guests. That's enough for engineer Moreno, who goes off to build a dam and immerse himself in "men's work" in the Argentine.

Garbo and her schizophrenic character follow: Earlier, she seemed aloof, pursued by the men. Now, arriving in the wilds of Argentina wearing a snazzy Parisian outfit, she gets down to the business of destroying every man in sight. Moreno, who had been trying hard to forget, confronts her with her vampdom. In return, she merely offers him a quizzical look that says, "Oh, well, if *that's* the way you feel about it. . . ." Later in her room, she consults a mirror and—satisfied with her fabulous beauty—goes downstairs for supper.

"This is not a country where people dress for dinner," says Moreno. "I shall always dress for dinner," she replies, and the men at table forget their food in favor of a stronger appetite. Braless and ravishing beneath their gaze, she nibbles, flirts, and stretches languidly, raising one arm high above her head to display an underarm whose erotic impact is almost palpably olfactory.

Lionel Barrymore is among the gauchos enthralled by her. So is Roy D'Arcy as Manos Duras ("Rough Hands"), a guitar-strumming villain who's about to make trouble. The film now turns into a Western: D'Arcy and Moreno trade insults, and Garbo's breast is soon heaving at the sight of their naked chests in a duel fought with whips. She savors the sadomasochism of it, and is soon washing Moreno's wounds, practically licking the blood from his chest—a daringly kinky scene for 1926.

The barefoot workmen, meanwhile, struggle to push their wagons through the mud at the dam site.* The job is long and tempers short. After an argument over Garbo, Barrymore stabs his best friend. In the climax, D'Arcy blows up part of the dam and a torrential storm finishes it off. Moreno's effort to find redemption through engineering has failed.

"Men have died and killed and been destroyed for you," he rages.

---

* It is the actual site of the Hoover Dam's construction. MGM could not resist the temptation to make use of its impressive size and shape for free.

Garbo and Antonio Moreno in a tender sadomasochistic moment after his whip-duel in The Temptress

"Not for me, but for my body," she replies. "Not for my happiness, but theirs."

The murder in his eyes changes to desire. But just when he gives in to her, *she* gives in to him—renouncing her love for the sake of his far nobler work.

Niblo had no magic cure for the script, but he and cameraman Tony Gaudio at least made certain to film Garbo stunningly, much like Genthe's *Vanity Fair* photo then on the stands. Garbo did the rest herself, overcoming many of the story's absurdities with her ambiguous performance. That she succeeded at all was amazing in view of the final cut—or cuts: Even more schizophrenic than the title character was MGM's bet-hedging double ending.

In the original, the seedy Temptress is down and out in a Paris café. Moreno, in town to be decorated for his engineering work, bumps into her, but she's too drunk to recognize him. ("I meet so many men. . . .") In her stupor, she mistakes the bearded artist at a nearby table for Jesus and hands him her one valuable possession, a ruby ring: "You will understand. You died for love." The grim message is that vampdom doesn't pay.

Too grim. MGM felt an alternative "happy" ending was called for, in which Moreno spots her in the crowd during his award ceremony, singles her out for credit and effects their happy-ever-after reconciliation on the spot. Exhibitors were given their choice; predictably, the real ending was shown in New York, California, and Europe, while the happier one was preferred in the hinterlands.

The making of the film had been traumatic for Garbo, reinforcing some of her neuroses while helping overcome others. "I used to make them laugh with my mistakes," she told screenwriter Val Lewton. "Once they tried to teach me to ride a horse for a scene in *The Temptress*. 'I am so unhappy on top of the horse,' I told them. That got a laugh. I used to keep still rather than be laughed at."

Director Niblo had seen that and tried to loosen her up. In midproduction, he called a meeting of the cast and crew at which, Garbo recalled, he "made a little speech for me, winding up by saying that I could speak no English. 'Can you?' he asked. Then it was my cue to reply, 'Not one word.' When the audience laughed, I suddenly realized that it was a friendly laugh, that they were doing their best to show a stranger from another country that she was welcome. . . . After that, I guess I really began to learn English properly. It meant more than just language then. It meant making friends."

Her American friends at that point were precious few, but one of them was Hubert Voight, her MGM greeter and first pal in Manhattan, who came to Hollywood in June 1926 and visited Garbo on the *Temptress* set. "Oh, Hoobert! Oh, darling!" she cried when she saw him, throwing her arms around his neck. For a while, they recalled the fun they had had together in New York, and then she said, very sadly, "I am so unhappy here, Hoobert, I think I would like New York [better]."

It was more than moodiness. Voight's visit came within a few days of the most shattering blow of Garbo's adult life: the death of her sister Alva, at age twenty-three, in Stockholm. Stiller handed her a cablegram with the awful news on the fourth day of *Temptress* shooting. Alva's health had been poor for some time, but Garbo had not suspected how seriously ill she really was. She died not of tuberculosis, as is often reported, but of cancer, which family members say was aggravated by a blow to the chest from an abusive boyfriend. Upon hearing of it, Lillian Gish sent flowers to Garbo, who came to thank her later at her MGM set. "Tears came to her eyes," Gish recalled.

Beautiful Alva Gustafson in Två Konungar
(Two Kings), *shortly before her death in 1925.*
The face was an uncanny cross between her sister's and Ingrid Bergman's.

"I couldn't speak Swedish so I put my arms around her and we both cried."

Doomed, tragic Alva was a beauty to rival her sister. Her death came just as her own embryonic film career was beginning to take shape: Alva Gustafson had recently played her first featured role in the historical romance *Två Konungar* (*Two Kings*, 1925), directed by Elis Ellis in Stockholm.

"My poor little sister," Garbo said later, with her habitual implication of their birth-order reversal. "I could hardly believe it. My sister was always so gay, so healthy, so beautiful! I always hoped she would come out to me in America. She had a try at pictures, and I believed in her future. I just couldn't believe she was dead—until I came home [in 1928] and found her gone."*

By Swedish or any other standards, they had been close, and the loss was unfathomable: Garbo could not come to grips either with the fact of it or with its emotional impact. She never fully did so. It remained with her

---

* The persistent claim that both Gustafson sisters appeared in *Two Kings* is unsubstantiated, and the film is lost. The confusion derives from a probable misquotation by Åke Sundborg in *Photoplay*, May 1930: "I have seen [*Two Kings*] here in Stockholm. I see my dead sister live again on the screen, with me at her side!"

Stiller with Valentino's doberman, Kabar,
on the Paramount lot, Hollywood, 1927

thereafter, and visible to all on screen, in a new and wrenchingly beautiful line of sorrow on her forehead.

Stiller's sorrows began with a cable from Sweden informing him of the death of his beloved dog Charlie. The loss was hardly comparable to Garbo's, but it further unnerved him at a time when his insecurities were already acute. He could console himself somewhat with Garbo's success, but it was now becoming obvious that his own situation at MGM was hopeless.

"He wasn't going to make it," said Irene Mayer Selznick. "It was no go. Because of Garbo, they tried. My father was tortured by the Stiller situation. It was heartbreaking. 'Give him another chance. . . .' Garbo wasn't going to leave, and it was a terrible burden on her. Whatever she did was wrong."

Without a strong cue from Stiller, Garbo was not one to take initiatives. So she did what she would most often do in a crisis: nothing. She and her mentor were both paralyzed, just as she was becoming a popular sensation. If the moment of stardom can be pinpointed, Garbo's did not follow *Torrent.* It came, rather, after *The Temptress* premiered in October 1926, to critical raves. But MGM had a secret. Everyone assumed—and the studio let everyone believe—that Garbo's recognition as a great actress was reflected by a box-office stampede. All contemporary accounts and subsequent Garbo books describe *The Temptress* as a smash success.

In fact, and carefully hidden, *The Temptress* was a financial failure, losing

$43,000. Without European sales, the loss would have been twice that. Stiller and the eighty-three production days were the reasons, and Mayer and Thalberg understood that Garbo herself could not be blamed. Accordingly, the studio took a big gamble on its Temptress's future: By declaration instead of acclamation, and with the unwitting aid of the press, MGM simply *proclaimed* her a great new star.

Romantic étude: Garbo and John Gilbert in an impromptu duet on the set of Flesh
and the Devil *(1927)*

CHAPTER 5

THE ICON IN SILENCE
1926–1929

Look at Johnny Gilbert,
Oh, isn't he a darbo,
With nose transfixed to collarbone,
Inhaling Greta Garbo.

—ANONYMOUS (1928)

For late-twentieth-century audiences bombarded daily by high-tech video images, it is difficult to imagine the captivating impact of Garbo's first Hollywood films. Equally captivating was her personal evolution in the midst of undreamed-of popularity, and the way MGM grappled with its puzzling inability to "type" a completely new kind of icon.

Garbo was basically unhappy in Hollywood from the moment she arrived until the day she left for good. But her unhappiness was especially intense in the beginning. "If you knew how ugly their studios are," she confided to a friend back home, shortly after settling in. "Everything is such confusion and a jumble, just like my poor head at times. I live in a dreary hotel in the quietest part. . . . Oh, my enchanting little Sweden, how happy I shall be to get home to you again!"

Private blues were matched by professional dissatisfaction with the whole process of American moviemaking and the type of scripts she was given, which related to the deeper question of "who" she was on film. Garbo herself was keenly aware of the problem: "They don't have a type like me out here," she wrote home in 1926, "so if I can't learn to act they'll soon tire of me, I expect." The tone and the theme were recurring throughout her career.

"Success," observed film historian Alexander Walker, "acted on Garbo like a depressant."

She was becoming wildly popular, but it was unnerving not to be able to put a finger on *why*, or on the kind of "new woman" she was supposed to represent. And she was right to worry about how long her vogue would last: Hollywood was full of overnight sensations who were gone tomorrow, many of them beautiful young women who for one reason or another attempted to buck typing.

To date, the evolution of American feminine film "types" was primitive and rigid. First came the virgins, in all their sweet innocence—the wounded Lillian Gish, the perky Mary Pickford, and the high-minded Mae Marsh, fighting for their purity and virtue. They reigned long but began to grow stale at the box office around 1913. An interlude or subgenre was the virtuous worldly woman: Edna Purviance, Florence Vidor, Aileen Pringle—alluring but too remote and mature to intrigue the public for long. Next came the vamps—passionate, sexy, and morally deadly to the opposite sex. Theda Bara, Pola Negri, and (later) Gloria Swanson were the greatest of them. Negri and Swanson would endure, to some extent, but after 1918 the vamps began to fade and give way to the flappers.

Social and economic changes at the end of World War I brought about the Jazz Age, the literary success of F. Scott Fitzgerald, and the phenomenon of feisty little working girls who acted and dressed in a bold new way— from the bobbed hair to the open-flapped shoes that gave them their name. As a film type, they held sway from Colleen Moore's *Flaming Youth* in 1923 through the fabulous pictures and persona of the " 'It' Girl," Clara Bow, in the late twenties. But by 1926, the youth-oriented flappers were not so fresh as they'd once been and not strong enough alone to hold the international film audience. If not to break the old molds, it was at least time to strike a new one.

The revolution in "type" actually began in 1925 when film censorship (in twenty-four states) was supplanted by Will Hays's voluntary moral code. The National Board of Review approved such sexually realistic new films as Chaplin's *A Woman of Paris* (1923), von Stroheim's *Greed* (1925), and Sternberg's *Salvation Hunters* (1925), which were accepted by the public along with a new kind of amoral hero on the order of Adolphe Menjou and John Gilbert—"an acceptance based on the proposition that practically all women are whores anyway," said Louise Brooks. But suddenly the producers were "pulled up short by the realization that they had no heroine with youth, beauty, and personality enough to make free love sympathetic."

Enter Garbo.

When Mayer first saw her in *Gösta Berling*, wrote Brooks, "he knew as sure as he was alive that he had found a sexual symbol beyond his or anyone else's imagining." Her face was as pure as Michelangelo's Mary of the *Pietà*, yet glowing with passion. Her pain was both moving and erotic, and Mayer and Thalberg would leave it to the public and the critics to define her appeal. Plots didn't matter with Garbo; through her face and eyes, filmgoers discerned thoughts and feelings far beyond the script. In *Torrent* and *Temptress*, the suffering of her soul was such that people could forgive any moral lapse. The relative virtues of marriage and sex could be finessed.

Those stunning Genthe pictures and her first two Hollywood films had inclined MGM to see Garbo as either the new Duse or the new Sarah Bernhardt. Gradually, the studio settled on a Bernhardt variation: the seductress who was warm, strong, and vulnerable at the same time.

Most of the established women stars would soon be swept away, and Garbo was the reason: "From the moment *Torrent* went into production, no contemporary actress was ever again to be quite happy in herself," declared Brooks. Garbo's "was such a gigantic shadow that people didn't speak of it. At parties, I would see Norma Shearer and Irving Thalberg, Hunt Stromberg, Paul Bern, Jack Conway, and Clarence Brown, all of whom worked at MGM. If, by chance, one of the men was so inhumane as to speak of a Garbo picture, one of the girls would say, 'Yes, isn't she divine?' and hurry on to a subject that created less despair."

Torrent opened in March of 1926, the same week as King Vidor's prestigious *La Bohème*, with Gish and Gilbert. *Torrent* packed the houses; *Bohème* did not. *The Temptress* revealed the spirituality within her sexuality—a certain enigmatic indolence, heightened by the mild anemia from which she suffered. Offscreen, her own withdrawn instincts and Stiller's orders not to reveal much about herself further fostered the image of a remote, mysterious being.

Garbo was the ultimate evolution of the vamp. The type stopped there, and the actress who newly embodied it was too real to remain a cardboard essence for long.

At the moment, this mysterious being was much annoyed with MGM over its treatment of Stiller and over her upcoming role—another seductress in another potboiler, *Flesh and the Devil*. Her performance in *The Temptress* had replaced MGM's fear that she might be just a fad with the hope that she represented in the feminine realm the same qualities possessed by John Gilbert in the masculine. MGM hit upon an idea: Why not star them together? But the actress balked.

"I did not like the part," she said.

John Gilbert likewise scorned his role in *Flesh and the Devil*, but he was curious about his new Swedish co-star and magnanimous in advance. When Thalberg approached him about giving Garbo opening title-card billing, Gilbert agreed without fuss—in the spirit of Thalberg's policy of keeping his own name off his films: "If you are in a position to give credit," Thalberg once said, "you don't need it."

Gilbert was born John Pringle in 1895 in Logan, Utah, the son of stock-company parents. He entered films in 1916 with the Thomas H. Ince Company and was soon playing leads—often unsympathetic ones. After a stint at Fox, he joined MGM in 1924 and quickly rose to fame. Though the 1926 *La Bohème* fared poorly at the box office, Gilbert's performance in it was riveting and, after Rudolph Valentino's death that year, he was second to no other male star. Writer Ben Hecht left a lyrical sketch of the actor at his peak:

> We met at a dinner party and Jack came home with me and talked all night. In Hollywood's most glittering days, he glittered the most. He received ten thousand dollars a week and could keep most of it. He lived in a castle on top of a hill. Thousands of letters poured in daily telling him how wonderful he was. . . . There were no enemies in his life. He was as unsnobbish as a happy child. He went wherever he was invited. . . . He drank with carpenters, danced with waitresses and made love to whores and movie queens alike. He swaggered and posed but it was never to impress anyone. He was being Jack Gilbert, prince, butterfly, Japanese lantern and the spirit of romance.

Hecht was not quite right. Gilbert had one powerful enemy: Louis B. Mayer. At MGM, Gilbert's friend and mentor Irving Thalberg served as buffer between the actor and his studio chief, who had a history of trouble. Once during a script discussion, Gilbert expressed interest in both *Anna Christie* and *Camille*, later to be two of Garbo's greatest triumphs. At that time, however, the moralistic Mayer said he objected to those stories because their heroines were essentially just prostitutes.

"What's wrong with that?" replied Gilbert, with his usual offhand candor. "My own mother was a whore." Mayer's rage at the affront to motherhood was such that he jumped up and nearly attacked Gilbert on the spot.

More recently, Mayer and much of Hollywood thought Gilbert a cad for divorcing the popular actress Leatrice Joy in August 1924, just sixteen months after their marriage. "Everyone was very romantic about Leatrice and Jack," Irene Selznick recalled. "People who knew them had been eager to see them get married, and they seemed to be yearning to get back together." Joy was

John Gilbert pre-moustache, c. 1922

reportedly heartbroken by the split, which occurred just three weeks before the birth of their daughter.*

Over Garbo's objections, Mayer insisted that *Flesh and the Devil* begin shooting right after *The Temptress*. "I told him I was tired and ill—that I felt I could not do justice to a new role without rest," said Garbo, "and that I felt sure the part was not suited to me. . . . I had just lost my sister, but it didn't seem to matter [to him]." Indeed, on August 4, 1926, the studio took a hard line, in insulting language:

> You are hereby notified and instructed to report at 4:30 p.m. today at the office of Mr. Irving G. Thalberg, for the purpose of receiving instructions with reference to the part to be portrayed by you in "The Flesh and the Devil." . . . Failure on your part to comply with this demand, particularly in view of the attitude heretofore displayed by you, and your general insubordination, will be treated by us as a breach of your contract of employment with us dated August 26th, 1925, and we shall take such action in the premises as may be necessary to protect our interests.
>
> In connection with the foregoing, your attention is called to the fact that you have attempted to reject the part of "Felicitas" which has been assigned to you in "The Flesh and the Devil," and that from time to time you have attempted to insist upon obtaining your wardrobe in a manner other than instructed by us.

After a token forty-eight hour boycott, Garbo reported for work. The man in charge was Clarence Brown, a reliable MGM house director. "He was a good executive who kept his eyes open and his mouth shut," said Irene Selznick, "—a dignified man, a solid citizen." Brown had apprenticed with Maurice Tourneur, who taught him everything he knew about composition, lighting, and tempo. Brown's *Smouldering Fires* (1924) with Pauline Frederick, *The Goose Woman* (1925) with Louise Dresser, and *The Eagle* (1925) with Valentino were of modest budget and good quality. He was also a Norma Talmadge specialist, having recently directed her in *Kiki* (1926), and Mayer felt he might bring out those Talmadge qualities he had initially detected in Garbo. In the end, Brown would direct no fewer than seven Garbo films—far more than any other director.

Flesh and the Devil was as lurid a title as the censors would allow for Benjamin Glazer's screenplay of *The Undying Past*, a nineteenth-century novel

---

* The daughter is Leatrice Gilbert Fountain, from whose paternal biography, *Dark Star*, this chapter draws heavily. Her parents' divorce took place before Gilbert met Garbo, who thus, contrary to myth, could not have been responsible for it.

by Hermann Sudermann, the Teutonic answer to Blasco Ibáñez. Its unabashed theme was sex, as heralded by the first title card: "When the Devil cannot reach us through the spirit, he creates a beautiful woman to tempt us through the Flesh." Thus begins a glorified "buddy film" in which two soldier pals fall in love with the fickle Felicitas. An Alpine matte provides Germany for the opening barracks sequence that, like much of the picture, concerns the bonding of John Gilbert and Lars Hanson. But then comes the electric meeting of Garbo's and Gilbert's eyes, followed by their first great love scene.*

Gilbert responded to Garbo with the hottest lovemaking in cinema history; they had barely been introduced before enacting a scene that would result in the most celebrated Hollywood romance of all time. She kissed so *thirstily*, said Kenneth Tynan, "cupping her man's head in both hands and seeming very nearly to drink from it." There were no retakes on the Garbo-Gilbert love scenes. "You can actually see these two terribly attractive people falling in love with each other on the screen," said Gilbert's daughter, and director Brown confirmed it:

> It was the damnedest thing you ever saw. It was the sort of thing Elinor Glyn used to write about. When they got into that first love scene . . . nobody else was even there. Those two were alone in a world of their own. It seemed like an intrusion to yell "cut!" I used to just motion the crew over to another part of the set and let them finish what they were doing. It was embarrassing.

Even the lumpy narrative could not detract from the stunning erotic naturalism. In a stroke, Garbo seemed to revise all existing concepts of screen acting: in her unique walk, leading with hip and shoulders; at the cottage fireside, throwing off her kerchief and shaking her hair; and most of all, in the love scenes, from invitation to the kiss through postcoital languor. This was neither virgin, vamp, nor flapper, but an entirely new female animal. For the first time in his career, John Gilbert was not the seducer but the seduced. Though technically "evil," Garbo circumvented the censors, and audiences saw her for what she really was: a passionate woman without a pose.

Among Brown's bold touches was one of the first horizontal love scenes ever filmed, at the end of which Garbo's husband (Marc MacDermott) bursts in on her and Gilbert. The resulting duel is shot in silhouette: The men

---

* Sixty years later, at the restored-print screening of *Flesh and the Devil* with live orchestra in Radio City Music Hall on March 6, 1987, an audience of three thousand burst into applause at that initial, sexually charged Garbo-Gilbert meeting.

Garbo, director Clarence Brown, and John Gilbert posing with Hermann Sudermann's The Undying Past, *on which* Flesh and the Devil *was based*

The photographer inadvertently reveals the tiny electric light—concealed in Gilbert's palm to simulate the chiaroscuro effect of a match—in an unreleased still shot from Flesh and the Devil.

start back-to-back and walk out of the frame. A burst of smoke rises from either side of the screen, followed by a dissolve to Garbo trying on a black hat at her milliner's—the slightest hint of a smile on her face. "That's how we told who was shot," said Brown. No title card or other explanation was needed. Gilbert is exiled, and for the later scene in which he speeds home to his lover, Brown fashioned a powerful montage:

"I synchronized the beat of the hoofs with the name of the girl . . . Fe-li-ci-tas . . . superimposed [over the images]. From the hoofs hitting the sod, we went to a steamer, and the pistons seemed to be saying 'Fe-li-ci-tas . . . Fe-li-ci-tas. . . .' A double exposure gave a close-up of Garbo's face. In the train, he's getting more excited at the thought of seeing her; *clucketty-cluck, clucketty-cluck*—Fe-li-ci-tas, Fe-li-ci-tas. Each cut was faster as the method of transportation became faster."

Most memorable is the film's communion-rail sequence, when Garbo turns the chalice back to the spot where Gilbert's lips have just moistened it. Audiences swooned.

"The hardest thing about that story was the ending," Brown told writer Scott Eyman. "How do you have the woman die and the two men embrace without making them look like a couple of fairies?" He did it by having Felicitas go down bubbling—as she morally must—beneath the ice. That was enough to satisfy the censors, but exhibitors were complaining about downbeat films, and MGM needed a *happy* ending even more than a moral one: After Garbo's wages-of-sin demise and the buddies' embrace, Gilbert and Barbara Kent (the Good Girl from reel one) were reunited.

"I had to shoot it and it killed me," said Brown.

But there was gold at the box office. Released on January 9, 1927, *Flesh and the Devil* was a sensation everywhere. In New York, it was held over for a rare third week and shattered all records at the Capitol Theater. The *National Board of Review Magazine* called it "another variation of the familiar vampire plot" but pegged Garbo as "a symbol of sexual appeal rather than any particular bad woman." The old film vamp was relentlessly cruel, "and wise and sober men could be on their guard against her. [But Garbo] shows a frail physique and a fragile, ethereal air. She is infinitely more civilized and all the more subtle for not being so deliberate. [Her] art is both instinctive and imaginative; it is therefore revealing and consistently right."

In addition to her beauty and subtlety, it was Garbo's unprecedented eroticism that transfixed audiences—those first open-mouthed screen kisses and photographer William Daniels's close-ups of them. The film came close to violating the Code with some of the most daring (yet fully clothed) love scenes ever filmed. Her co-star had risen to the occasion, as the *Herald Tribune* noted: "Never before has John Gilbert been so intense in his portrayal of a

Garbo and Gilbert
in a still shot for
the poster art and
lobby cards of
Flesh and the
Devil, *October 2,*
1926

Garbo goes to a
frigid grave in the
climax of Flesh
and the Devil.

man in love. . . . Frankly, we have never in our career seen [a] seduction scene so perfectly done."

Gilbert's effect on Garbo's performance was profound. Aside from providing inspirational chemistry, he deferred to her in camera angles and insisted on retakes whenever he felt she appeared to disadvantage. "Jack helped her enormously," said Clarence Brown. "He watched everything she did and corrected it. Garbo was so grateful. She recognized his long experience in the movies and she hung on his every word." She trusted him implicitly, as she later told journalist Åke Sundborg:

> I don't know how I should have managed if I had not been cast opposite John Gilbert. . . . Through him I seemed to establish my first real contact with the strange American world. If he had not come into my life at this time, I should probably have come home to Sweden at once, my American career over.

Instead, she went home with Gilbert. Audiences came away reeling from *Flesh and the Devil*, and so did Gilbert—smitten to the core. Even before the film's completion, he and Garbo were inseparable, and the fact that reporters followed them everywhere provided a good excuse to avoid public places and retreat to the privacy of Gilbert's house. Shooting on *Flesh and the Devil* ended on September 28, 1926; by Halloween, Garbo had moved in.

Gilbert's hillside home, directly above King Vidor's, was at 1400 Tower Grove Road, a narrow street winding high up into the eucalyptus-and-chaparral-covered area behind the Beverly Hills Hotel. It was a two-story, Spanish-style house with tennis court and swimming pool. An entrance hall and large party area occupied the first floor; upstairs, the rooms afforded terrific views of the city below. The furniture was carved walnut, faux seventeenth-century Spanish. Hedda Hopper was a frequent visitor: "He had the living room painted blood red, fireplace and andirons shaped like owls . . . their lighted eyes glowing, then mysteriously fading. The massive lock on Jack's bedroom door was from a medieval castle, and the house shook when he shot the bolt."

"The House That Jack Built" had only one spare bedroom—but no more were needed. Leatrice Joy thought this guest room "grotesque," for Gilbert had decorated it like a monk's cell, with narrow bed, ebony crucifix, prie-dieu, and missal—a replica of *The Merry Widow* bedroom in which he tried to seduce Mae Murray. Gilbert now called in his friend Harold Grieve to redesign it as a miniature Louis XVI boudoir in blue, ivory, gold, and black.

"When Mr. Gilbert started seeing Garbo in 1926, I installed black marble walls and a sunken black marble tub with gold fixtures in the master bedroom," recalled Grieve, a set decorator on the 1926 *Ben-Hur*. "But Garbo complained that the marble glistened too much. So workmen fluted the walls to remove the shine." The bathroom alone cost fifteen thousand dollars—an extravagance typical of the free-spending Yankee and horrific to the thrifty Swede. Gilbert also built a small cabin for her at the back of his property and planted a pine grove there because she missed the sight and smell of Swedish trees; he hoped the artificial waterfall and the sound of the wind in the pines might relieve her homesickness as well as her insomnia.

No one could have been more solicitous. Because of Garbo's ongoing difficulty with English, Gilbert opened a mail-order account for her with a bookstore in Stockholm. Like Jack, she was self-educated but an avid reader, hungry to learn almost anything. He taught her to play tennis and she worked hard at it, clutching the racket in peculiar fashion by the middle of the handle and playing a fast, slashing game. Her net game was especially ferocious. She stood so close to the net that her opponents feared a ball might damage her million-dollar face. When she lost, she never said, "You played well," but rather, "I played badly." King Vidor called her "a bulwark of strength, covering [the court] in long leaping gallops and strides, displaying a typical Swedish stubbornness and determination to let no shots get by her."

These days, she and Gilbert hosted a number of Sunday tennis parties whose core group consisted of Carey Wilson, Paul Bern, Thalberg, Vidor and Eleanor Boardman, Barney and Alice Glazer, Edmund Lowe and Lilyan Tashman, producer Arthur Hornblow, Jr., and writer Herman Mankiewicz and his wife, Sara. She liked Mankiewicz and laughed at his raucous jokes, whereupon he would tease her with, "You don't understand one word. What are you laughing at?" Garbo would protest, "I do, I do!" and sometimes try to explain the joke in her own eccentric English, to everyone's delight.

"Gilbert's was her only home," said Boardman. "The four of us used to play tennis, over the weekend, on Gilbert's court or on ours. In the pool, we'd wear bathing suits. She wouldn't. In her country, that was the custom. She'd get out of the pool and put her dressing gown over her shoulder, but she walked around nude and the Japanese gardener would gawk."

At the opening of *Bardelys the Magnificent*, starring Gilbert and Boardman, Eleanor and King Vidor were joined by Norma Shearer and Irving Thalberg and by Gilbert and Garbo—the one and only (photographically documented) film premiere Garbo ever attended, although she typically refused to go to the Cocoanut Grove afterward for dinner and dancing. Shortly before her death, the ninety-two-year-old Boardman summed up her impression of Garbo six decades earlier:

Norma Shearer, Irving Thalberg, Garbo, and John Gilbert at Bardelys the Magnificent *premiere—the only one Garbo ever attended*

Eleanor Boardman—Mrs. King Vidor —during the making of Bardelys the Magnificent *(1926)*

She was very selfish. I had a car and a chauffeur. She had just arrived and she didn't know how to drive, so I took her to town. Nothing was in Beverly Hills, so we went to a shoe store in Los Angeles and she tried on a thousand pairs before she finally said she'd take one. She left them on and we walked out of the store and crossed the street to another shop, walked around a bit, and then she said, "They hurt me." I said, "They won't take them back." She said, "We take them back." They took them back. . . . I took her downtown, a long way, brought her back, spent all day with her, never a word of thank you. Nothing. Garbo takes, you give—but she was fascinating. She was unique.

Stiller, meanwhile, was living in Santa Monica, in poor health and fighting to salvage something of his career. If he objected to his protégé's much-publicized passion for Gilbert, he made an effort to keep it to himself. Garbo, for her part, was trying to divide her time between the two men and failing to satisfy either of them. There seemed to be two conflicted Garbos: Gilbert's relatively sociable one and Stiller's brooding Ice Queen. When she disappeared for long hours, Gilbert always knew she had gone to Moje—and was much annoyed.

Jack was both "very impetuous and very immature," in Clarence Brown's opinion, "and she had him under her thumb. . . . They were in love, although he was more in love with her than she was with him. He was always proposing in front of people, trying to coerce her into accepting, but she always kept him at arm's length." Gilbert was so persistent in his proposals that Garbo finally gave in—or so he believed.

The epochal wedding of September 8, 1926, at Marion Davies's hacienda in Beverly Hills, was to be a double bill. The first couple consisted of Gilbert's friendly neighbors Vidor and Boardman, whose nuptials were long planned. Two weeks before the event, they had invited Gilbert and Garbo "up the hill" to dinner, during which the festive mood and drink led the effusive Gilbert again to propose to Garbo. Wouldn't it be grand, someone said— surely, one of the men—if they all got married together! To everyone's surprise, Garbo said yes—or, more likely, that it was a nice idea. Gilbert was delirious with joy. This time, with the Vidors as witnesses, he was sure she was serious.

In such a spectacular event, Garbo and Gilbert would be the main attraction, with the Vidors relegated to second feature. But Garbo loathed the prospect of a media circus, and it was decided to keep her part of the ceremony secret—a strategy that appealed to both Gilbert's sense of drama and Garbo's sense of privacy. But Vidor, a company man and good friend to Louis B.

Mayer, told him the news, and, coincidentally or not, within a few days, Garbo seemed to retreat.

Early on the wedding morn, Gilbert saw Garbo pull out of the driveway. As the appointed hour approached and she still hadn't returned, he called Davies, who said Garbo might be planning to come directly there, and Jack should come on over. Vidor stalled as long as possible, but finally Boardman took Gilbert aside and told him they could wait no longer. Gilbert was beside himself and now, on this most humiliating occasion, found himself face-to-face with Mayer. With four (or at least two) of MGM's biggest stars involved, Mayer was present and had just stepped out of a guest bathroom. According to Boardman, he walked up to the grieving Gilbert, slapped him on the back, and gave him a piece of earthy, man-to-man advice: "What's the matter with you, Gilbert? What do you have to marry her for? Why don't you just fuck her and forget about it?"

Mayer's daughter Irene, who was there but not in the room, denied the exchange took place. But others insist it did and that Gilbert turned and pushed Mayer backward into the bathroom, banging his head against the tile floor and breaking his glasses. Eddie Mannix, the MGM studio manager and ex-bouncer, reportedly pushed his way in and pulled them apart.

"You're finished, Gilbert!" Mayer shouted. "I'll destroy you if it costs me a million dollars!"

Had Gilbert really expected her to show up? "Oh, sure—expected and hoped," said Eleanor Boardman, who confirmed the Mayer-Gilbert brawl but said she did not hear Mayer's vow of vengeance. Conflicting accounts and the date of the event put the whole story in doubt: September 8 was in the middle of *Flesh and the Devil* shooting (August 9 to September 28). Garbo and Gilbert had known each other for only a few weeks at the time of Gilbert's proposal. It seems unlikely that the cautious, unimpulsive Garbo would have agreed to it.

In any case, if a vendetta hadn't existed before, Gilbert now acquired Mayer's permanent enmity, leading to a string of lousy star vehicles (*The Show*, *Desert Nights*, *The Cossacks*) and eventual doom in movies. But at the moment, he could see nothing except his own outrage at Garbo. He refused to speak to her when she eventually returned to his house, and he sent her a note suggesting it was time she pay rent. (She never did.) *Photoplay* summed up the situation in verse:

> Off again, on again, Greta and John again,
> How they have stirred up the news for a while.
> Making the critics first sigh with them, die with them,
> Making the cynical smile.

Two years and several films later, Garbo was forthright when asked about Gilbert: "It is a friendship. I will never marry. But you can say that I think Jack Gilbert is one of the finest men I have ever known. He has temperament, he gets excited, sometimes he has much to say that is good. I am very happy when I am told that I am to do a picture with Mr. Gilbert. He is a great artist. He lifts me up and carries me along with him. It is not scenes I am doing. I am living."

Shortly after his real or imagined jilting, Gilbert took a wound-licking trip to New York, expecting to find on his return that Garbo had moved out. If she hadn't, according to Richard Barthelmess, who was on the train with him, he would throw her out. He had had enough. But Garbo was still there. "He took one look at her and his resolve turned to smoke," says his daughter. "She'd missed him, she said. And she needed him."

Their cohabitation resumed as if nothing had ever happened.

She needed not only his companionship and his energizing film presence but also his professional advice in the matter of her contract renegotiation. To that point, all her dealings with MGM had been handled by a lawyer. "My direct need was for an intelligent, experienced person who could judge my position from a business point of view," Garbo later said. "One day a friend told me of just the sort of man I needed to handle my tangled life in motion pictures. He would understand that I wished no trouble—only to make good films."

The friend was Gilbert, and the greatest indication of Garbo's trust in him was her signing on, in late 1926, with Harry Edington, Gilbert's friend, agent, and business manager.* For most of the rest of her screen career, Edington handled all Garbo's business affairs *without fee*, simply for the prestige—although it appears that he later got a nice $20,000 "consultation fee" from MGM for each picture Garbo made, to sweeten his attitude toward the studio during negotiations.

"Most of my professional contentment," Garbo would say, "I owe to the

---

* The Garbo-Edington association was reinforced by Barbara Kent, who played Herthe in *Flesh and the Devil* and was married to Edington from 1932 until his death in 1949. Kent, today, denies the claims that she was Garbo's "confidante" but confirms that Garbo relied heavily on her husband. Edington's film work began in the accounting department of MGM on *Ben-Hur*, but he soon left to set up his own agency. Through his first client, writer-producer Carey Wilson, he met and represented Gilbert, for whom he eventually obtained the highest salary ever paid to a film actor. His later clients included Marlene Dietrich, Cary Grant, Claudette Colbert, and Charles Boyer.

guidance of this intelligent and understanding man, who took over my affairs when they were in an unhappy and precarious condition."

Edington's first act, in December 1926, was to notify Mayer that Garbo was receiving only a fraction of her worth and wanted a raise from her current $750 a week to $5,000. The money battle was going to be serious, and Mayer was apoplectic that Gilbert was aiding and abetting: "Now he's even inciting that damned Swede and it's going to cost a fortune." As any negotiator might in his first response, Mayer rejected her demands outright, and it was at that point, according to legend, that Garbo uttered her second-most-quoted line: "I tank I go home now." There are as many confirmations as denials of the actual words, but the gist was right—though the meaning has been misconstrued. She was not threatening to leave Hollywood: "Home" was not Sweden, but rather the Miramar and Gilbert's house on Tower Grove Road, which was even more galling to Mayer.

An epic battle of wills had been joined between Garbo and her boss, who made some none-too-subtle threats to have her deported; through Edington she countered that, if he tried, she could simply marry Gilbert and become an American citizen. Her real trump card was that if MGM wouldn't meet her monetary demands, many other studios happily would.

Money, however, was not the sole issue. Her new "type" was still embryonic; for the present, she was still getting and hating the same old roles. "Always the vamp, I am—always the woman of no heart!" she lamented. Her next MGM project was slated to be *Women Love Diamonds*, in which she was to play yet another one. "This upset me again," she told Åke Sundborg:

> I felt I simply could not do another such role. It seemed to me that my future in America was at stake. I went back to my hotel and waited. Next morning the studio called to ask me to look at some sketches for the film. I refused, and did not go.
>
> This was the first time I had actually disregarded the wishes of my company. . . . Then came the explosion!

It came in the form of a letter from MGM vice president L. B. Mayer, hand-delivered by messenger to Garbo at 7 p.m. on November 5, 1926:

> Yesterday you were notified by telegram as well as by letter to report at our studio this morning at the hour of ten o'clock. You have disobeyed this instruction and we have not heard from you either directly or indirectly. . . . [Thus] it will be impossible for us to cast you in [*Women Love Diamonds*]. We desire you to know at this time that it is

our intention to engage another artist to play the part assigned to you.*

Until further notice you are instructed to report daily at our studio at the hour of nine o'clock a.m. . . . . During the period of any insubordination on your part your compensation under said contract will be discontinued. . . . Your resulting idleness would be due purely to your attitude and to your wilful [sic] disobedience of instructions.

Thus began several months of no work and no salary, during which Garbo holed up at Gilbert's. *Flesh and the Devil* opened in January 1927, to sellout crowds, and turned a great profit of $466,000 for MGM. That bolstered Garbo's position but entrenched the studio's. Hostile news stories trumpeted "her refusal to accept the generous offer made her by Louis B. Mayer of $2,500 a week," and new deportation threats emanated from the MGM press office.

Many of her fans were alarmed—among them Robert Reud of Detroit, a thirty-year-old theatrical producer. He wrote her on March 31, 1927, with a proposed solution to her "doubly impossible situation of either playing minor roles for MGM or being deported in June"—marriage. "I am offering to 'lend' you the use of my name (a good one, and without blemish) until you may have ceased to need it as a shield." His impressive list of character references included Theophelus Wessen, the Swedish consul in New York, who would act as best man. "You would have to see me only the one time that a ceremony would be performed [and] could return to California immediately. You could readily divorce me, at any time, on the simple grounds of 'desertion and non-support,' which would immediately set you free. . . . The present 'offer' is one that I have not made before, and will not make again; I would not be making it now, save for the fact that I believe the only thing that matters in life is art." Though Reud's offer was declined, she was surprisingly grateful, and they kept in touch for many years.

Garbo was now convinced—surely by Gilbert—that Mayer himself was the stumbling block and that she should go over his head to Loew's Inc., MGM's parent company in New York, where the real purse strings were controlled. On March 6, 1927, she sent a soulful six-page telegram to Loew's chief counsel Robert Rubin (a friend of Gilbert's), defending herself and her position. Some of the language was Edington's, but much of it was clearly in the Garbo voice:

---

* The role was reassigned to Pauline Stark, with Lionel Barrymore and Douglas Fairbanks, Jr., in the supporting cast. *Women Love Diamonds*, directed by Edmund Goulding, got a disastrous critical reception and lost $30,000.

You no doubt already know that I have refused to sign the new five-year contract which Metro-Goldwyn offered me. Perhaps the New York office is not aware of the motive of my refusal to sign this contract and in order to stop false rumors I should like you to know what conditions really are. [MGM has] gone so far as to threaten me to the effect that I would not be given any good parts. . . . A five-year contract was ready several months ago, the terms of which were impossible and I immediately told them I could not sign it. The result was that every newspaper published long articles about my temperament and my refusal to play any roles. They also said that I refused to take the part of Anna Karenina which is indeed a false assertion as I asked them to let me take that part. . . . I was fighting to play three roles a year because my constitution is not strong and if I were to play as many roles as they see fit I know that I would break down under the strain and fail to do my work as it should be done. . . . To my deep regret I see that Metro-Goldwyn has no understanding nor consideration for my situation though I have always tried to do my best in my pictures.

—Garbo

By now, MGM was anxious to begin filming the Tolstoy novel and tried to call Garbo's bluff by announcing that Anna Karenina would be given to Jeanne Eagels, the new Broadway sensation as Sadie Thompson in *Rain*. But Garbo took Gilbert's cool advice to wait it out; *Flesh and the Devil* profits were soaring and Garbo's fan mail climbing toward five thousand letters a week, many demanding a reteaming of the Tower Road duo. By mid-April, Mayer was desperate. The exact impact of Garbo's telegram on MGM's internal politics is not known, but it was in Garbo's favor: in May, Mayer capitulated. The new five-year contract, drawn up by Edington and signed by both sides, gave her a weekly salary of $3,000 rising to $5,000 over the contract period.

MGM and its publicity department were about to lose a second battle with Garbo, though they would benefit from it hugely in the long run. At first, her resistance was polite, as in her response to an MGM publicity man who proposed that she allow her face to appear on the Palmolive soap wrapper and, thus, on the bathroom sinks of America. "I don't understand English very well," she replied innocently. "Wouldn't good movies be enough?" The studio thought not, and failed to grasp that Garbo's aversion was not just to advertising schemes but to *all* forms of personal publicity. That issue would soon come to a head.

For now, it was Garbo's salary that most rankled MGM, plus the public and intra-industry humiliation of having failed to bully her. "The studio had not reckoned on its defeat and the consequences," wrote Louise Brooks. "And the victory of one friendless girl in an alien land over the best brains of a great corporation rocked all Hollywood."

A salutary side effect of The Big Holdout was that Garbo had stalled through MGM's original casting of Ricardo Cortez as Vronsky in the Karenina film. The production had been originally conceived for Lillian Gish, then given to Garbo, and was now in disarray due to delays, jockeyings, and illnesses. Filming had already begun, as Cortez recalled to Kevin Brownlow:

"We were on [Karenina] for six weeks and she became ill and Mr. Thalberg asked me to wait around. [Then] he called me in and said, 'I don't know how long this girl's going to be out, and I'd like to put you in a film with Lon Chaney. It's a good part, entirely up to you.' She was down with anemia of sorts. So I went into [Mockery], and they threw out what I had taken with her and began [Karenina] all over again."

Anemia, indeed. By then, it was "a mess of a picture," said Louise Brooks. Mayer "tried to stick her with Dmitri Buchowetski [the original director], along with those two dummies, Cortez and Norman Kerry. But she held out till she got what she wanted: Goulding and Gilbert." That was also what her housemate wanted, and on May 18, 1927, just days after she signed her new contract, Variety announced that Gilbert would replace Cortez and that the title would be changed to the audaciously simple Love.

Thalberg was delighted with the obvious marquee, "Garbo and Gilbert in Love." Gilbert was back to his old cocky self. He and the MGM executives were not on speaking terms, he told a Los Angeles reporter: "We go around glaring at each other like a lot of spoiled children. I don't like the stories and the management I've had lately, and I've told them so." He was dissatisfied with his last picture, Twelve Miles Out, and had refused to attend its preview. Now, he griped, "We are making a Russian picture built around the splendor and lavishness of the days of the Czar. The appropriation is $125,000. It can't be done on this sum. That's all there is to it."

This was salt in Mayer's wounds, but of course Gilbert was right: the final tab for Love was $488,000, nearly four times the initial estimate. Frances Marion's scenario was a reductio almost ad absurdum of Tolstoy, rescued by Goulding's direction, William Daniels's chiaroscuro photography, and the tasteful sets and costumes of Cedric Gibbons and Gilbert Adrian.

Through the opening snowstorm and change of sleighs, Garbo's face remains veiled. But when Anna and Vronsky gaze upon each other for the first time, no intertitles intrude on the lust in Gilbert's eyes and the mesmeric fascination in Garbo's. A maid at the inn mixes up their luggage, and Gilbert

During the filming of Love *(1927): Director Edmund Goulding, left, his wife,
Marjorie Moss, behind him, Garbo, and Gilbert*

comes to her room to sort things out. It is their most powerful encounter
of the film: Gilbert fondles her negligee and Garbo looks on with a
kind of violation and ambivalence that he misinterprets. Clutching
her roughly, he intends to ravish her but is held in check by her icy, controlled
anger. At the end of a long, suspenseful staring match, he backs off—
for now.

In *Love*, as in *Flesh and the Devil*, the sexual chemistry between them is
real, but now it is more tense. Garbo's true tenderness is reserved for her
extraordinarily physical scenes with ten-year-old Philippe de Lacy as her son,
Seryozha, whom she constantly hugs and nuzzles and who responds sexily
to her touch. In no other film and with no other actor does Garbo cavort
so freely and naturally as with this boy. Certainly, she can have no feeling
for Karenin (Brandon Hurst), her codger of a husband, who rebuffs and
ridicules her. She kisses Seryozha again in their second scene, through a
pane of glass, prompting Vronsky in jealous vanity to make her choose
between himself and her child.

Gilbert's characterization was petulant by design, and he strove hard with
his flashing, expressive eyes to offset the bad haircut and high-collared uniform that made his head look like an apple on a stick. In a break from
tradition, easygoing Goulding granted Gilbert's request to direct some of the

love scenes. Also by way of precedent, the Garbo set was closed to visitors for the first time—by order of the cameraman, not the director: "No one present except the director and the crew," Daniels ordered. "She was so shy, so shy. I did it to protect her."

The shooting itself went smoothly. But Gilbert's deliberately unsympathetic Vronsky made Garbo's role harder, and midway in the film, her judgment or Goulding's failed her. In the race stands, with men and horses crashing down on the field, her passion for Vronsky is exposed, and she overacts in a hysterical frenzy. It is her sole lapse in carrying the burden of the film alone—or almost alone. With de Lacy's help, her magic is soon restored.

Anna is banished but steals home and strokes her son as he sleeps. When he wakes, the close-up of their faces is a thing of pure love. Delicately, the boy removes her hat, holds her face in his hands as an adult lover might, and plants a sumptuous kiss on her lips. In the next scene, de Lacy becomes the only person ever bathed, seminude, by Garbo on film. It is all the more sensual for the boy's prepubescent innocence—nightshirt off, flexing his muscles, showing Mother his bad tooth, wallowing in her caress—and for Garbo's own clear delight.*

In the final farewell with Gilbert, her hands again do the acting. As she waves goodbye, her fingers turn upward for a moment, clawlike, beseeching. And then the end—no, two ends: On Thalberg's orders, a happy one by Frances Marion was filmed to supplement the box-office drawback of Tolstoy's. In the latter, at the station, we glimpse Garbo's maniacal look as she steps in front of the train. In the "up-tempo" version (filmed later, as Gilbert's different haircut and make-up reveal), Vronsky goes back to his regiment, everyone drinks "To Love!" and Anna plunges not to her death but into his arms.

As with *The Temptress*, MGM democratically gave distributors their choice: East and West coasts went for Tolstoy, while most places in between voted the Marion ticket. Either way, it was the most profitable of all Garbo silents ($571,000), with reviews to match. "*Love* is certainly a poor translation of the title *Anna Karenina*," said *Time*. "It would be natural to suppose that

---

* Film historian Richard Corliss notes that Garbo was only twenty-two at the time she played this ten-year-old's mother: "De Lacy, who had already appeared in more films than Garbo, knew how to project a pre-Raphaelite sensuality that made him the perfect love object for a repressed and doting mother." A war orphan, de Lacy also appeared in *Don Juan* with John Barrymore, *Beau Geste* with Ronald Colman, and *Peter Pan* with Betty Bronson before disappearing from the screen in 1930 at age twelve. He reentered films as an adult, co-directed the epic *Cinerama Holiday* (1953–55), and later became an executive with the J. Walter Thompson Advertising Agency, from which he is now retired.

*Gilbert and Garbo as
Vronsky and Karenina in
an unretouched publicity
still for* Love, *July 29,
1927. Note Garbo's freckles.*

*Mother and son—Philippe
de Lacy as Sergei—in their
forbidden reunion of* Love

Garbo and Gilbert—decidedly bored and unpassionate—await their next call during the shooting of Love.

the rest of [the] novel would suffer similarly; that it does not, is due in part to the direction of Edmund Goulding and in even larger part to the acting of Greta Garbo, whose beauty infuses the picture with a cold white glow." Said *Photoplay:* "It isn't Tolstoy but it is John Gilbert and Greta Garbo, beautifully presented and magnificently acted." The bottom line from *Variety:* "They are in a fair way of becoming the biggest box office team this country has yet known."

Offscreen, too, the big team remained together—fondly, if not blissfully. Gilbert's ardor was clear. But now more than ever his friends wondered if Garbo truly loved him, in her way, or if she was merely using him and his home for a hotel.

The answer was both. Gilbert was the most affable and hospitable star in Hollywood. His congeniality was infectious and, despite their differences on the subject of marriage, Garbo was at her most outgoing and social with him. They went hiking together, and she even took up water polo briefly. She was frequently seen coming and going from Gilbert's in her little Ford coupé, dropping in at buffet suppers or parties now and then, including one at the home of her boss.

"My father was very conservative, by way of understatement," said Mayer's daughter Irene. "He was only social on Sundays, when we used to have a buffet supper, drinks, and a movie. The front door wasn't locked, and there was an elevator that brought up the guests into the living room, and on one of those Sundays it brought up Garbo and Eddie Mannix. She had on a black velvet suit with rhinestone buttons—charming, chic. They had a few drinks and it was old-home week. They only stayed fifteen or twenty minutes, turned the place upside down, and off they went. She'd never been in our house before, and she never came again."

She showed up once at Arthur Hornblow's home in late 1927. On that occasion, the ebullient guest of honor was Charles Chaplin and the acerbic recording secretary was Louise Brooks:

"I watched [Charlie] doing all his tricks—like a poodle—for Garbo, whom he had just met. She sat smugly on the arm of a chair leaning on the back, watching him under lashes (like centipedes) with her slight contemptuous smile while her feet pawed idly at the slippers she had cast on the floor. . . . Did I say poodle? Well, she did a jolly job of altering him!"

Then and later, Garbo and Chaplin had a great mutual respect, and he often proposed joint film ventures—impossible fantasies at heart—in which she humored him.

A tantalizing, one-minute piece of film—the fragment of a 1928 home movie—shows her laughing and playing at the home of Conrad Veidt during his daughter Kicki's birthday party, in the company of Dolores del Rio, Camilla Horn, and Emil Jannings. Another time, during a pool party at Jannings's, Norma Shearer remembered holding Garbo's attention, for about fifteen minutes, by diving gracefully into the pool and swimming vigorous laps:

"I could tell she admired the way I swam, so I kept on swimming for Garbo. Later that day we posed together for a photograph with Jannings. She was really very cordial with me—and then, after clasping my hand, she was suddenly gone."

More often, Garbo could be found at Gilbert's, on his tennis court or lying out in the sun—tame diversions for a man who, hitherto, felt tragically deprived if he couldn't play thirty-six, or at least eighteen, holes of golf daily. Gilbert's door was always open, and when his pal Carey Wilson moved in for a while around this time, he got to know Garbo well:

The flicka and I had many quiet long talks. We'd stay up half the night discussing anything from bookbinding to radio transmission to

Ibsen's plays. We never finished a conversation without my being utterly amazed. Few people knew the extent or the depth of her reading. . . .

She also tried hard to be a good hostess for Jack. Every Sunday, there would be an open house on Tower Road, with two dozen or so guests. Entertaining was second nature for Jack but agony for Garbo, at least at first. But when she realized that these people wanted only to exchange sociability and friendship, she did gradually relax and lose most of her shyness. . . . She entered heartily and effectively into all the games, from tennis to murder mysteries. She could clown with the best of them when clowning was in order. She was also perfectly capable of more than holding her own in some reasonably erudite discussions. Garbo made a lot of friends in this Sunday group.

Other friends confirmed it: "Garbo was at her best with Jack," said screenwriter Salka Viertel. "She came out in society, she laughed and went to parties. People will never forget how she was then, warm and vibrant and wildly beautiful." She went once to William Randolph Hearst's castle in San Simeon and, in San Francisco, visited the home of Robert Watt Miller, chairman of the board of Pacific Lighting Corp. If she knew the other guests, she might do playful imitations of other Hollywood stars; when strangers were present, she clammed up.

But not everyone felt she was much of a hostess at Gilbert's.

"More of a guest," said Eleanor Boardman. "After lunch, she made no attempt to go anywhere. She'd take a rest, loll around, and other people would come. She acted as if it were her home. It *was* her home, but she never 'socialized.' People had to go to her. She kept to herself. People tried to find out more about her, but she didn't want to come into the Hollywood life and say she was a soaper girl [in Sweden]. I guess she didn't trust people. She didn't *know* people. If she didn't like something, she'd say, 'I go home.' She managed to get things her way. She was supposed to come to my house once for dinner but she came around half past nine when dinner was over. God knows where she'd been. No apologies."

Romantically, these Gilbert days were a constant series of ups and downs. Said Joan Crawford, who worked with him in *Twelve Miles Out* in 1927: "He was still madly in love with Garbo, and the romance was not going well. He was like a caged lion. He resented every moment he was not with Garbo." Gilbert would arrive on the set, call Garbo, who was out or not answering, and that would set a negative tone for the day. One morning, Crawford claimed, he arrived nearly hysterical and told her, "She wouldn't sleep with me last night! . . . She hates Hollywood and everything in it. She wants to buy half of Montana or whatever state has no people in it and raise

At San Simeon. Back row, left to right, partially obscured: *King Vidor, Beatrice Lillie, Richard Barthelmess, Eleanor Boardman.* Middle row: *Frank Orsatti, E. B. Hatrick, Edmund Goulding, Mrs. Talmadge, Garbo, Nicholas Schenck, unidentified, Harry Rapf, Aileen Pringle, J. Robert Rubin, Norma Shearer.* Front row: *Hal Roach, Natalie Talmadge, Eddie Mannix, Constance Talmadge, Buster Keaton, Paul Bern, Irving Thalberg. John Gilbert reclines in foreground.*

wheat and children. She keeps saying, 'You're in love with Garbo the actress.' And I say, 'You're damn right!' "

A new marriage report had it that Garbo and Gilbert were on their way to an out-of-town justice of the peace when they stopped for gas, Garbo went to the washroom, locked the door, climbed out the window, and "escaped" back to Los Angeles. In April 1927, Gilbert called his actress friend Colleen Moore to announce that Garbo had again promised to marry him —for sure, this time. He was celebrating in his usual way:

"After a while he called [back] distraught to say that Garbo didn't appreciate him getting drunk on this occasion and had taken off to visit Mauritz Stiller," Moore recalled. "He said he was going over to visit the Donald Ogden Stewarts." There, Stewart tried to distract him with a discussion of Flemish painters, after which Gilbert rushed off to the Miramar Hotel to "find Garbo and tell her all he'd learned about Breughel. When she refused to let him in, he went around outside and tried to climb the wall to reach

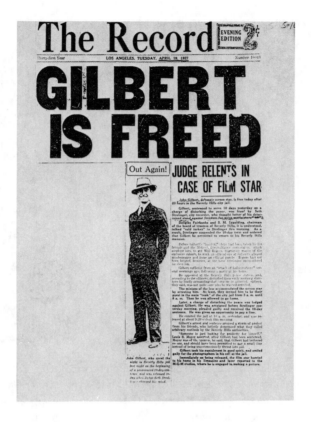

her balcony window. . . . Stiller stepped out on the balcony and told Jack to go home. Jack just kept climbing. When he reached the balcony, Stiller grabbed him by the shoulders and threw him back down to the ground."

Gilbert was stunned but not badly hurt. To Carey Wilson, who found him there, he said, "The son of a bitch tried to kill me!" Wilson got him home and Gilbert promised to go to bed and sleep it off, but later went out again—to the Beverly Hills police station, waving a revolver and demanding Stiller's arrest. They arrested Gilbert instead, and it hit all the front pages.

"JOHN GILBERT IN JAIL CELL" blared one headline. He pleaded guilty to a drunk-and-disorderly charge and was sentenced to ten days, taking it with a matter-of-fact grin. As he was led off to the Beverly Hills lockup, he said: "It's amazing, isn't it? The judge just asked me if I thought I could get away with such stunts in Beverly Hills. I replied, 'No, I didn't think so, and probably wouldn't do it again.' Then he said, 'Ten days.' Bang! Just like that, and here I am. Ought to be a nice quiet vacation, though."

"I mean to make an object lesson of this case," said a stern Judge Seth Strelinger. "Nobody, no matter who he is, is going to 'make a monkey' out of the Beverly Hills police and get away with it. The ten days will give Jack a good chance to reflect on the error of his ways."

As it turned out, convict Gilbert only had twenty-four hours to reflect on the error of his ways. He was due to start filming *Twelve Miles Out* the next day, and Mayer needed him as much as he hated him. MGM tried to get Will Rogers, the mayor of Beverly Hills, to wink an official eye at Gilbert's misdemeanor and issue a pardon, but Will could not be located. Failing that, Douglas Fairbanks intervened on his behalf, and Judge Strelinger suspended the rest of the sentence.

"GILBERT IS FREED" proclaimed a two-inch banner headline in the *Los Angeles Record* of April 19, 1927.

Photographer Cecil Beaton said Garbo once told him about another trauma around this time in which the drunken Gilbert pointed a revolver at her during a spat and she fled out into the night to a stranger's house. "I find I'm without a car," she told the people, who were kind to her, gave her a lift to her hotel, and never leaked the story to the newspapers.

Such incidents horrified Garbo and did nothing to convince her that a permanent alliance with Gilbert might be any more stable. But neither did they convince her to break off with him. By now, Gilbert had become Stiller's functional replacement in her life, psychologically if not Oedipally. He was no father figure—just a dashing complement to her own more self-possessed kind of energy. They were the most desirable man and woman in America, at the peak of their powers, and Garbo was finally adjusting to Hollywood. Life with Gilbert was exciting, and when he got out of control, there was always the Miramar and Stiller and her transplanted Swedish friends.

The Scandinavian colony was expanding so rapidly that "Americans," said the jingoists, now felt like outsiders in Santa Monica. The 1925 arrival of Garbo, Stiller, Lars Hanson, and his wife, Karin Molander, was followed by that of many others. Einar Hanson, who had been discovered by Stiller and had appeared with Garbo in *The Joyless Street*, was put under contract by Metro and then Paramount. Nils Asther came that same year, as did Norway's Greta Nissen. Danish imports included directors Svend Gade and Benjamin Christensen, whose *Witchcraft Through the Ages* (1922) led to his directing nine American features, and Karl Dane, whose memorable roles in Vidor's *The Big Parade* and Sjöström's *The Scarlet Letter* led nowhere.*

* Dane could not master English or cope with the later challenge of sound. Out of work, he was reduced to operating a hot-dog stand outside the MGM entrance and committed suicide on April 14, 1934, at the age of forty-seven.

Garbo was friendly with them all, but especially Sjöström, whose cozy bungalow at 425 Palisade Avenue in Santa Monica was the favorite gathering place of the Swedes-in-exile. Sjöström was a beloved figure, as generous as he was successful, and Stiller's close friend. Garbo revered him and his beautiful actress-wife, Edith Erastoff (1887–1945), who had starred in some of her husband's finest Swedish films, including *The Outlaw and His Wife*. During the Sjöströms' years in Hollywood (1923–30), Edith was den mother to the Swedish community and a woman in whom Garbo confided—usually about Stiller's tribulations at MGM and his jealousy over Gilbert. Only the Sjöströms understood Moje as Garbo did, though they, too, were frustrated by their inability to convert that understanding into any concrete assistance. By and large, most people considered Stiller a nuisance.

Unlike Stiller, Sjöström was flexible, fluent in English, and nowadays quite at home in Hollywood with his family. Garbo had grown very fond of his two young daughters, Greta and Guje, as well as his wife. On the set, Sjöström was adored because he never raised his voice, always knew what he wanted, and was efficient in getting it. "Louis B. Mayer used to call him Christ!" said Lars Hanson. "Everyone [admired him] both as an artist and as a human being." Sjöström would ultimately direct eight major films in America.

At the moment, in June 1927, he had just finished his masterpiece, *The Wind* (1928), with Lillian Gish. A fascinating production photo survives in which Garbo—looking elegant in a new fur coat—is talking with Gish, who stands with a broom in a dirty kitchen, like Cinderella. "It is tempting to see it in symbolic terms," says Swedish film historian Bengt Forslund. Gish was on her way out. *The Wind* was temporarily shelved and, with the onset of sound, Sjöström's Hollywood days were numbered. But he was presently riding high, and Garbo was riding with him. At his home, she could take refuge and be herself. Now, in addition to their friendship, came the chance to work together.

The Divine Woman, crudely derived from the life of Sarah Bernhardt, was a kind of all-Swedish production. Garbo asked for Sjöström as director and got him. She also got her choice of co-star, Lars Hanson, with whom she'd worked well in both *Gösta Berling* and *Flesh and the Devil*. The lingua franca on this set would be Swedish, and American audiences on the other side of the silent screen would be none the wiser. But Gladys Unger's Bernhardt drama, *Starlight*, was deadly. The playwright's own screenplay was rejected, and MGM's Dorothy Farnum was assigned to collaborate on a new draft with Sjöström. Their fifth version was approved by Thalberg, who then reversed himself and demanded three more drafts, for a total of eight. By then, little remained of the Divine Sarah: A simple country girl succumbs to a rich Don Juan, who turns her into a great star. Redemption comes in the form of an army deserter, whose love moves her to trade the footlights for a South American ranch.

Lillian Gish, director Victor Sjöström, and Garbo on the set of The Wind *(1927)*

Karin Molander, her husband, Lars Hanson, Garbo, and an ailing Mauritz Stiller,
shortly before three of the four of them left Hollywood forever

Shots of Garbo and Sjöström on the set show them beaming with affection
and reveal none of Garbo's usual tension. Sjöström was trying to make her
softer and more easygoing than she had yet appeared—more like the warm,
open person he knew in his home. Critic Paul Rotha thought he succeeded
in making her "less of a star and more of a woman than in any other of
her American films" but that Sjöström himself had "ceased to develop."

The Divine Woman, which opened on January 14, 1928, was a popular
and financial success ($354,000) and gained Sjöström his usual bonus of
$10,000. But it was, in fact, just a bread-and-butter project, and he was too
self-critical not to be aware of its slim artistry. "This picture is a huge
disappointment," said Delight Evans in *Screenland*. For Sjöström personally,
the most sobering verdict came from his faithful Edith. After the preview,
she said icily, "You mustn't do such films, Victor." Future generations will
not be able to judge for themselves: *The Divine Woman* is the only one of
Garbo's twenty-seven feature films that has not survived.*

* Some 90 percent of all silent films have been lost, but the one missing Garbo picture is an
especially tantalizing Holy Grail. Like Elvis and the Loch Ness monster, it is often sighted
but never quite found. Reports of its existence at the Czech film archive in Prague have
proven false. A short trailer of the film exists, but MGM-Turner holds out no hope for
discovery of the whole film: "*Divine Woman* was reconstituted for the silver content years
ago," a studio official told the author on November 20, 1990. Most silent films, in fact, were

To Garbo, the worst thing about the bad reviews was that she and the Swedish colony agreed with them: Her early Hollywood movies were crude in comparison with Sweden's films, and Garbo accepted the verdict of her Swedish friends who told her she was being misused and that her career was ruined. "They were good critics, but poor prophets," wrote Alexander Walker. "They overlooked what captivated American audiences: the wholly new way in which Garbo backed up her acting with her body."

The Swedes had brought their native love of the elements to Hollywood, and Garbo's writers tended to link her personality with the snow and ice and floods that were convenient metaphors for emotions too deep to be put on a title card. Garbo required fewer intertitles to convey her emotions than any other silent era performer, and if the film results thus far were not high art, it was clear that she was inventing a profoundly different woman through her face, her walk, and her subtle mannerisms.

"With Garbo you were aware less of an actress than of a soul exposed to life and to mankind," wrote film historian David Robinson. "The depth and intensity of her acting metamorphosed anything she played. She made ten silent films in Hollywood: if they were not novelette rubbish to begin with, they ended up that way after the Metro script department had done their stuff. . . . But Garbo gave them a little of her own divinity."

In some novelette rubbish called *The Mysterious Lady*, directed by Fred Niblo, Garbo played Tania Fedorovna, a Russian spy charged with stealing secrets from the Austrians, her lover Conrad Nagel among them. At its opening, the melancholy Garbo lounges in a Viennese opera box, her hair—fine as a baby's—exquisitely lit from behind to highlight every strand. Daniels's lens caresses her, particularly in the love scenes with Nagel, magnifying the erotic deception by which she operates.

Garbo, in short, has never looked better in a script that has never been worse. The sole sequence of dramatic interest begins when she crosses a crowded room, trying not to draw attention to her tryst with Nagel. When they are discovered by the villainous Gustav von Seyffertitz, she is forced to shoot him. Then comes the great Necrophiliac Scene: Garbo sits on the dead man's lap as if making love to him, in order to fool his bodyguards who come bursting in. The plot—similar to that of *Tosca*—is but an excuse for her visual presence.

"In our few contacts between scenes," said von Seyffertitz, "I found her

---

melted down to recover some of their expensive silver nitrate component. In the 1970s, when Garbo's friend David Diamond told her the Moscow Film Archives might have *Divine Woman*, her reply was characteristic: "Why do you think that's so important?"

to be most unassuming and fascinating, with a peculiar flavor of recherché."
Garbo, for her part, told a friend that the old actor had asked her, "Why
do you not wear a brassiere?" In many shots, in fact, her nipples are visible.
His question prompted Garbo's inspired nickname for him, "Safer Tits."

Of more lasting impact than the film itself was a six-minute still-photo
session on the *Mysterious Lady* set: Niblo and Garbo consented to allow
Edward Steichen to photograph her between scenes. "I made, in all, nine
pictures in the time allowed me," said Steichen. "I didn't ask her to do
anything. You would be either incompetent or a damned fool to ask that
woman to do anything." Garbo simply threw a black shawl over her costume
and straddled a straight-backed chair. Steichen told her, "It's too bad we're
doing this with that movie hairdo," and Garbo agreed. "Oh, that terrible
hair," she said, reaching up and covering it with her hands. She felt an
uncommon rapport with Steichen in that brief encounter. "Afterward," he
recalled, "she threw her arms around me and said, 'Ah, you should be a
motion-picture director.' " That was before she even saw his photographs
—arguably the best known and most beautiful ever taken of her.

Garbo's diffidence these days was observed at close range by actress Marion
Davies, who was making *Her Cardboard Lover*, under the direction of Robert
Z. ("Pop") Leonard, at the same time Garbo was making *The Mysterious
Lady* in June 1928. Allowing for its nasty edge and a few unlikely phrases
in the dialogue, Davies's strange interlude has a plausible ring of truth:

> On a very warm day I happened to go by [and] hear her say, "Why
> should I work? It's so silly and I'm hot. . . . Look at this hot dressing
> room; and not even a toilet."
>
> "You can use mine if you want to," [said Marion].
>
> "No, I've got mine." She had one of those pots. "It's very good for
> this reason—you can dump it out on top of the directors."
>
> "Aw, you wouldn't."
>
> "I wouldn't, eh? . . . I don't feel good. I don't know why people
> work like this, under these conditions. It's perfectly preposterous. . . ."
>
> Then she said, "Come and see me sometime on the set." Now that
> sounded very funny, because everyone knew she wouldn't allow anybody
> to see her on the set. I was doing my picture right on the same stage.
> Her half was all blocked off, but mine wasn't, and one day she came
> over. . . . When she went back to her set, I said to the director, Pop
> Leonard, "Have you got a scene you can do without me? I'd like to
> go over. . . ."
>
> She was in the middle of a scene, with Fred Niblo directing, but the

moment she heard me walking along, she said, "Stop the camera. . . . Who's there?"

Fred Niblo saw me and said, "Miss Garbo does not want anybody on the set." I said, "I know. But Miss Garbo came on my set and I thought I'd repay the compliment."

Greta said, "I've got to get my hair done—I'm terribly sorry." I said, "Can I go and help you get your hair done?" She said, "No, I have my own hairdresser. . . . Why don't you go back to your set?"

"Well," I said, "I thought I'd like to come over and see you. I understand you're a wonderful actress. You were nice enough to come to my set. I thought I'd repay the courtesy." I was dying to see how she worked.

"You're very funny. You make me laugh," she said. "I didn't come over to see you—I came over to see a great actress, Miss [Jetta] Goudal [Davies's co-star in *Her Cardboard Lover*]. She's a very good actress, but she's stealing my stuff, and I don't like it." Then she said, "They're calling you on your set."

"I don't hear any call."

"You're wasting my time. Get off before I have to kick you off. Go back to your set. I won't act. I don't like anybody watching me." I said, "Well, that goes both ways. Don't you come on my set, either."

"You're very funny, [but] I don't care about your acting. I just like to visit."

"Well, so do I. And I'm going to stay here."

"Oh, no you don't. It's going to cost the company money, and you're going to be blamed for it. They'll put it on your production."

"Then I'll leave."

Michael Arlen's novel *The Green Hat* symbolized the spirit of the time. That spirit, said Garbo's friend Mercedes de Acosta, went overboard in sentimental bravado: "The heroine was utterly reckless but always gallant. Gallant and dangerous were in a sense the passwords of the '20s. One could do anything, as long as one lived gallantly and dangerously."

Millions of de Acosta's generation were influenced by the story and its doomed protagonist, Iris March. Katherine Cornell played her in the 1925 Broadway version, and Garbo made known her desire to do so on film—asserting herself in a *positive* way with MGM for perhaps the first time. Iris is a free spirit, and her reputation suffers thereby, more so after her husband commits suicide on their wedding night. He died "for purity," is all she will say; everyone assumes he had learned and despaired of her promiscuity—a view she never contradicts. Only at the end is it revealed that he had syphilis and that she has destroyed her own life in order to protect her dead husband's name.

There were a dozen reasons why such a story would run afoul of the censors, and the Hays Office raised every one. All references to venereal disease had to go; the husband became an embezzler instead of a syphilitic; everything had to be sanitized—even the title and all characters' names changed. As British critic Robert Herring put it, director Clarence Brown and MGM "lacked the courage of their inhibitions."

In *A Woman of Affairs*, Iris March became Diana Merrick. Her true love is Neville (John Gilbert), but their romance is opposed by his father, who convinces her to give him up for the sake of the son's "honor." It is the first of many thwartings on his part, and the first of many sacrifices on hers. Neville departs for "two years of reckless living," says a title, leaving "a gallant lady trying to forget." Her method of forgetting is a series of empty affairs that enrage her brother (Douglas Fairbanks, Jr.). He worships the athletic David (John Mack Brown), who is "always there" for Diana. They finally marry, but just hours after the wedding, a police visit precipitates his shocking leap from a window. Garbo must endure not only her grief but also the guilt trip of Fairbanks, who rejects her (as her film brothers—in *Love* and *Conquest*, for example—so often do). Neville rejects her, too, and marries Constance (Dorothy Sebastian).

Sebastian, a former chorine with the George White *Scandals*, was then in love and in residence with director Clarence Brown. She and Garbo became friends during *A Woman of Affairs*, as Sebastian recalled:

> Everyone trembled when Garbo first came on the lot, [but] I decided that I would just be myself; that Greta must be only human and that she probably disliked all the kowtowing that greeted her from all sides. So when our director introduced us, I said, "Hello," casually. . . .
>
> Greta inquired, "How do you feel?"
>
> "Tired," I answered.
>
> "I do, too," said Greta. . . . "I'm glad that you are tired. I like tired people."

This was a powerful sympathy of the tired for the tired, though the source of Dorothy Sebastian's exhaustion was different from Garbo's. She was nick-named "Slam" for her tendency to get falling-down drunk and crash into things—something she did often, notably during a long affair with Buster Keaton. In any case, Garbo liked Sebastian and invited her to lunch in her dressing room that very day, and thereafter. She also had her cast in *The*

Garbo with Dorothy Sebastian filming a scene in A Woman of Affairs, *August 24, 1928*

Single Standard six months later. Once, when Sebastian rented a new house, Garbo asked to see it.

"When Greta dropped in," said Sebastian, "my chairs hadn't yet arrived and so we ate our luncheon—baked beans and Boston brown bread—sitting on the floor. Greta seemed to enjoy the grand confusion. It was really a lark for her, as she enjoys herself most when she can romp about and not have to give a thought to how she looks."

In *A Woman of Affairs*, Garbo is stunningly natural in every frame—even when picking a bit of tobacco off her tongue after lighting a cigarette. Two scenes in particular were classics. In the first, in Gilbert's bedroom, she plops down on the world's most inviting divan, absently twirls her loose ring, and says, "I've been told I am like this ring—apt to fall." Shot from below with neo-Expressionist lighting, Gilbert sinks slowly over her, they merge for the kiss, her hand drifts down—and the ring falls with a silent but heavy metaphorical clunk to the floor.

The second magical moment, and the film's highlight, occurs toward the end when Garbo—in the hospital after a nervous breakdown or an abortion or both—receives a bouquet of roses from Gilbert and fondles them in a

Director Clarence Brown and Garbo at the Victrola during a break while shooting A
Woman of Affairs

passionate pantomime of love and loss. Filmed again from a very low angle,
she transfers her desire to the flowers enveloping her face and fashions one
of the most poignant silent-film "arias" of all time.

For the two stars privately, however, things were not so feverishly romantic. Garbo had finally moved out of Gilbert's house but was still heavily
dependent on him. During shooting, she still wanted to know what Gilbert
thought about how she played this or that scene, and when they weren't
speaking, Douglas Fairbanks, Jr., often served as go-between.

"They would have little spats and then they'd make it up and then they'd
have little spats again," Fairbanks recalled. "I was a friend of both, so I'd
be taking notes from her to him. . . . I was a very respectable and decent
fellow. Give me a note folded up, and I didn't peek. I wanted to, but I
didn't."

Gilbert, to his credit, did not allow the offscreen emotional turmoil to
affect his work. Brown cited their first script discussion of *A Woman of Affairs*
as a consummate example of Gilbert's professionalism:

> Gilbert's part [was] a weak man, dominated by his father. I quite
> naturally thought that Gilbert might object to the short footage which
> he had in the picture. . . . Before even waiting for any objection from

Garbo in her Hispano-Suiza suicide vehicle, Clarence Brown standing, William Daniels behind the camera

him, I proposed that I add something to his part, making it a bigger and more manly role. [But he] said, "I'd rather you didn't touch my part a bit, Clarence. If you do, we might weaken our story. My character *is* weak and he's got to be handled that way. Footage doesn't matter. I'd rather play the part of a butler in a good picture than have every foot in a film that's a flop." That's what I call idealism in an actor, and God knows it's rare enough in Hollywood.

In truth, Gilbert was miscast and, once again, a victim of his barber and haberdasher. Also miscast was Lewis Stone (1879–1953) for the first of *seven* times in a Garbo film; his narrator character, merely inscrutable in the book, is totally baffling in the movie. But the compensation is Garbo, and others rose to the occasion, too. Daniels's camera work is the most artful of all Garbo silents, and Brown's direction exudes a rare "modern" energy befitting the potboiler. The novel's sensational wallop was largely censored, but what remained was a cross between *Franny and Zooey* and *Valley of the Dolls* in topical vogue.

A Woman of Affairs disappointed many purists but few Garbo fans. *Variety* called it "by long odds the best thing she has ever done," and at the box office—where MGM rang up a $417,000 profit—the Garbo-Gilbert reteaming was an unqualified success.

Mauritz Stiller did not live to see it. Fate and Hollywood had been much less kind to him than to his friend Sjöström. That Mayer originally wanted Stiller and took Garbo as part of the bargain was either a myth or a ploy; it was the other way around, and, in the end, Stiller never finished a picture for MGM. "Knowing his temper," said Louise Brooks, "Mayer let him play interpreter and assistant director for his find until, engulfed with rage, he settled his contract and fled."

He had fled some twenty-four months earlier, actually, with the aid of his old friend Erich Pommer, to Paramount. According to Howard Dietz, Garbo wanted to go with him, but MGM of course declined to release her and Stiller told her to stay put. Even after his break with MGM, Stiller continued to take a pathetically keen interest in Garbo's career there and to provide Louis Mayer with unsolicited advice. For example, one can imagine Mayer's reaction to the following Stiller letter:

> You doubtlessly know, Mr. Mayer, that Miss Garbo had a much better contract with UFA than the one she now has with your company, and it was I who persuaded her to accept the lower salary at Metro-Goldwyn-Mayer, because I was . . . convinced she would make a wonderful success in America. . . .
>
> The reason that Miss Garbo has been so unhappy here, notwithstanding her success, is simply a matter of the vamp roles she has been forced to play. . . . You saw her in "Gösta Berling" and you know that it was because of her great success in this production that you gave her a contract. In this picture she was an entirely different type—an innocent girl—not a vamp.

But he had his own career to think about, too, and Paramount and producer Pommer had given Stiller the break and the decent directing assignment he was looking for: *Hotel Imperial* (1927), starring Pola Negri, the World War I story of a servant girl in occupied Galicia who becomes involved with an enemy officer. It was a compelling narrative rendered with great beauty by Stiller, thanks to one of his most extraordinary innovations. The stage containing the hotel was one of the first and largest composite sets ever built—eight rooms in complete detail, four on either side of a lobby. Above it, he suspended rails along which a "flying" camera could move at will, allowing shots to be made from every angle and point of view—*in sequence*. It was a revolutionary new production method, soon picked up in Europe but not in

Mauritz Stiller and Pola Negri in an intimate conference during
The Woman on Trial *(1927)*

Garbo refused to see any visitors (royal or otherwise) on any set, and
when Crown Prince Gustav Adolf (center) and Princess Louise of
Sweden (far left) came to Hollywood, they visited Paramount instead
of MGM and were guests of Pola Negri (second from right). Others
in the photograph are, left to right: Mauritz Stiller, Jesse Lasky,
and Paramount executive Milton Hoffman, on the set of
Hotel Imperial *(1927)*.

Hollywood until years later. Because of it, *Hotel Imperial* took much longer than expected to produce, but Stiller and Pommer were perfectionists, and both men were determined to make their American reputations with this film.

The great German theatrical impresario Max Reinhardt, for one, thought they succeeded. Upon seeing it in Hollywood, he embraced Stiller and said, "I would give half my life if I could produce and direct a picture like that one." But typical of the mixed press reviews was Robert Sherwood's in *Life:* "Camera angles, lap dissolves and other photo-acrobatics are, in themselves, insufficient to make a picture a work of art."

Hotel Imperial, nevertheless, was one of the more successful films of 1927, and there were raves for the leading actress. All agreed that Stiller had deftly handled the "difficult" Negri—including Negri. She, unlike everyone else he ever worked with, found him "sensitive, patient, gentle." Their two troublesome personalities were somehow complementary, and when Negri's beloved Rudolph Valentino died in the middle of *Imperial* shooting, she was deeply touched by Stiller's response:

"This kindly man sympathized with me from the bottom of his heart. He was also experiencing the most awful unhappiness of his life. Things were going disastrously between Garbo and him. . . . He said gently, 'We must finish the picture, Pola. Let me know as soon as you are ready to come back to work.'" She was back on the set the next day. "His heart was broken when Greta Garbo transferred her affections to John Gilbert. . . . During this tragic period for both of us, we would often meet, knowing that in each other we would find understanding and consolation."

Thenceforth, Negri declared, she would make films with no other director; she considered *Hotel Imperial* one of the greatest pictures of her career. Stiller, for his part, finally seemed ready to face reality and abandon Garbo in favor of a more established goddess. It had been a good if belated start.

"Stiller was getting his bearings and coming into his own," said Garbo. "I could see that he was getting his chance. I was happy for him, and this helped me through my own troubles."

But Stiller's troubles continued. After *Hotel Imperial*, he directed Negri again in *The Woman on Trial*, co-starring Einar Hanson, for whom tragedy was looming: Hanson, in just eighteen months in America, had made nine films—seven in 1927. But he was dangerously volatile and part of a quarrelsome, heavy-drinking crowd. On the night of June 3, 1927, he persuaded Garbo and Stiller to accompany him to a party, where he got very drunk. Stiller and Garbo left, but Hanson learned of another party in progress at Clara Bow's, with whom he had just appeared in *Children of Divorce*. He jumped into his car and set off alone. His body was found in the wreckage the next morning.

Stiller next began *The Street of Sin*, written by Josef von Sternberg for Emil Jannings but—due to ill feeling between the latter two on *The Last Command*—turned over to Stiller. Halfway through, Stiller quarreled with Paramount over retakes, and Sternberg finished the picture. The great Stiller, assigned now to make episodes for other directors' films, had had enough. He could not bend his ways to Hollywood, or vice versa. In November 1927, depressed and ill, he left in defeat for Sweden. "His return was just like his arrival," said Hubert Voight, who handled the arrangements and served as Stiller's farewell party of one. "No MGM executives [in New York] wanted to think about him, let alone see him." The lonely man Voight escorted to his ship was far from the cocky, debonair figure who had danced with Garbo in the Manhattan speakeasies not so long before. Back in Stockholm, he signed on to direct a stage show—ironically titled *Broadway*—that December. It was well received and, for a time, seemed to herald a promising new direction in his career.

Garbo was distressed but distracted from his fate by being rushed immediately into production—before the final print of *Woman of Affairs* was dry—of *Wild Orchids*. This was the first of her two films in quick succession with Nils Asther, a fellow Swede, dark and exotically handsome, whose recent performance in *Sorrel and Son* (1927) was much praised. In *Wild Orchids*, his "Oriental" character would impress Frank Capra enough to get him the title role in *The Bitter Tea of General Yen* five years later. *Heat* was the original title of the picture at hand, but the prospect of "Garbo in *Heat*" on marquees called for a substitute. Only two other actors received screen credit—remarkable proof of Garbo's power to carry a film virtually alone.

Wild Orchids opens with Garbo and husband, Lewis Stone, boarding a ship for Java to inspect Stone's plantation there. Also on board is Javanese Prince De Gace (Asther), who takes an immediate interest in Garbo. During the voyage, she is shocked to discover the Prince cruelly beating his servant—shocked yet strangely attracted. In Java, the prince steps up his advances. "You are like the orchids of your country—cold," he says. "In Java, the orchids grow *wild*." Stone has assigned her and himself separate beds, and she is left to sleep alone with her S/M nightmare of Asther beating the servant. But she's a virtuous wife, and the next night, a long generic Polynesian dance show inspires her to obtain a Balinese costume in order to seduce her own husband. Stone takes one withering look and says, "You look silly, dear—take off all that junk and go to bed."*

He is unkind but correct. Garbo looks much sexier in her jodhpurs. One

---

* Many years later, when David Diamond mentioned that bizarre costume, Garbo's response was, "What a jo-o-o-ke."

*In Balinese dance costume,
preparing to seduce her own
husband in* Wild Orchids
(1928)

*Bored wife Garbo and dis-
interested husband Lewis
Stone, directed by Sidney
Franklin and photographed
by William Daniels on*
Wild Orchids

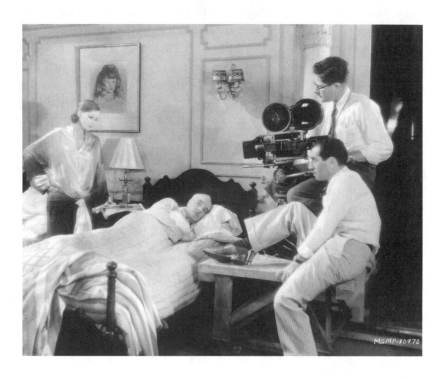

static scene follows another, Asther and Stone sparring over her until the husband's self-sacrificing decision to release her prompts the wife to remain faithful.

Not even the reliable trio of Daniels, Gibbons, and Adrian could overcome John Colton's screenplay (a derivative of Somerset Maugham's *Rain*, which Colton helped rewrite for the stage) or the handicapped direction of Sidney Franklin. Thalberg liked Franklin, said Louise Brooks, "because he was a quiet, neat director. Directors like Eddie Goulding were hard on Irving's rheumatic heart. Alfred Lunt and Lynn Fontanne shot *The Guardsman* [directed by Sidney Franklin] in 21 days, three weeks under schedule. Franklin simply held the book."

Garbo's concern about Stiller was ongoing, but she told herself (and him in letters) that she'd soon be home to see him at Christmas. During *Wild Orchids*, she had no idea that he was gravely ill and that, by late October 1928, he had been hospitalized. Sjöström learned of that in London and, hastening to Stockholm, immediately went to his bedside. "In spite of our sincere friendship I am not sure I ever knew him profoundly," said Sjöström. "I don't think anybody did." But Stiller wept with joy upon seeing him and kept him for hours at a time at the hospital. Sjöström had just arrived home from one such long vigil when he was summoned to return. Stiller was distraught and said he had to see him, Sjöström recalled.

I thought he wanted perhaps to talk to me about making his will. He had not made a will—so typical of him. I hurried back to the hospital again and was with him for more than an hour waiting eagerly for what he wanted to tell me. But he only talked about indifferent things. Then the nurse finally came in and said she could not allow me to stay longer. . . . Stiller suddenly got desperate. He grabbed my arm in despair and would not let me go. "No, no," he cried. "I haven't told him what I must tell him!" The nurse separated us and pushed me toward the door. I tried to quiet and comfort him, saying that he could tell it to me tomorrow. But he got more and more desperate, his face was wet with tears. And he said: "I want to tell you a story for a film, it will be a great film, it is about human beings and you are the only one who can do it." I was so moved I did not know what to say. "Yes, yes, Moje," was all I could stammer. "I will be with you the first thing in the morning and then you will tell me." I left him crying in the arms of the nurse. There was no morning.

Stiller died on November 8, 1928, at age forty-five. The cause was water in the lungs, according to his death certificate, not suicide, as some claim. Word reached Garbo on the *Wild Orchids* set, where she nearly collapsed.

She stayed home for the next two days, disconsolate, and begged to be allowed to return to Sweden immediately. But MGM said no. She had to finish the film, which her director called "a disaster."

"What I knew about Java you could put in your hat," said Franklin. Stiller's death "affected her profoundly—and it affected the picture. Our relationship, which wasn't too good to begin with, deteriorated. . . . It became so difficult that I went to see Irving to ask him to take me off the picture. [But] he refused to relieve me and I struggled on as best I could to the end. It was not a happy picture. The result showed it."

Stiller had fought many battles for artistic independence and lost more than he won in America. He was not the only emigré who felt Hollywood hired fine European directors just to keep them from making competitive films abroad. Garbo later told S. N. Behrman that she hated Louis Mayer not for anything he did to her (or even Gilbert), but for what he did to Stiller. Stiller's two great stylistic genres—dramas set against nature and elegant indoor comedies—assured his place in film history. But he would be remembered most for the discovery and development of Garbo's career, largely at the expense of his own.

"What shall we become?" Gösta Berling is asked in the Lagerlöf novel. "The same as we have been—dust," he replies. "We are fuel, surrounded by the fire of life. The fire goes from one fuel to the next. We are ignited, we flame up, and die."

Nils Asther had also planned to visit Sweden that Christmas to exchange the traditional "*God Jul!*" greeting with his loved ones. "When we get home," Garbo had told a friend cheerfully, "Nils will eat himself to death and I'll sleep so that I'll never wake up again!" But Asther changed his plans and now, a few weeks after Stiller's death, Garbo's homecoming was more somber than joyous. In late December 1928, she slipped out of California by train, her ticket and luggage marked "Alice Smith." To elude the press, she got off at Croton-Harmon, thirty-six miles north of New York, and motored into the city. Reporters had staked out every major hotel except the one she and Stiller occupied on their arrival in America three years before, and it was there that she put up. When finally cornered by the press on boarding the *Kungsholm*, Garbo's simple dignity was moving: She was going to visit the grave of Mauritz Stiller, she said. "He has meant a great deal in my life."

Also on board the *Kungsholm* that trip was her first film mentor, Ragnar Ring, who witnessed the newsmen's frantic attempts to get her to talk and criticized her avoidance of them (and evidently of himself): "Why can't she say a couple of friendly words to the reporters and show her enticing smile for a few seconds to the photographers? Then they wouldn't bother her. As a clever woman, she should know that."

During the crossing, MGM radioed her several times with instructions to return by the first ship for last-minute retakes on the as yet unreleased *A Woman of Affairs*. Those orders she ignored, concentrating instead on her new shipboard friendship with twenty-one-year-old Prince Sigvard, a bright and charming member of the Swedish royal family, with whom she passed the voyage enjoyably. She was sustained by the thought of spending Christmas among family and friends—of tasting the traditional Swedish lyefish and finding "the almond of luck" hidden in the Christmas rice pudding. The universal longing to spend the holiday at home was nowhere stronger than among Swedes, who jam the railways to Stockholm from far and wide. Those tending the home fires, for their part, eagerly awaited the Christmas ship from America at Göteborg and, in 1928, anticipation of the *Kungsholm*'s arrival was heightened by the knowledge that it carried not only a prince but the queen of the screen. Bad weather delayed the liner, and the suspense grew.

The welcome was tumultuous, but Garbo's friend Mimi Pollack and her actor-husband, Nils Lundell, somehow got her to the train for the final leg of the journey to Stockholm. Journalist Åke Sundborg had been tipped off and was at the little suburb of Södertälje, where Garbo's mother awaited her. "Now I think I am almost truly happy!" she said, and as the train crossed the bridge over the Mälar and passed through her girlhood neighborhood of Söder, Garbo's eyes filled with tears.

"Almost" truly happy—always the tinge of doubt.

An apartment had been rented for her at Karlbergsvägen 52, where Lars Hanson and Victor Sjöström had resided at different times. At first, the telephone drove her crazy: One day, sixty calls were logged by 2:00 p.m., most from total strangers. Why the number had been listed was unexplained, but it finally dawned on someone to have the phone disconnected. She had thought she could find the tranquility she was seeking in Sweden, that her countrymen would leave her in peace. But now the Swedish crowds instead of the American ones besieged her.

Among other distractions, the local theaters were begging her to appear, and in a rash moment, she agreed to appear as Katinka in a Stockholm stage version of Tolstoy's *Resurrection*. She evidently went so far as to study the part and memorize lines, but the night before the dress rehearsal she got so nervous she couldn't sleep. Predictably, she backed out, and no amount of pleading could change her mind.

Another day, she visited the Råsunda movie studio and watched filming for *The Triumph of the Heart*, with Carl Brisson, who made the doubtful

*Garbo, on her first visit
home to Sweden in 1928, is
reunited with her mother on
the train.*

claim that he never realized Garbo was Greta Gustafson until that Yuletide
reunion. They arranged to dine together. "After supper," he said, "we walked
mile after mile through the streets of Stockholm and back and forth under
the lights of the famous Strandvägen [Beach Street], still talking and laughing.
She remembered every one of the songs in 'Brisson's Blue Blondes,' and she
sang them all to me as we walked."

She maintained contact with Prince Sigvard, who introduced her to Wilhelm Sörensen, the son of a Swedish financier. A close friendship was begun
with him, and with Count and Countess Wachtmeister, with whom she
stayed several days at Tistad Castle, south of Stockholm. Toward the end
of the holiday, she met and befriended actress Märte Halldén at Stiller's
grave, but mostly she enjoyed just wandering the streets, window-shopping
and going off to dinner without having to change clothes. During her three

Mimi Pollack and Garbo accommodate a local photographer upon setting out for lunch in the Swedish capital.

Garbo en cloche *posing for student artists at the Palladium in Stockholm*

months in Sweden, Garbo corresponded with Gilbert and telephoned him once, to wish him a happy new year. She left Stockholm on March 9, 1929—a day ahead of schedule, to avoid attention.

The trip was bittersweet in every way. As a child, she had been especially fond of Uncle David—her father's generous brother—the one to whom she'd confided, "I'm going to become a prima donna or a princess, and when I'm rich I'll give all I can to poor children." David Gustafson saw his famous niece only briefly during her holiday visit. Afterward, he had trouble hiding his disappointment that she had forgotten to bring his daughter a Christmas gift.

Hubert Voight, the publicist, was on hand to greet her when she returned to New York. Everybody who had declined to meet her in 1925 now wanted to do so, MGM executive Nicholas Schenck among them. "He bought her a huge bouquet of flowers and trotted alongside like a schoolboy," said Voight. "[He] could hardly speak when he met her."

Voight had given a dock pass to a ten-year-old girl who had made a beautiful scrapbook of hundreds of Garbo pictures and clippings. Pale with excitement, the little girl gave the book to Garbo, glanced frantically at Voight, then at Garbo—and fell in a dead faint on the concrete. Kneeling beside her, Garbo rubbed her temples until she revived. "Give me a pen, somebody," she said, and—for the only time in public—signed her autograph in large letters across the first page of the girl's book.

In the turmoil, Garbo was pleased to see Voight's familiar face. "I am so popular now with all these people and I don't want to be," she told him. "Make them go away like a good boy, and we will go out later." Voight was thrilled and flattered but said he dreaded having to go back and tell his boss he had failed to line up the interviews he was to arrange. "O.K., Hoobert," Garbo replied, "I do it for you, but not for Mister Metro."

Chief among the interviewers was Mordaunt Hall of *The New York Times*, a paper whose importance—then, as now—was often out of proportion to the caliber of its personnel. Film critic Hall was one of the *Times*'s dullest lights, but he got his audience with Garbo at the Hotel Marguery the day after she arrived from Sweden. Hall found her "more amused than embarrassed by her none too extensive knowledge of English." She was willing to make talkies, she said. Asked what story she'd like to do, she puffed on her cigarette, lowered her eyelids and replied:

"Joan of Arc. But it probably wouldn't go so well. I would like to do something unusual, something that has not been done. . . . I don't see anything in silly love-making. I would like to do something all the other people are not doing. If I could get von Stroheim! Isn't he fine?"

Once the press obligations were over, she was free to enjoy herself a bit before returning to the grind. "We went to an apartment where Lawrence Tibbett and [his poet-wife] Margaret Sangster were being entertained," said Voight. "Garbo threw off her reserve in the center of all those charming people and laughed with more gaiety than the rest. She got a wee bit tipsy on champagne and she was singing in Swedish so adorably. . . . I saw a new sophistication—a polishing off of the rough corners—but there, underneath, not bothering to remain hidden was the real Garbo . . . marvelous friend and child of the sun. She was the most beautiful creature I have ever seen that night."

On her way down to the train that would take her back to Hollywood, she sang "Can't Help Lovin' Dat Man," the *Showboat* torch song she'd heard in a speakeasy the night before. Just before they parted, she begged "Hoobert" to send her a Swedish translation of Eugene O'Neill's *Anna Christie*—which he did.

John Gilbert, with a huge bouquet of roses, was at the San Bernardino station in his open-topped Ford to meet her train and help her evade the crowd waiting at Union Station in Los Angeles. On the drive into town, he told her how much he'd hated the past three months alone, especially the nights. The two insomniacs used to pad around together—she with a glass of warm milk, he with a stiff Scotch. Unlike the object of his affections, Gilbert never wanted to be alone for ten minutes. Nevertheless, they were made for each other, he declared. After more than two years, her detachment was driving him crazy, as he complained to Howard Dietz:

"When I said, 'I'm going out,' the only thing she said was, 'I'll leave the door open, Jack.' . . . I said, 'I'm going out to sleep with Anna May Wong.' She said, 'I'll leave the door open, Jack.' What in hell do I do?"

"That's obvious," Dietz answered. "You go sleep with Anna May Wong."

But it was Garbo that Gilbert wanted to sleep with, and he also wanted a commitment. He was thirty, she was twenty-four, and he now asked her for the last time to marry him. When she again said no, Gilbert pressed, becoming angrier and more frustrated. "You are a very foolish boy," Garbo told him. "You quarrel with me for nothing. I must do my way, but we need not part."

"Not this time," he replied ominously. "This time, it's going to be all or nothing."

Immediately upon her return, Garbo was whisked off to Catalina Island for location shooting on *The Single Standard*. Gilbert was alone again, drowning his sorrows in the bottle and the newfound companionship of actress

Ina Claire, as of May 9, 1929, Mrs. John Gilbert

Ina Claire. Whether for love or spite—or both—Gilbert suddenly announced his engagement to Claire, the marriage to take place in about a week.

The day before the wedding, screenwriter Lenore Coffee was visiting Harry Edington when he took a call from Garbo, whose voice was audible. She was sobbing, said Coffee, and telling Edington to stop the marriage: Gilbert belonged to her and they should never have separated. Edington asked why she'd waited so long to say so. Garbo said she'd been on a boat in Catalina and only just heard the news. Edington—who was to be Gilbert's best man in a few hours—said *she* was the only one who could stop the wedding. But melodramatic intervention and potential scandal did not appeal to Garbo who, typically, did nothing. On May 9, 1929, after a courtship of six weeks, John Gilbert married Ina Claire in Las Vegas. Afterward, Claire had an immortal line for a reporter who asked how it felt to be married to a great star. "I don't know," the bride replied sweetly. "Why don't you ask Mr. Gilbert?"

Claire and Gilbert sailed on the *Ile de France* to the Riviera, then Italy, Spain, and England. They stayed for a time with Noël Coward "in the course of a rather strained honeymoon," said the writer. Coward, who was also on their ship when they returned, recalled that the newlyweds enlivened that voyage "by their conjugal infelicities, quarrelling and making up and quarrelling and making up again unceasingly, all the way from Southampton to the Statue of Liberty." Claire's friend Laurence Olivier called the marriage "an unkind, empty gesture" on Gilbert's part, "taking advantage of [Ina's] flattered fascination simply in order to snap his fingers as he paraded her in front of Garbo."

Once back in California, the new Mrs. Gilbert had an understandable desire to remove some ghosts. Garbo had never fully moved out; rushing into production of *The Single Standard*, she never even had a chance to unpack her trunks from Sweden and had returned to Tower Road only once to collect a few things. It did not bode well that now, in late November, Jack and Ina took up separate residences until the remodeling of Gilbert's home could be finished. "Jack built this house some time ago . . . as a bachelor's home," Claire told the papers. "There's only one bedroom in it. There's really not room for both of us and all our servants." Added Gilbert: "I get up in the morning, and I have to say 'Good morning' to all the carpenters on the way to the bath. Just as I get to shaving, someone begins pounding on the door with a hammer. I come out and have to climb over a pile of lumber to find my underwear."

Garbo possessions and Garbo ghosts still occupied the house but at least —to Ina Claire's relief—Garbo herself did not. She had left Gilbert's home once and for all and moved into the Santa Monica Beach Hotel.

Wild Orchids's success was enough for MGM to justify Garbo's immediate reteaming with Nils Asther in *The Single Standard*, directed by John S. Robertson—now forgotten but then one of the best-liked directors in Hollywood. His big successes were John Barrymore's *Dr. Jekyll and Mr. Hyde* (1920) and Mary Pickford's *Tess of the Storm Country* (1922). Tasteful sentimentality was his forte, but his skills would be severely taxed.

The Single Standard was a vehicle rebuilt from Adela Rogers St. Johns's novel about a girl who demands sexual equality but settles for motherhood. It starts off on the theory that "men have always done as they pleased and women have done as men pleased." Garbo's role, initially intended for Joan Crawford, was her first truly American one: Arden Stuart is a San Francisco debutante whose chauffeur commits suicide when fired for dallying with her. Soon after, she meets Asther, a painter, sailor, and ex-prizefighter— three glamorous occupations rolled into one man. He is sailing for the South Seas tomorrow on his yacht, *The All Alone*, and she elects to go with him.

Asther was far sexier than most of Garbo's leading men, and there is convincing chemistry between them in numerous close-up kisses. His passion on the high seas shines as brightly as hers. But then comes the absurd St.

Garbo as "new woman" Arden Stuart, exquisitely posed by director John S. Robertson and photographed by Oliver Marsh—a rare change from William Daniels —in The Single Standard *(1929)*

Johns twist: Despite their shipboard bliss, Asther breaks it off for the reason that their *future* love could never be as perfect as it is now; he wants to freeze-dry it in his memory. Garbo returns to the Bay City an outcast, but long-suffering John Mack Brown makes an honest woman of her and they have a son. When Asther returns, Garbo is ready to abandon husband and child, just as in *Anna Karenina*, until brought to her senses by Brown's thoughtful offer to kill himself (in order to save their son's name).

The Single Standard was photographed not by William Daniels but by Oliver Marsh, who cleverly highlights Garbo's tendency to lounge against and make herself a part of any scenery. In this instance, the Art Deco sets are perfectly matched to the abstract-geometric pattern of her pajamas—a strikingly fine example of the collaboration between Adrian and Cedric Gibbons.

The film's most memorable scene, perhaps, is a funny one in which Garbo takes a stroll in the rain. She is savoring the experience until approached by a man who pesters her on the pretext of holding her umbrella. "I'm walking alone because I *want* to walk alone," she says. When that fails to discourage him, she simply hands over her umbrella to the boor and makes a quick

Bound for the South Seas on board The All Alone, *in* The Single Standard

stage-left exit. It is one of the few sight gags she was ever given, and nicely executed.

John Mack Brown was the oddest of her many odd co-stars. An all-American halfback and 1926 Rose Bowl hero, he was plucked from the gridiron and thrust before the cameras solely on the basis of his drop-dead good looks. *The Single Standard*, incredibly, was his third role opposite Garbo in eighteen months (after *The Divine Woman* and *A Woman of Affairs*), ranking him just below John Gilbert, Lewis Stone, and Melvyn Douglas as her most frequent male lead.

"Johnny was a sweet guy from Dothan, Alabama, with a southern accent you could cut with a knife," said Lina Basquette, star of Cecil B. DeMille's *The Godless Girl*. She and her second husband, Peverell Marley, DeMille's cameraman, were close friends with Brown. "He was flawlessly handsome and built like the Rock of Gibraltar. In Hollywood, women threw themselves at him—from Joan Crawford to Norma Shearer—even though he had a dear little high-school sweetheart wife, and they were both good Baptists. When his second film was with Garbo, everybody was amazed. They sent him to elocution teachers and tried to get rid of that overwhelming accent, but he 'honey-chiled' everybody—every woman was 'Sugah.' You walked

Garbo with fellow Swede Nils Asther during a lull in Single Standard *shooting*

in a room, and he picked you up like a toy. He was charming, but Garbo, I'm sure, could hardly even have *understood* him."*

As for the main co-star, Nils Asther, his propensity for "Garboesque" self-analysis epitomized the impact she had on her leading men:

> Like Garbo I have been given many labels by the newspapers. "Very nearly as handsome as Valentino" . . . "the masculine version of that mysterious fascination that is Garbo's." [But] I am tired of being just a screen lover, and I hope some day to get a chance to be myself. I am rather like Greta in that I like to be alone. I love peace and quiet. Hollywood is really no place for me. I stagnate there. . . . I only really feel awake when the air is fresh and crisp as in my native Scandinavia. I believe it is because Garbo is from Sweden that she feels the same.

* After success in King Vidor's *Billy the Kid* (1930) the following year, John Mack Brown made some two hundred cowboy films and was among Hollywood's top Western stars through 1950.

The rarely unveiled Garbo legs on the boat in Single Standard

Asther said Garbo had "always been shy" and that difficulty with English had increased that shyness in America. On the other hand, she could be nonchalant about things that upset other people. Asther had the rare privilege of being invited to her home, and when he informed her that a servant was letting paying customers watch her nude swims from a certain window, "she just laughed," he said. In her home, the only room she used was a combination sitting room and bedroom in a far end of the house. The curtains were usually drawn, and most of the rest of the house was undecorated.

They often went walking or climbing together—Garbo usually leaving Asther far behind. She visited him at Lake Arrowhead and was always up and swimming before anyone else was awake. Her compulsive physical exercise, she told him, was due in part to her fear of the diseases that had taken Stiller and her sister. The Garbo-Asther friendship was very intense for a time, and her presence had a lyrical effect on him. "When she laughs, it's a silent, breathless kind of laugh, that shakes her whole person but makes very little noise," he said. "She likes to be led and is easily influenced by anyone she admires." In his opinion, "she probably isn't very happy." Years later, he told Kevin Brownlow "she could have developed into a much more interesting actor, I'm sure, if Stiller had remained." Once when she seemed depressed, Asther asked her what the trouble was, and Garbo replied, "I had an awful row with God this morning."

A dip in profits from *Wild Orchids* ($380,000) to *The Single Standard* ($330,000) meant no more Garbo-Asther teamings. Despite some hot foreplay in the latter film, the critics found "no show, except a veiled peep at Arden's garters." They would get even less of a peep in *The Kiss* (1929), Garbo's thirteenth and final silent film.* It was also the last silent film made by MGM and—except for Chaplin's two die-hard gems, *City Lights* and *Modern Times*—the last in Hollywood history.

The Kiss was a trial drama made elegant by Belgian director Jacques Feyder's sensitive handling of Garbo and young Lew Ayres. Paul Bern, Ayres's former mentor at Pathé and now an MGM producer, had asked him to make a screen test for Garbo's approval. She loved his face the minute she saw it, and thus the twenty-year-old Ayres became her co-star just a few months before his breakthrough performance in *All Quiet on the Western Front*.

In *The Kiss*, Ayres falls in love with the wife of his father's partner. Garbo resists the boy's advances, but her husband thinks otherwise and, in an ensuing struggle, is killed by his own gun. Conrad Nagel, Garbo's former lover, defends her at the inevitable murder trial, where the jury—as one reviewer put it—"does just what it would do if you were on it."

The film's first intertitle, as Garbo and Nagel rendezvous at the Lyons art museum, contains the greatest cliché of all time: "Irene—we can't go on meeting like this."† The scene ends with a tracking shot of Garbo's brisk exit from the museum, with her trademark slouching walk. William Daniels was rarely so successful with Garbo in movement. His finest close-up comes in the film's second sequence as she is making up in front of a mirror: We *are* the mirror, and she makes intimate eye contact with us. The direct Garbo gaze is rare and jolting—a big visceral difference from the usual angled shots in which her eyes look just beyond, instead of boring into, our own.

When she meets Ayres on the tennis court the next day, he tells her that, if she won't love him, she must at least give him her picture. At home, she has a stack of 11-by-14 glossies for just such occasions. They debate which is best, moving closer and closer together. Can he have a kiss? "Yes," she says, "—at the door." The Kiss itself is not as exciting as the fight provoked

---

* Not counting *A Man's Man* (1929), directed by James Cruz, a comic vehicle for William Haines and Josephine Dunn in which Garbo appears briefly with Gilbert in documentary footage.

† Research by the fact checking department of *The New Yorker* indicates that *The Kiss* was where that line originated—in which case, it was a classic instead of a cliché.

by her jealous husband who witnesses it. A door shuts on the scuffling trio; we can't see who pulls the trigger. The truth remains ambiguous almost to the last moment: Irene beats the rap, and in the odd, pre-Code ending—crime pays.

Feyder brought an authentic European look and atmosphere to his first MGM picture and ably transformed his international cast into Gallic character types. He had an English interpreter for Ayres and the others who spoke no French, while his instructions to Garbo were always in German. Her sharp instincts and absence of "star" attitude on the set struck Feyder, as nearly all her directors and co-stars: "Garbo is exactitude incarnate."

"What do you mean, 'Woman of Mystery'?" said Conrad Nagel. "We worked in two pictures together, and the only mystery about Greta was in the title [of *The Mysterious Lady*]. I found her to be a thoroughly enjoyable person. Every day we would come to the studio with a new joke." Nagel, an ardent Christian Scientist, was not much liked in Hollywood, recalls Lina Basquette, "because he didn't carouse much and was too open about his religion." He was open, too, about why he liked Garbo:

"She always quits promptly at five-thirty, while many of us lesser souls sometimes have to work all night. Greta won't work one minute overtime. I admire her for it—and I'd do the same thing if I were important enough to get away with it!"

Lew Ayres, Garbo's last surviving co-star, was told years later that, when asked which of her leading men she most enjoyed, his was the name she cited. "I don't know if that's true," says Ayres today. But he confirms that he faltered in their first scene together, at which point Garbo took him to Feyder and said, "Please introduce us—we haven't met." The introduction helped.

During the title Kiss itself, Ayres said, "she threw the action so entirely my way that I actually dominated the scene. Throughout the picture she gave me hints that I could have known otherwise only through long experience. I shall always be grateful to her, for she helped me over the hurdles. . . . Even in the most trying situations she was always serenely calm, complete mistress of whatever problems came up."

There were reports that Garbo not only took Ayres under her wing during *The Kiss* but also that they became close friends. Ayres recalled:

I was a little greenhorn of twenty, bouncing my way around, and she was the most sophisticated performer on the screen. I worked with her for six weeks, that's all. I was a nobody, but she never tried to hog a scene—you know, that trick of backing up the other person, which brings them around so you only see their profile. None of that. Around

Helping to put young Lew Ayres at ease on the set of The Kiss
(1929), Garbo's—and MGM's—final silent movie

the set, in between shots, we sat and chatted with each other, or on location, many times, we played tennis or went out to lunch. But I couldn't expect to become her confidante, and I didn't.

Ayres saw Garbo only once again:

I was in my car on Sunset Boulevard about ten years later, and I saw her driving behind me. I honked and rolled the window down and yelled and kept ahead of her and turned around so she'd see it was me—just to say hello. Not once did she acknowledge me. It went on for four or five more blocks, and finally—you just had to laugh and let her be what she was. She was not going to look at *anyone*. It's funny. I know she'd have been glad to say hello and maybe talk for five minutes. But she was frightened and couldn't run the risk of an "encounter" with some fan, or something she couldn't control.

Jacques Feyder, far left, William Daniels at top, and co-star Conrad Nagel, below, in The Kiss

The Kiss opened in New York on November 15, 1929, just seventeen days after the stock market crash. For that reason, and because it was a silent, it was not expected to do very well. But to MGM's pleasant surprise, it made more money—$448,000—than any previous Garbo film except *Flesh and the Devil* and *Love*. By special dispensation of the public, her silent swan song was a success, but everyone knew it was now time for Garbo to speak.

Silent film, like pantomime and ballet, was stylized movement intensified by the absence of speech. The face and body did the work of the voice, as well as their own. The "shadow play," as silent film was often called, was a technique of surfaces—a thousand nuances magnified on a screen. But just when its complex sign language was perfected, it became obsolete, and so did many of its practitioners.

One reason why neither Greta Garbo nor John Gilbert was in a hurry to talk on screen was the taunting of the silent stars. When film magazines began to address the new sound reality of Hollywood in late 1928, they were often vicious about it.

Charles Farrell, for instance—teamed with Janet Gaynor for *Seventh Heaven* and *Street Angel*—was half of a hot pair of late-silent lovers. But insiders snickered about how badly his high-pitched voice and strong New England accent would record. Sure enough, when he finally talked, critics trounced the voice and made fun of his "audible osculation":

"Charles Farrell in *Sunny Side Up* draws many a giggle for his mush stuff," said *Variety*. "The normal kiss, delivered with the usual smack, sounds like an explosion. For that reason, kiss scenes in the early talkers have them rolling in the aisles." Thanks to "Little Caesar Microphone," said *Photoplay*, Farrell "faces the fight of his life in the picture business."

Such stories, multiplied by the hundreds during the sound transition, were part of the love-hate relationship between the stars and their fans. There was unmistakable jubilation at the new vulnerability of the pampered few, wrote Alexander Walker in *The Shattered Silents*, and the stars were now bombarded by "the latent sadism of the very magazines that had sucked up to them for interviewing and access privileges."

The greatest abuse and biggest fall were reserved for a likable young man of whom Greta Garbo was still fond—John Gilbert, the highest-paid man in the business. Due to the calculation of Irving Thalberg, MGM was the only major studio that refused to rush into sound. Despite pressure from the New York office, Thalberg insisted on studying his rivals' output, waiting for the technology to improve, and continuing to produce quality silents, thus buying time for his stars, of whom Gilbert shone brightest. His prospects seemed even brighter after his explosive on- and offscreen teaming with Garbo. Yet there was the matter of that feud with his boss.

"It really began when Irving hired Jack after Fox fired him," said Louise Brooks. "Mayer didn't want [him], but Irving insisted. . . . And then Jack was so silly and drunken, hamming it up, letting Mayer bait him into scenes, instead of minding Irving and staying away."

Mayer now had a golden opportunity for revenge. Gilbert was convinced that he was behind a malicious article in the May 1928 *Vanity Fair* by "hobo author" Jim Tully, who reportedly met with Mayer before writing it and was currying his favor at MGM:

"In *Flesh and the Devil*, he was merely a romantic prop upon which Miss Greta Garbo hung an American reputation," Tully wrote. "Mr. Gilbert is not a gifted actor. He plays every role the same. . . . Gilbert is blamed for much of the so-called temperament with which Miss Garbo punished [MGM]."

But it was the end of the piece that drove Gilbert wild:

"John Pringle, Gilbert's father, is now an extra player in Hollywood. His salary averages less than $50 a week. He traced his son to Hollywood, having seen him on the screen. They had not met in 20 years. This was said not to have pleased the young Mr. Gilbert. I saw John Pringle recently in the role of a convict. He stood head down in prison garb among other sad partakers of crumbs from producers' tables. I wonder what he was thinking. Perhaps of the vagaries of women . . . and children."

The rejection of the poverty-stricken father was a total fabrication, but the story was widely believed.* Among many who came to Gilbert's defense was James Quirk of *Photoplay*, who called Tully's piece "brutal, unfair, untrue" and persuaded Gilbert to set the record straight in a four-part *Photoplay* series. But the damage was done, and more was forthcoming— ironically, in the form of a huge salary increase. Gilbert was still one of MGM's two biggest stars (Lon Chaney, not Garbo, was the other), and his contract was due to expire. His friend Nicholas Schenck in the main office was worried by reports that Gilbert was looking elsewhere and might take Garbo with him.

Accordingly, Schenck signed Gilbert for an astonishing million-dollar deal—four pictures at $250,000 apiece—that infuriated Mayer, who had been bypassed in the negotiations. "It is a long-term agreement," said Schenck. "It definitely sets at rest those rumors of his future activities. Elaborate plans for his forthcoming productions will be started immediately."

There was little the vengeful Mayer could do to or about Gilbert—until now, when many studio chiefs were exploiting the sound turmoil. Gilbert's first talkie was *Redemption* with the popular Eleanor Boardman and Renée Adorée; his second was *His Glorious Night* with Catherine Dale Owen, a screen unknown from the New York theater. But the films were released in reverse order, so that as far as the public was concerned, *His Glorious Night* was Gilbert's first talkie and the one by which his voice would first be judged.

Because of his stage experience—and, some said, his friendship with Mayer—Lionel Barrymore was called in to direct. With scant directing experience in silents, let alone talkies, he seemed the worst choice in the world and had little to work with: *His Glorious Night* was a Ruritanian romance from the moldy pen of Ferenc Molnár. Most disastrous of the lines Gilbert had to deliver were the three most intimate words in the language: "I love you." Over and over, at one point three times in a row, he declared

---

* Eighteen months later, on February 10, 1930, a Hollywood nightclub brawl between Gilbert and Tully made big headlines. Tables were upset and blows exchanged.

his love in a voice that seemed humorously shrill and at odds with his virile image. When the film opened on October 5, 1929, audiences did the worst thing they could do to a serious actor: They laughed.*

Neither the public nor MGM nor Gilbert grasped a deeper problem that had more to do with the dialogue than with the delivery. People still new to the talkies found it embarrassing to hear a man declare his passion for a woman. The strangeness of hearing love uttered so bluntly, says Walker, had an effect on the audience similar to that of first hearing four-letter words spoken on a stage several decades later. It seemed like eavesdropping, and people felt like Listening Toms. The violation of that splendid privacy between viewer and actors—the essence of silent film—was producing acute discomfort.

Gilbert's voice was in the ear of the beholder. It wasn't *bad*, said director William de Mille, "It was just not the voice his audience had heard in their minds in *The Big Parade*, or the voice that made love to Garbo in *Flesh and the Devil*." The darker question was whether Gilbert was deliberately sandbagged. Gilbert thought so. Louise Brooks hadn't the slightest doubt:

> Gilbert had a well-trained actor's voice. *Redemption* was made by Fred Niblo. It was pretty good. They previewed it and Quirk gave it a good review. So they shelved it.† John was terribly unpopular with producers . . . always making a fuss. So when they [were] stuck with the guy, they figured all they had to do was give him a couple of bad pictures. The plot thickens with *His Glorious Night*. The title alone shows that it was twenty years out of date. They got Lionel Barrymore to direct it: "You make that picture, and make it *lousy*." And he certainly did. MGM was the most wickedly ruthless studio in Hollywood. Any director to last there had to be mixed up in some of their evil deeds.

Brooks further alleged that Barrymore, during both Gilbert movies, was addicted to morphine: "Sammy Colt [Ethel Barrymore's son] partially excused Lionel . . . on the grounds that Irene Fenwick (his wife) got him on drugs in the teens and he was henceforth too stoned to worry about anything but money, which Louis Mayer supplied in large, appreciative amounts."

P. G. Wodehouse, in a letter written on August 18, 1930, while he was a

---

* At least, according to legend. There are many subsequent claims that people laughed at Gilbert's I-love-yous, though no contemporary reviews mention the fact.

† Niblo only directed part of *Redemption*; midway, he was replaced by—Lionel Barrymore! In the Niblo sections, says Kevin Brownlow, "Gilbert is relaxed, his voice is strong (a light baritone). Then the lighting changes, and Barrymore's stuff takes over. Gilbert's elocution was a little too pear-shaped in Niblo's scenes, but in Barrymore's he is acutely embarrassing—like a parody of himself."

writer at MGM, supported the conspiracy theory: "Just before John Gilbert did that first talkie, MGM had signed him for four pictures at $250,000 apiece, and the thought of having to pay out those million smackers gashes them like a knife. The rumor goes that in order to avoid this they are straining every nerve to ensure that his next picture will be such a flop that he will consent to make a broken-hearted settlement and retire from the screen."

Hedda Hopper said, "I watched Jack Gilbert being destroyed on the sound stage by one man, Lionel Barrymore," who denied requests by sound engineer Douglas Shearer (Norma's brother) for retakes. Most damning is the account of Clarence Brown, who said, "I know what happened. Douglas Shearer told me himself. He said, 'We never turned up the bass when Gilbert spoke; all you heard was treble.' Of course it was a 'mistake.' "

Lionel's brother John Barrymore succinctly summed up Gilbert's personal and professional plight: "From Garbo to limbo."

Gilbert's tale of woe was not, of course, the only one, but most stars bided their time and passed the test of their sound debuts.* A whole new breed of sound actors, moreover, was impatiently pushing. They ranged from such distinguished stage types as George Arliss to such hot young newcomers as Muni Weisenfreund, better known as Paul Muni. Regardless of sound, the harsh new decade would have brought new faces. Gilbert's title as the leading screen lover gave way first to Ronald Colman in the transition period and then to a new King with a devastating face and voice to match—Clark Gable.

What killed Gilbert in talkies was not so much his voice, which sounded just fine in the brilliant *Downstairs* (1932) and in *Queen Christina* (1933). It was his feud with Louis B. Mayer, his drinking, and the repetition of those three fatal words. "After *His Glorious Night* it was a long time before any man, no matter what his voice register, said 'I love you' on the screen again," said Colleen Moore. John Gilbert had made more money for MGM than any other star in its history up to that time, but now he was mocked and ruined.

Watching it happen, Greta Garbo was horrified.

---

* The smartest waited as long as they could. Joan Crawford's *Untamed* (released November 29, 1929) stressed her dancing and bought time for her vocal improvement. Gloria Swanson waited for Edmund Goulding's help on *The Trespasser* (November 1, 1929). Lillian Gish's first talkie was another soggy but passable Molnár play, *One Romantic Night* (May 20, 1930). Norma Talmadge's delay was one of the few that didn't pay off: Her *Du Barry, Woman of Passion* (November 2, 1930) prompted a wire from sister Constance: "Quit while you've still got your looks and be thankful for the trust fund mother set up"—which advice Norma took.

Salka Viertel, center, and members of the "salon." Clockwise from top right: *Billy Wilder, Stella Adler, Sergei Eisenstein, Christopher Isherwood, Emil Jannings, Tallulah Bankhead, Max Reinhardt*

CHAPTER 6

SALKA'S SALON
1930–1931

Now that films were talking, she was more silent than ever. Everybody wanted to know when the great Garbo's sound debut would occur, and many secretly relished the prospect of her going the way of Gilbert. She would take the plunge soon enough, and it would coincide with the ripening of the deepest friendship of her life. But for the moment, Garbo still wasn't talking onscreen, nor was she talking about talking, or anything else, offscreen.

She hadn't been talking for a long time. The unparalleled MGM promotion machine of Howard Dietz found itself with the unique dilemma of a star who hated publicity of all kinds, wouldn't speak to reporters, never went to premieres or nightclubs, and banned all visitors—no matter how important, including the royalty of half a dozen countries—from her sets.

Dietz (1896–1983) had been publicity director at Goldwyn Pictures and kept that position when it merged with Metro and then Mayer to form MGM in 1924. He was credited with inventing the company's trademark lion, as well as its *Ars gratia artis* ("Art for art's sake") motto. In his spare time, he was a librettist and songwriter ("Dancing in the Dark" was his biggest hit). His department employed a hundred people, and he was one of the most powerful figures in the industry, accustomed to the fawning cooperation of all MGM performers. Garbo's recalcitrance he viewed as a rebellion to be put down.

"Garbo was not enchanted by the motion-picture people in Hollywood," said Dietz. "[She] spoke the approximate truth in her interviews and panned Hollywood. I wasn't paid to pan Hollywood, and it was important to harness this free spirit. I insisted that a member of the publicity department [Katherine Albert] be present at every interview. Garbo said if she weren't allowed to speak freely, she wouldn't have any interviews, and she didn't have any interviews for the next 48 years."*

That odious if honest admission of the goal of "taming" Garbo contained a revelation: It was the restraint on her free speech as much as the interviews per se to which Garbo objected. Katherine Albert was a former movie extra forced by finances into journalism and then studio promotion. At the time she was assigned to be Garbo's press aide, "she was a disappointed ham in MGM publicity and looked upon Garbo as a Swede peasant robbing her of a job," according to Louise Brooks. "In 1926, Garbo finally learned to speak and read English well enough to realize that it was Katherine Albert who was creating the 'stupid Swedish peasant with big feet and comical accent' image."

After Albert left MGM and became a regular contributor to *Photoplay*, the hostility of her Garbo coverage escalated, as in the 1931 article "Exploding the Garbo Myth":

> Excavate the Spanish torture chambers and do with me as you will. I've simply got to say it.
>
> I'm bored with Garbo! . . .
>
> In the early days when she was first beginning her amazing career and I was in the publicity department I used to go out on the set with what is called a symposium idea. This means that a writer for a magazine or newspaper had requested that I ask the stars for certain of their opinions on various subjects. I grant you that some of these "ideas" were pretty terrible, but others there were that might have promoted a little interesting discussion.
>
> Invariably Garbo said, "Oh, dot's silly. I do not want to be quoted. . . ."
>
> I saw her one evening at one of the most select and brilliant of gatherings. The few people there were the real intellectuals of the colony and not a word of banal chatter . . . was uttered. Garbo came. A hush fell across the group. She completely wet blanketed the crowd. She was obviously bored and went home early. . . .
>
> On the screen—well, I believe that it's a trick. That something about those lack lustre eyes, that sullen mouth, that high brow, that pale, clay-like skin appeals to the imaginations of people. Rudolph Valentino had

---

* Even with several borderline cases, there were no more than fourteen and technically only eleven bona fide interviews with Garbo in her entire lifetime. For the full listing, see Appendix B, "Documented Garbo Interviews: 1924–1990," pp. 565–6.

a dead nerve in one eyelid. It gave that eyelid a droop. And a nice, wholesome, Italian boy became the sinister, mysterious dream lover of a million women.

Garbo appeals in the same way. I do not want to hurt her, for she does care about the things written of her and she reads them, yet she must realize that her personality has now become public property. . . .

But the Garbo legend is a myth—and don't let anybody tell you anything else. And her "great art" is something quite outside herself like the art of Clara Bow and Lupe Velez and other emotional machines.

Dietz was frustrated but personally fascinated by Garbo. "She was sincere in everything she said," he recalled. "When she said she didn't want to be interviewed she meant it. She has no possessions." Those non sequitur facts were beyond his comprehension, but he was amused rather than offended by her term for him—"Vice President of Poetry."

Albert was never amused. She told film historian Kevin Brownlow that the MGM publicity department was "burned up about her. Every other star gave [us] details, but not Garbo." Angrily, the department thenceforth produced and disseminated Garbo press releases without consulting her at all. That negative—in fact, punitive—policy, by Dietz's own admission, "turned out to be the best publicity notion of the century."

Some claimed Harry Edington had specifically advised her to follow the example of Maude Adams (1872–1953), America's greatest stage actress, whose curious aloofness had boosted her popularity. Unlike her peers, Adams shunned publicity, insisted on full privacy away from the theater, and capitalized on that secrecy itself. (In later life, she lived quietly with a woman said to be her lover.)

No screen star had ever attempted that tack. Garbo, whether by accident or calculation, was the first who dared refuse to cooperate with Louella Parsons and Hedda Hopper—let alone her own promotion department. It was outrageous, and surely suicidal. Yet instead of a "blackout," the press coverage of Garbo became obsessive, and so did public curiosity. One who keenly admired the results was another legendary European import, now in the embryonic stage of her own Hollywood climb.

"I envy Garbo," said Marlene Dietrich. "Mystery is a woman's greatest charm. I wish I could be mysterious like her. I don't want people to know everything about me! Garbo never gives interviews. I wish I could do the same."

But, in fact, the screen's great "silent woman of mystery" was an accidental creation—a publicity formula she only gradually learned to manipulate for

her own ends. And Howard Dietz never forgave himself for making her a
fabulous star.

She thus cut herself off from the public, but not from the world. The dynamic
Salka Viertel (1889–1978) was becoming her closest friend, collaborator, and
link to Hollywood's sizable émigré colony. No one was more important to
Garbo's California existence in general, and to her impending entry into
sound film in particular, than the Viertel family—Salka, her husband Berthold (1885–1953), and their three sons. They would keep and play their
roles in her life permanently.

Garbo, Stiller, and the two Hansons, like Ernst Lubitsch and Emil Jannings, were part of the first wave of European film immigrants to Hollywood.
The talkies produced a rollback of that group and then a replacement wave
of artists geared to sound. At first, most were English, but the continentals
soon followed when the studios began making foreign-language versions of
certain films for Europe. Among the new group was Salka Viertel.

She was born Salomé Steuermann in Galicia, then part of Poland. Her
lawyer-father was the Jewish mayor of a town named Sambor on the Dniester
River. His practice was thriving and they lived on a grand scale. Salka
dreamed of becoming an actress; her brother Edward, a pianist. Latin, Greek,
and German were required at school, and they learned German and French
from governesses at home. Added to her native Polish and Ukrainian, and
later English, Salka knew eight languages and was well prepared to host an
international salon in Hollywood.

Her parents had an open-door policy for artists, some of whom stayed
months or years. "There were many beggars in the community," she recalled.
Twice a week they came to receive alms—Christians on Thursday, Jews on
Friday, the gypsies at irregular intervals—"a nightmarish procession of
misery."

Come evening, the Steuermanns gathered around Edward to perform
chorales and oratorios and the sensational new music of Richard Strauss and
Gustav Mahler. But Salka's obsession was theater. Garbo "vamped" privately
in her Swedish childhood; Salka dressed up like Cleopatra in hers. Her debut
as Medea in Pressburg led to a job in Teplitz, in the Bohemian Sudetenland,
where she played the title role in Schiller's *Maria Stuart*.

"A favorite pastime [there] was trying to shock me," she wrote in her
memoirs. "The comedian . . . never failed to tear open his trousers and
expose himself as soon as he caught sight of me. The elderly character actor
[chased] me all over the place, trying to force me into a dark corner. For-
tunately I was stronger and could defend myself. But sometimes the snide

remarks and dirty jokes were so funny that I laughed with the others. I was afraid of them but they fascinated me."

It was precisely the kind of rough-and-tumble theatrical experience her friend Garbo never had and would have hated.

Brother Edward took Salka to Max Reinhardt's theater in Berlin, where she met the young comic Ernst Lubitsch and, soon after, performed in Reinhardt's *Faust II* and the title role in Heinrich Kleist's *Penthesilea*, a wild expressionist Sturm und Drang part she loved "because of its extravagance. Penthesilea's bacchantic jubilations, her demented despair and maniacal ravings were enough to release any amount of pent-up passions."

In Berlin, Salka and Edward created their own "proto-salon" in a two-room apartment and nearby restaurant where artsy friends came to exchange animated conversation and "immoral" ideas. Edward was in the process of becoming Arnold Schoenberg's greatest apostle, sacrificing his own promising piano career to propagate the master's works, often with Alban Berg and Anton von Webern in tow. He premiered Schoenberg's *Pierrot Lunaire*.

Salka's bohemian life, meanwhile, included performing in a scandalous 1913 play about syphilis. When World War I began, she and her sister Rose enrolled as volunteer nurses and were soon caught between the Russians and the Germans, ending up as refugees in Vienna. There, in 1916, Salka played Vassilisa in a production of Gorky's *The Lower Depths* that was attended by Lieutenant Berthold Viertel, a poet and stage director on furlough. He was married but told Salka he planned to get a divorce and marry her instead. Berthold's poems had been published in *Die Fackel* by Karl Krauss, the great editor and passionate opponent of the war.

True to his word, when Viertel returned to civilian life in 1918, he got his divorce, married Salka, and began directing at the Royal Theater in Dresden, while inflation and the Spartacist revolt raged. "We were always hungry," recalled Salka, who doggedly pursued her own career after the birth of Hans and, in November 1920, her second son, Peter. Financial extremes were typical: The Viertels had their own repertory theater in Hamburg for a year, and the next year were so destitute they couldn't even afford a Christmas tree.

In 1922, Berthold was invited to direct for Reinhardt in Berlin, where—despite horrendous political violence and inflation (the dollar was then fluctuating between two and three billion marks)—artistic life flourished. Kandinsky and Klee exhibits vied for audiences with Schoenberg's music and Reinhardt's exciting theatricals. In film, Salka preferred Stiller's "wonderful Swedish tales"—*Gösta Berling* was then a Berlin sensation—to the expressionism of F. W. Murnau and Fritz Lang. In February 1925, six months before the birth of her third son, Thomas, Eisenstein's *Potemkin* created an uproar in Berlin. And, of course, everyone loved Chaplin best of all.

The Viertels were ever avant-garde and adventurous, and in late 1927, when director Murnau asked Berthold to come to Hollywood and write the screenplay for his American film *The Four Devils*, they were inclined to take the risk. Salka and Murnau had acted together at the Reinhardt theater; Murnau and Berthold had a long, complex relationship in which Berthold periodically rebelled against Murnau's authoritarian personality. Berthold thought Hollywood was changing for the better, making him less Prussian and more relaxed. Salka doubted it, but director Jacques Feyder and his wife, actress Françoise Rosay—who likewise had a Hollywood contract in hand and were taking three young sons to America—convinced her to say yes to the New World.

The adult Viertels sailed from Hamburg on February 22, 1928 (the children followed later with a nurse), and were met in New York by a German-speaking publicity man from Fox and three reporters—three more than had greeted Garbo and Stiller. In those first days, they were thrilled by Rouben Mamoulian's Theater Guild production of *Porgy* (1927) and by the magnificent stage show accompanying Murnau's *Sunrise* at the Roxy. But *The Jazz Singer* (1927) dwarfed everything else. "For a stage director and a writer," said Salka, "the talkies offered greater possibilities than the silent film."

After the cross-country train trip, they checked into the Hollywood Roosevelt Hotel, where they got their first taste of local culture. Coming downstairs for lunch, Salka recalled, "We heard a cacophony of shrill voices as if from an enormous, excited poultry yard. The lobby was packed with women of whom the youngest could not have been less than 70. About a hundred of them tottered around on high heels, in bright, flowered-chiffon dresses, orchid or gardenia corsages pinned to their bosoms. We wanted to know the purpose of the gathering but were told only that the ladies were Republicans."

The strangeness struck Salka as strongly as it had Garbo, but with a characteristic difference: from Salka, it elicited humor; from Garbo, horror. The Viertels rented a modest house on Fairfax Avenue in West Hollywood and jumped into the life of the German community. Many were leaving, but they still tended to stick together for protection: Emil Jannings threw a welcome party for the Viertels in his grand Hollywood Boulevard mansion (rented from Joseph Schenck), where the guests included Conrad Veidt, Ernst Lubitsch, Max Reinhardt, and director Ludwig Berger, whom Paramount had signed but didn't know what to do with.

"Throughout the evening the main topic of conversation was the catastrophic impact of the talking films upon the careers of foreign stars," said Salka. Afterward, she and Berthold agreed that "Conny Veidt was most handsome and a darling; Lubitsch inscrutable but worth knowing better; and Ludwig Berger's fate a warning to European directors."

On weekends, Salka took her boys to the beach or to "my beloved merry-go-round" at the Santa Monica Pier, while the Fox executives regarded Berthold as an eccentric but valuable acquisition. They sought his opinion on scripts and took his inventive advice on films that needed to be doctored. Berthold was as creative as he was impractical—forgetful of details, incapable of arriving anywhere on time. He looked more like a musician than a writer, with his long, thick wavy white hair. "He was gentle and sympathetic, extremely European and poetic," said Garbo's later friend Mercedes de Acosta. "I always felt he was like a fish out of water in Hollywood."

More an amphibian, really, in a world where the land-sea transition was no more challenging than the silent-sound one. Berthold's first directing assignment was Fox's last silent film, *The One Woman Idea* (1929), in which he cast the newly arrived Françoise Rosay. Feyder, for his part, got a plum first assignment directing Garbo in MGM's final silent, *The Kiss*. The Feyders and Viertels drew closer, and Berthold soon cast Françoise again in *The Magnificent Lie*, a Ruth Chatterton talking vehicle. Rosay, in turn, helped get her émigré friend Charles Boyer the part of a con man in that film, but Boyer hated it and thought Berthold—who was "Bertlevertle" to most of Hollywood—oblivious to characterization.*

Berthold's personality and directing style were not to everyone's taste, but he was fondly recalled in Christopher Isherwood's roman à clef, *Prater Violet* (1945), inspired by their film work together in England. Among its in-jokes are the delusions of a producer whose one great ambition is—"*Tosca*. With Garbo. Without music, of course. I'd do it absolutely straight. And to write it? Somerset Maugham. . . . If I can't get Maugham, I won't do it at all."

Prater Violet mostly concerns the Viertel character, a director, and his relationship to Isherwood, the writer-narrator: "He was my father. I was his son. I loved him very much." He smoked constantly, with a frantic nervous impatience, holding his cigarette like an accusing finger pointed at his partner. His discourse was brilliantly philosophical, especially on movies:

---

* *The Magnificent Lie* set Chatterton's career on a downward slide and was Rosay's last American picture for twenty years. Boyer was also cast—to his chagrin—in Viertel's *The Man from Yesterday*. As director, Berthold also made *Man Trouble* (1930), *The Spy* (1931), *The Wiser Sex* and *The Man from Yesterday* (both 1932) in America, and *Little Friend* (1934), *The Passing of the Third Floor Back* (1935), and his one commercial success, *Rhodes of Africa* (1936), in England.

"The film is an infernal machine. Once it is ignited and set in motion, it revolves with an enormous dynamism. It cannot pause. . . . It cannot wait for you to understand it. It cannot explain itself. It simply ripens to its inevitable explosion. This explosion we have to prepare, like anarchists, with the utmost ingenuity and malice. . . .

"The film studio of today is really the palace of the sixteenth century. There one sees what Shakespeare saw: the absolute power of the tyrant, the courtiers, the flatterers, the jesters, the cunningly ambitious intriguers. There are fantastically beautiful women, there are incompetent favorites. There are great men who are suddenly disgraced. There is the most insane extravagance [and] horrible squalor hidden behind the scenery. There are vast schemes, abandoned because of some caprice. There are secrets which everybody knows and no one speaks of. There are even two or three honest advisers. . . ."

His anger [always] subsided into philosophic doubt. He could never dismiss any suggestion, however fantastic, without hours of soul-searching. . . .

"You know what my wife tells me when I have these difficulties? 'Friedrich,' she says, 'Go and write your poems. When I have cooked the dinner, I will invent this idiotic story for you. After all, prostitution is a woman's business.'"

This last was the voice of Salka, loud and clear. She had a home, two careers, and three children to juggle.

So did the Feyders, who had a salon of their own. Their circle of friends included writers Jacques Deval, Yves Mirande, and the Viertels; directors Ernst Lubitsch, William Wyler, and Robert Florey; actors Arlette Marchal, Michele Morgan, Garbo, and Boyer. Jean Negulesco met Garbo there while he was painting a portrait of Feyder, which Garbo liked: "She posed willingly for some sketches and photos I made of her and Jacques." But when an actor she didn't know came in unexpectedly, she "suddenly acted like a caged wild animal. She hurried out onto the terrace and walked alone in the dark, in the rain, to her home."

Fox picked up Berthold's option and doubled his salary, but the Viertels kept prolonging their visitor permits instead of applying for immigration papers, vaguely still intending to go "home." In June 1928, they moved from Hollywood to a house just off the beach. "Contrary to predictions, moving to Santa Monica did not impair our social life," said Salka. "On the contrary, our [open house on] Sunday afternoons became very popular."

For émigrés, the Viertel house at 165 Mabery Road would become the most famous address in Los Angeles. Murnau, for one, came regularly, until

*165 Mabery Road, Santa Monica, with its peekaboo view of the Pacific Ocean at left
—the home of Salka and Berthold Viertel and their "salon"*

he saw Robert Flaherty's *Moana* and left for the South Seas to work on
Tabu. Salka saw him off with two pounds of Malosol caviar in late 1929,
around the same time the Janningses left. By then, most of the Germans
had disappeared, but other Central Europeans came to replace them, including director William Dieterle and nineteen-year-old Fred Zinnemann,
Berthold's new assistant, from Vienna. Billy Wilder arrived, with his abrasive
sense of humor; he didn't quite fit in with the grander circles but made
some good tennis friends at the Viertels'. Albert Einstein came to town and
asked Salka and Berthold to dinner.

Natives were welcome, too. When Tallulah Bankhead moved out from
New York, she joined the Viertels' "Sunday afternoons," as did Stella Adler
during her frequent visits west. Adler was one of the few who became as
fond of Berthold as of Salka over the years, due to Berthold's increasing
theatrical work and time spent in New York:

> Salka was a very close friend. I knew her well. I knew the boys. I
> knew her brother Edward, a great pianist. I knew her horrible dog.*
> I was there a lot. She didn't have any money, you know. She asked me

---

* Few who met "Prince" ever forgot him: He bit everybody, including Mercedes de Acosta,
Peter Viertel; and Garbo.

for money once. I didn't give her much, maybe $100. But I did help
her out. Is that immoral to say? She was extraordinary and she had an
extraordinary husband, a great poet and great friend. One day I was
sitting in the Russian Tea Room, and Berthold passed. I didn't see or
greet him, but he stopped and said, "Don't you know I'm your relative?"
You remember words that are so startling. He only connected with
certain people.

I remember one particular experience at their salon. I was introduced
to a young man and he said, "I don't want to talk to you." Now, let's
be honest, I was a beauty. I said, "Why?" He said, "There's nothing
written on your face." Isn't that great? I have no idea who he was.
Maybe a poet. I suppose only a poet would say something like that.

Among the new émigrés arriving around this time were Lya de Putti,
Camilla Horn, Greta Nissen, Dmitri Buchowetski, Paul Leni, E. A. Dupont,
and Erich Pommer. "The movie kings housed and fed these valued impor-
tations like prize cattle," says Paul Rotha, "and succeeded after some struggling in taming them for their needs." Most, but not all, of them came to
the Viertels, and most people, but not all, adored Salka.

"She was a busybody," said Irene Mayer Selznick. "I knew her a long
time, and she was up to all kinds of things—very strong physically and
hearty Mittel-Europa, very gemütlich. She made her husband's career possible
and was adept at getting things arranged. She was no more self-seeking than
anyone else, just a little more successful."

She and Berthold, in fact, helped each other. In *The Seven Faces* (1929),
a tale of waxwork characters that come to life, he cast Paul Muni as Jack
the Ripper and Salka as Catherine the Great, but "the experience did not
make me wish to become a movie actress," she said. "Acting in fragments
is like drinking from an eyedropper when you are parched." She couldn't
know that her next film acting assignment would be the most historic of
her career, due to its connection with the greatest Hollywood émigré of all.

When Salka first met Garbo at a Lubitsch party in late 1929, she confessed
that she had seen just one of her movies. "She told me she was pleased that
I had only seen *Gösta Berling*, as she did not care much for her other
films," Salka wrote. "She was very funny, caricaturing the repetitiousness of
the seduction techniques." They spoke of Berlin and Salka's work in the
theater—and then Garbo was gone.

The next day, Salka recalled, her doorbell rang "and in the open window
of the entrance appeared the unforgettable face. . . . Gaily she announced
she had come to continue the conversation of last night, and stayed all
afternoon. We went for a short walk on the beach and then sat in my room."

Salka found her "intelligent, simple, completely without pose, with a great sense of humor, joking about her inadequate German and English." Her English was better than her German, but she loved certain German words (such as *vervalos*, "slovenly") and never gave them up. She and Salka spoke in a mixture of the two tongues.

Everyone found Garbo's English charming, but not having a comprehensive command of the language was an inhibiting factor (on top of many others) for her. By 1930, she spoke it well but still missed some subtleties of rapid American speech. More important, the *movies* spoke English. Gone was the universality of the medium; overnight, films were national. The ability to handle English was a life-or-death challenge and a tremendous psychological hurdle for the émigrés. An accent limited any actor's roles, and any slight self-consciousness—even in fluency—could hamper his expressive skills. The merciless camera never failed to pick it up.

It was hard enough for Americans, as the Gilbert case demonstrated. But Garbo's distress over that was empathy for him personally. Sound per se neither impressed nor intimidated her. Unlike Clara Bow, she had no terror of the microphone itself.

"If they want me to talk, I'll talk," she said. "I'd love to act in a talking picture when they are better, but the ones I have seen are awful. It's no fun to look at a shadow, and somewhere out of the theatre a voice is coming."

As early as *Flesh and the Devil*, an experimental sound sequence had been prepared for her and Gilbert but then discarded as too dangerous. By late 1930, many of the great foreign actors, such as Vilma Banky—and not a few domestic ones, such as Corinne Griffith and Rod La Rocque—had bitten the dust in talkies. Garbo's fall was next, it was assumed. Rumor had it she was planning for failure and making arrangements to shut up her house and return to Sweden. Nobody's job was safe and, as Isherwood wrote, no one knew what was coming next: "Taste, perhaps, or Smell, or Stereoscopy, or some device that climbed right down out of the screen and ran around in the audience. Nothing seemed impossible."

MGM was deeply worried about sound in general and its ethereal Swede in particular. "Garbo's present contract is still a 'silent' one, as she has never signed an agreement to talk," according to an internal studio memorandum at the time. "In this respect, she is the one exception in our stock company. The question of her signing was discussed with the advent of sound pictures, but she declined to sign, giving as her reason, as I recall it, lack of proficiency in the English tongue."

Thalberg had wanted her to play Joan of Arc in her first talkie but was unable to persuade George Bernard Shaw to sell the rights to *Saint Joan*.

Blanche Sweet in the 1923 silent Anna Christie

For $570,000, Eugene O'Neill's *Anna Christie* was obtained instead. The transition of MGM's most valuable property to talkies had long been calculated: She would make it, finally, in the role of an immigrant whore with a Swedish accent.

Anna Christie (1930), Garbo's fourteenth film, was adapted by Frances Marion with surprising fidelity to the play. Richard Corliss called the drama "all scissors and paste, with a tacked-on happy ending," as if O'Neill had written it expressly to be made into a Hollywood movie. Pauline Lord had played Anna on the stage, and Blanche Sweet had done so in the John Griffith Wray silent film of 1923. It won a Pulitzer Prize in 1921 but by 1930 seemed a bit of the old malarkey:

Anna was abandoned in her Minnesota girlhood, raped by a cousin, and propelled into prostitution. Weary, disgusted, and broke, she returns to her father, Chris, and his broken-down coal barge in New York harbor, first encountering Marthy, his old dockside dame. For a while, Anna finds tranquility, but a more interesting find is Matt, the seaman she rescues from a storm.

It is sixteen minutes into the film before Garbo appears, slouch-walking

Cameraman William Daniels, unidentified light technician, Garbo, and director Clarence Brown on Anna Christie—*with the career-wrecking instrument above their heads*

through the "Ladies" entrance of a bar. The delay builds excitement for our first glimpse of her: Leading as always with her shoulder, she drags herself to a table, plops down in a hardback chair, and, to the bartender, utters her immortal first words on film: "Gimme a viskey, ginger ale on the side— and don' be stingy, baby!"

Both the line and the delivery were perfect, but no more so than the voice: deep, resonant, soulful—*real*. Comparisons were useless. Jeanne Eagels's and Tallulah Bankhead's somewhat similar pitches were known only in the theater. For millions, Garbo's was a vocal apotheosis—the richest, sexiest, most natural low. Reportedly, she had to retake certain *Anna Christie* scenes because her accent was not strong enough!

The voice was clear, piquant, and alluring. That it fit both the character and the actress's private self was a fortuitous delight. Marie Dressler, who played Marthy, described Garbo as:

> Phlegmatic! . . . She always seemed totally uninterested in her sur-
> roundings, even a trifle bored. [But] no one I have ever worked with

in pictures has made me work so hard. Greta works almost to the point of exhaustion, and her capacity for work is contagious. The fact is, an actor must put forth every last ounce of effort every minute of his working time, or his role will fall short miserably in comparison to Greta's uniformly splendid work. There are several actors, for this very reason, who have risen to great heights when playing opposite Garbo, only to fall back to their natural levels when appearing in other casts.

That veteran vaudevillian knew whereof she spoke. When Frances Marion first proposed her for Marthy, a studio official said, "There is no doubt that Miss Dressler was a great actress in her day. But her day is past. Nobody has heard of her in ten years." It was true—partly because of her bold activity in a Broadway labor dispute in the twenties—and Dressler, at sixty, was bitter about it. She was one of the most exploited comediennes of the Jazz Age, a fine actress subjected to stereotyped casting. In *Anna Christie*, she was a powerful wreck in the drunk part of a lifetime, and many felt she stole the show.

"Of course this was not true," said Dressler in her memoirs. "Nobody could steal a show from Garbo. What they meant was this: They were surprised that the part of a homely drunken old waterfront hag could be made a thing that pulled at your heartstrings. . . . After ten years on the shelf, how do you think I felt? Letters poured in. People liked me. They wanted to see me again. It didn't matter to the public that I was no longer young. The hurt in my heart was healed."*

Charles Bickford as Matt was too full of himself to pay much attention to Garbo, Dressler, or anyone else. He'd recently made his and Cecil B. DeMille's first talkie, *Dynamite* (1929), on which he served as dialogue coach and managed to intimidate even DeMille through his personality, his diction, and his stature in the New York theater.

The reviews, of course, focused on the unveiling of a single set of vocal cords—"the voice of a Viking's daughter, inherited from generations of seamen who spoke against the roar of the sea, and made themselves heard." Richard Watts, Jr., in the New York *Herald Tribune* described it as "a deep, husky, throaty contralto" with "fabulous poetic glamour." Norbert Lusk in *Picture Play* called it "The voice that shook the world!" A hinterlands critic observed: "Some of the strange mystery of the woman (you never visualize Garbo as saying words, and it is a breathless sort of shock when she speaks)

---

* After *Anna Christie*, there was no more doubt about parts for Dressler. Metro put her under contract at once, and she made a dozen more films between then and her death in 1934. She won an Oscar for best actress in *Min and Bill* (1930) and was the country's number-one box-office attraction in 1932 and 1933.

Garbo in the title role with Marie Dressler as Marthy in Anna Christie *(1930)*

Garbo with Salka Viertel as Marthy in the German version of Anna Christie
(1930)

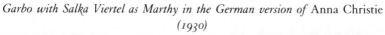

is gone, but the new Garbo is a greater actress than the old." There were a
dozen reasons why her voice should have "failed," but she overcame all of
them—simply by not *worrying* about it.

Had her voice proved unsatisfactory in *Anna Christie*, Garbo would have
been lost to the screen thereafter. But everyone went gaga. In Los Angeles,
even the Mexican puppet shows celebrated her triumph—and did a send-
up of it—at the Teatro Torrito on Olvera Street. She saw it several times,
once with Jacques Feyder, and laughed heartily at the Garbo marionette's
parody of the sea captain's lines:

> Dat old devil sea . . . was an angel to me.
> With photography misty, I did Anna Christie,
> and see what O'Neill did for me!
> I live as I please, with the world at my knees
> Singing "Skol!" to dat old devil sea.

Garbo's first talking picture was only Clarence Brown's second, and no
one was more impressed with her performance than he. Brown made an
amazing admission: "Her judgment on matters affecting screen technique
is excellent. So highly do I regard it that often, as in *Anna Christie*, I adopt
Garbo's ideas rather than my own. [It] made Garbo one of the greatest
talking picture stars, and it placed my name among the ten best directors
of the year—so I believe I have been justified in having done the picture
Garbo's way."

One day around this time, she trekked on foot from her home in Beverly
Hills to her friend Howard Greer's dress shop in Hollywood, where one of
his models told her, "I'm going downtown in a few minutes to see *Anna
Christie*." Garbo replied, "How would you like me to go with you?" They
climbed into the girl's roadster and drove into Los Angeles for the early
show, where she was unrecognized and could judge quietly for herself.
During its first week at the Capitol Theater in New York, *Anna Christie*
smashed the house record by $10,000. Huge lines stormed the theater, even
for the midnight shows. But Garbo's private assessment, expressed in a letter
to Mimi Pollack, was typical: "Isn't it terrible? Who ever saw Swedes act
like that?"

The twenty-seven feature films Garbo is always said to have made should
really be twenty-eight: *Anna Christie* was such a hit that MGM decided to
remake it in German. The success of Garbo's talkie debut made her doubly
valuable to the studio since now, in the early years of sound, many pictures
were being shot in alternative-language versions in an effort to hold on to
at least some of the foreign markets.

*One of the many still shots of Garbo smoking and
drinking from* Anna Christie *by Milton Browne.
Such photographs were morally disallowed in
America and sent off exclusively for foreign
distribution.*

In the case of *Anna Christie*, the result was a separate and very different film. Jacques Feyder was chosen to direct, German actors were imported, and under the velvet whip of producer Thalberg, it was cranked out in a lightninglike twenty days. The leading lady would thus make three films in the nine months between October 1929 and June 1930—two of them under Feyder's direction—and with the stock market crash as no small distraction.

"Garbo had to conquer the difficulty of still another language," said Salka Viertel. "She worked hard, with precision, and her German was almost without accent." No one was in a better position to observe that than Salka, who sat next to her in the same bar chair Marie Dressler had occupied. Under her maiden name Steuermann, it was now Salka's turn to play Marthy:

> Being 25 years younger [than Dressler], I was not too eager for the part, but Feyder persuaded me that Marthy could be of any age. Also he wanted me to help him with the German dialogue. . . . I was

frightened when my first scene had to be shot. I hated my costumes, my make-up seemed all wrong and there was no time to change it. But Feyder made everything easy. He made me play a long scene just as I would have done it in the theater, without interruption and, although blinded by the lights, I forgot that three cameras were shooting it from different angles.

At the end of her big scene, the stagehands burst into applause.

The crew was the same in this slightly longer foreign version (82 versus 74 minutes), but the performing ensemble and its dynamics were entirely different: Hans Junkermann was Matt, Theo Shall played Anna's father, and Salka was Marthy in Reinhardt theatrical style. This time, Garbo resembles Joan Crawford in the grand entrance, and her *"Whisky—aber nicht zu knapp!"* is a fine idiomatic rendering of the famous first line. Dressler was more authentic, but the interaction between Garbo and Salka is more intimate, from the first locking of their eyes through a subtle exchange of sidelong glances as they drink.

Garbo's German Anna is more relaxed, less declamatory—and a heavier smoker. Junkermann's Matt is sexier and less blustery than Bickford's. While Bickford tried to devour her, Junkermann just wants to get his *hands* on her, teasing her about knitting a sweater and using that as an excuse for physical contact. He turns on the charm instead of the brawn. One brief bit of business illustrates Garbo's attention to detail: In the Brown film, she slices some bread, downward, on a galley table; in the Feyder, she holds the loaf and cuts it upwardly, toward herself, European style. Her unique laugh—dry, quick, and rueful—is the same in any language but, in the Feyder version, conveys something closer to despair. She told friends privately that the German *Anna Christie* was the best thing she had ever done.

Bilingual viewers today can judge for themselves, for both versions survive in beautiful prints. Garbo, either way, was home free in talkies. It was *Salka's* career that was on the line: The second *Anna Christie* would make or break her in MGM's eyes. The bottom line—$1,013,000 in domestic earnings, $486,000 in foreign, and a profit of $576,000—is that it made her and, indirectly, her salon.

"I was very sad and lonely, the first year my husband and children and I spent in Hollywood," Salka later wrote. "We were strangers in a strange land." But she and Garbo "often poured out our lonely hearts to each other. . . . We discovered we had much in common—literature, music, painting, sculpture, the theater. Hollywood, we seldom discussed." What charmed her most was Garbo's attentiveness and canny assessment of people. "All that

*Garbo with Hans
Junkermann as seaman Matt in
the German version of* Anna
Christie *(1930)*

*Jacques Feyder, seated at center, directs
them in the Coney Island sequence;
William Daniels is at the camera.*

fame prevents her from living her real life," Salka told her husband. "It's a very high price to pay," Berthold replied.

Garbo's original circle of friends was shrinking and the Swedish colony breaking up. Soon after Stiller left in December 1927, so did Lars Hanson and Karin Molander. Victor Sjöström went off to Sweden for an extended holiday, and by the time he got back to Hollywood, Lillian Gish was gone and so was a historic opportunity: Garbo's first preference to direct *Anna Christie* had been Sjöström, but he lingered too long abroad. It might have established Sjöström, not Brown, as "The Garbo Director" of the future. Instead, after one talkie—adapted from a bad Broadway comedy called *A Lady to Love* (1930)—Sjöström returned to Sweden in April 1930 for good.

With the departure of the Sjöström family, Garbo nowadays came even more frequently to Salka's. They took long walks, usually in early morning when the beach was deserted, and discovered common bonds in their vastly different backgrounds. Salka told her that, as a child, the thing she most prayed for was that her father and mother wouldn't quarrel: "I was on my father's side, perhaps because my mother was always so much louder and more violent than he. It always seemed to me that Papa, this aloof, immaculate man, was being brutally dragged down from the pedestal upon which he justly belonged."

A lifelong soul-mate relationship—or the closest thing to it that Garbo would ever have—was flowering at a time when her triumph in sound seemed to exacerbate, not alleviate, her anxiety over the direction of her career.

The least appreciated film of that career was *Romance* (1930), Garbo's second talkie and far more representative than *Anna Christie* of what was to come. Directed by Clarence Brown with the familiar Daniels-Gibbons-Adrian team, it derived from a popular Edward Sheldon play based on the life of prima donna Lina Cavalieri. Garbo as an opera singer is phlegmatic beyond Marie Dressler's imagining, and the hints of music are few and far between; not only was her singing dubbed by a soprano (Diana Gaylen), but we never even see Garbo pretend to sing or move her lips. Yet her speaking voice and presence are riveting, from the first cynical speech:

"Sometimes I wish that I'd died before I ever heard those words, 'I love you.' What is love? It's made of kisses in the dark, and hot breaths on the face, and a heart that beats with terrible strong blows. Love is yust a beast that you feed all through the night, and when the morning comes—love dies."

The sentiment is Latin, the "yust" is Swedish, and the script is woeful.

In high Adrian fashions as Rita Cavallini, a diva modeled on Lina Cavalieri, in Romance *(1930). George Hurrell's were the only post-1929 Garbo portraits not taken by Clarence Bull. (See Chapter 8 for Garbo's opinion of the two photographers' diametrically opposite techniques.)*

Yet Garbo gets away with it because it's 1930 and she's game enough to enter Linguistic Bedlam. "O, mon dieu!" she exclaims. "The hours—they fly so fast!" Her French-cum-Italian English is full of rolled Scandinavian *r*'s. When she stomps her feet in a "hot-blooded" tantrum, it is not believable but thoroughly delightful. Her sad tale of having been sold at sixteen to a traveler is a bad speech, but speech *itself* was still a novelty—especially hers. The success of *Romance* is inexplicable unless we remember that talkies were still as new and marvelous as the sound of Garbo's voice.

Less marvelous was the rest of the cast, except for Clara Blandick in a short, hilarious scene with a monkey.* As Garbo's initial benefactor, Lewis Stone with speech is no more interesting than Lewis Stone mute, his wooden "dignity" again mistaken for acting. He is a dull authority figure, awaiting his cues like an impatient commuter at rush hour. But Garbo adored him, then and later, as a kind of father figure. Lina Basquette recalls that, offscreen, "Stone was very much the way he was in films—avuncular, kind." He made Garbo feel comfortable but was a canker on almost every movie she made with him.

Poor, panned Gavin Gordon (1901–70), on the other hand, was really no prissier than his part as a sexually repressed vicar required. (Garbo's first choice, Gary Cooper, was lamentably unavailable.) Gordon was a Kentucky hillbilly who never saw a movie until he was nineteen; after a modest bit of stage experience, he had come to Hollywood in 1928 and nurtured the fantastic dream of someday acting with Garbo. Lady Luck was with him: Among the dozens of prospective leading men whose screentests were run for her and director Clarence Brown, Gordon's was the one they both liked best.

The first day of shooting was to be the greatest of his life, but as Gordon was driving along Washington Boulevard toward Culver City, another car turned out of a side street and smashed into his. He was thrown out onto the pavement, landing on his left shoulder. Though the pain was excruciating, his only thought was, "If they know I'm hurt, they'll never let me start."

Somehow he made it to the studio, struggled into his costume and makeup, and at the end of his first scene fainted dead away. He came to in the hospital with a fractured collarbone, a dislocated shoulder, and a bedside visitor named Garbo. When he struggled to get up, she said, "Please do not do that. You are hurt, Mr. Gordon. . . . But if you will be good and take care of yourself, we will wait for you."

She made good on her promise, opposing the studio's desire to find a

---

* Best known as Judy Garland's Auntie Em in *The Wizard of Oz* nine years later, Blandick committed suicide in 1962 at the age of eighty-two.

replacement and arranging with Brown to give Gordon time to recuperate by first filming all the scenes in which he did not appear.

Impaired in more ways than one, Gordon struggled with the vicar's part as best he could. When she begs him to elope, he laments, "But I've got a meeting of the Board of Charities tomorrow at eleven and a funeral at twelve." It is not Gordon's fault that his character is a cardboard zombie until awakened by lust, at which point Garbo shames him to his senses.

At the end of *Romance*, she poses in angelic self-sacrifice, celestial choir in the background. An epilogue informs us that she died in a convent. It is the penultimate absurdity; the ultimate one is Gordon's final advice as an old man to his nephew: "Don't lose it, my boy, it's the greatest thing in the world—ROMANCE!"

The script was matched by Clarence Brown's lame direction. Mesmerized by what Garbo could do by herself, he failed to supplement her performance with any ideas of his own:

"She is original," he enthused. "Her acting finesse is very nearly perfect. Although the term is popularly misused, I must say that Greta Garbo is a genius. . . . In talking over the script of *Romance*, I thought she showed more brains and good judgment than anyone on the set."

That wasn't saying much. But Brown was right in that Garbo was dazzling despite all handicaps, striving so hard and magically that audiences succumbed to her spell. "Her performance is a thing of pure beauty, an inspiring blend of intellect and emotion," said *Picture Play*. "The Garbo voice itself is not of Italian quality or inflection, but for all anyone cares [she] might as well be Portuguese or Roumanian, for it is her emotions that are conveyed to the spectator, and her nativity counts for nothing at all."

Garbo was Oscar-nominated for both *Anna Christie* and *Romance* in 1930, which split her vote and brought victory to Norma Shearer's tear-jerking performance in *The Divorcee*. But *Romance* was of far-reaching importance to star and studio alike—the epitome of early sound soap operas. Its $287,000 profit assured MGM's continuation of the same basic formula and character, of which her next was a carbon copy.

Inspiration (1931) imitated neither life nor art but only the artifice of *Romance*. The screenplay was based on Alphonse Daudet's mildly scandalous 1884 play, *Sappho*. This time, Garbo is Yvonne Valbret, "inspiration of all the artists in the Latin Quarter." In the beautiful opening shot, a champagne fountain fills five glasses simultaneously at a gala soiree. As Garbo smokes seductively, men hurl themselves at her feet. Sculptors, painters, poets—she's tired of them all.

"Are you really as heartless as you seem?" asks Lewis Stone, her mentor–father figure yet again.

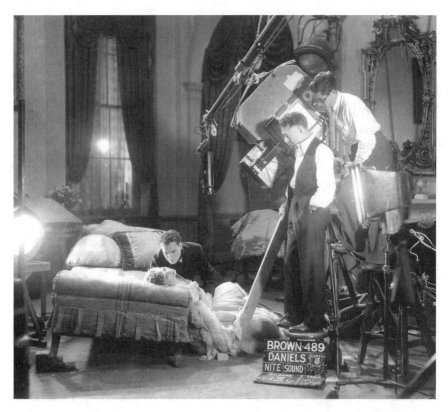

Clarence Brown directs Garbo and amorous vicar Gavin Gordon in Romance, *William Daniels photographing. The intense lights and tightly soundproofed room produced 104-degree temperatures during the filming of this scene.*

"You're all alike, you men," she replies. "You only want the satisfaction of being through with us first, that's all. So far, I have the good fortune of beating you to it—so I am heartless. . . . Who's the boy over there?"

He is André—a very awkward Robert Montgomery—and he's studying for the consular service. And who is she?

"I'm just a nice young woman," she says after they are introduced, "—not too young and not too nice."

They leave the party, drive to his apartment, climb the stairs, he carries her into his room. Later, they look out the window at Paris through the mist. "There's something magic about the first dawn two people see together," she says. It is a sexy sequence—the only one. The film then plunges into improbable melodrama: Montgomery refuses to let her meet his family. He's a priggish cad, simultaneously hypocritical and "innocent."

Marjorie Rambeau is one of three fine supporting players, warning Garbo she will end up in the gutter. ("I've known some very nice people in the gutter," Garbo replies.) The second is Beryl Mercer as Garbo's long-suffering maid. Best of all is Karen Morley as Stone's mistress. He gives her a check upon dismissing her, tiptoes off sheepishly, slowly descends several flights of steps—and then discovers her body at the foot of the staircase: the quietest suicide leap of all time.

Montgomery, with fabulous male ego, now worries that Garbo might kill herself over *him*, as Morley did over Stone. But Garbo just wants to hear those three words, "I love you," and finally he says them. "That makes up for all the misery," she sighs.

Not for the audience. The film was a shameless rehash that in the current era would have been titled *Romance II*. Vapidly directed by Clarence Brown, it is the worst by far of all Garbo talkies. Rarely was sex appeal so synthetic, drama so dull, and dialogue so bum. But in America, *Inspiration* got decent notices—or rather, Garbo did. "Miss Garbo has never looked or played better than in this picture," said *Variety*.

Katherine Albert, however, was on her case again in a *Photoplay* story clearly based on inside information about the tensions among Garbo and her colleagues:

> Garbo did not like her role in *Inspiration*. She did not like her lines. She did not like the conception of the woman she played. She did not like working in the picture.
>
> ["Sappho"] is now old-fashioned. . . . A new script had to be written and neither Garbo nor Brown was entirely satisfied with it, but there was nothing to do but experiment on the set and see how it read. In order to get anything out of it they must rehearse and rehearse and change and change. There's where the trouble began.
>
> Garbo would not rehearse. . . . Garbo believed that she knew more about dialogue and the reading of lines than the producers. . . . Because she would not learn at home the lines she did not like, the set was turned into a school room. While the other members of the cast . . . waited, Garbo was taught her speeches.
>
> [Said Clarence Brown]:
>
> "I would not direct Miss Garbo again under the same conditions that prevailed during the last picture."

If there were flashes between Garbo and Brown, there was little spark between Garbo and Robert Montgomery. At the time, he was grateful: "It is the secret wish of every young actor to play in a picture with Greta Garbo. To work with Garbo is an education in screen art." But over the years, a certain haughty embarrassment set in. Asked about *Inspiration* in the sixties, Montgomery replied, "I'm not interested in discussing Garbo."*

In 1927, Garbo defied a mighty company with her folkloric "I tank I go home now," or some variation thereof. Now in June 1931, with a year left in her contract, she was said to be going back to Sweden—not as a result of any talkie failure or as a negotiation ploy, but for good. It might have been dismissed had it come from any source other than her manager, Harry Edington:

> Naturally, I shall attempt to persuade her to remain in motion pictures, but the rumors of her retirement originated with Garbo herself. She has frequently referred to her plan of going home. And she can quit whenever she wants to. She has saved enough to be financially independent for life. Her money is all invested in substantial American securities.
>
> If Garbo retires, it will not be because of a loss of popularity. She may be restless. But if she does go back to Sweden—I say "if"—my bet is that some day she will return and make the greatest picture of her career.

Edington laughed off the idea that she was upset about the "second Garbo" hullabaloo surrounding Marlene Dietrich's recent Hollywood debut. ("She must think that I am trying to imitate her, but there is nobody like Garbo," Marlene said at the time.) Edington said Garbo admired Dietrich, though he denied the reports that she played Dietrich's records over and over. That story was started, he said, "after I brought a couple of records of the German girl's songs and played them for Garbo on the set."

So much for that issue. On a weightier one, *Motion Picture Classic* reported that "Hollywood is betting pro and con that Greta and John Gilbert will co-star again in *The Fall and Rise of Susan Lenox* . . . and John is eager." Indeed, ten months earlier, Irving Thalberg personally told Gilbert he intended to team him again with Garbo in *Susan Lenox*. Down on his luck, Gilbert relished his potential comeback but, in the end, the dark handsome face opposite Garbo's would be Clark Gable's.

Susan Lenox: Her Fall and Rise was the hot, two-volume masterwork of

---

* Robert Montgomery (1904–81), a four-time president of the Screen Actors Guild in the thirties, helped expose labor racketeering in the industry. He was a decorated World War II hero and, in 1947, a "friendly witness" for the House Un-American Activities Committee's effort to purge Hollywood of Communists. An active Republican, he worked hard for Dwight Eisenhower in 1952 and served as his media consultant. His daughter, Elizabeth Montgomery, was the star of the TV series "Bewitched."

David Graham Phillips, who was murdered in 1911—shortly before its publication—by a crazed reader who believed Phillips had maligned his sister in a previous novel. This one was a servant-girl story of the type that produced many film scripts in the Depression. They were wish fulfillment for women who could only hope to achieve luxury and adventure through some morally sanctioned form of sex.

Garbo's director, for the first time in sound would finally be someone other than Brown: Robert Z. Leonard (1889–1968) had made scores of films in the silent period, many of them starring his first wife, Mae Murray. His later films often featured second wife Gertrude Olmstead, who was among the Scandinavians welcoming Garbo and Stiller the day they arrived in Hollywood. Olmstead was evidently Leonard's entrée to Garbo at MGM, where he specialized in slick romances over three decades.

In the romance at hand, Garbo is Helga, with origins much like Anna Christie's. Her unmarried mother dies in childbirth, leaving her a slave to farmer Jean Hersholt, who gives her to hideous "fiancé" Alan Hale. William Daniels's lighting and photography are brilliant in these first scenes, ominous shadows framing Hale's attempt to ravish her. She escapes in a rainstorm and seeks shelter in a cabin belonging to engineer Rodney Spencer—Gable, premoustache. He had just turned thirty, and 1931 was the most astonishing year of his or any film novice's life.

Gable had first come to Hollywood in 1924, after marrying Josephine Dillon (he was twenty-three, she was thirty-seven), the actress-manager of his road show touring company. She tried to groom him for movies, and he made some screen tests. Viewing one for Warners, Darryl Zanuck made the famous pronouncement: "His ears are too big. He looks like an ape."

Even so, early in 1931, Gable got a nice villain's role in Pathé's *The Painted Desert*. MGM then signed him to play heavies, and his manhandling of Joan Crawford in *Dance, Fools, Dance* and Norma Shearer in *A Free Soul* brought him sensational notices. Within weeks, he was cast opposite Garbo, and before 1931 was out, he had become a new MGM star.

In his first scene of *Susan Lenox*, Gable is the world's most easygoing guy, discovering the world's wariest gal—half-drowned from the rain and cornered by his German shepherd.

"Your dog will bite me!" she whimpers.

"You better take off your clothes," he says.

"No."

"Aw, I didn't mean it that way. I meant change your clothes."

There will be no ravishing by Rodney, but *Garbo* is ravishing—even in Gable's striped pajamas. Once assured he's a Good Samaritan instead of a Don Juan, her personality undergoes a complete change. The caviar he serves

Garbo in the clutches of engineer Clark Gable in Susan Lenox: Her Fall and Rise *(1931)*

William Daniels behind and director Robert Z. Leonard in front of the camera for a moodily lit, early shot of Garbo as Helga in Susan Lenox

her "looks like buckshot!" she says, with a nervous giggle. Gable takes her fishing the next day, a scene ending in their first lovely clinch. Back at the house, as he packs for a trip, she playfully makes him chase her around a chair before rewarding him with a second, more passionate kiss. Sans exotic costume for once, Garbo seems natural and contemporary. Her hands roam sensually over Gable's face and arms as he departs.

But their embryonic love—like the film's first reel—is too good to last. The minute Gable leaves, fiancé Hale shows up in pursuit, necessitating her flight. She hops a circus train and becomes "Susie from Lenoxville," the sideshow beauty. Gable tracks her down, finds her "taken" by circus manager John Miljan, and—rather than hear out her explanation—rejects her. She, in turn, becomes "hard" and ends up the mistress of a crooked politician in an elegant New York penthouse, where she invites Gable to a dinner party in order to humiliate him. He leaves in a huff.

She runs off in search of him, the train wheels superimposed over "Philadelphia," "St. Louis," "New Orleans" . . . all the way to "Puerto Sacate" and the Paradise Cafe, where she becomes a dancer in the hope that Gable might show up. Sure enough he does, mean and drunk and dirty (but actually better looking with his growth of beard). She begs forgiveness: "This hurt that we have inflicted on one another has become a bond that neither of us can break." Only Garbo can pull off, or almost pull off, such lines.* "Every time a man would come along, I'd wonder," Gable pouts. Her response— "I'll make you believe in me!"—serves as the film's abrupt, implausible ending to a crescendo from Tchaikovsky's *Pathétique* Symphony.†

In *Susan Lenox*, wrote critic James Agate, "Neither hero nor heroine at any moment behaves like a sentient human being, because any straight answer to any straight question would have brought the film to an end at any moment." But the fond and realistic Garbo-Gable interplay of its first half made the movie a considerable success. "If you were mad about her before," said *Photoplay*, "just wait until you see her teamed up with this manifestation of masculine S.A. called Clark Gable."

They were so mismatched that they clicked. And because they got along so well, Garbo and Gable were almost paired again, in the forthcoming *Red Dust*. Production notes indicate the casting evolved from Garbo and Adolphe Menjou at first, to Garbo-Gilbert, then Garbo-Gable, and finally to Gable and Jean Harlow.

---

* Years later, viewing her films with Richard Griffith at the Museum of Modern Art, this was the one that most amused her. Said Griffith: "She loved to mimic herself saying, 'R-r-rodney, when will this painful love of ours ever die?'"

† MGM's most lackluster composer, Herbert Stothart, employed the same uncredited Tchaikovsky motif for the ending of *Conquest*, among many other films.

But much as Garbo liked Gable, she was miserable during the making of their only film together. A friend visiting her at home one day was told, "You will have to leave soon. I am very tired and I have to shoot again tomorrow very early on that ghastly *Susan Lenox*."

"Aren't you happy about the film?" the woman asked.

"Happy?" she replied. "*Who* is happy? No one making films can be happy."

Her fellow stars could attest to that unhappiness, or at least to a stand-offishness that was more pathological than ever. "I made several friendly gestures," recalled Myrna Loy, who shared an MGM dressing area with her. "Garbo never responded. One day we ran into each other in the hall, and there was no way she could avoid me. I looked at her and smiled. She lowered her head, and in that low, lingering voice, said, 'Halloo . . . ,' and hurried on by. That was my only exchange with Greta Garbo."

That jibed with her habit, when people knocked at her dressing-room door, of calling out, "Not in!" And it was consistent with her reply to Howard Dietz (and others over the years), who asked her to dine on, say, the following Wednesday: "How do I know I'll be hungry on Wednesday?" Upon arriving at a restaurant where she'd made reservations, her infallible radar informed her whether the press had been alerted and, if so, she would immediately order her chauffeur to drive away. She turned down an urgent personal request from Douglas Fairbanks to attend his and Mary Pickford's party for Lady Louis Mountbatten. For the London opening of *Anna Christie*, she declined an honor that even the reclusive Charles Lindbergh had accepted —to speak in a live broadcast over transatlantic radio.

Even those she trusted were constantly in doubt as to whether or not she wanted to see them. One of the few allowed on Garbo's sets was editor Margaret Booth, who did the cutting of *Mysterious Lady*, *Susan Lenox*, and *Camille*. "In the early days, before she had lost Stiller and her sister, Garbo was quite gay," said Booth, who perceived a change in personality after that. "One day I was at Bullock's inspecting some yard goods, and there at my side was Garbo. She was wearing her large floppy hat and I thought she probably didn't want to be recognized so I said nothing. The next day at the studio she came over to me and said, 'Margaret, why didn't you speak to me yesterday?' "

If generally unhappy with Hollywood, she was particularly unhappy with her homes and forever in search of a new one. The first was 1027 Chevy Chase Drive, a house with a huge ten-foot cypress hedge lining its driveway and hiding all evidence of habitation. Once, when house hunting, she asked MGM hairstylist Sidney Guilaroff to come along and bring his two children

The official publicity photo of "Sven Garbo," Garbo's brother Sven Gustafson, in 1931, looking much like Robert Young (or Montgomery)

on the theory that they would look like a family and nobody would recognize her. The kids came, but the cover didn't work.

All in all, Garbo moved eleven times in California, but those homes were just houses. *Real* home still felt like Sweden, and she remained close to her family in Stockholm—perhaps a little too close, professionally, to brother Sven.

Inspired by his sister—both sisters, really—Sven Gustafson (1898–1967) had set forth in 1929 on a film career of his own. At thirty-one, he had the smashing good looks for it, and certainly the entrée, but not the name. That problem he solved by billing himself as "Sven Garbo" in several Swedish and English pictures. He played in *Konstgjorda Svensson* (1929), directed by Gustaf Edgren and premiered in Stockholm on October 14, 1929. His biggest role—and one shot as a romantic lead—was as Anatole in *När rosorna slå ut* (1930, *When the Roses Bloom*), a British Paramount production, directed by Edvin Adolphson in London, which had the distinction of being the first Swedish talkie. His final appearance was in *Charlotte Löwensköld* (1930), directed by Garbo's old champion from the Royal Dramatic Theater, Gustaf Molander.

He was not greeted warmly by the critics, nor was the name "Sven Garbo" by his sister. She dreaded the embarrassment to both of them in case he failed. Which, of course, he did. When *När rosorna slå ut* was released in America (retitled *The Hole in the Wall*), the April 1931 *Photoplay* notice was brutal: "This Swedish talking picture is reviewed here because Sven Gustafson, brother of Greta Garbo, makes his American debut in it. He's a tall, limp, black-haired boy with a minute moustache, and doesn't bear the faintest resemblance to his famous sister. And he's a punk actor, if this is a sample."

Swedish film authority Lars Lundstrom maintains that MGM thereafter paid him *not* to make movies. In any case, Sven's movie career was soon aborted in favor of painting and a series of art-related sojourns to France, where he studied with the influential painter-teacher André Lhôte (1885–1962). On a 1930 London trip, he met an attractive young American named Marguerite Baltzer, whom he married in 1931. Their daughter Gray was born in 1932.

Sven Gustafson dearly wanted to come to Hollywood and finally did so a few years later. If his sister was angry with him for filching her stage name, she was quick to forgive and the sibling relationship stayed fond. "The happiest times in my family," says Garbo's niece, "were when my aunt and my father were together—the clowning, the verbal repartee and the storytelling. Both of them were charismatic. They'd start with a funny situation—something that happened during the day or at the market—and it developed from there. He could make cutting down a cactus the longest story in the world. . . . Later, he advised her a great deal in business affairs and on painting, but mostly, they just enjoyed being together."

Few people understood how traditionally family-oriented Garbo was, in selective ways; how she longed for an idealized hearth and home; how much of her life was spent in search of a kind of nonmarital domesticity that didn't involve having babies or cooking meals. During her hectic years as a superstar in California, she never found such a thing, nor could have. But in Salka Viertel's family, she found a reasonable facsimile, complete with a lively trio of boys whom she loved and who were the objects of such maternal feelings as she had or cared to express.

She liked Berthold Viertel, too, but Garbo's greatest fondness was for Salka: trusted confidante, soulful artist, and surely the world's most generous friend. "Thank you for everything you have done for me," she cabled Salka around this time, having left her with a list of chores to tend to while she was away, "but above all thank heaven that you exist. Auf Wiedersehen, liebe Salka. Hope to God you had a chance to pay [the maid and chauffeur]."

They were a dyad. What Salka gave Garbo is obvious. What Garbo gave in return, less so; most likely it was her ear, with which Salka had much to fill. Her expanding circle now included an even more eminent group of European artists and musicians seeking refuge from totalitarianism.

In June 1930, just as she finished shooting the German *Anna Christie*, Salka
—and everyone else in the Hollywood émigré community—was riveted by
the arrival of Sergei Eisenstein, Russia's foremost film genius. He had signed a
one-year contract with Paramount and, with his two great collaborators, Edward Tissé and Grigori Alexandrov, settled into a house in Coldwater Canyon. Upton Sinclair gave them a picnic welcome at the ranch of King Camp
Gillette, the razor-blade millionaire, where Salka met and became enthralled
with Eisenstein. Under her tutelage, he soon learned to avoid the endless
round of Hollywood parties and to follow Garbo's sensible advice: "Never
refuse. Accept and then don't go. Nobody ever misses anybody." Salka became
his mentor, champion, and chief Hollywood guide, as she later wrote:

> Eisenstein and his friends wanted to explore the religious and the
> sinful Los Angeles, and the first stop on our itinerary was Aimee Semple
> McPherson's Angelus Temple, which promised to combine both. We
> were lucky in hitting upon one of Aimee's most glamorous productions.
> . . . Her sermon appealed to the senses. She assured her audience that
> the Lord is sweet, and made gourmet sounds, tasting Jesus on her
> tongue—the congregation drooled and smacked their lips. The Russians
> were delighted.

Some sources maintain Salka also became his lover, thanks to Berthold's
frequent absences on New York theater assignments. Her son Peter—who
was a watchful twelve-year-old then—denies there was any time or place
for a romance but confirms that for two years his mother was passionately
devoted to Eisenstein's film cause in America.

Eisenstein's two scenarios for Paramount, *The Glass House* and *Sutter's
Gold*, are still gathering dust in that studio's files. In late 1930, he left
Hollywood for Mexico to make a grandiose, four-part historical epic called
Que Viva Mexico!, which soon ran into all sorts of political and budget crises.
Eisenstein asked Salka to be his representative when rushes were shown in
Los Angeles and cried out to her from Mexico on January 27, 1932: "Help
us, Zalka! No, not us, help our work, save it from mutilation! . . . Your
Sergei." But not even the resourceful Salka could save the project, and no
one, including Eisenstein, ever saw the assembled film in the form he planned.
It remained, in Salka's words, a magnificent "mutilated stump with the heart
cut out." Eisenstein wrote her before leaving America to say, "You and
Berthold have been our best friends in the stormy and hard times."

Eisenstein's American directing career was as doomed as Salka's acting
career. She played in only two more films—William Dieterle's *The Flood*
and the German remake of Somerset Maugham's *The Sacred Flame*, directed
by Berthold.

"I was neither beautiful nor young enough for a film career," she wrote in her memoirs. "If I had been 60 and an American, I could have played the so-called 'earthy' character parts. Probably I would have had a chance in the theater in New York, but we were tied to Hollywood. It made me miserable that I, who had started to act at the age of 17, had to be idle in my best years."

But Salka was resilient and unself-pitying. Realizing that her acting career was over, she now turned seriously to scriptwriting. In that field, she was destined for prominence, her star fixed to that of a Swedish friend.

Adrian and Garbo at their high-fashion peak, 1931

CHAPTER 7

THE ICON IN SOUND
1931–1932

Secure as she would ever be under Salka's wing, Garbo was now approaching the midpoint, if not the summit, of her career. Through the late twenties and into the new decade, she was "Garbo the Star" in something called "the movies." Now that the medium had settled down, and settled in, to its definitive talking form, she was becoming "Garbo the Icon," in something called "the cinema"—a greater phenomenon that magnified both her myth and her cult.

"I'm a woman who's unfaithful to a million men," she said. Proof of that, and of the fast progress of her iconization, lay in her next (and first truly campy) role in a film that is most fascinating for the way she is packaged in it. *Mata Hari* is the greatest example of the fact that Garbo's worst pictures often got the best receptions: Its windfall $879,000 profit for MGM was larger than that of all but one of the films she ever made.

Directed by George Fitzmaurice (1885–1940), *Mata*'s story was concocted by Benjamin Glazer and Leo Birinski. Pola Negri had planned on the same vehicle as her talkie debut for RKO, but MGM and Garbo beat her to the punch. It opens with the grisly execution of three French collaborators, followed by Mata's appearance in a Parisian cabaret. "Shiva, I dance for you tonight as the Bayadères dance in the sacred temples of Java!" says Garbo, and then shimmies around a huge Polynesian idol, balancing a triple-tiered hat much like a Christmas tree on her head. *Variety* called the routine "a polite cooch," but it is enough to kindle the tinderbox of Ramon Novarro, a Russian lieutenant whose war plans Mata must filch for the Germans.

Lionel Barrymore plays Mata's old lover, General Shubin, whose American

Garbo at the end of her "polite cooch"
in Mata Hari *(1930)*

accent rivals Novarro's Spanish one for unconvincing Russian. Enslaved and guilt ridden, Barrymore tells Mata he is close to confessing his treason.

"Do you want to die so badly?" she asks.

"I'm dead now—just as surely as though there were a bullet in my heart. . . . *You* killed me!"

"Then why don't you give me up?" she replies.

"I will!" he declares.

"Well, *do!*" she dares.

For the moment, they're at an impasse, and Mata turns her attention to the seduction of Novarro. When they are alone together in his bedroom, he rhapsodizes about "God, country, honor, you!"

"I come last?" she asks.

"No."

"That's how you said it."

"You come first, before anything."

"There's so much light in here."

Novarro extinguishes all but the votive candle that burns perpetually beneath an image of the Madonna in honor of his mother.

"Put out that one too," she demands, and he does—his moral resolve broken. Novarro's soft good looks and manner suit his character, but any chemistry between him and Garbo is strictly inert.* The morning after, she relights the Virgin's shrine, and her subtle expression reveals a qualm or two—but no more—in this most overtly evil role Garbo ever played.

Yet she seems constricted throughout. When in love, she throws her head back; when worried, she looks furtively to the side. Those are her two basic gestures, and activities, in *Mata Hari*. Near the end, Novarro is shot down and lies blinded in his hospital bed as the strains of "Ave Maria" on a violin drive home his betrayal of the Madonna. When he insists on visiting her, Garbo—by now convicted of treason—participates in the absurd pretense that her death-row cell is a sanitorium.

In the first days of shooting, Novarro was shocked by Garbo's reluctance to rehearse but soon discovered the compensation: "The moment she began acting her whole being changed, and the force she radiated electrified those acting with her."

He got little help from director Fitzmaurice, who was born and trained in Paris as an artist and prided himself—like Murnau—on rarely looking through a camera, concentrating instead on preproduction work. "I even carry out this initial supervision so far as to accompany the women of the cast to the stores where they purchase their gowns," said Fitzmaurice, "in order to be perfectly sure before I start work that everything is in harmony."

He must have spent weeks with the local milliners: In *Mata Hari*, Garbo appears in a long and progressively more bizarre series of hats—starting with the Christmas tree and moving on to a sequined cloche, a hypnotist's bonnet with spirals in the forehead, a Friar Tuck–style cap, a bishop's-miter pillbox, and, finally, a black yarmulke in her trial scene.

Fitzmaurice was laissez-faire about composition. "I never bother about

* British censors objected to Novarro's choice of profane love for Garbo over sacred love for the Virgin, and a retake, substituting his mother's photo for the icon, was edited into the British version. At the time, Ramon Novarro (1899–1968) was one of Hollywood's most eligible offscreen bachelors. During *Mata Hari*, rumors abounded that he'd fallen madly in love: "Greta Garbo is my ideal woman, but I shall never marry." Artists shouldn't marry, in general, he said. Asked what he'd most want if he *weren't* an artist, he replied: "Greta Garbo."

As Novarro's career declined in the sound era, he became less cautious about his homosexuality. In later years, he drank heavily and lived alone in the Hollywood Hills. On Halloween in 1968, he was beaten to death in his home by two teenaged brothers—hustlers and petty thieves—from Chicago.

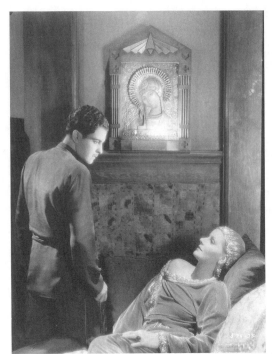

*Garbo with Russian officer
Ramon Novarro during the
moment of truth beneath his
mother's shrine*

The bizarre line of Mata
Hari *millinery: from Friar
Tuck skullcap, top left, to se-
quined-cloche helmet by
Adrian, center, to modified
bishop's-mitre pillbox, middle
left, to triple-tiered Christmas
tree*

it," he said, "except to notice when it is wrong." He left that to William Daniels, whose photography is downright German Expressionist. The few high spots are due to Daniels's chiaroscuro lighting and Adrian's dazzling costumes—a backless lamé gown with metallic leggings, for example, and a host of other furbelows. Only the final scene is inspired: Hair severely pulled back, Garbo marches stoically to the firing squad—the wicked obverse of Joan of Arc—with an escort of weeping nuns.

Her friend Mercedes de Acosta took credit for Garbo's visual impact in that finale: "She [took] me to Adrian's house [and] he showed me his sketches for Greta's clothes. I suggested that she wear a long black cape for the scene at the end when she is shot, and that she should brush her hair absolutely straight back. . . . Adrian agreed and was delighted with the suggestion."

Mata's deceptions continued even after her execution. The real-life spy, Margaretha Zelle (1876–1917), was Dutch, and as part of its promotion, MGM promised exhibitors in the Netherlands and Indonesia that Garbo would make an international call to the opening-night audience in Java. Not surprisingly, when the time came, the star refused to comply. But a certain MGM secretary named Pilkington was known around the studio for her great vocal imitation of Garbo. With very little urging, Miss Pilkington placed the call, and nobody in Java was the wiser.*

With the exception of *Anna Christie*, Garbo's roles largely broke down into two types of male fantasies: the vamp for whom men lust, as in *Flesh and the Devil*, *Romance*, and *Inspiration*; or the virtuous woman in a love triangle, who ends up repentant or dead, as in *A Woman of Affairs*, *Wild Orchids*, and *The Kiss*.

Now, finally, came a more sophisticated concept: Vicki Baum's *Grand Hotel*, the great breakthrough in how to maximize star resources. Borrowing its structural device from the Renaissance satirical poem *Ship of Fools* (1494), Baum's novel would prove that a multiple-story format could work just as well on stage and screen, without confusing audiences. Its formula was quickly copied—in Paramount's *If I Had a Million* (1932), MGM's *Dinner at Eight* (1933), and dozens of subsequent films—and provided an enduring subgenre that is still popular, especially in disaster variants (*Airport*, *The Poseidon Adventure*, *Earthquake*).

Thalberg personally supervised the script and casting of *Grand Hotel*, then turned production over to Paul Bern, who had first suggested buying the

---

* The brothers of Margaretha Zelle filed suit in Rotterdam on October 17, 1932, demanding the withdrawal of *Mata Hari* on the grounds that their sister never murdered a Russian general and was never even proven to have been a spy. They lost the case eight days later.

property with Garbo in mind. The setting is Berlin, where the curtain rises on everyone checking in: John Barrymore looks suspicious, as a baron-turned-key-thief well might. Brother Lionel plays the underling of Prussian tycoon Wallace Beery, and immediately hams it up. Joan Crawford as Flaemmchen, Beery's stenographer-and-then-some, looks great and acts tough. Garbo is the fading, suicidal ballerina Grushinskaya.*

A year earlier, Crawford had been talking with columnist Sara Hamilton at MGM one day when Garbo strode across a nearby set: "There goes my ambition," she said quietly. "My ambition is to fit myself so that when Garbo leaves—and you mark my words, she'll go one of these days without a word of warning—I'll be able to take over. . . . I want to do a Garbo!"

MGM wardrobe man Jerry Asher now witnessed the first Garbo-Crawford encounter: As Crawford came out of her dressing room and was walking downstairs to the set, Garbo was coming up. Crawford was flustered and lowered her eyes, but Garbo held out her arm to block the way and said, "I am glad we are working in the same picture. How are you getting along?" Crawford managed a reply, and after a few more pleasantries, Garbo said goodbye. The subsequent reports of snubbing and hostility were groundless.

Among the all-stars of *Grand Hotel*, Garbo got first billing, followed by John Barrymore, Crawford, Beery, and Lionel. Garbo's entrance as the ballerina comes a full twenty minutes into the film. She is too exhausted to perform, she says—too close to despair. Art imitated life in her repeated moan, "I want to be alone . . ." Life has become so "threadbare." She was twenty-six years old, with the weariness of a century in her voice. But when Barrymore woos her—first as a ruse to steal her jewels, then as a man truly in love—she comes to life unforgettably.

Some thought it self-parody; most thought it a soulful performance and that the film overall—however melodramatic—was captivating. Director Edmund Goulding gave it a smooth flow and pace, and of all stars in attendance, the Garbo-Barrymore interaction was by far the most electric. How many mediocre leading men had she been saddled with? Thank God, said the critics, she was finally opposite someone of her own stature.

Garbo thought so, too. After their intense love scene, she surprised the crew by giving Barrymore a serious off-screen kiss and telling him, "You have no idea what it means to me to play opposite so perfect an artist." Later, she said he was "one of the very few who had that divine madness without which a great artist cannot work or live."

In fact, he got the role only because John Gilbert was fussing with MGM

---

* Marie Dressler reportedly volunteered for the part of Garbo's maid *at no salary*—just to be in the picture—but MGM wouldn't allow her to play such a small role.

about his contract at the time. Garbo loved performing with Barrymore and acquiesced to the request that his "better side" (the left) be on view in their close-ups. "If you stay in front of that camera long enough," Barrymore once said, "it will show you not only what you had for breakfast but who your ancestors were." She was much amused when he told her his secret solution for bloodshot eyes—an over-the-counter product called Oculine. With the possible exceptions of Gilbert and later Charles Boyer, the world-weary John Barrymore was the only actor who really gave the world-weary Garbo a run for her money in dramatic ability and personal magnetism. The two-shots of their locked embrace inspire rhapsodies to this day.

"Who's holding onto whom? Who holds sway?" asks novelist Rachel Gallagher in *The Girl Who Loved Garbo*. "The thrust of her head, the challenge in her eyes as they gaze at one another, the set of her mouth and jaw, all indicate challenge. Her character seems to meet Barrymore's on an equal footing. It's a portrait of true love and grand passion, and something more than just equality: surrender that is both mutual and consummate."

Barrymore also rhapsodized: "She takes us out of ourselves by the mere accident of her presence. It isn't acting; it is a kind of magic." Their joint magic even carried over to her scene with an *imaginary* Barrymore—the telephone—in which she employs her erotic shorthand, fondling the phone with an eager, "stylized sexuality" that animates everything around her.

It carried over into folklore, too, inspiring one of the few Will Rogers jokes that backfired. America's favorite humorist was master of ceremonies at the April 29, 1932, Grauman's Chinese Theater opening of *Grand Hotel*, as he recounted a few days later in his syndicated newspaper column (all spelling *sic*):

> Mr. Louie B. Mayer asked me and I was tickled to do it. The whole thing is the biggest "hooey" out here. . . . This was an especially big one for it was the biggest cast picture ever made. . . . They have an intermission and everybody goes out and looks at each other and you can't get 'em back in again. They would rather look at each other than the show. . . .
>
> My job was to introduce the cast. . . . Well of course you all know Greta Garbo never goes anywhere. When she come to America that is the only thing she ever went to. Nobody has ever met her. John Barrymore who played with her in the picture, he has never seen her, that was all done with mirrors. . . . She is a fantom, the minute you look at her, she's not there, she is in Sweeden, or Norway, or Denmark, or wherever it is these Swedes come from. . . .
>
> She don't go anywhere, [but] I announced that on account of the

Garbo with John Barrymore, dancer and thief, in MGM's epochal Grand Hotel *(1932) "Who's holding onto whom? Who holds sway?"*

*Director Edmund Goulding and Garbo as fading ballerina Grushinskaya share
the melancholy of a coffee break.*

importance of the occasion, Miss Garbo would break her rule and be there, and that immediately after the picture was over [she would] come on stage and take a bow. . . .

Well, I had framed up a gag with Wally Berry [in] some "dame" clothes. He was my Greta Garbo. Sounds kinder funny don't it? Well it wasent to them. Wally did it fine. He even looked like her, but not enough to satisfy that crowd. Now they should have known that Garbo wasent going to be there any more than Coolidge, but they go and believe it and then get sore at themselves for believing it. I dident mean any harm. Gosh, us comedians must get laughs. But these first nighters don't want us to get 'em at their expense. They want to be the ones that do all the laughing. I think they got their waitings worth by seeing Wally Berry in skirts. [But] they threw old wedding rings, marriage certificates, they tore up their overhauled ermines, they were so sore they had been fooled.

Grand Hotel, aside from the star salaries, hadn't really cost a fortune to make ($700,000—only $120,000 more than *Susan Lenox*). But it *looked* expensive and so in London, for example, the Palace Theater charged double the usual ticket price. It is arguably Garbo's best-known film, and the one in which we see her the least—in just two long scenes, isolated from all her co-stars except Barrymore. She was like the most expensive perfume, to be kept bottled and used ever so sparingly.

A few, such as critic Sydney Carroll, thought the whole thing "only worth seeing as a drum-beating exhibition of stars—each and all of them miscast." But most thought otherwise, and *Grand Hotel* won the 1932 Academy Award for best picture.

The Will and Wally spoof gives an idea of Garbo's elusive celebrity—already legendary by 1932—and the awe she inspired among her greatest colleagues, as well as the fun-poking that she didn't always appreciate.* But she had made herself ripe for it; her mysterious behavior was often more annoying than fascinating.

One morning, Garbo and Mercedes de Acosta were sunbathing on

---

* Marion Davies did a Garbo parody in King Vidor's *The Patsy* (1928), but it was removed from the final cut. Kay Francis turned in a wicked Garbo imitation in *Madame Satan* (1930), directed by C. B. DeMille. In *Blondie of the Follies* (1932), Davies and Jimmy Durante did a hilarious spoof of the Garbo-Barrymore love scene from *Grand Hotel*, and it stayed in—probably because *Blondie*'s director was Edmund Goulding. ("I vant to be alone," says Davies. Durante pleads for a little time with her. "Vell, maybe for a veek," she agrees.) Years later, Norma Shearer told biographer Gavin Lambert that she was "doing a Garbo" in *Idiot's Delight* (1939), which was directed by none other than Clarence Brown.

Mercedes's balcony when the doorbell rang. Garbo instantly assumed her startled-fawn expression. A maid appeared and took Mercedes out of the room to tell her it was Katharine Cornell, then in Los Angeles on a tour of *The Barretts of Wimpole Street*.

"Who is downstairs?" Garbo called out nervously.

"It's Kit Cornell," Mercedes replied. Garbo advised sending her away, but Mercedes said she couldn't be rude: "If you don't want to meet her, stay here in the sun." Soon enough, Garbo descended the stairs, leaned over the bannister, and in her most beguiling voice said, "Hello, may I join you?"—followed by drinks all around, and a good time. "Greta gave the impression she had always been longing to meet Kit," said Mercedes.

That incident is more amazing since—unbeknownst to Mercedes—Garbo had seen *The Barretts of Wimpole Street* and met Cornell in 1931, in New York.

"One Wednesday matinee a woman with her coat collar up, hat pulled down, hands held across her face, walked up to the box office and bought a ticket," Cornell recalled in her memoirs. After the show, at the stage door, that deep-voiced lady asked, "Would Miss Cornell see a stranger?" But the stranger wouldn't give her name, and Cornell figured it was a joke. After waiting a few minutes, the fan turned and left, remarking on her way out, "Miss Cornell, I see, does not like strangers."

The next day, when Cornell discovered the truth, she sent Garbo a note of apology and an invitation to supper which Garbo accepted. Ten days later, they "sat and talked, easily and comfortably, until about four o'clock in the morning."

Even more legendary was Garbo's one and only encounter with Groucho Marx. Meeting her in an MGM elevator one day, he tipped up the brim of her slouch hat and said, "Oh, I'm sorry. I thought you were a fella I knew in Pittsburgh." He never recorded her reaction, if any.

She was not really such a total recluse or sourpuss. Many old émigré friends were now gone—Emil and Gussie Jannings, Ludwig Berger, Erich Pommer, Conrad Veidt, the Feyders, and Victor Varconi (1896–1976), the smooth Hungarian actor. But Lubitsch and the Viertels remained, and Garbo frequented their homes and a select few others, such as Cedric Gibbons's gorgeous Art Deco house, where—typically—a tennis court was the draw.

Tallulah Bankhead, having met her at Salka's in 1931, lost no time inviting her to dinner. "I was pleased when she showed up in jodhpurs," said Tallu. Ethel Barrymore was there—she, too, had been eager to meet the Swede—and they all played charades, danced to phonograph records, and got slightly drunk. Garbo complimented the cook, who replied, "Next to Miss Bankhead I think you're the finest actress on the screen."

Tallulah later beat her soundly at tennis on Clifton Webb's court, but such outings were infrequent. Film actors in general had to give themselves totally to their jobs, and Garbo, more than most, was easily exhausted. Garbo, after working, went home to bed. Despite the increasingly long stretches between films, it was her screen work that occupied her—as it occupied her fans, her studio, and her directors.

Much has been written about how those directors molded Garbo's performances, but little about the paradoxical way she molded *them*, and a new standard of film heroine in the process. Among her early sound directors, two in particular left valuable impressions of Garbo at work—never at play.

"Socially, I don't know her at all," said Clarence Brown in 1931. "Only when she invited me to her home to work on a script, did I learn that I had been living directly across the street from her for more than a year! We had a homey relationship. I was not afraid of her, and she was not afraid of me. I love her and love to work with her. She is perfect to direct. She knows her business. Not strong physically, she works very hard, giving everything she's got, quits promptly [at 5:30 p.m.] and feels that when her work is done she should be free to go where she pleases and do what she pleases."

Brown directed seven of her twenty-four American films, far more than any other director. Garbo, he said, "had something that nobody ever had on the screen. Nobody. I don't know whether she even knew she had it, but she did. And I can explain it in a few words." Those words related to his belief that "silent pictures were more of an art than talkies ever have been." To Kevin Brownlow and, later, Scott Eyman, Brown elaborated:

> I would take a scene with Garbo . . . three or four times. It was pretty good, but I was never quite satisfied. When I saw that same scene on the screen, however, it had something that it just didn't have on the set. Garbo had something behind the eyes that you couldn't see until you photographed it in close-up. You could see thought. If she had to look at one person with jealousy, and another with love, she didn't have to change her expression. You could see it in her eyes as she looked from one to the other. And nobody else has been able to do that on the screen. Garbo did it without the command of the English language.
>
> For me, Garbo starts where they all leave off. She was a shy person; her lack of English gave her a slight inferiority complex. I used to direct her very quietly. I never gave her a direction above a whisper. Nobody on the set ever knew what I said to her; she liked that. She hated to rehearse. She would have preferred to stay away until everyone else was rehearsed, then come in and do the scene. . . . In silent days, the

lights were so bright she couldn't see off the set; when sound came in, new lights were used and were dim enough so she could see everybody around. The sight of an electrician or carpenter watching her act would put her off balance. . . . She didn't act for anybody but the camera. [Later], I saw her in Switzerland and she was just the same: the life of the party if she knew you, but let one stranger enter the room and she goes and sits in the corner.

We could never get her to look at the rushes, and I don't think she ever looked at any of her pictures until many years later. When sound arrived, we had a projector on the set. This projector ran backward and forward so that we could match scenes and check continuity. When you run a talking picture in reverse, the sound is like nothing on earth. That's what Garbo enjoyed. She would sit there shaking with laughter, watching the film running backward and the sound going *yakablom-yakablom*. But as soon as we ran it forward, she wouldn't watch it.

"In his repressed way," Louise Brooks later wrote Brownlow, "Clarence Brown was a great director [even though] he never reveals himself in his films." Tolstoy, Dickens, Proust, and Joyce in literature; Griffith, Stroheim, Pabst, and currently Mike Nichols in film—all were self-revelatory, she believed. But Brown's films were the works of a man who was afraid to expose his passion—"and it is only passion that makes a work of art. I am speaking of sexual passion. Brown who detested lesbians and adored Garbo; who hated whores and adored Dorothy Sebastian; who abominated drunkards and adored his wife, Alice Joyce." But despite all failings, "He perfected the Garbo face."

Brown also understood camera work and lighting. "Whenever we saw a painting with an interesting lighting effect, we'd copy it," he said. " 'Rembrandt couldn't be wrong,' we'd say. At least we stole from the best!" One secret he figured out early was "never to shoot an exterior between 10 a.m. and 3 p.m. The lousiest photography you can get is around high noon when the sun's directly overhead. You can only get depth on black-and-white exteriors with backlight or three-quarter light and a fill light . . . on the face."

By the time of his Garbo sound films, Brown was growing complacent, his style alternating between artful and artless. Still, his basic sweetness and innocence made him what Eyman calls "the last Romantic Idealist" of the movies.

Quantitatively, Brown was Garbo's most important director. For quality, it was Goulding. "Why does no one appreciate Eddie Goulding?" asked

Louise Brooks. "He was a brilliant director and could sing, write, compose, and act, besides being the most delightfully corrupt man ever born. Everything was easy for him. Perhaps that is why he is overlooked." The irony of Garbo's obsessive shyness was that she chose to hide in front of a camera—in the "public solitude" of playing a role. Among the few who understood the amazing change that came over her when she acted was the director of *Love* and *Grand Hotel:*

"In the studios she is nervous," said Goulding. "Rather like a racehorse at the post—actually trembling, hating onlookers. At the first click of the camera, she starts literally pouring forth Garbo into the lens."

Goulding was a Renaissance man in the arts and in the practice of his vices, of which sexual promiscuity was high on the list. He once left Louise Brooks—at seventeen—waiting in a cab while he ran in to visit a prostitute, emerging twenty minutes later to tell her about it. But he adored talking to women as much as making love to them, and figuring out just how they liked to be treated in order to perform magic for him when the camera rolled. Garbo responded deeply to his inventive, sympathetic methods and gave him two of her best performances. Goulding reciprocated with a fine complementary grace: In *Grand Hotel*, his visual choreography and skillful manipulation of the multiple plots showcased Garbo's own unique phrasing. He did much the same for Crawford and Swanson and would later do so for Bette Davis in *Dark Victory* (1939), Joan Fontaine in *The Constant Nymph* (1943), and Tyrone Power in *The Razor's Edge* (1946).

George Fitzmaurice had a similar theory but less successful practice. "A comprehensive knowledge of psychology in all its branches is a necessary complement of good directorship," said Fitzmaurice. That was certainly a key to directing Garbo and to the working principles of those "women's directors"—Brown, Goulding, Stiller, von Sternberg, Dorothy Arzner, George Cukor—who, in conventional film history, are said to have had a special "way" with problematic actresses.

But feminine psychology was perhaps not so different from masculine; actors of both sexes responded to the coddling of their neuroses. With a few notable exceptions, Garbo's directors were serviceable technicians who were not monumentally inspired in the handling of women *or* men, and who were often unaware of what she was doing. Either way, they were not just aided but in fact often *rescued* by William Daniels.

Daniels photographed nineteen of her twenty-four American movies and all but two of her sound films, and the way he lit and filmed her was paramount to keying the mood of her peak dramatic moments. Daniels's eye became the world's. "The close-up is such a valuable thing," Billy Wilder once said, "—like a trump at bridge." Daniels made certain she was "always taken in close-ups or long shots, hardly ever intermediate or full figure." In a rare interview in 1935, he explained why:

> I don't think she is conscious of movement, voice or expression; she just seems to think her part, and everything about her expresses it to perfection. That is why we use so many close-ups. She can tell so much with the subtlest glance of an eye, and put so much meaning into a fleeting expression. In a more distant shot, these subtleties will be lost. [But] Garbo's walk is one of the most entrancingly graceful movements I have ever seen, and it naturally shows up best in full-figure shots.

Daniels thought her "the most sensible woman I have ever known," smart, simple, and sincere. "Best of all, she has the gift of winning—and keeping —the affection and respect of [colleagues]. The most enthusiastic Garbo fans are the people who work with her."

She was bored by the endless preludes and preparations and hairdressers and makeup sessions. Unlike other actors who gradually revved themselves up during those procedures, she felt pulled down by them. But even so, she had a sense of humor about it that charmed Daniels: "Often, she will grow restive when I take longer than usual to get ready for a scene. Waiting in her portable dressing room, she will send her maid out to haunt me: 'Go out and look at that man Daniels,' she will say. 'Stare at him! Make his conscience prickle!'" Daniels had a bicycle horn mounted on his camera, and when a scene was lit to his satisfaction, he squeezed the bulb. That one loud honk was the signal for director, technicians, and actors to take their places. Sometimes when she grew impatient, Garbo would creep up behind him and blow the horn herself, scaring him to death.

Daniels had an indispensable executive ally in Irving Thalberg and MGM's costly but artistically wise retake policy. "We always made a picture with the idea that we were going to retake at least 25 percent of it," said Clarence Brown. "We made the picture, then took it out to an audience, previewed it, and found the weak spots. We then rewrote and redid them. . . . It paid off in the long run. . . . Nobody has ever touched Thalberg." That view was the consensus, but director Edward Sutherland dissented from the general adulation of Thalberg:

> He would tell the director all the thoughts he had. Then he'd look at the result on film and decide he could do it better, and do a lot of retakes. This had never been heard of [before]. But the Metro system was: "Let the producers make it till they're happy," which is expensive, incompetent, and makes for mass regimentation of pictures. MGM's

studios at Culver City became known as Retake Valley. I think that when the producer came in as, theoretically, the artistic head of production, pictures started to deteriorate.

But Thalberg's active involvement with the men who directed Garbo's pictures seems to have been limited. The bottom line, says film historian David Robinson, is that, "She worked with good directors and bad ones, was happy with some and miserable with others. But none of them ever really affected her extraordinary, radiant, indefinable talent."

Indefinable and radiant, all right—but poetry encased in a prosaic routine. Her friend Mercedes de Acosta, who observed her at close range for a decade, described Garbo's work methods in 1931 and 1932 during the making of *Mata Hari* and *Grand Hotel:*

> At five o'clock Greta would meet me outside the studio, and we would go to the beach or walk in the hills. Sometimes during the walks she would discuss various scenes she had shot during the day or intended to shoot the next day, or some problem presented by the picture. . . . Unlike other actresses, she did not plan ahead what she intended to do in a scene. . . . She *brooded* on the part or on a scene or particular situation that she had to play. She never thoroughly read a script before the first day of shooting, when she went onto the set and became the part.

"Great actresses like Garbo and Duse used the same technique," said Louise Brooks. "They learned their roles so perfectly, developing everything to such an extent, that they were able to think of their role on [the level] of real life. Their thought was no longer linked to 'learned' gestures. Hence the timing of great actresses is the same as that which marks the rhythm of their real lives. You can neither teach nor learn to act according to any timing other than your own."

If interior thought was the main thing, it was only accessible to audiences through external expression. "The sensual side of acting is too often underrated," wrote Kenneth Tynan. "Too much is written about how actors feel, too little about how they look." Garbo's androgynous physique was most fully revealed in that *Mata Hari* cooch; Adrian's costumes normally only afforded a view of its outlines. "The broad ivory yoke of her shoulders belongs to a javelin-thrower," said Tynan. There were sexier feminine forms, but Garbo's special allure lay in the awareness "that we are watching a real, imperfectly shaped human being, and not a market-fattened glamour-symbol."

That what she did was instinctive, not cerebral, was why she was so uncomfortable with anyone who wanted to talk about her acting. She was at a loss to articulate it; and the body that enthralled millions did not enthrall its owner. At the Swedish dramatic academy, she'd been ashamed to dance because "I was so big—so very big." In fact, she was only 5'7" and about 126 pounds. But that was considered large at a time when actresses were expected to be petite, in movies and theater alike. Of the two fields, however, size was much less a "problem" in film.

"In repose, Garbo was ungainly," wrote Alexander Walker. But when she moved, "her awkward proportions shifted into sensuous adjustment to each other, and gave the Americans a kind of animal movement that they had never before seen." Perhaps only a dancer could explain it:

"Everything is built on movement," said Louise Brooks, and "Garbo is all movement. First she gets the emotion, and out of the emotion comes the movement and out of the movement comes the dialogue. She's so perfect that people say she can't act."

More than anything else, Garbo's screen movement was distinguished by her walk. "She walked obliquely," said Tynan, "seeming to sidle even when she strode, like a middle-weight boxer approaching an opponent." She led with her shoulder in a kind of S-shaped undulation—not the sashay of a coquette but a natural liquidity, quirky and seductive. David Diamond thought it was her right leg—"the right *foot*, actually, slightly splayed out"—that distinguished her unique walk.

Those folkloric feet were, in fact, a perfectly median length for a woman of her size: Garbo's shoe size was 7AA, according to no less reliable a source than Salvatore Ferragamo, the well-heeled cobbler who made seventy pairs for her in later years.* "Garbo's feet were beautifully shaped and long, in correct proportion to her height," testified actor David Niven, a yachting friend of later years who had many occasions for firsthand observation, "but she had an unfortunate habit of encasing them in huge brown loafers that gave the impression that she wore landing craft."

On the set, she liked to wear carpet slippers for comfort, no matter what the rest of her costume. In her early films, before a take, she would inquire, "Is the feet in?" If so, the slippers would go; if not, they'd stay. "Is the feet in?" became a popular and permanent expression around MGM, long after she corrected the verb. By and large, on- and offscreen, "she usually wore flats," says her niece. "She believed things should make sense, and it didn't make sense to hobble around in heels."

---

* For more on the compelling subject of Garbo's feet and conflicting claims of her shoe size, see chapter 9, page 299.

In her films, this most sensible and unexcitable actress so rarely moved *fast* that it's almost a shock when she does—falling through the ice at the end of *Flesh and the Devil*, for example, or being chased around the table by Gable in *Susan Lenox*. Those were the exceptions. For the most part, a certain serene melancholy, or melancholy serenity, was reflected in the movements of her body and—most of all—in The Face.

Stella Adler recalled the first and last time she saw it, in person, on a railroad journey from California to New York. Garbo and Salka Viertel were on the same train, and Salka asked Stella if she wanted to meet Garbo. Adler said yes and waited in the corridor while Salka went to pave the way. Permission was granted. "I went in to her stateroom and she was in bed," Adler recalled. "I couldn't talk. I can't remember any conversation. I just couldn't take my eyes off her face, her physiognomy. I spent much of my life in Europe looking at art, and when I saw Garbo's face, it was sculptured beyond all of it."

The first thing that struck Louise Brooks when she met Garbo was "the perfection of her features and the petal loveliness of her skin."* Though audiences could never see their color, her eyes were a translucent grayish blue. The famous eyelashes were quite real (Tallulah once pulled them to make sure); the nose, slightly large for any other face but hers; the mouth and lips, classically severe and slightly drooping at the corners in a hint of sorrow that would increase with age. The *geometry* of the face transcended its components and gave it a haunting blend of intensity and detachment, as if there were two people behind it—observer and participant—and the observer was always mildly amused by the strange behavior of the participant.

Very little make-up ever adorned it. Offscreen, just a dash of powder, a little lipstick, and eyebrow pencil.† On screen, she wore not much more. Except for MGM employees during a shoot, no hairdresser ever laid a hand on her. Jewelry? Never. Yet Garbo had a greater influence on the appearance of her peers and her public than any other actress who ever lived. Even store mannequins began to resemble her. The great film critic Otis Ferguson put it wryly: "I found her more lovely in the straight-cut clothes . . . than in the

---

* William Daniels confirmed it in 1935: "Her complexion is remarkable, both to the camera and the eye. She has the clearest, finest skin-texture in pictures. It is a joy to photograph; it will be a revelation if she ever makes a color-film." In 1969, he lamented: "The saddest thing in my career is that I was never able to photograph her in color. I begged the studio. I felt I had to get those incredible blue eyes in color but they said no. The process at the time was cumbersome and expensive, and the pictures were already making money. I still feel sad about it."

† "If she only knew it, her best disguise would be to use no mascara," said her friend and co-star Nils Asther. "Her eyebrows and eyelashes are almost white, and without mascara she looks like a different person."

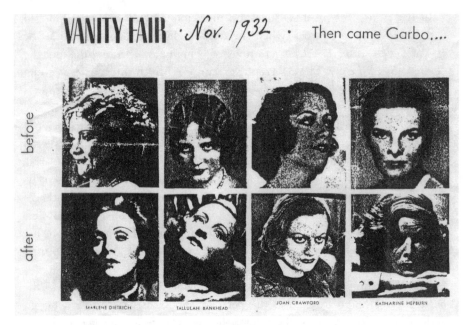

VANITY FAIR · *Nov. 1932* · Then came Garbo....

before

after

MARLENE DIETRICH   TALLULAH BANKHEAD   JOAN CRAWFORD   KATHARINE HEPBURN

Vanity Fair *(November 1932):* "*Anthropologists of the future, when bending their beards over cinema archives, are going to unearth a perplexing phenomenon in relation to the Twentieth Century woman. They are going to discover that, . . . about 1931–32, they suddenly all began to look alike. . . . The upper row depicts them in the sunny days of their earlier, pre-Nordic innocence. Then along came Garbo. Below are shown the ensuing metamorphoses.*"

later 'creations,' for while I am strictly anti-nudist, I should say that a real and commanding beauty is clearest without clutter—all you need on the outside is a stretch of burlap and a bath."

A wonderful illustration of her impact appeared in the November 1932 *Vanity Fair* photo feature, "Then Came Garbo," depicting Crawford, Bankhead, Dietrich, and other actresses in early and recent photos. In the pre-Garbo shots, they all look coquettish and much "done up." Post-Garbo, they wear minimal make-up, their hair is straight, their eyebrows thin, their cheeks sucked in, and their expressions "uniformly languorous and inscrutable, as if they were brooding over some abiding sorrow," said John Bainbridge. "Perhaps they are only brooding over their inability to look even more like Garbo."

Garbo, of course, had undergone a major transition of her own. It was an "unretouched Swedish dumpling" who first arrived in Hollywood, with the shadow of a double chin, frizzy hair, and slightly bucked teeth. Was she as much a product of the beauty factory as all the rest? Yes and no. The chubbiness was "puppy fat"; she was still a very young woman in the process of gaining control over her body and her make-up. At MGM, the weight was taken off, the eye sockets (and possibly nostrils) were darkened for depth, and the pulling back of her hair would beautifully "lift" her face. If she was just an average pretty girl to start with, her perfect bone structure made perfect beauty possible.

The evolution of her teeth—slightly irregular at first, and later corrected, but never "capped"—is fascinating. But on film, we rarely saw her teeth. We saw much more of her hands, not just because of their greater visibility but because she *acted* with them. Her nails were simply buffed, never manicured. "People forget what extraordinary hands Garbo had," says David Diamond, "particularly when dealing with children." On a man's face, hers were the most expressive fingers in the world. Like few other actresses, Garbo's emotional responses often began in her hands, as Arnold Genthe had observed in New York: "With a single gesture of her hands, Greta Garbo can express more than can most actresses after hours of emoting. Just look at her hands! [They] really say more than her words."

Features, limbs, movement—all were made more dazzling, of course, by the clothes that encased them. Gilbert Adrian designed Garbo's wardrobe for seventeen of her twenty-four American films and warrants as much credit as William Daniels for how marvelous she invariably appeared. Adrian's role in creating the Garbo "look" cannot be overestimated. She spent dozens of hours with him on every film, not just choosing and modeling his fashions but figuring out how they would *move*. Garbo integrated costumes, as everything else, into her performances; Adrian was essential to helping her do it. He was tall, thin, handsome, and sympathetic. From her earliest days on the lot, they enjoyed a personal if problematic friendship. The fondness between them was mutual and genuine, and they were of deep, symbiotic importance to each other professionally. But Garbo's volatility was maddening, and Adrian was forever having to adjust to her mixed signals.

She could arrive at his studio in a foul mood or a lighthearted one—Adrian never knew which to expect. Either way, her grubby sweater, slacks, tennis shoes, and disheveled hair were handicaps to his glamorous "vision." But even at her scruffiest, she was the greatest imaginable model and inspiration for his stunning designs, and Adrian knew she would showcase them with the utmost panache. Though they often battled, she almost invariably capitulated to his wishes, after which a nearly unanimous chorus of critics and public would hail his latest rendering of her. To survive the creation process and pull off each new coup, Adrian's good humor was crucial—but so, for that matter, was Garbo's, as MGM wardrobe man Jerry Asher recalled:

One day she came in to try on a costume [for *Grand Hotel*]. Milliners, fitters and tailors stood back in a respectful half-circle, waiting for her decision. Slowly Garbo walked up and down. She would stop, survey herself in the full-length mirror and then start walking again. She did not utter a sound. Her face didn't betray a single emotion. The tension became unbearable. . . . Garbo continued her pacing. Suddenly she stopped, whirled around and faced herself in the mirror. Slowly but surely, she opened her mouth, put out her tongue and gave herself a huge razzberry.

Through 1929, the visual presentation was all that mattered. As of 1930, audio was required. The most mesmerizing quality of Garbo's voice was its deep, rich, contralto tone—"a low-keyed Swedish foghorn," Anita Loos called it—with an accent to match. "Have you noticed how her English grows better and more natural with each successive picture?" said William Daniels in 1935. But at some point, she seemed to stop honing and simply let it "hang out." Garbo's English was a modified British with American elements—lovely and easy to understand—and much of her impact was derived from its exoticism. It was the first and probably only Swedish voice millions of Americans ever heard. Overseas, Europeans voiced their affection for her in many tongues. The British had a song called "I Dreamed That I Was Kissed By Greta Garbo," while the Germans sang "Du Bist Meine Greta Garbo."

But there were dissenters. Documentarist-critic Pare Lorentz confessed in a 1929 issue of *Judge*:

"I have never been able to understand the universal palpitation that has followed [Garbo's] slow but stupid appearance on the great American screen—sex appeal, unfortunately, is a matter of opinion."

Lorentz, one of the rare Garbophobes of his day, was in the minority. Films depicting intelligent women in love were (and still are) uncommon; few actresses were able to portray love and brains at the same time. "What matter if the picture as a whole is slow, even draggy, and lacks climaxes?" wrote one critic of *Romance*. "It is nevertheless absorbing because of Garbo—her inescapable magnetism, her sure intelligence."

Intelligence, without which beauty was just beauty, leavened everything Garbo did. "Don't act, think!" F. W. Murnau once declared. That was what elevated Garbo's eroticism, along with something more metaphysical—her soul.

The feminine film ideal was always the *male's* ideal of the female, of course, and changed according to masculine tastes and commerce: Essentially, it was a matter of selling Woman as one might sell soap or dental floss, but with more glamour and profit. The film heroine evolved, as we have seen, from virgins to vamps to flapper working girls and now to the Love Goddess, of whom Garbo was the ultimate exponent.

Woman as sorceress, casting a spell over man, is an ancient, universal myth. In film, Garbo and Dietrich were the "enigmatic incarnations of all that is mysterious to man—all that he wants to conquer, subjugate and destroy," wrote Marjorie Rosen. Garbo didn't devour men as the silent vamps did. She drew them like a magnet in spite of herself: "She said no; they said yes—and ultimately they changed her mind." Her grief corresponded to her reluctance to capitulate:

> When Garbo made love, her partner seemed invisible. . . . It was as if she were caught up on a crest of autoerotic intimacy, a self-caress, with her public as keyhole voyeurs. Her curious duality served to appease and compel men and women alike. For men, her aloofness made the effort of conquest . . . worthwhile. Indeed, isn't the man who tames the temptress infinitely virile? Isn't her imprisonment his freedom? For women, she suggested . . . strength, a quiet self-awareness usually equated with masculinity. Woman admired her toughness and were fascinated by her willingness to acknowledge her sensuality, not through clothes or nakedness, but through her voice and eyes. . . .

> But inevitably the Garbo character's ephemeral spirit was broken and her bravado punctured. She exuded splendid élan and soul while going down, but her ship always sank.

A lot of ships were then sinking in America, which made Garbo even more the woman of her escapist time and place. Though many of them were out of work, seventy-seven million Americans went to the movies every week. Desperate for diversion and with no native royalty of their own, folks manufactured surrogate kings and queens from the choices offered them by Hollywood.

Garbo was an unusual queen candidate in that audiences could identify with her but also—as with Bette Davis later—bear to see her slain or punished. "Garbo was the only one we could kill off," said MGM's Robert Rubin. "The Shearer and Crawford pictures had to end in a church, but the public seemed to enjoy watching Garbo die." In the Depression, glamour plus suffering was a surefire formula. Beyond sex and suffering, Garbo treated everyone "with perhaps too much care at the moment, because she knows what's going to happen to them in a year or two," wrote film critic Alistair Cooke.

The ethereal Swede had little in common with most Depression victims,

but her intoxicating image temporarily took them out of themselves, even
as it evaded definition.

Just as well, perhaps, not to define it. "How cleverly the trappings of
mystery and illusion cloak a vacuum, the embryo of a personality that has
never developed—or been allowed to," says Rosen. "And how expiating of
man to elevate mystery if he is the force which has prevented the embryo's
development." Garbo acted without regard to men; Dietrich, by contrast,
was ever aware of men's weaknesses and ever ready to take advantage of
them. But both reflected the Josef von Sternberg notion of 1930:

> It is the nature of a woman to be passive, receptive, dependent on
> male aggression, and capable of enduring pain. In other words, she is
> not normally outraged by being manipulated; on the contrary, she
> usually enjoys it. I have plenty of evidence to assume that no woman,
> as opposed to the male, has ever failed to enjoy this possibly mortifying
> experience of being reorganized in the course of incarnating my version
> of her.

When Sternberg first met Dietrich, neither her plumpness nor her previous
mediocre films deterred him from conceptualizing the Ideal Woman he could
mold. Stiller had done the same with Garbo, cleverly helping her blend her
real self with her roles. Most often, she was cast as an exile. "The displaced
person always inspires curiosity," wrote Kenneth Tynan. "Who displaced
her, what forces drove her from her native land?" Her screenplays exploited
a "melancholy, sexually enigmatic, neurotically shy Swede, who relaxed in
men's clothes, viewed life fatalistically and talked of 'going home,'" wrote
Alexander Walker. Those traits were worked into films that supplied historical or romantic reasons for them and tossed in her intrinsic indolence
for good measure.

"What she did was like nobody else," said Eleanor Boardman, at age
ninety-two still marveling at a woman she did not much like. "You could
hardly distinguish the screen character from the real one. Don't you see?
She could never have had two personalities."

So much of that indivisible personality and its expression on- and offscreen
was owed to an accident of Nature—the tabula rasa face that mirrored a
thousand subtleties. When those two "worry" lines in her forehead were
added, on command, that face became all-tragic, all-feminine, all-human, in
its ability to convey emotion and in its unprecedented photogeneity.

In her films, "the plot and the dialogue are for the censors," wrote Charles
Affron. "The face, Garbo's ultimate field of sexuality, is for us." The *real*
communication lay there. Garbo always appeared eager to make love. She
was, in fact, so timid that she banned all visitors and most technicians from

the set, but where the activity of her face was concerned, no code or censor could inhibit an actress "whose most cherished fetish is a movie camera."

Few were consciously aware of that, but millions felt it viscerally. Garbo was the first to touch the erotic depths of men and women everywhere, crossing all national and cultural boundaries. "What, when drunk, one sees in other women, one sees in Garbo sober," wrote Tynan in the most famous Garbo paean. She was all objects of desire at once—innocence, experience, strength, and tenderness.

Feminists have a more political interpretation of the scopophilia—sexual pleasure through looking—that lay at the heart of Garbo's impact, and of all film viewing. Freud called the "controlling erotic gaze" a basic sexual instinct in which man is the looker and woman the looked-at. "From pin-ups to strip-tease, Ziegfeld to Busby Berkeley, [woman] plays to and signifies male desire," wrote Laura Mulvey, positing that the high-Hollywood style was geared to male voyeurism and fantasy relations with women on screen.*

Whatever its psychoanalytic explanation, Garbo's power was a social and emotional function of the pre-TV moviegoing experience itself, as illuminated by Meyer Levin, *Esquire*'s astute film critic of the thirties:

> I know I'm not alone in feeling this hypnotic, habit-forming need for the movie. The motion picture is a necessity, rather than a luxury. . . . An escape once a week into the other-world of the films, and the heart is able to go on. [But] I think there is something more involved than simple escape; I think the need for congregation is there, the need to feel one's self in a room with other folks, sharing a common experience; and also a kind of religious experience in confronting the un-natural together. . . . Maybe it is simple hypnotism. The hypnotist holds an object before the eye. . . . The willing subject [is soon] in a trance state, freed of responsibility, freed of himself, happily guided by an outside force. . . . Each time the trance is deeper, because you have comfortably given up suspicion, you know the litany, you know the ritual will never be betrayed. That's the movie in its most essential form.

---

* The radical extension of this theory holds that fragmented close-ups of the female body—say, of Garbo's face or Dietrich's legs—augment her eroticism while, by contrast, the male almost always requires a three-dimensional space. Examples abound in Garbo films but most pathologically in the oeuvre of Alfred Hitchcock, notably *Psycho*, *Marnie*, and *The Birds*, where the woman's sexuality is a threat to be reduced through "the pleasure of seeing the woman's body in pieces," which thus reassures the totality of the man's. (See photo and caption of Garbo "decapitated," p. 291.)

With Garbo, the relationship between hypnosis and film viewing was more intense because her personal erotic modality—iconic, ironic, laconic—was so original. But the real secret to Garbo as actress and icon was secrecy itself: What exactly was she holding back? No one quite knew. But they sensed the spirituality within the sexuality—the tragic soul that lifted Garbo above banal melodrama toward something more immortal.

Garbo at Silver Lake, the Sierra Nevadas,
1932; snapshot by her companion Mercedes de
Acosta

CHAPTER 8

SEX AND PSYCHOLOGY
1932

Intelligence was its secret ingredient, but since Eros was the open essence of Garbo's screen soul her private sex life intrigued millions. Whom she was sleeping with was only the most crass and common question; speculation on all aspects of the subject would continue unabated for sixty years. And since Garbo's conflicted sexuality was the thing she most wanted to conceal, the insistent probing of it was a key factor in her increasing public and private withdrawal. There was never any necessary correlation between the on- and offscreen love life of film stars, least of all Garbo's. But the more she withdrew, the more she reinforced the image of the cold, aloof Snow Princess, whose secret sex life must surely match the fantasies of her fans.

Most galling to Garbo was that the subject was fully in the public domain, seriously and in jest. Everyone was amused, for example, by the report that actor Wayne Morris had labeled his bathroom faucets "Ann Sheridan" and "Greta Garbo" instead of Hot and Cold. The running-hot-and-cold metaphor was particularly apt, of course, in relation to those many alleged "marriage plans" with John Gilbert, largely fabricated by the press with and without MGM's help. "Gilbert managed to lure her to the marriage license bureau at Santa Ana," said one report. "The story is that she broke away from him and hid in the railroad station until a train for Hollywood arrived." Wrote Louella Parsons another day: "Garbo and Gilbert slipped quietly out of Los Angeles last Friday and were married in a nearby village. San Jose or Ventura are mentioned as the county seats where the license was obtained."

Garbo's true feelings about Gilbert and his proposals have been the subject of debate for half a century. "It was a love affair from the very beginning," insisted Eleanor Boardman, and not just hype from the MGM publicity department. "The studio had nothing to say about it; they had no control over that part of her life. She was always herself."

The few statements reliably attributed to Garbo are inconsistent. "It is a friendship," she told writer Rilla Page Palmborg. "I will never marry." A reporter caught her leaving her hotel on February 23, 1927, and asked about the Louella Parsons report. "Ridiculous," she replied. "We are not even engaged." Years afterward, however, she told her friend Nicholas Turner, "I was in love with him. But I froze. I was afraid he would tell me what to do and boss me. I always wanted to be the boss." Gilbert Adrian, from the male perspective, felt "Garbo did not bring out a sense of gallantry in a man. She tried, too soon, to force him into her way of living. She made the rules. No man was allowed to remain himself. He soon was a leash dog, and the tugging that went on did not always lead to a pleasant walk."

But another friend was startled one day to hear her say, "You are aware I was in love with John Gilbert; he was a fine man. I can never answer the question, 'Why weren't you married then?'" But later on she added, "God, I wonder what I ever saw in him. Oh, well, I guess he was pretty."

He was pretty, he was sexy, he was fun to be with, and he adored her. He was also immature, self-pitying, indiscreet, manic-depressive, and prone to fights and drunken scenes.

"I cannot bear to fight or argue, and I can't stand people who get drunk," she said at the time, in a not very veiled reference to Gilbert. "If I see an accident or hear two people quarreling, I am just sick all over. I never fight myself and I won't do any fighting in pictures."

In Hubert Voight's opinion, "She was flattered pink by his ardor and his passionate expressions of undying love. [But] he did not measure up to her intellectually at all. He did not have a great mind. Neither did she, in fact, but she was a hell of a lot smarter than Jack." Stiller was furious that she should fall "for anyone so half-witted as Gilbert," according to Garbo's friend Mercedes de Acosta, who said their affair was a result of Garbo's intimate contact with a *young* man for the first time. Louise Brooks, as usual, had an iconoclastic sexual take:

> Almost all men disliked Gilbert. He was a kind of disgrace to their sex—feminine, not homo, but wildly emotional. The only two men I knew who were fond of Jack were [directors] Jack Conway and Eddie Sutherland, [who] made him relax and laugh at himself. . . . There is enough dyke in me to know that Garbo must have detested him. . . . She did what every actress has done since the word whore has been changed to the word actress. She went out with him and gave him a

casual lay from time to time for the sake of her career. On safe ground, she gave him a fast broom.

That was a brutal but arguable assessment. At first, Garbo found Gilbert a kindred soul who knew the MGM ropes and taught her how to negotiate them, literally. She trusted him and moved in with him. But she did nothing to enlighten him about Stiller's sexual preferences, and Gilbert—in his jealous frustration—was convinced that Stiller was behind her insistent refusals to marry him. The abortive "double wedding" was neither the first nor last time Garbo backed out of marriage, the idea of which was always more Gilbert's wishful thinking than Garbo's intent. Did she deliberately lead him on?

"No, she just didn't contradict him," said Boardman, who co-starred with Gilbert in *Bardelys the Magnificent* (1926) and later *Redemption* (1930). "She did the right thing. She balked. She wouldn't do it. She never should have been married and she said she never would be and she never was. When it came right down to it, she knew what she was doing." Gilbert's spite marriage to Ina Claire took place on schedule, and so did the divorce.*

Many felt there was never a real love relationship between them at all. Their affair was "definitely overrated," said photographer Cecil Beaton years later. "When Garbo did speak of Gilbert, it was as though she were discussing a brother."† The truth, as so often, seems to lie in the middle: They were poor lovers but passionate friends.

Of all the men in her life, Garbo loved Gilbert perhaps as much as she was capable of loving any man. With her, everything was so very relative. "Love?" she mused, with a little laugh, in 1928. "It is the beginning and ending of a woman's education. How can one express love if one has never experienced it? Who has not been in love? [But] marriage? I have said over and over again that I do not know. There is always my overwhelming desire to be alone."

Certainly, to *live* alone. After finally disengaging from Gilbert, she had moved first to a Santa Monica beach hotel, because it was cheap, and then to the

---

* Gilbert and Ina Claire separated on August 31, 1930, and divorced August 4, 1931. Paul Bern was Claire's witness for the couple's incompatibility, Gilbert's "cruelty," and Claire's complaint that Jack told her she "had too much intellect." Gilbert married Virginia Bruce in August 1932 and divorced her on May 25, 1934: In court, Bruce alleged that he "belittled her intelligence and ability, insisted that she stay at home, told her she was extravagant, used profanity in her presence and was violent and abusive."

† Asked during that same interview how Gilbert lost his film career, Beaton replied: "He crossed one of the Higher Powers. I don't recall if it was an M, a G, or an M."

Beverly Hills Hotel after Edington lectured her on the proper residence for a movie queen. (It was bad enough she drove a used Packard, he told her.) But her stay at the Beverly Hills didn't last long. She was in the habit of asking the management to clear the lobby whenever she wanted to take a walk, and they were glad to see her leave when she bought her first house, a few blocks away, at 1027 Chevy Chase Drive. Not content with the ten-foot cypresses there, she wanted to build a wall around the property, but the neighbors—more concerned with their own vista than with her privacy—objected. In late 1930, she signed a six-hundred-dollar-a-month lease to rent actress Marie Prevost's former home on Camden Drive, but it proved too noisy and she only stayed a few weeks. In August 1931, she moved to 1717 San Vicente Boulevard, in Santa Monica, and, from there, in 1932, to North Rockingham Road in Brentwood. Next it was North Cliffwood Avenue, also in the Brentwood–Bel Air area, then back to San Vicente, and then to North Carmelina Drive. The mailman couldn't keep up with her, which was fine by Garbo.

In any case, and house, Garbo finally had the freedom to do as she pleased, which did not include playing Great Lover in private. The perfect romantic illusion she created onscreen was not transferable to life; on the contrary, it only aggravated her fear of personal intimacy. Psychobiography is a dubious approach to be eschewed in favor of Dr. Johnson's dictum: "What you do not know and cannot ascertain, leave out." But sexuality affects everything and is at the heart of the incessant demand to know "what made Garbo tick." That demand will never be met. Yet an informed theory can be offered:

Garbo's ego boundaries and personal identity were never very strong. Hers was an empty-vessel syndrome common to many great actors: "Make me into what you will" went the message (see discussion of *As You Desire Me*, pp. 270–3), and directors did so. She was a textbook case of dazzling exterior far removed from inner self. The seductiveness was *acting*; she didn't really *feel* seductive. Her empty vessel was also open to the projected illusions of millions who viewed her as the ultimate desirable female. But there was no connection between those projections and a reserved, sexually ambivalent young woman, who was neither self-deluded nor self-reflective. Garbo was baffled and frightened by the reactions of the outside world. By now, she was receiving some fifteen thousand fan letters a week, many of which were pornographic and none of which she read. She was not a highly sexual person, and the constant sexual fantasies projected on her—full of subjugation and transsexuality—gave her a power over people she never wanted.

"Who are all these people who write?" she said. "I don't know them. They don't know me. What have we to write each other about? Why do they want my picture? I'm not their relative." It was an amusing example of the simple, literal-minded worldview she never shed: Serious Swedish people didn't do such things. It was undignified. And there was a darker, metaphysical aspect: If you can make a person turn around by staring at the back of his head, what is the psychic impact of *millions* of thoughts directed at someone so hypersensitive as Garbo? Garbo's psyche was not well equipped to withstand such assaults. Her self-identity was a thin membrane, easily punctured. Her terror of being *probed* was revealed by reporter Ruth Biery four years after obtaining one of the last bona fide interviews Garbo ever gave. In the January 1932 *Photoplay*, Biery recalled:

"She spent many hours giving me the material. I was fascinated by her sincerity, her warm, earthy qualities; her utter lack of affectation. After my story was printed, she said to me, 'I do not like your story. I do not like to see my soul laid bare upon paper.'

"After that she decided not to see writers. . . . I have seldom met anyone more timid than Garbo. When I first went to interview her she kept me waiting in the lobby of her hotel for fifteen minutes. When she arrived she was all apologies—hesitating, nervous ones. She was sincerely frightened [then and in general]. She told me that she packed her trunk more than once and that only the restraining hands of Jack Gilbert and Mr. Edington kept her from returning to Europe."

The outside threats she perceived were not all paranoiac. On February 24, 1932, Representative Samuel Dickstein of New York, chairman of the House Immigration Committee, demanded in Congress that Garbo, Maurice Chevalier, "and other foreign movie stars" become American citizens or face deportation. Meanwhile, newsmen camped outside her house almost daily. One of them waited patiently until opportunity came one evening when she was backing her car, rather crookedly, out of her driveway. He jumped on the running board and startled her terribly. "Damn!" she said, and jerked into gear with such force that he toppled off as she sped away. The resulting story—titled, "A One-Word Interview"—was considered a coup in journalism circles.

Beneath her Swedish cool was a slowly building anger at the world. In a later day, celebrities hired publicists to manufacture their public images for the press and leave them their privacy, but it was beyond Garbo's ethos and basic honesty to do such inventing. The only way she knew to cope was to cut off publicity entirely, which was interpreted as playing "hard to get" and further fueled everyone's fascination. Cannibalistic fans and reporters reinforced her misanthropic, lone-wolf, Ishmael-like quality. "I never said, 'I want to be alone,'" she told her friend Allen Porter of the Museum of

Modern Art, in a famous clarification of many years later. "I only said, 'I want to be left alone.'" Her sociophobia predated her film career, and she articulated it bluntly: "People make me nervous."

That nervousness ruled her life and was continually reinforced. A friend recalled her genuine terror one day, outside an art gallery, when surrounded by a crowd of children seeking her autograph: "If they had been lions about to tear her to pieces she could not have been more frightened." By this point, in 1932, Garbo was less social and more of a recluse than ever. She lived in fear that her new home in Bel Air would be discovered by the mob, and she was isolating herself more, even from her friends in the depleted German colony.

"Her Nordic blood may be a reason for her tendency towards morbidity," Cecil Beaton speculated after their first meeting that year, "and being so highly strung, together with her sadness at finding herself in a trap, she periodically gives way to bouts of complete despair. It is then that she locks herself up without seeing even her maid for days; for two years no one crossed the threshold of her home." On the other hand, when happy, "she is childishly uninhibited, walking on chairs and tables, climbing trees and hanging from the branches. She enjoys reciting fragments of poetry and mystical catchphrases, and uses romantic similes: 'The moon's face tonight is soft, like moss with white violets in it.'"

But suspicious moments outnumbered the carefree ones. Once she wanted to reject a bouquet of flowers sent by Louis Mayer. Fear of offending him never entered her mind; she just thought it inappropriate for anyone she didn't consider a personal friend to send her a present. Even if one *was* accepted as her friend, he never knew how he might be greeted or treated on any given day. Designer Adrian often complained about her mistrust of people and the neurotic set of rules she imposed: never to discuss her with anyone else; never to mention any mutual friends (which would imply you'd been talking about her with them); and never to pin her down for a definite date. On the other hand, if *she* wanted the date, one was obliged to cancel all prior plans.

Adrian was deeply annoyed by such behavior. Salka Viertel was empathetic. Garbo's need for solitude, said Salka, stemmed from a "deepening introspective quality" and ever-greater concentration:

> Garbo is of a very serious nature and does not view life or her work lightly. . . . There never was a human being more sincere in her hatred of publicity and more frightened by public adoration. Sometimes the irony of it strikes me strongly—that so sensitive a type as Greta should

have become a tremendous entity in an art medium [of such appeal to] the masses from whom she shrinks.

It is amazing to me that Garbo has succeeded in achieving the isolation [she seeks]. But it is much more amazing that the influence of Hollywood [hasn't] touched her. She remains, and always will remain, a great, solitary, distinctive individual. . . . She makes it a point to stay very close to Mother Earth. No truly deep lover of the out-of-doors was ever talkative.

Garbo spoke more than once of loving "to trudge about in a boy's coat and shoes and ride horseback [and] watch the sun set over the ocean. I am still a bit of a tomboy. Most hostesses disapprove of this attitude to life, so I do not inflict it upon them." Marie Dressler, observing her at close range during *Anna Christie*, came to a penetrating conclusion:

Garbo is lonely. She always has been and she always will be. She lives in the core of a vast aching aloneness. She is a great artist, but it is both her supreme glory and her supreme tragedy that art is to her the only reality. The figures of living men and women, the events of everyday existence, move about her, shadowy, unsubstantial. It is only when she breathes the breath of life into a part, clothes with her own flesh and blood the concept of a playwright, that she herself is fully awake, fully alive.

It was a combination of isolationism and chronic indecision that produced her standard reply to invitations: "How do I know I'll be hungry on Wednesday?" That semihumorous response revealed her peculiar "commitophobia"—a pathological fear of obligating herself even for a dinner date, let alone romance.

Garbo's temperament ruled out live-in lovers and husbands alike. With her parents' and a depressing variety of other negative marriage models all around, it didn't take Freud to explain why she preferred the limbo of loneliness to marital hell. As early as 1929, a medical psychiatrist named Dr. Louis E. Bisch published an unusual article titled "Why Garbo is the World's Love Ideal" in which he declared that Garbo "is harboring a powerful father complex. Her father died when she was only fourteen [and] she was left with a highly idealized memory of him. No doubt, he soon became a sort of dream hero—a man who never, never could really be duplicated again in actual life." This seems literally to have been the case: Decades later, she told her composer-friend David Diamond she often had dreams about her father.

Posthumous "shrinking" aside, it is safe to say that her relationship with her father had been intense, and that the pedestal Karl Gustafson occupied in her life was selectively "loaned out" later on in the form of a reverence for father types that served her well in the film business: When an older male authority figure told her what to do, she usually did it. She had to be pushed or at least nudged, externally motivated out of a passivity rooted in Stockholm, where she mooned outside stage doors for several years until an avuncular male finally told her to go to the Royal dramatic school and helped her do it. She had a good intellect but didn't know how to break a pattern and move forward. She lacked a capacity to visualize the first step, but picked up on it quickly when someone else showed the way.

Garbo's perception of helplessness explains much about her withdrawal and her life: She never understood that she could control things—except by withdrawing, which worked in certain situations and made her look canny. But by and large, decision making was a nightmare for her. She preferred to be led, within a firm set of rules, one of which was that the man at the top knew more rules than she and it was usually safe to do as he said.

No one epitomized that principle in her life more than Stiller, on whom she had relied totally. If their private relationship was "romantic" in an emotional sense, physically it was chaste. Stiller had a strong sense of propriety toward the young women in his charge. When he and Garbo traveled together, which they did often for two years, their accommodations were always separate and inviolable. She had spoken of "the bliss of perfect solitude" on her ocean voyage to America in 1926—further indication that Stiller did not disturb her, literally or sexually, when he had his best opportunity to do so. Some sources insist they had erotic encounters, which was possible but unlikely: Given Garbo's father complex—not to mention her reticence—it would have been highly incestuous.

Stiller's dalliances with men were known. In Germany after the Constantinople disaster, for example, not all his time was devoted to film deals. Later in Los Angeles, he received a letter dated January 12, 1927—preserved by the Swedish Film Institute and never before published—from a man named Edgar Sirmont on Martin Luther Street in Berlin:

I think often of the nice time we had, the reveillon [New Year celebration] two years ago at the Adlon and my little visits at the Esplanade. . . . "Hotel [Imperial]" was one of the biggest successes out, playing at the Gloria Palast, a wonderful, elegant kino theatre. . . . I am quite sure you have a great deal to do, [but] have your secretaries?

(Why did I not become one?) You know I would have loved to come along, yet I know you went over there, not knowing how things would turn out and even sort of afraid. . . .

Am looking for a lodger and have as usual no money. If you have a lot . . . be a dear and send me a couple of hundred dollars, I would be so very grateful, you would hardly notice it. . . .

Berlin has improved a great deal, more kinos, restaurants. . . . One can so nicely disappear and have one's little pleasures if one is careful. . . . Please be a dear and give my special love to Greta, whom I admire a great deal, and also to Hansen and if you want to be exceptional nice send me those $200 dollars—they would be such a help till my next payday in April. . . . Xmas was so expensive etc. and now I am just a poor little lassie . . . and I know you could help, you big strong man. I just felt like being in a fairy play. Put [it] in an envelloppe with a nice letter from you and have it registered and send it to me.

What Garbo initially felt for Stiller, she said, was "the adoration of a student for her teacher, of a timid girl for a mastermind." What she felt for him later, in Hollywood, was largely fear for his well-being, and not just as an artist. In European fashion, Stiller's friends in the Swedish-German colony spoke casually of his homosexuality until they learned that he and his more openly gay colleague F. W. Murnau were picking up young male prostitutes on Santa Monica Boulevard. To a friend, Garbo expressed shock that the two eminent directors would stoop to street boys—adding, "Moje only had the best in Berlin."

By this time, it was all ancient history. Murnau had returned to Hollywood in 1931 from filming *Tabu* in the South Seas. Only there had Germany's greatest director found some peace and happiness in an exuberant culture untouched by European morals and guilt. Murnau had brought back a handsome, fourteen-year-old Polynesian as his "valet-chauffeur," despite the boy's total ignorance of American highways. He was at the wheel of Murnau's Packard during the fatal trip from Los Angeles to Monterey—and Murnau was allegedly performing oral sex on him—when he swerved to avoid a truck and crashed down a thirty-foot embankment. Murnau died in Santa Barbara Hospital the next day, March 11, 1931, at the age of forty-two. *Tabu* was scheduled to open six days later in New York.

True or untrue, the scandalous gossip surrounding Murnau's death had such a chilling effect on Hollywood that only eleven people were brave enough to attend his funeral. Janet Gaynor, whom he'd recently directed in two important films (*Sunrise* and Berthold Viertel's *Four Devils* screenplay), was not among them, but Garbo was. Such was her fondness for Murnau

Director F. W. Murnau in Hollywood,
1930, shortly before his death in a car wreck

—and the memory of Stiller's—that she reportedly commissioned a death mask and kept it for years on her desk.

Stiller had died in Sweden three years earlier, and the amazing thing was that Garbo had managed so well, emotionally and psychologically, since. But at the time it occurred, Stiller's death devastated her and coincided almost precisely with the break-off of her relationship with Gilbert. Parted by death from the one and conflict from the other, she became even more aloof and love-leery. Of the two sexes, men somehow seemed to bring her greater and more frequent heartache.

Many years later, the last film role Garbo sought to play was the title character of Balzac's *La Duchesse de Langeais*, and the Duchess's lament on the relative costs of sexual love to women and men was one reason why she wanted to play it:

> I am in despair that God should not have invented some nobler way for a man to confirm the gift of his heart than by the manifestation of his most vulgar desires. [Women] become bond-slaves when we give

ourselves body and soul, but a man is bound to nothing by accepting the gift. . . . Our persistent coldness of heart is the cause of an unfailing passion in some of you; other men ask for an untiring devotion, to be idolized at every moment, some for gentleness, others for tyranny. No woman in this world has as yet really read the riddle of a man's heart.

Garbo, for one, was tired of trying. To understand her sexual pathology is, first, to grasp that of the powerful, self-indulgent men around her, who burned not just to love but to *possess* the most dazzling woman in the world, with scant awareness of their own sexual neuroses, let alone Garbo's. Such men, typically, were madly in love until the object of their desire was obtained. Garbo intuited this keenly. She might placate them on a case-by-case basis, and they might usefully reciprocate with support and guidance. But sex with men was dangerous in many ways—not least of the dangers being pregnancy. Various sources maintain that, in an era of primitive contraception, Garbo and many other actresses underwent abortions at the hands of a doctor discreetly engaged by MGM for that purpose (on a shared-cost basis with other studios); writer S. N. Behrman said she had had "a couple" of them and that the procedure had given her an ever greater "terror of sex."

Equal to a fear of pregnancy was the fear of betrayal, private and public, deliberate or accidental. Gilbert's passion for her, and the resulting headlines, had caused her more embarrassment and chagrin than any other experience in Hollywood, with the possible exception of Stiller's dilemma. Her troubled ties with both men at the same time had been an ongoing agony.

Not until 1928 did Garbo's independent sexuality really begin, after the death of Stiller and the end of her liaison with Gilbert. That double separation marked the end of her life with, and sexual domination by, men—in a real sense, the end of heterosexuality or its pretense. Enough of men for a while. She would now move on, discreetly, to women. Socially, she was always more comfortable with women and homosexual men anyway. Romantically, she preferred women, which is not to say she often acted upon this preference.

Virtually all the reports and "common knowledge" of Garbo's affairs with women (or men, for that matter) are gossip. The unabridged *Sex Life of Greta Garbo* would be a slim tome, indeed, and a great disappointment to voyeurs: Four years of research on two continents—hundreds of interviews and two hundred thousand pages of documents—unearthed qualified proof of a single Garbo sex affair and provided circumstantial evidence for only three others. There may have been more, or there may have been none.

With regard to her own sex, Garbo's relationships were not unlike those of nineteenth-century Englishwomen who "never married" but didn't necessarily "do" anything else. The current notion that everyone wants sexual fulfillment and has numerous experiences in pursuit of it was not the prevailing sentiment in early-twentieth-century Stockholm, nor in the mind of someone raised in that time and place, when people didn't necessarily want to think, let alone talk, much about sex.

In preadolescence, Garbo reportedly had physical encounters with certain girlfriends and possibly also with her sister, Alva. In any case, for her, the sexual theme was set at least by age fourteen, as indicated in her letters to Eva Blomgren that hint at lesbianism. It was more clearly manifested three years later in her relationship with fellow apprentice Mona Mårtenson. Their mutual infatuation was well known on and off the set of *Gösta Berling*. Later, in America, when a friend asked about Mona, Garbo replied, "None of your business!" But on another occasion, she confided that she had told Mona "I love you" in so many words, adding that she had wanted to return to Sweden and act on the stage with Mona but that she could never do so.

In Hollywood, Garbo's muted interest in women continued quietly—or as quietly as possible, considering that two of the beautiful actresses with whom she associated were Lilyan Tashman and Fifi D'Orsay. Louise Brooks, always the sexual-conspiracy theorist, believed there was more to MGM's publicity blackout on Garbo than just her mistrust of the press:

"After finally freeing herself from Stiller's disgusting homosexual games, she relaxed happily among the Hollywood lesbians until stories spread by those notorious gossips, Lilyan Tashman and Fifi D'Orsay, forced [MGM publicity chief Howard] Dietz to yank back Garbo with the invention of the Gilbert-Garbo romance."

The trumpeting of male "lovers" was a standard device "to fight off 'les' publicity," said Brooks. Later, when MGM was ready to dispose of Garbo and switched tactics, the disaffected Katherine Albert was "the perfect gal to write all the lesbian-slanted gossip":

> [After Garbo left MGM,] Howard did endless talk shows on radio explaining that all Garbo pictures, after Gilbert, lost money because she appealed only to women—the lesbian cult. [But] the attempted "annihilation by lesbianism" never worked because Garbo's fans didn't *believe* in lesbians.

The existence of such a conscious, active conspiracy was improbable. But it was a fact that Garbo's bonding took place almost exclusively with women. By the late twenties, she was "out of the closet" as much as she would ever be, and one of the women who most lured and allured her was Lilyan Tashman.

Garbo was a great Ernst Lubitsch fan and did not fail to catch *So This Is Paris* (1926), his sparkling spoof of continental infidelities and the male "adagio dancers" then in vogue. Patsy Ruth Miller and Monte Blue were the nominal stars of this farce (derived from the same play that inspired Strauss to write *Die Fledermaus*), but the show was stolen by Lilyan Tashman as a comic vamp. In the film's hilarious opening, Tashman and a shirtless sheik (André de Beranger) wrestle violently to the death. Only when she scratches her head after being killed do we realize it's a rehearsal. Their subsequent "Dance of Despair" is even funnier, thanks to the duo's deadpan tableaux. Garbo was delighted by the film's state-of-the-art special effects in several dream and fantasy sequences, but most of·all by the slinky blond Tashman (1899–1934), a former Ziegfeld girl who was now a popular second lead in Hollywood, playing sarcastic sophisticates in such pictures as *Man-handled* (1924) and *No, No, Nanette* (1930).

"Lilyan wasn't a great beauty—tall, skinny and with masculine kind of features—but she was a good comedienne and she had great *style*," recalls silent-film actress Lina Basquette. "She was a leader of fashion, too, always beautifully dressed, and an important part of that social caste system in Hollywood that wasn't always based on money. She was one of the first women I ever heard use obscene language. She tried to corner me in the ladies' room once when I was seventeen."

Many lesbian actresses were married, of course, often amid great studio fanfare. Tashman's second husband was actor Edmund Lowe (1892–1971) —one of Hollywood's most overt homosexuals. His preference for men and hers for women made their marriage a convenient and convivial one, and invitations to their glittering parties were much coveted. Tashman and Lowe were close friends of Gilbert's, and she and Garbo saw each other often. Tashman, who owed her svelte figure at least partly to bulimia, was rivaled only by Constance Bennett as the best-dressed woman in movies. Exclusive Fifth Avenue shops advertised "Lilyan Tashman gowns" and Tashman hats, coats, pajamas, and trousers. She was once reported to have spent $50,000 on a single dress. Among other things, Tashman gave Garbo fashion advice and Garbo, surprisingly, took it. In late 1928, Tashman helped her select a new wardrobe for her long-postponed trip to Sweden.*

"She really has bought some divine things," Tashman told a reporter at that time. "Several smart tweed traveling suits, two lovely velvet dresses, heavenly evening gowns in which she will look—well, as only Garbo can look. She bought a gorgeous gray fur coat. We have had a lot of fun shopping.

---

* A bit later, when Hedda Hopper played a small part in *As You Desire Me*, she obtained an inside scoop about those clothes: "Garbo never wore them."

*A Cecil Beaton portrait of
Lilyan Tashman. The
onscreen comic vamp
was the offscreen queen
of fashion.*

*She and her husband,
Edmund Lowe, hosted
Hollywood's most
glittering parties.*

*Fifi D'Orsay, the sexy little Fox actress who never set
foot in France, Beverly Hills, 1930*

She can't tell real lace from machine made. She will turn to me and ask,
'How do you *know* it is hand made, Tashman?' "

Garbo, of course, loathed to have her name and private activities linked
with anyone in print, but Tashman got away with those revelations because
Garbo was out of the country by the time they were published. When she
returned, their relations were broken off for a while, and one of the reasons
was a plucky little Montreal girl named Fifi D'Orsay (1904–1983).

Though she'd never set foot in France, D'Orsay was billed as the new
Parisian sex symbol. Will Rogers had discovered her in a Vaudeville show
at the Palace, where she sang and danced and became famous for her
trademark phrase, " 'Allo, beeg boy!" before breaking into movies. Garbo
had been much taken with her cavortings in *Hot for Paris* (1929). She wanted
to meet her, and it was arranged for them to dine together with Jacques
Feyder at the Russian Eagle. Garbo and D'Orsay dined together alone several
times after that and enjoyed each other's company a great deal. Though

D'Orsay never went to Garbo's house, she had The Phone Number and called often. Reported one of the Los Angeles dailies in February 1930:

> Greta Garbo and Fifi D'Orsay have become inseparable friends. Everywhere that Greta goes, Fifi is sure to tag along and vice versa. Greta stays in her shell and is so reserved that Hollywood has been greatly amused and interested in this dalliance. Fifi is Greta's first pal since Lilyan Tashman and Greta parted company. Greta sings the songs Fifi sang in *They Had to See Paris* [1929] and Fifi retaliates by trying to talk Swedish. Just how long it will last no one knows, but the two "gals" are certainly a colorful pair—so different and both so foreign.

The implications raised eyebrows, and the source of the leak was obvious: Fifi had made the mistake of speaking with reporters as Garbo's intimate, after which she couldn't seem to get through to her friend on the phone. She then tried to repair the damage and "come clean" in the manner least likely to succeed—another newspaper interview:

> I nevair played tennees with Greta Garbo! . . . Most of ze intair-viewairs say theengs I nevair say. Like saying I am from Folies Bergère, when I nevair have been in Paris. And zat I am zee insepairable friend of Greta Garbo!
>
> All zat ees a big lie. I have seen Greta Garbo maybe four times in my whole life. I like her. I theenk she ees zee greatest of all actresses. You can tell everybody Fifi say that. But I am not her . . . insepairable friend, even eef I would like to be.

Garbo, unplacated, would see her no more. "She liked Fifi D'Orsay," wrote Ruth Biery. "Fifi was young, impulsive, unable to understand upon such a brief acquaintance the reasons for Garbo's reticence. She gabbled all she knew." Fifi was as sweetly empty-headed as the parts she played, and the brevity of her Garbo liaison surprised no one.*

Tashman, on the other hand, was smart, fascinating, and a force to be reckoned with—prototypical of the strong women to whom Garbo was attracted. "I suppose she is not strictly beautiful," said Cecil Beaton, who often photographed her and was charmed by her outrageousness. "But I love her nose!" She once got into a public hair-pulling bout with Constance

---

* D'Orsay soon walked out on her Fox contract and was thereafter blacklisted by the major studios. Decades later, she resurfaced on American television as the mother superior on "Adventures in Paradise" and the drunken cook on "Pete and Gladys." She also had small roles later in the Tony Curtis film *Wild and Wonderful* and in *French Connection II* and made her Broadway debut at the age of sixty-six in *Follies* (1970).

Bennett and was highly aggressive in general, as attested by Irene Mayer Selznick, who had a story to confirm Lina Basquette's:

"When Lilyan had some drinks, it was best not to go into the powder room with her. I did once and was never so startled in my life. I'd known Lil from way back, but nothing like that had ever happened to me in my life. So overt. I'd never seen anything like it—couldn't believe it was happening. Didn't know it *ever* happened."

Ultimately, Tashman was simply too much for Garbo. Her high profile was nerve-wracking over the three years (1927–1930) of their closeness, but it was her emotional insecurity that finally put Garbo to flight. In the end, says a mutual friend, "Garbo couldn't stand always having to reassure her and tell her she was beautiful and help her deal with the weird situations she got herself into." There was no dramatic break, just a quiet disengagement on Garbo's part—and a tragic ending. Neither woman knew that Tashman's problems and volatility were partly physiological: She died in 1934, at thirty-five, following an emergency brain-tumor operation.

Mercedes de Acosta—the mentor who introduced Garbo to the haut monde and to vegetarianism, among many other things—was many things herself: a pure Spanish aristocrat raised in America and France, a poet and dramatist, an avowed lesbian, and a serious devotee of astral projection and primal moaning. From an early age, she said, "I had violent attacks of psychological suffering and, going into a corner of the room, put my face to the wall and moaned." Anxiety attacks were a common trait and source of extinction in her family. Her father committed suicide by jumping off a mountain in the Adirondacks and her brother Enriqué also took his own life. Mercedes and Enriqué were both "desperately unhappy and unadjusted people, centered in our own despair and unable to help one another," she said. "[We] lived in an inner state of melancholia."

The Acosta family history was *Candide*-like. Her grandparents shuttled back and forth among Spain, Cuba, and France with violent misadventures—revolutions, imprisonments—and large new inheritances for consolation along the way. Mercedes's sister Maria was married to composer Theodore Chanler; her beautiful sister, Rita Lydig, became a beloved *saloniste* and patroness of the arts in New York. In Paris, they were called "The Sisters Karamazov." Rita introduced Mercedes to, among others, Auguste Rodin, Anatole France, Edith Wharton, Gabriele D'Annunzio, and Sarah Bernhardt. But her deepest friendships would be with Eleonora Duse and Isadora Duncan.

Mercedes (1893–1968) was one of the great celebrity collectors of the century. By page 75 of her autobiography, she had befriended Maud Addams,

*Mercedes de Acosta, c. 1932, in a snapshot taken
by her friend Marlene Dietrich*

Kahlil Gibran, Jean Cocteau, Sergei Diaghilev, Vaslav Nijinsky, Igor Stravinsky, Miguel de Unamuno, Pablo Picasso, Henri Matisse, Edna St. Vincent
Millay, Ezra Pound, Robert Frost, and Dorothy Parker. Her guest list for
a 1928 dinner party included Mrs. Patrick Campbell, Jeanne Eagels, Alla
Nazimova, Constance Collier, Helen Hayes, Helen Menken, and Katharine
Cornell—all eyeing each other suspiciously. Even in grief, Mercedes could
not be distracted from name-dropping: When Rita died, "Friends were kind
to me, especially my theatre friends Noël Coward, Harold Ross, Alex Woollcott, Alfred Lunt, Lynn Fontanne, Clifton Webb, Kit Cornell. . . ."

Mercedes was what a later generation might have called a space cadet.
She studied astrology and yoga with Natasha Rambova, Rudolph Valentino's
eccentric, bisexual second wife. Kahlil Gibran led her to the *Bhagavad Gita*
and other Hindu epics, and Krishnamurti's influence was likewise heavy.
She claimed she once got rid of a colony of ants by chanting Vedic mantras
and "Please leave the house" over and over—until the ants complied. "In
my own experience," she said, "I believe I have gone out so far on the astral
plane that it has been hard for me to find my way back." No one who knew
her would have disagreed.

On the other hand, in the earthly realm, she was an active feminist who
labored ceaselessly on behalf of women's suffrage and related causes. Upon
marrying artist Abram Poole in 1920, she insisted on retaining her family
name—her *mother's* rather than her father's. She was also a playwright and
novelist—extravagantly romantic in all genres, on the order of D. H. Lawrence's Hermione in *Women in Love* or Marie D'Agoult, the overbearing

patroness of Chopin and Sand in Sarah Kernochan's brilliant screenplay *Impromptu:* "I have only a little talent, but I have a *lot* of time."

Mercedes was in love with Garbo and felt linked to her by destiny, long before they even met. She had missed her first chance in Constantinople, and a second in New York in 1925 when Arnold Genthe invited her to watch a photo session one day (she declined) and later sent her one of the pictures "to make you regret that you did not meet Greta Garbo." In July 1931, she moved to Hollywood to work on the script of a Pola Negri film and, as usual, wasted no time. On her second day in town, she met Mary Pickford and on the third day, Salka Viertel, who invited her to have tea with a friend who wanted to meet her. When it turned out to be Garbo, Mercedes was swept away:

"She was dressed in white jumper and dark blue sailor pants. Her feet were bare and, like her hands, slender and sensitive. Her beautifully straight hair hung to her shoulders and she wore a white tennis visor pulled well down over her face in an effort to hide her extraordinary eyes which held in them a look of eternity."

Garbo was sufficiently pleased with Mercedes for Salka to invite her back, just two days later, this time for breakfast, with Garbo—and a more extraordinary encounter. After the meal, Berthold was expecting a business associate and Salka suggested Garbo and Mercedes go next door to the seaside home of Oliver Garrett, the Paramount scenario writer (and Salka's future lover), who was away. They did so—and had a helluva time.

"We put records on the phonograph, pushed back the rug in the living room and danced," Mercedes said. " 'Daisy, You're Driving Me Crazy' we sang and danced over and over again. I loved Greta's deep voice, and I made her repeat and repeat it, until she said, 'We will wear the record out, not to mention my poor throat.' For waltz time we put on 'Ramona' and 'Goodnight, Sweetheart.' Finally for a tango we wound up with 'Schöne Gigolo'—which was all the rage at this time."

Delighted with her new playmate, Garbo announced, "I will take you home to lunch with me," but Mercedes replied that she already had a lunch date with Pola Negri. "What of it?" said Garbo. "Just telephone Pola and say you can't come." Mercedes said she couldn't be so rude at the last moment since it was an intimate lunch for six, whereupon Garbo roared with laughter: "More likely six hundred! . . . I see you don't know Hollywood, but go to Pola's today and learn your lesson."

There was an intimate gathering of a hundred at Pola's, and, in the middle of it, Mercedes got a phone call. "Well," said the low voice, "are there six people or six hundred?" The answer was followed by Garbo's instruction, "Now, make for your car and come to my house and no more nonsense about being polite to Pola." Mercedes sped to 1717 San Vicente Boulevard, where Garbo was waiting for her outside in a black silk dressing gown and men's bedroom slippers, looking tired and dreading the fact that she was due on the *Susan Lenox* set early the next day:

> Only a few hours ago I had seen her radiant. When I came to know her well, I realized how easily her moods and looks could change. She could be gay and look well and within five minutes she would be desperately depressed. . . .
> "You were happy this morning, weren't you, when we were dancing and singing?"
> "Yes, thanks to you I had a few minutes' gaiety this morning. But now it is nearly evening. Soon it will be night, and I will not sleep, and then it will be morning, and I will have to go again to that terrible studio. Let's not talk. It is so useless talking and trying to explain things. Let's just sit and not speak at all.

At sunset beneath her eucalyptus trees, Garbo finally sighed and broke the silence: "Now you must go home," she said, and the day created a pattern for their relationship. "It is a joke between us," said Mercedes. "She always has to remind me to go home." On her next visit, she found Garbo in a lighter mood. "My present prison term is over," she said upon greeting Mercedes in the driveway. "I have finished shooting [*Susan Lenox*]." She then announced ceremoniously: "I never invite anyone to my house but today, as a great exception, I am inviting you."

Her living room struck Mercedes as gloomy and unlived in, and Garbo caught her thought. "I never use this room," she said. "I live in my bedroom," which contained only a bed, dressing table, desk, and several uncomfortable straight-backed chairs, all in heavy oak. "There was not a single personal thing in it," Mercedes said. Garbo walked to her window and pointed to a slim, dead tree—"my one joy in Hollywood," she said. "I call it my 'winter tree.' When my loneliness for Sweden gets unbearable I look at it and it comforts me. I imagine that the cold has made it leafless and that soon there will be snow on its branches." She turned away sadly and added, "I have never told anyone before about this tree." It took much less than this to reduce Mercedes to tears, and she was weeping as she now asked Garbo about her early life. Garbo spoke hesitantly, but she *spoke*—of her childhood, her dreams, her great love for Alva.

By then it was time for a mood swing. "Let's go out to the beach," she said suddenly. They got into her old black Packard, which Garbo called "the bus," and drove along the coast to Casa del Mare, parked, climbed to the top of a small mountain, and looked out over the moonlit sea.

"What do you believe about God?" Garbo suddenly asked.

If anyone was prepared for such a question, it was Mercedes, who at length gave Garbo the benefit of her pantheistic view that God was more or less everything. "Then finally, as the moon sank and disappeared and a tiny streak of light fell across the sky in the east, we were silent," Mercedes related. "Slowly the dawn came. As the sun rose we walked down the mountain and picked rambler roses as we went along."

They had literally spent the night together, outdoors, in a deep intimacy that was not necessarily physical but did not necessarily rule it out, either. From now on, they grew steadily closer and Mercedes took on great importance in Garbo's mental and emotional life, with an impact on her performing life, too. Garbo at the time still spoke English "quite incorrectly," in de Acosta's opinion, but her accent and mispronunciations were enchanting and her mistakes often more expressive than the proper words would have been. ("I trotteled down to see you.") Mercedes's own English was flawless, and over the next few years she gently helped modulate Garbo's, leading her to adopt a more cultivated accent and to eschew Yankee slang. "George Cukor used to say that I taught Greta her beautiful English and it was generally accredited to me that I did," wrote Mercedes, demurring that "this was not really true. It is possible that her English was in some small way influenced by mine, but she has such innate taste that she could never speak any language other than beautifully."

In Hollywood during the thirties, Garbo had a total of three long-suffering servants, two maids—Ettie (nicknamed "Whistler") and Gertrude ("the Dragon")—and a black chauffeur named James Rogers. Garbo was afraid of Gertrude, worried about being tyrannized by her, and always tried to be out when she was in. But unlike their predecessors, this trio remained loyal, resisting fabulous bribes and never tattling to the press.

Mercedes grew very fond of Garbo's domestics, who were as eccentric as their mistress. James had come as a window cleaner, and because he was so quiet Garbo asked him to be her driver, in which post he served her faithfully for nine years. "He never made the slightest comment about anything and he never moved faster than a snail," Mercedes wrote. "Besides chauffeuring, he was also supposed to clean the house. This he would do in slow motion, taking at least half an hour to polish one doorknob, and when Greta would say to him, 'James, you are very lazy,' far from disagreeing with her he would answer, 'Yes, ma'am,' in a soft drawling voice."

In the car, James never drove faster than twenty miles an hour—a crawl of a pace that Garbo liked. He also did not know right from left, and he never asked where they were headed.

"He would start off in a straight line and follow it indefinitely unless we told him otherwise. Greta would say to me in an undertone, 'Let's just see how long he will drive without asking where we are going.' Finally, as we were about to drive into the ocean or up some mountain, she would say, 'James, do you know where we are going?' 'No, ma'am,' he would answer." Sometimes Garbo would have James drive her as far away as Lake Arrowhead, where she would hire a canoe, row out to the middle of the lake, and read a book for hours while he waited.

The apotheosis of the Garbo–de Acosta relationship was a long vacation they took together—the account of which, in Mercedes's autobiography, is the primary source of Garbo's presumed lesbianism. It began when Garbo solemnly informed Mercedes that she was leaving for six weeks to be "utterly alone" on an island in a lake in the Sierra Nevadas. No one could reach her there, and only Mercedes was to know about it. She and James then drove off. Two nights later, Mercedes's phone rang and Garbo's voice said, "I am on the way back. I have been to the island but I am returning for you." Toward midnight the next day, a black limo pulled into her driveway with weary James and Greta. They had driven straight through the 120-degree Mojave heat, stopping only for food. The lake was gorgeous, said Garbo, but "I had to come back for you because I could not be such a pig as to enjoy all that beauty alone."

The duo, now a trio, repeated the journey the next day with the uncomplaining James at the wheel. The desert temperature had now risen to 140, and the hot wind and sand stung their faces at each refueling stop. Finally, after the long climb, they saw Silver Lake in the distance between two mountain peaks, and Garbo grew very excited: "There is our lake and there, that little island in the center, is our island!"

The lake was fourteen miles long and three miles wide, and the island was about half a mile from shore. It contained a little house—not much more than a shack—belonging to Wallace Beery, who had given the keys to Garbo. James transferred their provisions to a boat and then Garbo sent him off, telling him not to come back until the last second of six weeks had elapsed. "If you turn up one second earlier I will throw you into the lake," she told him. "And mind you, absolutely *no one* is to know where we are. Not even Whistler, and certainly *not* Louis B. Mayer!"

Garbo took up the oars, and Mercedes was amazed to see how well she rowed, with smooth, steady strokes, to the island. On all sides stood the majestic, snow-covered mountains in grand silence, as Mercedes rhapsodized:

How to describe the next six enchanted weeks? Even recapturing them in memory makes me realize how lucky I am to have had them. Six perfect weeks out of a lifetime. . . . In all this time there was not

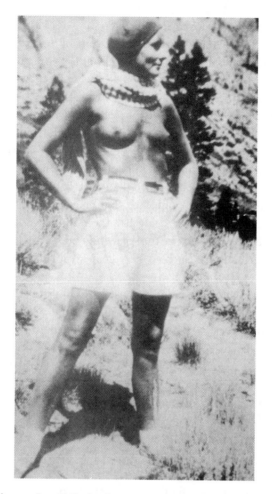

De Acosta's snapshot of Garbo during their idyllic Silver Lake vacation. "I would see her above me, her face and body outlined against the sky, looking like some radiant, elemental, glorious god and goddess melted into one."

a second of disharmony between Greta and me or in nature around us. Not once did it rain and we had brilliant sunshine every day. . . .

The little house could not have been simpler. It was only a log cabin but neat and clean with windows all around it. Greta said, "We must be baptized at once." Throwing off her clothes she made a magnificent dive into the water and followed it with the long, powerful strokes of an expert swimmer. . . . "Isn't there anything you do badly?" I called out to her. . . . The water was icy cold and I had to keep going or freeze. Greta swam beside me. . . .

That evening she cooked dinner. Along the way we had bought

mountain trout. She poached it and made the wonderful strong coffee that Spaniards and Swedes like to drink. "None of this American coffee, just hot-water business," she said, adding proudly, "I make *good* coffee." And indeed she did.

The days and hours flew past far too quickly. . . . There was no sense of time at all. It is generally accepted that Greta is morose and serious. . . . Metro-Goldwyn-Mayer employed her from 1925 to 1938 before they discovered she could play comedy. . . . She can play high comedy and low comedy and she can play the clown when she wishes. . . . On Silver Lake I laughed more than ever before in my life and it was Greta who made me laugh. . . . No one can really know Greta unless they have seen her as I saw her there in Silver Lake. She is a creature of the elements. A creature of wind and storms and rocks and trees and water. A spirit such as hers cooped up in a city is a tragic sight.

There in the Sierra Nevadas she used to climb ahead of me, and with her hair blown back, her face turned to the wind and sun, she would leap from rock to rock on her bare Hellenic feet. I would see her above me, her face and body outlined against the sky, looking like some radiant, elemental, glorious god and goddess melted into one.

Often she rowed me across the lake to a lumber camp a few miles away. Here we bought milk and eggs and talked to the lumbermen, who thought we were schoolgirls on a holiday. At night in a fantastic silence with dark mountains towering around us we would go out in the boat and just drift. . . .

Somehow, six weeks that seemed only six minutes wound itself round and came to an end. We had almost come to believe that we would never return to civilization. Then one day across the lake we heard James' horn. Greta turned deadly white and fled into the house. "I can't—I *can't* go back to Hollywood and that studio life!" she cried.

But we packed our things and, without a word between us, got into the boat. Slowly, and as though a great sadness had befallen her, she rowed to the other shore.

Garbo's domestic life now involved Mercedes on a daily basis. In late 1932, soon after the Sierra Nevada trip, she moved from San Vicente Boulevard to North Rockingham Road in Brentwood, just half a block from Mercedes. Her new home came with a garden, a fine vista of the canyon, and a tennis court (de Acosta played a decent game but Garbo always beat her). Often they hired horses at the exclusive Bel Air Riding School nearby, where

Garbo's favorite was a mare named Elizabeth. Though she had never ridden before coming to Hollywood, she rode the hills like a natural, according to stableman Roy Davis.

Rockingham Road ran up through wild country to the San Fernando Valley ten miles away, and they sometimes walked that distance, to be met by James with the car on the other side. "We thought very little of such a walk and most days did at least six or seven miles, played several sets of tennis, swam in the sea and sometimes rode," said Mercedes. "Our day often started at five and never later than six. Greta would come down to my house just after the sun was up and whistle under my window. I'd dash into my clothes and we would be off over the hills. Sometimes we took picnic lunches and spent the whole day on the beach far up toward Malibu. We went to bed very early." When shooting, Garbo retired at seven—otherwise, around eight or nine.

Mercedes soon moved even closer—to a house on Rockingham Road right next to Garbo. On Christmas, 1931, Garbo closed all the curtains "so that we could have candlelight and pretend it was snowing outside" as they sat around the tree and opened presents. Garbo gave her a raincoat, boots, and sou'wester hat, saying the rains would soon come, which they did. "We would put on our raincoats, hats and boots and make for the hills," Mercedes wrote. "Sometimes terrific thunderstorms came up and we would rush out to the highest peak overlooking the sea to watch the lightning break through the sky like great cracks of fire, and hear the thunder crashing down on us. We were always happy and stimulated in a storm."

Erotic imagery was employed, and activity implied, by Mercedes—but hardly proven. Independent of her attachment to Garbo, she was part of an elite and chic set of Hollywood lesbians in a "Sewing Circle" that included Aldous Huxley's wife, Maria, and, on the fringe, alleged bisexuals such as Salka Viertel and members of Alla Nazimova's old entourage (known as "Gillette blades" because they cut both ways).

"Salka was AC/DC," Irene Selznick firmly declared. "Lots of people knew about that. She was quite masculine, I thought—overweight and unappetizing, but charming." She, as everyone, might well have been attracted to Garbo, but the reverse was unlikely, and none of the many claims that they were "lovers" offers anything but conjecture to back it up. Says Salka's son Peter, an ever-present teenager during these years, along with two other brothers: "When would she have had time? Where would they have gone?"

On a typical afternoon, Maria Huxley would drop off Aldous at a bookshop or museum, then meet up with Salka, Mercedes, and sometimes Garbo. Without Garbo, they were more likely to attend a poetry reading or perhaps a séance at the Hotel Brevort. Salka was peripheral but Mercedes was integral to the sorority, often sporting a tuxedo after her other great friend, Marlene Dietrich, was so attired in *Morocco*. Despite a nominal husband, Mercedes was one of Hollywood's most visible lesbians. Irene Selznick called her "fascinating, bizarre, a little distasteful, yet very cultivated—very outré."

Mercedes's elegant dress modes did not impress Tallulah Bankhead, who said she always looked like "a mouse in a topcoat," but most thought her highly fashionable. It was, in fact, Mercedes more than Tashman who cultivated Garbo's interest in clothes. Though overly eager to add Garbo to her celebrity collection, Mercedes possessed the high breeding and cultural sophistication that Garbo lacked and was quite willing to exploit. The result was a pathetic danse macabre: When Garbo wished to see her, Mercedes was ecstatic. But more often, Mercedes's elaborate plans would end with Garbo's failure to materialize and the distraught hostess in tears.*

"Mercedes was so *persistent*," says Peter Viertel, adding that Garbo made fun of her and used her but also truly liked her. Many years later, Mercedes was the first and only woman to write—albeit guardedly—of something close to an "affair" with Garbo. When Salka read Mercedes's book, *Here Lies the Heart*, her comment to actor Jack Larson was: "Here lies the heart—and lies and lies and lies!"

Was Mercedes de Acosta Garbo's lover or her passionate friend? Alice B. Toklas, who met them together, wrote Anita Loos: "You can't dispose of Mercedes lightly. She has had the two most important women in the U.S. —Greta Garbo and Marlene Dietrich." But Garbo's friend Nicholas Turner claims she told him explicitly that they were *not* lovers.

Garbo's niece, Gray Reisfield, sums up Mercedes as "an hysteric." But for all her oddity, she had certain gifts of insight and eloquence. "To know Greta one must know the North," she wrote. "She may live the rest of her life in a Southern climate, but she will always be Nordic, with all its sober and introvert characteristics. To know her one must know—really know— wind, rain, and dark brooding skies. She is of the elements—actually and symbolically. Forever, in this present incarnation, she will be a Viking's child—troubled by a dream of snow."

A full inventory of Garbo's alleged affairs with women would be long and pointless, but one of the few worth noting was supposedly with Marie Dressler. Dressler's own comments about Garbo always sounded more maternal than passionate: "I consider her a charming young person, with the

---

* There are 181 letters from Garbo to Mercedes de Acosta—an amazing total—in repository at the Rosenbach Museum in Philadelphia. They would shed much further light on their relationship but are sealed until the year 2000.

same mysterious sort of appeal that attracts you to her screen personality—together with a lot of common sense that one seldom finds in the youth of today." Dressler was a well-known lesbian, says composer David Diamond, "but at that stage of her life [she was sixty-one], admiration was as far as she would go with anyone, especially with the most beautiful woman in the world. Garbo had great admiration for her and thought she was extraordinary in *Anna Christie*, but what sexual attraction could there have been and who would have known? Garbo, of course, never told *anyone* whom she went to bed with."

People knew only that she had many lesbian friends and a keen interest in women's sexuality. She treasured, for instance, a copy of Edouard Bourdet's *La Prisonnière (The Captive)*, a then-shocking lesbian drama, signed by Helen Menken, who played the title role on Broadway in 1926. Garbo was said to have been a friend to—and to have had a brief involvement with—Eva von Berne,* the short-lived "second Garbo" discovered by Thalberg in Vienna, who appeared with John Gilbert in *The Masks of the Devil* and then disappeared. It was possible, and more possibly mythical.

More fascinating, because of its firsthand account, is Garbo's close encounter of the Louise Brooks kind. The two beauties were never friends, but Brooks knew John Gilbert and occasionally showed up at his house to find Garbo playing tennis. She was as much in awe of Garbo as everyone else.

"From the age of fifteen," wrote Brooks by way of preface, "I was pursued by lesbians and I was strongly attracted by them, but not much sexually. By the time I got to Hollywood, everyone thought I was a lesbian. In 1928 when I met Garbo at Alice Glazer's, we sat facing each other closely across a

---

* Eva von Berne (1910–1929) was born Eva von Plentzner in Sarajevo, moved to Vienna after World War I broke out, and met Thalberg there at age sixteen. It was decided to name her after MGM executive Paul Bern but to tack on an "e" and keep the aristocratic sounding "von." When she arrived in New York, Hubert Voight made up for all he had been unable to do with Garbo. He spent lavishly and introduced Eva to all the studio executives. There were daily press conferences and nightly parties. Her first film, *Masks of the Devil*, would be directed by Victor Sjöström and star John Gilbert.

Thalberg and everyone else at MGM had overlooked only one thing: They all had assumed she could act. But Eva could neither take direction, emote, nor move properly. Self-conscious and wooden, she also looked heavy. The makeup and wardrobe staffs helped her appear more beautiful but could do nothing about her acting.

MGM implied that if she lost weight, as Garbo had done, and returned home to get more training, she could make a comeback. It was a ruse to get her to leave without a fuss. On October 24, 1928, she asked to be released from her contract, and Thalberg gladly agreed. The studio gave her a farewell check for three hundred dollars. The publicity department was ordered to permit no interviews, just to make sure that she left the country. She did so on November 1, 1928, and was never heard from again.

narrow breakfast table. Her gaze was so intense and so eloquent that I left
after an hour although I had intended to spend the afternoon." They only
met a few times, she told film writer John Kobal, adding offhandedly: "She
made a pass at me." She claimed they spent a night together, and that Garbo
had been both charming and tender. If so, it was not repeated. Brooks never
ceased to admire and analyze Garbo in her irreverent way:

"Garbo was a completely masculine dyke, which makes her films even
more wonderful. She did the chasing, except for Mercedes de Acosta, whom
she took on for snob reasons and gave a hell of a beating—the daughter of
a butcher abusing a descendant of the Duke of Alba! When somebody like
Dietrich or Bankhead went after her, Garbo took it on the lam."

Garbo liked to confuse people, or at least not clear up their confusion, and
mysteriousness was both instinctive to her, inside, and part of everyone's
projections, outside. The assumption of her lesbianism or bisexuality was
fueled by her gender confusion in speech and dress, on and off the screen.

In fact, there was as much humor as sexual revelation in Garbo's constantly
masculine self-references. "I have been smoking since I was a small boy,"
she often said, and she regularly excused herself from parties with, "He's
got to be in bed by 9:30." Once, over drinks with a friend, she broke a long
silence with a baffling non sequitur: "I am a lonely man circling the earth."
When her host asked what she meant, she only sipped her vodka, said
"Someday I will tell you," and smiled. In later years, she would drop by
friends' apartments with the greeting, "Give an ooold man a warm cup of
tea."

With such words went the visuals: Garbo's offscreen wardrobe of "men's
clothes" defined her androgynously in the popular mind and made a powerful
fashion statement emulated by millions. It was, as Mercedes distilled it, "the
era when many young women wanted to look masculine and many young
men wanted to look feminine." Garbo had recently created a stir by attending
a film—not one of her own—in beret, sweater, and tweed skirt. But that
was nothing compared to the commotion for which de Acosta claimed
responsibility:

When I had known Greta a little while I got her to exchange her
sailor pants for slacks. Looking back it seems difficult to believe that
at this time people were still shocked to see women in trousers. Once
we were photographed in them on Hollywood Boulevard [and it was
published with the caption]: "GARBO IN PANTS! Innocent bystanders
gasped in amazement to see Mercedes de Acosta and Greta Garbo
striding swiftly along Hollywood Boulevard dressed in men's clothes."

Considering what walks down Hollywood Boulevard now, it seems strange that Greta and I should have caused a sensation such a comparatively short time ago.

Garbo's most celebrated "drag" appearance was at a legendary costume party of April 27, 1929, soon after she returned from Sweden to begin work on *The Single Standard*. The story reveals much about her relationship with Adrian: She came in for a fitting one day and found him designing a disguise for himself to wear to a gala hosted by Basil Rathbone and his wife, Ouida Bergere. Costume parties were the Rathbones' passion; they had recently hosted one at the Victor Hugo restaurant as Henry VIII and Anne Boleyn. Garbo, in Cinderella fashion, sighed pathetically and said she wished she too might go, but the thought of so many people. . . . Adrian pleaded with her to no avail, but she asked him to stop by her house and show her the finished costume on his way to the party. He did so—having taken a chance and fashioned a Hamlet costume for her in the hope of luring her along. Garbo tried it on, added the mask, and Adrian assured her she'd never be recognized.

Garbo went to the Beverly Hills Hotel in her Adrian-designed black satin trousers, full-sleeved blouse, and circular collar—the melancholy Swede disguised as the melancholy Dane. All evening, fellow stars tried to guess the identity of the slender young man clutching protectively at the dagger in his belt, while Garbo moved unknown among them, perhaps eavesdropping on some gossip about herself (and perhaps also flashing to that fatal masked ball of King Gustav III). In any case, she was happily into the spirit of the occasion when Lilyan Tashman walked up, tapped her shoulder, and said, "Well, look who's here—if it isn't Garbo in person!"

Annoyed and disappointed, she sought out a corner and soon slipped away. The added subplot was that John Gilbert was also there, parading his bride Ina Claire. When Garbo's presence was revealed, everyone assumed (and relished the idea) that she had come in a kind of retaliation.

In larger fashion terms, Garbo was on record with, "I care nothing about clothes. . . . When I am off the set I don't want to have to think of clothes at all. . . . I like to live simply, dress simply. I like to have time for doing nothing."

The whole second half of her life, for instance. But the irony was as unintended as the fashion influence. Garbo's broad-shouldered suits, for example, produced major reverberations at the time Adrian designed them for her (and later, when adapted more severely to Joan Crawford). Yet Adrian's brilliance was not the real essence of the phenomenon. At heart, the crazes Garbo inspired grew out of her private, idiosyncratic preferences, the way she wore things, and the rakish angularity of her posture—the jutting hip, the cocked elbow, the "space-straddle" of her stance, the unique walk. All these would be appropriated by designers and models throughout the late twenties and thirties. She was unlike anyone else and could *dress* unlike anyone else: Everything Adrian created for her—from the high-necked evening gowns (in that era of décolletage) to the boyish casual attire—set international fashion standards beyond his imaginings. She herself, meanwhile, seemed truly unaware of, or disinterested in, the enormous impact of what she wore on and off the screen.

Garbo's niece, Gray Reisfield, views her aunt's relatively masculine dress as a statement, all right, but not a sexual one: "She simply *liked* men's clothes—she found it easier to move in them. No man understands how ridiculous it is, for instance, getting in and out of a car in a skirt, especially if you have three photographers snapping away at you."

So Garbo was not personally interested in fashion at all?

"Wrong," says her niece. "She had a great interest in fashion, but it was her *own* fashion. She was very fussy about it, in fact. The pants, the walking suits, the lack of jewelry—all that contributed to what was thought of as 'masculine' but what was really just uniquely *her*. She ran her own train; she didn't feel she had to get married; she wore her hair and makeup the way she wanted to; she furnished her home the way she wanted to—she did *everything* the way she wanted to."

Transvestism is differently interpreted for the two sexes: Male transvestites generally find women's clothing arousing. Female transvestites tend to be turned on more by the relative liberty and authority men's clothing represents—what Louisa May Alcott called "the freedom of male experience and possibility." Carolyn Heilbrun, in *Writing a Woman's Life*, notes that women who go beyond conventional expectations usually run up against gender barriers, of which dress is the most onerous. George Sand had made Gray Reisfield's point a century earlier:

> I had legs as strong as [my young male friends'], and good feet which had learned to walk sturdily in their great clogs upon the rutted roads of [the country]. Yet on the [city] pavement I was like a boat on ice. My delicate shoes cracked open in two days, my pattens sent me spilling, and I always forgot to lift my dress.

Gender-assigned speech restrictions annoyed Sand, too, and the people who wrote about her. "What a brave man she was, and what a good woman," said Turgenev, one of many to describe her as both male and female without any sexual implications. Much as she wanted to, Garbo never got to play George Sand on screen but often got to play with pronouns. In one of her most cryptic lines, she once told her art-dealer friend Sam Green, "I'm a kept woman but somebody missed a good man in me." As Reisfield dismisses her "transvestism," Green similarly discounts a sexual reading of her speech. Such references were not an expression of sexual preference, he says, but "a way of removing herself" from a story and becoming another person in another time, place, and gender, especially when speaking of Hollywood, where she was deeply alienated.

"It was hell working in California—what a nightmare," she once told him. "I could never go anywhere. I was never free to be myself. All I did was work. Sometimes it was too much to bear and I had to get away. I would get in the car and drive all the way to Santa Barbara. But when I got there, I realized there was no place I could go even to have coffee, and I would drive all the way back to purgatory. It's a sad life."

Garbo's sexual ambivalence was confirmed over the years, in both the public and the Hollywood mind, by the male roles she always said she wanted to play—Dorian Gray, Hamlet, and St. Francis of Assisi, to mention a few— and by her periodic, losing battles with MGM to play them.*

Mercedes was dying to work professionally with her beloved friend and was thrilled one day in late 1931 when Garbo burst into her house excitedly to say she had obtained Thalberg's approval for Mercedes to write a vehicle for her. Mercedes came up with *Desperate*, a romantic story with Garbo as a wild Iris March–type heroine and an escape scene in which she was disguised as a boy. Thalberg liked the idea well enough at first to put Mercedes under contract, but later he declared that Garbo could not wear men's clothes on the screen.

"Do you want to put all America and all the women's clubs against her?" he asked Mercedes. "You must be out of your mind." When Mercedes said Garbo liked it, Thalberg replied, "She must be out of her mind, too. I simply won't have that sequence in. . . . We have been building Garbo up for years as a great glamorous actress, and now you come along and try to put her into pants and make a monkey out of her. The story is out."

Garbo, as usual, exhibited sangfroid about it. She had another bright idea, she said. She wanted Mercedes to write the Dorian Gray scenario. Replied de Acosta: "You go and tell Irving that idea and have him throw *you* out the window—not me!"

There was another potential Garbo-Acosta collaboration that was much dearer to Mercedes's heart: the film version of Mercedes's play *Jehanne d'Arc*, which had been performed in 1925 at the Odéon in Paris with her friend

---

* When asked to write a St. Francis screenplay for Garbo, Aldous Huxley's response was: "What—complete with beard?"

Eva la Gallienne in the title role. Now, in 1932, a few months after his rejection of *Desperate*, Thalberg again asked Mercedes for Garbo ideas. She said she wanted her for once to play a role where beautiful clothes would not stand between Garbo and her acting. "I also told him I thought Greta should play the roles of saints," she said. Thalberg asked which saints—the question and the cue Mercedes had been waiting for.

St. Teresa of Avila was one possibility, she replied, and of course Joan of Arc. . . . Thalberg seemed interested and asked for more information. Mercedes happily complied, suggesting the Joan of Arc story could be shot in France in all its actual locations. According to her, "He became so excited and interested about this that he assigned me to write a scenario of Jehanne d'Arc."

The life of Joan of Arc had been filmed many times, but Thalberg and everyone else agreed that Garbo would be most spectacular in the part. Mercedes worked passionately for nine solid months on turning her drama into a film scenario. When Thalberg read it, he praised it extravagantly, she said, but he called her back that same night with grim news: "Garbo does not want to do this film," he told her. "I'm as disappointed as you are."*

Mercedes was devastated but, for some reason, could not bring herself to speak directly with Garbo about it. The next day at MGM, Thalberg told her, "Greta is being influenced by someone. She would not make this decision on her own." The implied "someone" was Salka, supposedly motivated by the fact that she would have no part in the writing of it. But Thalberg may have been disingenuous with de Acosta; others maintained "the terminator" was Mayer, who was appalled when he found out that Garbo planned to do the part without makeup and with her hair cut off.

"Of all the disappointments I had in Hollywood, this hit me the hardest," said Mercedes. "For some time after this when I was with Greta a ghost seemed to stand between us—the ghost of Jehanne d'Arc. But I never again mentioned a word to her or to anyone else about it."

In any case, it was a great loss not just to Mercedes but to film history, especially in view of the problematic new Garbo script approved in its stead: Luigi Pirandello's *As You Desire Me* (recently starring Judith Anderson in the stage version) about a woman who may or may not be another man's long-lost wife. Garbo would play Zara, the amnesiac cabaret singer from Budapest, whose memory loss is a result of shock during the war. Since then, she has been the prisoner of a sadistic novelist until an Italian count

---

* When Mercedes wrote to lament this turn of events to Marlene Dietrich, Dietrich told her husband, "What stupidity! Can't you just see Garbo—hearing voices? Being ever so religious *à la* Swede?"

(Melvyn Douglas) discovers her, claims to be her husband, and takes her back to Florence so she can regain her memory. Is she or isn't she his wife? No one knows, least of all herself. In her most explicit tabula rasa line—applicable to Garbo's whole film career if not her life—she makes an agonized declaration: "There is nothing in me, nothing of me; take me—take me and make me as you desire me."

The film had been fully cast except for the role of the sinister writer, when Garbo herself suddenly thought of Erich von Stroheim. Stiller had called him the most important man in American movies; shortly after their arrival in New York in 1925, they had gone together to see his virtuosic direction of *The Merry Widow*. Garbo was impressed with the film (and its star, John Gilbert) and made a point of seeing all subsequent von Stroheim pictures and appearances as an actor. "If I could get von Stroheim!" she had told *The New York Times* back in 1929. But the extravagant Prussian was nearly as antisocial as Garbo, and they had as yet never met.

Salka now solved that easily by inviting "The Man You Love to Hate" to Mabery Road to meet Garbo and discuss *As You Desire Me*. The role interested him because it caricatured the Hungarian playwright Ferenc Molnár, he said, but there was a big stumbling block in Irving Thalberg, whose career von Stroheim had haunted at every turn.* Like Orson Welles twenty years later, he was no longer employable as a director, but his acting talents were sufficiently potent at the box office to enable him to ask for $1,000 a day. Thalberg, von Stroheim told Garbo, had vowed that he would never work at MGM again, and Mayer had once literally thrown him out of his office for remarking, "All women are whores." But *the* reigning MGM star of 1932 merely laughed and said she'd make Thalberg give von Stroheim the part, or threaten to go on strike.

Garbo, as always, was as good as her word, and a few days later von Stroheim entered the forbidden MGM portals. Mayer and Thalberg gritted their teeth; they and the rest of the company resented his friendship with Garbo, who sat at his feet and chatted between scenes. Director George Fitzmaurice—this was his second Garbo film of that year—could barely

---

* As the young production chief of Universal in 1922, Thalberg had watched von Stroheim spend an unheard-of million dollars on *Foolish Wives* (he demanded a life-size replica of Monte Carlo and historically authentic underwear for his Austrian troops). The next year, Thalberg fired him in midproduction of *Merry-Go-Round*. *Greed* (1923–1925) was begun at Goldwyn, but when Goldwyn merged to form MGM, von Stroheim was again working for Thalberg, who was appalled by the forty-two-reel extravaganza and removed it from von Stroheim's control, releasing a "streamlined" ten reels. MGM thought it had him under tight control on *The Merry Widow*, but von Stroheim turned that fluffy operetta into an orgiastic black comedy. The greatest von Stroheim fiasco was *Queen Kelly* (1928), but at least that was Gloria Swanson's and Joseph Kennedy's nightmare, not Thalberg's.

Two great profiles merge for the topsy-turvy eroticism of Pirandello: Garbo and Erich von Stroheim in As You Desire Me *(1932).*

tolerate von Stroheim and his two most infuriating traits as an actor: He couldn't remember his lines, and he was an unpluggable fountain of un-solicited script ideas, camera angles, and "business."

Melvyn Douglas was disillusioned: "I had looked forward to meeting him, regarding him as a true genius for *Foolish Wives* and *Greed.* . . . But he was rude and common, and had such a hopeless stutter that his scenes had to be shot over and over again—angle by angle, phrase by phrase. I was surprised that a man who had shown such gifts had no subtlety, no savoir-faire."

Von Stroheim, for his part, was miserable. Not yet recuperated from a recent operation, he was often ill and his frequent absences might have led to dismissal, had Garbo not been protective. She told him to phone her if he couldn't report to work, on which days she told the studio that *she* was indisposed.

The film opens at the nightclub where Zara's dubbed singing voice sounds "pretty much the way Garbo might—and exactly the way Dietrich did," according to Richard Corliss, who maintains that Zara was "clearly Garbo's playful parody of Marlene Dietrich." In *As You Desire Me*, she appeared for the first and last time as a not very convincing platinum blonde. Among its highlights is her first scene with von Stroheim—a heavy kiss, shot from above and behind for erotic effect.

Also of interest is a minor supporting performance by actress-turned-gossip-columnist Hedda Hopper, who worked with Garbo for seven weeks: "It took me three weeks to break through her wall of reserve. She was the only member of the cast who, at the first rehearsal, was letter-perfect." The film's best scene is the one in which Garbo knocks on Douglas's door after he has virtuously declined to exercise his conjugal rights. "Got a cigarette?" she says when he lets her in, then lights it from his own, very suggestively, and lets it fall to the floor in the ensuing passionate clinch.

Mercedes de Acosta felt Zara was the least appreciated of all Garbo roles—especially the scene in which she gets drunk: "It is rare for an actress to play an intoxicated scene without appearing either vulgar or absurd. She was neither of these, but instead, gave a sense of being lost, like a person taking the wrong turn of a road and trying to grope her way back onto the right one. [She said] she was worried about giving it a sense of reality. She asked if she could rehearse it for me and suddenly, right there in my room, she became the character [and] I felt the influence of drink taking over her personality."

Melvyn Douglas, in this first of his three films with her, said, "Her acting made you feel here was a woman who knew all there was to know about all aspects of love." Scenarist Gene Markey observed that "she absorbs dialogue and situation instantly. She needs very little rehearsing and nearly always improves on the material she is given."

The compliment to Garbo was a backhanded insult to himself; Markey's dialogue was lame. Garbo's cerebral performance was much praised; von Stroheim's villainous one was not. But Garbo herself liked the film, in spite of its sappy-happy ending. She quoted, with amusement, von Stroheim's remark when she took off her shoes before a certain shot. Looking at her feet, he observed, "I don't think they're as ugly as everyone says."

The "take me—make me" theme was "intriguingly relevant to the creation of Garbo the star," wrote Corliss. "Indeed, the film has everything going for it but good writing, acting, and directing." He is right. In their final embrace, Melvyn Douglas—for no rational reason—obscures his leading lady completely. Notwithstanding Mercedes's opinion, *As You Desire Me* is one of the true oddities of Garbo's oeuvre. Far greater drama was to be found in what, if anything, she would do next.

Garbo's career, said Alexander Walker, profited from the curiosity that the mysterious, independent woman always aroused. Lines like "I am Mata

Cecil Beaton, photographed by George Platt-Lynes

Hari—I am my own master" sounded like an oblique reference to her own life or a coded ad in the personals: dominatrix on the outside, potential dream mate underneath.

In reality, a married Garbo was as hard to imagine as a wifely Queen Elizabeth I. Both women converted their enigmatic sexual status (and relative sexual inexperience) into power, and marriage would have made them vulnerable. Lovers made bad husbands, and vice versa. John Gilbert had challenged that assumption, to no avail. Another equally intense and persistent young man would now do the same.

Photographer Cecil Beaton (1904–1980) entered Garbo's life in a most romantic way in 1932. He had long been desperate to meet her and, as the current Hollywood houseguest of Edmund Goulding and his wife, Marjorie Moss, he had asked them to arrange it. They tried, but Garbo said no, on the grounds that "he talks to newspapers." Beaton was in despair, but on the last day of his visit he looked out the Gouldings' upstairs window to see Garbo below casually chatting with his hosts.

"If a unicorn had suddenly appeared in the late afternoon light of this ugly, ordinary garden, I could have been neither more surprised nor more amazed by the beauty of this exotic creature," he wrote. At their introduction, "she pervaded a scent of new-mown hay, and of freshly-washed children." They hit it off beyond his wildest dream. "You're so beautiful," she told him. "But *you're* so beautiful," he replied. "No," she said, "you should never return a compliment."

She spoke lightheartedly of "her coloured maid, whose husband had cold feet at night" and of "a woman who had an oversize Adam's apple." A vase of freshly sprayed roses was on the bar, and Garbo asked, "Oh, who put the dew on them?" She picked one out, kissing and fondling it "with an infinite variety of caresses." Later, she became extremely interested in the sex of two cold chickens on the buffet.

Suddenly, the air was electric. Garbo hated off-color jokes—most of all, for some reason, those related to the posterior. Goulding, said Beaton, had "idiotically proclaimed that if Garbo didn't do his bidding as director he'd turn her upside down and give her a smacking where she sits upon." Garbo reprimanded him sharply, and to help breach the gaffe Beaton asked her upstairs to look at his photographs. She went.

"Are you happy?" she asked him there.

"Yes."

"It's so easy to say Yes."

"And you?"

She sighed, and gave a deeply soulful reply: "Tomorrow I go to work with a lot of people who are dead. It's so sad. I'm an onlooker. I've passed being active in life. It's not a question of time and age—it's just what you are yourself."

By then it was past twilight, and the mood shifted again. They went downstairs, and everyone was soon dancing to the radio. Garbo imitated Douglas Fairbanks, swinging from the cross beams. They all did improvisations to Strauss waltzes, Rachmaninoff and "Wunderbar." "Garbo, as a policeman, arrested me for some importunity," said Beaton. "The lights were turned out and our bacchanalia became wilder in the firelight."

Suddenly, she announced she was leaving; she had to be at the studio in a few hours. As she sat at the wheel of her car, Beaton held her hand through the window and told her he was due to leave California but if she'd see him again, he would stay. Could he come and eat spinach with her at the studio that day?

"No."

In desperation, he grabbed a feather duster that was lying by her side and asked if he could keep it as a memento.

"No."

Then this was goodbye?

"Yes. I'm afraid so. *C'est la vie!*"

It was better than *The Green Hat* or any movie script. Poor Garbo—Prey Girl of the Western World. Everyone was in *pursuit* of her, physically and emotionally. And poor Beaton—so honest and direct about it, and so neurotic. It was no secret that he used photography as a means of social entrée, career advancement, and personal ends. Jean Cocteau referred to him and his Hollywood articles as "Malice in Wonderland." Beaton's Garbo accounts, then and later, were extremely revealing, to his own detriment but to the benefit of history.

In terms of men, Garbo was both cautious and cavalier these days. Cameraman Karl Freund, whom she had met in Berlin (and who would photograph *Conquest* a few years later), had emigrated to Hollywood and renewed their friendship. One day, wickedly, he asked her what she did about sex. Her reply was tongue-in-cheek, in view of the fact that her Swedish maid had long since quit, but basically true nonetheless:

> Once in a while I go out, when I meet a man I like who enjoys me. When he arrives I peek out at him to see what he's wearing and then I dress accordingly. Many of the men who ask me out go crazy about my Swedish maid, who is very pretty. They pat her on the cheek and flirt with her, but for me, at the end of the evening they say, "Thank you, Miss Garbo," and they tell me how wonderful it was, but not one ever says, "Let's go to bed."

In terms of women, Mercedes was the only (relatively) known quantity. Garbo's many other alleged affairs with women either never happened or are forever hidden beneath a unique sorority of silence. Both things are possible—but so is simple love and friendship without sex. How often have outstanding women loved other women and been loved and sustained by them in return. How invariably and irrelevantly are such intimate female friendships considered proof that they are lesbians.

More significant than with whom and with which sex Garbo slept is how sex was integrated into her life and psyche and—by way of revelation—her films. Many of her best love scenes were played alone or with props. "She was in need less of leading men than of altar boys," says Corliss. Her melancholy self-absorption was constant: People could adore her from afar, but at close range they made her nervous. She was always desperate for privacy and chagrined to be deprived of it.

Or was she? For all her professed loathing of publicity, Garbo was "crazy about pictures of herself," according to her friends. For one man alone, she sat still for some four thousand photographs. He was Clarence Sinclair Bull, her sole portrait photographer at MGM from 1929 to the end of her career. It was the longest and greatest collaboration of its kind in Hollywood history.

Their first major session was during *The Kiss:* "The great Garbo walked into my portrait gallery looking like a frightened schoolgirl," said Bull. A new photographer after three very comfortable years with Ruth Harriet Louise was upsetting. At the end, she said, "I'll do better next time, Mr. Bull. I was quite nervous." He patted her hand and replied, "So will I."

Garbo invariably arrived at his gallery at 9 a.m. sharp, completely made up, and quit precisely at 5 p.m.—exactly the same as when filming. Few of Bull's other subjects were ever so professional; many had to be eased into the mood with a martini or two. Not Garbo. Virgil Apger, Bull's assistant, recalled that she would arrive quietly and walk barefoot around the gallery for a while: "We would be getting things ready and setting up lights, and maybe an hour would pass and we wouldn't realize she was there. She liked one sort of lighting, high-key and very little fill. One key light and one top light." That was it. She moved freely about. Bull did the rest:

> When the pose was to my liking, I quickly adjusted the lights and made the picture. Garbo read my face out of the corner of her eye and when she saw that I liked an expression there was no need to say "Still" or "Hold it." All I did was light the face and wait. And watch. [She was] the easiest of all stars to photograph, having no bad side and no bad angles—the most cooperative star I ever worked with, always willing to try unusual lighting effects and expressions of inner feelings and conflicts. She never seem[ed] to tire of posing. I have known her to hold a pose, either in glaring lights or by the dimmest ones, for more than a minute and a half.

"The Swedish Sphinx" was Bull's idea: In a 1931 darkroom experiment, he superimposed a close-up of her face over a photo of the Egyptian Sphinx, having first airbrushed out its face. He was afraid Garbo might be offended, but she laughed heartily at the result and approved its wide release. Normally, their sessions produced about two hundred negatives, all of which Garbo examined and most of which she approved for publicity use.

"Her face," said Bull, "was the most inspirational I ever photographed."* His pictures of her are timeless.

But for many connoisseurs of the Garbo image, Ruth Harriet Louise's

---

* The one exception to Bull's post-1929 monopoly on Garbo portraits was a 1930 sitting for *Romance* with George Hurrell. Hurrell's technique was the opposite of Bull's. He gabbed incessantly, hopped about and crawled around the floor looking for angles. After a few shots, Garbo came out of the studio and said, "There's a crazy man in there."

"The Swedish Sphinx," 1931, photographed by Clarence Sinclair Bull. Garbo's face on the monument at Giza. The photograph became one of the most popular and widely reproduced images of her ever.

1926–1929 Garbo portraits are more revealing. Louise had been John Gilbert's favorite MGM portrait photographer, and soon became Garbo's. That she was the sole woman in a man's field—and almost exactly Garbo's age—were not insignificant facts. Louise captured a girlish Garbo quite different from Genthe's "woeful woman" or Bull's later icon. Garbo smiled often for Louise and seemed more casual and more sexual—face unmasked, blouse unbuttoned—than she ever did for a male photographer. Louise was at the top of her profession when she left the studio suddenly to marry director Leigh Jason. She died in 1944.

In all her still pictures, as well as her moving ones, Garbo exhibited what Marjorie Rosen called an "autoerotic intimacy, a self-caress." Her films were geared to people's fantasies with her on screen, but the obverse was the pleasure of being looked at. Such was the symbiotic essence of Garbo's relationship to the camera and to her audience. *Scopophilia*—that "primordial wish for pleasurable looking"—is satisfied by film, even as it simultaneously reflects the narcissism of the subject.

Garbo was technically bisexual, predominantly lesbian, and increasingly asexual as the years went by. Critic Charles Affron noted "her pervasive orality, aggressively open-mouthed kissing and interminable puckering over a cigarette and communion cup." But that was onscreen. In life, Garbo the sexual creature was above all *passive*. She was a woman who could have almost any man or woman on earth, and yet she was so terribly reticent that she never sought out lovers. They came to her—essentially, to worship. Deified, she and her sexuality were hopelessly tangled up in her inescapable egoism.

The irony is that the egoism was accompanied by very low self-awareness. She couldn't stand to be criticized. She was not in the habit of philosophical questioning in general, of examining her own sexual boundaries in particular. The adult did not go much beyond the child's understanding of her own psyche and religious demons. Her sexuality was more repressed than developed. As in so many areas of her life, she basically didn't want to have to deal with it. One close friend claims she was "strictly, exclusively lesbian." Many things point to that, but in Garbo's case—for that very reason—perhaps it wasn't true. Even Mercedes, who desperately wanted to believe otherwise, led Beaton to record in his February 2, 1930, diary entry, "she isn't so far a lesbian, but might easily become one." Another friend declares with even greater conviction, "She wasn't lesbian. She wasn't *anything*."

Garbo was hardly alone among beautiful actresses assaulted by the romantic fantasies of friends and fans. But unlike many who had been treated as sex objects from childhood and felt "complete" only with a man, the young Garbo was a gawky loner who then and later preferred the company of other solitary and sexually unthreatening people—housekeepers, relatives, homosexual men, father figures, and maternal women.

What did she "do" sexually?

"Probably not a helluva lot, and possibly nothing," says one analyst. "If she did, those Lutheran goblins would have chased her so badly that it wouldn't have been worth it. I doubt she ever had a functional sexual relationship, male or female." Despite those liberal Scandinavian attitudes, wrote Parker Tyler, "something in Garbo wanted to be where sex wasn't."

From adolescence, her recurring trauma was abandonment—by death, in the case of her father, sister, and Stiller—and in adulthood, she was determined to avoid being abandoned by the living. "She associated sex with betrayal," said a friend. Sexual intimacy was the ultimate violation of her privacy. She had an extremely low threshold of embarrassment, on and off the screen. (She would allow her single "bomb" in the movies to end her film career.) How much more *personally* threatening was any kind of sexual activity, let alone intercourse?

In Selma Lagerlöf's *Saga of Gösta Berling*, there is an "old maid" of forty with whom Garbo might have identified: "Miss Marie thought that love was the root and origin of all evil in this world. Every evening, before she fell asleep, she used to clasp her hands and say her evening prayers. After she had said 'Our Father' and 'The Lord bless us' she always ended by praying that God would guard her from love."

The more Garbo became a sex symbol in America, the less she understood or adjusted to it, and the more abstinent she became: Sexually and psychologically, Garbo was a largely celibate narcissist.

In Gallagher's *The Girl Who Loved Garbo*, the narrator finally thinks she understands why Garbo was always wandering and searching and referring to herself in the masculine gender: "I imagine Garbo's astonishment to discover many years later that she is and always has been that which she seeks."

In the realm of nonfiction, however disappointing it may be to her fans in search of titillation, Garbo's sexual activity was close to nil, despite the fact that sex was at the center of her image and appeal. "How does a woman cope with the fact that her value is determined by how attractive men find her?" asks Heilbrun. In Garbo's case, not well. But the fact that she couldn't fulfill the social-sexual script the world prepared for her was the *world's* problem, not hers. At a time when sex roles were unambiguous, Garbo was complex and ambivalent: "She gives to each onlooker what he needs," wrote critic Kenneth Tynan—an idea borrowed from Dr. Bisch's article of thirty years before: "To any man she may be anything. From the parts she plays, they fill in the gaps in their imagination and construct for themselves an ideal love to their own liking."

Her haunting look, her brooding loneliness, her "mystery" made her the embodiment of the nameless strivings of both sexes. Her farm ancestry had come out in those long limbs and "broad yoke of collarbone that looks as if it was meant for harnessing to Mother Courage's wagon," says Walker. "From birth, Garbo's physique united the two sides of her nature, the feminine and the masculine," which she deployed brilliantly in her acting. Her unique, androgynous movement was especially potent in love scenes, "where the almost male intensity of her attack was played off strongly against the feminine spirituality of her looks."

In the last analysis, "Her independence of either sex is responsible for the cryptic amorality of her performances," said Tynan. Dietrich "has sex but no gender," and in a modified way, the same was true of Katharine Hepburn. But "Garbo transcends both of them. Neither [of them] could have played Garbo's scenes with her son in *Anna Karenina*. . . . Garbo alone can be intoxicated by innocence."

Garbo's own innocence was as real as it appeared onscreen, and it was a quality that had to do with love, not sex. In thirteen of her fifteen talkies, she played "bad women" ranging in badness from promiscuity to prostitution. Yet she did so more decorously than any other leading lady of the time. An exposed knee and occasional peekaboo dance outfit were the most that filmgoers ever saw of her body. Her fans, by and large, did not fantasize about sleeping with her: Garbo transcended the sex act itself—to a large extent offscreen as well as on.

The metabolism that photographed as listless sensuality was really closer to fatigue; what looked like a migraine on Joan Crawford was, on Garbo, "an intense form of sexual yearning." Few could believe the simple truth—that the connection between Garbo's erotic screen essence and her private sexuality was nonexistent.

Queen Christina *(1933)*

CHAPTER 9

GARBONOMICS
1933—1937

You're the top!
You're the National Gallery,
You're the top!
You're Garbo's salary . . .
—COLE PORTER

Aside from her MGM contracts, a single slip of paper in the Swedish
Film Institute archives constitutes the only irrefutable evidence of
Greta Garbo's finances of this time. It is a form memo from her then "business
administrator," Charles A. Greene, with the cautionary instruction "Please
Destroy After Noting." But she neglected to do so, which is why we know
that, on April 16, 1931: "Your balance this morning after depositing your
check for last week and deducting all checks drawn to date, is $1,046.92
(Beverly Hills First National) and $73,505.78 (Beverly Hills First National
Savings). $74,552.70 total."

There were other accounts, of course, and the sum in this one was not
gigantic. But it was quite respectable in a time of bank closings, unemployment, bread lines, Herbert Hoover's ineptitude, and a fast-worsening Depression. The country was in horrendous shape—but Garbo was not.

How much money she really had, and what she did with it, were subjects
almost as secret as Garbo's sex life. So were the details of her next victory
over MGM, which was accomplished not by a holdout or any strategic ploy
other than making her private life a higher priority than moviemaking. As
her contract was expiring in 1932, Garbo's fear of losing her secrets was

equalled only by MGM's fear of losing the profits she generated. At this point, with Garbo at her peak, Mayer and MGM dreaded the one headline potentially bigger than "Garbo Talks": "Garbo Walks."

In her contract battle five years earlier, when the terms were not to Garbo's mind adequate, her famous response, "I tank I go home now," had rocked Metro. Now it wasn't even necessary to say it; she just went ahead and quietly did it—arranging for a sabbatical, with no threats or howls of outrage from the studio. Her great weapon was indifference to whether she won or not—"the triumph of the apathetic will," Alexander Walker called it. Mayer had learned the hard way that one couldn't get Garbo to sign by strong-arming her, only by finding out what she wanted.

Nowadays, it wasn't money—which removed MGM's main bargaining chip. As her old contract ticked away, she was disenchanted with the movie business in general, Hollywood in particular, had openly discussed "retire-ment," and was in a financial position to do it. With no new contract in sight, there was a frenzy of press speculation about MGM's multiple fears: that Garbo might quit outright, as she told many she wished to do; that she might move back to Europe and make films more happily there; or—worst of all—that she might desert MGM for one of its many rivals who were clamoring for her. "Other studios made fantastic offers," said Salka Viertel. "She had only to choose." She was by now the greatest money-making proposition ever put on the screen, and she knew it. She had no need to accommodate anybody or any corporation unless she felt like it. Mayer had to find something other than money to lure her, and eventually he did: *control*.

Garbo's MGM contract was due to expire in June 1932, which was why the studio rushed her into production of *As You Desire Me*. Despite von Stroheim's anxiety attacks, it had been shot quickly (forty-two days), within the confines of her time remaining. Both Garbo and MGM were taking her contract down to the wire. Just forty-eight hours before it expired, Harry Edington announced that she was leaving for an indefinite vacation in Swe-den. Surreptitiously, he was also responsible for a widely circulated report that Garbo was negotiating with Max Reinhardt to appear in a Berlin stage play that would subsequently be brought to Broadway. But there was no indication of future movie plans.

Not publicly, that is. For half a century, it was believed that Garbo left MGM up in the air, letting the studio fret for eight months while she lounged abroad. The truth was that—before she left—frantic, behind-the-scenes ne-gotiations had produced a new agreement that was unprecedented at MGM or, for that matter, in Hollywood history.

This top-secret, two-picture deal, signed by Garbo on July 8, 1932, bound the studio to set up a special production company for her at MGM—production schedules to be determined largely by herself. Garbo was to designate a starting date for the first picture by July 6, 1933; the second would be set within six to ten months after wrapping the first. She would get $250,000 per film ($100,000 on signing, $30,000 on reporting to work, $15,000 per week for four weeks, $60,000 upon completion). As if those terms weren't generous enough, an addendum of February 4, 1933, gave her director and co-star approval, too. MGM was to submit the names of two directors and four co-stars for her to choose from. So eager was MGM to sign her before she left America that names, dates, film subjects—virtually everything was to be filled in later.

Garbo's secrecy about the arrangement was predictable, but MGM's silence was unusually sly: Let public speculation about Garbo's future continue and thus build up suspense for her next picture—whatever and whenever it might be. Mayer was also in no hurry to publicize the new terms for fear of provoking an insurrection by his other stars.

Garbo's own account, as told to Cecil Beaton, is delicious:

> When I had finished the [previous] contract I said to [Mayer]: "This is the end. I don't want to continue: I want to get out of pictures." He and his minions were all so worried. They had these long discussions with me, and we walked up and down outside the sound stage, and they said, "You can't quit now. We won't let you. You're at the very peak of your career." But I was all set. I was so unhappy. . . . Somebody joked that Mr. Mayer made my bank fail so that he could get me back. I had to sign another contract, but I told him to do pictures that I liked, and he agreed to pay me [half of] my next picture in advance. He wrote out the highest cheque I have ever seen. But I had nowhere to put it —no pocket, no bag, so I tucked it into my open shirt, and went home to Sweden while they prepared my next film.

Indeed, Garbo calmly vacationed, first for a month in California, then with Mercedes for a few days in New York, where they evaded the press by staying at the Gramatan Hotel in Bronxville instead of in Manhattan. On July 29, 1932, Garbo boarded the *Gripsholm* for Sweden, two Burns guards stationed outside her stateroom door to ward off intruders. The belief that she might never return was bolstered by a presumably symbolic going-away present from her MGM technician friends—a suitcase. Harry Edington lied outright to the press: "Miss Garbo has not made any definite plans as to her future in motion pictures. When she leaves she will do so without having signed with any Hollywood company. She affixed her signature to no contract of any nature or sort."

Will Rogers, meanwhile, was still on her case. "Hollywood is all excited, they hear Greta Garbo is going home," he wrote. "She is supposed to go home now and take up this match king job." The reference was to her friend Ivar Kreuger, the industrialist, film financier, and wheeler-dealer who turned the Swedish Match Company into a powerful international monopoly but whose empire had been collapsing in the wake of the stock market crash. "He was the biggest man over there. And she is the biggest woman. Just think of running a little tiny stick of wood, with some phospherous [*sic*] on the end of it, into an establishment that controlled the finances of a dozen nations."

The levity was macabre in view of the fact that Kreuger had just committed suicide, and Garbo was known to be upset about it. Chalk it up to typical Yankee insensitivity. Her own nation welcomed her home warmly, and more respectfully. The crowds of adoring fans were smaller and somehow less threatening in Sweden, and she could disappear from public view more easily.

She spent several weeks on an island in the Stockholm archipelago with her mother, brother, and his recent bride, Marguerite, whom Garbo immediately liked. They swam and sunbathed in typical Swedish family fashion, and the experience was sufficiently relaxing for Garbo to muse about building her "dream house" there, someday, on one of the hundreds of little islands dotting the Baltic Sea east of the Swedish capital.

By September, when the warm weather was exhausted, she was back in Stockholm, renting a modest one-bedroom apartment. She saw a few friends and entertained even fewer, until the arrival of Mercedes for a visit during which they went to the Comedy Theater, where Garbo's old friend Karl Gerhard was performing. She and Mercedes dined at such elegant establishments as the Operakällaren, located next to the Swedish Royal Opera Theater, with its high ceilings, chandeliers, baroque murals, and upper-crust clientele who noted her presence but left her largely unmolested. The home folks were much disappointed, however, on September 13, 1932, when she failed to show up at the Stockholm premiere of *Susan Lenox*, even though her mother, brother, and sister-in-law were proud members of that capacity audience.

All in all, said one press account, "she continues her Hollywood-style. seclusion in Sweden, which the Swedes find puzzling and at variance with the old outgoing Garbo who used to go out to clubs." There were new reports of never-to-be Garbo stage productions: Prince Lennart, who recently renounced his title to marry a commoner, had written a play for Garbo. "It is uncertain whether she will appear in the production," said the dispatches. Uncertain indeed. Gösta Ekman, the Swedish stage and film star, announced he wanted to do a theatrical version of *Grand Hotel* with Garbo in the role she had played on screen. All uncertain, to say the least.

But the bulk of Garbo's time in Sweden was spent alone or in the company of two very private friends. The first was Max Gumpel, the self-made construction baron whom she'd met as a clerk at PUB years before and hadn't seen since her days at the dramatic academy. Gumpel was now divorced, and Garbo phoned him one day at his office, playfully making him guess who she was. When he failed and she identified herself, he thought it was a joke but sportingly invited her to dine at his home. She said she didn't have an evening gown, but he replied, "Never mind, just make yourself look as much like Garbo as you can." She arrived wearing the diamond ring he had given her eight years earlier, and thenceforth they were often seen around Stockholm, playing tennis and inspiring marriage rumors.

She spent even more time with Countess Ingrid ("Hörke") Wachtmeister, whom she met through Wilhelm Sörensen. The countess, a descendant of Queen Christina's "master of the royal horse," was an accomplished equestrienne and skier who, like Garbo, preferred men's boots and trousers. They took long hikes together at Tistad, the huge Wachtmeister estate southeast of Stockholm, where Garbo was a frequent guest in the family's seventy-five-room, sixteenth-century castle.

One of their adventures came close to disaster. They had gone for a walk on a frozen lake when, suddenly, the ice broke and they found themselves up to their necks in the icy water. With her walking stick, Garbo pulled herself and her companion to shore. But now what to do to avoid pneumonia? They were miles from home. Should they go to some nearby house and risk press stories? "I couldn't face that," Garbo told Cecil Beaton, "so we decided to run. We ran all the way home, and when [her] husband came back he found me in bed with his wife drinking hot whisky, and he laughed so much!"

When winter set in, she and Countess Wachtmeister repaired to London and then Paris for a change of scenery, but Garbo's disguise as a school teacher failed to fool the Parisians. Her hotel was jammed with journalists and photographers, traffic in the street was blocked outside, and extra police labored to control a mob of fans. She tried to escape to another hotel—a modest one near the British embassy—but that didn't work either. A photographer jumped on the running board of her taxi and, though he soon fell off, reporters followed and easily discovered her new location at the Hôtel Castiglione in rue Faubourg-St.-Honoré, where she registered as "Madame Gustafson" in a dark wig and sunglasses.

Two nights later, Garbo and the countess and an unidentified male escort went to what one paper called "one of the most lurid nightclubs in Montmartre, frequented by hard-boiled women of the Paris demimonde, who go there attired in mannish costumes to give lady tourists the shock they are looking for by asking them to dance. The girls attached to the establishment used all their wiles trying to persuade Greta to follow the example of her more enterprising friend, who amused herself by dancing with some of the female gigolos, but the actress did not appear interested, at least this evening, and instead remained at the table chatting and talking with her boy friend."

Forty-eight hours later, Garbo—in an unconvincing black wig—and Countess Wachtmeister took the night train back to Stockholm, where she wrote Salka that she was "tired and frustrated. I've been so hounded I don't want to travel any more." Spring was approaching, her new contract beckoned, and she was ready to go back to California—at her own pace. She would avoid New York completely this time. "I am going to try to go secretly again. God knows how well I succeeded [in the past]." On March 26, 1933, she embarked on her most unorthodox voyage to America, as one of just four passengers on a slow freighter, the *Annie Johnson*, bound for San Diego by way of the isthmus.

"I sailed on a freighter through the Panama Canal as a strapping young boy," she said years later. The *Annie Johnson*'s accommodations were not luxurious, but the slow passage of time was, and she adored the opportunity to indulge her solitary eccentricities. She had her meals delivered in a lifeboat—a *different* one each day—and thus avoided the common dining room. She rarely ran into the other passengers and spent her time reading, walking alone on the deck, and speaking now and then with the captain, who delighted her by saying she would have made a fine sailor.

Thoughts of Ibsen's *Lady from the Sea* were running through her mind, including her audition speech as Ellida for the Royal Dramatic Academy nine years before: "If only men had chosen from the very beginning to live on the sea—or even *in* the sea—we should have reached a perfection quite different from our present state—both better and happier."

But her peace of mind could never be complete. It was invaded by her obsession with evading the press and, as she got closer to California, with Mata Harian plotting about how to do so. From the Canal Zone on April 17, 1933, she scribbled a cryptic set of instructions to Salka in German:

> Do you want to meet me on the pier? I will take a little boat in.
> . . . The *Annie Johnson* itself will remain out in the ocean because there's no harbor to dock. You probably don't understand what I'm saying. A man will [phone] you in San Diego from the *Annie Johnson* and will explain everything and say when and at what hour we will arrive. I believe that if I go to San Pedro, there will be no newspapers there.

. . . If it's too far for you to drive, telegraph me, I can get a car through
code telegraph Emerson. . . . I have lied to Edington, and I hope he
doesn't go [to meet me]. Dearest, if you believe it is possible to get to
San Pedro to meet me, please tell me. I don't want the papers again.
. . . It's such a peculiar wanderer who comes to you. The only thing
that matters is that you're there. Otherwise—I don't know what.

For all that, she was also engaged during her voyage in the important
activity of studying for her next screen role—arguably her finest and certainly
the dearest to her heart. Of the many accounts of that film's genesis, the
evidence favors an unlikely source: Marie Dressler. In the 1931 interview,
in which that old trouper had called Garbo "phlegmatic," she added, "I have
never known her to exhibit a lively interest in anything, except once, when
I suggested the life of Christina, the madcap Queen of Sweden, as a splendid
Garbo screen vehicle. She was really enthusiastic about that."

Only Dressler would have described Christina as "madcap." But hers
predates other claims to the film idea.* Salka said she had read and mentioned
a biography of Christina to Garbo during *Anna Christie* and that Garbo
agreed "it would be a wonderful role for her" and "should be produced in
Europe, preferably Sweden." Mercedes maintained she had often thought of
Christina as a Garbo role and had written a story outline and discussed it
with Garbo, "but as things often go in Hollywood, the idea was taken
from me."

---

* Except one—in an unpublished letter to Mauritz Stiller from writer Inga Gaate, whose
"embarrassing" interview with Garbo at the time of *Gösta Berling* (1924) had incensed him.
Stiller ordered Garbo to stay away from Gaate but didn't practice what he preached. From
Sweden, on February 17, 1927, Gaate wrote him:

"Permit me to remind you of our last rendezvous at the Grand Hotel in Stockholm where
you had the kindness to say that you were interested in my idea for the film about Christina.
[Are] you still . . . interested in it? If so, I will provide you with a manuscript in English.
. . . I have [a] friend in Rome who is a chamberlain to the Pope and married to his niece. If
introduced in the proper way—that the Christina film could be a Catholic propaganda movie,
which of course it isn't—we could get His Holiness interested and perhaps take some authentic
scenes within the walls of the Vatican. [It] has top-notch psychological and dramatic material.
A fate and a life like Christinia's are like a fairy tale, a thrilling adventure, a wonderful
mosaic, the arabesque of which consists of a woman's strong and strange personality . . .
tragic, comic, grotesque, poetic, and grandiose.

"Oh, and most important! As Christina, you can choose between Pola Negri and Greta
Garbo. Both would make wonderful Christinas under your direction. For my own part, I
only ask to become your assistant and to collaborate on the manuscript with you. . . . I can
come over in October."

But Gaate's proposal arrived just as Stiller was quitting Hollywood, and there is no evidence
that he ever told Garbo about it. [Gaate letter, courtesy of the Swedish Film Institute.
Translation, courtesy of Ann Sitrick.]

In fact, even before leaving America, Garbo had given MGM the go-ahead to draft a script, which Salka completed and sent to Sweden and which Garbo was reading (and liking) on the slow boat home. But there would be no European mise-en-scène. "Salka, I know that I am an impossible human being but I can't make *Christina* in Europe," she wrote before boarding the *Annie Johnson*. "When you've trafficked so much in film as I [have], you would understand that. I am very sorry, Salka. . . . If I had money, I'd go on to an island to rest for years. . . . I've never in my life been so poor as I am now."

The connection between her inability to make the film in Europe and her poor-mouthing was obscure. The former was a matter of logistics; the latter was disingenuous. Meanwhile, back in Hollywood, the question was whether Queen Christina was really such an important and popular figure in history. The simplified answer was—important, yes; popular, no.*

Christina inherited the throne in 1632 at age six upon the death of her warrior-father, King Gustavus II Adolphus, at the battle of Lützen. At eighteen, she took the formal coronation oath, insisting on the word "king" rather than "queen." She was a brilliant linguist, thoroughly trained in philosophy, theology, and art, not to mention history and statecraft. Intellectually and physically, she had little in common with the actress of three centuries later, but there were certain other striking similarities between the two.

Christina was a solitary, fatherless woman locked in a royal cage from which she was desperate to escape. She had great strength of will and spoke from an early age of "the power I have over myself and my passions." She was adept at concealing her own feelings while getting others to reveal theirs, even as she was tormented by yearnings that could scarcely be discussed, let alone resolved. In her *Apothegms*, she wrote that God had given her "a heart that nothing could satisfy."

Most problematic, for a seventeenth-century monarch, was her sexuality. At birth, she said in her memoirs, "my body was entirely covered with hair, and I had a deep, loud voice. This led the midwives attending me to take me for a boy."† The King's reaction was as graceful as could be expected: "I hope this daughter will be as dear to me as a boy would have been." As for her mother, "There was a delay in informing the queen of my sex until she was able to bear such a disappointment." Christina herself thanked God

---

* The following account relies on the authoritative biography, *Christina of Sweden*, by Sven Stolpe (New York: Macmillan, 1966).

† Garbo once made a cryptic, remarkably similar statement to her friend Sam Green: "I looked like a boy when I was born, and I'll never tell you who told me so."

An engraving of Queen Christina from a contemporary portrait, c. 1650

The Garbo-Christina. In feminist Jane Gaines's view: "The collar which slices the head off at the neck carries connotations of the guillotine and the rack."

for having endowed her with a soul as "masculine as was the remainder of my body."

Medical experts today believe Christina was a "pseudo-hermaphrodite"—a person with the internal reproductive organs of one sex and external sex traits of the other—and that she probably had a related condition called adrenogenital syndrome. Her father suffered from a "profound melancholy," aggravated by his marriage. Queen Maria Eleanora was a high-strung illiterate, whose chief occupation was stuffing herself with sweets in the company of dwarfs. The King ordered that, in the event of his death, she was to have no part in governing Sweden, and Christina always held her in contempt as a woman, mother, and regent.

Christina felt, in her own words, "an ineradicable prejudice against everything that women like to talk about or do." Her mannish behavior was known and remarked upon throughout northern Europe. She paid no attention to clothes or personal adornment, wore men's boots, and, when riding, dressed as a cavalier or cavalry officer in order to disguise her sex.

When she reached her majority, the pressure to marry and produce an heir was intense. "I am just as likely to give birth to a Nero as to an Augustus," she said, but the issue lay deeper, in her aversion to intercourse and childbirth. She would not be "a field for a man to plough," and her unwavering refusal to marry flew in the face of all the prevailing norms. Not unlike Garbo, Christina felt powerfully attracted to beautiful women but her attachments were more emotional than physical—an aesthetic more than a sexual kind of love. She sympathized with *les Précieuses*, the French female intellectuals who were then championing the dignity of women and deploring male tyranny.

Christina's pride and royal position made it impossible for her to submit to anyone, with the exception of a beautiful young noblewoman named Ebba Sparre, who played Venus in the magnificent court ballets Christina loved. The queen was openly passionate toward her and, after she left Sweden, revealed herself more freely. "I am condemned forever to love and adore you," she wrote Ebba, and, from Italy in 1657: "It is now twelve years since I had the good fortune to be loved by you. . . . I belong to you in a way that makes it impossible for you to reject me. Only when my life ends shall I cease to love you."*

---

* The authenticity of these letters has been confirmed, but Christina's reputation was later besmirched by the circulation of fake pornographic letters she was said to have written to Ebba Sparre, and by her interest in libertine literature. "Libertine" then meant freethinking, not sexually licentious, but the sensuous paintings and nude statues in Christina's superb art collection bolstered the myth of her promiscuity.

Christina's passion for Ebba Sparre—who was married—was not reciprocated to her satisfaction. Her painfully unrequited love for Ebba helps explain why she was so unhappy in Sweden. But there was another, greater reason.

"I did not believe the religion in which I was brought up," Christina wrote. As a girl, she had been terrified by a Lutheran sermon on the Last Judgment, "in which the preacher described the cataclysm so vividly that I was filled with dread. . . . I began to weep bitterly, for I was convinced my end was near." The experience sowed doubt instead of belief in the young princess. Her father had called the Pope a "son of the devil" and permitted the persecution of Catholics in Sweden, but Christina as queen put a stop to that and fostered religious tolerance. She surrounded herself with liberal French Catholic freethinkers, whom the Swedish Lutherans hated, and she found Catholic doctrine to have the unity and consistency which the squabbling Protestant sects lacked. From girlhood on, she was deeply interested in the holy virgins, especially Joan of Arc, and by Catholicism's concept of virginity as a virtue, not a defect. Protestant Swedes resented their queen's celibacy for depriving them of an heir and a secure line of succession. Increasingly, Christina saw the conflict between her duty as queen and her private sexuality as irrevocable.

"I am unable to marry," she declared. "That is how it is. . . . I have earnestly prayed God to let me change my attitude, but I have not been able to do so."

How much clearer could she be? To Garbo reading that statement in the middle of an ocean, it had to hit home, and so did Christina's solution after years of brooding: Since she would not marry or produce an heir, she must abdicate. By 1650, she contrived for her cousin Carl Gustav to be designated heir and to make the monarch's ultimate sacrifice. "Not many have renounced their kingdoms," she later wrote. "I can only think of Diocletian, Almansor [the Moor], Charles V [of Spain] and Christina." In our own century, many kings have lost or given up their thrones, but three hundred years ago the resignation of a monarch was a fantastic and baffling event that upset an entire continent. Christina stepped down at twenty-eight, exactly Garbo's age when she played her. At her abdication, in 1654, she said:

"I am not keen on applause. I know that the part I have played cannot be governed by ordinary stage rules. . . . Others know nothing of my motives and little or nothing of my character and way of life, for I let no one look inside me. . . . Without being arrogant or vainglorious, I exerted my power, and [now] I lay it down painlessly and with ease."

A few years later, those exact sentiments could have come from Garbo.

For now, she was empathetic to and spellbound by Christina on her own departure from Sweden.

MGM's first director-cast suggestions reached Garbo at sea, by cable, on March 29, 1933. Robert Z. Leonard (*Susan Lenox*) and Eddie Goulding (*Love, Grand Hotel*) were proposed, and Garbo took only twenty-four of her allotted seventy-two hours to reply: "Goulding. Regards. Garbo." The next day, Mayer cabled back: "Think there is opportunity of getting Lubitsch. . . . Advise if [acceptable] and will try borrow from Paramount." Garbo's answer on April 1: "Prefer Lubitsch. Also happy for Goulding." But neither Goulding nor Lubitsch turned out to be available, and Mayer scrambled for an alternate—possibly Clarence Brown or Rouben Mamoulian. Even von Sternberg was under consideration.

Mrs. Viertel now had a crucial script conference with Mr. Thalberg: "Abruptly he asked if I had seen the German film *Mädchen im Uniform* [which] dealt with a lesbian relationship. Thalberg asked: 'Does not Christina's affection for her lady-in-waiting indicate something like that?' He wanted me to 'keep it in mind,' and perhaps if 'handled with taste it would give us very interesting scenes.' Pleasantly surprised by his broadmindedness, I began to like him very much."

When Garbo's ship docked in San Diego on April 29, 1933, Salka was there to meet her, and together they drove up the coast to Los Angeles with much talk of Queen Christina. It would be their first of four collaborations, and of great significance to both women, for different reasons.* FDR's and Garbo's New Deal were beginning in tandem: Salka informed her that her new dressing-room suite at MGM would have its own private entrance and driveway. The press said Garbo and Harry Edington "have now parted company and Greta talks for herself, assisted by Mrs. Berthold Viertel, [who] will manage the amazing Swede's screen fortunes [from now on]." Such reports were premature but contained more than a grain of truth.

Garbo had a writer and counselor but still no director or co-stars. Edington had notified MGM that she would be ready for work on May 15 and that

---

* Salka had dramatized the first part of Christina's life in German. The job of translating it into English was offered to Margaret Le Vino, who, said Salka, "was unimpressed with the idea until learning that Garbo was to play the lead." Salka got co-credit for the story (with Le Vino) and the screenplay (with H. M. Harwood). After filming began, S. N. Behrman was engaged on a loan-out from Fox and credited with "additional dialogue." Eventually the script was "completely rewritten," said Behrman. "I was to keep a day ahead of the shooting."

The other three Garbo-Viertel film projects would be *Anna Karenina* (1935), *Conquest* (1937), and *Two-Faced Woman* (1941).

—to everyone's amazement—she wanted to make the second film with only a month's rest after the first. Finally, on May 17, Mamoulian was approved and signed for *Queen Christina*. Everyone was happy with the choice of that creative, Falstaffian stage man, newly converted to film direction, who had helped liberate talkies from their paralysis by restoring the camera's mobility in such films as *Applause* (1929), *City Streets* (1931), and *Dr. Jekyll and Mr. Hyde* (1931).

It was ten more weeks before Garbo approved MGM stable horses Ian Keith, Lewis Stone, and Reginald Owen as Christina's suitor, chancellor, and successor. Ebba Sparre would be played by Elizabeth Young. But who for the leading man? Leslie Howard had turned it down. Subsequent contenders Fredric March, Clark Gable, Nils Asther, Victor Jory, and Franchot Tone gave way to the dark-horse candidacy of a young British actor: Laurence Olivier was the surprise announcement to play Spanish ambassador Don Antonio Pimentel de Prado, the love of whom fuels the screen queen's (but not the real queen's) decision to quit her throne.

Olivier, reportedly, had been Garbo's own idea after she saw and liked him (and his slight resemblance to John Gilbert) in RKO's weepy Ann Harding romance *Westward Passage*—the best of Olivier's three mediocre Hollywood "debut films," made the previous year. He was delighted by his good fortune to be cast opposite Garbo but, in retrospect, "casting" was the wrong term. He was *testing* for the part, according to Mamoulian:

> I was thinking of having John Barrymore do the part, and Barrymore was very anxious to do it, and then on second thought it seemed that he would be a little too old. And then I had this crazy idea—there was a young Englishman on the lot who had never done anything to my knowledge. . . . I could not possibly decide on him without making a very thorough test, and the test would have to involve Garbo because there's no point in testing him with somebody else—he has to keep his weight balanced against this enormous authority of Greta Garbo on the screen. So I asked her if she would make the test and she said yes. And then I worked on this test, it was a very thorough test, and I looked at the screen and the fellow wasn't there. He was young and callow, you see.

Olivier thought he was performing, not testing. In either case, his delight was brief:

> I realized in the first two weeks with ever-increasing apprehension that I was not by any means making the best of myself; something was stopping me. I was too nervous and scared of my leading lady. I knew

I was lightweight for her and nowhere near her stature, and began to feel more and more certain that I was for the chop. I made up my mind that I must make a big effort to get along with her and find some way to get on friendlier terms.

Before work had started one morning, I found her sitting on an old chest on the set. I went boldly up to her and said the three or four sentences that I had made up and practiced; but no utterance came from her. I began to flounder and grab at anything that came into my head; some sayings of Will Rogers, of Noël—anybody—anything at all, until I came to a wretched end and stopped, pale and panting. After a breathless pause, she slid herself off the chest sideways saying, "Oh, vell, life's a pain, anyway." I knew then that the end was not far off.

Olivier took it in stride and, for years, regaled friends with an imitation of the executive who peered at him, put his finger to Olivier's face, and said, "What am I going to do about this actor's uuuuug-ly face?" Mamoulian later claimed that "Sir Laurence and I laugh about it to this day. He told me in London recently, 'I resented it for a long time, but you were absolutely right.'"

Olivier's startling replacement by John Gilbert took place over the furious objection of Louis B. Mayer, a man whose few defeats were mostly by Garbo. He hated Gilbert as no other studio chief ever hated one of his own top stars, and had until very recently (July 31, 1932) been stuck with his expensive contract. Assigning him few decent roles, he'd cut off Gilbert's nose to spite MGM's face, and Gilbert had retaliated by telling the press that his own troubles were minor compared with the studios': Paramount and RKO had gone into receivership in January 1933. MGM and Warners, he predicted, weren't far behind.

"The Depression has finally caught up with them," Gilbert told *The New York Times*. "They never thought it would. As a result, it looks as if the days of the big studios are over and that a chance for individual expression may come out of the general reorganization now being undertaken."* Gilbert was speaking in April 1933, on the pier where he and his new bride, Virginia

---

* Gilbert, also a writer and aspiring director, meant this very much in terms of himself. His one post-talkie break at MGM came when Thalberg approved his original story *Downstairs* (1932) for filming by Monta Bell. Gilbert played the antihero—a mean, conniving butler—brilliantly (and, as was his wont, fell in love on the set). His voice recorded just fine in the film, which inspired the television series *Upstairs, Downstairs* decades later. *Downstairs* was a critical succès d'estime but not a box-office hit, and it failed to revitalize Gilbert's career.

Bruce, had just disembarked after a cruise from California to New York—
via the Panama Canal. His and Garbo's ships literally passed each other in
the night.

Enter producer Walter Wanger—who, in an unusual reversal, had been
selected by the director instead of the other way around. Mamoulian knew
that MGM producers usually had a great deal to do with cutting. When
invited to direct *Queen Christina*, he said, "I told Mr. Mayer that I would
have to have Walter Wanger [as] producer for the very simple reason that
I had known Walter through Paramount and he knew how I worked and
I knew that I would have no interference from him."

That wisdom now paid off. Wanger phoned Gilbert, told him of Garbo's
difficulties with Olivier, and asked him to come to the *Christina* set and "see
if he might help Garbo relax." They had scarcely seen one another for three
years, but Gilbert agreed and, once there, was asked to don a costume for
a kind of dress rehearsal. Garbo seemed more at ease than she'd been in
weeks. The scene was "rehearsed" with cameras and microphones on, and
without quite realizing it, Gilbert had made a screen test. The next day,
when Wanger told him he had the part, Gilbert hooted—Mayer would never
allow it, he said. "Get down here," Wanger replied. "Mayer's already approved." Some thought Harry Edington, out of loyalty to an old client, had
a hand in it. But it was Garbo's doing, motivated by *her* loyalty to Gilbert
and by the knowledge that she could play comfortably with him.

"She knew Jack was having trouble finding work and that his spirits were
down," said actress Colleen Moore, a close friend of Gilbert's. "Garbo had
a long memory. She knew Jack had given her equal billing when she was
barely established and she remembered all the times he'd helped her career.
So she simply marched into Louis B. Mayer's office and said it would be
Gilbert or nobody. Mayer went through the roof, of course. They'd just
gotten rid of Jack a few months before; they certainly didn't want him back
again. Mayer screamed and ranted, and Garbo, as always, said nothing until
he was finished. Mayer knew it was useless to argue with her. You can't
really argue with someone who's just as happy to go home if she doesn't get
her way."

Mayer swallowed his rage and let it be put out that "Gilbert, who a few
weeks ago announced his retirement from acting, was a surprise move made
by studio officials in response to fan and exhibitor demand. The romantic
lead opposite Miss Garbo was originally intended for Laurence Olivier. . . .
But a deluge of letters urging that Gilbert's services be obtained resulted in
negotiations being opened with him."

In actress Barbara Barondess's view, "Having Gilbert in that picture is the only decent, giving thing Garbo ever did. She insisted he be given the chance because she'd jilted him—and because he was nearly finished."*

In her first shot in *Queen Christina*, a hat hides Garbo's exquisite face. It is a lovely idea, followed by a lovelier one: Garbo laughs—six years before *Ninotchka*! She does so gaily, at the sight of Ambassador Gilbert's carriage stuck in the Swedish snow.† For that matter, she carries off a lot of humor in this tragedy, as when Gilbert presents the Spanish king's portrait along with his marriage proposal: "Oh! Does he really look like that?" she asks. "My suitors usually come in oil."

Garbo not only gets to laugh but to *move* in this film, unlike most others. She strides and struts about animatedly, indoors and out, trim and fit in costumes that—for once—reveal legs to rival Dietrich's. Her dialogue "moves," too, thanks largely to S. N. Behrman. "This is the first time that anyone has troubled to write speech that really represents Garbo," wrote critic C. A. Lejeune.

Of the two most memorable scenes in *Queen Christina*, the first takes place at a wayside inn where a snowstorm‡ and a shortage of rooms force the queen—in male disguise—to share a bedroom with the Spanish envoy. Gilbert innocently inquires of his sexy roommate, "Aren't you going to undress?" His perplexity at the "gay" attraction is palpable and funny—and then his eyes tell us that her breasts have given Garbo away. The overt sexual

---

* Gilbert was an extremely generous person himself. Among his countless acts of generosity to Garbo and others was a $2,500 gift to his friend Dorothy Parker for a serious operation she couldn't afford. When to his surprise she repaid it in 1932, his note of reply said, "Thank you, Miss Finland"—a nice allusion to the only nation that ever repaid its World War I debts.

† Mamoulian told Charles Higham how he did it: "They said to me at the studio, 'She cannot laugh.' And I said, 'Well, that's odd, because in life she has a very childlike infectious laugh, the laugh of a little girl.' She herself told me she couldn't do it, too. [But] I had to get her to laugh at . . . the Spanish ambassador stuck in the snow. So I went to John Gilbert and Akim Tamiroff and two others and I took them aside and said, 'You know the child's game of making faces? . . . When she comes up, you're under the carriage trying to free it; you look at her and hold that face.' I said to Garbo, 'No matter what happens, go through with the scene. Go into the dialogue, and get it done.' And she asked me, 'What's going to happen?' I said, '[Just] go ahead.' She rode in and I kept the camera on her; the others were out of the frame, of course. And when she saw the four faces, she threw her head back and laughed like a lark."

‡ For years, MGM let the public believe that the beautiful snow scenes in *Queen Christina* were filmed on location, probably in Sweden itself. "Did you like that snow, on the castle, the parapets and the yard?" Mamoulian inquired of Kevin Brownlow in 1970. "It was shot in the middle of summer, about 97-degree heat, and what you think is snow is tons of oatmeal."

nature of the joke is one of Hollywood's more daring moments, perfectly executed by Garbo and Gilbert, with the aid of Barbara Barondess as Elsa, the sluttish servant girl.

Barondess had just previously played a featured role with Jean Harlow and Clark Gable in *Hold Your Man*. When Mamoulian offered her the *Christina* bit part, she at first declined, but at $1,500 a week for six weeks in the middle of the Depression—she decided to take it.* Once on the set, she observed Garbo astutely ("she had a frightened gazelle spiritual quality"), but when it came time for her own big scene, Barondess clutched:

> In part of that scene, I was to take her boots off and run my hands up and down her legs, and it drove me crazy. I knew a little about her reputation, and I didn't want to be pawing her in 10 or 15 takes. But I had to try to seduce her, and I was so self-conscious in rehearsal that Mamoulian said, "Barbara, I never saw you so stiff. What are you afraid of?" I got red in the face. I couldn't say, "I don't want to be making love to her 35 times—she's liable to like it." . . . . So I said, "I'm so overwhelmed by playing a scene with Miss Garbo, please forgive me. When you do the take, I'll do it right." So he laughed and she laughed, and then, to put me at ease, she told me a story about the time she went into a shoe store and asked for moccasins and the clerk recognized her and came back with sizes 8 and 9. She said, "These are too big for me," and he looked at her, very disappointed, and said, "Oh, I thought you were Garbo."†

No one, including the great Garbo herself, was excepted from Mamoulian's rehearsal policy, as he told Kevin Brownlow:

* Someone else wanted a bit part and didn't get it. According to film writer Jimmy Fidler at the time: "Katharine Hepburn worships Garbo to such an extent that she went to her own studio executives and begged permission to work as an 'extra' in *Queen Christina*, in order that she might observe at close range the mysterious Garbo charm and technique." Permission was denied.

† Garbo's shoe size was 7AA, according to Ferragamo; 7½, according to her niece, Gray Reisfield; 7AAA, according to David Diamond; but 6½ AA, according to Barondess—which discovery related to why Garbo's shoe story so delighted her. In 1929, when Barondess was writing the "Little Bo-Peep on Broadway" column for the New York *Morning Telegraph*, Walter Winchell bet her five hundred dollars that she couldn't get an interview with Garbo and find out her shoe size. He gave her five years to do it. Four years later, in 1933, "I Act With Garbo," by Barbara Barondess, ran in *Motion Picture Magazine*. The good news was that she had won the bet. The bad news was that she received no screen credit in *Queen Christina* because her agent forgot to ask for it in her contract. And after all her trouble shooting it, the scene in which Barondess ran her hands up and down Garbo's legs ended up on the cutting-room floor.

She said, "Oh, I can't rehearse." I said, "What do you mean?" She says, "I never rehearse, I can't rehearse—if I rehearse I'll be no good." I said, "Well, how do you do it?" She said, "Well, you tell me what you want me to do . . . and then we make a take. And usually the first take is my best." And I said, "Well, look, if this is true and it works that way, it's marvelous because it saves me an awful lot of time, [but] if it is not satisfactory you'll have to do it my way." And she said, "It will be satisfactory." So I rehearsed the two actors and I told her what she would be doing and we made a take [and] I said, "How do you feel about it?" She said, "Fine." I didn't say anything. And she said, "Don't you like it?" I said, "No, I don't like it." Her face fell. She said, "Why?" I said, "I can't begin to tell you, I have to rehearse. There are so many things [that] are not there." And she said, "Well, then, we're lost because if I rehearse I'll be worse, I'll never be better than this." I said, "I took it your way, now you do it my way." So we rehearsed for two hours. And she said, "I'm completely gone, this is going to be terrible." So I made a second take, third take, fourth take—she says it's getting worse and worse. Eighth take—I said, "That's it. Take No. 8. . . . I'm going to print Take 1, and then I'm going to print Take 8, and you are going to come to the projection room in the morning at eight o'clock. I won't even be there. You run the two scenes, then you tell me which would you like to be in the film. And I promise you I'll take your judgment. She leaned over and she whispered, "Please don't print Take 1." And that was it.

The best-loved sequence in *Queen Christina*, apart from its ending, is "the morning after" that night in the inn—perhaps the single most sublime illustration of Garbo's acting. It is a classic Method exercise in the art of relating emotionally to physical objects: Garbo moves dreamily around the room as the mesmerized Gilbert watches. She strokes the walls, the objects on the mantle, a spinning wheel, the pillow on the bed, and then hugs the bedpost as sensually as if it were her lover. What is she doing? he asks. "I have been memorizing this room," she replies. "In the future, in my memory, I shall live a great deal in this room." She plays the scene for joy and sorrow at the same time, longing to preserve rapture but preparing for loss.

Mamoulian (1897–1987) a product of the Moscow Art Theater, was a modified believer in the Stanislavskian sense-memory system and encouraged Garbo to "draw upon" things from her own life. Four years earlier in Sweden, shortly after Stiller's death, she had asked to be taken to the place where his effects were stored, according to Stiller's lawyer, who was present:

I remember vividly how she walked about the room, touching this item and that. "This was the suitcase he bought in America," she said, picking up the bag. "And those rugs—I remember when he bought them in Turkey." We stayed quite a time, while she walked round the furniture and paintings and all the other things and made sad little comments.

The immortal "touching scene" in *Queen Christina* was performed to the beat of a metronome—a tempo device that Mamoulian had used to good effect in *Porgy* (on stage) and *Love Me Tonight* (on film). "Garbo works intuitively," he said. "She caught on right away. The scene was choreographed. [She had to] move around the room in what was a kind of sonnet in action. I explained to her: 'This has to be sheer poetry and feeling. The movement must be like a dance. Treat it the way you would do it to music.' "*

She did so brilliantly, although the scene was nearly ruined in post-production by Herbert Stothart's clippity-clop music, emulating the metronomic rhythm. The film is marred throughout by Stothart's treacly score, but even that talentless composer could not wreck her magic. Garbo's sense of touch afforded what Walker calls an "emotional illumination, like Braille to the blind," that overcame everything else.

In both bedroom scenes, there was "no reason to censor and every reason to try," wrote one critic at the time. All the sexual innuendos were tastefully handled, including Garbo's revelation of her identity to Gilbert at court. "We admire greatly the prowess of your country," she declares, with just the slightest movement of one eyebrow.†

During the first week of shooting in August 1933, both Gilbert and Garbo reportedly came down with flu, which held up production for several costly days. There was a surprise interruption in the form of a visit to the set by American prizefighter Max Baer who, contrary to her rules, was allowed to stay for a whole hour. But no matter what, the prompt 5:30 arrival of Alma, her dressing-room attendant, with a cup of tea signalled the end of Garbo's

---

* "I always divide the world into two: those who like the scene and those who don't," said Mamoulian. He claimed that *Queen Christina* was the favorite movie of both Stalin and Mussolini. Stalin's daughter Svetlana Alliluyeva testified to its impact in Russia in her book, *Twenty Letters to a Friend*.

† Some moralists, however, objected. A monarch caressing a bedpost was not only "pornographic" but downright "dangerous," fumed Martin Quigley, assigning *Queen Christina* to the category of "Pictures Typical of Wrong Standards" in his book *Decency in Motion Pictures* (1937).

working day, even if she was in midscene. "An actress is no good after eight hours on the set," Garbo explained to Elizabeth Young, who was startled by that abrupt practice at first. "Making a picture without Alma is like being in New York without dark glasses."

Gilbert had been drinking heavily and sometimes needed a day or so to dry out. He and Garbo may or may not have had any flu; more likely, she timed her own indispositions to his, as she had done for von Stroheim during *As You Desire Me.*

"She was magnificent to me while we were working together," said Gilbert. "She knew that I was nervous, raw, almost sick with excitement and the thrill of the thing. And never once did she fail in consideration of me, in tact, in saying and doing the right thing at the right moment. . . . She sensed every one of my feelings and was tender toward them. [I was] gunshy. I felt that only Garbo wanted me there."

Gilbert was also experiencing a reawakening of some of the old feeling between them. After one especially passionate love scene, Garbo took Mamoulian aside and reminded him that Jack was a married man with a new baby. She thought it might be more appropriate if their scenes were played with a bit less fervor. When Mamoulian reported this to Gilbert, he smiled and said, "Backward, turn backward, O Time, in your flight."

Garbo and Salka sometimes dropped in for tea at S. N. Behrman's house in Beverly Hills on days "when Garbo couldn't work, because the leading man had not shown up." On one such occasion, they were "in a state" about it and Behrman boldly asked how she got mixed up with a fellow like Gilbert in the first place.

"It was a rhetorical question," said Behrman. "I expected no answer. But I got one. Garbo meditated; it was a considered reply, as if she were making an effort to explain it to herself. Very slowly, in her cello voice, she said, 'I was lonely—and I couldn't speak English.' "

Historians have long quibbled about discrepancies between *Queen Christina* and history. They agree the abdication scene is accurate, down to such details as Christina's white dress and the fact that, when her loyal aides refused to remove her crown, she had to do so herself.* Don Antonio, however, was not Christina's lover but an agent of Spain and the Jesuits, sent to Stockholm to make sure she carried through on becoming a Catholic. Unanswered was the deeper question of whether she was really so noble and self-sacrificing,

---

* Cedric Gibbons created an exact replica of Christina's throne. He also searched hard for the queen's original globe, long missing from Sweden, and finally located it—at the Huntington Library in Pasadena, fifteen miles from MGM.

Garbo and John Gilbert with director Rouben Mamoulian during shooting of the inn scene in Queen Christina

Garbo in a publicity shot for Queen Christina, *October 25, 1933: "I have a great longing for trousers," she wrote Salka Viertel.*

or just, as a Swedish contemporary called her, an "egocentric neuropath."*

If historians cared, audiences did not. Nor did the film's political content seem to disturb people. "Must we live for the dead?" asks Christina of her warmongering parliament. She insists on peace and demonstrates that a woman can govern as well as a man. And, of course, she stubbornly refuses to marry.

"You can't die an old maid," Lewis Stone intones.

"I have no intention to, Chancellor," she replies. "I shall die a bachelor."

She declares that "the public won't dictate my love life" and fights to preserve her singularity: "Must I smile for the masses?" The similarities between the queen and the actress culminated in the film character's whimsical remark (borrowed from Molière), "How is it possible to endure the thought of sleeping, with a man in the room?"

Garbo could utter such sentiments with great conviction, aided by the best-yet photography of William Daniels. "I'm tired of being a symbol—I long to be a human being," she says, as the angle and light on her face intensify the yearning. Just when she and her lover are to sail away together, he is fatally wounded in a duel. Daniels's final shot—the long, slow zoom onto Garbo's face at the prow of her departing ship—closes the picture with one of the most exquisite images in film history. Barbara Barondess was present when it was shot:

> I was sitting there, crocheting a scarf, because I got bored waiting around for set-ups, and they were happy to have me because she enjoyed talking to me and there was a good atmosphere on the set. She was notorious for kicking people out, but that mostly applied to visitors. She couldn't stop the script girl or hairdressers or lighting and cameramen and technicians who hung around. So I watched her during takes of the final shot, and it didn't bother her. They set it up and were ready for the first take, and she turned around and said to Mamoulian, "Rouben, what should I think about in this scene?" And he said,

---

* The real epilogue: Christina went to Rome and was quickly disillusioned. Italian Catholicism contrasted sharply with the French ideas of reconciling faith and science. Rome had crushed Copernicus and recently Galileo, in 1633. Christina scandalized Italy, as she had Sweden, by dressing as a man and entertaining artists at all hours in her palace. But she was a dominant force in Roman artistic life until her death in 1689, championing the music of Corelli and Scarlatti (who dedicated many works to her) and the "dangerous" dramas of Molière and Racine; she founded academies and dazzled even the popes with her erudition. She also became heavily involved in Italian political intrigues with the apparent object of becoming Queen of Naples. Her legacy in Sweden was bitter: After her abdication, Swedish law was changed to prevent the succession of a woman to the throne—a ban not lifted until 1980, to permit Princess Viktoria to succeed the present-day King Carl XVI Gustaf.

Garbo, William Daniels, and Mamoulian filming the exquisite final shot of Queen
Christina

"Darling, just make your face a blank." She looked at him and just
said, "Oh." And there she stood with her eyes on the horizon which
wasn't there—a blank looking into a void.

Just before shooting of that final scene began, Mamoulian got an emergency
call summoning him to Mayer's office. There, he was informed that Mayer
and all his producers had unanimously concluded that the ending was too
unhappy and would have to be changed. Why did it take until now to
discover that? Mamoulian wanted to know. Somehow it had been overlooked,
replied Mayer, but he was now certain that audiences would come away
depressed by it. Mamoulian carefully disagreed:

I said, "Mr. Mayer, you know Greek tragedy?" He said, "Oh, yes,
I know Greek tragedy." I said, "Well, usually it has an unhappy ending
but it never depresses the audience. It exhilarates them. I would like
to shoot it just the way it is, and if it depresses the [preview] audience,
if they walk away miserable, then I'll do something about it [in just]
three days' retakes." So he said, "All right, that's fair—[but] what *is*
the ending?" I said, "I can't describe it because it's mostly visual imagery.
There are sails, there is Garbo, practically no dialogue. But I'll guarantee

you will not be depressed." So I shot the ending and then we ran it for the executives before any preview. Nicholas Schenck came from New York, Thalberg was there, Mayer, everybody [came] to see how depressing this was going to be. And they all walked out on cloud nine. Not a word was spoken—they didn't even wait for a preview. [It showed] that you have to actually see it. How can you discuss a painting or a piece of music ahead of time?

[I told Garbo], "Just be completely passive, don't think about anything, express nothing, and preferably don't even blink your eyes. Just be a mask, and then the audience will write in whatever emotion they feel should be there. If you were to cry, some people will say, 'Ah, she's a small woman.' If you didn't cry, some would say, 'What's the matter with her? Her lover is dead.' If she smiles they'll say she's crazy." And so on. So that's what she did—she stood there, just a blank face but it happens to be GARBO's face. And each critic had his own interpretation. Everybody wrote his own ending—which is a valid principle in the theater and more so on the screen.*

In *Gösta Berling* and *Joyless Street*, Garbo had demonstrated her ability to sustain a complex role, but in the years since then had played nothing so difficult or rewarding. Of her American films to date, wrote Robert Payne in *The Great Garbo*, "she could legitimately be proud of perhaps ten minutes of *Flesh and the Devil*, a quarter of an hour of *Anna Christie*, twenty-five minutes of *Grand Hotel*, and a single minute of *Mata Hari*. The rest [was] kitsch." Harsh, but largely true—until now.

MGM's trailer billed *Christina* as Garbo's "triumphant return to the screen," capitalizing on public uncertainty that she might quit. It was her first screen appearance in a year and a half—her longest absence to that time—and the praise for Garbo was lavish, though she herself was dissatisfied, as always. "I tried to be Swedish," she said later in Sweden, "but it's difficult in Hollywood to be allowed to try anything. It's all a terrible compromise. There is no time for art."

Gilbert had turned in a solid, restrained performance despite his bad make-up, goatee, and slicked-down hair; there were no vocal problems. He and the film took a few lumps, such as the following from Otis Ferguson: "In the end, it reduces the complex circumstances surrounding the abdication of a homosexual queen to a quick and wholesome elopement with the Gentle-

---

* A final footnote on that final shot: Many noticed that the wind blowing Garbo's hair was going the right way for the shot but the wrong way for a sailing ship. "Oh, God," Mamoulian said years later, "people were so delighted to catch me on that."

The gargantuan, block-long billboard and marquee for Queen Christina *at the Astor Theatre in New York*

man from Spain. And here it reaps no profit from the fact that under the ambassadorial mustachios you can perceive the lineaments of Mr. John Gilbert, made up like the devil in a musical comedy and loving to beat anything." But most of Gilbert's notices were good, and in a moment of euphoria, he made a conciliatory phone call to Mayer. "I was feeling on top of the world and I thought I'd call up just to say 'thank you' for the part," he said. "I'd hardly opened my mouth before he opened up on me and let me have it, foul abuse, threats, damnation, and all hell broke loose. I tried to scream into the phone that I was just trying to say thanks. I didn't want any more dough."

If there had been any doubt before that only Garbo's insistence got him the part, it was now erased. So, too, was Gilbert's comeback dream. In the sixty years since, it has been repeatedly stated—even by Gilbert's devoted daughter and biographer—that the Garbo-Gilbert team had "lost its drawing power" and that, however much revisionists may revere it, *Queen Christina* was a financial failure. The recently learned truth is otherwise: Eddie Mannix, Mayer's top assistant, kept a top-secret "register" of every MGM film's cost and earnings, in which it is revealed that *Queen Christina*'s $632,000 profit

Queen Christina promotion merchandise for exhibitors ranged from posters and papier-mâché heads to the name "Garbo" in "4 × 7 feet block letters" and even a spare-tire cover accessory.

was greater than that of all other Garbo films except *Mata Hari* and *Grand Hotel*. But—tragically, for her future—Garbo herself either never realized or never took advantage of that fact.

Gilbert's own tragedy, meanwhile, was drawing to a close. In order to do *Christina*, he had signed a standard, seven-year MGM contract (at one-tenth of his former salary), which meant he and MGM were now stuck with each other again. Even before *Christina* opened, he was in California Superior Court seeking relief from MGM's refusal to assign him a new film. Three months later, in March 1934, he took out a full-page ad in the *Hollywood Reporter:*

> METRO-GOLDWYN-MAYER
> will neither
> offer me work
>   nor
> release me from
> my contract.
>   —JACK GILBERT

Release finally came when Gilbert's old friend, director Lewis Milestone, went to bat for him with Harry Cohn at Columbia. There, Gilbert made *The Captain Hates the Sea* (1934)—a kind of seagoing *Grand Hotel* with an all-star cast, among whom Gilbert gave a fine if painfully ironic performance as a heavy drinker. But by then it was too late. *The Captain Hates the Sea* was his last film. The sad truth was that it didn't matter how good or bad he had been in *Queen Christina*.

Any time Garbo went anywhere with a man—especially out of town—it was a "romance," and the press inevitably reported her friendship with Mamoulian that way. They had often dined together, during and after *Christina*, and they now went on an ill-fated vacation by car to Arizona that further torched the love-and-marriage rumors. Reporters—and other obstacles—hounded them at every leg of the journey.

The long-suffering James was at the wheel, as always, when the first problem arose. According to January 13, 1934, news accounts, Garbo, Mamoulian, and James spent their first night in Needles, "after being delayed in an inspection station on the California-Arizona state border. The patrolmen said the actress and her director, bound for the Grand Canyon, sailed across the border line at considerable speed without the formality of stopping for the customary examination of tourists."

From that point on, thanks to publicity surrounding the incident, they were met by noisy little crowds all along the route. Nobody was fooled by "Mary Jones" and "Robert Bonji," the names under which they registered at the El Tovar Hotel, where they took a suite of three rooms and immediately went off hiking to the rim of the Grand Canyon in ski caps and dark glasses. The tourists weren't fooled, either, and less than a day after reaching the Grand Canyon, they turned around and headed back to Los Angeles.

All this was big news in the sleepy Southwest. "Garbo never has been off on such a long trip with an admirer, as far as anyone recalls," said one report. No detail was left uncovered. On the way back, they stopped at the Beale Hotel in Kingman, Arizona. The next morning, Garbo and Mamoulian had breakfast in their separate rooms (Nos. 12 and 17) in an effort to avoid being seen. Mrs. Ella Hall, the proprietor, revealed that the meal was "substantial" and that "both tipped the waitress well. The Negro chauffeur had risen early, refueled the car and was waiting for Garbo and her companion when they continued their flight shortly before 10 a.m."

By January 17, they were home again. The disastrous trip took its toll on the Garbo-Mamoulian "romance." But nothing could detract from the fact that, on *Queen Christina*, they had collaborated beautifully; that she was enthralled with his direction, and he with her consummate acting. Surely they would want to work together again—yet it never happened.

"Mamoulian was important to her at the time," says Barbara Barondess, "but she was cooperative and friendly with anybody who was important to her. Afterward, she always went back to being Garbo."

Newsflash! Los Angeles *Examiner*, Thursday, May 10, 1934: "Greta Garbo's 'Double' Kills Herself—Leaves Note Telling Despair at Not Being Star":

> Beneath a mirror that had told a bitter truth, Sigrun Solvason, the girl who was known in Hollywood as "Greta Garbo's double," lay dead yesterday.
>
> She had taken poison, police said. All about the room were photographs of herself and Garbo, mute evidence of the resemblance that raised her hopes so high she could not bear the pain when Hollywood dashed them to earth. . . . She had always stated she could be as great a star as Greta Garbo if she had a chance.

The headline was deliberately misleading: The woman was a Garbo look-alike, not her stand-in.* So was the photo caption: "Sigrun Solvason, film actress, a suicide, whose body was found amidst photographs of herself and

_____

* Her MGM stand-in was Geraldine de Vorak, who subbed for Garbo in the operatic scenes of *Romance*, the snow scenes in *Love*, and the car crash in *Woman of Affairs*, among others, and was sometimes called upon to pose as Garbo at film premieres. It was said that over the many years she did stand-ins for Garbo—all the long-shot scenes and all the light and camera setups—de Vorak never met her.

Greta Garbo." The photos were of Garbo and Solvason *separately*, not together. Nevertheless, Solvason's suicide aggravated Garbo's melancholia.

After *Queen Christina*, she moved again, this time to a house in Brentwood
near Mercedes on North Carmelina Drive. In that snowy winter of 1933,
they decided to go to Yosemite, where Garbo registered at their hotel as
Harriet Brown. So no one would recognize her when they went skating,
she donned dark glasses, pulled a lumberman's cap down over her head,
and wore multiple layers of heavy sweaters, trousers, and woolen stockings.

"When I saw her on the ice, I roared with laughter," said Mercedes.
"There was no trace of her beauty. She looked like a Michelin tire."

People stared and laughed, not because she was Garbo but because she
looked so strange. That prompted her refusal to skate anymore and her
decision to get away from people and go into the forest. It was just before
sunset, and they were soon plunged in total darkness amid thick trees and
underbrush. With the temperature falling fast, they held hands but got
hopelessly lost, stumbling and scratching their hands and faces—numb from
the cold and trying to keep from panicking.

Suddenly, Garbo shouted, "There's a light!" and they followed it to a
small house, where an old man opened the door. They had been walking
for four hours in near-zero weather and would soon have frozen, said
Mercedes. Provided with coffee in tin mugs, they stretched out on his floor
in front of a fire and were taken back to their hotel in the morning.

Back in civilization, Mercedes had a meeting with Thalberg during which
she again expressed her dream of working on a film with Garbo. In June
1934, it was reported that Garbo would next play writer George Sand, but
that was just the first of many proposed Sand films that never materialized.
A dozen other historical figures and literary properties were considered in
the attempt to find a project worthy of following the bold and original
Christina. But MGM eventually reverted to type, and the booby prize at the
end of the search was a dirge by Somerset Maugham.

The melodrama of *The Painted Veil* only worked on the page if one kept
its Orientalia to a minimum of mental images. It couldn't, and didn't, work
on screen where the impossible pagodas and faux Chinese ceremonies encased
a set of dull characters uttering self-pitying clichés for eighty-three minutes.
After *The Letter*, *Rain*, and *Of Human Bondage*, Hollywood's love affair with
Maugham outlived the usefulness of his stories. His treatment of women
was based more on his fear of their sexuality than on their real jockeyings
for power.

The Painted Veil was no exception, and Salka Viertel's script made it rather
worse than better, eliminating its biting probe of expatriate white society—
the book's more interesting *raison d'etre*. Garbo had to play the restless wife

of Herbert Marshall, who drags her along for his medical-missionary work in China. There, she is sexually reawakened by George Brent, menaced by Warner Oland and Jean Hersholt, and finally redeemed by Marshall. The plot, resembling that of *Wild Orchids*, was expected to be salvaged by Richard Boleslawski, a thoughtful "new" stage-based director and Stanislavsky disciple. He was a former actor at the Moscow Art Theater and the recent author of *Acting: The First Six Lessons* (1933), a modified Method approach that would have twenty-five printings but no discernible influence on the star of his current film.

The single word "GARBO" is the first thing on screen, and it stays there in a monolithic bas relief behind and during all the other credits. This was Harry Edington's idea, and it was not lost on audiences or on Hollywood that "Garbo" was now akin to "Duse" and "Bernhardt"—only the surname was needed. And it was up to that surname to camouflage the weaknesses of *The Painted Veil* by the sheer force of its presence.

To some extent, she succeeds: She is full of nervous energy in her early scenes with Marshall, making no attempt to repress her thick "Austrian" accent. At her sister's wedding, she plants no fewer than four kisses on the bride's lips, and hears her mother's advice to "wait for the perfect man like your father." The look on her face tells us exactly what she thinks of that idea, and of her father, but she finally resigns herself to Marshall and, with a sigh, delivers her best line of the film: "Better to have something to absorb oneself than—[big pause]—*not* to have something to absorb oneself."

In Shanghai and Hong Kong, Marshall is busy battling a cholera epidemic and she is a medical widow who must entertain herself as best she can with the local ethnic stereotypes, the odd Caucasian tea party, some horse riding—and diplomat George Brent. After resisting Marshall's amorous advances, she welcomes Brent's, and it is only a matter of time (the time required for one of the worst "Chinese" production numbers MGM ever filmed) before Marshall finds out.

Maugham's stiffly British "romantic" dialogue always seemed to require some exotic locale, and Marshall was considered an expert Maugham interpreter. Critics who called him a "wooden" performer made an unwittingly cruel joke: He had lost a leg in World War I, and the artificial one made him walk with a noticeable limp. The supreme analysis was Graham Greene's in 1935: "Marshall [is] intractably British [and represents] some genuine national characteristics, if not those one wishes to see exported: characteristics which it is necessary to describe in terms of inanimate objects: a kind of tobacco, a kind of tweed, a kind of pipe; or in terms of dogs, something large, sentimental and moulting, something which confirms one's preference for cats."

Garbo found his tweedy British qualities appealing. She was more sociable than usual, frequently lingering on the set to converse with Marshall, share a laugh with Brent, or discuss Oriental matters with young Keye Luke and other Chinese members of the cast. Marshall, for his part, had nothing but positive things to say about her. During several drenching rain scenes, he said, "Miss Garbo displayed keen concern for several elderly ladies in the mob, actresses who had been more important at an earlier time. Of one in particular, Miss Garbo was a little annoyed at herself because she could not recall the lady's name. She called to an assistant to get the name, and then requested a comfortable chair in a dry spot for the elderly actress."

She displayed similar concern for himself, Marshall said, telling him at one point, "If your make-up is wrong, I will change mine." He noted "a freedom from hysteria in Miss Garbo's company," adding that "I have never met a more natural woman. [When problems arise with] dialogue or wardrobe, she does not condemn or disapprove. She will only tell you that she is anxious about it."

On- and offscreen, Marshall was charming and intelligent and could deliver almost any line with conviction.

"I despise myself for ever caring anything about you," he says in the film, dismissing Garbo, who will soon be abandoned by Brent, too. Then finally, some action: Marshall torches the Chinese village for its own good, what with the epidemic and all; the villagers don't quite see it that way and, in the ensuing riot, he is stabbed to death. Garbo had only just reconciled with him and become a cholera nurse strongly resembling a nun.

"Everything he does is love," she sighs over the body as the final theme builds. "It's another language, it's another world."

It's another disappointment.

One of many Hollywood puzzles of this period is the appeal, let alone the sex appeal, of George Brent (1904–1979), who was a consistently uninteresting performer in more than a hundred films. But thousands of hearts throbbed over him and, for a while, Garbo's was evidently one of them. Rumors of a romance between them were rife throughout the filming and continued long after. At the least, they became close friends.

A month or so after they met on the set, Brent built a wall around his Taluca Lake mansion so Garbo could lie about, unseen and unmolested, and play tennis and swim with him in privacy. She did so often, intrigued by his outdoorsmanship (he was a skilled horseman, a polo player, and a stable owner) and by his colorful past.

Born in the west Irish town of Shannonsbridge, Brent was orphaned at age eleven. In his early teens, he became involved in the Irish Rebellion as

ABOVE: *George Brent and
Garbo in* The Painted Veil
(1934)
BELOW: *In redemptive mode*

a trusted dispatch carrier of Sinn Féin leader Michael Collins. It was possibly the most dangerous post of the uprising and, when Collins was killed in 1922, Brent was smuggled aboard a freighter to Canada a step ahead of the authorities seeking him for subversive activities.

Brent's 6'1" good looks and some stage experience in Ireland led him to theater work in New York and finally to Hollywood, where his twenty-month marriage to actress Ruth Chatterton conveniently ended around the time *The Painted Veil* shooting began. Chatterton was a social butterfly, while Brent was a semirecluse who detested parties and Hollywood nightlife. "I'm free and I'm going to stay free," he said after the divorce. "Any man likes his freedom. . . . He can read his newspaper at the table; he doesn't have to dress for dinner; and he doesn't have to talk when he gets home from the studio dead tired."

Those views nicely mirrored Garbo's, whose experience with Gilbert matched Brent's with Chatterton. The press called him "the male edition of Garbo." Both were loners who came straight home from the studio and were in bed by ten. Brent's athleticism and introversion were much like—and compatible with—the Swede's. He had trained with "Mushy" Callahan, the junior welterweight champ; he and Garbo sometimes boxed together in Brent's backyard! Over his living-room mantel hung a large marine painting she gave him. He also smoked a lot, played the piano well, and said if he ever married again it would be to a film actress: "I'd rather have a screwball around my house any day than a solid something from Pasadena."

Sometimes they sought out secluded restaurants or side-street movie houses in unlikely parts of Los Angeles, but most often they dined in, tête-à-tête, at Brent's. He said she was the most fascinating woman he had ever known or known *of*. Privately, he told intimates they would soon be married.

George Brent was as mistaken in thinking he could talk Garbo into marriage as David O. Selznick was in thinking he could talk her out of *Anna Karenina*. Selznick, the producer of her next film, was disturbed by her preoccupation with historical and "literary" dramas—equally bad screen sources, in his opinion. Selznick begged her to release him and MGM from the Tolstoy remake "following the disappointment of *Queen Christina* and *The Painted Veil*."* "I do hope you will not force us to proceed [with *Karenina*]," he wrote Garbo, adding that her approved co-star, Fredric March, was "fed up" with costume dramas and would only do *Karenina* if "forced." In a

---

* Selznick didn't know—because Mayer hadn't told him—how profitable *Queen Christina* really was.

hand-delivered letter to Salka Viertel, Selznick made it clear that his strong preference was for Garbo to do *Dark Victory* instead.

Garbo was, in fact, seriously considering that 1934 play and other Selznick suggestions for a good "modern" vehicle, including the life of Isadora Duncan. Playwright Philip Barry had agreed to write either the Isadora or the *Dark Victory* screenplay for her and was so enthusiastic about working with Garbo that he sent a barrage of backup suggestions to Selznick: Henry James's *Golden Bowl*, Joseph Conrad's *Arrow of Gold*, Scott Fitzgerald's *Tender Is the Night*, Willa Cather's *My Ántonia* or *Song of the Lark*—any of which he was willing to convert to the screen for her.

Garbo pondered and agonized but leaned toward *Karenina*, partly because George Cukor was supposed to direct it and possibly because of Salka Viertel. Salka had a pre-existing contract to write the Tolstoy script, whereas Selznick had signed Barry to write *Dark Victory* (or any of the alternatives). According to the first of the Salka "conspiracy" theories (see Chapter 10, pp. 372–73), to avoid being cut out of a job she allegedly hindered communication and "talked down" all the other options with her indecisive friend. Garbo's ultimate reasons for rejecting *Dark Victory* (which was snapped up by Bette Davis) are forever clouded, but Salka's crucial importance as her chief intermediary was now clearer than ever.

In any case, nine years after *Love*, Tolstoy got the nod again. "Karenina Talks!" said the wags. Reliable Clarence Brown would direct. Salka's screenplay was doctored by Clemence Dane and S. N. Behrman, and MGM's top technicians went to work—Daniels behind the camera, Gibbons on set designs, Adrian on costumes, and Stothart on stealing his score from Tchaikovsky.

They all did their jobs, but Garbo—or more precisely, her face—carried off the film and the audience from first shot to last; one notices little else, except Brown's fabulous long reverse-tracking shot of the Karenins' banquet table to open the picture.* After that, from the moment Vronsky first glimpses that Face through billowing white steam at the railway station, he and we are in her thrall. It is a sound film, but it is pure, visual Garbo: This Anna

---

* Brown explained how he did it. In *The Eagle* (1925), he had made an elaborate effect shot—a long track down a banquet table. The camera started at one end, then traveled backward the full length of the table, which was sixty feet long: "To get the camera in that position was very difficult; no equipment existed to do it. So we made two perambulators. We put one on each side of the table and constructed a bridge, with stressbeams so that it was rigid. Then we dropped a crosspiece and fastened the camera from the top, so that the bottom of the camera could travel along the top of the table. Nothing could obstruct the movement of the camera, so we had prop boys putting candelabra in place just before the camera picked them up. I liked the effect so well I did it again in *Anna Karenina*."

was most eloquent with her face and body. May Robson as Vronsky's mother speaks beyond the novel when she tells her, "You, my dear, have the divine gift of silence."

Dialogue is unimportant; the attitude of Garbo's head reveals precisely how she feels about every man, woman, and child she encounters. Her greatest warmth is reserved for Freddie Bartholomew as her son. Older and prissier than Philippe de Lacy in the silent version (child actors were better seen than heard), Bartholomew lacks the sexual but provides the emotional spark to ignite their scenes together. In their bedside nimbus, the mutual adoration of mother and child is something greater than the passion of man and woman. In both versions of *Anna Karenina*, Garbo's main lovemaking is directed toward her child. But in the talkie, it is virtually the *only* lovemaking she does.

S. N. Behrman recalled that the one and only time he ever saw Garbo cry was on the set of *Anna Karenina* when "she was having trouble with the scene with her son." Bartholomew's memory of her was more bitter than sweet: "My aunt Cissy [said], 'Greta Garbo loves you. She doesn't give autographs, but she will [for] you—get her to sign this picture.' I knocked on her dressing-room door and she came and I said, 'Would you please sign this for me?' And she said, 'No,' and closed the door."

Fredric March's initial reluctance carried over to the production itself: Anna's lover is as dull as her husband, and the idea that she would wreck her life for him is never believable. "I'm sick and tired of love," he tells her, and so are we of him. Basil Rathbone, miscast as Karenin and ill at ease playing such a weak character, is likewise unconvincing. But Garbo makes us forget them by a quick gurgle of laughter; by quietly telling Vronsky's friend Reginald Denny, "I think it's very generous of you not to hate me." Her wrenching visit to her son on his birthday, against Karenin's orders, ends in his fierce harangue, banishing her from her own home.

Adultery must pay, and we see the price in Garbo's stricken face. There was no need for the denouement or even, really, for the suicide scene. Anna's death is clear in the last, haunting agitation of Garbo's eyes. Alistair Cooke wrote the best elegy:

> An actress is usually said to be mature at the time when her daughters threaten to take over the parts she made her name in. But Garbo's maturity is not the maturity of her career, it's a wise ageing of her outlook. The old, bold, slick disdain has given way to a sort of amused grandeur. Physically, this means simply a new balance between two features—a softening of the eyes, a hardening of the mouth. . . . In *Anna Karenina* she moves a plane higher. Before she has even chosen

The camera crew positions Garbo and Freddie Bartholomew in Anna
Karenina *(1935).*

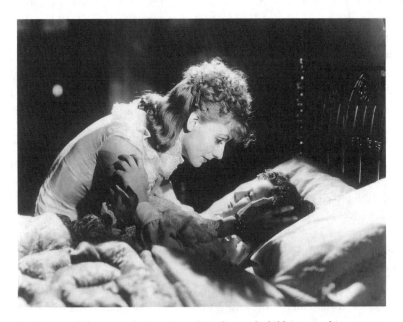

*In close-up. The mutual adoration of mother and child is something greater
than the passion of man and woman.*

her lover, her look tells you it doesn't much matter who he is, they all go the same way home. . . . This tolerant goddess wraps everybody in the film round in a protective tenderness. She sees not only her own life, but everybody else's, before it has been lived. . . . She has suddenly and decisively passed out of her twenties. [Her] quality of gentleness, a gift usually of women over fifty, is an overwhelming thing when it goes with the appearance of a beautiful woman of thirty.

It's no use to talk about the others or even much about the direction. [Everyone else's] acting gets referred back to the way Garbo looks at people these days, the way she implies that the least you can do for people in this stupid, brawling world is to keep them warm and give them a share of comfort before the end comes.

Behrman drove to Riverside with the Selznicks, Salka, and Garbo for the preview. "The delicacy and distinction of Garbo's performance affected me, as they did the audience," he wrote. "I felt, as I always did watching her, that she was the most patrician artist in the world." But on the way home in the car, Garbo sat silent. Selznick, finally, asked how she felt. "Oh," she said, "if once, only once, I could see a preview and come home feeling satisfied."

Back at the Selznicks', her mood improved. "Nothing mattered to Garbo but the tennis," Irene Selznick recalled. "Everybody got a drink and we turned the outside lights on and went down to the court. Garbo didn't have the right shoes, but she tried on some extras we had and finally got her big feet into the most suitable ones and went out and played mixed doubles. [Garbo beat Cedric Gibbons, 6–2, and Selznick, 6–love.] We were in high spirits because the movie was so good."

David Selznick's spirits were even higher when *Anna Karenina*'s profit turned out to be $320,000, more than double that of *The Painted Veil*.

Maureen O'Sullivan, who played Garbo's little sister in the film, said that "when working with her, one felt that she was doing nothing really, that she wasn't even very good, until you saw the results on the screen." But not everyone found the film, or Garbo, enchanting. Fredric March's negative experience was made complete by an offscreen exchange in midproduction after he had observed her from the sidelines during a shot and then complimented her on it. "Do you mean you watched me acting? You should not have done that," she said, and fled to her dressing room. The much-miffed March later opined that she always appealed more to women than to men and that "co-starring with Garbo hardly constituted an introduction."

———

She still appealed very much to George Brent, however, who begged her not to go back to Sweden, as planned. Undeterred, she was in New York by May 24, 1935. There, she bought three tickets to *Three Men on a Horse*, sitting alone in the middle seat so as not to be bothered, as part of her customary pre-cruise theater week. Manhattan always indulged her more than Hollywood: She would receive the New York Film Critics' best-actress award (but no Oscar nomination) for *Anna Karenina*.

By the time the movie opened in August, she was long out of the country, traveling under the aliases Mary Holmquist and Karin Lund. The surprise was not that she rejected Brent's pleas to forgo Sweden but that she stayed there for the better part of a year. In Stockholm, she was quoted as saying that she wanted to settle down and raise potatoes: "The things which have to do with the soil are the only things which are pure, fine and wonderful." A later report said she was dissatisfied with "the Hollywood compromise between art and box office" and intended to form her own film company, à la Chaplin.

What was she *really* up to? It was the job of a certain Mr. Prinzmetal to find out. He was one of MGM's veteran European distributors, and he was spying on her. This was a routine company policy to make sure the studio was the first to learn if its stars got in trouble and—in Garbo's case—to be certain that Immigration let her back in.

Mr. Prinzmetal's task was made easy by the newspapers, which gave hysterical coverage to the fact that Noël Coward was now in Stockholm, dancing the rhumba with Garbo. Coward shared neither her discretion nor her aversion to the press. He later quoted a talk they had about her refusal to let people watch her act on the set. "It's a public profession we're in, after all," Coward told her, to which she replied, "If I am by myself, my face will do things I cannot do with it otherwise." As for the inevitable rumors of romance, an aide responded archly with: "Mr. Coward is *only* interested in his art." Still, the papers insisted they would announce their engagement at any moment, while Coward refused to accommodate her penchant for secret meetings in dark glasses. Instead, he coaxed or bullied her into various outings, including a party given by actor Gösta Ekman. On that occasion, he got her as far as Ekman's door, at which point she panicked and tried to bail out.

"Believe me, Noël, I really and truly cannot go in," she said. "I cannot face it." According to Coward, he shook her and said, "You bloody well *are* going in," and pushed her inside. Once there, she enjoyed herself and stayed until 3 a.m. Afterward, they exchanged fond telegrams and phone calls, referring to each other—in the spirit of the wedding stories—as "my little bridegroom" and "my little bride."

"Noël Coward was very charming to me," she wrote Salka. The letter also contained a guilt trip. "This is my last attempt to try and get an answer from you. Are you ill—or has something else happened? I have asked you much little things which can't take you more then [sic] ten minutes to write me about. Perhaps my letters haven't reached you, or you are perhaps angry at something. If you will let me know, I shall try and correct it. . . . Yesterday I got a wire from 'Swartzweise' [their code name for Mercedes] who wants to come here and wait and accompany me back. She is indeed amazing. I shall not answer."

But she changed her mind and eventually wrote Mercedes a letter in which she said, jokingly, "I will meet you for dinner a week from Tuesday at 8 o'clock in the dining room of the Grand Hotel." Within hours of receiving it, Mercedes booked passage on the S.S. *Europa*, arranged to fly from Bremen to Malmö (Sweden's only airfield), and from there to reach Stockholm by train, just in time for the dinner date.

Garbo was stunned—possibly horrified, possibly pleased. Who knew? One didn't suggest such a rendezvous to Mercedes unless one was prepared for her to accept! Garbo's approach-avoidance of de Acosta was classic. Whether or not she really wanted this interlude, she was about to have it.

There was no such ambivalence on the part of Mercedes, who was still wildly in love. "The evening was a sentimental one," wrote de Acosta. "We sat at the [corner table] she had described to me so many times in Hollywood . . . ordering caviar, champagne, and our favorite tunes from the orchestra. In that rococo room with its pink-shaded lights, its soft string orchestra and its old-world atmosphere, I felt that I was moving in a dream within a dream."

The White Horse Inn was then playing in Stockholm, and after dinner they went to see it. The next day, Garbo took her to the Wachtmeisters' Tistad. In their long walks through the fields, Mercedes was a spellbound witness to Garbo's deep affinity for the little red farmhouses with their piles of fir cones in the courtyards. Back in Stockholm, Garbo took her to see the house where she was born. "She made no comment as we stood looking at it—nor did I," wrote Mercedes. "I knew that such a gesture meant much to her. As we moved away neither of us spoke."

By the time Mercedes left, Garbo was exhausted and ill:

"I am in bed most of the time and so stupified [sic]," she wrote Salka on November 22, 1935. "I have been in bed for years, I feel. So you have had troubles. . . . I have no lovers but I have troubles just the same. Mercedes has been here as you know by now. I took her to Tistad as I didn't know what else to do. She is more quiet than before but otherwise the same. I was a wreck after she went and I told her she must not write me. We had a sad farewell."

Her illness was not feigned. Mayer heard of it from Laudy L. Lawrence, head of MGM's Paris office, to whom Garbo had written about a film job for her brother Sven. After meeting him, Lawrence wrote Mayer on December 3: "Sven is a nice boy, but that is all. His health is very bad. Incidentally, the entire family is in bad health, including Garbo. . . . Her younger sister died from TB long ago and Sven is in bed a whole lot more than out of it. Garbo is rather seriously ill."

The press was calling it a heavy cold or influenza. On December 8, 1935, Garbo wrote a long, touching letter to Mayer. She thanked him for his efforts on her brother's behalf. She said she'd been ill since September, largely confined to bed, but that even so, her thoughts were on work. There was a certain pathetic resonance of *Camille*, the film she and· MGM were now planning; she asked for an extra month's recuperation. Mayer cabled on January 10, 1936, to say he was "terribly distressed" and to assure her "all contract obligations would be suspended for a month." Five days later, she replied: "Agreed. Thank you. Feeling better. Greetings. Garbo."

That exchange was less amazing for its content than its omission: Neither party mentioned that the day before Mayer's cable, on January 9, 1936, John Gilbert had died of a heart attack at age thirty-eight. He had been restricted to home for two months after a diagnosis of myocarditis, aggravated by too many years of hard drinking, attended by his new "closest friend" and reputed lover, Marlene Dietrich. Shortly before he died, Gilbert had said, "There's never been a day since [Garbo] and I parted that I haven't been lonely for her."

The news reached Garbo in the foyer of a Stockholm theater during the intermission of Schiller's *Maria Stuart*. She returned briefly to her seat, then left soon after the curtain rose, avoiding the press. A report, spitefully invented by one of the eluded newsmen, claimed she said, "What is that to me?" It was widely circulated and so distressed her that she broke her rule of silence and said it was "vicious misquoting" about a man for whom she felt deeply.

The emotional upset did not speed her recovery, but finally she felt well enough to return to America. Before leaving Sweden, she took a seclusionary cue from George Brent and instructed Mercedes by mail to have a ten-foot fence installed around her house in Brentwood.

Brent and Brentwood had both been on her mind during the year abroad. She had written him regularly, and he was the main topic of interest for the reporters who greeted her in June 1936, when the *Gripsholm* docked in New York. The scribes, to their shock, were ushered into the ship's smoking room, where Garbo agreed to answer questions for ten minutes. "I do not

Garbo at the Wachtmeisters' Tistad estate in Sweden, early spring 1936

know why I should talk to people I do not know, but I am beginning to learn that it is necessary," she said with the frankness she could summon when she wished. A report that she was shipping a whole Swedish castle to be reassembled stone by stone on her own property amused her: "Always when I come back I hear some beautiful story. This is the loveliest of all. Can you imagine what a lot of little parcels, all neatly tied up, a castle would make? Mr. Hearst can do many things that Garbo cannot!"

She had hoped her little conference would satisfy the press, but it only satisfied the New York press. Diligent reporters in California got word of her itinerary and raced to board the Santa Fe *Chief* before Garbo disembarked. Kay Proctor of *Screen Guide* got on in Barstow and obtained a scoop quote from a porter: "That missy shore am a light eater. She's hardly ate enough to keep a bird alive." Garbo was traveling with Berthold Viertel, who was irate about the coast-to-coast hounding "of my poor little rabbit. It is inhuman the way they dog her. No wonder she is frightened of people. . . . It is like a pack of hungry dogs chasing one poor little scared fox! Why do they insist she belongs to the public like—like a park? She has her rights!" But Proctor was insistent, and Garbo wearily agreed to answer her dull questions. (No, she had no plans to build on property she bought in Beverly Hills.) Her only interesting statement was a heartfelt one on an old subject:

Garbo, bolstered by and beneath the ship's motto ("If God is for us, who is against us?"), grants a ten-minute press conference aboard the Gripsholm.

It is not that I do not like people. I do. Believe me. But it does frighten me when hordes of strangers rush at me, pull at me, stare at me. It is a dreadful feeling. It is—it is humiliating! I do not want to be ungracious, but they make it impossible for me to do anything but shut myself away where they cannot reach and tear at me.

In San Bernardino, Jim Mason of *Photoplay* had some equally uninspired queries, including the perennial one about her current romance. A trace of a smile crossed her features, he reported, as she parried him: "Well, I cannot say. That is a personal thing. We like to keep some things to ourselves."

That said, and the *Chief* having pulled into its station, she went "like a homing pigeon" straight from the train to see George Brent—who thereafter disappeared from her life completely.

Everybody has two professions, Gottfried Reinhardt liked to say: his own and the movies. It was especially applicable to Hollywood's European immigrants, of whom Reinhardt and his father, Max, were notably two. The first wave, which included Garbo and the Viertels, had come for economic and professional reasons. The Reinhardts were part of the second wave, larger and more desperate, who came for the same reasons as the first group plus two overriding ones: political freedom and sheer survival.

The exile community, out of shared trauma, tended to stick together. Hollywood's romantic rough-and-tumble period was over; sound had systematized everything. The studios reigned over a town where movies offered everyone a real or imagined livelihood and where the widespread illusion among immigrants was that they were superior to the Americans, most of whom were recent settlers themselves. So amorphous was the emigré intellectual ghetto-in-exile, "that many occupants did not perceive it at all."

By 1935, half of the Europeans and most of the Germans lived within a ten-square-mile coastal strip of Southern California. The breathtaking new wave of Austrians, French, Slavs, and Britons would include composers Arnold Schoenberg, Erich Korngold, and Igor Stravinsky; Arthur Rubinstein, Nathan Milstein, Gregor Piatigorsky, and countless other musicians from the Vienna, Paris, and Berlin philharmonics, including conductors Bruno Walter and Otto Klemperer. Among the stage and film people were Fritz Lang, Otto Preminger, Billy Wilder, Peter Lorre, Hedy Lamarr, Robert Siodmak, Lilli Palmer, Lotte Lenya and Kurt Weill, Jean Renoir, and Jean Gabin. The philosophers and writers included Christopher Isherwood, Herbert Marcuse, Lion Feuchtwanger, and Franz Werfel—plus a thousand lesser-known artists, doctors, scholars, educators, and technicians with nothing in common but the venue of their exile.

For Europe, said the younger Reinhardt, it was "the most suicidal bloodletting of a civilization since Spain's expulsion of the Jews and Moors in 1492." For America, it was an extraordinary influx of talent—the unprecedented mass immigration of an elite. And Salka Viertel provided them a gathering place.

"It *was* a salon," Gottfried recalled. "In her house in Santa Monica, George Sand, Chopin, Liszt, Musset, Delacroix would have felt comfortable." It was a place where Garbo would tell Max Reinhardt how she wanted to play Hamlet; where Max Reinhardt would finally meet Bertolt Brecht; where Chaplin would recruit his musical ghostwriter, Hanns Eisler. Salka was more than a great hostess. She was an active friend to individuals in need and "to the ghetto as a whole, for she was one of the few who knew and faced the fact that it was a ghetto. Hers was one of the few clearinghouses between the inmates and the guardians. It was neutral ground where, for a few hours, everything was allowed and many an opportunity was created." A hundred artistic collaborations had their genesis in her living room.

Salka's own importance as an MGM scriptwriter was largely tied to her friendship with Garbo, of whom the immigrants no less than the natives were in awe. "The conversation would cease when she came in," says Peter Viertel, "especially among the Germans and if it was highly political. It would be an event."

Berthold's film projects these days often took him to England, where he fretted about the worsening situation in Europe. Isherwood recalled in *Prater Violet* that his "personal trouble gave way to political anxiety and anger, which grew from day to day." In Austria, the socialist leaders were by now arrested or in hiding, and Berthold "listened eagerly to every news broadcast, bought every special edition, [and] seemed to be possessed by a devil. He tried to quarrel with everybody."

In private life, he and Salka had drifted into an amicable separation, and she was pursuing the affairs to which she had alluded in her letters to Garbo in Stockholm. The first was with writer Oliver Garrett, her next-door neighbor who hailed from a wealthy New England family, wrote action films, drove a convertible, and wore a beret and loud sport coats. Her second, and more significant liaison was with Gottfried Reinhardt, who often took over the hosting duties at her Sunday-afternoon open house. Drop-ins included the Schoenbergs, Klemperer, composers Dmitri Tiomkin and Bronislaw Kaper (both then working at MGM), and such unlikely Yankees as Johnny Weissmuller, Oscar Levant, and Miriam Hopkins.

At those gatherings, Salka wrote, "Political discussions, verging on personal bitterness, were unavoidable among the Europeans and amazed the Americans." But in another breath she could write, "Sam [Behrman] arrived, as dear and whimsical as ever, and in spite of the Spanish Civil War, which broke out in July, Hitler's threats, and the appeasement policy of England and France, we finished in a reasonably short time a very good screenplay." Since this was *Marie Walewska*, a politically irrelevant period piece, some felt that even Salka—typical of everybody who came to Hollywood—viewed what was happening in the world as just a backdrop to her movie work.

But that was unfair. All the Viertels were committed activists: Berthold and Salka were staunch antifascists, and publicly outspoken about it; sons Peter, Thomas, and Hans were a New Dealer, a Democrat, and a Trotskyite, respectively. Hans Viertel's activity with a radical group that picketed Stalinist meetings earned him several physical beatings. The Viertels had helped to organize the controversial 1934 reading by Fredric March and Florence-Eldridge of a new antiwar play, *Bury the Dead*, by Peter Viertel's friend Irwin Shaw, after which writer Donald Ogden Stewart made a speech urging the film industry to become active in the anti-Nazi movement:

"Let us have no more million-dollar revolving staircases, no more star-filled symposiums of billion-dollar entertainment—but let us have some simple truths . . . on a bare stage, against nothing but a plain background," said Stewart's manifesto. His call to arms was largely ignored, of course, and it was observed that he himself was then working on the script of a Joan Crawford comedy called *No More Ladies*.

In the 1934 California gubernatorial election, Upton Sinclair advocated federal control of the film industry, greater taxation of the rich, and studio unionizing—pure Bolshevism to the movie tycoons, who united behind Republican Frank E. Merriam and produced phony newsreels showing how thugs and Communists would invade California under Sinclair's radical utopia.

"What does Sinclair know about anything?" said Mayer. "He's just a writer." Indeed, at this point no group in Hollywood was more mistrusted than the writers, especially foreign ones. Salka was active in the Screen Writers' Guild, which MGM considered subversive. She was also a founding member of the Anti-Nazi League and stuck by it when others, such as her close but more politically cautious friend Ernst Lubitsch, warned her in 1936 that it was under Communist control and he was bailing out. Salka pooh-poohed that idea: "Ernst, what all these people do is sit around their swimming pools, drinking highballs and talking about movies, while the wives complain about their Philipino [*sic*] butlers."

In a naïve way, she *did* tend to view politics, if not life, in movie terms: Thirty years before the rest of the country, Hollywood understood the principle that everything, including politics, depended more on star quality than on platforms. When André Malraux and Ernest Hemingway came to speak for the Spanish Republicans at select gatherings, including Salka's, many celebrities and contributions were drawn to the cause. Without charismatic presentation, one's political or artistic dream was doomed, and at the bottom of everything was money, as Max Reinhardt soon learned. At a lavish house-warming for George Cukor, Reinhardt marveled to Irving Thalberg that a director could afford such luxury. Thalberg replied, "I encourage personal extravagance in the talent working for me. It makes them dependent."

While Reinhardt lived in Los Angeles, from 1934 to 1942, everyone loved him but few went to the Max Reinhardt Workshop. Max and Gottfried both adored Garbo and dined with her often at the Cafe Trocadero (once seated two tables away from Dietrich, but the women never spoke). Max now took the small liberty of sending Garbo a telegram asking, "Please come to the Workshop today or tomorrow and take a look at the old *Everyman* in a modern version with a number of young talents. It would make me very happy to see you again." But Garbo didn't come. He sent the same telegram to Chaplin, Sam Goldwyn, Harry and Jack Warner, Harold Lloyd, Joe Schenck, Darryl Zanuck, Aldous Huxley, C. B. DeMille, Frank Capra, Walt

Disney, Walter Wanger, Norma Shearer, Charles Boyer, and Bette Davis—
and they didn't come either. "The Europeans would rather wallow in a rich
Reinhardt past than enjoy a more modest Reinhardt present," said his son.
The Americans would do neither.

But Reinhardt pressed on, with one great Hollywood project that came
to fruition—the 1935 film version of *A Midsummer Night's Dream*. The
previous summer, Max had instructed Gottfried to secure his dream cast:
Garbo (Titania), Chaplin (Bottom), Clark Gable (Demetrius), Gary Cooper
(Lysander), John Barrymore (Oberon), W. C. Fields (Thisbe), Wallace Beery
(Lion), Walter Huston (Theseus), Joan Crawford (Hermia), Myrna Loy (Hel-
ena), and Fred Astaire (Puck). The film was made with a Warners instead
of an MGM cast, and with Anita Louise instead of Garbo as Titania.

Reinhardt never gave up. But he could never get the cooperation of Garbo,
in particular, or Los Angeles, in general: Despite its steadily increasing
population and fabulous pool of artists, theater simply never took root there.

Max Reinhardt got no less and perhaps more respect than Arnold Schoenberg, on whose behalf Salka petitioned Thalberg to write the score for *The
Good Earth*. Thalberg agreed to meet him; Schoenberg was late, his embryonic English having gotten him into a studio tour instead of Thalberg's office.
Even so, they got along well and discussed Schoenberg's ideas for the key
musical moments in the Pearl Buck story. Then Schoenberg said he would
require full control not only of the music but of the whole soundtrack,
including dialogue, which should be delivered in the *Sprechstimme* style of
Pierrot Lunaire—a technique he would teach the actors. Thalberg hadn't the
faintest notion of what he was talking about, so Salka gave a helpful but
frightening demonstration of German "speech-song," an operatic cross between speaking and singing. The composer later demanded a fee of fifty
thousand dollars—twice the studio's norm. That was it for Thalberg. Schoenberg went back to teaching and composition.

For Salka and her salon, the focus of activity continued to career wildly
from high art to practical employment to politics, often mixing up the three.
Thalberg now suggested that Donald Ogden Stewart sit in on an MGM
story conference with Sam Behrman and Salka on that long-moldering Garbo
script about Napoleon and his Polish lover, Marie Walewska.

"The first conference, however, concerned nothing but the [Screen Writers'] Guild," said Stewart, "and to my delight Salka joined forces with me
against Napoleon Thalberg. It was a tough fight but we held our own. We
also held our jobs, and Salka and I even baited Irving about the advantages
of Socialism. . . . Irving disclosed that in his Brooklyn high school days he
had been a member of the Young Peoples' Socialist League and had made

streetcorner speeches. But now he merely regarded us with the sad re-
proachful eyes of a betrayed parent."

Stewart called Salka's house "a rallying point for all rebels," especially in
the struggle for the Guild, which had been formed in 1931 but rendered
impotent by the producers' refusal to recognize it. Now, under Roosevelt,
the mood was more favorable toward unionizing and the Guild revitalized
by an influx of such "name" writers from New York as Lillian Hellman,
Dashiell Hammett, and Dorothy Parker. The producers retaliated with a
company union called "Screen Playwrights" and with a threatened blacklist
of Guild-connected writers.

Stewart and Salka were on thin MGM ice as they labored over the Napoleon story and as Garbo labored over whether and when she wanted to
do it. As always, there was a dizzying array of other offers, including the
Algerian femme fatale in Richard Boleslawski's *The Garden of Allah*, which
she wisely turned down and Dietrich unwisely accepted. The most serious
alternative was *La Dame aux Camélias*, Dumas *fils*'s ultimate challenge for
all actresses. It was the one role Garbo truly wanted to play and proposed
to the studio herself. But she didn't want to do it *next*. From Sweden, she
had written Salka an amazing letter, actively (but sneakily) involving herself
in the production process more than usual:

> I do not understand why they are not going to do Walewska first.
> And are you not doing anything on *Camille*? . . . Perhaps [Mayer] could
> let Selznick [produce] *Camille* [instead of Thalberg]. I shall write another
> sheat of paper and if you wish you can show it to Thalberg. Please ask
> Thalberg to think very carefully about *Camille*. It's so like *Anna* [*Kar-
> enina*] that I am afraid. . . . It's devastating to do the same story again.
> . . . The Waleska story [is] a newer thing—because Napoleon isn't a
> usual figur on the screen, like my other fifty thousand lovers. . . . Is
> Sam Berman around the lot now? I hope you and Sam will be on
> *Camille*. . . . I am very nervous as you see in my silly letter. But every
> time, the studio goes thru the same misstakes and one's heart goes
> fluttering again.

Within three weeks of her return from Sweden in 1936, MGM made the
unusual announcement that the next two Garbo films would be *Marie Walewska* and *Camille* but that, owing to "difficulties of casting," it was not yet
sure which would come first. Adding to the uncertainty was the report that
she planned to go back to Sweden for good after those pictures were made.
"She would prefer to make only one, or, better still, none at all," said an
anonymous MGM official.

Garbo, at thirty, had a life and soul beyond the movies. Her melancholia in Sweden, increased by sickness and by Gilbert's death, had given her more cause to reflect on the dubious value of fame and film—on life's innate tragedy and brevity, and on how she was conducting hers. In the summer of 1936, she wanted to move again. Mercedes had her eye on a house rented to Jeannette MacDonald, and Garbo liked it too, but MacDonald had no plans to vacate until Mercedes called upon her psychic forces to spook the singer into moving out. Garbo got the house.

As for playing the Dumas heroine, her indecision went down to the wire: "She is such a tragic figure. I do not know. I have not yet read the script. It may please me very much."

Then again, it might not. Garbo would suit herself these days. But the movie that finally suited her was *Camille*.

In the gay half-world of Paris, the gentlemen of the day met the girls of the moment at certain theatres, balls and gambling clubs, where the code was discretion—but the game was romance.

At the center of that 1847 world, described in the film's introductory title above, was Marie Duplessis, the real-life "Camille"—mistress of Dumas and Liszt. In the Garbo rendering, she was Marguerite Gautier. In all renderings, she was the most dazzling and cultivated courtesan of the day, her legend enhanced by a consumptive death at twenty-two.

Camille production began in September 1936, and even among seasoned MGM veterans there was a sense of something epochal in the works. Garbo's beauty and skill were at their peak. She established an immediate rapport with director George Cukor. The screenplay by Zoë Atkins, Frances Marion, and James Hilton was luminous. The Daniels-Adrian-Gibbons team could be counted on for the best photography, costumes, and sets money could buy. Thalberg visited the set during the first week of shooting and came away awed. "Don't you understand?" he said impatiently, "she is completely *unguarded*." His premature death a few days later, on September 14, 1936, was a great shock to all, but the gloom it evoked was eerily appropriate to the film at hand.

The unguarded quality that so struck Thalberg is evident in Garbo's every naturalistic nuance, starting with the film's opening theater scenes, which are surprisingly funny as well. This very *knowing* Camille is on the prowl, spying Armand through her opera glasses: "I didn't know rich men could ever look like that." She is bitchy perfection when sparring with Olympe (Lenore Ulric) and old Prudence (Laura Hope Crews) over who stays and who leaves their box. Yet something ominous always lurks beneath the

A portrait by E. Vienot of the original Lady of the Camellias, Alphonsine Plessis, who upgraded her name to Marie Duplessis

With George Cukor on the set of Camille *(1936)*

surface. She dislikes sad thoughts, she says, but moments later, when complimented, replies, "I always look well when I'm near death."

"I thought you didn't like sad thoughts," she is reminded.

"I don't, but they come sometimes."

Upon meeting Armand, she issues a semiplayful warning: "I'm not always sincere." Those subtle degrees of sincerity shape her performance as well as our response to it.

The casting of her leading man had been as problematic as always, ending in the selection of the strikingly handsome Robert Taylor. He is a shallow Armand, indeed, which works to his advantage in certain moments, as when a loudly laughed-at dirty joke shocks him at the dinner table. But the chemistry between him and Garbo is minimal through much of the film.

English actor Rex O'Malley, on the other hand, had an upbeat experience with her in this, his first Hollywood film, as Armand's friend Gaston: "I liked her sense of humor. Once when we were dancing in a scene she started giving way, and over she went. I fell too, as gently as possible, right on top of her. She burst into laughter. 'It's my little feet,' she said."

By far the finest male performance in *Camille* is Henry Daniell's as Baron de Varville, the lame-duck lover who knows something's up—another role originally intended for John Barrymore. The baron is a man "whose lips have been locked in sarcasm for so long that he cannot unpurse them even to kiss his mistress." The tension of every Daniell-Garbo encounter is electric. In their most brilliant scene, at his piano, she stretches her beads in symbolic complement to stretching the truth—lying, in fact, about why the bell has rung. They bait each other with the film's best barbed dialogue, she knowing (he suspecting) that her new lover is outside. Their nervous laughter and barely controlled hysteria mount as Daniell pounds out Chopin to a furious musical and emotional crescendo.

Daniell was one of very few actors who could or ever did steal a scene from Garbo. His suavity always made him appear completely at ease, but in fact he was decidedly nervous about acting with her. Before this critical scene, he confessed, "I am terribly worried about it. You see, I don't laugh very easily."

"Neither do I," she replied, and the mutual admission was no more or less than they needed to do it superbly.

Far from superb as Armand's doting father was Lionel Barrymore, who overacts worse than ever and at one point invokes God's blessing on "Margaret" instead of "Marguerite" Gautier.

Most superb, behind the scenes, was Adrian, whose costume designs switch from white in the carefree beginning, to grey as the tragedy gathers momentum, to black toward the bitter end. It was Adrian's idea, too, that her

*Garbo as Marguerite and
Henry Daniell as the
Baron de Varville, her
lame-duck lover, sparring
by the piano in* Camille

*Henry Daniell with his
chow, Nemo, in an MGM
publicity shot by Clarence
Bull. Daniell was far and
away the suavest of
villains, and even here
transcends the linoleum
floor and plywood mantel.*

hairstyles evolve from elaborate ringlets and curls at first to simpler, straighter arrangements as she neared death. He also decreed that her jewels be *real* diamonds and emeralds so that she might "feel" them as such while acting. They argued sharply over the ornate jewelry in *Camille*: She maintained that in Sweden of the period, no ladies—or even courtesans—wore such gaudy gems. But Adrian insisted and, in the end, she acquiesced.*

Authenticity aside, the film's production values provided a sumptuous frame for the restraint of Garbo's playing, especially in what is perhaps the most memorable death on-screen. Garbo died in six of her films, but only in *Camille* did she have the protracted death scene beloved of all actresses —executed in an aura of sublime and ravishing tranquility. She had been sick a great deal during the filming and strongly identified with her tubercular character. Many times on the set, said Mercedes, "she could barely stand on her feet. Often she came directly from the studio to my house, looking deadly white and sometimes scarcely able to drag herself up the stairs." The psychological factor was obvious.

It was well known that Garbo never looked at rushes, and she told Cukor why: "I have some idea, some notion of what I'm doing, and every time I see it, it falls so short that it throws me." Mercedes thought that watching herself on the screen broke "some dream quality she had created within her own psyche." Rushes and previews "caused her great suffering [because] she always felt she could have done much better."

But there was one exception—one piece of film she watched the day after shooting and perhaps the only one with which she was ever satisfied: The last ten minutes of *Camille* constituted the only rushes Greta Garbo ever asked to see. "She told me she was baffled by what she had done," said David Diamond, "and by the peak she'd reached. She couldn't explain it."

It had been reached without much help from Robert Taylor, whom one critic described as "deeply hygienic." Before *Camille* filming began, Garbo called him "a fine actor—and handsome, too." Fifty years later, to Diamond, she put her view of Taylor a little differently: "So beautiful—and so dumb."

George Cukor later defended Taylor and his performance:

> Armand is historically a terrible part. It was usually played by middle-aged men. As a result he seemed stupid doing the things he did. When you get someone really young playing Armand, you understand him; he becomes appealing, with a kind of real youthful passion; whereas if he were thirty-eight years old you'd think, "Oh, you ass, why do you

* Adrian won, but Garbo's instinct was correct. The real fashions of Camille's period were far less extravagant than those designed by Adrian. Her costumes were so heavy that ice-cooled fans were required to keep her from fainting on the set.

Robert Taylor photographed by Ted Allan, 1936

do that?" So that very crudity, that intensity of young passion made Robert Taylor an extremely good Armand. [But to get herself in character, Garbo] was rather distant with him and he was rather hurt. She told me, "If I got to know him too well it would only confuse the images I've been making of myself as [Camille] and of Armand."

Cukor was "staggered by her lightness of touch—the wantonness, the perversity of the way she played it." *Camille* proved that the restrictions of the Code could be made to work to an intelligent performer's and director's advantage. Garbo and the film functioned on two sexual levels: The obvious one was in the depiction of the demimonde (excused by virtue of the play's literary status); the second was Garbo's "highly pitched emotional vibrato" that broke through her sophistication, in the piano scene with Daniell, for instance, to provide an added erotic dimension.

Camille was Garbo's first, last, and only "pure" classic—her most enduring gift to film, unequalled in the range it allowed her to express. She won the New York Film Critics's best-actress award and a third Oscar nomination, but, for the second year in a row, Luise Rainer took home the statuette, this

Camille: *Multiple angles and dimensions of erotic subtlety*

time for *The Good Earth*, a melodramatic performance (with or without Schoenberg's music) to which time has not been kind.

For a little while afterward, with Cukor's delicate prodding, Garbo was more social. She had heard about Katharine Hepburn's luxurious new home on Angelo Drive, above Benedict Canyon, and asked to see it. Cukor, who had recently directed Hepburn to pass for a boy in *Sylvia Scarlett*, arranged a visit. Hepburn took her upstairs to show her the bedroom: "She walked over to my bed. There was a lump on the bed (obviously a hot-water bottle). She looked at me, patted it and sighed. 'Yes, I have one too. Vat is wrong vid us?'"

Shortly thereafter, Garbo attended a small party where an elderly guest gushed that her Camille was greater than Duse's. Without a word, Garbo got up and left the room. "She went home alone right afterward," said another guest. "It broke up the party, but she couldn't help herself." She must have valued the compliment, but her self-consciousness made the hearing of it unbearable.

Half a century later, actor Jack Larson recalled seeing Garbo on Lexington Avenue in New York. They were having a good chat about mutual friends in Switzerland until she noticed a small crowd gathering, quickly disengaged, and left. As he walked on, Larson remembered a letter that Salka Viertel once showed him, written to her by Garbo from New York where she had just been mobbed after the release of *Camille:*

"She described the unpleasantness, but ended the letter with a little drawing of herself as a tightrope-walker with a parasol in one hand and the final sentence, 'I guess I can't complain because after all, I'm only a circus lady.' "

The circus lady now readied herself quickly for another sort of French tragedy—the story of Napoleon's most intriguing mistress, a patriotic Polish countess whose affair with Bonaparte produced a son whom he could never acknowledge.

The film's title alone had caused endless debate and serious division at MGM over whether the film was aimed at Americans or Europeans. The final compromise was *Conquest* for North American distribution and *Marie Walewska* for Europe. The scenario, from the novel *Pani Walewska* by Waclaw Gasiorowski, was credited to Samuel Hoffenstein, Salka Viertel, and S. N. Behrman, but they were only three of *seventeen* writers who had a hand in it.

The idea had been languishing for years among more than a hundred other story properties MGM had purchased as possible Garbo vehicles. MGM had yet to find a suitable Napoleon who wouldn't wither in Garbo's presence and who, ironically, was *short* enough. Claude Rains was seriously considered but finally rejected as too old to make love to Garbo. Then, in the summer of 1937, came the American release of Anatole Litvak's *Mayerling*, the most successful foreign-language film of the decade and the picture that brought Charles Boyer into the star ranks.

Boyer had serious doubts about playing Napoleon:

"I would have been less hesitant if someone had asked me to play Jesus. I mean no disrespect to the Christ, but Napoleon has a more powerful historical presence, where Jesus is a powerful spiritual presence. Which would be the harder role to play? For a Frenchman, I believe it would be Napoleon. I was fearful that to the French people, no performance of Napoleon Bonaparte, not even a *perfect* one, would be satisfactory."

But MGM wanted him badly and signed him on at a huge fee. The ho-hum choice to direct was Clarence Brown; William Daniels's replacement by Karl Freund, the Oscar-winning photographer of *The Good Earth*, was also unhelpful.* Freund helped Brown execute a fine opening in which the invading Russians smash up the home of Polish Count Walewski (Henry Stephenson), stopping just short of raping Garbo, his wife. But that is virtually the only action in the film, which then goes into the drawing room as a kind of heavy-footed cross between *Anna Karenina* and *Camille*.

For the only time in her American career, Garbo's lover's role was more compelling than her own. Her consolation prize was that Boyer was very good, indeed—perhaps her best co-star ever. His truly Gallic Napoleon is a bulldozer even at cards, equally believable when dreaming of his United States of Europe, when telling his own reflection in the shaving mirror, "I am a man in love!" and, later, when changing his tune and his character into a tyrant's.

Marie Walewska's interest in him is reluctant. "The destiny of Poland is in your hands!" she is told, but actually it lay elsewhere on her person. She is a virtuous wife who gives in out of duty, and her reward—as in *Karenina*—is rejection by all the male moralists around her, including her husband and brother. The latter is played by Leif Erickson, who never for a moment resembles anything but a gung-ho American.

The great Maria Ouspenskaya has a nice turn as Marie's senile old aunt, Countess Pelagia, who neither knows nor cares about Napoleon and catches him cheating at cards. But the other characters are uncompelling. As the love child of Napoleon and Marie, little Scotty Beckett's robotic performance makes one long for Philippe de Lacy or even Freddie Bartholomew: Beckett's climactic reunion scene with Boyer and Garbo has all the poignancy of a corporate board meeting.†

---

* Freund (1890–1969) was one of the geniuses of German Expressionist film of the twenties. His masterful angles, chiaroscuro lighting, and "mobile camera" work were legendary in F. W. Murnau's *The Last Laugh*, E. A. Dupont's *Variety*, and Fritz Lang's *Metropolis*. Some called him "the Giotto of the screen." After emigrating to Hollywood, his career continued through the fifties. But *Conquest* reflected little of his talent or past glory. He ended his career as chief cameraman for Desilu Productions, shooting "I Love Lucy" episodes.

† Scotty Beckett (1929–1968) began his film career as a sweet-faced boy of three in the Our Gang comedies. He played in *Anthony Adverse* and *The Charge of the Light Brigade* (both 1936) and later *Marie Antoinette* (1938), *King's Row* (1942), and *The Jolson Story* (1946), after which his career began to falter. In 1954, he was arrested for firearms violations, robbery, and passing bad checks. His first narcotics arrest was in 1957, his first suicide attempt in 1958. In 1962, his own mother had him arrested for drunkenness and "despondency." Another suicide attempt, by wrist slashing, took place in 1963. "It's a tough thing to be washed up at twenty-five," he said. Beckett died of a pill overdose on May 13, 1968.

*Scotty Beckett as Napoleon's "love child" and
Garbo as Marie Walewska in an MGM
publicity photo by William Grimes for*
Conquest *(1937)*

Normally the production values might have compensated for such failings, but they were curiously absent this time. Little of the huge budget was spent on war scenes: The Battle of Waterloo consists of two cannon shots and a map. And, once again, the terrible music of Herbert Stothart adds nothing even as it steals rampantly, and without credit, from Tchaikovsky.

The most serious problem was the screenplay. Even Behrman, who did the revisions, admitted that "the Emperor is not fully or satisfactorily developed." What Boyer accomplished was due to "his own intelligence and his own magic. He didn't have a lot of help from the script, although he had help, or inspiration, from Garbo." *Conquest* should have been much better. Garbo and Boyer struggled valiantly against Brown's dull direction and a script crippled by censorship. Among its few good passages is Napoleon's announcement that he intends to marry a Hapsburg princess to get a royal heir. Garbo responds with a beautifully delivered reproach: "Ancient blood—thin, cold, watery—a dead house and you are going to live in it, with a bride that hates you. What a pity. The liberator of Europe has become—a son-in-law!" But overall, the dialogue lacked bravura.

*Clarence Brown gives advice to Garbo during the
ballroom scene of* Conquest.

So did the role of Marie. It was too bad Salka or MGM did not heed
Garbo's own advice, as expressed in a delightfully literary allusion, to Salka
from Stockholm, on July 10, 1935:

> I was thinking about the Napoleon story and was going to ask you
> something that you probably would not like. I have a great longing for
> trousers and if I ask you in time maybe you can put in a little sequence
> with the trousers, maybe her dressed as soldier, going to Napoleon's
> tent, at night, or something. I am sorry not to contribute anything more,
> but it is merely to remind you about the trousers—/trousers, girls in
> trousers, pressed trousers, girls, trousers, trousers./ By G. Stein.

That extraordinary letter was soon followed by another. Garbo rarely
revealed her emotions on paper—except to Salka, quite vulnerably, during
the preparation of *Conquest*:

> Can it help in any way that I tell you again that I am glad God
> made me so intellegent that I can understand *wie begabt sie sind* [how
> gifted you are]? You don't like me as mutsh as you should because you

don't understand me (sounds like Mercedes). That is the one big fault you have but one person can't have everything. What I really wanted to say was, even if you do not like me as mutsh as you should, think of the moment when I [will] read you *Walewska*, and my sad face registers nothing, but a little later when I have a chance I shall grab you and say, "blessed be the God that made you." I don't suppose that is mutsh of an inspiration to give you, but its all I have for the moment.

Salka tried but failed, personally and professionally, to reassure her. So did Charles Boyer, who made it a point to get acquainted with her before production so they would feel at ease together. He found her "guarded mystery" enchanting and said there was no other actress like her in the world: "You could read on [her face] all the thoughts that came to her. Her ability to project what was within was unique." But the two of them could only do so much. The script, the censors, and Clarence Brown's direction had combined to achieve the impossible: to make Garbo uninteresting. It was as if, in the wake of Cukor's *Camille*, Brown wanted to make his own version of it, with Garbo still recovering from consumption. His pacing and continuity are constantly off.

Conquest was his last picture with Garbo, "and I enjoyed every minute of it," Brown said later. Her hypersensitivity even at this late date—in her third-to-last film, and final dramatic role ever—convinced him "not to do anything aggressive" with her. In deference to that, as all Garbo wishes, he made the decision to do nothing at all. Solely concerned with making her feel comfortable, he made her so comfortable that he eliminated all tension—erotic and dramatic—from his film. Brown may have enjoyed every minute of *Conquest*, but audiences and critics did not. It premiered in November 1937, largely to yawns. Wrote John Mosher in *The New Yorker:*

> Madame Garbo's elegant anemia, I fear, can pall a little. Her performance seems static. Beautiful, fragile, and tired, she stands in the first scene among the Cossacks invading her husband's house; and quite unchanged, fragile and tired still, she waves her last farewell to Napoleon, as though . . . loyalty is but a symptom of exhaustion. I think that for the first time Madame Garbo has a leading man who contributes more to the interest and vitality of the film than she does. She is, we may assume, grateful for such assistance.

Indeed, this last of Brown's seven Garbo films was less a Garbo vehicle than any other. Boyer earned an Oscar nomination (losing to Spencer Tracy for *Captains Courageous*, as Garbo was losing to Luise Rainer). In addition to her fee of $250,000, MGM had to pay Garbo an additional $100,000 because

A final touch-up with Charles Boyer
at left

Brown advises Garbo and Boyer
about placement—and not much else
—during the making of Conquest.

the film's 127 shooting days were way beyond schedule. *Conquest* failed to recoup its whopping $2.7 million cost—the first and only of her sound films to end up in the red, with a serious loss of $1,397,000.

But if that was an ominous sign for Garbo's film future, her financial present was just fine.

Garbo represented a staggering sum of money both for her studio and herself. In her first seven years in Hollywood, her personal earnings exceeded $1.3 million; her total income in 1932 alone was $312,000—a sum worth millions, by today's rate, in Depression-era purchasing power. The income-tax rate for her bracket (the top one) was then a mere 25 percent and her lifestyle was modest. The gross earnings of her twenty-two American films thus far exceeded $35 million. But even so, Garbonomics were neither simple nor ideal for MGM.

"She had a fanatical following in the United States, but unfortunately all those fans were not enough," said Clarence Brown. "Her pictures opened to bigger grosses than any other pictures we handled, but they didn't hold the extended run. Once the fanaticism was over, the box-office takings went way down. On the other hand, in Europe, Garbo was queen. Over there, Garbo was first, second, third and fourth."

As early as 1931, during one of the periodic MGM contract maneuverings, her business manager, Harry Edington, had said, "She has saved enough to be financially independent for life. Her money is all invested in substantial American securities."

The details of those investments are no easier to come by today than in 1931. She lost nearly a quarter million of her savings in the 1929 crash, after which Edington would not allow her to play the stock market. Some of her earnings had been invested in Sweden, and she thus escaped a total wipeout. But the specifics of where Garbo put her money—the trust funds, stocks, and real-estate investments in America and abroad—were among her most closely guarded secrets. Even her family and her lawyers never knew the full picture. Neither did her various "business administrators" and advisers, each of whom thought he was her sole handler. Max Gumpel was a good example. Aside from his personal affection for her, Gumpel was one of the shrewdest businessmen in Europe, and he gave Garbo some useful investment advice concerning Stockholm real estate.

Garbo and her studio were not the only parties concerned with her finances. She was a multimillion-dollar industry worldwide far beyond her control. To MGM fell the thankless task of policing the Garbo name and its commercial use. Several years earlier, J. Robert Rubin in MGM's New York office was panicked to learn of a trademarked product called "Garbo," which turned out to be a newfangled garbage unit. The final cable from head-quarters in Culver City concluded: "It would be fairly hard to stop the word 'Garbo' in connection with a refuse container. . . . It does not seem anyone is going to confuse the two."

Throughout her lifetime, Garbo and MGM had little choice but to ignore the plethora of minor infringements—the countless stores and restaurants and products that employed her name. "Garbo" dress designs, beauty products, hair salons, jewelry lines, and cabarets existed around the world. There was even a brand of Swedish fancy chocolate sporting her name and signature. She knew of it, but the litigation necessary to stop it was too expensive and fraught with publicity.

She was not avaricious but, unlike many other high-salaried film stars, she was shrewd enough to make certain that her current fortune would generate income-to-be. That $73,505 in the Beverly Hills First National savings account was the equivalent of perhaps ten times as much in mid-1990s dollars, and it was earning interest every day. These days she was playing it safe. Not until the Depression finally wore off in the forties would she reenter the markets; by the end of that decade, her portfolio would contain $100,000 in grade-A stocks (worth $9.8 million in 1990).* Other revenues would come in later from real estate bought and sold in Stockholm, Palm Springs, Chicago, and elsewhere; a monthly rental income of $10,000 would be generated by one property alone in Beverly Hills ("fifty feet of Rodeo Drive"). By the early fifties, trust funds would mature and pay her annuities variously estimated at between $3,500 and $100,000. Her art collection—not yet begun—would later add more millions to her worth.

With such wealth, the question of her tightness or generosity was always on people's lips. One friend answered it with the old Jack Benny joke:

STICK-UP MAN: Your money or your life!
BENNY: [Silence]
STICK-UP MAN: I said, your money or your life!
BENNY: I'm thinking, I'm thinking . . .

"She was very stingy," said Eleanor Boardman. "Of course, she didn't make much money at MGM when she first started. And when they gave her big money, she was still stingy."

Tales of Garbo's penny-pinching are legion. Her friend John Loder, the actor, accompanied her one day in 1930 to her favorite Chinese store in Hollywood. She was interested in two carved Buddhas but told the shop-keeper they were too expensive. "When he refused to come down on his

---

* For a full accounting of Garbo's worth at the time of her death, see Chapter 13, pp. 540–1.

price she walked out the door," said Loder. "She sauntered up the street a little way, turned around, and went back into the shop again. She did this three times before he came down on his price. Then she bought the two pieces. As she came out of the store with them she laughed: 'You have to do it every time or they will cheat you.'"

Once, upon checking out of a New York hotel, she asked Hubert Voight, the MGM publicist, how much she ought to tip two attendants at the front desk. He suggested five dollars each. "That's too much money for me," she said. (Voight's solution: "Write them a check—they'll frame it.") She had just returned from Stockholm and had some Swedish money that she wanted to exchange. Voight went out to take care of it for her, "but the only way I could cash it at that time of the night was to lose one-twentieth of its value." Rather than sustain the loss, she delayed returning to Hollywood over the weekend in order to cash in the currency at full value during banking hours. The difference was a total of about four dollars.

"She was terribly tight," says Barbara Barondess. "She's one of the three people in Hollywood who refused to give one-half of one percent of their salary—which was automatically taken out of all our salaries—to the Motion Picture Relief Fund. The other two were Noah Beery and Charlie Chaplin. She just didn't want to. She was full of fear that her money would disappear."

Some years later, however, a counteropinion came from her Swedish friend Kerstin Bernadotte: "If you want to pay your own way you have to be quick about it, because Garbo is generosity itself and has the skill of a conjurer when it comes to getting up her wallet first." Her miserliness, overall, was exaggerated. Garbo's caution about money reflected native Swedish conservatism and the typical Depression-era behavior of those who lost their savings and were determined never to let it happen again. "She truly never considered herself wealthy," her friend Sam Green said. "She didn't think she was going to end up in the poorhouse, but at the same time, she believed that wasting money was not the thing to do."

Her notion of thrift extended to others. At the Russian Eagle on Vine Street, for example, she liked the gypsy trio and red-smocked waiters and would always sit in the flickering candlelight of the far right corner, consuming fresh Beluga caviar. The proprietor, General Theodor Lodijensky, reported in 1934 that "Garbo is very considerate. When she is someone's guest, she always orders the dinner, table d'hôte, with no specialties. But when she is alone or the hostess, she orders anything she chooses, because she will pay the check."

Howard Dietz, who was no great friend or flatterer of Garbo, provided a more substantial revelation of her financial integrity: When one of her pictures ran six weeks over schedule, she was paid the $10,000-per-week surcharge that her contract stipulated. Garbo returned the $60,000 to MGM. She was really quite choosy about what money she would accept: In 1933 alone, she turned down $25,000 for a magazine interview, $150,000 for a series of ten short radio broadcasts, $50,000 for a one-week stage engagement in New York, and $25,000 for a cigarette endorsement. Total rejected earnings: $250,000.

Garbo's money neither came in nor went out indiscriminately. Some claimed she gave large sums, anonymously, to charitable institutions, but nobody could name them, and in general her reluctance to support any cause diminishes her. "My God!" exclaimed one of her friends. "Doesn't she *ever* think of anybody but herself?"

The basic answer was no.

It was too bad that David O. Selznick felt the need to separate once and for all from his overbearing father-in-law, Louis B. Mayer—too bad for Garbo, not Selznick. He had been brought back into MGM three years earlier as a vice president and producer when Thalberg's illness turned serious. In 1936, after *Anna Karenina* and other successes, he left to form Selznick International; *Gone With the Wind* wasn't yet a gleam in his eye. "When it became known that I was leaving," wrote Selznick, "she came to see me and pleaded with me to stay and said that I could produce all her pictures."

Selznick had been smart enough to see and blame MGM's early mishandling of Garbo for her pathological mistrust of the press. He had a heightened awareness of her psychology and a much more refined taste in scripts than his MGM colleagues, and Garbo knew it. They could have worked more and well together. Instead, Garbo after *Conquest* was increasingly on her own, and both the movie business and the world were rapidly changing. Garbo's triumphs of the apathetic will endeared her to no one in authority. Louise Brooks claimed that Garbo was marked for destruction because her independent ways threatened the moguls' power. It was less a conspiracy than a kind of inevitability: MGM would never "kick out" Garbo so long as she was a top meal ticket. Yet ominous signs, such as the following news item, would soon appear: "Reports that Metro is dropping Greta Garbo, Joan Crawford and Norma Shearer as being too expensive have been current the last two days."

For the time being, that was premature. But in Garbo's war with MGM, if that's what it was, General Brooks's battlefield analysis contained a profound truth: On the rare occasions when they attained power in Hollywood, women such as Garbo deeply frightened the men in charge. Power was even more important to them than sex or money—though money, of course, was always at the heart of power.

On one of her many transatlantic voyages

Garbo with Gayelord Hauser at his house in Coldwater Canyon, Los Angeles, 1939

CHAPTER 10

HEALTH, EDUCATION, AND
WARFARE
1938–1945

As the 1930s drew to a close, money and movies were equally tiresome subjects for Garbo. By and large, she had enough of both to last quite a while, and it was dawning on her that there were other things in life to which she might more enjoyably turn her attention. Educating Miss Garbo—the cultivation of her nonfilm interests—would be a function of her friendships with a variety of artists in other fields, many of whom wondered, then and later, if she was a closet intellectual.

Garbo herself didn't know, but she was at least and at last giving herself time to find out. The two years separating the premieres of *Conquest* in 1937 and *Ninotchka* in 1939 constituted the longest stretch ever between Garbo films. But her own leisurely work schedule was coinciding with a deadly rush of global events in which she herself would become a kind of casualty. The warning signs were there, but they were largely on the other side of the Atlantic, and Garbo was among a great majority in Hollywood who found the signals easy to ignore.

If she was not fiddling while Europe burned, she was at least consorting with the conductor. While making *Camille* in 1936, Garbo had paid a rare visit to Universal, where juvenile star Deanna Durbin was filming *One Hundred Men and a Girl*. In that charming Depression tale—Hedda Hopper called it "the one perfect musical picture"—Durbin as the daughter of an unemployed musician pesters Leopold Stokowski to give Dad a job. Garbo liked Durbin's singing voice, and the teenager was thrilled to meet the queen of the movies. On Durbin's set that day, Garbo met Stokowski—then enjoying great popularity as the first "crossover" star from the symphonic hall to films. Anita Loos claimed that "Stokowski had it in mind to have an

Mischa Auer, conductor Leopold Stokowski,
Adolphe Menjou, and Deanna Durbin in a
publicity shot for Universal's One Hundred Men
and a Girl *(1936)*

affair with Garbo" and that he enlisted Loos in the matchmaking. Asked to arrange a small dinner party with Garbo as one of the guests, she obliged. "Stoky didn't waste much time on the overture," said Loos. "He told Garbo they were destined to have a history-making romance, like Wagner's with Cosima. It was written in the stars. . . . The gods had made their decision."

It seems unlikely that such a hard sell would have suited Garbo, but they delighted one another and soon began "dating" and pairing off at Salka's salon. Gottfried Reinhardt recalled that, one evening there, "Garbo knelt before Stokowski and listened, enraptured, to such tales as when he spent an entire day—from sunrise to sunset—with a native sage on an Indian mountaintop, gazing at the landscape spread out below and discussing the eschatological problems of the world, only to realize, after taking leave of each other, that his interlocutor had spoken no English and he did not know a single word of any Hindu dialect, and yet they had understood each other completely."

The maestro could be very otherworldly. But he was worldly, too, and he and Garbo began to appear more frequently in public and in the news-

Garbo with friend Robert Reud, who once offered to marry her so she could thwart deportation, in New York, 1938. She was quick on the draw with her hat, but forgot about the mirror behind her.

papers. Reports of romance multiplied greatly in October 1937, when Stokowski's second wife, Evangeline, took up residence in Nevada. On December 1, she filed for divorce,* and a few days later, reporter Jim Simmons of the Los Angeles *Examiner* ambushed Garbo in Hollywood as she was getting out of her car in front of George Cukor's house. Garbo was furious, but for some reason she answered The Big Question:

"No, no—I will not marry Mr. Stokowski. These rumors are absurd. I won't deny that Mr. Stokowski and I are very good friends. But as for marriage to him—no. That is out of the question."

Soon after his divorce was granted, Stokowski was present for dockside farewells when Garbo left to spend Christmas in Sweden. On February 5, 1938, Stokowski, too, crossed the Atlantic, on the *Conte di Savoia*, which reached Naples seven days later. Garbo was then staying at Hårby, the beautiful thousand-acre forested estate with fifteen-room manor house, which

---

* Garbo was a catalyst but not the cause of the breakup. Just six weeks later, on January 27, 1938, Evangeline Stokowski married the former Prince Alexis Zalstem-Zalessky of Russia.

she had purchased for her mother, brother Sven, and his family in 1937. The Wachtmeisters had helped to find the place, situated on Lake Sillen outside the town of Gnesta in the county of Södermanland, an hour's train ride southwest of Stockholm. It was income producing, with farmland and with timber to be harvested from the groves of larches, birches, firs, and poplars.

This was, in fact, the first time Garbo had seen Hårby; she had sent the money to buy it from California. The typically Swedish house was cream colored with wooden shutters and pointed gables highlighted by bright touches of green, red, and blue. She was greeted upon arrival by a picturesque sight and a warm, traditional welcome: Her mother and brother had lined the snow-covered drive from the road to their door with dozens of torches, and the curtains of every window had been drawn to reveal lamps shining brightly within. Garbo had said more than once that the things she missed most in Hollywood were smorgasbords and snow.

The long Swedish winter "slows down the tempo of daily life to a quiet pace incredible to those who have never experienced it," wrote Hettie Grimstead, who gained access and information from the servants. "[The] white and blue bathroom is surely the smallest ever owned by a famous film star. It has no provision for cosmetics." When the quiet pace became too dull, Garbo sometimes went in to Stockholm:

> On these days she leaves Hårby alone in a modest car whose chained wheels lumber slowly along the snow-stacked country roads and stays at the apartment of a woman painter she has known for many years. Together they go to watch the winter sports, the ice-yachting and skate-sailing on the frozen waters of the great Archipelago, the hockey matches at the Stadium and the skiing on the hill at Fiskartorpet. Like most Swedish women, Garbo is an accomplished skater.
>
> One night Garbo went to her own cinema in Stockholm. She is the only star in the world who has a motion picture theater named after her: "The Garbioscope" stands in what Garbo often describes unaffectedly as "my part of the city"—the densely populated working class district. . . .
>
> She was the center of a gay informal dinner party at the Grand Hotel one night, sitting in the Winter Garden restaurant. . . . She wore an ankle-length gown of midnight blue velvet. Over it went a sweeping blue velvet cloak which pulled the fur-lined collar across her head exactly like a becoming monk's hood. . . .
>
> She buys all the American and European film magazines and takes them back to Hårby to peruse as she lounges beside the stove.

After two months, melancholia set in, as ever. Sven's hapless farming efforts and mismanagement saddened her. And Salka had just written of romantic woes with Gottfried Reinhardt back home. But a legendary rendezvous was in the works, as Garbo confided in her soulful, four-page reply to Salka:

> I do not believe in sorrow. Having been my companion all my life, I definitely do not believe in it. . . .
>
> I live in my brothers place which is a "mess". I tryed to find something that would have helped him in life but it is not right. He can't take care of it and now I don't know anymore what to do. I have been trying to find furnitures for the house, otherwise I go nowhere, see no one. Just like in Brentwood. . . .
>
> Soon I am going to see Stoky with the help of divine power. God help me if the [reporters] catch me. But I must try. I always sit in a corner somewhere and I don't see anything. So I am really going to try this time. . . . Is Gottfrid still with you or have you sent him away from you? It is hard and sad to be alone but sometimes its even more difficult to be with someone. . . .
>
> But somewhere in this world are a few beengs who do not have it as we have. Of that I am certain. And if I would stop making film I could go and see if I could find out a little about it. And from the sublime [to—] *Walewska* opens here in a few days and I'm not glad that it does. . . .
>
> Live well, dear sir—and will you greet your children and my and your Hardt.

Fearfully but according to plan, Garbo left Sweden and joined Stokowski in Rome on February 24. The next day, they set out by car for what was to be an idyllic month in Ravello at the medieval Villa Cimbrone, whose picture-perfect cloisters and gardens overlooked the Bay of Salerno. *The New Yorker* normally eschewed celebrity-travel reports but couldn't resist this time. E. W. Selsey got the Villa Cimbrone staff to tell all:

> [Garbo's] luggage consisted of a small, worn suitcase containing no dress, no dressing gown, no bedroom slippers, one pair of blue espadrilles, one pair of coarse flannel sleeping pajamas, and several pots of some sort of special jam. . . . The Italian cook was never able to discover what kind of fruit the jam was made of, since Miss Garbo kept it locked in her bedroom all day, brought it down to the breakfast table at eight-thirty sharp, scooped it onto her corn flakes, and poured her coffee over

the mixture.* Before breakfast, she and Leopold Stokowski had already done half an hour of Swedish exercises on the belvedere [which was] built nine centuries ago in the solid rock, dominating the whole Mediterranean Gulf of Salerno and the little city of Amalfi, a sheer fifteen hundred feet below.

[During the exercises], an eavesdropping gardener caught the conductor of The Philadelphia Orchestra being reproved with the words, "Vun, two, vun, two, Mister-r Sto-kovf-ski, vy can't you keep time, vun, two."

The romantic element was real, but the sexual element doubtful. Garbo's quarters, as always, were quite separate from those of her host. She went to bed promptly at eight; Stokowski did not. They did not sleep together literally or figuratively. "His role was that of escort," says a mutual friend. "He may have wanted more, but he would never have set himself up for any sexual rejection. He was the most vain man I ever knew."

In any case, the only "idyllic" days were the first three or four before their presence was discovered. From then on, the villa was besieged by reporters and photographers from Naples and by hundreds of local villagers hoping for a glimpse of the one they called *la Donna Misteriosa*, and the ongoing circus was unconducive to *l'amour*. Four carabinieri and three police dogs had to be posted at the gate. Sacks of letters and parcels arrived daily for Garbo, who ordered them all thrown into the incinerator—manuscripts, plays, books, poems, the whole lot. One package contained a brassiere and a request for Garbo to wear it, sign it, and then return to sender. MGM's Rome office didn't help: It reported marriage was imminent and that Wallace Beery was coming to serve as Stokowski's best man! Hitler's upcoming visit to Rome and most other international news stories were wiped off the front pages in favor of the Garbo-Stokowski "romance."

Stokowski was fairly blasé about it, but Garbo was beside herself. What to do? After two weeks under siege, the conductor convinced her that if she gave them what they wanted—an interview and a "photo opportunity"— they would go away. He was wrong, of course, but Garbo consented and held a scolding press conference in the Villa Cimbrone library on March 17, 1938. Her first words to the assembled reporters suggested her mood: "Well, what do you want?"

They wanted to know if she and Stokowski were already married or planning to marry. She shook her head no to both.

"There are some people who want to get married, and there are others

---

* As she had come to Italy from Sweden, the mysterious jam was undoubtedly lingonberry, her favorite Swedish delicacy.

who do not," she said. "I never had any impulse to go to the altar." Then, after a pause, she surprised them all with a long and deep-felt reflection:

> I haven't many friends. I haven't seen much of the world, either. My friend, Mr. Stokowski, who has been very much to me, offered to take me around to see some beautiful things. I optimistically accepted. I was naïve enough to think that I could travel without being discovered and without being hunted. Why can't we avoid being followed and examined? It is cruel to bother people who want to be left in peace. This kills beauty for me. I live in a corner. I am typically alone, but there are so many beautiful things in the world that I would like to see before they are destroyed. . . . I wish I could be otherwise, but I cannot. I don't like this. I only want to be left alone.

With a sigh and another few words, she left. So did the wire-service reporters, but other writers and photographers failed to keep their end of Stokowski's bargain and remained to hound the couple to the end of their stay. For Garbo, it was thoroughly spoiled. They left Ravello for a week in Rome, stopping in Pompeii and Naples on the way, then sailed to North Africa for a fortnight of touring before returning to Italy—with the press in hot pursuit.*

From Italy, they drove to Sweden, arriving in early May and staying three months at Hårby. There they took their walks and vegetable-dominated meals, with occasional visits to Gnesta (where Stokowski mailed a letter to Jean Sibelius) and to Stockholm for concerts and antique browsing in the Old Town. The two artists had long philosophical discussions during their stay at Hårby, but there were also long silences, with which the actress was more comfortable than the conductor.

Stokowski left Sweden at the end of July. Garbo remained for two more months, disappearing into the true solitude she liked best. The honeymoon was over, and—if it ever existed—so was the romance. Thereafter, they spoke by phone on a number of occasions and she took him up on an offer of his West Coast home as her temporary residence. But Garbo and Leopold Stokowski never saw each other again.

Upon his return arrival in New York, Stokowski was Garboesque in his secrecy about a project called *Fantasia*. He admitted that he would soon

---

* Cecil Beaton claimed Stokowski sent telegrams to the UPI at every stop along the way. Ernst Lubitsch recalled Garbo's telling him "about her affair with Stokowski, about traveling with him—and she was so funny! About how Stokowski would try to play the idea of wanting to hide from the crowd, and then becoming furious when no one recognized him."

travel to the West Coast, "not to meet Miss Garbo but to discuss with Walt Disney some cartoon pictures for which he will arrange the music," said the New York *Post* on August 15, 1938. "It was reported some time ago that a picture based on Paul Dukas' composition, 'The Sorcerer's Apprentice,' would be made under the Mickey Mouse imprint with Stokowski accompaniment. But even that the conductor wouldn't confirm. 'You will have to ask Mr. Disney,' he said."

Garbo returned to America on the *Kungsholm*, arriving October 7 after having agreed unexpectedly to a shipboard press conference filled with more questions about Stokowski and marriage. When asked if she'd enjoyed her vacation, she replied, "You cannot have a vacation without peace, and you cannot have peace unless you are left alone."

She had several days in New York before boarding her train to Los Angeles, and she spent them seeing shows—and enraging the hairdressers' convention then in progress. At the Coiffure Guild's "World's Fair Night," model Syd Semmelman wore her hair shaped like the trylon obelisk and perisphere symbols of the 1939 World's Fair, but Syd was upstaged by the absent Garbo as reported in the October 19, 1938, *New York Times:*

> The International Master Ladies Hairdressers Assn. and the Coiffure Guild of New York, which are strenuously fostering the upswing hair style, adopted yesterday a joint resolution criticizing Greta Garbo for wearing her hair not only down but straight.
>
> The hair style with which Miss Garbo returned from Europe ten days ago was characterized by the resolution as "wholly unsuited for wear by her or by the women of this country." It was said further that if it should be popularized by Miss Garbo's adoption it "would have the effect of working vast injury to the hair stylists and hairdressers of the United States [due to Garbo's] tremendous personal influence over hair and other styles."

Cosmopolitan New York could be just as silly as Hollywood when it wanted to. For a change, she was almost eager to get back to California, where—at her request—Salka and George Cukor (recently fired from *Gone With the Wind*) were trying to develop her next film project. On the day of the hairdressers' flap, she mailed Salka the claim checks for her steamer trunks, which had been sent ahead, and asked her to collect them. Among the instructions:

"If you have my trunks I can take some things and go right to Stokis place. . . . Please don't tell Cukor where we will meet. And ask if he will be silent about my coming if it is not in the newspapers. Let us meet in Pasadena. I will wire 'meet Bieler'—that means Pasadena."*

Faithful Salka did her bidding, as always. Nothing came of the Cukor talks. Some of her friends thought she seemed mellower in the wake of her trip and that the Stokowski interlude had kindled her musical interests; others said he'd had no influence at all on her musical tastes, which remained as quirky as ever. "Turn that music off," she once told a host who was shocked at her rejection of the Mozart on his phonograph. "I never listen to anything as nice as that!" To an opera-buff friend, she was equally dismissive but self-deprecating: "You just accumulate culture," she told him. "I'm accumulating nothing—no culture of any kind." And she was certainly no friend to dance: "I must have seen it some time or another," she said of *Giselle*, then added categorically, "I loathe ballet."

Music is the most abstract art form, and Garbo was concrete. Even so, her musical horizons were expanded these days through discussions with composers Miklos Rozsa, Bronislaw Kaper, and David Diamond, and especially with Edward Steuermann, a pioneer interpreter of Schoenberg's twelve-tone music. Steuermann was often to be found at the home of his sister, Salka Viertel—and so was Garbo, who became very fond of him and once presented him with a "musical necktie" (which he hated and gave to Salka, who gave it to Schoenberg, who loved it). "She was in great awe of him," says David Diamond, and she seemed to find the difficult, dissonant music he championed more compelling than that of the classical or romantic composers. Others found it less compelling. Peter Viertel recalls the evening his uncle played "Fifty Variations on a Theme by Webern": "Oscar Levant was there, and he kept counting them. It was two hours long, at the end of which he said, 'You go out whistling the tunes.' "

The flow of German, Austrian, and other Central European refugees was now increasing from a trickle to a stream, and most of those who came to Los Angeles passed through Salka's open door. On a given evening, Schoenberg or Igor Stravinsky might be there, recalls Diamond, "and they were always talking about anything but movies. That's why Garbo enjoyed stopping in so often, though she also enjoyed the food. But mostly it was the conversation—the situation in Europe, the latest essay by Karl Kraus—one talked about everything at Salka's."

Bertolt Brecht and Aldous Huxley were among many writers at the Viertel salon, and in company with them Garbo rarely spoke and never competed for the conversational floor. But she was a careful listener, and her interest

* For the identity of "Bieler," see footnote, page 371.

in books was not restricted to Salka's house or guests. Her preference was for the nineteenth-century Russians: Tolstoy fascinated her even before *Love* and *Anna Karenina*, and more afterward. She knew Dostoyevsky's works, but she most loved Turgenev and sometimes, at intimate gatherings, she could even be persuaded to read from such essays as "The Execution of Troppmann" in the *Literary Reminiscences*, an esoteric volume she knew well. Turgenev's *Nest of Gentlefolk* perhaps most appealed to her—a novel about the impossibility of happiness: "You only understand someone close to you fully when you've parted from him," says one character. Another leaves the room during a musical soiree because "Beethoven agitated her nerves too much."

Garbo also loved Goethe and was a frequent reader of Heine and of other German, English, and Swedish poets. "She has no set reading habits," her friend George Schlee said years later. "She will read anything suggested by someone she respects. [She] is avid for information [and] likes to be led. Same goes for theater and movies. She will see anything a friend recommends as being particularly good."

At about this time, Garbo met Erich Maria Remarque, whose *All Quiet on the Western Front* had moved her deeply. They saw each other subsequently in Europe and New York, and—according to Remarque's wife, actress Paulette Goddard—had a brief affair. Goddard was not among Garbo's admirers; her reliability (and her husband's) can be questioned in later quoting him on Garbo as saying, "She was lousy in bed."

Among writers in English, Garbo knew and liked the poetry of Marianne Moore and often quoted Hemingway and Emily Brontë, but a peculiar psychological glitch made novel reading problematic for her. "*Gatsby* is short, but I couldn't finish it," she told her friend Raymond Daum. "I read thirty-five pages in two months' time. Dangerous things started to come up and I couldn't read it, I had to put it down. Then I picked up Conrad—*The Secret Sharer*." That eerie tale of a sea captain who harbors a murderer made her so nervous that she couldn't finish it. "When I read, I get afraid that something terrible will happen." On the other hand, "If nothing terrible happens, I don't remember it."

In reading, as all else—diffident.

Meanwhile, she was the unwitting inspiration of writers she did not know. "Tell Madame Garbo that I had her in mind when I wrote about Elisabeth in *Les Enfants terribles*," Jean Cocteau wrote to Roland Caillaud, who was Garbo's neighbor in California for a time. But one author she inspired at closer range.

In February of 1938, Aldous and Maria Huxley were lured back to Hollywood. They were welcomed by Mercedes de Acosta, who was very fond of Maria—"Belgian, fragile, charming, smart"—and very pleased that Aldous was now eating only naturally prepared food, cooked by the sun's reflection in a mirror. One of the first "new" people he met was Salka, whose influence was such that *less than a week later* he was asked to write a film script for MGM based on the life of Marie Curie—Garbo to star, George Cukor to direct. When Huxley's contract was signed in July ($15,000 for eight weeks' work), he, Cukor, and Salka met to thrash out a story at the home of MGM executive Bernie Hyman. The discovery of radium was both photogenic and dramatic, Huxley said, with all those glass tubes bubbling and glowing in the dark. Hyman wanted him to spice up the story, but Salka privately urged Huxley to stick with the facts and with his family's innate gift for presenting science to the public. This literary-scientific project indeed suited him perfectly, and he even found a sex angle: Madame Curie chose her lab assistants for their looks and made love to them in a bed over which hung a picture of her husband, Pierre.

Huxley's novelistic, 145-page treatment, dated August 26, 1938, portrayed Curie as the protofeminist she was, journeying from her one-room laboratory to the first woman's lecture chair at the Sorbonne. He waited for the studio's response. When none came, he went on to other things. Scott Fitzgerald later worked on the story. So did Salka, who revealed its fate:

"It was instantly forgotten. . . . On the next occasion, I asked Bernie what happened to [the Huxley script]. Embarrassed, he admitted that he had had no time to read it but had given it to Goldie, his secretary, who told him, 'It stinks.'"

Garbo's professional plans were formulating in her own slow, circuitous way. While abroad, she had said she would like to appear in a Swedish film, if and when she stopped working in America, and that she was much impressed with two recent British historical pictures, *Rembrandt* (1936), with Charles Laughton, and *Fire Over England* (1937), with Flora Robson. She thought Robson "magnificent" as Queen Elizabeth:

I would have been very proud to give such a performance myself. [But] I am tired of period pictures and I want to do something modern now. My next film is to be a comedy. . . . Will I be allowed to keep my lover in it? Certainly I am hoping so. Don't you think it is high time they let me end a picture happily with a kiss? I do. I seem to have lost so many attractive men in the final scenes.

Both her mood and her statement were unusually cheerful in that Swedish autumn of 1938. It appears as though she knew all along what her next project would be; that poor Huxley and Marie Curie were never really seriously in the running. In any case, now, in early 1939, she took the biggest gamble of her career: a comedy—her first in Hollywood—at a salary less than half that she'd been paid for *Anna Karenina*.

For years, Garbo had admired the films of Ernst Lubitsch. After meeting the ebullient director at Salka's, she dropped by several times, unannounced, at his house on Camden Avenue. Lubitsch, for his part, was eager to work with her and to be the first to take the screen's biggest star into the realm of comedy.

One afternoon while walking with Mercedes on the Santa Monica beach, Garbo said, "That's Ernst Lubitsch's house. He is the only great director out here. Let's go and see him." It was a rare impulse for Garbo, who knocked on the window until actress Ona Munson—then Lubitsch's paramour—came and invited them in. When Lubitsch found them in the living room, he let out a joyful whoop. Mercedes recalled:

> He was a small man with dark hair brushed down straight over his brow. He had a large black cigar in his mouth—a man of enormous energy. He spoke English with a strong German-Jewish accent. "Mein Gott, mein Gott, Greta!" he cried as he seized her in his arms and kissed her wildly. "Gott, such a surprise . . . Greta, Greta, sit down and never go away." He pushed her onto the sofa and sat beside her holding her hand. . . .
>
> "Greta, why don't you tell those idiots in your studio to let us do a picture together? Gott, how I vould love to direct a picture for you." Greta answered, "Ernst, you tell them. I am far too tired to have a conversation with any studio executive." She said this very sadly but for some reason we all laughed. Lubitsch shook his head. "What fools they are. How vunderful Greta and I vould be together. Ve vould make a vunderful picture."

That visit had taken place before Garbo's six-month Swedish holiday. MGM, since then, had told Lubitsch he could direct a film called *Ninotchka* if he could persuade Garbo to star in it, and Salka Viertel arranged another meeting. Screenwriter Walter Reisch was also present and recalled:

> Garbo arrived, said she was on a diet and would just listen as he discussed the film. Poor Lubitsch had ordered an immense meal—the antipasto, a dozen special dishes, and the chianti, and the frutti, and the cheeses were already on the table.
>
> "I never touch lunch," Garbo said.

"All right," said Lubitsch. "I will eat and you listen." He started telling Garbo the story. He got more excited with each line, and forgot the food. An hour later, when he had finished talking, he looked at the table—it was cleaned out. Garbo had been so carried away by his enthusiasm that she had forgotten her diet and put away the whole meal.

The basic comic idea was rather similar to Anatole Litvak's *Tovarich* (1937), with Claudette Colbert and Charles Boyer, a tale of Russian exiles in Paris—the stage version of which Garbo had seen and liked in Stockholm. Lubitsch was convinced that the commissar's role in the story could be feminized and tailored to Garbo.

Ninotchka, actually, did not start out to be a political satire. It began when Salka told writer Melchior Lengyel that MGM wanted to make a comedy it could advertise with "Garbo Laughs!" as *Anna Christie* had been promoted with "Garbo Talks!" The next day, Lengyel had an idea: "Russian girl saturated with Bolshevist ideals goes to . . . Paris. She meets romance and has an uproarious good time. Capitalism not so bad, after all." MGM would eventually pay him fifteen thousand dollars for those three sentences.

But first he had to sell the idea to Garbo. Soon enough, he was summoned to Salka's. "When I arrived," Lengyel said, "Miss Garbo was in the swimming pool. I was introduced to her at the edge of the pool. 'You have a comedy for me?' she asked. I told her that it was yet but an idea and I read the memo from my notebook. She was highly amused. In fact she laughed out loud at the possibilities the idea offered. 'I like it. I will do it.' Then she turned and dived back into the pool."

Viertel and Lengyel were to write. Both of them failed. So did S. N. Behrman, though he did come up with the notion that their tough female Bolshevik should fall in love with a French gigolo. Lubitsch put Walter Reisch on the script and soon added Charles Brackett and Billy Wilder for good measure.

Wilder was the most politically radical of the writers, but that did not prevent him from poking fun at Communism. "That idea of rigid, ice-cold lady commissar who softens under the onslaught of our corrupt capitalistic world is especially funny when you think what's happening now," says Wilder today.

The trick, he knew, was that it had to be funny but at the same time realistic. If she was to be a real woman with brains, she (and the film) had to address the reality of Soviet life. Thus did *Ninotchka* break the primary film taboo of its day: It was a "serious satire," teeming with references to five-year plans and purge trials and other things requiring no little political sophistication to grasp.*

The well-known plot has Garbo as a humorless Communist sent from Moscow to check up on three inept male comrades, one of whom—Felix Bressart—bears an uncanny resemblance to the wrong Marx, Groucho. They have been assigned to recover the jewels smuggled out of Russia by Grand Duchess Swana (Ina Claire), whose aristocratic boyfriend (Melvyn Douglas) agrees to deflect Ninotchka by romancing her.

Garbo's inherently fine timing is aided by lines that might well have come out of her own mouth. "Don't make an issue of my womanhood," she tells her agents when they apologize for not greeting her with flowers. With a cold stare at the three cigarette girls in their room, she observes, "Comrades, you seem to have been smoking a lot."

How are things in Moscow? they ask nervously.

"Very good," she replies. "The last mass trials were a great success. There are going to be fewer but better Russians."

But her best moments are reserved for Melvyn Douglas and his shameless advances.

"Must you flirt?" she asks.

"I don't have to, but I find it natural," he answers.

"Suppress it," she returns.

Later, she listens with a steely gaze as Douglas delivers a long declaration of love, then waits a perfect beat before the noncommittal reply: "You are very talkative."

He is determined to crack her humorlessness, and it finally happens, no thanks to his bad jokes but rather to his accidental pratfall—falling off his chair in a bistro. Garbo was very nervous about the famous nightclub sequence in which she gets drunk on champagne and laughs "with abandon," but Lubitsch worked with her calmly and patiently. Asked by writer Garson Kanin why he put her in a comedy in the first place, Lubitsch replied:

> Because she was funny. You couldn't see it? You didn't know how funny she was off the screen? . . . And I knew she could be funny on the screen. . . . Most of them are so heavy. Heavy! But she was light, light always, and for comedy, nothing matters more. When someone has a light touch, they can play comedy, and it doesn't hurt if they're beautiful. There was only one thing worried me a little. I wondered if she could laugh, because I didn't have a finish if she didn't have a laugh. She had the most beautiful smile. What am I saying? She had

---

* Nine years later, the U.S. State Department sent thirty-five prints of the film to Italy for wide distribution during the "Red-threatened" elections of 1948.

a whole collection of smiles. . . . Warm, motherly, friendly, polite, sexy, amused, mysterious. Beautiful smiles. But a smile is not a laugh. . . .

I said to her one day, "Can you laugh?" and she said, "I think so." I said to her, "Do you often laugh?" And she said, "Not often." And I said, "Could you laugh right now?" And she said, "Let me come back tomorrow." And then next day she came back and she said, "All right. I'm ready to laugh." So I said, "Go ahead." And she laughed and it was beautiful! And she made me laugh, and there we sat in my office like two loonies, laughing for about ten minutes. From that moment on, I knew I had a picture.

Lubitsch thought Garbo the least vain actress he ever knew. "Having worked with many women stars, I have found that one of the difficulties in working with them is their slavish devotion to the mirror," he said. "In the eight weeks during which I worked with Garbo she never looked into the mirror once unless I told her to do so. Nobody but the film director can appreciate the significance of that." But she was also full of inhibitions— "probably the most inhibited person I ever worked with," he said—and when it came time to laugh, she made it clear that "she disliked playing the scene in front of all the extras."

Lubitsch's solution was simple: He cleared the set and later intercut the takes of her and Douglas with the crowd scenes. As a result, Garbo laughs—long and loud and a bit forced, but charmingly. The rumor that it was dubbed is absurd, says Wilder. There was no need; her real laugh was wonderful.

Lubitsch did everything to assist her. Between scenes, he let her retire to her dressing room and lie down until needed again, whereupon a soft buzzer would summon her. Wilder recalled only one time when Lubitsch ever changed a line on the set—for Garbo. She was orating against capitalist trains: The first-class section has velvet chairs, the second-class leather seats, the third-class wooden benches. "We Communists," she was to say, "will change this from the bottom up."

It may be recalled that Garbo was always peculiarly offended by jokes related to the posterior. She objected. Lubitsch took it out.

Mercedes described the spring and summer of 1939 as one of the happiest times of Garbo's life:

Never since I had known her had she been in such good spirits. She had been shooting the first gay picture she had ever done, and Lubitsch was directing it. "[It is] the first time I have had a great director since

ABOVE: *With Melvyn Douglas (and Ernst Lubitsch's hands at right)*
during a rehearsal on the set of Ninotchka *(1939)*
BELOW: *And her three visiting comrades from Moscow, Sig Rumann, Felix*
Bressart, and Alexander Granach, in Ninotchka

I am in Hollywood," she said.* Greta was a changed person; [she] laughed constantly. She would imitate Lubitsch's accent. . . . It was fascinating to see how by playing a gay role rather than a sad one her whole personality changed.

Not entirely. Garbo, as always, would not let strangers watch her being filmed—even screenwriters—but Wilder contrived now and then to sneak onto the set and hide behind a flat. "The face, what was it about that face?" he said. "You could read into it all the secrets of a woman's soul. She became all women on the screen. Not on the sound stage. *The miracle happened in that film emulsion*. Who knows why?"

Co-star Ina Claire, similarly, once coaxed the stagehands into letting her peek for one of Garbo's most emotional scenes.

"Are you ready, Miss Garbo?" asked Lubitsch.

"As soon as Miss Claire gets from behind that curtain, yes," said Garbo, whose instinct for detecting voyeurs was uncanny.

Ina moved to a more concealed location and, in fact, watched the take. "I am here to tell you that scene was one of the most extraordinary things I've ever seen," she told Garbo when it was over. "And damn you, I saw you cry."

"Very unmanly of me, wasn't it?" said Garbo, and returned to her dressing room.

At the beginning of production, there had been concern about possible tension between Garbo and Claire—the ex–Mrs. John Gilbert—but the two women became friends from the start. Ina, a former variety artist, amused Garbo between scenes by tap dancing, among other things, and Garbo's dresser, Hazel, once found her in her dressing room trying to imitate the steps.

Melvyn Douglas was competent, but it is a Cary Grant role, and we miss him in it for Garbo's sake as well as our own. The laughs diminish sharply midway in the film, once she and Douglas fall in love. Claire as the comic villainess—with her bizarre hairdo and accent—temporarily steals the show. But Garbo steals it back in time for the touching final scene in Moscow: "Bombs will fall, civilizations will crumble—but *not yet . . . Give us our moment!*"

Ninotchka completed shooting on July 27, 1939. Between then and its premiere at Grauman's Chinese on October 6, 1939, the USSR and Nazi Germany signed a treaty of friendship. The Lubitsch Touch is more of a

---

* *Sic transit* Hollywood: Lubitsch was available to direct *Ninotchka* only because he had been removed from *The Women* and replaced with George Cukor—who was available to direct *The Women* only because he had been removed from *Gone With the Wind*.

fingerprint in *Ninotchka*, but for Garbo in 1939 it was a triumphant success. "Garbo Laughs!" the ads promised, and she delivered.

When Mercedes saw the advertisements, she was shocked that the mere fact of Garbo's laughing was so ballyhooed and considered so remarkable: "MGM employed her from 1925 to 1938 before they discovered she could play comedy. . . . It is a sad commentary on the stupidity of the studio that they did not discover this until it was too late. Had they given her happy and fun-making roles, she might still be in pictures." Garbo didn't have "an ounce of humor in her," said Melvyn Douglas later, but Lubitsch had cleverly utilized "all her eccentricities for comic effect."

Frank Nugent in the *New York Times* enthused: "Garbo's *Ninotchka* is one of the sprightliest comedies of the year, a gay and impertinent and malicious show which never pulls the punch lines (no matter how far below the belt they may land) and finds the screen's austere first lady of drama playing in deadpan comedy with the assurance of a Buster Keaton."

Otis Ferguson called it "neither heavy with Thought nor absurd with venom; it is partly true and possibly beautiful, but it is certainly good." Others were critical of Lubitsch in general and *Ninotchka* in particular. "I would never impose a performance on any actor," said Garbo's most frequent director, Clarence Brown. "That was one of the troubles with Lubitsch's pictures. He was one of the greatest directors, but every player that ever worked for him played Ernst Lubitsch. He used to show them how to do everything, right down to the minutest detail. . . . He knew his art better than anybody. But his actors followed his performance. They had no chance to give one of their own."

Garbo herself had no complaints. *Ninotchka* earned her her fourth and last Academy Award nomination. Bette Davis had snapped up the role she declined in *Dark Victory*, but neither Davis nor Garbo took home the Oscar. It was Vivien Leigh's year, and *Gone With the Wind* swept everything and everyone else away.

Miss Leigh, on the other hand, was not swept away by Miss Garbo. Some months earlier, George Cukor hosted a luncheon in honor of the recently arrived Scarlett O'Hara and her boyfriend, Laurence Olivier. Garbo was among the guests, and after lunch she and Olivier strolled off together into Cukor's beautiful gardens to converse and bury the *Queen Christina* hatchet. Leigh was left behind, smoldering.

"Look at him," she fumed to Garson Kanin. "He's behaving like a ninny. . . . Why he's sucking up to her, I simply can't fathom. She once had him sacked." When the strollers returned, Leigh switched on a dazzling smile and said, "Ah, there you are! *Bon promenade?*" After Garbo disengaged, a major spat ensued. Leigh demanded to know the subject "of your *enthralling* little tête-à-tête." It was about *gardens*, for God's sake, Olivier replied, and when Leigh wouldn't believe him, he reconstructed the conversation with a perfect imitation of Garbo's voice:

"We have gardens in Sweden."

"Yes, you must have . . ."

"In some of our Swedish gardens, we grow fruit. Apples."

"We have apples in England, too . . ."

"Do you have oranges?"

"No. No oranges. But we have peaches."

"We have peaches in Sweden."

"Oh, I'm so glad! And do you have nectarines?"

"No. No nectarines—cabbages . . ."

"Gooseberries?"

"What are gooseberries?"

"Gooseberries. You know. To make gooseberry jam with. Or a pie. Or a gooseberry fool."

"What is a gooseberry fool?"

"Well, it's the same as a raspberry fool or a damson fool, except that it's made with gooseberries."

"Do you have artichoke?"

"We have them but I don't think we grow them. We import them. However, we do have asparagus."

"We have asparagus, too. But no Cranshaw melon."

"Nor do we."

"Cranshaw melon is good."

"Watermelon is good."

"And cantaloupe?"

"I don't like cantaloupe."

"I like this garden. It's a nice garden."

"Yes, it is. A very nice garden."

And that was it until you said, "Ah, there you are."

Events in Europe were no longer possible for a transplanted European to ignore. A few weeks before *Ninotchka* opened, Germany invaded Poland, and Garbo sent a radiogram to her mother and brother and his family instructing them to come immediately to the United States and wiring the money needed to do so.

They came by ship and, after a three-day, cross-country train ride, arrived in California. The reunion was more somber than joyous, but Anna, Sven, and Marguerite Gustafson, and their seven-year-old daughter, Gray, now settled in with Garbo on Bedford Drive in Beverly Hills for the next six months and began to make a new life for themselves.

Her mother spoke no English, but Sven knew a little and sister-in-law Marguerite was an American. If anyone thought Garbo's little niece was in for a fairy-tale experience, they were wrong. "I never went to the studio with her or thought much about it," says Gray Gustafson Reisfield. "She was just a part of the family." Later reports of squabbling and discord in Garbo's new domestic arrangement are debunked by Reisfield with a simple, ironclad declaration: "You never fought with my aunt in my family."

The other addition to Garbo's family circle at this time was not a blood relation, but he was an important one for life. The nutritionist Gayelord Hauser would soon be writing numerous books on diet and beauty, of which *Look Younger, Live Longer* (1950) and *Be Happier, Be Healthier: New Guide To Intelligent Reducing* (1952) were the greatest successes.* Food, he said, "has to look good, taste good and do good." Hauser was no quack and his theory of health no passing fad: Exercise and diet are the keys to longevity, and one's diet should be largely but not militantly vegetarian. His basic ideas have been modified and embellished by many others but never much improved upon.

Among various people who claim to have introduced Garbo to Hauser are Barbara Barondess, who was then decorating Hauser's apartment, and Mercedes de Acosta, a health-food fanatic who was devoted to Hauser's principles. Hauser's own devotion was to such diverse celebrity clients as Clara Bow, Adele Astaire, Albert Schweitzer, Eva and Juan Perón, and the Duchess of Windsor, whom he induced to drink garlic juice—regularly.

In late summer of 1939, after Garbo finished shooting *Ninotchka*, Mercedes took her to Hauser's beautiful Sunrise Hill estate high up in Coldwater Canyon, where he lived with his "manager," Frey Brown. Garbo didn't want to go, but Mercedes tempted her with the promise of a vegetarian feast. Garbo liked the gregarious, handsome, six-foot-three-inch Hauser, whose first meal for her was veggie-burgers, consisting of wild rice and chopped hazelnuts, mixed with an egg and fried in soybean oil. Dessert was broiled grapefruit with molasses in the center. One of the few ways to Garbo's heart was through her stomach. She loved the food, she already loved physical exercise, and so her friendship with Hauser was cemented in short order. Soon after, the foursome took a trip to Reno, where they attended a rodeo, which the women disliked. They hated to see the steers and calves mistreated but enjoyed the outing anyway.

"She eats intelligently," said Hauser of his prize pupil. "One of my favorite

---

* Hauser's books have sold more than forty million copies to date.

Garbo with nutritionist Gayelord Hauser, early 1940s

lunches, and hers, is a cup of chicken broth with chives, cottage cheese, half a ripe avocado with a vinegar, herb and oil dressing, a slice of pineapple and one piece of toasted and buttered dark bread." Hauser changed Garbo's eating habits for life. Thereafter, she patronized health-food stores and subsisted largely—but not exclusively—on chicken, dried apricots, and whole milk, with brown beans and biscuits for snacks. She became "ferocious" about the punctuality and adequate content of meals, said actress Dana Wynter, who met her during one of Garbo's visits to Hauser's home that continued for the next forty years.

Unlike Stokowski, Hauser refused to indulge her melancholy and did everything to talk, trick, or force her out of it. They walked, swam, sunned, and ate together—always vigorously—and he fostered her gradual metamorphosis from full-time recluse to part-time cosmopolite. In November 1939, he gave her a diamond ring. So convinced was he of their impending marriage, during a yacht cruise to the Bahamas, that he "confided" it beforehand to the International News Service wire.

Tactically, this was not the way to get Garbo to the altar. Their close friendship was never an affair, despite the gossip columnists, and it was seriously jeopardized for a while by Hauser's publicity-minded courting.

Hauser was, in fact, a homosexual bachelor who lived with Frey Brown from the early forties until the end of his life in the same Coldwater Canyon house. But once or twice a year, for an extended period, Garbo lived there, too, as if it were her own.

Hauser actually provided Garbo with not one but two getaway homes. The second was in Palm Springs, a safer distance from prying eyes—but not completely safe. In 1940, Ray Daum's father, who rented a cottage next door to the Hauser hideaway, wrote, "That skinny Swedish actress and her fancy boyfriend are always running around naked in their backyard." Hauser's Palm Springs hospitality came equipped with his own "family" there, which welcomed her warmly—a set of gay friends including Roy Bradley (Tyrone Power's lover), Danny Aikman (an adagio dancer and onetime Tennessee Williams boyfriend), and others. Garbo was especially fond of Bradley, at whose home she, Hauser, and Frey Brown spent a great deal of time.

That trio was often together in Los Angeles as well. A typical escapade involved one of Garbo's countless searches for a new home. Before inspecting a house one day, she told Brown to introduce her as Harriet Brown, and she wore comedy false teeth as a disguise. The real-estate agent wasn't fooled. With the addition of Mercedes, the trio often turned into a quartet for picnics on secluded beaches. The two odd couples once sailed to Jamaica "to dine on pineapple, papaya and coconuts," according to *The Hollywood Reporter*. In later years, Garbo and Hauser also enjoyed visiting Pamela Mason (the wife of actor James), who had interviewed Hauser on radio and knew him well.

"They were obviously very good friends," Mason recalls. "He was an awfully reasonable master of nutrition. He said, 'Don't go on a diet, just eat less of what you like.' The thing was to cut down. He said, 'No one will ever give up anything they really like for life. You'll only give it up for three weeks, so it doesn't do any good. Have two martinis but don't have four.' Garbo did everything, of course—drank, smoked—but she exercised and clearly wanted to keep her shape."

Garbo had always been health concerned, if not health obsessed, and had a lifelong interest in health foods and alternative medicines. Commanded by Stiller and Mayer to lose weight, she had become a diet fanatic by age nineteen. From age twenty-one, she worried that she might be subject to the cancer or tuberculosis that took her sister's life. Stiller, too, had suffered from a TB-like lung ailment that led to his premature death and, like Stiller, Garbo was a heavy smoker.

Garbo tapped into Hauser's affinity for health, and he into hers. Though angry about his leaks to the press, she forgave him—not once but on several occasions when he appeared to be exploiting his relationship with her on his lecture tours. Such clemency was rare on her part; most offenders never got a second chance, let alone a third. One friend said she excused Hauser's "media mouth" because "she credited him with saving her health, which was always her biggest concern."

She also prized and utilized his business acumen. In addition to those matters handled by Frey Brown, some of Hauser's financial interests—such as his line of health-food products—were managed by Anthony Palermo of Milwaukee, and the services of both those men were made available to Garbo. Over the years, she and Hauser invested separately and jointly in certain Beverly Hills properties. Hermès and Gucci were among the exclusive shops to which Hauser played landlord, while Garbo was the landlady of that ten-thousand-dollar-a-month Rodeo Drive parcel.

Most of all, though, she simply liked Hauser's company and the way he took charge of things, including her. She looked forward to their visits and the regularity of them, whether at Coldwater Canyon, Palm Springs, or his beautiful home in Palermo. She never gave up her caviar, her two measured vodkas or Cutty Sarks, or her daily pack of cigarettes, and she liked the fact that Hauser didn't harp on her smoking. Like all food faddists, she had her own rules, alternately denying and indulging herself. But by and large, she stuck to Hauser's notions of diet and fitness for life, and whatever else is said of them they worked for her.*

Another of Garbo's odd-shaped sets of friends of this period was the singer Jessica Dragonette, her sister Nadea Loftus, and Jessica's husband, Nicholas Meredith Turner. Dragonette—now largely forgotten—had an audience of some fifty million weekly listeners on NBC and was one of the most popular radio performers of the late thirties. She was the first to sing light opera on the air, and Gayelord Hauser was among her devoted fans. One day in the fall of 1939, he announced that he was bringing Garbo to brunch at Drag-

---

* Mercedes challenged Hauser's seminal dietary influence on Garbo, noting that Dr. Harold Bieler, a Pasadena doctor and dietician, was the first to prescribe a vegetarian diet for them both: "[Garbo] went to Dr. Bieler and began to live on vegetables and fruit. He is the only person, regardless of what others may claim, who has had the slightest influence on her health and physical manner of living. She has continually consulted him about her diet and health for many years." One day on the set of *Conquest*, a sound technician complained that some strange noise was interfering with the recording. It turned out to be Garbo in her dressing room, puréeing vegetables in a blender—long before she met Hauser. Raymond Daum quoted Garbo in the sixties as saying, "I wish I had Bieler here. If I had Bieler, he'd give me yeast and water for two days, no food, no mercy." Said her friend Eleanor Colt: "Garbo lived on 'Bieler Broth.' It's such a lovely, simple soup, a purée of zucchini, an onion, some other kind of squash, and potatoes." The only book Garbo ever endorsed was Bieler's *Food Is Your Best Medicine* (1965).

onette's apartment on Fifty-seventh Street in New York. In her memoirs, Dragonette recounted that first visit:

"A series of half-hourly telephone calls ensued in which Gayelord announced the status quo. 'Yes, she will come.' Then, 'No, I don't think she can make it.' Again, 'She has changed her mind.' And finally, 'She will come if you can assure her that no one but yourselves alone will be there.'"

The suspense was frenzied, but Garbo indeed showed up. When she arrived she said, "I eat only poached eggs." She then produced a small packet and handed it to Adelaide, the maid: "I drink only Postum. Here, I brought some." Adelaide was indignant and said, "Miss Jess' has Postum, thank you."

Dragonette's spacious apartment was a mini-salon of its own for such diverse friends as Oscar Levant, Edgar Lee Masters, and Bishop Fulton Sheen. With Garbo, the sisters never pried or asked questions, as a result of which she felt comfortable and sometimes even prankish. Dragonette recalled that one evening before the 1940 elections, she jumped up on a bench before the fireplace and said, "Will you vote for me as President of the United States?" Then, patting herself on the chest and flashing a broad smile, she declared, "I'm a good man. Besides I'll have to do something important after having been in the films."

At this point, Garbo's private life was as rich and as happy as it would ever be, with or without "romance." In professional life, too, she could still savor the success of her last picture. But it was time to start thinking of the next one, and she could not know that the triumph of *Ninotchka* would lead to defeat. The problem lay in script selection. With Garbo, that process was always compounded by her own indecision, the studio's lack of imagination, and conflicting advice from friends. MGM now had a comedienne and tragedienne in one—as problems went, a "good" one. Salka's intercession was called for again, and she now joined the search for Garbo's next vehicle.

After 1932, Garbo had been in the enviable position of being able to choose her films, but except for *Queen Christina*, she rarely asserted that power. Lubitsch, with *Ninotchka*, had opened up a whole new world of comedy roles and had several new ideas to propose to her. But the difficulty, he told S. N. Behrman, was that he couldn't get her on the telephone. "I spoke to Salka Viertel about this," said Behrman. "She told me that Garbo had really not been happy on the set with Ernst. There was no *Stimmung* there, Garbo said. It was never patched up."

Privately, Behrman thought Salka resented the fact that she had been cut out of writing *Ninotchka* and was thwarting further contact between Lubitsch and Garbo. Others complained of similar communication problems: Max Reinhardt had wanted her for the role of the Madonna in a production of

Maeterlinck's *Sister Beatrice* but lamented in a note to his son, "A pity that we cannot reach Garbo."

Salka denied the degree of her power over Garbo: "Contrary to all the gossip, I have never been Garbo's 'advisor' in her dealings with the film industry. I had no mind whatsoever for business and what I could grasp of it either horrified or bored me. This defect in my character . . . was most detrimental to my own career. Money was something I never valued excessively as long as it was there, and I tried to ignore it as gallantly as possible when it was gone. I had inherited from Mama a touch of 'Oblomovism' when financial matters had to be faced."*

Salka's defense was a bit disingenuous. It was not business acumen that people attributed to her. "She was the only one with genuine access," said Irene Mayer Selznick. "If you were trying to get to Garbo, the shortcut was Salka. She was sort of her broker and had enormous control over her, and she was nobody's fool. She was Miss Fix-It—discreet and shrewd. You could talk to her. 'All right, Salka, come on, put the cards on the table. What is it you really want?' She had a good story sense and she could talk Garbo into something she didn't want."

The Salka-as-villain theory in terms of Lubitsch may or may not be true. Garbo, at this point, could have made a one-picture deal with almost any studio for any price. But she elected to stay with Metro, and after eighteen months' consideration of a myriad of comedies and tragedies for the screen's greatest star, the worst possible decision was made: The war in Europe called for frothy comedy at home; audiences wanted to escape, and MGM would oblige them by turning Garbo into a fun-loving sex kitten. The goddess would become the girl-next-door.

Two-Faced Woman was a cheap story with a cheap $316,000 budget.† The script by S. N. Behrman, Salka Viertel, and George Oppenheimer was based on a moldy Viennese play, *The Twin Sister*, by Ludwig Fulda, which even producer Gottfried Reinhardt called "a featherbrained comedy." Salka herself suggested it—"halfheartedly," she later maintained. Her own preoccupation

---

* Oblomov was the title character of Ivan Goncharov's 1859 play about a man whose dreams and talents are forever buried in lethargy. His name became a Russian synonym for inertia.
† The original working title, *Turns*, was the first of many tortured gropings for a name. Among the others considered and discarded: *I Love Your Sister*, *The Twins*, *Anna and Anita*, *Her Naughty Sister*, *Her Weekend Sister*, *Her Wicked Sister*, *Naughty Today and Nice Tomorrow*, *Nice Little Hussy*, *It's Nice to Be Naughty*, *Her Sister's Husband*, *Double Meaning*, *A Double Life*, *Beside Herself*, *The Gay Twin*, *The Adorable Twin*, *Her Gay Sister*, *Happily Married*, *Twin Wives*, *The Shadow Wife*, and *One-Day Bride*. Ruth Gordon, who had a featured role in the film, recalled that "Sam Behrman wanted to call it *Ubiquitous Lady*. He said everyone would know what it meant." Howard Dietz claimed he was the one who finally came up with the *Two-Faced Woman* title.

A pre-production photo taken before the filming
of Two-Faced Woman *(1941). It was rejected*
and never released.

during the film's production seems to have been with its stress on her relationship with Reinhardt.

The screenwriters were charged with transplanting the tale from Renaissance Italy to contemporary America—no mean task in itself—and with turning the heavy-handed German humor into witty English. Nobody's heart was in it. "At the time when each day brought news more horrible than one could bear, it was not easy to manufacture a silly comedy," said Salka. What they finally manufactured was a yarn about a priggish ski instructor who poses as her sexy twin sister in order to seduce and win back her own husband.

"In those days, cinematized sexual intercourse was—well, it just wasn't," said Gottfried Reinhardt. "The edicts of the Breen Office, the industry's self-elected censor, were complied with so rigidly that no major studio would consider shooting a script without its seal of approval. The script for *Two-Faced Woman* was turned down by the Breen Office on the grounds that it conveyed implications of a premarital carnal relationship. . . . The offending scenes were rewritten."

In charge was George Cukor, whose direction of *Camille* had been stellar. In the interim, the prolific Cukor had made six films, four of them hits: *Holiday* (1938), *The Women* (1939), *The Philadelphia Story* (1940), and *A Woman's Face* (1941). If anyone could make something of nothing—stylish film comedy out of decrepit stage farce—it was he. But Cukor's problems were manifold, starting with casting. Garbo was neither sexy enough as the one twin (Katherine) nor unsexy enough as the other (Karin). Melvyn Douglas played yet another "devilish" role that cried out even more loudly for Cary Grant, who had just performed brilliantly for Cukor in *Holiday* and *Philadelphia Story*.

There was one bright spot, by the name of Constance Bennett. As Douglas's former flame whose torch still burns, Bennett has the film's best role and makes the most of it. She is Griselda Vaughn, star of the hit Broadway musical *Nostalgia in Chromium*. When she discovers during a phone call that Douglas is married, she discreetly covers the receiver and lets out a fabulous scream. It is the funniest moment to that point in the film, and for a long time to come. The delayed-reaction scream is later reprised to good effect at the end of her tête-à-tête with Garbo in a ladies' room. In the following scene, Griselda gathers up her aplomb to declare: "You made me lose my poise, and for that I shall never forgive you!" It is one of Bennett's most polished comic turns, with Garbo largely serving as her foil.

(Bennett provided Garbo with some subversive "assistance" during production: Garbo's costumes in the film were supposed to be "high fashion," but no one liked them. Desperate, MGM sought advice from Bennett, who, after years of stardom, was now playing supporting roles and was better known as a fashion plate than as an actress. Bennett's obliging costume suggestions were adopted, and—if anything—made Garbo look even worse.)

In the infamous swimming-pool scene of *Two-Faced Woman*, not even Garbo could look alluring in the world's ugliest rubber bathing cap—a disaster, wet or dry. It was the first time she had been required to appear in a swimsuit since *Peter the Tramp* in Sweden at age seventeen. But at least Garbo was a swimmer. She was not a dancer, yet the film's big musical number called for her to "improvise" a hot new dance step—a modified rhumba called the "chica-choca." The teaching of it to Garbo went no more smoothly than any other aspect of the production. MGM dance director Robert Alton was sent to Garbo's house in Brentwood to coach her in the routine. He rang the bell, banged at the front and back doors, knocked on windows—no answer. As he was about to drive off, he suddenly glimpsed Garbo treed like a cat, not a sex kitten, in one of her cypress trees. "Go away, Rhumba!" she called down to him. "Go away!"*

---

* Garbo was always honest about her terpsichorean deficiencies. Emmett Davis recalls the night in the 1970s when he met her at the penthouse home of producer James Pendleton in New York. There was music playing, and he asked her to dance. "Thank you," she said, "but I can't dance." Davis protested, "But you danced in *Ninotchka*," to which she replied, "For one minute—and it took them three weeks to teach me."

ABOVE: *Constance Bennett (with an agenda of her own) and Garbo prepare for the restaurant scene in* Two-Faced Woman. BELOW: *Cukor coaches Garbo, a slightly long-in-the-tooth bathing beauty, before the swimming-pool scene of* Two Faced-Woman.

Garbo, with choreographer-partner Robert Alton at right, dances the infamous chica-choca in Two-Faced Woman.

The appointment was rescheduled and, in the end, Garbo did the minimalist rhumba quite passably, with Alton himself as her partner. But she was not exactly sylphlike, and the reckless "spontaneity" of the scene is never for a moment credible. Yet when the script gave her half a chance, she was on the mark. When Douglas accuses her of rejecting him because of his age, she replies sweetly, "I like older men—they're so grateful." Later she mentions an Englishman she met in Singapore.

"What happened to him?" asks Douglas.

"He killed himself," Garbo answers.

"Over you? Oh, look here, men don't kill themselves over women anymore."

"I hope so, because incidents like that depress me."

Her deadpan delivery, as in *Ninotchka*, is unbeatable, but the witty exchanges are rare, and the dazzling Garbo smile seems awkward on this two-faced and too-forced woman. For the first and last time, the normally top-notch MGM costume and make-up departments let her down. The five inches lopped off her hair for this picture set off a fashion controversy in the press akin to that crisis at the New York Coiffure Convention three years earlier. Her unflattering new "bob" appeared to be held in place by two butterflies on either side of her head. Constance Bennett's sly agenda was reflected in her gowns, as the film's photographer, Joe Ruttenberg, recalled:

> Two days before we were to start shooting a party sequence, Garbo nixed the dress she was supposed to wear. After being shown dozens more, she picked one—the worst possible choice. It had shoulder pads and was low-cut and she didn't have much of a chest. They tried to put some jewelry on her, but it just didn't look right. . . . If her clothes were on the severe side, with clean lines, it would simplify things. Unfortunately, she had a taste for bulky, ugly clothes that made her look much older than she was. It was like she couldn't stand to look beautiful, she only felt comfortable frumpy.

On an interpersonal level, Garbo was consistent to the end: Co-star Roland Young was charmed by her and recalled that—even at this late date in her stardom—she kindly helped fellow players with their lines. But when Young asked her to autograph a photo, she declined. Young framed the photograph anyway.

She was moody and ill at ease throughout the shooting, as though she sensed something ominous. "They are trying to kill me," she told Mercedes de Acosta. Both the film and its advertising campaign were aimed at the lowbrow American market for the first time: "Who is the screen's rhumba queen—who no longer wants to be alone?—a gayer, GRANDER, GREATER Greta . . . Every other inch a lady—with every other man!"

An unexpected source put the final nail in *Two-Faced Woman*'s coffin and produced the nearest thing to scandal in Garbo's career. The "morally offensive" scenes to which the Breen Office initially objected had been rewritten. The censors were satisfied, but the Legion of Decency—cinematic watchdog of the Catholic Church—was not. After an advance screening, the Legion gave the film its dreaded "Condemned" rating, with horrific box-office implications, on the grounds that it was adulterous for a man to have sex with his sister-in-law. It was the first such condemnation of a major studio film in years.

"My counterargument that his sister-in-law was, in truth, his wife they dismissed as Hollywood sophistry," said producer Reinhardt. Francis Cardinal Spellman, Archbishop of New York, "took time off from shepherding X-million souls to wage a one-man crusade—in a world torn by strife, with his own country on the brink of it—against my sinful *Two-Faced Woman*. He whispered his caveat into the ear of . . . Louis B. Mayer, and Mayer thundered into mine to 'flush the filth down the drain where it belongs.'"

On Sunday morning, December 7, 1941—three weeks before the film's opening—Reinhardt was in an MGM dubbing room mixing soundtracks for *Two-Faced Woman* and listening to the weekly New York Philharmonic broadcast. Artur Rubinstein had just struck up the opening of Brahms's Piano Concerto No. 2 when an announcer interrupted with a bulletin from Pearl Harbor.

"Every last one of us in the room, as everyone in America . . . realized instinctively that life and its pursuits had been radically changed," said Reinhardt. "Everyone save New York's Prince of the Church, who [opposed *Two-Faced Woman*] up until the very day of Los Angeles's first air-raid alarm, when he flew in and asked for a viewing of the expurgated version. I ran it for him and gained the sanction my employers set such store by."

Spellman had demanded a new scene showing that Melvyn Douglas knew all along that the sexy "twin" was his wife. That, of course, completely ruined the joke, and Cukor would not do it. But the additional scene was duly filmed by Andrew Marton and Charles Dorian, and an already weak story was thereby made even more illogical and unfunny.* Even so, it was still banned in such places as Boston, Buffalo, and St. Louis, and Republican

---

* Gottfried Reinhardt said large sums of money changed hands between Louis B. Mayer and Cardinal Spellman. The MGM boss was so appreciative of the clergyman's "help" over the years and so fond of him as a person that, in his will, "Louis B. Mayer left $10 million to Cardinal Spellman."

Congressman Martin J. Kennedy of New York introduced a bill to halt its distribution nationally. The Catholic Interest Committee of the Knights of Columbus of Manhattan and the Bronx called it "a challenge to every decent man and woman."

Primarily, it was a challenge to stay awake through. The initial blame belonged to Reinhardt, Viertel, and Garbo herself for the story selection, especially in view of the fact that Garbo had a choice between *Two-Faced Woman* and another MGM film for which Cukor was under contract: *A Woman's Face*, a remake of the Swedish *En Kvinnas Ansikte* (1938), with Ingrid Bergman. MGM's version would co-star Conrad Veidt—with whom Garbo had always wanted to work—as the cool villain of a story in which the Swedish heroine's scarred face turns her into a "bad woman," until she is redeemed by a plastic surgeon (Melvyn Douglas!).

But Garbo didn't "do" bad women or women with deformities. Virtually every role she played from *Love* through the end of her career was both romantic and sympathetic. She didn't understand (and no one, including Cukor, ever explained to her) that the deformity was a minor matter; becoming a character lead was the real issue. The "Swedish" role in *A Woman's Face* went by default to Joan Crawford, whose career it helped revive.

Garbo picked *Two-Faced Woman*. Once under way, its most blameworthy participant was George Cukor, who, as director, could have bailed himself and Garbo out and cut the studio's losses once he saw how hopeless it was; failing that, he had the power and talent to rework it radically. But distracted by his own rising star, he made it in a hurry and moved on to *Her Cardboard Lover* (1942), Norma Shearer's equally disastrous final film, made within six months of *Two-Faced Woman*. Both failed at the box office and caused their stars to abandon their careers.

Louise Brooks, for one, railed against Cukor's reputation as a "woman's director" (much beloved by Vivien Leigh and Olivia de Havilland, who consulted him in secret even after he was replaced by macho Victor Fleming on *Gone With the Wind*) and against the "simple-minded idea that a pansy understands women":

"The best performance Clara Bow ever gave was in Fleming's *Man Trap*. And in *The Wizard of Oz*, Fleming made Judy Garland the most adorable creature we will ever see in films. Yet Garbo allowed Cukor to destroy her in *Two-Faced Woman*. It is no more reasonable to think that pansies love women than to think that cats like birds."

Said Cukor himself, years later: "We really had no script [and] the film didn't work at all." Garbo took it "very seriously, very personally" and lost faith in the studio because of it. In retrospect, he admitted, the attempted makeover of Garbo "was a shitty decision."

Critics had a field day lambasting the picture, but the main reason people stayed home in droves had little to do with the quality of the film, which opened December 31, 1941: Who was interested in movies three weeks after Pearl Harbor? But Garbo, totally unnerved by the film's hostile reception, was convinced that, at thirty-six, her box-office appeal was on the wane.

"Serious people naturally want Miss Greta Garbo to be serious," wrote Otis Ferguson. "She ought to go with the guy that brought her, that is. . . . She was a brilliant success in *Ninotchka* and allowed to be such by special dispensation from even the serious [because of a] stunning screenplay. . . .

"Now Miss Garbo is in another comedy, but with the direction of George Cukor [who takes his time] following the tortuosities of a script that wastes the audience's. [But Garbo herself] is a pleasure to watch. . . . Unless you are determined to be grumpy you will probably enjoy it."

Most audiences were determined to be grumpy; most critics were determined—like Ferguson—to show a respectful sympathy toward Garbo personally. But *Time* on December 22, 1941, summed up the impact: It was "like seeing Sarah Bernhardt swatted with a bladder."

"Greta was humiliated by the reviews and by the furor created by the women's clubs," wrote Mercedes. ". . . But I think Greta's regret was more in her own soul for having allowed herself to be influenced into lowering her own high standards. She said, 'I will never act in another film.'"

One person who saw it coming and took a position of principle was Gilbert Adrian. When ordered by MGM to produce designs for a new, modern, "American" Garbo, he said the public would never buy it. When his protests were ignored, Adrian stunned the studio by resigning. On the day of his departure from MGM, he went to bid a final farewell to Garbo, who was silent and melancholy for some moments (Adrian later told Irene Selznick) before astounding him with her parting words:

"I'm very sorry that you're leaving," said Garbo to the man largely responsible for her glorious image on screen. "But, you know, I never really liked most of the clothes you made me wear."

Still, there was no real thought of retirement in Garbo's or MGM's corporate mind at this point. She was under contract for one more picture, and it was assumed she would take a break while MGM went about searching for her next project—a problematic process now made more so by the disastrous *Two-Faced Woman*.

Garbo was depressed, and Gayelord Hauser decided to shake her out of it. A few days after *Two-Faced Woman* premiered to its pans, he had her in New York City and took her out on the town three nights in a row, once to the Chevy Chase Room of Clara May Downey's Olney Inn on East Forty-ninth Street.

Marriage rumors abounded as usual in the columns, to her annoyance, but Hauser's social therapy seemed to be working. Under much pressure, including a phone call from Eleanor Roosevelt, she agreed to a rare charity engagement and on January 24, 1942, made her radio debut with Ronald Colman and Bob Hope in a benefit broadcast for the "March of Dimes" antipolio campaign. A few weeks later, still making the rounds imposed by Hauser, she mistook Vincent Astor for a Vanderbilt (in conversation with *Mrs*. Astor)—but what the hell, she had at least shown up.

In April, she saw Alfred Lunt and Lynn Fontanne in *Idiot's Delight* and accepted an invitation to dine at their home. Another guest there, Russel Crouse, told her a novel called *The Paradine Case* would be a perfect new vehicle for her and later sent her a copy of it. But as 1942 drew to a close, she still had no new film project, despite many reports.

"Greta Garbo would like to star in *Empress Elizabeth* (of Austria), and a certain rich financier is about ready to put up the bankroll to make the picture," wrote Louella Parsons on December 10. Parsons, for once, was more or less correct. Then and later, Garbo discussed the Elizabeth film with Salka and others, and David Selznick was one of the "rich financiers" who seriously considered producing. But nothing came of it.

Developing a Garbo film was further complicated these days by the fact that Leland Hayward was her new agent. Harry Edington had recently resigned that duty to embark on a producing career of his own.* Hayward and Garbo had reached a representation agreement on December 6, 1941, but Salka still seemed to carry the most weight in negotiations with her. Even within MGM, there was confusion about whom to approach (and how) with a Garbo project. Finally, in December 1942, a decision was made, or so it seemed: Garbo signed a contract to play a Russian resistance heroine in a war story called *The Girl from Leningrad*. She was to receive $70,000 up front and another $80,000 upon completion—much less than her previous quarter-million per picture. But *The Girl* never got beyond the script stage.

Another grim year dragged by, and at the end of 1943, with no end to the war or Garbo's indecision in sight, she decided to take herself and MGM off the hook. On the subject of integrity, Mayer once said he'd rather have Garbo's word than the signature of anybody else, and the way she conducted herself in her final dealing with MGM shows why. Garbo's films in America provided big box-office returns initially but then depended on the second-

---

* Edington became an executive producer at RKO for the Ginger Rogers films *Lucky Partners* and *Kitty Foyle* (1940) and Alfred Hitchcock's *Mr. and Mrs. Smith* and *Suspicion* (1941).

tier profits from Europe. *Two-Faced Woman* had shattered both parts of that magic formula, and the savage reviews shattered Garbo. Now, said Clarence Brown, after two years of flailing about for a follow-up project:

> Garbo did the greatest thing for a company that any star, living or dead, has ever done. . . . Under the terms of her contract, MGM was obliged to pay her whether they made another picture or not—win, lose or draw. The company couldn't afford to make another Garbo film without the vital European market, and she understood the situation. She went to Mr. Mayer and released him from the contract for $250,000. She never took a nickel of the rest of the money she was entitled to under the contract. Is there a motion-picture star in the world who would do that? I wouldn't. But that's Garbo.

Film historian Jan Wahl wrote that she moved like a sleepwalker through most of her films but that "it was a Hollywood-weariness, not a world-weariness, that caused her to withdraw." Garbo, "the proud somnambulist, dutifully fulfilled her association with MGM, was exploited and wrung dry, then by mutual agreement she was let go."

George Cukor's assessment was defensive: "People often say glibly that the failure of *Two-Faced Woman* finished Garbo's career. That's a grotesque oversimplification. . . . It certainly threw her, but I think what really happened was that she just gave up; she didn't want to go on." S. N. Behrman was more honest. Asked why Garbo quit after *Two-Faced Woman*, Behrman replied, "Because the movie was so terrible," adding that he felt he helped assassinate her.

Neither of them was quite right. The end of Garbo's association with MGM need not have signified the end of her film career. Her "crash" in popularity was neither inexplicable nor irreversible. Rarely did a major Hollywood star stay at the top for more than ten years, and she had been there for fifteen. Wartime audiences needed Betty Grable's great legs more than Greta Garbo's great art. Withdrawal from films now was a tactical response to the evaporation of the European market: Garbo would simply go on hiatus until the war was over.

The most haunting scene in Charles Chaplin's *The Great Dictator* is the "globe ballet," in which Adenoid Hynkel cavorts choreographically with a balloon of the world. Less remembered is the preceding scene between Chaplin and Henry Daniell as "Garbitsch," at the end of which the dictator dismisses his stooge with a line of unmistakable origins: "Leave me—I want to be alone." The chuckle was at Garbo's expense, of course, at a time when the world had precious little to laugh about.

"I don't think many people have seen Garbo cry, but I did," recalled
Walter Reisch:

> It was in June of 1940. Mussolini had just announced that Italy would
> enter the war and Roosevelt was going to make a speech at the University
> of Virginia. I was in producer Gottfried Reinhardt's office listening to
> the radio. Salka Viertel was there, too, [with] composers Arthur Good-
> man and Dr. Bronislaw Kaper and also John McLain. We were all
> surprised when Garbo appeared at the door. She was wearing blue
> slacks and a sweater, one of her enormous straw hats, sandals, no
> makeup. She had heard the radio and asked if she could come in. She
> sat and when Roosevelt started talking she listened very intently. . . .
> "On this tenth day of June 1940 the hand that held the dagger has
> stuck it into the back of its neighbor . . ."
> FDR's voice so moved Garbo that she dissolved into tears. We were
> all looking at her to see her reaction, but she didn't seem to care.

With time on her hands, Garbo might now have been expected to do as
many of her colleagues and become involved in troop-morale projects and
war-bond drives. But she could not bring herself to engage in such public
activities. The war disturbed her deeply, but she practiced a childlike (some
said unpatriotic) avoidance of the subject, preferring that it not even be
brought up. She was depressed, rather than pleased, by news reports from
Nazi-occupied Paris that the French were crowding into illicit "speakeasy"
screenings of her films.

Repression was her way of dealing with the war, and with her career,
though she was by no means abandoned. One of her most energetic cham-
pions was Lubitsch. Garbo was always in the back and often in the front of
his mind, as in late 1944 when he was producing *A Royal Scandal* for
Twentieth Century–Fox. Lubitsch was recovering from a heart attack and
had asked Otto Preminger to direct. Tallulah Bankhead was contracted for
the starring role of Catherine the Great. Soon after rehearsals began, Lubitsch
rushed into Preminger's office, as Preminger recalled:

> "Otto, I have wonderful news!" he said. "I had dinner last night
> with Garbo. I told her our story and she wants to play the part of
> Catherine."
> "But Ernst," I protested, "what about Tallulah?"
> "Forget Tallulah," he said impatiently. "We'll pay her off. *We can
> get Garbo!*"
> I said, "Ernst, please STOP!" I told him how Tallulah rescued my
> family when they were facing deportation. I could never participate in

anything that would hurt her. If Tallulah was removed from the picture I would resign too.

Lubitsch refused to listen to me. He insisted there would be some way to get around the situation. He took me to see [production chief Darryl F.] Zanuck, [but he too] showed no excitement.

"I don't know that I prefer her to Tallulah," he said. He was using the standard yardstick of Hollywood: How successful was your last picture? Garbo's *Two-Faced Woman* had made no money, while Tallulah had just appeared in Alfred Hitchcock's *Lifeboat*, a box office winner.*

But *Two-Faced Woman* was just a catalyst. What really derailed her career—the only thing big enough to do so—was World War II, whose human tragedy so dwarfed any "professional" tragedy that, in good conscience, she couldn't even mourn the career loss.

If Garbo was paralyzed by the war, Salka Viertel was not, and neither was Lubitsch. In October 1939, just after the Nazi invasion of Poland, they had founded the European Film Fund for the aid of artists in Germany and elsewhere who were soon to be refugees. Co-founder was agent Paul Kohner, and the organizing committee included William Dieterle, Lothar Mendes, Gottfried Reinhardt, Erika Mann, Walter Reisch, and Conrad Veidt. In war and peace, it was salon business as usual: On May 2, 1941, Salka hosted Heinrich Mann's seventieth birthday party, the greatest gathering in the history of Hollywood's "New Weimar." Among the guests were Herbert Marcuse, Bruno Frank, and all the other major émigré literary figures. The evening climaxed in an exchange of speeches between Thomas and Heinrich Mann—a ritual reconciliation which the bickersome brothers evidently performed every ten years.

Christopher Isherwood was another refugee who came to Los Angeles—and to Salka's—and became a part of the "New Weimar" set. He lived on Amalfi Drive near the Viertels and he later worked on various MGM film scripts, contributing scenes and bits of dialogue (without screen credit) to such pictures as *A Woman's Face* and *Free and Easy* (both 1941). Isherwood's million-word diary contains an account of the big social event of autumn 1939—an all-star picnic organized by the Huxleys at Tujunga Canyon for thirty guests, including Bertrand Russell, Krishnamurti, Salka, and Garbo:

---

* Lubitsch was so bitter over the rejection of Garbo that he took it out on Bankhead, behaving rudely and accusing her of stealing scenes from Anne Baxter. He eventually withdrew from *A Royal Scandal* altogether.

I had seen Garbo [before], but we had only been together for a few minutes at a time. She was always full of secrets to be discussed in private. . . . She wore the famous straw gardening hat, with slacks, and a tiny patch of plaster between her eyebrows, to prevent wrinkles from forming. She was kittenish, in a rather embarrassing way; and her lack of makeup and general untidiness were obviously calculated. Just the same, I liked her and felt quite at ease in her company. She climbed the fig tree in the Viertels' garden to get me some specially ripe figs. I remember that she referred to some business dealings with the studio, and said that one must always pretend to be a child when talking to the Front Office. She had her own kind of little-girl slyness.

Garbo . . . was anxious to meet Krishnamurti. She was naturally drawn to prophets—genuine and otherwise. Salka said that she was very unhappy, restless and frightened. She wanted to be told the secret of eternal youth, the meaning of life—but quickly, in one lesson, before her butterfly attention wandered away again. . . .

As we started out [for a walk], Garbo said: "As long as we're on this side of the fence, let's pretend we're two other people—quite, quite different." "You know," I announced solemnly, "I really wish you *weren't* Garbo. I like you. I think we could have been great friends." At this, Garbo let out a mocking, Mata Hari laugh: "But we *are* friends! You are my dear little brother." "Oh, shut up!" I exclaimed, enormously flattered.

I suppose everybody who meets Garbo dreams of saving her—either from herself, or from Metro-Goldwyn-Mayer, or from some friend or lover. And she always eludes them by going into an act. This is what has made her a universal figure. She is the woman whose life everyone wants to interfere with.

Garbo was already planning to move away from Hollywood, according to composer David Diamond, who met her in the early months of 1942 at Salka's. He had been sitting morosely in a corner, downcast about a love affair, when someone sat down next to him and said, "Why do you look so glum?" He looked up into the Face of the Century. Diamond and Garbo talked at length that night and remained friends for life. Their conversations ranged widely and freely, within the Garbo caveat to steer clear of movies. But once in a while, she could be led accidentally or indirectly into the subject. Diamond recalls one evening in late 1942 when they were chatting outside in Salka's side garden:

I said perhaps, someday, she might consider theater again, and she let out a little yelp. I said, "Wouldn't it be wonderful to do Ibsen—

The Lady from the Sea?" and she said, "But I *did*—that was one of my exercises in Sweden at the Royal Academy." One other time, when I mentioned Mercedes's *Joan of Arc*, she said, "Oh, I know all about that. I would like maybe someday to do that as a film and I talked to [MGM] about it and Salka has talked, but—no go." She said she begged Mayer to let her do it, and submitted a list of other plays she'd like to do, including *Lady from the Sea*, but the studio said no to all of them.

The careers of many other major artists who came to Salka's were likewise on hold or in transition. Diamond met Conrad Veidt there in 1942 when the actor came back to Hollywood from England to play his immortal Nazi in *Casablanca*. "Garbo very much wanted to make a film with him," says Diamond, "but again, it was 'nothing doing' with Mayer." Veidt died later that year of a heart attack at age fifty. The Viertel home continued to be a haven for the geographically and creatively displaced, and Diamond rhapsodizes about its atmosphere:

> All those wonderful people were there—most of the German colony. Franz Lederer and Brecht came and Stella Adler. In the black-out period, you had to be home early, but you'd come and stay for as long as you could. Most of the actors and writers were glad not to have to talk film, except for something like Lombard's being killed [in a plane crash on a 1942 war-bond tour]. From dawn til dusk, film was the obsession, so that when they got home or went to a party it was, "Please—anything but movies." Dorothy Parker was there once and I remember her saying, "If anyone brings up film, I'll tell them how to spell it"—just like that other four-letter word. She was among the first to say "fuck," and she said it a lot because it always got such a rise out of people.

"I walked in the back door one day," recalled writer Robert Parrish, who was new to the scene, "and there was a guy with short hair cooking at the stove. In the living room, Arthur Rubinstein was tinkling on the piano. Greta Garbo was lying on the sofa, and Christopher Isherwood was lounging in a chair. 'Who's the guy cooking in the kitchen,' I asked no one in particular. 'Bertolt Brecht,' came the reply."

Salka's assemblies always glittered, but after *Two-Faced Woman* and Garbo's unofficial retirement, her professional importance was much reduced and Hollywood émigré social life, in general, became fragmented by grievances and rivalries.

"There was always a split between those who liked to go to Salka's and those who preferred going to Frau Mahler-Werfel's [widow of composer

Gustav]," Diamond recalls. Schoenberg belonged to Club Salka, in firm allegiance with the woman who tried so hard to sell him to Thalberg for *The Good Earth* in 1937. Stravinsky, on the other hand, more often frequented Alma Mahler's or the soirees of Mercedes de Acosta, who had her own mini-salon. She and Stravinsky were devoted to each other; Mercedes and Garbo were still friendly but not so devoted.

Garbo was spending more time in New York these days—sometimes, by Salka's arrangement, in S. N. Behrman's apartment. Behrman's secretary came in one day to find the phonograph blasting and Garbo dancing barefoot around the living room. Garbo embraced her and said, "I'm so happy here," and later sent Behrman a giant mass of flowers.

There were many reasons why Garbo welcomed her wartime break from moviemaking and the chance to spend more time in New York, but not least of them was the excuse to learn more about art and assemble a collection of her own. Garbo did not cultivate friendships with any major artists, but she had some fascinating encounters with several of them.

Salvador Dalí biographer Meredith Etherington-Smith reports that in 1942, when Dalí was the Hollywood guest of Jack Warner, he told his host he was dying to meet Garbo, and Warner set up a meeting. After agonizing over what to wear, Dalí finally settled on a white suit, lilac silk shirt, and extraheavy waxing of the moustache. Garbo showed up in trousers and tennis shoes and, when introduced to Dalí, took a long look at him and said: "One of us has got it wrong." She then left.

In New York, she attended one or two parties thrown by Dalí and his wife Gala at the St. Regis Hotel, but their carryings-on appalled her. She never bought a Dalí painting but prized her copy of a 1945 Maurice Sandoz novel, *The Maze*, for which Dalí did the drawings. Her impact on the artists of her time was way beyond her ken: In 1942, the great constructivist Joseph Cornell included a Garbo box in his "Twentieth Century Portraits" exhibit at the Museum of Modern Art. Garbo saw the show, but when Cornell learned that she didn't like "her" box, he destroyed it.

Garbo's treks to the art galleries of Manhattan increased, though they always involved more browsing than buying. She made repeated visits to Kirk Askew's Durlacher Gallery because she was fascinated by the surreal theatrical paintings of Tchelitchew, whom Askew handled. The seriousness of her art interests was difficult to assay, but toward the end of 1942 she made some uncharacteristically bold moves.

Barbara Barondess MacLean—the saucy maid in *Queen Christina*—had quit movies in 1938 to become a decorator and art-and-antiques broker. Garbo often visited her shop in Los Angeles; MacLean decorated Garbo's house and made her blackout curtains, too. A year later, Garbo was in

MacLean's New York City office when a dealer called to say he was pushing two Renoirs into an important Sotheby's sale of Otto Preminger's art and antiques that day. In MacLean's words:

> When she heard it was Preminger's paintings, she said, "Can I come with you?" I said, "This is not for your temperament—you take six months to decide to buy a piece of furniture that costs $300." I wasn't afraid to talk to her that way, and she used to laugh when I did, because she knew it was true. She'd bought two little 18th-century tables from my shop—very fine pieces, $285 apiece—and she'd looked at them for six months! But she came and sat with me and I bought 12 paintings that day, and she almost had a heart attack when I bid $14,500 for one Renoir and then $18,500 for the other. When I saw her face turn white, I said, "You don't have to take them, I have other clients for them," but she caught her breath and decided to buy them. She paid for them on the spot—the only check I ever saw her make out—and handed it to the boy when we picked them up. That way, she didn't have to pay me a commission, and I never sent her a bill for it.

Had Garbo always been partial to Renoir?

"No," says MacLean, "she just thought they were pretty and she knew the name. She wasn't educated, but she wasn't stupid. I liked her, but she was mostly a nuisance to me."

The month of November 1942 was the most amazing of Garbo's life as an art collector: During the week of November 9 to 16, she bought not only the two Renoirs through MacLean (*Confidence* [1897], an atypical Renoir of a woman whispering a secret to a man, and *Léontine et Coco* [1909]), but a third one, from Jacques Seligmann & Co., *Enfant en Robe Bleue* (1889), the ghostly portrait of Renoir's nephew Edmond, looking for all the world like a beautiful little long-haired girl—an example of Garbo's taste for the androgynous in art as in life. Nine days later, she purchased a superb Pierre Bonnard still life, *Les Coquelicots* (1915), and, soon after that, the first of two Rouaults.

"She looked at pictures patiently," said Howard Dietz, himself an amateur painter whose canvases she summarily dismissed. But most intriguing was her later encounter with actor-artist-collector Edward G. Robinson, who wrote:

> I never played with Garbo. She was as mysterious and unreachable to me as she was to you—except that one day [when] the bell rang, and against all my principles, I answered the door myself. There,

through the peephole, I saw a lady with a floppy hat holding a package. And the lady said, "Is Mr. Robinson in? My name is Garbo."

I opened the door. She came in, shook hands with me stiffly in the European manner, asked my pardon for intruding, but there was a matter of some importance she wished to discuss with me if I could spare her a moment or two. Greta Garbo in my house! I was overwhelmed, awed, and as nervous as a cat.

I took her into the living room; she glanced at the pictures on the wall approvingly but did not look at them closely. She refused to sit down, toyed with the string on her package, having some trouble with the knots, refused to let me help her, and finally unveiled a painting.

Was it worth buying?

It was a landscape by an artist I had never heard of. It had quite a decent feeling about it, though far from masterly.

"Is it worth—?" she started to ask, and I interrupted, I hope, politely.

"Don't tell me the price yet," I said. "Tell me if you like it."

"I do at night," she said. "In the morning I am not so sure."

"Then," I said, "live with it for a few weeks before making up your mind."

"You are right, Mr. Robinson," she said. "I do not like to be forced until I am certain. Yet, he needs the money."

"The artist?"

"No, the man who bought it from the artist and now needs to sell it in order to eat."

"In that case," I said, "you are not buying a picture; you are giving charity. How much charity does he want?"

"Two hundred dollars," she said.

"For two hundred dollars," I told her, "you are getting a very nice picture. And if you find you do not like it, you can always give it away or put it in a closet."

"That is excellent advice, Mr. Robinson," she said, "but two hundred dollars is still quite a lot of money. Can I take it off my tax?"

"I don't know, Miss Garbo," I said. "I suggest you talk to your accountant."

"He will charge me," she said. Again refusing help, she wrapped the picture again. "I will buy it. It is nice. It is about forests. And I like forests."

She started for the door. I followed her and opened it for her.

"Thank you very much for your time, Mr. Robinson," she said, and then suddenly she smiled that *Ninotchka* smile. "You also have nice pictures. Very nice. Thank you. Goodbye."

I never saw her again.

I'm wrong. Once again. On Fifty-sixth Street. She didn't know me.

Garbo tucked away her new art treasures in storage in New York and returned to the West Coast, where she learned that Salka had been dismissed from MGM for bringing in "leftist" agent Paul Kohner to renegotiate her contract. A less obvious but no less significant factor in her dismissal was that Garbo was no longer under MGM contract.

"Salka was horribly shattered," says David Diamond, "and Garbo saw that. She never said another word to Mayer after that and resolved never to go back there again. There was terrible treatment of many others, too. To GG, it seemed to come full circle back to the treatment of Stiller."

Though she grieved for Salka, Garbo's own position was so weak she could be of little assistance. Her traumas mounted. In July 1944, her home was burglarized while she was awake—and terrified—inside. She escaped by sliding down a rain pipe from the second floor. The police found some of her things—two coats, some ration cards, and a watch—discarded in a neighbor's yard. California seemed more odious by the day. "Swedish film interests want Garbo in Stockholm for *Countess Julia* by Strindberg and are in negotiations with Leland Hayward for her services," said a November 1944 report. "She is said to be interested in returning to Sweden after the war."

But she was most interested in getting out of Hollywood, and she now closed up shop there for the better part of a year and moved to the Ritz Tower in New York. The person made happiest by that move was Mercedes de Acosta, who maintained an apartment at 471 Park Avenue, from which she could see Garbo's rooms in the Ritz Tower, facing north. During the blackouts, said Mercedes, "We used to signal to each other at night with lighted candles. Why we weren't arrested for showing lights I will never know."

Having abandoned the safety of Salka's salon, Garbo now had to find a new one in New York, and she did so with relative ease. It included Valeska Gert's lesbian nightclub in Greenwich Village, where she enjoyed the company of Muriel Rukeyser, the Berlin *diseuse* Marianne Oswald, and dancers Harold Kreisberg and his partner, Gyorga. David Diamond was also in New York then and achieving considerable success. He had composed the songs and incidental music for a sensational new production of *The Tempest* at the Alvin Theater in January 1945, and was conducting, too.

"I turned around and there she was, sitting with one of the Rothschild barons," Diamond recalls. "It threw me off a bit. I saw her afterwards, and she said she thought Vera Zorina [as Ariel] was wonderful."

Garbo was no less mysterious in Manhattan than in Hollywood. Her presence and the probability of it were always unpredictable. On September 14, 1944, Marcia Davenport, whose *Valley of Decision* was a best-selling novel the year before, co-hosted a party with Madeline Sherwood, the wife of playwright Robert, at Davenport's East End Avenue apartment. Many notable New York writers and musicians were invited, and one of them—John Gunther—asked if he might bring Greta Garbo along. Davenport recalls:

> At that time, I had the best cook in New York. She had worked for my mother [soprano Alma Gluck] and she was in our family for at least 25 years, so the food was phenomenal. There was a whole poached fish, a great big 8- or 10-pound striped bass or salmon, with all the sauces that went with it. Garbo came, and I cannot remember that she said a word. But she was beautiful. Everybody had the supper and it was very fine. And when it was quite late in the evening, by one device or another, I got them all out of the dining room so the servants could clear up and not be kept any later than necessary. As a hostess, I began to feel, "Gee, I wish they'd start to leave." Then I looked around and thought, "I don't see Garbo. Well, if she left, she left."
>
> So finally, when most of the guests had gone, I wanted to speak to one of the servants. I slipped into the dining room on my way to the kitchen, and the pièce-de-résistance, or what was left of it, was still on the table. And there stood Garbo, all alone at the remains, having a fine time calmly devouring the fish.

But what did they *say* to one another?

"Nothing, of course," Davenport replies. "I pretended I didn't see her, which is just as she would have had it. You don't think I would have intruded on her at a point like that? No. I just went about my business and left her to hers."

Early in World War II, Garbo was told that Adolf Hitler loved her films and admired *Camille* so much that he allowed its wide distribution in Germany, despite the "racial impurity" of director Cukor. Garbo, in turn, reportedly said she wanted to meet him and try to convince him to stop the war. She felt the power of her personality could alter the course of history, but "if not—I could shoot him."

The romantic idea that Garbo was willing to martyr herself by assassinating Hitler sounds apocryphal, but her friend Sam Green confirms it:

"Once she said, 'Mr. Hitler was big on me. He kept writing and inviting me to come to Germany, and if the war hadn't started when it did, I would have gone and I would have taken a gun out of my purse and shot him, because I'm the only person who would not have been searched.' That's a direct quote. She said it to me over dinner, and it was so out of character. It wasn't her habit to make up such a story to stop a dinner party."

Or maybe not so out of character. As a child, she had had fantasies that "I might shorten the life of a cruel king and replace him by a romantic knight."

Garbo's low level of political sophistication was mirrored by those around her: Mercedes, for example, was upset by the internment of Japanese in California—lamenting not the loss of their civil rights but, rather, of her gardener. Louis B. Mayer constantly worried about what the Hitler government would think of his new movies and was quite willing to make changes. As late as 1941, he called in William Wyler to complain that the early rushes of *Mrs. Miniver* showed an anti-German bias:

"This is a big corporation," Mayer told Wyler. "I'm responsible to my stockholders. We have theaters all over the world, including a couple in Berlin. . . . We don't hate anybody. We're not at war." Even Chaplin was worried about hostile reaction to *The Great Dictator*, while Charles Lindbergh was calling Jews the "principal war agitators." "Their greatest danger to this country," Lindbergh told a crowd of eight thousand in Des Moines in September 1941, "lies in their large ownership and influence in our motion pictures, our press, our radio and our government."

Meanwhile, what was Garbo doing? By Cecil Beaton's account, something traditional for a woman in wartime: A California man, by stealth, had obtained her phone number from a tailor and called her. She thought he had a house for sale and went to see it. "He answered the door," said Beaton. "They talked. They saw the garden together, the downstairs room. Greta thought to herself, 'Why not?' so she asked, 'Have you a very beautiful view from your bedroom?' Next day he went to war."

Maybe, or maybe not.

Beyond that, there is evidence to suggest that Garbo played a small role in the Allies' wartime intelligence apparatus. Due to its neutrality, Sweden was a hotbed of espionage activity on all sides, and Hitler's war machine—especially in the early years of the struggle—depended on the crucial assistance of the Swedish steel industry and its agents. British spy chief William Stephenson maintained that Garbo identified important Nazi collaborators in Stockholm to British agents there. Author Charles Higham, after examining a thousand declassified U.S. government files, said Garbo became involved with the British secret service in 1939 through director Alexander Korda, a middleman for recruiting celebrities to the war effort. She reportedly served as go-between for the British with shipping magnate Axel Johnson and members of the Swedish royal family. She was also credited with helping obtain the release of physicist Niels Bohr from occupied Denmark to Sweden and later to America, where he worked on the Manhattan Project.

If those claims are true, they are a redemptive manifestation of Garbo as real-life Mata Hari.

"When my husband asked her about that, she didn't deny it," says her niece.

In later years, Garbo made puzzling references to Dag Hammarskjöld, the Swedish diplomat and United Nations secretary-general, who had intimate knowledge of Allied intelligence operations in Scandinavia. She and Hammarskjöld subsequently met in New York City, after which she told Ray Daum, "There were some things that happened a long time ago that we had to talk about. We spoke Swedish to each other. It was very painful for me—but I can't tell you that story."

Known for a fact is that on December 12, 1939, she wrote a five-thousand-dollar check to the Finnish Relief Fund for its war-orphans program during the "Winter War" in which Stalin overran Finland. But the donation was made under a strict condition of anonymity, and as the war progressed there was increasing criticism in the press of her apparent uninvolvement and her failure to join the great majority of other stars in war-bond drives and in entertaining the troops. One published story claimed she had even refused a GI amputee's request for her autograph—and it was true. Actor-director Orson Welles was a witness to that most mindless faux pas. As neighbors in Brentwood during the war, he and Garbo were good acquaintances and spent a few evenings together. One night, he told biographer Barbara Leaming, they emerged from a restaurant to find "a soldier in uniform without a leg, standing on his crutches with an autograph book and she refused it. That is how dumb she was! She refused him, in front of my eyes!" Faithful Salka came to her defense: "If anyone has made the suggestion that Garbo isn't selling bonds because her sympathies are on the wrong side, it's too preposterous even to be discussed. There are some people who just cannot face crowds, no matter for what cause. Garbo is such a person. Instead she buys many bonds herself [and] has done her utmost to help me in my work of rescuing anti-Fascist refugees from Europe."

But there could be no pretending that the war was one of Garbo's foremost concerns. She mostly muddled through it in a daze and, once it was over, took up a wandering, self-imposed exile—not unlike Queen Christina's—that would characterize the rest of her life.

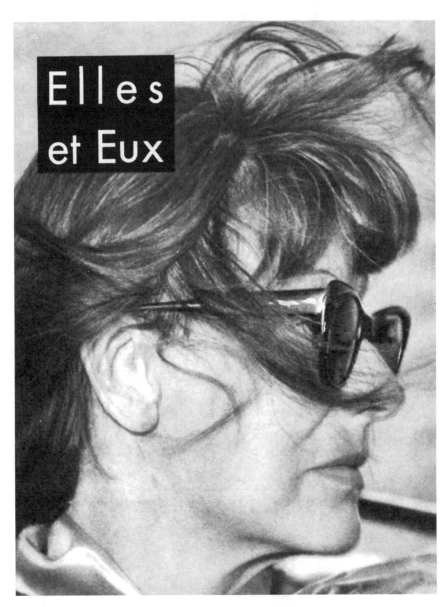

**Elles
et Eux**

*On her return to Idlewild airport from France (Paris Match, October 4, 1958), a
reporter asked, "What brings you to New York?" Garbo replied, "I live here."*

CHAPTER 11

MADEMOISELLE HAMLET
1946–1959

The lanky, attractive, solidly built "Miss Hanson" walked down the gangplank of the *Queen Mary* at Southampton on August 25, 1947, her large sunglasses attracting more attention than the absence of them would have, in a port where shades are truly necessary on maybe three out of 365 days. In her ongoing game with the news media, she was about to lose a round—not a terribly important one, just one of the most improbable.

Garbo was in England to dispose of a rather large sum of money left to her by a secret admirer named Edgar Donne, an eccentric hermit and descendant of poet John Donne. He had been banished as a youth by his family to wander America and ended up an invalid in a ramshackle cottage, where he slept on an oak table, quoted from the Bible, and dreamed of Greta Garbo. Edgar's money was in England but his mortal coil was in Dorr, Michigan (population: 500). When he threw it off, in October 1946, his will astounded everyone:

"I, Edgar H. Donne, bequeath my entire fortune of $75,000, inclusive of securities and jewelry, to Greta Lovisa Gustafson, by profession film star and known under the name of Garbo. Should she agree to become my wife, my house and land similarly go to Greta Lovisa Donne."

Donne left Garbo 160 acres, $700 in war bonds, $180 in U.S. postal savings bonds, and "all securities and jewelry and cash in the bank"—a total of about $210,000, including land which engineers said would yield $700 a day in oil.

More surprising than the gift itself was the fact that Garbo accepted it. "I do not know Mr. Donne," she said. "I vaguely recall that he once sent me a letter some years ago which was returned to him. I don't recall anything he said in it. . . . I'm told that he once made a trip in Los Angeles to see me. I didn't see him, nor did I ever talk to him."

Miss Garbo never became Mrs. Donne, except in the fantasy of Mr. Donne. Thousands of men and not a few women had fallen in love with her, but none had made Edgar's ultimate display of devotion. Of all the millions of dollars and admirers she had ignored over the years, what secret reason did she have to concern herself now with this? The solution is like that of many other Garbo "mysteries"—on and not beneath the surface: She was a pragmatic Swede, and if a man she never knew was fool enough to leave her a large sum of cash with no strings attached, and if it fit in with her travel plans, why not collect it?

As it turned out, after probate in America and England, most of the money was eaten up by inheritance taxes, and the remainder of Donne's assets could not be taken out of England. Garbo donated the balance to an unnamed British charity—by one account, the Sister Kenny Foundation—and went on to a holiday in Cannes.

"She drinks champagne, does not dance and is in a very bad temper," said the French papers. Her restless traveling often brought her to France these days, where Mercedes de Acosta took charge and care of her. Their separate rooms at the Crillon had fine views of the Eiffel Tower, and they went for long walks in the Bois and Tuilleries Gardens.

A greater fascination—perhaps the most fascinating of Garbo's postfilm life—was Cecil Beaton, who could be relied on to snatch her up and amuse her in a way that no one else ever could. Their suspended relationship had been renewed the year before, on March 15, 1946, at a small gathering in the Manhattan apartment of Beaton's friend Margaret Case, as he recorded in his diary:

"At the sight of Garbo I felt knocked back—as if suddenly someone had opened a furnace door on to me: I had almost to gasp for the next breath. . . . I held on to the back of a chair. Garbo made no definite sign of recognition but seemed to glean amusement from the mere sight of me. She took it for granted that once again I had immediately fallen in love with her. . . .

"Her eyes were still like an eagle's—blue-mauve and brilliant, the lids the color of a mushroom—but there were a few delicate lines at the corners. The face having become thinner, the nose appeared spikier which made the modelling of its tip and the nostrils more sensitive. The hair, that had appeared golden in the California sun, was now an uncompromising, but beautiful, cinder-mouse. The bold, workmanlike hands were a little weatherbeaten. . . . She remarked with a smile: 'I didn't wear lipstick when you knew me before.' I noticed now that her mouth was too generously daubed with carmine, but the effect was charming—as if a child had been at the jam jar."

After smoking five Old Golds, she abruptly rose to leave, and Beaton was panicked at the thought that another decade might elapse before they met again. He asked her to come out onto the roof garden to see the skyline, "determined that she should remain there until I struck a chord of intimacy," which he achieved by a stream of eloquent babble and by touching "the knobbles of her spine." He made her promise to phone him, and at the beginning of April, she did so—to say she was coming right over. She arrived out of breath, having been chased by a crowd of autograph hunters on the way; she praised Beaton for keeping his rooms at a chilly temperature: "Ah, fresh air! British Empire!" When Beaton asked where she lived most of the year, she replied, "Oh, I follow the fleet. I don't quite know what that means, but I often say things like that. . . ."

Her talk had "a rather wacky, inconsequential quality," he said, but "one automatically and willingly accepted the idiom imposed by her. This wackiness took the place of wit and would change erratically from gay to sad. 'A doctor once [asked me], "Are you bored?" I don't know why he used so violent a word!'"

They began to take walks together in Central Park—long and fast, all the way around the reservoir—during which her mood often became euphoric: "To be part of nature gives her the same elation as champagne to a novice," Beaton wrote. "She strides, leaps, laughs, becomes as lithe as a gazelle." And then in mid-April came the conversation that would change his life—if not hers—for two decades. Apropos of nothing one day, she said: "My bed is very small and chaste. I hate it. I've never thought of any particular person in connection with marriage; but, just lately, I have been thinking that as age advances we all become more lonely, and perhaps I have made rather a mistake . . . and should settle down to some permanent companionship." That gave Beaton the opportunity he had been waiting for. "Why don't you marry me?" he asked.

I had never before asked anyone to marry me, and yet to make this proposal now seemed the most natural and easy thing to do. I was not even surprised at myself. But Garbo looked completely astounded. "Good heavens, but this is so sudden! . . . Really, this is very frivolous of you . . ."

"But I mean it. I've never been more serious."

"But you hardly know me."

"I know all about you, and I want to take you and teach you to be much happier."

"But we would never be able to get along together and, besides, you wouldn't like to see me in the mornings in an old man's pyjamas."

"I would be wearing an old man's pyjamas, too. And I think we would get along well together—unless my whistling in the bathroom got on your nerves?"

"You're being very superficial: one doesn't plan one's life on other people's bathroom habits. Besides, you'd worry about my being so gloomy and sad."

"Oh, no—you'd have to worry about why I was so happy, and you'd be the reason."

"It's a funny thing, but I don't let anyone except you touch my vertebrae—they so easily get out of place."

Encouraged by that discussion, Beaton later called her at the Ritz and asked: "Is that my beloved?" With a laugh, she said yes. "Do you love me?" he asked, and to his astonishment, she said yes. "I then stretched my luck by repeating the question—and again she said: 'Yes.'"

One day soon after, she started to ask him something, faltered, and began again hesitantly, "If only you were not such a grand and elegant photographer . . ." Beaton finished the sentence for her: ". . . you'd ask me to take your passport photograph." She looked astounded—forgetting she'd told him she was leaving soon for a holiday in Sweden. "It would have been impossible for her to go to any ordinary passport photographer without the results being displayed far and wide," Beaton wrote—ironically, as it turned out:

> The sitter arrived wearing a biscuit-coloured suit and polo-collared sweater, her hair a lion's mane. At first she stood stiffly to attention, facing my Rolleiflex full-face as if it were a firing squad. But, by degrees, she started to assume all sorts of poses and many changes of mood. The artist in her suddenly came into flower. She was enjoying the return to an aspect of the métier that had been her life's work. Could I believe my luck? By degrees I was emboldened enough to ask if she would take off her habitual sweater. Then I brought out some "prop" clothes—a pierrot's ruff and white pointed hat. . . .

Garbo was pleased with the results, pronouncing the pictures "strong" and pencilling an X on the back of those she approved for publication in *Vogue*—or so Beaton chose to believe. When shown the quantity and variety of moods, Alexander Liberman, art editor at *Vogue*, could hardly believe his eyes. Garbo picked the least arty one for her passport and, on July 6, 1946, boarded the *Gripsholm* for her first postwar visit to Sweden. An army of reporters awaited her at the dock with questions, and one or two of them

Cecil Beaton took these photographs for Garbo's passport—and more—in his rooms at the Plaza Hotel in New York, April 1946.

even got an answer. Asked if she was planning to affiliate with a newly organized Swedish film corporation, she replied: "Oo-la-la, no, nothing like that."

Meanwhile, word of Beaton's photo scoop was circulating. But a week before the magazine hit the stands, Garbo cabled from Sweden to say, according to Beaton, that "if more than one of the photographs were to appear I would never be forgiven. Frantic calls to my friends at *Vogue:* 'Stop everything!' It was too late: the copies were already bound and on their way throughout the country. Greta's telegram was later followed by a letter saying she was deeply distressed at the idea of having any costume pictures of herself published unless they had to do with her work. . . . It was now impossible to prevent her from feeling completely betrayed. My abject cables, letters, telephone calls, and flowers sent to her in Sweden went by unanswered. I felt as if I had committed a murder."

She felt that he had, too. Their mutual friend Sam Green says there were two reasons why Beaton published the Garbo pictures:

> Number one, he thought they were very good photographs, and they were. Number two, they got him back to Condé Nast, where he had been blackballed for ten years because of a 1938 *Vogue* drawing he did—an illustration of a Paris cafe scene with some anti-Semitic remarks that nobody noticed until it ran. I think he bought his way back into a career there by selling her out, thinking he could get away with it or that she would understand if he explained. He was desperate to get published again in the United States.

When she returned to New York on September 4, 1946, Garbo refused to take Beaton's calls at the Ritz. A month later, he finally reached her in Hollywood, but she treated him as a tiresome burden to be disposed of once and for all, as Beaton recalled:

> "This is no good," she said. "We are too different. By your action you have deprived me of a friend." "Who is the friend?" "You were!" She did not wish me to phone. . . . "I'm not being cruel or vindictive, but things have changed." "I haven't changed—have you?" I asked. "No. I'm a very strange person," she replied, "and I can't change— and I don't think I want to very much either, so you had better not call any more." I was fighting for my life. "Then may I write?" "What's the point?" This was pretty near to disaster, but by banter and repartee we eventually returned to better terms. Greta suddenly showed that she was curious [about a new production of *Lady Windemere's Fan* he had

Beaton's perfect lighting shows off Garbo's profile to best advantage, taken during the same afternoon "passport" session.

designed]. "Are you shocked with me for exhibiting myself on the stage?"

"No—not interested," she replied.

Beaton was not one to give up easily. For the next year and a half, he kept up a relentless barrage of calls, letters, and telegrams—to none of which she responded. "I am in despair," he wrote in his diary in October 1947. Later that month, he got through to her at the Ritz, but she was frosty and put off seeing him. In December, he confided his agony to his New York friend, Mona [Mrs. Harrison] Williams, who had some Machiavellian advice:

> You're being a dope. Stop it—it's not getting you anywhere. Surely you know what a bore it is to have someone waiting for you—always at your beck and call. Just play her game. . . . Don't call her up, and when she calls you, say you've been busy. Be nice to her, of course, but be rather casual. . . . I don't wish to be a traitor to my sex, [but] you're my friend and I see her game so clearly. . . . You've got to get her worried: you've got to get her mind, and her mind's got to worry about what's going on in your mind. . . . Don't have any mercy. Why do you think I've been able to keep Harrison interested all these years? . . . He's guessing all the time.

With nothing to lose, Beaton tried silence. After four days, his telephone at the Plaza rang.

"Can I come around now?" Garbo asked.

"It's too rainy," he said, "and I've got to go out."

"I'll be right over," she replied.

It worked like a charm. He savored his "pathetic little victory" and took every opportunity over the next weeks to annoy Garbo by mentioning his outings with other women. One night during an hour-long phone talk, Beaton punctuated some remark with, "So put that in your pipe and smoke it." Garbo replied: "You're not to use such rough expressions to me—I'm feeling downtrodden enough as it is." Once on a walk, they dropped into a bookshop, where Beaton pointed out a picture of her in an album of cinema stars. "I don't give a damn," Garbo laughed. Then, putting her arm through his, she said: "I like you—it's not a big word, but I like you, and whenever I say goodbye I want to see you again."

According to his diaries, Beaton's physical affair with Garbo began with a back massage at the Plaza on November 3, 1947. She rose and drew the curtains. "I was completely surprised at what was happening," he wrote, remembering "when in my wildest dreams I had invented the scenes that were now taking place." A few days later, after a walk, they made it a point to enter the Plaza separately but Garbo was anguished when caught by a hotel employee sneaking up the back stairs. Once in Beaton's room, she drank some tea and slowly relaxed. "Suddenly," said Beaton, "as if it were the most ordinary question in the world she stretched out her arm towards the other room and asked with such disarming and natural frankness, 'Do you want to go to bed?' "

Their intimacies continued. One night, she criticized the way he "draped" himself when he stood, hand on hip. "She said firmly that 'She wanted to make a man out of me.' " In her opinion, "The homosexual life is a 'cut up' without a sense of responsibility." Another day, it was his turn to be critical. "You're so unreliable," he told her. "I could never marry you. You're not serious about me." To which she replied: "What a rebuff, and I love you, Cecil. . . . I'm in love with you."

That was "to date," he wrote on December 8, 1947, "my greatest triumph." One night they discussed Mercedes de Acosta and Garbo said, "She's done me such harm, such mischief, has gossiped so and been so vulgar. She's always trying to scheme and find out things and you can't shut her up." When Beaton said Mercedes had asked him if he and Garbo were having an affair, she replied, "That's just like her. It's so vulgar."

Nothing turned her off so much as "vulgarity," a recurring problem between them. But for now he was in a state of bliss. On December 29 at the Plaza, "We enjoyed ourselves in a quite uninhibited and unshy way," he wrote. On New Year's Eve, he and Garbo ushered in 1948 by drinking a bottle of 1840 whiskey in Beaton's room: "I gave a toast to our marriage, our life together, but Greta did not elaborate on this theme, and smiled a little diffidently." Their lovemaking was particularly "wild and tender" that night, he said. Often Garbo would say "I must be going" as a prelude to sex. Cecil could not believe his luck: "Here I was with someone whom I'd always wanted to love me and here she was loving me." When Garbo admired Christian Bérard's portrait sketch of him, Beaton gave it to her. At times, he told his diary:

> I feel that the possibility is within sight that one day I might get her worked up sufficiently to rush off to a registrar. For myself I am not only willing, but desperate, and confident that we could have the infinite joy of making a new and successful life together. What was there to stop our living the rest of our lives together? It was so easy: it was indicated. "No, it's not easy," said Greta. "You have not had a difficult life as I have. Everything has been smooth for you. . . . Occasionally

When Garbo admired Christian Bérard's
sketch of Beaton, he gave it to her.

you may have been sad, when someone has not loved you as much as you loved them. But life has been difficult for me. You must realize I am a sad person: I am a misfit in life."

From England, he dared to write, "If you come to be my wife I trust you will allow me to sleep in the sitting- or dressing-room, if not in the large room." And a bit later: "It is really terrible that you should spend your time hiding from imbecilic film fans on Madison Avenue or Sunset Boulevard. All of which is a long way of extending an invitation to you to come and build your nest here at Reddish House."

He felt he had a sexual hold on her and attributed it to the fact that "I am so unexpectedly violent and have such unlicensed energy when called upon. It baffles and intrigues and even shocks her. May this last a long time!!" Whether he meant the bafflement or the energy—or both—is unclear.

"To make my winter's conquest complete," he wrote March 3, 1948, "I must see her in her own home. I must be able to spend the days uninterruptedly with her, just to stay from morning until bedtime without her looking at her watch and saying 'Got to go now.'" That very day, he left New York for California, ostensibly on a *Vogue* photo assignment but primarily to spend twelve days with Garbo.

She met him upon his arrival and took him—timorously—to her Benedict Canyon home for the first time, on the condition that "when we do go in, you're not to look! Promise to put on blinkers! I'm ashamed. . . . I'm a perfectionist, and this is far beneath what I would like it to be." Once inside, they embraced at length and then:

> We suddenly looked at each other in startled amazement. "You really want to in the middle of the morning?" In a trance I went upstairs through her sitting-room up the circular steps to [the] bedroom. We were both very happy in our fervour and something very violent had overtaken us both. Our reunion was most passionate and ended in a serenity that was most beautiful. We came downstairs the tenderest of friends.

"Curiously enough, Cecil was one of the few people who gave her any physical satisfaction," claimed Truman Capote, a twenty-three-year-old confidant of Beaton's then. For the first time in his life, Beaton thought maybe he was being used for his body.*

Garbo's greatest joy at home was working in the back garden; her Japanese gardener was permitted to work only in the front. It's "the one thing that thrills her," Beaton wrote, "and she works frenetically," doing the heavy labor such as fence mending herself, "quite naked," until she discovered that people could peer through the gaps. He accompanied her to buy wood and manure, and she rose "at screech of dawn to spread the stuff over the front lawn before the neighbours are awake to watch her." Afternoons, they lay in the sun, watching the hummingbirds, with Garbo in white shorts and brassière, smoking Old Golds. Now and then, she would look furtively toward the house and wonder if "the Dragon" had gone yet—Gertrude, her hardly dragonlike maid. "She went to a door and listened with an expression of fear on her face," wrote Beaton. "It is obvious that she does not know how to handle servants and that 'the Dragon' holds her in terror."

Inside, they spent hours in the big sitting room, where the best of her Impressionist paintings hung: two Renoirs, a Rouault, and a Bonnard. "I bought them as investments before I knew anything much about painting,"

---

* Aside from such secondhand reports as Capote's, the sole source of the Garbo-Beaton sex relationship is Beaton's diaries, which his meticulous biographer Hugo Vickers has verified as factually reliable in almost every instance. His fervid obsession with Garbo, however, raises the possibility that the predominantly homosexual Beaton fantasized his carnal knowledge of her in his diary with an eye to his post-mortem reputation. When writer Boze Hadleigh asked if Garbo was the first woman to whom he was romantically attracted, Beaton was evasive: "She was the only one I wanted to marry. . . . It would have been an achievement. It was an achievement just to keep in touch with her."

she told him. "They're rather boring ones, I think." She said she wished the Impressionists hadn't been so bourgeois in their choice of subjects. But even during her most relaxed moments—if a noise came from outside—she was suddenly a frightened animal on the alert, peering through the blinds. "Beaton thought this "a most pathetic sight, for she spends hours at the windows trying to see if anyone is about."

Sometimes they motored to the mountains, then got out at a summit to walk. After one such occasion, Beaton wrote:

> She was in high spirits and started reciting poetry, singing old songs and being the most companionable of human beings. When she wishes she has the capacity to talk by the hour, and her brain is alert and quick. She recounted how she used to walk alone for miles in the mountains. She would talk to herself, and shout and sing, and "go to the little boys' room," thinking she was all alone and free to do anything. But one day she saw a photograph of herself [in one of those isolated spots], taken by someone hiding in some bushes: "When I saw it I got such a fright. I thought maybe I'd be followed and attacked. . . . Since the burglary I'm afraid to be alone."

Newspaper attacks were on her mind, too. With Beaton that day, she spoke of the time she declined to appear at a charity benefit, after which Louella Parsons wrote that she should be deported. As they walked, they came to an isolated house whose construction Garbo had watched over some months. Numerous dogs ran out to greet her, "and she was ecstatically happy patting them and playing with them, although some were so large that they jumped up to her shoulders. Greta said, after fondling a pet donkey: 'These must be nice people who live here—so close to nature. People can exist like this in California if they want to—oblivious of the movies and Miss Parsons.'"

She told him about her long chauffeured drives to Lake Arrowhead, just to read a book, and of the pointless five-hour journeys to Santa Barbara for a cup of tea: "What a waste of the best years of my life—always alone—it was so stupid not being able to partake more. Now I'm just a gypsy, living a life apart, but I know my ways and I must not see people." Nowadays, she said, Gertrude served her dinner in bed at six-thirty, "and three-quarters of an hour later I'm asleep."

But there were exceptions, such as a dinner party at the Palisades home of writer Winifred (Clemence) Dane, a friend of Beaton's. Constance Collier led the way at a fast clip, while Garbo drove behind with Beaton until "a sexily-dressed police officer" on motorbike pulled them over and yelled, "You're going pretty fast, young lady!" Chaplin was at Dane's that night, imitating Elinor Glyn's denture problems and doing an excruciatingly funny ballet of Christian Scientists who, despite their afflictions, "leapt into the air with terrible limps in the most grotesque but dreadfully comic *arabesques*." Garbo, too, performed with a grace and ease that surprised Beaton—especially when she imitated his own absurdly British walk: "I sometimes forget how professional an artist she is. The pantomime was brilliant and received the applause it deserved." Yet the evening took a lot out of her; on the way home, she said: "It's awful to be bored, but really for once I was. If I saw these people every day I'd perish."

Soon after, Beaton's agent, Carlton Allsop, arranged for him to see *Anna Karenina* at a private MGM screening, and after much coaxing Garbo decided to come along. "It takes Beaton to get me to the studios for the first time in six years!" she said as they approached, becoming increasingly nervous. It was an emotional experience for her. MGM had been "for so long her prison [that] to return after such an interval made her feel self-conscious." In a little projection room, the lights went down and Garbo lit an Old Gold. During the running, she interjected: "Those were real Russians. . . . Those were feathers [a snowstorm]." She was pleased by how little it had dated.

Beaton wanted to stay with her forever but could not postpone his return to New York past March 14. He had a precious half-hour reserved for her just before leaving, and he asked for a last tour of the garden. "With arms linked, we walked a few paces," he wrote. "Suddenly, I realized that there was to be a break. . . . My cheeks became wet. . . . Life held no immediate prospects. I knew that, in some ways, I had scored a victory over Greta: I knew that I had made her love me. Yet I had failed to give her the strength to act. . . . In spite of our closeness, I realized that there was nothing more concrete about our future: I had no hold over her. She had for so long designed her life to protect herself . . . that even I could get no closer than before. I had won the battle, but the main campaign had been lost."

It was true, but not solely due to Garbo's neuroses. It was also, in no small measure, because Beaton in his egoism always thought in terms of "conquest" and "victory."

Garbo was still a part—however peripheral—of the film elite and still much sought not just for her social presence but for a variety of stage and movie roles. Tennessee Williams, for example, had spoken to George Cukor in Beverly Hills about the possibility of her playing Blanche Du Bois in the film version of *A Streetcar Named Desire*. Cukor introduced them, but she found the character too difficult and unsympathetic. "I'm an honest clear-cut person and see things very lucidly," she told Beaton afterward. "I could never be an involved and complicated person: I'm too direct and too mas-

culine. I couldn't bear to tell lies, and see things round corners, like that girl
in the play." Her idea of a comeback role was not an aging Southern belle
on the verge of madness. She wanted a sexless, androgynous role on the
order of Peter Pan or Dorian Gray*—as far from Blanche as one could get.

Undaunted, Williams told Cukor he'd written a film script called *The
Pink Bedroom* with a perfect part for Miss G, and in July 1947 Cukor arranged
a meeting at her apartment in the Ritz—"very carefully and privately like
an audience with someone superior to the Pope," said Williams, who had
several drinks along the way to fortify himself. Once there, he drank more
vodka and launched into a monologue of his screenplay:

> I got a big high and began to tell her [the story]. . . . She kept
> whispering "Wonderful!" leaning toward me with a look of entrance-
> ment in her eyes. I thought to myself, She will do it, she'll return to
> the screen! After an hour when I had finished telling the scenario, she
> still said "Wonderful!" But then she sighed and leaned back on her
> sofa. "Yes, it's wonderful, but not for me. Give it to Joan Crawford."†

The Pink Bedroom perhaps hit too close to home: Its eerie story concerned
a famous actress and her mentor-director "Michael Stiller," who discovers
her with a new manager-lover and kills himself in her boudoir. She takes
up with a drag queen, and—Williams never finished it. Garbo later startled
him by coming with Helen Hayes to a party he gave in Chelsea before the
December 1947 opening of *Streetcar*, during a terrible blizzard:

> Garbo arrived all bundled up with a hat pulled down over her ears.
> All you could see were her eyes. . . . On this cold night I had a fire
> going. Garbo stayed by the fire, she didn't take off her coat or even her
> gloves. . . . I was very nervous. She is the only actress that always
> intimidates me. Whenever I have seen her, I cannot really believe she
> is there, you know? She is the greatest actress we have ever had. . . .
> As we stood by the fireplace talking, a guest of one of my guests came
> over to us. He held a Kodak camera in front of his face and pointed
> it at Garbo like a gun. Garbo went pale. She stiffened. Before I could
> prevent the calamity, this guest of a guest had taken her picture. It was

---

* A few years later, she told Katharine Cornell that she still wanted to play Dorian, with
Marilyn Monroe as the young girl ruined by him.
† When a friend later quoted this anecdote to her, Garbo replied, "Oh, well, I probably never
said it." But she was always interested in *A Streetcar Named Desire*. Harry Mines, publicist
for the 1951 film, recalled going to the back of the screening room to admit Garbo in the
dark, just as it began, and helping her dart out before the lights came up at the end.

like he shot her. She fled into the night. I think she believed I had put him up to it.

Tennessee Williams observed that Garbo alone of the great film goddesses never inspired a good drag act; her femininity was too unique and difficult for impersonators to play off: "She is really hermaphroditic, with the cold quality of a mermaid."

In the early forties, as part of his campaign to spiff up her appearance, Gayelord Hauser and Eleanor Lambert had taken Garbo to the exclusive dress shop of Valentina Schlee in the Sherry-Netherland, above the Fabergé egg boutique A La Vieille Russie. Valentina called herself "an architect of clothes" and was famous for her pronouncements ("Mink is for football, ermine is for bathrobes") as well as her fashions. During their initial encounter, Garbo met her husband and partner, George, who was amazed when Garbo stood casually naked in front of him.

Schlee's colorful background began in St. Petersburg, from which his wealthy family was driven south after the Bolshevik revolution. He ran a newspaper in Sevastopol until the White Army's collapse forced him to flee the country in 1920 with the beautiful Valentina Sanina, whom he allegedly met at a railway station and married when she was just fifteen. "I can't give you love," Valentina told him then, "but if you want friendship, then I'll marry you." That was fine with Schlee. "If you marry me," he told her, "I'll look after you for the rest of your life." And so he did, at least for the next four decades.

They had come to America in 1923—two talented, ambitious émigrés— and straightaway met Mercedes de Acosta and her artist-husband, Abram Poole. Valentina, whose reddish gold hair trailed the floor when loose, became one of Poole's models. By 1928, with George's help, she opened her own Madison Avenue shop, Valentina Gowns, where her creations soon drew fashionable ladies as well as the theatrical trade. Her Broadway designs included Lynn Fontanne's as the dubious Russian "countess" in *Idiot's Delight* (1936)—a character that playwright Robert Sherwood was said to have modeled on Valentina herself. Among her customers in the forties were Queen Marie of Rumania, the Duchess of Windsor, Rosalind Russell, Norma Shearer, and a host of other stage and film stars.

"There was nothing grander than a simple Valentina dress," said Irene Selznick, noting Valentina was the first to design clothes in which a woman could throw her arms around a man's neck without her dress riding up in the back.

Valentina Schlee, Gladys Swarthout, and "The Little Man," George Schlee, at El Morocco in the late forties

By the time they met Garbo, the Schlees were quite successful and Valentina had some three dozen people working for her. In later years, the life-size mannequin that greeted all visitors at the entrance of her studio bore a remarkable resemblance to Garbo. At the moment, under the Schlees' diplomatic tutelage, the real-life Garbo suddenly began to look more fashionable and the columnists were writing of how much Valentina loved working with her. George, for his part, "had terrible nerves but could be very charming," said Selznick. "Valentina couldn't have run the business without him. He knew how to make money, and he didn't mind appearing as someone who was living off his wife."

Before long, an odd ménage à trois developed. "I think at one point it was the ladies—a three-way street is my guess—but it wound up the other way," said Selznick. So it seemed, and yet the reality was something else. The ménage was odd, but not sexual. Valentina was not attracted to Garbo, and Garbo was drawn to George in other than sexual ways. He reminded her of Stiller, with his Russian blood, large hands and features, and cosmopolitan savoir faire. He gave everyone, including Garbo, orders—and she always took direction well. It used to be Hauser who told her to put on her hat and prepare for a walk; now it was Schlee who bought the steamship tickets and said, "We sail for Europe next Friday." Soon enough, he would take over her life and become the Stiller of her middle age.

Among other things, Schlee seriously cultivated her interest in art. He introduced her to Baron Erich von Goldschmidt-Rothschild, a tall, silver-haired patrician with cultivated manners and tastes and, like Garbo, full leisure. In New York, they dined at expensive restaurants, attended art exhibits, and, in the summer of 1952, even motored together through Austria with the baron's former wife and mother-in-law! He had owned a major art collection in Germany before Hitler came to power and barely got out in time—*sans* art—as a penniless refugee. After war's end, with a little help from his relatives, he was soon back on his feet as a prominent art and antiques consultant and man-about-town in Paris as well as New York. Garbo often accompanied him to Parke-Bernet's Saturday-afternoon auctions, and though neither of them ever bought much, he helped her hone her tastes.

Once, in April 1946, after a walk through Central Park, Garbo and Beaton dropped in at the Cloisters to see an Apocalypse tapestries exhibit. Garbo was transported, said Beaton. "She whistled and sighed in admiration, while other visitors stared at her. She made birdlike noises of delight at the rabbits and butterflies and other small animals and insects woven into the needlework grounds of wild flowers in the 'Unicorn' tapestries. Pointing to some draperies done in reds and rose and dull pink: 'Those are now my most beloved colours. It's incredible that human-beings can do such things!' "

A less charming vignette of Garbo's art outings concerns the first major American exhibition of Toulouse-Lautrec's work, in the fall of 1946, on the ground floor of the Wildenstein Gallery, co-sponsored by the Goddard Neighborhood Center, which served needy New Yorkers. Board member Rachel Townsend was stationed at a desk in the lobby to collect the entrance-fee donations. "On every day that my mother was on duty," says her son David, "Garbo took the elevator to an upper floor gallery (open to the public, but unrelated to the main exhibition) and walked down the stairs into the gallery showing the Toulouse-Lautrecs, thus avoiding paying the gargantuan sum of $2 to a charity."

Parsimony notwithstanding, Garbo was now assumed to be a serious art aficionado, but Mercedes and Beaton thought otherwise after the summer evening in 1952 when they took her to the Paris apartment of Alice Toklas to see Gertrude Stein's early Picassos, including *Young Girl with Basket of Flowers* and *Nude with Clasped Hands*. Toklas received them with great ceremony, seated her guests, and turned on the sidelights to show off the canvases. Without rising, Garbo took a cursory circular glance around the room and said, "Thank you very much." No further comment. The visit ended a few minutes later. Toklas afterward characterized Garbo as "Mademoiselle Hamlet."*

It was Garbo's way of saying, "I'm annoyed, I want to get out of here," says her friend Sam Green. "That would have been her 'statement' on the pomposity of the occasion."

Almost half a century later at Sotheby's, on November 13, 1990, one observer, reacting to one of too many sad-eyed harlequins in her collection, described Garbo's tastes in art as "the cutting edge of banal." The Renoirs suggested otherwise, and yet clowns, dogs, and pink flowers did dominate the subject matter of her paintings; obscurity, or downright anonymity, characterized most—but not all—of the artists.†

Neither logic nor whimsicality seemed to dictate Garbo's buying impulses, but something else did: color. She loved salmon, pink, and rose, of which there was a great preponderance not only in her paintings but in her living quarters. Walls, curtains (often drawn over the Renoirs), Savonnerie carpets, upholstery—everything was coming up rose or shades thereof. Conformity to those colors was a—or the—primary criterion in her art. Blues and greens, by and large, need not apply.

A tape-recorded conversation with her friend Raymond Daum years later in New York illuminates her approach. She had gone to a gallery one day and been struck by a certain painting:

> I thought, "What's the matter with me?" I can't stand horror, and some of the pictures I buy are horror things. They stare at you. . . .‡
> A salesgirl told me the price, and I said, "Well, there's no discussing

---

* An oft-quoted tale is that Garbo had a Picasso of her own—hung upside down. David Nash of Sotheby's, in Derek Reisfield's documentary on Garbo's apartment, clarifies that she had a Picasso on loan for a while in the fifties but returned it—and that it was hung right side up on her living-room wall.

† At the auction, Garbo's thirteen blue-chip paintings—three Renoirs, a Bonnard, seven Jawlenskys, and two Rouaults—brought $16,580,000. (One Renoir was withdrawn.) The provenance of her canvases hugely magnified the selling prices: A rustic watercolor attributed to Jean-Baptiste Leprince (valued at $1,000) sold for $11,000. An unsigned Neapolitan landscape ($5,000) went for $30,000. A seven-inch terrier of the nineteenth-century French school ($700) commanded $17,000. Albert André's *Dame en Blanc, Assise* ($35,000) fetched $170,000. *Embracing Couple*, an abstract by Garbo's brother Sven ($400), sold for $8,500. A harlequin by Gabriel Dauchot ($750) brought ten times its estimate. A vase of reddish flowers, *Les Anemones* by Elisabeth Faure ($5,000), sold for $80,000.

‡ The "horror things" were the German Expressionists, about whom she had educated herself. Among Garbo's many art books was a prized tome featuring the tormented works of Emil Nolde (1867–1956), the "decadent" paintings of Max Beckmann (1884–1950), and—her favorite—the bold works of Alexej von Jawlensky (1864–1941), who once declared, "Art is nostalgia for God."

it." I don't like it anyway. It's really a goofy painting. . . . But I took
it. I don't even sign for them. I take them home and hang them up.
They trust me. . . . My girl came to work and said, "Don't tell me it's
one of those again." And I said, "Yeah, it's one of those again." And
she said, "Now really, you can't, Miss Garbo. What do you want these
things staring at you for?" . . . I took it back and told the owner I
liked it but that it was too much. The price is indecent, and I'm a lone
woman. . . . Oh well, maybe I'll get it. I don't know who the hell else
would buy it. It's really very strange. I'll probably regret it. No—they're
my colors. I do like it. They're my colors.

Erich von Goldschmidt-Rothschild found her "a woman of every contra-
diction. One moment a serious-minded bluestocking, the next a Nordic gypsy
dancing on top of the world." A mutual friend who insists on anonymity
declares, "Erich definitely went to bed with GG—he told me so himself,
and I never knew him to lie or boast." The baron and Schlee adored everything Garbo did, and so did Mrs. Schlee—for a time. Once or twice she and
Garbo even dressed identically and made social rounds on George's right
and left arm.

In the high theater seasons, Schlee was a busy man with a repertory system
of his own. On February 18, 1948, for example, he took Garbo to the premiere
of *Mr. Roberts* at the Alvin, and the following evening escorted Valentina
to the opening of *Tonight at 8:30*. But more and more, only one of Schlee's
arms was occupied, and the occupant was Garbo. Finally, Schlee made a
rather too honest admission, not unlike the one Valentina had made to him
before they were married: "I love [Garbo] but I'm quite sure she won't want
to get married," he told his wife. "And you and I have so much in common."

Valentina took it badly and, in search of commiseration, told a friend,
who in turn told columnist Dorothy Kilgallen, who quoted George's words
in a 1948 *Saturday Home Magazine* piece—thus making Valentina's rage and
humiliation complete.

Noël Coward, when in New York, rarely missed a Schlee party, as his
numerous diary entries of this period indicate: "Drinks with Valentina, who
bared her soul a little over George and Garbo. Poor dear, I am afraid she
is having a dreary time." On another occasion, he noted in his journal:
"Russian Easter party at Valentina's, fairly dull but enlivened by Garbo who
was in an unusually merry mood."

In the fifties, Schlee regularly accompanied Garbo to the Riviera, Capri,
and the Greek islands, often aboard Aristotle Onassis's yacht. Their usual destination was "Le Roc," Schlee's villa in Cap d'Ail ("Cape of Garlic"), a tiny village just three miles from Monte Carlo. The fifteen-room, Mediterranean-

style house, set amid palms and cypresses overlooking the sea, had been built
by King Farouk for one of his mistresses (and was reputedly the site of many
royal orgies). Schlee was said to have purchased it with Garbo's money. In
July of 1957, Onassis arranged for fireworks to greet her when he deposited
her there—which much annoyed her. She and Schlee preferred to spend
time there quietly, and alone. Few people were ever invited to visit.

Writer John Gunther called Schlee "a connoisseur of the art of living."
Cecil Beaton, on the other hand, called him "that horrible little man" and
"that Russian sturgeon, [always] on duty as Cerberus to keep reality at bay,"
and was wildly jealous of his claim on Garbo's life and time.

With Schlee, "she possesses a new gaiety and an almost teen-age type of
flirtatiousness," wrote a reporter who spied on them during a transatlantic
voyage. "She rewards him with an amorousness [that is] surprising. When
he bends over her chair to ask a question, she throws her head back and
rubs her cheek against his chin like a kitten, asking, 'What is it, darling?' "

By 1951, Garbo had moved from the Ritz to a four-room suite on the
thirtieth floor of the Hampshire House at 150 Central Park South. In October
1953, she made the last and most important residential move of her life: At
Schlee's urging, she bought a seven-room, fifth-floor apartment at 450 East
Fifty-second Street, one story above his and Valentina's, for $38,000. Built
in 1927, that select cooperative (sometimes called the "Campanile" after the
Beekman Campanile, Inc., company that owned it) is situated in a cul-de-
sac overlooking FDR Drive and the East River. It was dubbed "Wit's End"
by Dorothy Parker when it housed the likes of Alexander Woollcott and
novelist Alice Duer Miller. Otto Kahn's daughter Nin Ryan and actors Rex
Harrison and Mary Martin were among its tenants.

"Garbo moved in and took Schlee right away from Valentina," claimed
Garbo's friend Nicholas Turner. "He knew all the best people. She told me,
'He really works for me. I give him 10 percent and pay for everything and
he breaks it all open. He's very good at that.' "

If so, she kept Schlee as off guard as she did everyone else, playing him
and Beaton and Hauser against one another for her affections and for the
privilege of running her life. On their trips together, says Turner, Schlee
was tyrannical:

> He had absolute control. When he didn't want to do something, they
> didn't do it, no matter how she felt about it. . . . She liked very much
> to get compliments from men. This made Schlee very upset. He was
> as jealous as the devil. I don't think he could tolerate having her exposed
> to other people, especially interesting or attractive men. Whenever that
> happened—and it happened several times—he would invent some ex-

cuse for cutting the trip short. He'd say he had forgotten about having to get back to meet a lawyer or a banker or something of the sort. So we would put into a port, and they would hire a car to take them back to their place. She never objected, never said a contrary word. Schlee dominated her completely.

Schlee, at least, never harried her with marriage proposals, as did Beaton, Hauser, and the other bachelors in her life. From Garbo's standpoint, he was almost perfect; Garbo, from his, was a deep mystery to which he thought he had the key. "She will not fight with an author or producer," he said. "If there's a script she thinks might be good with changes, and people scream about changes, she says forget it, and walks out. She hates conflict, [which] could be the reason for no pictures recently." But a different reason was intuited by Elsa Maxwell, the columnist and professional party-giver, who stumbled upon a private Garbo moment around this time:

> I came into the powder room and saw this woman studying herself in the mirror. She held her hands tightly to her cheeks as if to lift them. She gazed at herself a long time, then turned away from the mirror. I knew immediately that it was Garbo, but pretended not to notice. She left the room silently, but had a sad look on her face. . . . I had the feeling that she wasn't pleased at what she saw in the mirror. . . . I knew then and there that she'd never make another film.

Schlee knew no such thing. "She reminds me of Duse," he said, "[who] had been in retirement eleven years and returned to greater triumphs than ever. This will happen to Garbo." He was convinced she would return to the screen—and that only he could get her to do it.

When she came back from Europe in 1946, Garbo was asked by reporters about her film plans and, to their surprise, gave an answer: "I have no plans, not for the movies, not for the stage, not for anything, and I haven't even got a place to live. I'm sort of drifting." It was a poignantly honest reply. Garbo's aborted movie projects pepper the papers of the late forties. Always, there were obstacles.

"I was quite anxious to do *Mourning Becomes Electra* with Garbo and with George Cukor directing," said Katharine Hepburn of that 1947 film, but "we didn't get anywhere with Mayer." In the end, Dudley Nichols directed, Rosalind Russell played the cold-blooded daughter, and Katina Paxinou played the hot-blooded mother instead of Garbo, who was initially interested but, at forty-two, decided she didn't want to portray the thirty-nine-year-old Russell's insane mom.

But as early as 1943, she had indicated an eagerness to go back to work. "I continue to get all kinds of messages from Garbo asking if I won't make a picture with her," says a David Selznick memo of January 4 that year to an associate. "There is no particular reason why we should make a Garbo picture with all the women stars we have under contract—particularly Ingrid Bergman, but I will call it to your attention now only in case we run into a good piece of material."

In 1947, it was announced that she would star in Selznick's *The Paradine Case*, a property he'd bought with Garbo in mind way back in 1932. In addition, Selznick was talking with Leland Hayward about meeting "GG's eccentric demands and worries re: a deal for the two things about which she's excited, *Bernhardt* and *The Scarlet Lily*." He cited "the extremes to which I am going to meet her problems, show my respect for her, demonstrate a confidence in her possessed by no one else—treating her as though she were still a great drawing card, which no one in the industry will concede and which indeed is denied by all the so-called experts."

Selznick's confidence was slightly shaken by a Gallup poll ranking of the most popular stars in which Garbo's low standing "indicates pretty clearly that she would be outrageously overpaid at $100,000," he wrote in an internal memo. Around the same time, a bitchy but funny Irish critic had declared, "If Miss Garbo *really* wants to be alone, she should come to a performance of one of her films in Dublin."

Nevertheless, Selznick, like Schlee, believed "she could be an even bigger star than ever before," her comeback on a par with Bernhardt's and Duse's, and that the courtroom drama at hand, under Alfred Hitchcock's direction, was the vehicle by which she could do it. But there were story problems galore.

"For *The Paradine Case* we had a pile of scripts two feet high," said Hitchcock. "My wife, Alma Reville, did the first one, based on the novel. [Selznick] wrote the final shooting-script himself. That was his great ambition—to be a writer—and I think he should have stuck to producing. . . . He also cast the picture, to my mind unsatisfactorily."

At the last minute, Garbo backed out. Hitchcock said it was because her character was a barbershop lady in Stockholm—too close to home— and a murderess to boot.* But in a letter to Salka from the Ritz, she

* Her part went to Alida Valli, and the film, even with Charles Laughton, Ethel Barrymore, and Leo G. Carroll in support, turned out to be one of Hitchcock's dullest. In this 1947–1948 period of *The Paradine Case*, Garbo also turned down the title role in RKO's *I Remember Mama* with a classic four-word telegram that succinctly covered both: "No mamas, no murderesses." It was the worst of all her film-rejection mistakes. Irene Dunne took the part and, under George Stevens's direction, turned that well-written, evocative Scandinavian role into one of the most beloved film characters of the decade.

still sounded pathetically eager to make a film: "I spoke to Hayward and told him to talk to you of Sarah Bernhardt story. Did he? You were going to write me, but perhaps you don't feel like it. I am so sorry that it is so difficult for us to get started. Perhaps 'they' don't like us! [Have] you heard from Mannix or from anybody? . . . Darling Mrs. Viertel, will you let me know if there is something new. Please talk to Hayward about the S.B. story."

Salka did so. Before and after the *Paradine* negotiations, Selznick was trying to revive the Sarah Bernhardt project, while complaining about the time and fortune he had invested in it over the decades. In April 1946, he sent Garbo the expensive script he had commissioned from Ben Hecht, with a note asking her to read it quickly: "I hope this will be the clinching argument [for] a continuing association between us. . . . I should like to have Gregory Peck do this with you, [but] if we lose him for this summer . . . we may not get him for another year."

In November, Hedda Hopper reported that the Bernhardt story, starring Garbo, would soon be filmed by Selznick on a $5 million budget. By January 1947, it had progressed to the point that Selznick had decided to make it in color and was "absolutely positive" of its success. In July, he happily declared, "Schlee has agreed that Garbo will sign with us exclusively."

If so, Schlee deceived him, as various other negotiations were in the works. *Ninotchka* writers Billy Wilder and Walter Reisch were among many who were determined to interest her in a comeback. One day Wilder asked her if she would come over for a drink and discuss the possibilities:

> She said, "Yes, I vould like a drink." Very Viking. So we went to my house at 704 North Beverly Drive. I remember vividly, she came in and my wife was upstairs in her bedroom and I called up to her, "Come on down, we've got a visitor." And she said, "Who?" I said, "Greta Garbo." And my wife said, "Oh, fuck off."

Garbo either did not or pretended not to hear. In any case, once that awkward little moment was past Audrey Wilder came downstairs, and Wilder and Reisch alternated in telling her story ideas, as Reisch recalled:

> Billy started with the *Inconnue de la Seine*, the famous death mask in the Louvre, and developed the story of an unknown girl, drowned, reconstructing her life as the wife of a banker.
> "I do not want to play the wife of a banker," Garbo said.
> Billy's wife offered refreshments.
> "I will haf a nikolaiječek," said Garbo, referring to a drink made by

slipping a slice of lemon on the tongue, dissolving sugar on that same spot, and washing it down with a light brandy.

Then I took my turn, telling the story of Elizabeth of Austria, the most beautiful woman of the nineteenth century, an empress whose one temptation as a woman was to run away, abdicate and be herself.

"Another nikolaiječek," said Garbo.

"But what about the story?"

"I haf played Queen Christina already and I do not want to play another empress," she said.

I drove Garbo home and on the way tried one more approach: "Greta, if you ever wanted to make a comeback, give us one hint of what you would like to do. Do you want to play an actress, a spy, a coquette, a scientist?"

"A clown. A male clown."

"The most desired woman on earth wants to play a clown? Who will buy that?"

"Under the makeup and the silk pants, the clown is a woman. And all the admiring girls in the audience who write him letters are wondering why he does not respond. They cannot understand."

"It will never do," I said.

We never got any further.

Wilder felt she had become afraid of what the camera might see: "She wanted to hide behind greasepaint. She could play the clown in white makeup, so no one would be able to see her face." Unable to get past their own incredulity, Wilder and Reisch failed to see that her "ridiculous" idea was also stunningly original and might have changed Garbo's life and film history.

In France, there was much excitement over a report that Garbo would appear in a Serge Lifar production of *Phèdre* at the Paris Opéra, miming her role, but that performance remained a figment of the producers' imaginations. The French were always after her: Jean Cocteau was still begging Mercedes de Acosta to intercede for him in his desire to write and direct a Garbo film. (As late as 1960, Cocteau invited her to appear in a scene with Picasso in his *Le Testament d'Orphée*.) But she was as indifferent to those as to most other ideas.

Until Wanger and Balzac.

Walter Wanger (1894–1967) was one of the most colorful and sophisticated producers of all time. As a young man at the end of World War I, he was an aide-de-camp to the American delegation at the Versailles peace conference and claimed to be the first to announce the armistice. His early film career was spent mostly at Paramount, but his important later pictures were independently produced, including *Shanghai* (1935), *Blockade* and *Trade Winds* (1938), *Stage Coach* (1939), his recent *Joan of Arc* (1948), and the current *Reckless Moment*, starring his wife, Joan Bennett.

Wanger had produced the film closest to Garbo's heart, *Queen Christina*, during which they got on well. He had bided his time since her "retirement" to snag her for the comeback film he felt certain would be triumphant. The biggest of many hurdles was financing. The film he had in mind was to be made in Italy or France, largely with Italian money. Securing investors in Italy was problematic, though not insurmountable in view of his own skills and the magic name of Garbo. To that end, he formed Walter Wanger International Productions, with his friend Eugene Frenke in charge of funding.* Aside from money, there were many other things to attend to, not least the story selection—and Balzac's *La Duchesse de Langeais* was not yet even in the running.

"I'm meeting with Miss G. and Salka this afternoon at 3 o'clock to discuss [a film about] George Sand," Wanger wrote Frenke on September 14, 1948, adding that Garbo was still screening films of the directors and actors who were candidates to work with her, including Wanger's *The Lost Moment* with Robert Cummings, whom Wanger was pushing for the role of Sand's lover, Alfred de Musset. Salka told Wanger the same thing she'd recently told George Cukor:

"Greta will have a terrific success as George Sand. She would have a terrific success in anything because she is more beautiful than ever and a great artist, but her artistic integrity is something Hollywood will never understand and never value until she has made a foreign film."

Cecil Beaton agreed: "I could see Greta wearing velvet trousers and smoking a cigar. From Joan of Arc to Christina of Sweden, the idea of women in cavalier clothes has a visual aspect that is appealing to her. . . . *Travesti* has obviously titillated her and . . . she has enjoyed wearing the more romantic of men's apparel in her films. Ventriloquists' dolls and pierrots possess an ambiguity that delights her sense of the perverse."

But it had been seven years since her last film, and Garbo was more nervous and indecisive than ever. Wanger now cabled Frenke: "Star most excited about Pabst picture." He had just shown her and Salka the new Pabst film, *Der Prozess* (*The Trial*), a searing murder drama that reduced both women to tears: "This film is really wonderful, the first true and great

---

* Wanger's two other principal partners were accountant G. R. Mercader and actor Robert Cummings.

film about anti-Semitism," Salka wrote Cukor. "Greta was deeply moved and shaken. She said afterward, 'When one sees such a film, one realizes what a medium the screen can be.' Alas, Hollywood has forgotten it."

Knowing and revering Pabst two decades earlier on *Joyless Street*, the prospect of working with him again was as exciting to Garbo as the fresh evidence of his creative power. *The New York Times* was now belatedly hailing him as one of "the ten directors who most shaped the language of the film." At this very moment he was incubating a lavish new project with Garbo as the centerpiece: a modern adaptation of Homer's *Odyssey*, to be filmed in Italy with Garbo in the dual roles of Penelope and Circe, and either Clark Gable or Orson Welles as Ulysses.

But Pabst and *Ulysses* were quickly squelched by Frenke, who wired Wanger from Paris: "Pabst has a very bad reputation in France. He is tabu in this country. They won't let him in because of his former pro-Nazi activities. . . . The French producers are enthused about the Sand story." Pabst's "pro-Nazism" was a vicious but widely believed lie, sufficient to knock him out of the running.

Wanger had given up Cummings and was now "very keen to get Montgomery Clift to play Alfred de Musset," Salka reported. "I have seen a great deal of Monty lately [and] this part will make a great star out of him." Indeed, Clift came often to Salka's. He admired her courage in the face of political blacklisting. She was giving acting lessons to get by these days, but her "Sundays" continued, and she introduced Clift to Garbo. "Salka became another mother figure to Monty," says Peter Viertel. "She listened to him pour out his troubles." She also kept plugging for him hard—but uselessly—with Cukor:

"Every studio wants him. . . . He is modest, simple, and I think he would be very good as Alfred, if *you* work with him. All this, of course, is very premature. Still, it wouldn't be bad to secure a first-rate actor now so that Miss Brown doesn't end up with Melvyn Douglas, as she usually does." Salka saw Garbo almost daily and described her as "impatient to work [yet] afraid of it. I understand this very well, after all these years of idleness. Work is a habit and she lost it."

Poor Salka was laboring under three illusions: that the Sand story was a "go"; that Clift could be Garbo's co-star; and that Cukor would direct. Her own contract to write the Sand script was signed and she was ever optimistic—until she smelled a rat in the form of Leland Hayward, who had told Frenke, "You can have Garbo. Nobody wants her. I don't give a damn." Frenke relayed that to Salka, who was furious.

"I couldn't tell Greta this because it would have hurt her pride and ego terribly," she wrote Cukor, "but I implored her to get somebody else to represent her—Minna Wallis, anybody, only not Leland." Hayward not only denigrated Garbo for the Wanger project but bad-mouthed her to others who were interested in hiring her, as well.

Frenke plodded on, cabling Wanger from Rome that financing "will not be any problem." But there was a thorn in his side named George Schlee, now making the European rounds as Garbo's manager. After Salka alerted her to the Hayward problem, Garbo had turned that job over to Schlee on the erroneous theory that he could do no worse.

"I did not negotiate with any of the French writers," Frenke told Wanger, "because Schlee took such a pride in doing this and made such a big fuss that I did not want to hurt his feelings and show him any distrust. From the way he described trying to meet Coqteux [*sic*] and Sascha Guitry it would seem easier to arrange a meeting with the Pope himself."* There was even talk of getting Jean-Paul Sartre to write Garbo's screenplay.

By October 1948, the star was chomping at the bit. "Garbo anxious to get going," Wanger telegrammed. Frenke cabled that Dorothy Parker was working on the Sand script, but Wanger now wanted a backup: "When can I look at *Duchesse de Langeais*?"

Garbo was also still considering Empress Elizabeth of Austria—the subject of Cocteau's current play, *The Eagle Has Two Heads* (with Tallulah Bankhead), which Garbo had liked. Its atmosphere appealed to her, she told Beaton, who suggested it to his friend Alexander Korda. Korda loved the idea: "We do it right away in Shepperton [studios in London] in June."

Beaton, as ever, had ulterior motives. "I saw before me a whole new vista with Greta in England," he told his diary. "Everything went well [with Korda]. They were more or less decided they would make the picture. Greta would come to England for the studio work." She told Beaton: "I'll do it, but I've got to start preparing—getting fit right away, coaxing my body back in shape, exercising my arms—and if I'm going to wear *décolletage* there's a lot to arrange. Yes, I know I'm going to do this film—I feel it. I've never been as close to anything before."

Garbo asked Beaton endless questions about how she would live in England. Where was the studio? Could she rent a small house nearby and take walks in the evening? She wouldn't want to live London. She even called Korda and discussed certain script changes, to which he agreed. But then came a telegram: Korda was unable to make *The Eagle*, due to "previous commitments." The next day, she told Beaton: "It seems the Almighty doesn't want me to do a picture: every time I think I'm going to start again, something

---

* Salka flatly refused to collaborate with Guitry because of "his previous collaborators" from 1940 through 1945—the Nazis.

goes wrong. . . . I really thought this time we would be doing *Elizabeth*. *Oy veh!* But somehow I'm never surprised by the most unexpected things. . . . If they're bad things, then I'm sad—but never surprised."

Korda, as a kind of consolation prize, asked her to do a stage production of Chekhov's *Cherry Orchard*. It was Beaton's most beloved play and he would design her costumes and settings. "I would give almost anything to see Greta as Madame Ranevska," he wrote, "—a part that in many aspects resembles her. (The indecision, the incapability to face facts now.)" But she thought people would think her a lesser star in such a role. She had the urge, said Beaton, "yet she harks back to the safety of old-time directors and her former cameraman."

As 1948 ended, Salka said that Schlee "disliked George Sand, de Musset, and my story intensely." That signalled its death knell, but it was not until March of 1949 that Garbo finally abandoned Sand for Balzac. Contracts were signed and reported in the press, tying in the film to the Balzac centennial of 1950.

La Duchesse de Langeais was one of three stories comprising Balzac's swashbuckling novel *The Thirteen* (1834). It is the tale of capricious Antoinette, "loved to frenzy" by the Marquis de Montriveau. She flirts with him but rejects his suit and is then kidnapped by the fanatic fraternity of Masonic adventurers to which he belongs—leading her to a broken heart, a near-branding, a nunnery, and disaster. It is the Fiction of Frustration, defying credibility at every turn, but its breathless narrative had a certain screen potential. "The heart weighs the fall of a fourteen-year-old Empire and the dropping of a woman's glove in the same scales," Balzac begins, "and the glove is nearly always the heavier of the two."

It would be up to Garbo's subtlety to temper the romantic excess. Certainly, she identified with the part, for she was a kind of duchess-turned-nun herself. She, like the character, was "a woman whose instincts and feelings were lofty, while the thought which should have controlled them was wanting. . . . You might sit near her through an evening, she would be gay and melancholy in turn. She was anything that she wished to be or to seem. Like some straight-growing reed, she made a show of independence; yet, like the reed, she was ready to bend to a strong hand. She trusted nothing and no one, yet there were times when she traded her skeptical attitude for a submissive credulity." Balzac embellished that description with a grand sexist analogy: "Nations, like women, love strength in those who rule them; they refuse utterly to obey those of whom they do not stand in awe."

Garbo obeyed and stood in awe of George Schlee as no other man since Stiller, and when she came to Rome in April 1949 it was under Schlee's watchful eye. Her job was to meet and charm the financiers, a demeaning thing to which she had never been reduced before. Schlee fussed and hovered and aired his creative ideas and made everyone more nervous. Wanger called him her "embarrassing constant companion" and said he was "a barrier for direct contact with Garbo" unless such contact furthered his own initiatives.

Shortly before they left for Europe, for example, Schlee had taken her to see the new Broadway hit *South Pacific*. She liked it so much that she sent director Joshua Logan two red venetian-glass ashtrays—a symbolic substitute, she said, for two of Bloody Mary's shrunken heads. Schlee thought Logan should direct *Duchesse* and asked if he would meet with her to explore the idea, in great secrecy, at the little town of Vezelay outside Paris. Indeed he would, Logan recalled:

> I drove there and wandered the streets on the lookout for a glamorous lady wearing a billowing dotted Swiss skirt and a big picture hat. I almost bumped into a gangling boy in very short pants, the fabulous Garbo herself, walking with Schlee. She was so lean and beautiful that it was hard to believe she was not the fourteen-year-old she looked.
>
> Over aperitifs, we talked for hours about the Flea Market, about paintings and antiques, with only an occasional mention of *La Duchesse de Langeais*. I promised to read the story as soon as possible and told Garbo that it would be a fine honor to direct her.
>
> That day I never felt I was talking with a grown person. She had a child's laugh, and the things that amused her were childish things. Here was doomed Camille and noble Queen Christina and tragic Anna Karenina suddenly transformed into Huck Finn. I defy anyone to make the person she is fit the women she has played on the screen.

Back in California, Wanger was upset about slow progress, mounting costs, and the presence of Schlee, who billed him for $2,451 in European expenses. He had already paid $3,700 to Salka, $800 to Dorothy Parker, and $2,000 to other writers for the now-useless Sand script. He was currently paying $13,500 to writer Sally Benson for a *Duchesse* scenario "in progress" (and she would soon be suing him for an additional $15,000).

Frenke had spent many more thousands; the budget was $224,000 and climbing. Worse news was that the money men—chiefly, Angelo Rizzoli of the publishing family—had not been satisfied by their brief glimpse of *la Divina* in her hotel room. She had drawn all the blinds and worn a big hat, and the Italians were convinced she was hiding something like smallpox. No checks would be signed until they saw a screen test.

A *screen test*? Of *Garbo*?

It was insulting and outrageous, but Wanger was trapped. He and Frenke had come too far to dump the Italians now. The surprise was that Garbo,

William Daniels's screen test of Garbo for La Duchesse de Langeais. *The footage was thought to have been lost, until its rediscovery in 1990.*

when informed, offhandedly agreed. Attended by two of the best cinematographers in the business, James Wong Howe and her own William Daniels, she made the black-and-white tests in Hollywood on May 5 and May 25, 1949, in the Chaplin Studio on La Brea. For forty years, that footage was thought to have been lost, until its rediscovery in 1990 by film historians Leonard Maltin of ABC-TV and Jeanine Basinger of the Wesleyan University film archives: Gorgeously lit in close-up, Garbo pivots slowly in silence, her eyelashes sweeping the air. A fan plays on her hair. She smokes, she frowns, and then she cannot suppress a smile. For thirteen exquisite minutes, she proves that she has lost none of her riveting photogeneity.

There is no sound, but several times we can lip-read her question, "Enough?" To Daniels at one point, she smiles and clearly articulates the words, "Anything for you."

Howe thought the purpose of the exercise was to test *cameramen*, not Garbo; whoever did the better shots would get the job. In fact, both the actress and the photographers were auditioning and, beforehand, Garbo admitted she was scared.

James Wong Howe's screen test of Garbo for Duchesse

"She was like a horse on the track—nothing, and then the bell goes, and something happens," said Howe. "When the camera started to roll, she started to come to life. You could see her personality come out, her mood change; and she became more beautiful. We shot for several hours, a couple of thousand feet of film, from different angles and with different lighting. When we were through, she said, 'Thank you. I go back to the beach.'"

If Garbo felt humiliated by having to do the test, she never showed it but was professionalism incarnate. The results were so stunning that not even the cretinous financiers could deny it, and they now let loose some money. The script moved forward, and so did the selection of director. Logan and Cukor were ruled out. Finally chosen was the virtuosic Max Ophuls.

Next came the critical matter of co-star. In his sleek film noir *Caught* (1948), Ophuls had cast newcomer James Mason and did so again in his next American film, *The Reckless Moment*, a stylish Wanger production in which Joan Bennett saves her daughter from Mason's blackmail. Garbo liked it and gave him tentative approval for the role of Montriveau, who "despises himself for his weakness"—something Mason did often and well in films. But first she wanted to meet him. In spring 1949, Garbo and Wanger visited Mason's home—once Buster Keaton's—in Beverly Hills, as Pamela Mason recalls:

She was very outgoing, quite the opposite of everything they always said about her. She came to approve James—to look at him and see if he was tall enough. People always thought James was short, but he was six feet. So she came over and was delightful and never mentioned the film once. Walter had said to us before, "Don't scare her off by talking about the film unless she brings it up," which she didn't. She was sitting in the sunlight in the garden with no make-up, looking absolutely gorgeous. Most of the time she played with the animals, while Walter and James talked. She was full of laughter and fun and most surprisingly open. I wouldn't have called her shy at all.

Garbo liked both Masons and returned several times to visit, never discussing movies. "James wasn't much of a film-talker himself," says Pamela, who debunks the claim that Garbo had a "crush" on her husband. "She hardly saw him—just that first day, really. Most of the times she played with the children at the pool and he wasn't around. If she had had an interest in him, she could have easily promoted it. But she didn't make any real effort to get to know him, and he was a rather reserved person, anyway. He was far more Garboish than she." As for *Duchesse*, James Mason thought "it wasn't a very interesting script but it was a very interesting co-star. It would have been an interesting match for faces."

Wanger thought so, too. He was unwilling to meet Mason's "regular" fee of $150,000 but agreed to half that figure—which was 50 percent more than the $50,000 he was paying Garbo. It was amazing evidence of their relative value in the eyes of the 1949 film industry.

Things were humming along now; sets were under construction in Italy. But then came trouble. By the end of July, the budget estimate had soared to $490,000. In August, Wanger wired Frenke in Rome: "Garbo does not understand contract. Schlee must be misinterpreting it to her." And then, suddenly, in September, the Italians pulled out of the deal completely.

The papers said Rizzoli was withdrawning his offer to put up 300 million lire (about $522,000) because Garbo had imposed impossible conditions. The *Duchesse* project was described as a catch-22 situation in which she refused to commit herself until it was financed and the financiers refused to put up money until she committed. James Mason, in 1979, said: "They probably cancelled because they just couldn't deal with this crazy dame." But, in fact, none of those charges was true. Garbo, for once, did not remain aloof. She had actually signed several contracts, and in late September when things were worsening she not only agreed to a reduced fee but to waive it until the production got on its feet.

A new scramble for funds was on. Frenke cabled Wanger that Howard Hughes was now interested. Wanger did not reply. Frenke cabled again. Still no answer. Frenke again, on November 21: "I am very surprised not to have had a reply to any of my letters or telegrams. I am surely at a loss to understand your silence."

Wanger finally broke it on November 28:

"I don't know why you are surprised that I don't reply to your letters or telegrams. . . . Where is Garbo? I have not had a single word from you regarding her whereabouts or attitude. . . . Stop writing meaningless letters that impress no one and let me know (1) what the Garbo status is? (2) what your propositions are from Columbia and RKO?"

Wanger was getting testier by the minute. The above cable was toned down considerably from two previous versions he dictated—and saved for possible future use:

> Draft #1: "Dear Gene: I see no cause for alarm at your end as to why I have not answered your cables or letters. The answer is very simple—neither your cables nor your letters have been intelligible. Point of fact, the cause for alarm rests with me at your sloppy handling and wasted money on this project . . ."

> Draft #2: "Dear Gene: You stink. I don't want any part of you or Miss Garbo unless it's a legitimate deal. And as I am sure you are not legitimate and Miss Garbo only wants to remain in the limelight one way or another but certainly not to appear in a picture—goodbye!"

Culpability for the eleventh-hour collapse of *La Duchesse de Langeais* has been variously assigned to everyone connected with the project, including Garbo. Actress Dana Wynter, Wanger's friend, claimed it was all set to go until Garbo "asked for her usual clause: to be allowed three or four days each month when [she] would not be at her best [and] the shooting schedule would be arranged to accommodate that. . . . The head of the studio refused, thinking the lady would retreat from her position. She did not, he did not, and that was the end of her career."

But there was no "head of the studio." This was Wanger's independent production. Nor is any "period clause" to be found in any of Garbo's MGM contracts. "I never heard of it," says Pamela Mason. "Ginger Rogers and others had to work through [menstruation], and nobody ever thought twice about it."

Wanger himself dissembled even to the Masons. "Walter always told us the film fell through because Garbo refused to make a photographic test," said Pamela Mason, who believed that until she saw the test aired in 1990 by Leonard Maltin on national television. "This was obviously a lie. When I saw it the other night—she was so extraordinarily beautiful! They must all have seen the film and couldn't have been anything but thrilled by it."

The truth involved many mistakes within and beyond Wanger's control. Most serious was entrusting money matters to Frenke, a charming émigré who knew his way around Europe but was a neophyte at fund-raising. The Italians strung him along, mostly just to meet Garbo, by which time it was too late to improvise a replacement deal. Also, the financial failure of Wanger's expensive *Joan of Arc* with Ingrid Bergman a year earlier now hindered his ability to find investors for an even riskier Swede.

But the greatest "mistake" was George Schlee, an abrasive amateur whose ignorance of the business complicated Wanger's efforts. On January 22, 1950, as *Duchesse* was dying but still drawing breath, Sheilah Graham said in her radio broadcast, "One of the conditions [of continuing] is that Garbo leave her dressmaker-boyfriend, George Schlee, behind in America." In Paris, meanwhile, Schlee told Beaton how clever he had been to *extricate* her from the deal.

One by one, after a few more depressing weeks of waiting, the participants began trickling home—first Garbo and Schlee and then the rest. Only Ophuls got a lucky break. At a total loss for job or money, he was unexpectedly asked to direct a film in France: *La Ronde* (1950), one of the most beautiful and successful films of postwar Europe. In a sense, it was the film *The Duchess of Langeais* might have been.

Back home in New York, Garbo was stunned as to why the money couldn't be raised and then devastated when she came to grips with the reality: No one was sure she could still "draw" in 1950. Players rise and fall "according to how well they are managed [and] to the caprice of the public," Irving Thalberg once said, as if with Garbo and Schlee in mind. Even the devoted S. N. Behrman, who wanted her for *Quo Vadis* (1951) but was discouraged by George Schlee, would soon say, "I haven't mentioned her to a producer for years. If you do they leave the room. They say she's death at the box office."

Nicholas Turner went to see her at her apartment and asked what happened. "She came over to me, put her head on my shoulder, tears came down from her eyes, and she said, 'It was a fiasco,'" he recalled. "'I will never make or try to make a moving picture again. This is the end.'"

She had so *wanted* to do it, and it was so close. "Beauty," wrote Balzac in *Duchesse*, "is a woman's parachute." But Garbo's matchless beauty and all her past glory and present connections in the film industry failed her, even as—simultaneously—a much less likely "comeback" was in the works.

There were people in Hollywood who actually thought they could resurrect Gloria Swanson in something called *Sunset Boulevard*.*

On February 9, 1951, Greta Garbo stood with 150 others at the Bureau of Immigration and Naturalization in New York to take the oath of allegiance and become an American citizen—at a time when her new countrymen were regarding her, or at least her film presence, as an anachronism. The collapse of the Wanger film was a personal and artistic defeat that bitterly reaffirmed all the reasons why she left movies in the first place. If she hadn't been a recluse earlier, she was further motivated to become one now.

The "comeback" reports continued, some containing grains of truth. In March 1950, Pabst arrived in New York to drum up support for his *Odyssey* but was unable to get the two things he most needed: funding and Garbo. Around the same time, Clarence Brown suggested a remake of *Flesh and the Devil*. Garbo and MGM both liked the idea, said Brown, but two weeks later, "I was informed that there'd been some changes; instead of Germany, it was going to take place in South America, so they could use some frozen funds in Argentina. And didn't I think Ava Gardner was a better idea than Garbo? I walked out."

Salka Viertel was having trouble with the House Committee on Un-American Activities but was still negotiating with the long-suffering Selznick on Garbo's behalf—this time for a joint production of *Lady Chatterley's Lover* with Svensk Filmindustri. "Garbo still Garbo in all ways good and bad," wrote Selznick in March 1950—"terrified" of commiting herself. Even so, he proposed a "censor-proof adaptation" of *Chatterley* to Garbo as one of two pictures he planned to coproduce with her old friend Gustaf Molander. By making it in Sweden, they would overcome censorship problems and get great publicity from her return "home." But when the Breen Office refused even to consider it for release in America, Selznick abandoned the idea.

His last Garbo effort was an attempt to revive the Duse story through Charles Feldman, who had taken on some of her agenting duties. "Feldman tried to talk me into letting her do [a Billy] Wilder picture first," Selznick wrote Gottfried Reinhardt in November 1950. "But I told him I didn't think two Garbo pictures [were likely and that] she would have to make a choice. [I think] Charlie Feldman is a friend. . . . But strange things happen in this town and I therefore think you ought to get to her without delay [and say]

---

* In Billy Wilder's *Sunset Boulevard*, Swanson as the has-been star says, "In those days we had faces," and Garbo's is among the names she mentions. After seeing the film, Garbo—disturbed by the past-tense reference—told a friend, "I thought Billy Wilder was a friend of mine."

*Garbo in 1951, around the time she became an American citizen, photographed by
George Hoyningen-Huene*

I am counting upon her to sign no other deals. . . . If this works out as I hope, it will be the beginning of what she and I so often talked about—her career from this point on would be exclusively in my hands."

After two weeks of silence, Selznick wrote Reinhardt again:

"Tell her frankly that I am very much annoyed. . . . I want her to understand that I have no intention of being kept on the hook indefinitely while she and/or Feldman see what else they can put together. . . . Please kept this in front of you when you talk with her and don't mince any words."

Feldman, in all probability, was doing just what Selznick suspected: shopping for the proverbial "best offer." Garbo herself was still depressed and demoralized from the collapse of *Duchesse*, while Selznick was becoming increasingly annoyed by not knowing whether Feldman or Schlee really spoke for her. The result, by her usual "pocket veto," was the final demise of all three glossy projects—Bernhardt, Sand, and Duse—that David O. Selznick had for so long tried to make with her.

If true, as reported in July 1951, that Garbo had signed a formal contract with Feldman, he failed to bring off a single deal for her. A $25,000 offer from producer Irving Mansfield to appear on the CBS program "This Is Show Business" was declined because she was averse to appearing before a studio audience. Similarly, in mid-1951, she turned down $20,000 for a four-minute appearance on Kate Smith's TV show. She also said no that year to Salvador Dalí's request to star in a film about Saint Teresa of Ávila and to John Gunther's comeback offer in the form of a screen adaptation of *Death Be Not Proud*, his memoir to his son.

George Cukor was excited in 1952 when she agreed to make the film of Daphne du Maurier's best-seller *My Cousin Rachel*. But a day after her acceptance, she changed her mind. "I'm sorry," Cukor quoted her. "I can't go through with it." ("I could never be Cornish," she told a friend.) Money wasn't the issue: That same year she turned down $50,000 for a seven-minute spot on the "Omnibus" series. Ironically, her wealth worked against her. Other veteran stars overcame their ambivalence about making films and TV shows past their prime—Bette Davis and Joan Crawford, for example. Like them, Garbo wanted to work but, unlike them, she had no monetary incentive to do so.

Orson Welles wrote a screen scenario for her and Chaplin, *The Loves of D'Annunzio and Duse*—"two crazy monsters, degenerate hyper-romanticism . . . but neither would do it." In 1952, Ida Lupino and Collier Young had the bright idea of a drama called *The House of Seven Garbos*, about a Hollywood boardinghouse and its resident aspiring actresses, but Garbo never answered their letters. In 1954, she rejected Stanley Kramer's offer to star in *Not as a Stranger*, even as the newspapers were reviving rumors of the movie about George Sand and Chopin, claiming that Garbo was about to agree to star in it opposite Liberace. When someone mentioned that precious celebrity pianist to her, she replied, "Liberace? What's that? It's a restaurant?"

In 1955, it was Darryl Zanuck making an all-out but useless effort to get her to star in *Anastasia*. In 1956, she declined a $100,000 offer to play Catherine the Great on TV. On and on, the offers came and went.

The Garbo comeback got less likely as every new set of circumstances— and her growing indifference—worked to defeat it. Each year it became harder to measure up to her own myth. "I think she would have to be ever so dotty to make another film," said her almost-co-star James Mason. "Her memory is so gorgeous." Though many now believe that leaving films in 1941 was her coolest act, her friends at the time thought otherwise. "She just throws away her days," said one. "She talks about her last picture as her grave, and that is so foolish. . . . It is almost criminal." Said Jessica Dragonette: "She languishes in the best years of her life."

Garbo felt it herself, and her melancholy deepened. It was as hard for her as anyone else to grasp that so trivial a thing as *Two-Faced Woman* could destroy her self-confidence and that all her subsequent efforts could be ruined by what Gayelord Hauser summed up as "bad advice, poor scripts." But actor Roddy McDowall clarifies both the cultural and the psychological dilemmas she faced:

> It's amazing when you stop to think about it. Just two years earlier, she was completely *au courant*—"Garbo laughs!"—in *Ninotchka*. But people thought of her rather like a hemline: Her "statement" was so indelible that once it went out, it *really* went out, or so they thought until too late, when they realized how much they missed her. The way she reacted after *Two-Faced Woman* was like Joe Mankiewicz, who never recovered from what he considered the humiliation of *Cleopatra*, or Billy Wilder after *One, Two, Three*. People who've been sacrosanct are often unable to handle a flop—especially their first—the mocking and making fun of them.

She was a running gag, for instance, in the correspondence of Groucho Marx and E. B. White. Groucho had recently accused White of becoming a Garboesque recluse "who lives in a spirit world." Replied White on April 12, 1954: "It is nice here in the spirit world and if you get here I would like to buy you a drink. Garbo is here. We maintain separate residences, for appearances' sake."

Many of the jokes were public. One day on Fifth Avenue, she spotted a sign in I. Miller's shoe store: "We Can Fit Anybody's Feet, Even Garbo's." Her feelings were hurt, and she took—well, an unusual step, entreating her lawyer-friend Eustace Seligman to ask that the sign be removed. (It was.)

"She seems to be perpetually frightened, of people and of disapproval," said Barbara Barondess in March 1952, when Garbo was consulting her on interior decorating. "She wants friendship but hasn't matured much through the years or added a great deal to herself. Now and then she comes out of her shell when someone offers new interest or excitement, then after a while she goes back in again. Mostly, she just broods or makes slipcovers."

Barondess was unaware of the important friendship Garbo was then cementing—perhaps the deepest of the last half of her life—with Jane Gunther, second wife of John Gunther, the author and foreign correspondent. Several years earlier, Schlee had introduced Garbo to the Gunthers, who gently induced her to socialize at their 1 East End Avenue apartment, not far from Garbo's own.

"They were very gregarious and good hosts," recalls novelist Marcia Davenport, "and in those days when they had a party, she was there." The Gunthers were said to have an arrangement of bells and a concealed passageway so that Garbo could escape unseen if some "stranger" unexpectedly appeared. That was apocryphal, but it was a fact that they were extremely fond and protective of her. Jane saw her often at home and for lunch at the Colony. "She has a poetic magic, so difficult to describe," said Jane, "and all one knows is that one wants this in one's life."

Mrs. Gunther, née Jane Perry, was a former editor at Duell, Sloan & Pierce and *Reader's Digest* when she married John Gunther in 1948. She had a poetic magic of her own, especially with Garbo, to whom she remained devoted for the next forty years.

Aside from Schlee and the Gunthers, few others in New York could lure Garbo out of her Fifty-second Street lair, but one who did was Montgomery Clift. In 1955, he included her and Schlee in a dinner party with Libby Holman, Thornton Wilder, and Arthur Miller. Throughout the meal, Schlee kept baiting Holman about the mysterious death of her husband until Garbo, sensing everyone's embarrassment, muttered, "Shut up"—and Schlee did. Clift had "a violent crush" on her and subsequently took her out several times alone. At the end of one date, he managed to kiss her good night. "Her lips are chapped," he reported.

Her forays continued to the West Coast, where she was friendly with David Niven and his Swedish wife, Hjördis, recently featured on the cover of *Life* as one of the "ten most beautiful women in Hollywood." Niven recalled that among the "highly decorative Scandinavian ladies" who graced their gatherings were Viveca Lindfors, Signe Hasso, Anita Ekberg, and "the first naked female my sons ever saw—Greta Garbo swimming happily in our pool." The Nivens once chartered a small sloop and set off for Catalina

Island, with Garbo serving as cook. When the wind died and the boat's engine broke down, "the Swedish members of the expedition drank schnapps and made crude Nordic jokes at our expense. Garbo during the weekend made up for some patchy and uninspired cooking by exuding sparkling fun and swimming, unself-consciously, every day Swedish style."

During that same period, she attended a performance of David Diamond's Fourth Symphony by the Los Angeles Philharmonic. In these years, she also saw Diamond in Rome and later Florence, where he mischievously defied her no-film-talk taboo:

"Once I told her I was still upset about Janet Gaynor's wig in Murnau's *Sunrise*, and she said, 'Why do you talk about silly things like wigs? Yes, she looked ridiculous, but why do you talk about it?' "

But travel plans always paralyzed her, as indicated in a May 6, 1954, letter to Salka: "I usually go somewhere with Schlee for summer [but] I don't want to go to Europe. I feel so tired and listless. I would like just to go somewhere in fresh air and have no clothes on. . . . Schlee doesn't like Calif. very much and one does not know of any other place in America where it would be easy to play."

That year, and many others, she ended up on the Riviera with "Schleesky" more or less by default. In July 1957, Noël Coward recorded in his diary: "The high spot of the week has been a lovely evening with Garbo. We picked her up at her beautifully situated but hideous villa [La Roc] and dined at a little restaurant on the port at Villefranche. Garbo was bright as a button and, of course, fabulously beautiful."

A few months later, she was back in California for an extended stay through spring of 1958 at the Marmont Hotel in Santa Monica. She had tea one day with Rose de Haulleville, the Marmont's assistant manager, whom she'd met years before through her sister, Maria Huxley. Rose was in Garbo's suite for a long time and, when she emerged, hotel employee Carmel Volti asked how it went. Rose shrugged and said, "Oh, Greta just sat there and repeated, 'How flime ties'—and that was about it."

Garbo's Marmont days were often but not always solitary. Hauser came to visit, and there were dinners with Cukor at his home in the nearby hills. One evening, she breezed by the front desk in a floor-length black velvet cape on her way out. "She hadn't picked up her mail in ages, and I wanted to catch her," said Volti. "So I took the things from her box, held them out for her, and said, 'Miss Garbo, here are your messages and rent receipts.' She looked at me sweetly and, as she continued on her way, replied, 'That's all right. We trust each other.' "

Maurice Chevalier was also staying at the Marmont then, and one night they found themselves together at Cukor's. Chevalier tried to follow Garbo's mood, which changed abruptly from "gay, witty brilliance to deep sadness or a kind of mysterious despair," he said. They chatted easily, "and as the evening progressed I began to wonder why I had ever found it difficult to converse with this fascinating woman. Then, out of the blue . . . she asked me if I liked to swim in the ocean. It seemed like an odd, disconnected question, but I smiled and nodded. 'Good,' she said firmly, 'shall we now go to the beach?' I looked at her rather startled and replied, 'Now?' It was almost midnight and the icy Pacific in March held little appeal for me. . . . Instantly our warm, friendly conversation was over. The lady still sat beside me, but for the remainder of the party she was so remote and withdrawn and far away that I felt almost alone."

It was the last Garbo and Chevalier saw of each other.

Shortly thereafter, the Italian magazine *L'Europeo* made the most dramatic announcement of all: "Greta Garbo will enter a convent." She never took the veil, but she took to the road. There was one Garbo venue these days that neither the press nor anyone else ever caught on to: her brother's home in New Mexico. From "Desertland," circa 1954, she wrote Salka: "I have disappeared in the wilderness. I am sitting in a little home made house . . . practically a prisoner because I don't want anyone to know I am here. It is very unprotected and if someone should know they might come upon me and then no peace again. The air is good here and I have been working a little in the ground. . . . If you feel like writing to me, you can write to Occupant (that's my name) 1672 Cerro Gordo Road, Santa Fe, New Mexico. Please don't mix up things and put my name on the enveloppe. Because then I will have to leave."

There seemed to be two kinds of men in her life: the tyrannical organizer type who could make decisions, such as Stiller and Schlee, and the entertaining but emotionally immature kind, such as John Gilbert and Cecil Beaton, whom she could more easily handle.

"I think she encouraged Cecil's proposals," says their mutual friend Sam Green. "She felt at home and comfortable at his place—a cozy little cottage with a lot of sophisticated friends around. Right up her alley. She could have been Lady Beaton in Wiltshire in a very pretty house with a country garden, where nobody made a fuss. Everybody would have stopped bothering her because she was Cecil's wife. It was a viable possibility, and she would have been much happier."

But did Beaton really believe it would happen? Says Green:

Beaton and every other male, because she was so incredibly alluring. Sex wasn't a big thing to her. Penetration may have been, but closeness was not. Nudity was not. Physical togetherness was not. That misled not just Beaton, but everybody. Me included. I didn't want to marry her or sleep with her, but she was the ideal romantic companion. She led all of us on. You wanted to put your head on her lap or bury your face between her breasts or have her kiss you. It didn't matter how old she was. It was always a privilege to be with her. I was having fantasies all the time—not in the *Playboy* sense, but this was the ultimate courtship anybody could ever have.

Beaton certainly thought so. In the summer of 1951, she was his guest for six weeks at Reddish House in Broadchalke, near Salisbury. During that time, "the arty lensman"—as the British press called him—treated her to a social whirl that included a meeting with Princess Margaret, with whom she "got along like a palace on fire." She also got on famously with the local vicar and shopkeepers, whose Wiltshire accents and quirky personalities she loved. "It was a revelation to watch her coming to life [and] taking to Wiltshire ways as if this was where she belonged," Beaton wrote. "The transformation I had hoped for was, in fact, taking place." His only worry was the press, which badgered her and kept printing marriage reports, and his mother, who resented Garbo's threat to Cecil's affections and made no secret of it. His friend James Pope-Hennessy met Garbo there and later observed:

"She has the most inexplicable powers of fascination which she uses freely on all and sundry; but whether it is deliberate or not, nobody knows. . . . And then it gradually dawns on one that she is entirely uneducated, interested in theosophy, dieting and all other cranky subjects, has conversation so dull that you could scream. . . . Cecil Beaton guarded her like an eagle, and nobody was ever allowed alone with her."

When Stephen Tennant brought Julian and Juliette Huxley to dine with Beaton and Garbo, she sat at Huxley's feet and asked him to tell her "something interesting about animals." The biologist detailed the male-eating courtship habits of the female praying mantis, to Garbo's delight. Huxley was struck by her intelligence and thought her "not imaginative" but "astute and hard-headed."

During her previous visit, Beaton one day found Garbo looking somber in her room, having just received a letter from "the little man" in New York. "He's very clever," she said. At the end of a long guilt trip, Schlee had written, "There's nothing left now but to announce your good news" —her supposed marriage to Cecil. Garbo left quickly, and Beaton brooded: "The way he has managed to take control of Greta's interests is quite alarming, and I see no possibility of her getting free of him, for although they are no longer stimulated by each other's company and are apt to eat in silence, she gives a feeling of importance to his dreary existence and he is not likely to let her slip from his clutches. She, meanwhile, is touched by his loyal devotion and his efforts on her part, and thus they are bound together."

Beaton was violently jealous of everyone who laid any claims to Garbo's time or affection, including the Gunthers. He was particularly incensed when rival photographer Anthony Beauchamp, the husband of Sarah Churchill, persuaded Garbo to sit for her first-ever color portraits in California in 1951. But it was Schlee on whom he was most fixated.

"Try and mention my name to him glibly from time to time," he advised Garbo in a letter. "It only makes me seem like a ghoul if nothing is ever said." Perhaps she did, for the next summer Schlee took her back to England and delivered her to "Beatie" for three weeks. They also saw each other in New York, once attending the new *Camille* ballet Beaton had designed. (On that occasion, she was upset that he jumped up to take a curtain call, and he was ashamed of "how vulgar my self-display had been.")

As the years wore on, however, the relationship and Beaton's patience both began to fray. Persistence and obsession were the keys to his success with Garbo—and to his undoing, as well. In October 1956, he took her to the Bolshoi Ballet's performance of *Romeo and Juliet* in Covent Garden and then to tea at No. 10 Downing Street. But instead of invigorating her, those outings left Garbo edgier than ever. Their New York reunion of 1956 ended in an emotional argument. He'd been drinking heavily and she'd raised some offense of long ago. "I became uncontrollably angry," he wrote, and told her, "If after all these years you can't forget that, then I'm a failure and our friendship means nothing!" He stormed out of her apartment and she followed him to the elevator, joking, "Then you won't marry me?"

Beaton wasn't amused. The fact that he could never get her to—or even near—the altar was driving him crazy. The night before he left New York, he went to her apartment to say goodbye. Suddenly, she said, "I do love you, and I think you're a flop! You should have taken me by the scruff of the neck and made an honest boy of me. I think you could have been the Salvation Army."

"Thank you for telling me that," he managed to reply, in his despair.

In 1954, Beaton had introduced Garbo to critic Kenneth Tynan, who'd spent years trying to meet her. She was then in her premature oblivion, but Tynan's enthusiastic rapture in *Sight and Sound* helped spur an international reappraisal of her films and of the woman:

Fame, by insulating her against a multitude of experiences which we take for granted, has increased rather than diminished her capacity for wonder. . . . She visited Westminster Abbey, early one morning when no one was about, and in this most public of places found an enormous private enchantment. A walk along a busy street is for her a semi-mystical adventure. Like a Martian guest, she questions you about your everyday life, infecting you with her eagerness, shaming you into a heightened sensitivity.

Tynan wasn't the only one with a renewed interest in Garbo. Hollywood was also making a belated reassessment and, in contrition for past neglect, the Motion Picture Academy voted her a special Oscar in 1954. "I knew that Garbo would never make an appearance to accept the Oscar," said Jean Negulesco, who produced the Academy Awards show that year and hoped she would let him come to New York and make a short acceptance film in her apartment, or anywhere else. Her answer was, "Thank you, but no," and Nancy Kelly accepted the Oscar for her.

Years later, in conversation with Sam Green, she said she had read in *TV Guide* that "Garbo never got an Oscar" and that it wasn't true. "I have one in a cupboard," she said. "They picked someone I didn't know to receive it for me, and the wife of Mr. Wallis [Minna] kept it for two years before sending it on." Green suggested she make a lamp out of it, but she replied, "I have enough lamps."

It was now time for Garbo herself to take stock of her own work, which she had always deprecated. She began to cultivate a quiet interest in reviewing her films through her friendship with Allen Porter, film curator of the Museum of Modern Art, who ran her pictures for her in the museum's fourth-floor screening room. One of the first was *Joyless Street*, which she decided she liked a great deal. She came back for more and provided running commentary, always referring to herself in the third person. "Look—," she would say, "now she's going to ask for money," or, "Isn't that an awful dress she's wearing?" While a film was running, she was animated and talkative. When it was over, she reverted to her pensive self. Sometimes—as with *Romance*—she got up and walked out in the middle, filled with some sudden disgust.

"She doesn't consider herself a particularly good actress," said Porter in the fifties, "and is only now beginning to believe she did a good job in *Camille*. She thinks she overacted in *Grand Hotel*." Porter wanted to do her life story for a MoMA series of monographs, and said it would be a way to straighten out such misconceptions as those concerning her relationship with

John Gilbert, but her answer was, "Maybe people don't want to be put straight."

The Porter bio of Garbo, predictably, was never written, but she came to trust him. In 1950, she showed up at a party he gave for Gian Carlo Menotti, who was then preparing the New York premiere of *The Consul* after his recent success with *The Medium*. Apropos of the latter, the evening's entertainment was an appearance by the celebrated hypnotist Polgar, who fascinated Garbo with his astonishing memory tricks. Menotti had a Hollywood contract to make a film version of *The Medium* and tried to persuade Garbo to take the lead—with the usual results.

Garbo continued to view her films at MoMA with Porter's successor, Richard Griffith. Eventually, the public—and finally even MGM—caught on: The ever-cautious studio insisted on test-marketing *Camille*'s revival in Philadelphia and Miami Beach before approving its first major rerelease of a Garbo film.

"The fact that *Camille* is doing capacity business is the talk of the entertainment world," wrote Ed Sullivan in February 1955. "Garbo's box office appeal apparently is indestructible." The manager of the Normandie Trans-Lux Theatre in Manhattan said he was most surprised by the number of young people who packed his theater six times a day and made it a record-breaking engagement. The rereleased *Camille* ultimately grossed a cool $300,000 bonanza for MGM.

Two years later, when the George Eastman House in Rochester presented awards to the all-time great silent-film performers, Garbo was a recipient in absentia, while Ramon Novarro was her apologist: "She wanted so much to come. It meant so much to her to have been given this honor. I spoke to her, and she was in a torment of indecision. Finally her eagerness to be a part of this wonderful occasion won out over her shyness, and she agreed. And, having agreed, she immediately broke out in a psychosomatic rash. The doctor put her to bed for a week."

In 1963, the Empire Theatre in London slated a five-week season of Garbo films that broke all its box-office records. That same year, the state-subsidized TV network in Italy showed *Anna Karenina*, *Camille*, and three other Garbo films on successive Sunday evenings. The films were watched by ten million people and Italian movie houses were suddenly empty on Sunday nights, usually the busiest of the week. The 75 percent drop in attendance was so precipitous that exhibitors in Rome staged a twenty-four-hour "anti-Garbo-on-TV" strike.

Similar results were obtained at Garbo festivals from Paris to Los Angeles. The most ambitious American revival was staged in 1968 by MoMA in New

New York newspaper advertisement for the 1955 re-release of Camille

York—the first-ever complete retrospective, beginning with her short PUB pictures of 1921. Garbo asked John Gunther to help her obtain tickets for two of the films she had never seen. The museum was delighted and offered to run a special midnight screening for her. Within four days of the announcement of the festival, all twelve thousand tickets were sold out.

A friend of Garbo's, unable to restrain himself, committed the faux pas of bringing up the subject over drinks. It must be thrilling, he enthused, to be the toast of the film world again. Garbo's reply was brief and characteristic.

"I don't get a penny out of it," she said.

A telephoto lens captures Garbo with Winston Churchill on Aristotle Onassis's yacht, August 1958.

CHAPTER 12

GARBO LOST
1960–1979

I don't have to live in New York. I could live in hell.

—GARBO

Not that she sorely needed the income. It was true that Garbo never received royalties from all the revival screenings, broadcasts, video-tape sales, or rentals of her films. But by the 1960s, interest on her investments was in the six-figure ballpark; at any time, she could have liquidated or dipped into those holdings, though the thought of doing so threw her into a state. Her anxieties, as always, concerned her finances and her health. Although both were in good condition, her increasing wealth was matched by increasing anomie.

More and more, she felt lost—"drifting" was the word she often used. Whether she welcomed or lamented the end of her career, she had to do something to fill the hours and the years in its absence. Fate gave her precisely a half century of leisure time, and her only job was to figure out what to do with it. That challenge turned out to be more difficult than any other. It took her spirally around and between two continents, but the physical peregrinations are easy to chart compared with the inner journey: The last, "lost" years of Hollywood's most invisible star are a maze of internal melancholy.

Garbo's inner search, like the last half of her life, took place largely on the East Side of New York City, inside that apartment at 450 East Fifty-second Street. One of her funniest remarks was either terribly wry or terribly naïve: "I'm lucky to be in my building. They don't like actresses there."

She would live in that apartment for thirty-seven years. Contrary to the persistent reports that most of the rooms were closed off, she furnished all seven of them in tasteful style. The large, L-shaped living room featured a stunning assortment of signed eighteenth-century French antiques —Louis XV and Regency sofas, chairs, and ottomans upholstered in shades of her favorite dusty rose. Damask curtains complemented a huge, eighteenth-century Aubusson rug purchased from Consuelo Vanderbilt Balsan. Five windows, and a door to her terrace, looked east onto the river and south toward lower Manhattan. The paneled fireplace wall held sets of leather-bound classics, decidedly decorative, while Renoir's *Leontine et Coco* hung over the fireplace itself. At the end of that room was an alcove whose walls were lined with her bright Jawlensky canvases and a Robert Delaunay abstract.

The bedroom, which also had a river view, contained her painted eighteenth-century Swedish furniture. The double bed's head- and footboards were upholstered in Fortuny fabric matched by purple-and-dusty-rose curtains. Down a hall was the sparsely furnished guest room her niece used when she visited.

The formal dining room gave the impression she might once have considered entertaining: Needlepoint-upholstered French chairs lined one wall, but the table, which could seat twelve theoretical guests, was covered with protective pink oilcloth and served as a catchall. This room, says Sam Green, held the only reference to her former occupation: "On the serving console was a stack of coffee table books with titles like *Great Stars of Hollywood*." Garbo dismissed them as just "junk people send me."

Most of the walls were stippled with a coral-shaded glaze. Designer Billy Baldwin said Garbo described the color she wanted by lighting a candle and holding it behind a silk lampshade she had pinched years before from the dining car of a Swedish train; Mercedes said it was inspired by the pink-shaded lights in Stockholm's Grand Hotel. Baldwin called it a mulberry pink and said he deserved a Nobel Prize for replicating it.

"It had to be just this side of salmon, that side of dusty rose," says Green. "There was never to be white anywhere. White could not be seen in her environment, even in the background. She thought white spoiled colors, and color was terribly important to her." Another friend recalled her saying: "I was thinking maybe I should get a new color scheme in here—I mean for the phones. I only have black telephones. That'll keep me awake at night, trying to decide the color scheme. I do so little telephoning it really doesn't matter. Still, every little bit of color counts. Maybe I would use the telephones more if they were bright."

Once when Baldwin and his assistant, Edward Zajac, were at her apartment for a consultation, she mortified Zajac by telling him, "There's no point in looking at the telephones—all the numbers have been removed." Baldwin never forgot his first glimpse of her in the early sixties. He was entertaining two women friends and waiting for Cecil Beaton, who arrived unexpectedly with Garbo: She scampered "like a ballet dancer into my living room [and] pirouetted around the room laughing and sparkling in the firelight. The other two women sat speechless with shock. Suddenly, Garbo became aware of them watching her, and her face hardened from laughter to fright. Like a beautiful silent moth she ran from the room, down the stairs and out into the winter's night. . . . She refused to be in the same room with anyone she had not expected to see there."

In her own castle, she was more relaxed. Escorting Baldwin through her apartment one day, Garbo led the decorator into a room lined on three sides by closets, which she opened to reveal racks containing hundreds of dresses. "I have never worn a single one," she said. Her kitchen and pantry were the only rooms in which the shades weren't drawn: Their shocking-pink curtains were "so bright that if you were in a taxi coming down FDR Drive, you could spot them fifteen blocks away," Green recalls.

Her art made every room a miniature gallery. David Diamond called her apartment "le Petite Musée," a term that amused her when he exclaimed it upon entering. Like its owner, her home was elegant but not extravagant.

Garbo came to like both the neighborhood and the neighbors, one of whom was actress Mary Martin. Martin had purchased a bizarre Japanese exercise gadget called "The Wheel"—a huge twelve-foot iron machine with a suspended stretcher to which one was bound in a harness and moved around circularly. It was said to be marvelous for the circulation, and Martin spent many happy hours upside down in it. Garbo, on one of her rare visits, watched her spinning around. "You arrrrh a crazy woman," she told Martin, but a few days later she came back to try it out herself. With the help of George Schlee, Martin recalled, "We put her into it. After one tip backward she had had enough."

Says Nin Ryan, the daughter of Otto Kahn: "We lived in the same building for thirty years and never said anything but 'good afternoon.' " Once and only once, Ryan invited Garbo to see her apartment. Garbo came up, looked around, and said, "Very nice. I would never ask you to come to mine. It's too ugly."

Above all for Garbo, 450 East Fifty-second was comfortable, and she grew to love it so much that once when the staff went on strike she spent part of a day running the elevators. Over the years, she turned her space there into a womblike refuge that precisely suited her Spartan requirements: a place to hide, a place to eat, and—most important—a place from which to make her walks, the forays that were essential to her mind and body.

"Sometimes I put on my coat at 10 a.m. and follow people," she said of her daily routine. "I just go where they're going—I mill around." It was an ingenious way to be alone and with people, simultaneously, without having to interact.

Garbo Walks, for the most part. But sometimes, Garbo Flies. Her adoptive family in Paris—globally, for that matter—was one by whom adoption was devoutly to be wished: the Rothschilds. Through Baron Erich, she had met his cousins, Cécile and her sister-in-law Liliane de Rothschild. Almost immediately, Garbo and the unmarried Cécile became friends and remained so, ever closer, to the end of Garbo's life.* She spent several weeks a year in Paris, invariably staying—after 1965—with Cécile at her eighteenth-century "town palace" on the rue Faubourg-St.-Honoré's embassy row, next to the Elysée Palace. Cécile's *vin ordinaire* was Château Lafite, and it was she who initiated their bustling rounds of Parisian art galleries and cultural events—having to overcome Garbo's reluctance and lethargy first. Castles and gardens were Cécile's passion, and there was always a new one to which Garbo, with some eye rolling, must accompany her.

"Cécile just bullied her into things," recalls Sam Green, who met Garbo through her and spent a decade in their joint company. "Cécile's life was not going to stop for a month. G would be taken by the scruff of the neck. Otherwise she wouldn't go anywhere. When she'd say, 'I'm not sure I'm going to be hungry tomorrow,' Cécile would just laugh and say, 'Of course you're going to be hungry. The car is picking us up at a quarter after twelve . . . and that's that.' "

The annual summer cruise with Cécile—several weeks of Mediterranean sunning and swimming—became integral to Garbo's health regime. They would set out from Saint-Raphaël on brother Élie's yacht or a rented one. Garbo's obsessive concern was about "strangers" in the traveling party and protection from photographers, but Cécile was a master of such details. During many cruises together—to Greece, Cyprus, Malta, Corsica—their relationship grew fonder and funnier, as suggested by Garbo's efforts to compose a Christmas telegram to Cécile one year.

"[The Rothschilds] don't have Christmas, I know," she told Sam, who was to do the wiring. "Well, they do in a funny way, I suppose, because

---

* No such closeness developed with Liliane. At one of their early encounters, Garbo asked, "Which Rothschild is keeping Pamela Churchill?" Liliane's answer: "My husband."

they have a lot of Gentiles there, too, on the staff. After all, Jesus was Jewish
. . . Oh, well, just say, 'Warmest greetings, dear boy.' "

Some thought Garbo was just using the Rothschilds and would soon
discard them. "If you had something, she'd come and take that fruit from
you," said Jessica Dragonette's husband, Nicholas Turner. "Erich [Roth-
schild] taught her everything about eighteenth-century French furniture—
it gave Schlee a rest. But he went nuts. He fell in love with her. He was
getting too much. Out he went."

But Cécile felt just the opposite. "People have always tried to take from
her, not give to her," she said. Cécile knew Garbo could not function as a
regular tourist and that she could only see and go out into the world under
the aegis of the rich. She made her considerable resources available to Garbo
and introduced her to others who could do the same, such as Betty Estevez,
at whose home in Paris Garbo met Betty Spiegel, wife of the great independent film producer Sam Spiegel.*

"There was a camaraderie of those three ladies—Cécile, Estevez, and
Spiegel—in Paris and later in New York," says Sam Green. "It didn't have
anything to do with sex. When the Bettys would come to town, G would
ask me to accompany her, and there would be three tough women in the
room: Estevez, her current girlfriend, and Betty Spiegel at Spiegel's apartment. When she was with them, Garbo was 'one of the girls'—a great
character type, if not quite really herself."

Garbo was fond of both Bettys and of Sam Spiegel, one of the few who
got away with talking to her about films. She liked his garrulous honesty
and sense of humor. (Once asked why nobody made films for a million
dollars anymore, Spiegel replied: "How can you steal a million on a million-
dollar budget?")

Garbo had met Aristotle Onassis at Schlee's Le Roc on the French Riviera
in 1955. That fall, she sailed on the famed *Christina*, not just to Athens but
all the way to Saudi Arabia, and was subsequently seen with Onassis at
Maud Chez Elle and El Morocco in New York. Press reports the next summer
trumpeted the fact that Onassis had personally intervened to secure her entry
into the Monte Carlo Sporting Club and casino *in pants*—the first such
shocking exception in its history. (Marlene Dietrich had recently been turned
away and was furious.) As Onassis was a co-owner of the club and casino,
and much else in Monte Carlo, this was perhaps not such a remarkable
achievement on his part.

In any case, Garbo enjoyed Onassis's cosmopolitan charm as well as his

---

* Three of Spiegel's films, *On the Waterfront* (1954), *The Bridge on the River Kwai* (1957), and
Lawrence of Arabia (1962), won best-picture Oscars.

*With Aristotle Onassis at a
party in Monte Carlo's
Sporting Club*

*On the Isle of Capri with
Christina Onassis, July 16,
1955. George Schlee is
close behind.*

fabulous wealth—in particular, the *Christina*. That floating palace boasted a crew of fifty, the finest food and wine, a marble bathroom modeled on King Minos's of Knossos, the El Greco canvas *Ascension*, and nine staterooms named for Greek islands. (Garbo picked "Lesbos" on cruises to Capri, Nice, and Venice with the likes of Winston Churchill in the party.)*

Around this time, director Jean Negulesco and his wife, who had bought Garbo's last house in Beverly Hills, found themselves on the same transatlantic flight with her, and when she asked them to dine with her that night in New York, they happily agreed. "Do you mind if a friend of mine joins us?" Garbo asked. "His name is Aristotle Onassis, but he likes to be called Ari." The Greek shipping magnate's vast fortune offered both the movement and the security she craved. Garbo found Onassis's restrained flattery and smart conversation as appealing as his silences, and the admiration was mutual.

"[She is] refreshing," said Onassis in a rare comment to the press. "A simple, delicious, utterly natural woman, never calculating, never flirtatious, direct and honest as a young boy." Interviewer Jhan Robbins noted that "Onassis offers annually to finance Garbo's own movie company in any film she cares to undertake. But this is clearly too free-wheeling a proposition for her to accept. She seems to need more guidance, more support, more specific suggestion." Onassis, who had his hands full with Maria Callas at the time, was more willing than able to provide such guidance. Besides which, Garbo was not unanimously popular among his Euro set, many of whom looked down on her because she dressed so badly.

Garbo's Swedish friend Kerstin Bernadotte recalled "a warm and scented night when some forty guests were assembled around the deck-bar of Ari Onassis's yacht *Christina*. Everything was beauty and elegance. The women were dressed by Givenchy and Dior, the bank vaults had been emptied of their jewels. Talk and laughter drowned the tinkle from the piano. Suddenly there was silence as if in church. A lonely, slender figure glided across the gangway, dressed in a simple short dress of emerald green satin. On her feet, low-heeled sandals in the same material. . . . No jewels except a single gold ring on one finger, not a wave in the ash-colored pageboy hair."

The other women were furious.

"She couldn't compete with those clotheshorses," says Sam Green. "To true snobs, clothes mean everything, and they thought she was sloppy."

* In 1958, Garbo and Churchill played cards—at great length—on Onassis's yacht in Monaco Harbor. The press was frantic for information. When she finally returned to the United States, a reporter intercepted her at Idlewild Airport and asked what brought her to New York. "I live here," she replied.

But the Rothschilds were above that, and it was to them that Garbo turned in the most dire emergency of her life. Her relationship with George Schlee had intensified through the fifties and into the new decade. Garbo's "management" had become his full-time occupation. His possessiveness knew no bounds, and Garbo was always nervously aware of it.

"I have to leave you now," she once told Billy Baldwin, in a great hurry. "He knows where I am, and I'd rather not be seen with you or anybody here because he is a gentleman and it wouldn't be a good idea."

The Garbo-Schlee dependency was, in fact, a two-way street. "My little friend G.S. has had trouble healthwise a long time," she wrote Salka in 1961. "He is in the hospital and has been operated on." And soon after: "I am leaving for California. . . . Schlee is getting along fine so it will be all right for me to leave. Since it is a matter of time to gain back strength, he does not need me so desperately."

For Valentina, the novelty of sharing her husband with the world's greatest screen idol had long worn off. In summers, she vacationed at the Gritti in Venice while Garbo and George repaired to Le Roc in the south of France. In New York, Schlee and Garbo dined out frequently, often at Maud Chez Elle on West Fifty-third Street, which stocked the lady's favorite *fromage de chèvre*—a mild, creamy goat cheese. The threesome was now a twosome. Never mind that it was not sexual; what Schlee had with Garbo was not so much a romance as *custody*. But enough tongues wagged to the contrary for Valentina to find it increasingly unendurable.

The evening of October 3, 1964, began typically for Schlee and Garbo in Paris. They dined with Cécile, then returned to their suite at the Hotel Crillon. Schlee did not feel well and thought a walk might help. They went out together, but as they walked he began to feel worse—and then terribly sick. Minutes later, he collapsed with a heart attack. Garbo frantically sought aid from a passerby and an ambulance was summoned, but Schlee was beyond help. He was taken to the hospital, where he died later that night.*

Garbo was beside herself, her grief augmented by the knowledge of the sordid way in which the press would play up her presence. She threw herself on the mercy of Cécile, who took charge. Whisked off to the Rothschilds, Garbo evaded the press and simply disappeared.

It fell to Valentina to fly to Paris and collect her husband's body with

---

* A different account from the reliable Hugo Vickers: Schlee left alone for his walk while Garbo went back to the Crillon with Cecile. Upon suffering the attack, he staggered into a bistro and asked someone to ring Garbo, who couldn't understand what the caller was saying and turned the call over to Cecile.

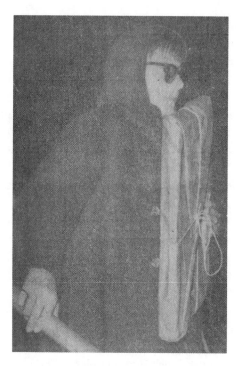

Garbo tries to hide behind a bundled-up painting as she de-planes at Kennedy Airport, October 6, 1964, after the death of George Schlee.

no help from Garbo, who was banned from the Russian Orthodox service held at Universal Funeral Chapel on East Fifty-second Street a few days later. Among the mourners there were Noël Coward, Bennett Cerf, Anita Loos, and Lillian Gish. Eulogies were delivered by John Gunther, Alfred Frankfurter of *ARTnews* (quoting Pushkin), and Schlee's friend and attorney, Eustace Seligman. After the burial at Ferncliff Cemetery in Westchester County, Valentina ordered the custodians to turn Garbo away if she ever tried to enter the premises.

"Valentina doesn't feel she has to put on a show any longer," said a friend. First, she rid the villa of all Garbo photos and mementos, stuffing all her possessions (including antiques) into crates and burning them. When she loaned the place to Diana Vreeland the following summer, Valentina told her, "I have had it exorcised. There will be no trace of that woman." Shortly thereafter, she sold it.

In New York, likewise, she called in an Orthodox priest to exorcise Garbo's presence from her own apartment. "The exorcising was very thorough," said her friend, "including even the refrigerator. Apparently Garbo was in the habit of looking in there for snacks."

Valentina's bitterness might have been cushioned by a long-range view. "The public defeat infuriated her, but I think she profited greatly from Garbo's dalliance with her husband," says Sam Green. Aside from years of Garbo-based publicity for her couturier business, Valentina also reaped the benefit of Garbo's aversion to signing things: At Garbo's request, Schlee had put a number of her major purchases in his own name—all of which his widow now inherited.

But for two women who lived a few hundred feet apart, there now began the twenty-five-year hell of having to avoid each other. Valentina thereafter referred to her former friend as "that vampire"—or, more generically, as just "the fifth floor." Said Garbo to a friend years later: "Madame V. [is] forever praying and lighting candles and crossing herself. But how can she behave the way she does? If I had kept seeing her, I wouldn't be alive today."

Cécile de Rothschild, to a considerable extent, took Schlee's place as the main "fixer" in the life of Greta Garbo. But Cécile was not her closest friend, and Paris could never again be such a happy place. The nearest thing to a soul mate for Garbo was always Salka Viertel.

"You would never know that I love you when you never hear anything from me, but I do—and forever," she wrote Salka on July 10, 1962. "I am in a state that is no longer human but I cannot describe it on a piece of paper—it would not look pretty. I do think of you very very often and would give anything to be back in the days when I could take my buggy and drive to Mabery Road and see you—the vibrant, wonderful person that is you. Now I am almost afraid to face you. . . . This little note is mostly to tell you that I love you."

Salka's home was now in Klosters, Switzerland, where her arms remained as open to Garbo as they had been thirty years earlier in Santa Monica. It was to Klosters that Garbo repaired annually, beginning in the midfifties. But getting there was never easy, logistically or psychologically.

"It has been so hot here," she once wrote from New York. "I suppose I was hoping for a miracle that a place with swimming would turn up out of the clear sky. Perhaps when I am in Klosters we could get a car and go somewhere for a few days just to have a little change. Oh Salka lilla! I was just about to go into a long thing about myself. But I changed my mind. . . . Hoping you can hardly wait to see me. Love, Tuscha."

"Salka lilla"—little Salka, in Swedish—was Garbo's term of endearment for her friend. The meaning of "Tuscha"—with which most of her sixty-six letters to Salka are signed—remains a mystery. The flurry of correspondence before Garbo's visits usually ended with something like her 1967 note: "Will arrive in Zürich, flight Swissair 101, July 10th Monday. Please be a good boy and [meet me]."

In 1968, her concern was about groceries:

"I shall wire when I am leaving, hoping Salka lilla will send a car to fetch me at the airport. May I also ask you to have enough food for me in the apartment for a couple of days—and my bread and cake from the bakery? . . . What I need in the way of food is: milk, coffee, eggs, margarine, a little butter, bananas and apples, a couple of vegetables, some cheese, honey, and two little steaks. Maybe a little spaghetti and grated cheese. I hope my credit is still good at the store! I thank you in advance for all this help you will give me and hope to pay you back with some of my kindness."

The fine Swiss mountain air was an antidote to Garbo's loathing of air-conditioning, which made summers in Manhattan intolerable for her. The main human attraction was of course Salka, but Garbo was also very fond of her son, Peter, and his wife, actress Deborah Kerr, who were married at the Klosters town hall in 1960 and lived in a big hillside house, surrounded by fir trees, south of town. It was Peter who had "discovered" Klosters on a ski trip in the late forties. He was also the one who first arranged for Garbo to rent the house of director Anatole Litvak there. When she had to surrender it to the new owner, Gore Vidal, Peter made a more permanent arrangement for her to borrow a place belonging to Count Frédéric Chandon de Briailles of the Moët et Chandon champagne firm.

"She used to pay him a token $150 a month," Viertel recalls. "I remember giving him her check once and saying, 'If I were you, I wouldn't cash it, because her signature will be worth a lot more.' It was just a small, two-bedroom flat, not a chalet, but she was very happy with it because it was secluded."

There, close to the village centrum, Garbo took up her regular residency in late summer before the ski season began, always departing on or about her birthday, September 18. Klosters—a winter society—was devoid of tourists at that time of year. By most standards, it was dull if not downright dead, but Garbo could roam the village and its environs at will with little fear of molestation, adhering to a regimen much like the one by which she lived in New York: An early rising, forty-five minutes of exercises, a light breakfast, a walk to town at ten-thirty. After window-shopping, she might stop in at Spiess's butcher shop for a single steak, walk to the tobacconist's for a magazine, and then head home. Her route took her past—but never into—the Cinema Rex. After lunch, she set out for her big afternoon walk on one of many picturesque mountain paths, followed by a short rest, and then on to Salka's for the late-afternoon tea that was generally the high spot of her day.

It was clear to all who saw her on those walks that the objective was *exercise*, not scenery—and certainly not social intercourse. But Salka was a highly social creature who loved company and whose home, wherever it might be, was always frequented by smart, interesting people who could be trusted not to frighten Garbo when she appeared, which Salka made certain she did often. "For Garbo, Salka is like a nanny," said a friend. "She looks after her. In a way, it's like a daughter coming home."

Salka's court in Klosters was not so different from that of Santa Monica. Not least among the artists, musicians, and writers who visited her regularly were her son and his wife. Peter had written *White Hunter, Black Heart* there—his much-acclaimed roman à clef based on the writing and filming of *The African Queen* with John Huston in the Congo. That unflattering portrait painted the director as an egomaniacal rogue and reckless drunk, but Huston didn't seem to mind.

Other "regulars" at Salka's included agent Swifty Lazar, writer Harry Kurnitz (who wrote *A Shot in the Dark* at Klosters), and novelist Irwin Shaw—better known for *The Young Lions* than for *The Survivors*, a play he co-authored with Peter Viertel in 1948.

Of Salka's many writer-*salonistes* in Klosters, Garbo most enjoyed Shaw (1913–1984). He had a jolly, flirtatious way with her—which she liked—and he sometimes took her and Salka to lunch at the Chesa Grischuna, Klosters's most fashionable hotel, where the menu featured a dish called "Trout à la Shaw." She also enjoyed Robert Parrish and his wife, Kathy.

"We'd all go to Salka's place," said Parrish. "You'd look at the window, and there would be Greta, peeking in to be sure no one else was there."

What she most enjoyed was the private company of Salka and a few of her local women friends, from whom a cryptic Garbo anecdote sometimes escaped:

"[Once] she told us that on her walk, she had met a woman with a moustache. She said, 'She was one of the most beautiful women I have ever seen.' We didn't know if this was supposed to be a joke, or what. Nobody laughed."

During his touring days in *The Barretts of Wimpole Street* long before, actor Brian Aherne had befriended Garbo. He was now divorced from Joan Fontaine and married to Eleonore de Liagre. The Ahernes lived in Vevey, Switzerland, and visited Garbo from time to time. In July 1964, they took her to supper with Noël Coward, who saw them again a few days later at the Geneva airport:

"Brian, Eleonore and Garbo (quivering with neurosis) were on the plane."

Eleonore once asked Jean Negulesco if he would mind dining with three ladies—the other two being Garbo and Dietrich. "GG complained about the neighbor living in the apartment over hers," Negulesco recalled. "He was building a new bath. Noise and copper pipes came through her ceiling. Marlene was comparing the rising prices from day to day on fruit and fresh vegetables. Two of the most famous women in the world exchanging banalities and kitchen talk!"

One of Salka's tea companions reported:

"She talks only about herself, but she doesn't talk about herself at all. In other words, she talks about things that relate to herself, but only in an impersonal way—her walks, her shopping plans, and so forth—but never a word about her thoughts or ideas or hopes or plans or anything self-revealing."

Garbo's normal day in Klosters ended with Salka's tea, but occasionally she could be coaxed into attending a small party at night, such as one champagne-and-caviar soirée at the old Litvak house. She had an acquired taste for all three of the delicacies on hand—the champagne, the caviar, and Gore Vidal.

"She flirted with Gore, the way she did with a lot of people," Peter Viertel recalls, asking him to sit by her near a front window and then speaking of her own days there. "This is where I used to curl up every night and have a whiskey and watch the people of Klosters," she said, but, as always, she wanted to leave early, and Peter and Gore dutifully escorted her home in Viertel's Jeep.

She once puzzled a Klosters friend by remarking that she didn't know where any of the light switches were in Chandon's apartment. He later figured out it was because she was always in bed before dark and rarely ever turned the lights on or off—an index to the life she led there: When in Klosters, she often seemed to be bored; when not there, she often wanted to be.

"I am here with my pains and you are there with yours," she wrote Salka at Christmas 1971. "Oh dear, I wonder if it's full of snow, if it is very very pretty, if your children are all there, if your work has been finished, if lots of people come to disturb you or distract you. I wish I was there."

The following year, she told Salka, "I am living in my usual rut again, seeing nobody. The Gunthers are away, so there is no one really to see. I feel rather tired all the time but it could be from living such a monotonous life, never wanting anything. . . . I want to do things in my mind, but I always postphone things till tomorrow and tomorrow is the same story."

The lovely verb "postphone" was, indeed, what she spent a lot of her time doing in New York.

In 1977, Frederick Sands and photographer Eckard Nitsche laid an elaborate trap to interview and photograph her in Klosters for a book called *The Divine Garbo*. After visiting Salka for several days running, Sands finally encountered Garbo there. "So you're a writer," she said. "I don't like writers. They're dangerous people." But Sands won her over and they took drives and walks together, during which she revealed herself as a prisoner of her fears. The train trip from Klosters to Davos took twenty-five minutes. "Many times I went to the station and turned back at the last moment," she told Sands. "Heaven knows how many tickets I bought, but each time the train pulled into the station I was frightened and walked away. It took me two years before I finally ventured on it the first time."

To Ray Daum, she said: "I spend three months in Switzerland, living exactly as I do [in New York], making my own meals, staying in a little apartment. There's hardly anybody who could take that, but I'm so abnormal. I just [see] one friend, every day, and the rest I'm alone." She later told Sam Green why she liked it: "It's so boring year after year, but at least they don't make a fuss. Even now that I stay in a hotel, they still don't bother me. I found an old couple who like to eat as early as I do, so I take my meals with them. They're boring, but [if] people see you eating alone, they feel sorry for you." Now and then, she said, an existential happening enlivened the tedium:

> The strangest thing happened to me this last time. Nobody would believe it, but the couple I eat with there are my witness: I was adopted by a fly—yes, sir, right there in the hotel dining room. Every time I would come in and sit down, he would fly over to me. The first few times, I used to shoo him away, but he would always come back, until finally I realized he didn't want my food, because sometimes there wasn't any, and he wasn't trying to bite me or anything, he just wanted to be my friend! So I let him be, and he did tricks for me—that couple was flabbergasted, I tell you. He wouldn't fly away if he was in my palm and I closed my hand and opened it up again. He would hop from one of my fingers to the next one—he was an acrobat. What makes me think he was a "he"? But I bet he was. Every day he came and played with me. It was amazing. But one day he didn't come anymore. I guess somebody killed him. The Swiss don't like flies in their restaurants, even if they're your pet. But I was sad, because he was my friend.

One friend she never lost was Deborah Kerr, whose quiet, thoughtful ways always charmed her. Kerr was a gifted painter as well as a six-time Oscar-nominated actress, and Garbo once asked for the loan of one of her small landscapes. "I'll give it back to you if I decide I don't want it," she said, and never did.

"She could be so funny and had such a wonderful way of knocking herself," remembers Kerr, whose lilting soprano voice downshifts at will into a perfect imitation of Garbo's baritone. "Once in the late afternoon, we were about to have a glass of wine and I asked, 'Miss G, would you like red or white?' She gave me the most tragic look and said, 'Ooooh, De-bo-rah—that is a *terrrrible* decision!' You never knew with her, whether she was sending you up or not. Peter, on the other hand, was never deferential. He would say, 'C'mon, Greta—just make up your mind!' "

A lyrical portrait of Garbo in Klosters was painted by actor Jack Larson, best known as Jimmy Olson in the popular "Superman" TV series of the fifties. He first met her in late summer of 1965, while visiting his friends Peter and Salka. They were to meet her halfway up a hill on the way back from her walk. Garbo was precisely where she said she would be, at a bench beside a stream, as Larson recalls:

> She couldn't have been friendlier, and as we continued our walk to the Viertels, she described some of the sights and sounds (many cowbells) of her long morning walk. In the sunlight, the most astonishing thing about her was the glow of her hair. Now she was graying but instead of streaks of gray, every fifth hair seemed to have turned white, evenly throughout, and gave the effect of highlighting the natural brown. She seemed to be walking in MGM keylights. . . .
>
> Salka then was in her late seventies, white-haired and vibrant, as loving and concerned about art, lives, and politics as ever. Peter, a romantic guy in the Hemingway mold, was a Marine Corps officer in World War II and treated everyone including Garbo humorously, with just a tinge of boot camp. She loved it and laughed at him teasing her. She seemed in her element.

"Salka was a very *true* friend," says Garbo's niece, in contrast to certain noble persons of her own country. Despite popular belief, she never maintained a second residence in Stockholm (or anywhere else) for the simple reason that it wasn't practical. But in 1975, she visited Sweden, for the first time in a decade, at the invitation of a royal couple she had met twenty-five years earlier on the French Riviera: Count Carl Johan Bernadotte, the uncle of King Carl XVI Gustaf, and his commoner wife, Countess Kerstin, for whom he had renounced his title.

She stayed at the Bernadottes' beautiful villa outside Bastad, a coastal resort in southwest Sweden, just across the water from Denmark. Three dogs accompanied her and the countess on their long, aimless walks through the beech woods, stopping in at farmhouses along the way. Garbo grew fond of farmer Ivar Nilsson and his housekeeper and one day was thrilled to see a calf that had been born there during the night. ("If only I had a camera," she said. Kerstin thought it perhaps the first time she ever mentioned "such a hellish invention" with pleasure.) They spent one beautiful day on the island of Hallands Väderö, where Garbo said, "One should not go to places like this—nothing can be as perfect." On July 30, 1975, they sailed over to Copenhagen to attend a Birgit Nilsson concert at Tivoli Gardens, and, soon after, the Bernadottes arranged a dinner for her with Nilsson and her husband, Bertil Nicklasson, as the only other guests.

On the subject of cameras, she had felt sufficiently comfortable—and off guard—to let her hostess photograph her. The countess claimed she made a true confession of her true profession to Garbo, who winced but accepted it. Others said Garbo was unaware that Kerstin Bernadotte was a photojournalist until her pictures appeared in the April 1976 *Ladies' Home Journal*, and around the world. At that time, with great bitterness, Garbo reflected that not even the aristocracy could resist the temptation to exploit her.

She never went back to Sweden again.

France and Switzerland were not Garbo's only safe way stations in Europe during these years, and Aristotle Onassis was not her only Greek playmate. In 1971, she was headed for the Adriatic to meet her friend Tina Lavranos—a member of the Niarchos family, archrivals to Onassis—and stopped over in Rome, checking in at the Minerva Hotel, for a top secret mission: a screen test for the Luchino Visconti production of Proust's *Remembrance of Things Past*. The test was reportedly in color and her part was to be a single scene as the Queen of Naples.

"I am very pleased [that Garbo], with her severe and authoritarian presence, should figure in the decadent and rarefied climate of the world described by Proust," said Visconti. Two decades after the abortive *Duchesse de Langeais*, it would have been enormously difficult for Garbo to work herself up for another attempt at age sixty-five. If, in fact, she did, the test has not survived. In any case, funds could not be raised, and Visconti's Proust went the way of Wanger's Balzac.

George Cukor, for one, wouldn't believe it. "She knew when to quit," he said in 1972. "She is much too intelligent to want to try to come back now."

Among her dozens of other offers these days was the title role in *Modjeska*, by Polish writer Antoni Gronowicz, who would come back to haunt her soon enough. The countless cameos, for which she was offered millions, included that of an aging film actress in *Airport 1975*, to which Garbo's response was both funny and predictable: "What could be worse than playing a movie star?"

Gloria Swanson took the part.

Europe was the escape, the retreat, the home-away-from-home. *Real* home —and as close as she could get to anonymity—was New York City. "Entering it from the greater reality of elsewhere," wrote Truman Capote, one could find "a place to hide, to lose or discover oneself." That observation led him to these:

> Have seen Garbo twice in the last week, once at the theatre, where she sat in the next seat, and again at a Third Avenue antique shop. When I was twelve I had a tiresome series of mishaps, and so stayed a good deal in bed, spending most of my time in the writing of a play that was to star the most beautiful woman in the world, which is how I described Miss Garbo in the letter accompanying my script. But neither play nor letter were ever acknowledged, and for a long time I bore a desperate grudge . . . until the other night when, with an absolute turning over of the heart, I identified the woman in the adjoining seat. . . .
>
> Yesterday, at the antique store, she roamed around, quite intent about everything, not really interested in anything, and for one mad moment I thought I might speak to her, just to hear her voice, you know; the moment passed, thank heaven, and presently she was out the door.

Capote's restraint—at least at that time—made him a member of New York's confederacy of Garbo watchers, a group not without its violators but largely united by the good manners not to disturb the object of its affection. Hundreds recognized her every time she left her building, but only a few would approach or pester.

Writer Alan Levy was trailing her one day on Second Avenue when, as she waited for a red light, a look-before-you-cross safety poster caught her eye. "Garbo appeared fascinated by its illustration of three alert giraffes, each peering in a different direction," Levy said. She studied them so intently that she missed two green lights. When she looked up and noticed that a small crowd had collected, she flinched and hurried on. In the short time he spent observing her, Levy counted forty-one people who recognized her. Garbo now noticed Levy and tried to lose him. He kept following, ever more closely, until she turned around suddenly and said, "If you follow me any more, I am going to call a cop." He stammered out an apology, mentioning his admiration for her, after which her voice softened a bit: "Then why do you follow me? Please don't at all."

One walking companion felt she had "an invisible protective shield around her. If we stumbled upon my friends, they knew to pass by without stopping. With most strangers, there'd be some quick jerk of recognition and then they'd turn away. She communicated how she wanted to be treated without saying a word." *The New York Times* reported the case of a young man who was crossing Fifth Avenue and saw Garbo approaching from the opposite side. Recognition and awe were written all over his face as they met in the middle of the crosswalk, whereupon she lifted a finger to her lips and mimed a soundless "Shhh!"—which he obeyed. It was a tribute to "the rudest city in the world" that most of its inhabitants left her alone. But they got scant credit for it, since the boors—and Garbo's fear of them—were always foremost in her mind.

"The story of my life," she once said, "is about back entrances and side doors and secret elevators and other ways of getting in and out of places so that people won't bother you."

Ambivalence characterized her attitude toward New York, as to everything else. "What are we doing racing through the soot and asphalt all the time?" she said to a friend. "Isn't it fantastic, the way we live—human beings, born from nature to walk around where there's grass and trees and birdies? . . . Why we have to spend our whole lives on asphalt, I don't know."

This particular recluse had chosen to make her home on a crowded urban island—in part, of course, for the anonymity of the crowd. Perhaps, too, she needed the hubbub. She was so enervated herself that she required the energy of others; in New York, one could live vicariously through the activity all around. But there was a more practical reason why she stayed in New York City, in Sam Green's opinion:

"New York is the only place where you can go out and get food any time and bring it back. The basic problem was, 'How do you feed yourself?' She would have adored being in the country, but she would've been under the scrutiny of the man who drove or the woman who cooked—domestics living with her. Not possible. She couldn't *wait* till Claire went home at 4:30."

The mechanics of reclusion were these: From the day she moved in to the day she died, Garbo lived at 450 East Fifty-second Street alone, attended only on weekdays—from 9 a.m. to 4:30 p.m.—by the faithful Claire Koger, her housekeeper and cook of thirty-one years. Claire was Swiss and almost exactly Garbo's age, which might have given them a thing or two in common, but in three decades they never went beyond a strict employer-employee relationship—or so it seemed on the surface.* Primarily, Claire shopped for food, kept the place tidy, and made dinner.

"I did most of the cooking, but the lady could do it herself, too," she says today, her heavily accented voice still reverential at the mention of Garbo's name. Claire also did a lot of sewing, for "the lady" was very fussy about the fit of her clothes—her pants in particular: "She kept me busy for a long time, letting out all her slacks." Claire's other key chore was answering the phone, which she was required to unplug every day before leaving. On weekends and even during the week, Garbo did a lot of cooking, cleaning, and errand-running herself.

"*Claire* was the one who had the arthritis," says Green. "She couldn't get down and clean much, so Garbo spent a lot of time doing that. In Klosters, I watched her clean everything in the Chandon apartment—with rubber gloves and Ajax. I was helping her pack her few measly belongings in cardboard boxes to put in the basement, so when Chandon came back he'd find an immaculate rental unit. I mean, she *scoured*. She put paper towels in the sink and poured in Clorox, let it soak overnight so the sink was really white. She knew how to do all that. And in her own kitchen, I know she got up on a ladder to wash the windows and change light bulbs. That occupied a certain amount of her time."

She couldn't stand to have domestics around, not just because of her nerves but because they sold their stories to the tabloids. "She has to live so alone because everyone except Claire tattles on her," said David Diamond a year before she died. Claire was "a downtrodden, honest Swiss woman who wouldn't do that," says Green. "She had to show up on icy days, despite her age, walking from about fourteen blocks away. I'd say, 'God, don't let her come in today. The sidewalks are awful. If she slipped and broke her hip, what in hell would you do?' She'd say, 'Claire will wear rubber boots,' or, 'I gave her Christmas off.' " One day she told Sam, "My girl is coming— the one that makes things miserable," then laughed at her own unfair characterization and added, "I don't have to sit with her, but I have to see her for a short bit."

Her life bore more and more resemblance to that of an elderly Swedish hausfrau. "I just listen to mediocre television," she told Daum. "I'm caught

---

* Born July 11, 1906, in Basel, Claire Koger was raised in Switzerland and moved to Germany when she was in her twenties. Before the outbreak of World War II, she made her way to England where, for a while, she cared for the children of actor John Mills. After the war, she returned to Switzerland and, in the early 1950s, left for better-paying domestic work in the United States, first in Washington and then in New York. It was there that Valentina Schlee discovered her through an agency and recommended her to Garbo. Her average salary over the years was about $150 per week.

in it. But my reception is bad. I look at Channel 13 and it's completely goofy.
. . . Channel 2 comes in well—the lower ones come in better. See, if you
cater to the lower things in life, you get somewhere." The TV, like the
phone, was shut off early lest the elusive "Sandman" be scared off.

She refused to hire a chauffeur because "they sit there and wait, and that
drives you crazy—to have a man sitting there spending his life waiting in
the street for you." Such hypersensitivity left her in a kind of constant state
of siege, as she once lamented to Daum when he came for a visit:

"It's all so silly. We ought to have a nice, lovely, silent Hindu man, who
comes and serves [dinner], who comes on absolutely soundless feet and puts
it on the table. Preferably, I wish he would come from the sky. But we
haven't got a Hindu that comes on soundless feet, so we'll have to do the
best we can. It's a bloody bore."

Pamela Mason remembered her expressing similar thoughts at age forty-
five, rather than seventy, and empathized strongly:

> It can be terribly embarrassing to be as celebrated as she was. You
> can't go anywhere, you can't shop, you can't go to the supermarket. If
> you go to a restaurant, somebody comes up and sits down at your
> table—"Do you mind? I just want to tell you about my life." People
> like Garbo and Frank Sinatra either surround themselves with body-
> guards or run like hares when they see an escape, to avoid the endless
> curiosity. Jacqueline Onassis had to marry a Greek to avoid being on
> show at all times. The whole thing becomes such a production that
> they just hide at home, which doesn't mean they necessarily hide at
> home *alone*. In Hollywood, I remember someone asking Cary Grant,
> "Why do you live out here?" He said, "Where the hell else could I
> live? Where could I go without attracting attention?" Garbo's equivalent
> was New York, where she could put on those hats and a raincoat and
> hope people thought she was a hobo.

If she was a royal prisoner in her Tower, she at least had stroll-parole. Her
wardens were "the walkers"—friends of varying degrees but all created
equal when it came to providing company and protection on her forays
outside the gilded cage.

Though Garbo often walked alone, she had many walking companions
over the years. One of the most steadfast was Raymond Daum, a United
Nations film producer when George Schlee introduced him to Garbo at a
1963 New Year's Day affair given by actor Zachary Scott and his wife, actress
Ruth Ford. Their subsequent walks—as often as thrice weekly—began in
1964 and continued until Daum moved to Texas in 1982. Garbo alone

The embryonic continental beauty at eighteen, around the time of
Gösta Berling's *premiere. Olaf Ekstrand, Stockholm, 1924*

A mysterious erotic subtlety no MGM executive had seen before.
Arnold Genthe, New York, 1925

Photographed by Ruth Harriet Louise in 1927,
the only female photographer in a "man's field" in Hollywood

During the making of Victor Sjöström's "all-Swedish" The Divine Woman.
Ruth Harriet Louise, 1928

One of the nine photos in a legendary six-minute session between scenes of
The Mysterious Lady. *Edward Steichen, New York, 1928*

Suffering beautifully in Inspiration *as "just a nice young woman—*
not too young and not too nice." Clarence Bull, 1930

Severely coiffed for the firing squad before the finale of Mata Hari.
Clarence Bull, 1931

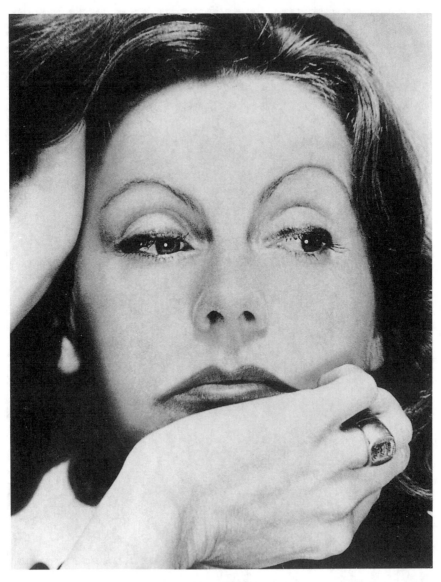

The melancholy retiree at forty-five, shortly after becoming an American citizen.
George Hoyningen-Huene, 1951

initiated the outings. Daum's phone would ring and the unmistakable voice would say, simply and peremptorily, "Let's go." In eighteen years, she never gave Daum her own phone number. Their conversations were bound by her strict caveat: "Don't ever ask me about the movies—especially why I left them."

There were perhaps a dozen old friends in New York with whom she was relaxed and in fairly frequent contact. One of them was Joseph Lombardo, antique dealer and brother of bandleader Guy. Another was Charles "Geza" Korvin, the cultivated Czech actor best known in America as the captain in *Ship of Fools* (1965).

She continued to see the trio of Jessica Dragonette, Nicholas Turner, and Nadea Loftus—"three days a week, nine months a year, for thirty-three years," according to Turner. Often, before moving to New York, she would implore Jessica tragically, "Won't you sing for me? I'll have nothing but the burned-out hills when I return to California. Besides, when you write your memoirs, you can tell how you sang for the world-weary." In New York, during one of many breakfast visits, she asked Jessica for a copy of Walt Whitman's *Leaves of Grass* "and to our utter surprise began reading one of the obscure poems in her eloquent contralto." Another day, she amused them with her own rendition of "True to You in My Fashion" from *Kiss Me, Kate*, which she'd seen the night before.

"Everyone who knows Garbo thinks he understands her," said Dragonette. "I rather think people misunderstand her natural curiosity, her meticulous thoroughness, her suggestibility." The singer recalled sitting on her roof terrace with Garbo when suddenly "she became aware that people on the terraces two blocks away might see her, and she was terrified. I assured her they were all too busy with their own thoughts to be looking our way." Even after Jessica's death in 1980, Garbo kept up the visits to her husband and sister. According to Turner, "Garbo was hot after me. *I* was the guy in New York. She cooked boiled beef for me. I made lemon sole for her."

In the late sixties, Salka came to New York for the publication of her autobiography and stayed with Kitty Carlisle Hart for ten days. Garbo had sent flowers to greet Salka's arrival and visited her at Hart's every day of her stay there—for tea and sympathy concerning back problems.

"She was interested in my exercises," Hart recalls. "I looked at her exercises and said, 'Miss G, if you keep on doing those exercises, you're going to have a bad back all your life. My doctor told me, never, ever, do exercises with straight knees.' She was very proud of the fact that she could put her palm down on the floor with straight knees. I said, 'You mustn't do that anymore.' The last time I saw her, she was walking past my building and I said, 'Hi, Miss G,' and she just walked right by me. We got to the corner and we both had to wait for the traffic, and she said, 'Which way are you going? We walk together.' She was very unpredictable."

Her last encounter of the Truman Capote kind was a literary one in his withering and cynical short story, "La Côte Basque 1965," in the November 1972 *Esquire:*

"I saw [Garbo] last night at the Gunthers', and I must say the whole set-up has taken on a very weathered look, dry and drafty, like an abandoned temple, something lost in the jungles at Angkor Wat; but that's what happens when you spend most of a life loving only yourself, and that not very much."

Capote would later describe her apartment as a "disconnected jumble" of chairs, tables, and couches. "The overall impression is astonishing, but pleasant in a somewhat gaga way." The inference was that he had been there, which he had not. His source for the details was Cecil Beaton, who had called Garbo's apartment "a dreadful hotchpotch of colours." Garbo never knew that. "That little Mr. Capote never came to this place," she complained.

"Truman Capote isn't first class, believe me," she told Beaton. "Nobody criticizes people for their private life. That's each individual's own business." She didn't know the half of it. In a November 8, 1952, letter to Beaton, Capote opined: "[Garbo] will never be a satisfactory person, because she is so dissatisfied with herself, and dissatisfied people can never be emotionally serious. They simply don't believe in anything—except their own limitations."

She was still seeing Beaton, who in spring 1959 told her he was contemplating marriage to June Osborn, the widow of pianist Franz Osborn. "I'll be right over to stop it," Garbo told him. "I'll come over to cut her head off. . . . Give me another chance." She was teasing, of course; neither the Garbo visit nor the wedding materialized.

In 1960, Beaton was devastated by the marriage of his rival Anthony Armstrong-Jones to Princess Margaret. Sick with envy, he confided to his diary that only by marrying Garbo could he one-up Jones. But he was soon consoled by his appointment as royal photographer and by his fabulously successful designs for the 1964 film version of *My Fair Lady*. In August 1965, when Beaton and Garbo saw each other on Cécile's yacht for the first time in two years, he thought her more childishly difficult than ever; he was miffed that she wouldn't say a word about *My Fair Lady* or about his designs for the 1963 ballet *Marguerite and Armand*, both of which he knew she had seen in New York.* But Beaton himself, to some extent, had switched

---

* Garbo, indeed, had attended the New York premiere of Frederick Ashton's Royal Ballet production of the *Camille* story, a showcase for Margot Fonteyn and Rudolf Nureyev. The reason for her silence on the subject was that she didn't like it—but then Garbo didn't like any ballet. "Those poor fellows," she said, "having to lift all those big girls. It's so silly."

Though he hadn't seen her in two years and was angry with her, Cecil Beaton did not fail to snap a fine photo of a happy, windblown Garbo in 1965, then age sixty.

allegiances these days—often visiting Valentina Schlee at 450 East Fifty-second Street without calling on Garbo, a few feet away.

More solicitous, in Garbo's life of the sixties, were Eustace Seligman, of the Sullivan & Cromwell law firm, and his wife, Maud, social registrants who knew how to treat celebrities. Garbo enjoyed the quiet swimming and reading at their Greenwich, Connecticut, estate and loved walking through their private woods. They introduced her to an unlikely new friend, cartoonist Charles Addams. Garbo liked the Seligmans but was not above making private fun of their social ways. "The lawyer" had once visited her and been shocked by her attitude, she told Sam Green:

He liked to give cocktail parties. He knew so many people, he traveled around, and whenever he met somebody, he took down their phone number and then he invited them—200 people was nothing—in the month of January, or whatever. He knew where he was going to have lunch in July. He wrote it down. He loved people. He said, "Oh, my, you could give parties here!" "Yeah," I said, "well, I don't." "It's too bad," he said. And then the phone rang and I didn't answer it, and he was in an absolute state that anybody could not answer the phone. That's beyond him. He was in agony about all these things—that I wouldn't invite anybody, wouldn't answer the phone, wouldn't do anything.

By and large, none of Garbo's friends knew much if anything about the others. "She kept us all in compartments," says Ray Daum. "Like Commie cells—one didn't know the next." When speaking of a trip or plan of any kind, no matter how trivial, she rarely disclosed a name.

Maximum secrecy was reserved for her contacts with Jacqueline Kennedy, who as First Lady had invited her to several White House functions, which Garbo politely declined. A reticent person herself, Mrs. Kennedy understood her reluctance to socialize. On October 21, 1963, however, Garbo attended a show of Irene Galitzine fashions at the Regency Hotel, renewing an acquaintance with Galitzine, with whom she had once cruised the Greek islands on Onassis's yacht. Galitzine and Mrs. Kennedy were also friends, and the fashion show seems to have been catalytic: A *private* White House invitation now came Garbo's way, and curiosity overcame her. She accepted on condition the event be small and secret. Both terms were met. In addition to President and Mrs. Kennedy, there were only four others, as she revealed fourteen years later to a friend who asked about the other guests:

"Well," Garbo replied, "there was a lady [presumably Galitzine] who was instrumental in getting us there by hook or crook, a White House friend, a man who was a friend of the President [Lem Billings], and some other lady, I've forgotten, a princess or somebody [Lee Radziwill]. That's all."

Did she get a tour?

"Oh, yes," said Garbo. "I went on top of Lincoln's bed. Took my shoes off. My, I was very careful."

Did she sleep there?

"No, not at the White House, [though] that could have been done—and then had a visit from the President in the night," she laughed. "The President visited a lot of ladies [at night]."

She slept, instead, at a hotel. Garbo later said she was afraid she had made a bad impression because of her "unruliness." One guest reported that she rose and said jokingly, "I must go. I am getting intoxicated," and that, after she left, Jacqueline Kennedy said, "I think she was." But Garbo was enormously pleased that, instead of withdrawing to his study as usual, John Kennedy had stayed with his guests after dinner—"longer than I have ever done since I became president," he said.

The one other account of that historic visit holds that it was a mischievous

joke at the expense of JFK's old Choate friend and adviser, K. LeMoyne
("Lem") Billings, who had returned from the Riviera that summer with the
hot news that he had met and befriended Greta Garbo there. They'd had a
lot of laughs, Billings told Kennedy, who listened with interest—and privately decided to get Garbo's version of the story. It was planned for Garbo
to arrive before Billings, giving her and the president a chance to chat and
make some "special arrangements," according to David Michaelis in *The
Best of Friends:*

> Lem was sure it was going to be a perfect evening. He arrived at
> the White House, glowing with anticipation, and was greeted by the
> President in the family dining room on the second floor. Then Jacqueline
> came in with Garbo at her side. The President ushered Lem over to
> say hello to their guest, saying, in effect, how happy he was to have
> them both to dinner since they were already so well acquainted. With
> a spring in his step, Lem greeted her: "Greta!"
>
> There was a ghastly pause. Garbo looked at Lem blankly. She turned,
> puzzled, to the President.
>
> "I have never seen this man before," said Garbo.
>
> Thereupon followed the most disorienting half-hour Lem had en-
> dured since World War II. The foursome sat down to dinner. Lem
> was unable to eat. He was in shock. He could not fathom the inexplicable
> amnesia that had overcome Garbo. She repeated that she was quite
> certain she had never met Mr. Billings before this evening. . . . Lem
> rattled off the names of places they had been together, the people they
> had seen, the approximate *dates*, for crying out loud. . . . Nothing seemed
> to refresh Garbo's memory about the enchanting times they had shared
> on the Italian Riviera.
>
> The President was full of earnest curiosity about how such a mix-
> up could have occurred. Perhaps Lem had become friends with someone
> who *looked* like Garbo. Lem testily declared that that was impossible.
> . . . He was mystified. In his befuddlement, the one possibility he did
> not consider was that Garbo's amnesia had been recently contrived by
> the President of the United States. The actress kept up the ruse until
> the second course.

The murder of John F. Kennedy just weeks later, on November 22, upset
Garbo terribly. She wrote his widow a letter of condolence—in Garbo's life,
a rare instance of reaching out. Their subsequent contacts were infrequent
but affectionate; separately, the two most famous women in the world continued to be yachting guests of Aristotle Onassis, who was still a favorite of
Garbo's in spite of her private complaint that the *Christina* was "too small

—I couldn't go for my walks." Mrs. Kennedy's decision in 1968 to marry Onassis could not have surprised her; they both valued the same appealing qualities in him, and, contrary to rumors, there is no evidence that Garbo was annoyed about it. Onassis had reportedly proposed to Garbo first, and she had declined for the same reasons she declined all marriage proposals. But reports of her romantic involvement with Onassis persisted and included the claim that "after his death she repeatedly asked her psychic to contact his spirit."

"Psychic-to-the-Stars" Kenny Kingston says Gayelord Hauser asked him to do readings for Garbo as early as 1952. She first participated in séances at the home of Clifton Webb in the fifties, Kingston maintains, "but she was afraid of them." He was last in her apartment in 1988, when she requested a séance to make contact with Onassis and Hauser—successfully, he says.

Garbo's family doubts the séances took place or that she put any stock in them if they did. "She liked Onassis," says her niece, "but not *that* much. He had a habit of pushing people into pools, which she thought gross." Nor was Garbo amused by one of Onassis's standard gags on the yacht. After seating a new guest on a barstool upholstered with whales' foreskins, he would ask, "How does it feel to be sitting on the world's biggest prick?"

The precious few in possession of Garbo's telephone number guarded it with their lives, used it with discretion, and savored every resonant utterance that came through the wires and caressed their ears. Garbo's voice: Everyone knew it well from the movies—a cultural treasure in the public domain. In private conversation, it was exactly the same: a kind of earthy drawl, an unhurried purr, a hypnotic source of unexpected phrases in a hard-to-define accent that was light one moment and heavy the next—a seductive instrument full of surprises and sudden silence.

One who heard it often for a decade was art dealer Sam Green. He met her in 1970 at the home of his friend Cécile de Rothschild in Saint-Raphaël on the Riviera, and it had not been his idea. Cécile "recruited" him after first screening him for two years on yacht cruises to make sure he would be acceptable to the world's fussiest recluse, who—Cécile felt—needed a new friend and helpmate back home in New York.

"I knew little and cared less about Garbo, and I'd never seen any of her films," says Green, which made him a perfect candidate for her friendship. Even so, on the day of their introduction—September 18, her birthday— he was jittery. Like a teenager on his first date, he rehearsed what he would say, but before he could speak she disarmed him with, "Mr. Green, I've heard so much about you. I know we'll be friends."

Green was then thirty. Garbo was sixty-five. To Sam, she was without airs and eager to put a nervous new acquaintance at ease. The only thing that jolted him was her clothes: "They were almost plain enough to be ugly. Everything was the same awful mustard-color—sweater, pants, socks. Even her honey-colored hair seemed a little like mustard. It was a shade I'd never seen before." At dinner that evening she rejected the perfectly prepared lobster and chastised Cécile for forgetting that she had an allergy to shellfish. Then she reached into the plastic shopping bag she always carried around (instead of a purse) and pulled out an apple. "She ate that," says Green, "and nothing else except two helpings of the prune soufflé. Then, at precisely nine p.m., she got up and announced it was past her bedtime and she had to retire 'or the Sandman won't come.' "*

Not until the following winter did Green see Garbo again—in Cécile's suite at the Regency in New York. Garbo shook his hand firmly as if they were meeting for the first time and said she hadn't been well. "I have bronchitis," she told him and, with that, pulled out a pack of Marlboros from her plastic bag.

Green walked her home that day and began to understand why she was a different person in New York: She was bundled up in a fur coat whose collar was turned up so high that it nearly touched her sunglasses—less due to the cold than to the autograph seekers and photographers encountered along the way. They had little in common but a love of walking and of silliness. "We developed a little language of our own on those walks and played childish games like kick the can and imitate the passersby. Once she said, 'I should stick with you. I haven't had a laugh like this in years.' We'd sit and talk for hours about nothing. I was never bored with her."

They walked twice a week. When Cécile came to visit, it was every day. "Cécile seemed to give her a sense of security," Green remembers. "With her, she was less worried about being recognized, for some reason. Sometimes we'd end up as far down as Fourteenth Street on some silly errand. We covered a lot of territory—her house to Fourteenth and back again was a four-hour trek."

Garbo's stamina amazed him; the weather never fazed her. Even in sub-

---

* There is no better or worse place than this to inform the reader of an ancient Scandinavian folktale that may relate to Garbo's lifelong sleeping disorders. According to several friends, she half-believed—from childhood—in "Mara, the Nightmare." Jacqueline Simpson's book on Swedish myths describes Mara as a beautiful woman in appearance, "but in her actions she is like a most evil spirit. She passes through locked doors and attacks sleepers, sometimes by sitting astride them and tormenting them with horrible dreams, and sometimes by lying down on them and twisting their hearts within them."

zero winter temperatures, she went out to walk—encased in many layers: two hats, two scarves, earmuffs, two pairs of gloves, three layers of underwear, two sweaters. On warm spring days in Central Park, she would say, "Mr. Green, why must we walk on the macadam when we have God's earth right here? Let's take off our shoes and go barefoot." If she saw a tree she liked, she ran to hug it. But no matter where they were or how lost in conversation, she was always on the lookout for "customers"—people who might "make a fuss."

Since Green was an art dealer and Cécile the owner of one of the world's finest private collections, Garbo sometimes ended up with them at a gallery. But art was not usually on the agenda. More often, the goal was something more like a shoe sale. "She was obsessed with finding comfortable shoes," he says, "but the clerks in the shops would recognize her. 'When they start to make a fuss, I always go,' she'd say. I went to hundreds of stores with her in New York and Europe and watched her leave empty-handed almost every time."

With mock formality, they always referred to one another as "Mr. Green" and "Miss G" but were becoming increasingly close. By 1972, the one thing that still eluded him was an invitation to her apartment, which—in typical Garbo fashion—was extended when he least expected it, on a wintry afternoon after a marathon walk through slushy streets. Green complained that his feet were soaked. She asked him in for a drink and the loan of a pair of socks "that looked like they'd been darned a dozen times." After the whiskey, she gave him a tour of the apartment, which seemed to him "unfinished," except for the living room and bedroom.

Green noticed that many of her paintings were covered with cheesecloth, and he asked her about it. "I would just have to wrap them up again when I go away," she replied. He inquired later, periodically, if she had unwrapped them.

"Only two of them," she said. "Nobody comes here but you, and you don't have to see them. You can look at the wrapping. And I don't want people looking at them when I'm away. People in the building come in when I'm gone. Last year, they stole all my silver. I had to borrow a knife, fork, and spoon. But I won't be giving any dinner parties, anyway."

Once he'd been inside, she no longer had anything to hide and, from then on, Green often went in when he took her home, waiting in the living room while she fixed their Cutty Sarks or vodka on the rocks, scanning the room for details. There was never a photograph or a vase of flowers. "What's the point?" she would say. "They'd only die."

But their relationship was largely telephonic. "There was a phone call almost every morning in which I'd tell her where I'd been and what I'd done the night before," Green recalls. "You had to ring once, hang up, and ring again. Claire would then pick up the phone and say nothing. You'd identify yourself into the void, and your name would be relayed to Garbo, who was standing by to give Claire the thumbs-up or -down sign." Over the years, their long, idle chats ranged from lampshades to mutual friends Cécile and Cecil to spiritualism. But the purpose was often to arrange a walk, during which Sam's chief duty was to protect Garbo from both the intrusion and the kindness of strangers.

"Oh-oh, Mr. Green," she would say as they trekked down Madison Avenue, "here comes another customer." That was Green's signal to get between her and the offender. Film collector Peter Hanson was one such customer. On a day when Green was not with her, Hanson spotted Garbo alone on a street in Greenwich Village, came up alongside, and begged leave to ask her a question. "Well, as long as we are taking a walk together," she replied in mild annoyance, without breaking stride. Hanson pulled out a blank card and said he had a friend "who would love me forever if I could get you to sign this for him." Garbo stopped, grabbed his lapel, and said, "That I cannot do, but you must tell your friend that he should like you just as much because you asked."

A less playful response was delivered to writer Thyra Samter Winslow, who was lunching one day with reporter Radie Harris at a chic Manhattan restaurant when she spotted Garbo at a corner table. Winslow sprinted over to Garbo's table, noisily introduced herself, and gushed, "Oh, Miss Garbo, I've always wanted to meet you, and now, at last, I can tell all my friends I finally [did]!" Garbo gave her a frosty stare and corrected, "You can tell all your friends it was an accident."

The day after another such encounter, Garbo was so ruffled that she declined to go out at all. Green suggested they pick an inconspicuous corner, but she snapped, "It has nothing to do with the conspicuousness of the corner. It can be any corner. It's just as bad." It was not only her privacy that was always violated; it was her sense of propriety. Sam once asked her to join him for lunch, unannounced, with some Wall Street friends and got the following lecture in response:

> That's not the way to do things. If a gentleman says, "Would it amuse Miss Garbo perhaps to come to lunch?" [that's one thing]. But to put on my hat and coat and go down uninvited, like you'd just bring along an extra man! I'm not in the habit of going that way. I'm not in the habit of going, *period*. . . . If they were crazy about having me come

join the three of you, that's a different story. It has to come from them.
I'm not a stickler as a rule, but neither would I ever [go anywhere]
uninvited. . . . But I can't go anyway.*

Though manners and errands were often their superficial content, the
Garbo-Green conversations shed bright light on her mind and speech in
general. "She turned almost every sentence into a joke on the one before,"
he says. "It was fascinating the way she wove her verbal tapestry. She had
a real gift for language and for discovering a new word. Once she learned
'unruly,' she used it fifty times a day for a while and then not again for a
year. She had a deep sense of irony and mimicry, and of course she was a
consummate entertainer. You could never talk about movies, but now and
then she'd speak of herself as a 'former entertainment person.' She almost
never used the words 'I,' 'me,' or 'my.' She said that when people used those
words, it meant the subject was of interest only to the speaker. It's very hard
to avoid first-person pronouns, but she managed to do it day after day. It's
a feat—and it's effete—but she did it as a kind of exercise in language
control."

There is a treasure trove of wordplay in the Garbo-Green recordings: One
day in 1975, she speaks of having just had some wooden cabinets installed
and of the need to sandpaper them herself—but, oh, the prospect of going
out and buying the sandpaper and shellac. Would she need one can or two?
And what about a brush?

It was Mission Nearly Impossible:

GG: What do I buy? Tell me what to do. I don't know. I'm in bed,
lying here in a state. It's very unhealthy to sit around here with nerves
on edge, wondering why all the workmen are taking advantage of
you. . . .
SG: Do you want to go for a walk in the park?
GG: Well . . . How can I decide on anything when I'm lying here and
haven't even shaved? I have to shave first . . . get rid of the stubs.

* This and all subsequent Garbo-Green exchanges are taken from the most important record
of Garbo's last fifty years. The verbatim authenticity of her words is guaranteed by the fact
that they were not "remembered" but tape-recorded. Early on, Green informed Garbo that,
as an art dealer working out of his home, he routinely recorded all phone calls. Garbo made
no protest then or later, and Green never violated the understanding that the recordings
would not be exploited in any way during (or, for that matter, after) her lifetime. Their
disclosure and quotation for the first time in this book are by courtesy of Sam Green and
the Greta Garbo Estate and have involved no financial transaction of any kind. The Garbo-
Green tapes—some one hundred hours of conversation in all—have been placed in repository
at the Cinema Archives of Wesleyan University in Middletown, Connecticut.

SG: The stubble?

GG: Yes, stubble. . . . If I have to be ready at one, I have to start shaving now. You know it takes me forever. A lot of stubs. You call it that?

SG: Stubble.

GG: Stubble? Like bubble? If I say stub, that wouldn't do?

SG: That wouldn't do.

GG: What did I say?

SG: You said stubs.

GG: Well, why did you have to change it? [Laughs] I'll have to put muck on my face, too, before you come. I don't go out without muck, [and] I couldn't have you sitting here with me putting mascara on and stuff. . . .

SG: I hope it's not a big job.

GG: Oh, it always is. It's horrible.

In this case, she was both amused and amusing about her imperfect English. She spoke the language quite well, her misusages always minor and charming. Once when Sam was leaving town she said, "I wish you a speedy journey"—slightly missing the mark, with "Godspeed" in mind. Sam gently corrected her, and Garbo took no offense.

Sometimes the subtleties of rapid American speech eluded her. She often had difficulty coming up with the exact English word she was looking for "because I don't get out and talk to people enough, just to myself—and I don't answer."

It was touchingly honest. Rather than ask for clarification of something she didn't catch, she often gave up and moved on (or back) to a more manageable subject such as the weather. But with Sam Green, she was comfortable enough to confront the problem, as in a chat about apartment maintenance:

GG: You may-tain.

SG: Maintain?

GG: Maintain? It's an *n*? I can't spell anything. . . . You pronounce the *n*?

SG: Main.

GG: Main. May-tenance. How do you say it?

SG: Maintenance.

GG: I thought that's what I said, but I guess I didn't.

SG: It sounded more like may-tenance.

GG: Well, I have a slight accent and I tried to get rid of it, but it creeps up once in a while.

Ray Daum "may-tains" that her apartment was always stocked with newspapers and magazines and that there was no doubt from her conversation that she read them. She never took sleeping pills for her insomnia but, instead, read voraciously. Her niece says that, during their annual spring cruises in the Caribbean, "I was ashamed of my Louis L'Amour when she was reading Sartre. She also read a great many books about art, historical novels, biographies, and lots of poetry, too."

Claire Koger also attests to Garbo's active reading. ("She had to do *something*!") Yet even that laudable, uncontroversial activity was not to be admitted—or "revealed"—under questioning. When Sam Green once asked her, simply and directly, "Do you read much?" she replied:

"No. I should. But I don't seem to have time."

The answer was so absurd that Garbo herself had to laugh. What else did she have but time? Sam laughed, too. He had a way of laughing with and even *at* her, without scoffing.

"Should I be artificially jolly?" he asked her one day.

"No," she replied. "Never be anything with me."

"You see through it?"

"You bet I do," she said.

The Garbo-Green friendship, for the dozen years it lasted, was unique. To few others did she reveal the details of her domestic life, albeit in stream-of-consciousness fashion, with many non sequiturs on both ends of the phone wire:

SG: Did you get up before dawn?

GG: Oh, yes, it's dark and handsome. It doesn't get light until seven. I look out and I see how many people in the big building to the left of me are up—not many, but there is always one or two. They're early birds. They catch no worms anyway. I know [when the sun comes up] because I always go in to the living room, where the sun comes up over the river. It shines in my face and it's not what I want at that time. That room is very bright when the sun is shining [and] I cannot stand strong light. So I tell it to go away for a bit [and] I go back [to the bedroom] and draw the blinds because I look at television while I'm eating my meager breakfast. . . .

SG: Do you ever have a fire?

GG: No, never. I'm hardly ever in the living room. Only when my girl makes the bedroom, I have to go and sit there. Otherwise, I am not in the living room. I have a little television in the bedroom, and there I am.

sg: A color television, I hope.

gg: No. No color. . . . I just don't care. . . .

sg: How easily satisfied you are.

gg: No, I just can't stand the bother of [buying a new one]. As long as it works, there it stays. I have another one in the big room. That's black and white, too, and it stays there. . . . No change, no. I can't bother with those things. As long as it works.

In the mornings, she did her stretching exercises on a floor mat that lay folded in front of the glass doors leading to her balcony. If she had trouble sleeping and awoke at three or four a.m., she would go out onto that balcony, squat down so as not to be seen, and watch the traffic below. She told Sam she often waited there in the dark, in high anticipation, watching for the trucks that brought the morning newspapers across the bridge into the city from the printing plants in Brooklyn.

Her invariable breakfast consisted of whole-wheat toast (unbuttered, with jam) and two cups of coffee. In midmorning, she took her first walk and shopped for lunch (vegetables and fruit). She then rested briefly in preparation for the afternoon hike, after which she indulged in her "two slugs" of whiskey or vodka—never more. Dinner, pre-prepared by Claire, was eaten on a tray in her bedroom in front of the television: grilled beef or chicken, perhaps a steamed green vegetable, and boiled potatoes. She was a creature of habit, and there was a truly monastic quality to her routine.

"I have to be home by five-thirty," she told Sam many times, "otherwise, the Sandman won't come." Aside from her walks, sleep was Garbo's chief requirement. "I'm a very sleepless man," she once said to Ray Daum. But there was more than just the Sandman involved. The day Sam took her to meet Diana Vreeland, the two women enjoyed each other a great deal, and their visit lasted much longer than anticipated, as Green relates:

It was dark by the time we got to Fifty-second Street, and I saw an elderly lady coming towards us. Garbo saw her too and said, "Oh God, I told you to get me back before five-thirty!" She just lost it—scuttled sideways like a crab, put her shoulder up, pulled her hat down, put her hand in front of her face. She got more and more distraught as the woman got closer. As we passed, Valentina looked at Garbo trying to hide and then at me and just tipped her hat and walked on. But Garbo was undone. They both knew the routine: Garbo was to be home by 5:30 before Valentina went out at 6, and they were never to meet. *That's* why she had to be home at 5:30—as much as for the Sandman.

One evening, Sam was worried when Garbo failed to answer his pre-arranged call. The next day she explained that those cabinetmakers were still invading her space; she had retired early and turned the phone off:

GG: Sometimes somebody will call here at night, one o'clock or something, some crazy person or the wrong number. So you have to turn your button off, and sometimes I forget to put it back on for days. . . . Well, anyway, there are very few people that can call me, but that's the most important thing to me, this button. . . .

SG: Claire is off tomorrow [Presidents' Day]?

GG: Oh, yes. It's not a real holiday. The shops are open. You can have food sent, everything. I give my girl every holiday off. She shouldn't have it because domestic people don't get holidays off. What the hell, take an opportunity to be left in peace. But I'm afraid I have to baby-sit here tomorrow a bit with these strange men in here.

SG: Claire can't do that?

GG: She doesn't know what to do with men. I don't either.

Green found her "a woman incapable of doing things by herself." There were few she trusted—Gray Reisfield, Jane Gunther, and not many others. Since she was loath to let strangers into her apartment, it was often Sam's job to fix a leaky faucet or rehang a venetian blind. Her calls to him involved such things as a light fixture over which she agonized for weeks:

I have no idea what I want. I don't like black and I don't like white. I saw one on Third Avenue and I stood there and thought, maybe I have to have it but—I need somebody to tell me if it's horrible or not. Maybe you can tell me. Wait a minute—can you wait a second? [Leaves phone, returns.] First, you have to put on the glasses. It's Third Avenue at the corner of Seventy-fourth—Light and Shade Company. It's hanging in the window right as you come in. It's pink and it's very funny-looking. It's like mother-of-pearl a bit. You can't miss it because it's right as you come into the door, the first one is pinky. . . . If you think it's absolutely divine, I could buy it and put a big bulb in it, if you have a chance to look.

Even more staggering was the thought, let alone the reality, of buying a certain pair of shoes—the logistics of which once occupied Garbo and Green for more than an hour in three separate phone calls. The transcript reads like a Samuel Beckett play, or a ZaSu Pitts improvisation:

SG: Is there anything I can do? . . .

GG: Yes, buy me a pair of shoes. [But] you'd have to come here and get one shoe. It's at Lord and Taylor, in Chinatown. You have to pass by the library, that's all I know. I've never been in the library. No, I'm not going to bother you with my shoes. I hope to God I'll be able to go out on Monday, [but] then, how can I go into Lord and Taylor, full of gawking humanity—it's dangerous.

SG: It's time to think of the sun.

GG: Yes, but I want shoes before. I hate being indoors. Hate it! . . . If I can think of something to make you get to Lord and Taylor to get me those shoes, I will. But if I can't—we'll see what develops over the weekend. I've got to get those shoes. I've *got* to get them.

SG: Why don't you just put one down with the doorman in a little package and say, "Mr. Green will pick it up," and I'll go and see if I can get something close.

GG: Not close, *only* that shoe. It *is* the shoe.

SG: Okay. Then just ring for the elevator man.

GG: Oh, no, I can't face the elevator man. No. . . . I'd rather face you than the elevator man.

SG: Why?

GG: I don't know.

SG: Then *telephone* the elevator man.

GG: If your lung hurts, is it in the back of the chest or in the front?

SG: Probably the front. . . . Where does it hurt?

GG: It hurts in the front and in the back. [Laughs] . . . Why did I bring that up?

SG: Cut down on the smoking.

GG: I can't cut down. You can. . . . Don't give me any more ideas, please. . . .

SG: Now they have something that you just inhale—

GG: Inhale? I'm not going to inhale. That's horrible. Yuk. It's terrible. I have Vicks. You put that in hot water with a cloth over your head. Then your poor hair gets wet. Then you have to dry your head. . . .

SG: You're in bed?

GG: I certainly am, with everything on me. . . . I have two sweaters on and long woolen underwear and socks. So if I should stagger out to open the door and let you in, I would have to disguise some of this, and today I decided I wouldn't put any make-up on at all because I have to take it off if I put it on. For two days now, I put make-up on.

SG: For Claire?

GG: No. Just for the hell of it. I thought, "Maybe Mr. Green will come over."

SG: I'm going to come over and get that shoe. Put it in a brown paper bag in your hallway, perhaps with the advertisement from the newspaper, and then telephone downstairs for the elevator man and say, "I've left a package for Mr. Green in my hallway."

GG: He will never understand.

SG: He gets the message.

GG: I'm not going to do it. Maybe it isn't the same shoe, anyway.

SG: Well, if it isn't, I wouldn't get it. . . .

GG: Maybe you can call me later. I think it's stupid for you to go and get them, because if they're not right, it's an awful lot of trouble for me. Goodbye.

An awful lot of trouble for *her*?

That was how she viewed it. Her clothes problems were constant—nothing fit, the styles weren't right. Since he knew Halston, Sam arranged for Garbo to have a private look at the designer's new line of cashmere turtlenecks and men's jackets that seemed her type. He specified that no one else be present and no "fuss" be made, and on the appointed day in 1977, he, Garbo, and Cécile arrived at Halston's showroom at Sixty-eighth Street and Madison Avenue. Halston was ecstatic. "You're the model of the kind of person I design for," he told her. "I'm so pleased you came, and I hope you come back soon, and I'll give you anything you want."

It had been a great success, thought Sam, until his phone rang the next morning at nine. "Mr. Green, you don't realize these things," said the deep voice. "I can't go anywhere." A full account of their visit was on the front page of *Women's Wear Daily*—and Halston lost an important customer.

Among Sam Green's services for Garbo was the composing of thank-you notes which she felt, or feigned, an inability to do herself. "It's stupid," she complained one day. "Why do you have to sit down and write a long note? What you should do is write a short thing saying, 'I'm sorry I'm so late but I've been running like crazy, and all of the sudden my conscience bothered me and I have to send this off fast and furiously, and as soon as things are clearing up, I will write you a long nice letter and tell you how much I like you.' " When she told Sam she felt guilty about owing Cécile a letter, he suggested sending a telegram instead. "You send it on the phone?" she inquired. "I wouldn't know how to do any of that. I get so nervous when they say, 'How do you spell it?' Then I have to think, is it *e* or *i*? I have a heck of a time with *e* or *i*. . . . You wouldn't understand, but it's the way foreigners have."

Telegrams were easy compared to providing medical advice and services. Her aches and pains occupied many of their talks. One day she called Sam with the shattering news that "I've got a wart on my toe." He knew a good wart doctor. "No," she said, "I'm so scared of the air-conditioning in these doctors' offices." There was a tragic sigh worthy of Camille before she added, "Oh, Mr. Green, that isn't all of my woes."

The most bizarre incident was dental. In 1978, she had a front tooth that was bothering her—but no dentist. Sam offered to make her an appointment with his own dentist, but she worried about the air-conditioning. It would be turned off, Sam assured her. Yes, but she couldn't sit in a waiting room, someone might accost her. The obstacles were endless, and the upshot was unprecedented in the annals of Manhattan dentistry: Sam Green deposited her on a bench at Central Park West and Seventy-second Street, where a disgruntled Dr. Irving Schultz examined the teeth of Greta Garbo alfresco.

Green claimed no special knowledge of medicine, but he was intrigued by various movements in holistic health, psychic well-being, and spiritual enlightenment—acupuncture, transcendental meditation, and reincarnation among them. When he plunged into such things (with friends Andy Warhol, John Lennon and Yoko Ono), he went all the way, and sometimes he took Garbo with him. Meditation was the one that "took." Garbo was so fascinated by Green's description of its benefits that, in April 1975, she agreed to two home visits by a certified TM instructor of the Maharishi Foundation. She meditated twenty minutes daily for several years thereafter, though she often complained of having difficulty emptying her mind and rising to a higher level.

One day in London, Green devilishly asked Garbo what her mantra was. "I can't tell—it's supposed to be a secret," she said. But he wormed it out of her, and it turned out to be the same as his. "That shattered the whole illusion," Green recalls. "She loved it while she did it, but nobody ever meditated again once we found out we were given the same mantra."

Acupuncture terrified her, though she submitted to it once or twice. "I'm frightened," she told Green after a treatment. "I don't like the idea of going and sitting in that dark hole getting needles stuck into me." In view of her timidity, it was amazing she had even dared to try it. But she was open to some amazing things. She surprised Sam one day with the news that she had checked out Rolfing long before he did*:

SG: You went to Ida Rolf?

GG: Years ago, and you be careful. . . . It's a drastic thing. What I was put through has done me harm for the rest of my life. . . . Got a hip

---

* Named for its inventor, physiotherapist Ida P. Rolf (1897–1979), Rolfing is a rugged—rather brutal—massage therapy involving intensive manipulation of the muscles and internal organs to relieve physical and emotional tension.

out of business, and I can never sit in Hindu fashion anymore. . . . It's too drastic, unless they've changed their methods. They take your flesh [and] just knead the jesus out of it, and it's dangerous.

sg: Did you go through the whole thing?

gg: I don't even want to go into it. It makes me sick. I suffered so terribly—it scared the life out of me. I saw her here in New York— this is probably twenty years ago. I thought she was in jail. Maybe I just had bad luck. I knew somebody else that went there, and she died.

When not rendering such warnings to Sam, Garbo was rendering unto Caesar, and none too willingly. By the midseventies, the complexity of her investments was such that only a professional could sort it out—the kind of professional she never liked to deal with. All she knew, and resented, was that much of her income went to pay taxes, and that she dreaded the few meetings she was forced to endure each year with her financial handlers.

Chief among them was Anthony A. Palermo of Milwaukee, who co-owned the profitable Modern Products natural-food company that Gayelord Hauser built. He had been Hauser's business manager and was happy to take on similar duties for Garbo. "I am the mystery man behind the scenes," he later claimed—the adviser and confidant who "paid Garbo's bills" from 1976 on. Palermo handled the bulk of her affairs, free of charge, and all he asked in return was an annual consultation in New York to review matters and bask in her presence. To this she acceded most grudgingly. If merely sending a telegram baffled her, her attitude toward high finance, taxes, and accountants can be guessed. Green heard many lamentations on the subject:

> I have tax that hasn't been paid and the government is drowning me with letters. . . . I don't have any secretary. I don't want any secretary. I'm going to try to arrange things differently. This way is too nerve-wracking. I can't stand it. My apartment [is] a mess, and I'm a mess. I couldn't face having a stranger coming here. . . . I loathe my hand-writing so, and I had to write out some checks by myself here. I made these poor little checks, and they look like a chicken has been walking on them. I have a new [bill] this morning. Maybe I'll wait till Friday and let somebody else do that one. That is Edison, Con Edison. Is that electricity?

And a week later:

> I don't know about stocks and bonds. I hate it. I never had anything to do with it, but I'm in it. This broker wants to know something by the end of the year. . . . I have to do something, otherwise everything

will go to the devil. I'll have the whole United States after me—they'll send the Army and lock me up. You can't just shovel it aside, and that's what I'm doing. I have to start the ball rolling, but I don't like to play ball. I'm not interested. . . . I have no deductions, no nothing. Everything goes *out*. I have no Medicare, nothing. . . . It's too awful, the whole thing. So I pay.

Helpful as usual, Sam suggested a tax specialist and, as usual, was rebuffed. "I don't want to go through that, no, sir," she told him. "I want to get *out* of things instead of in."

Green always began his conversations with Garbo by taking a barometric reading of her mood, his own being invariably cheerful. Hers was up and down, bright and dark, and Sam was at pains to assess and react the right way. Anything resembling pity was perilous, and so was any implied criticism—even the harmless suggestion that she might compensate for her sleeplessness by taking a nap during the day.

"I can't do that," she replied irritably. "You're different, totally different. You're not subject to stupid little laws, but I am."

"You sound down in the dumps a bit," he said. After a long silence, he added, "I'm sorry"—at which her anger flared. "If you don't stop it, I think we have to cut out everything," she said. "You can call [my habits] anything you like, but it's a way of life and it's a way of being . . . and cut it out!"

"Keep reminding me," he said, abashed.

"I don't want to," she shot back. "I'm not your *kinderfräulein*, if you know what that is."

Dealing with Garbo was epitomized by an exchange that capped numerous efforts on Green's part to cheer her up:

SG: I wish my good mood was infectious.
GG: Well, it isn't.
SG: Now, what I think we ought to do is—
GG: Whatever you suggest, it's no.

Garbo's avoidance of fellow celebrities defied a pattern. She would ignore invitations, accept and then fail to show, or shock a host by simply showing up with no prior indication of doing so. An instance of the last mode took place in the midfifties when she and Minna Wallis were in Palm Springs visiting Gayelord Hauser. After several days, Wallis asked her friend Ava Gardner if she and Garbo might spend the weekend at the Gardner-Sinatra residence there. Gardner said of course—when did they want to arrive? "In about five minutes," was the answer. When Gardner opened her door, Garbo swept past without so much as a handshake, asking, "Where is my room?"

and complaining about the air-conditioning. Gardner was sure she was in for the Guest from Hell, but Garbo soon materialized—topless—by the pool, all smiles. "She changed into a dress after that, accepted our offer of vodka, and began a memorable weekend of drinking, eating, laughing, and more eating," wrote Gardner, who privately told a friend, "She ate a whole fucking chicken!"

A few years later, on the Riviera, Garbo was introduced to John Gielgud as "Harriet Brown." After several days in her company, Gielgud finally said, "Don't you think it's time we stopped this 'Miss Brown' nonsense? May I call you Harriet?"

The most legendary encounter of all took place in May 1968 at the West Hollywood home of George Cukor. It was a small, carefully plotted dinner party in honor of two special guests: Garbo and Mae West—the alpha and omega of film femininity. The only others present were Gayelord Hauser, Frey Brown, and Roddy McDowall. Garbo came dressed very simply in a pink pantsuit. West was swathed in a slinky, sequined-and-flowered evening gown and, by her own account, did most of the talking:

> I got there first and when Garbo came in I said, "Oh, hello dear," and kissed her on the cheek to make her feel at home. And when she was loosened up she sat down on a very low chair. And I thought, "Oh, she's down low and there's a window open in back of her—she'll catch cold." So they closed the windows. And I said to her, "Do you like that low chair?" She said, "Oh, I'd like to sit on the floor." I told her, "No, you look good right there."

Diet and fitness regimes dominated the conversation. Roddy McDowall remembers hardly saying a word, just taking in the scene:

> George's way of choreographing an evening was masterful. He had a marvelous manner—earthy but sophisticated. Mae was just emerging from a period of retirement of about twenty-five years, and Garbo wanted to meet her, more than the other way around, or it wouldn't have happened. At one point George left the room to get a drink and said to Mae, "Tell G about the time you went to jail in the twenties" —about her being arrested for her play, *Sex*. She gave a real performance, and Garbo was fascinated—for a while.
>
> At dinner, they sat next to each other, and Garbo kept taking hold of her and saying things like, "Oh, look at her little hands—no spots! Look at her arms!" Mae said, in her best Mae voice, "Yeah, and they go *all* the way *up!*"

The mutual examination continued throughout the evening. Garbo wanted to see the famous spiked shoes which made the 4′11″ West look taller, while West confirmed with her own eyes that Garbo's feet weren't so big after all. There was evidently only one exchange of professional shop-talk. "She said that she loved my pictures, and I said the same about hers," West later told a newspaper reporter. "I said to her, 'You know, you really ought to make another picture. You look great!' She said, 'I dunno. I'll think it over.'"

Richard Burton was as star-struck by Garbo as any other fan, and when an opportunity presented itself he seized it: "While attending a party at which one of the guests was Garbo, I curiously asked her, 'Could you do me a great favor? May I kiss your knee?' She replied, 'Certainly,' and I leaned over and did so. It was an experience I'll never forget."

Not all fellow thespians came away from their Garbo encounters so fulfilled. "Garbo did not want to meet me," Ingrid Bergman declared in her memoirs. "Maybe she thought I was there to compete with her." When she first came to Hollywood in 1939, Bergman sent her flowers as a gesture of respect. Garbo replied by telegram on July 19, 1939: "Thank you. I would like to see you when I am free. If you would be willing, could you give me your phone number. Best regards. Greta Garbo." But there was a little problem in the timing.

"I was there for three months and I sent the flowers the very first week I arrived, but the telegram came only a few days before I left," said Bergman. Later, she told this to Cukor, who laughed and said, "But of course Greta wouldn't have sent the telegram unless she were certain you were leaving." The first and only meeting of two great actresses with so much in common did not take place until decades later in Barbados, where Bergman and her husband Lars Schmidt were vacationing.

"She came down into the garden and sat down beside me," said Bergman. "I didn't know what to say I was so nervous. But she opened the conversation. 'I understand you're in love with Barbados, and you're going to buy a piece of land here?'" Yes, said Bergman, they had plans for a little house.

"Oh, I wouldn't do that because here they steal everything," said Garbo. Bergman said it would just be a humble place with rough wooden furniture, to which Garbo replied, "Yes, but they'll steal your clothes." Bergman was incredulous. All she had in Barbados was a swimsuit, shorts, and pair of long pants, she told Garbo, who said nothing—then stood up and walked away.

Another Nordic woman had even less luck. One day in 1977, Garbo and Sam Green were walking near Sixty-seventh Street on Central Park West when a long chauffeured limousine suddenly screeched to a halt, and out jumped an attractive, wild-eyed young woman, who rushed toward them.

Green turned and planted himself between the pursuer and Garbo's getaway route—preordained, in such emergencies, as four left or right turns around the nearest block.

"That was Garbo, I know it was, I must meet her!" the woman cried, trying to get around Green, but he held his ground and Garbo was quickly out of sight and lost in the crowd. "Please tell her Liv Ullmann would like so much to meet her!" The Norwegian actress—brilliant star of a half dozen of Ingmar Bergman's greatest films and of a sequel to *Queen Christina* called *The Abdication*—explained to Sam that she would be appearing in a new Broadway production of *Anna Christie*, set to open just days later, and that she revered the Garbo film version. Ullmann recalls:

"I wanted to express how much she had meant to me as a fellow Scandinavian and . . . as an actress, as well as what to me was such a strange coincidence: here I was rehearsing *Anna Christie* and there she was walking on the street. Poor Garbo saw this 'madwoman' running out of a car after her, so obviously she had only one choice and that was to run. So she ran and I ran. After a while I understood that I was frightening her [and] I was both ashamed and sad. . . . In the end, she ran quicker than me."

Once he recognized her, Green was apologetic and promised to relay Ullmann's message and try to arrange a proper meeting. Upon catching up with Garbo, he told her the woman's identity. Garbo paused and then said with what Green remembers as great sadness: "She must think I am the rudest man in the world—and she's right."

Ullmann and Garbo never got together.

Tennessee Williams's last meeting with her was not much happier. His career was not going well and, in 1975, he had taken the role of Doc in *Small Craft Warnings*, which was dying at the box office and needed his presence as an audience draw. During its run, he was walking up Fifth Avenue with writer Dotson Rader, who spotted Garbo at Thirty-fifth Street. "Miss Garbo, it's Tennessee Williams," he said. Williams told her he was acting in his own play and would be honored if she would come and see him.

"How wonderful," she said. "But I can't accept. You see, I do not go out anymore," turning quickly and entering the store.

"As he watched her disappear," said Rader, "Tennessee commented, more to himself than to me, that she was the saddest of creatures, an artist who abandoned her art. And that was worse than death, he said, it was worse than anything, to live on without your art."

"I do not go out anymore" was not quite right, of course. More accurate was the anonymous wag's characterization of her as a "hermit-about-town."

Everyone in New York, it seemed, had a Garbo story—a sighting to be told and cherished—and some of the most famous New Yorkers were the most obsessed with her. Andy Warhol trailed her for years and took pictures on the sly. Fellow recluse John Lennon often referred to himself as (and signed his name) "Greta Hughes."

Jackson Pollock was once walking with a friend on Third Avenue when Garbo strode by in the opposite direction. "I've only experienced [love] three times," he said, and "one of them was when we passed that woman." With that, Pollock did an about-face and was not seen again all day.

One acquaintance compared her to a hummingbird: "She lights on your hand, and there is this vivid creature, and then she flies away." Her brief visits were like the appearance of a unicorn. But *planned* outings rattled her, even with such old friends as Gayelord Hauser. In 1975, he was in New York and insisted she go to dinner. Garbo told Sam she was agonized about it; as always, she hated the thought of going out in the evening: "People don't understand that. Some people go out and have a lovely time, they can't wait until they can get out. I wish I was like that—you want to go somewhere, you just pick up your hat and go. I don't even pick up the hat."

She did better on short notice or on impulse, when the anticipation was minimized. In bad weather, she sometimes slipped into a neighborhood movie house such as the Plaza Theatre on East Fifty-eighth Street, whose manager would quietly offer her a seat. Her film tastes were fussy. She had a strong aversion to violence and obscenity. One picture she loved was *Becket* (1964). "I was in a trance," she told Ray Daum. "I thought it was absolutely beautiful, in a haunting way. It's obviously homosexual between the two men. . . . I always wanted to see *Becket* again, but they put it on television so late at night that I can't watch it, because I'm a limited man."

Once in the early sixties, she was coaxed by Cecil Beaton into checking out the Peppermint Lounge ("Home of the Twist") on a lark. She decided she would be "with it," said Kerstin Bernadotte, who was in the party that night, and they arrived "just as the dance orgies were in full swing." Joey Dee and the Starlighters were the main attraction, and Garbo watched and applauded with delight, letting down her guard and unaware of the clicking cameras. She was sad and sobered the next day to find her picture all over the newspapers.

The only outings she relished unreservedly were her beloved walks. "I trotted out to get some things and looked at the human beings today," she would say. "Often I just go where the man in front of me is going." Walking with Ray Daum, she sometimes broke into a rendition of "Deep in the Heart of Texas" or "It's a Long Way to Tipperary" or some TV jingle, with charming errors ("You've come a far way, baby"). Once, when Daum was exhausted after 120 blocks, she reminded him, "The best thing is not to think, just trot." Another companion accompanied her one day to St. Patrick's Cathedral, where she prayed to St. Bridget, the patron saint of Sweden.

Major museum exhibits she attended rarely due to the crowds, but painter Michael J. W. Green was electrified one day at the Guggenheim when he overheard an employee exclaim that Garbo was there. Somehow, he knew she would go against the norm and walk *up* the spiral walkway that everyone else walked *down*. He too started up on foot, and soon she came into sight, dipping in and out of the exhibit bays at a leisurely pace. Green was careful to take his time before catching up and daring to enter the same bay and steal his glance:

> What I saw was so completely natural. There was no artifice. The skin was free of any make-up, or powder even. There was an exquisitely fine criss-crossing of lines over it, fine crow's feet, like the hairline cracking of a rare Chinese porcelain that gives to that rarity its unique sheen of time. The hair on another head would have been mousy; on hers it was silky fine and the colors were no colors at all, ash-blonde greys mixed with darker and whiter shadows. It was the structure of that face I most remember, what lay under the skin. The carving of it, the bones. No angle of it could have been modelled for improvement.

In 1974, Garbo attended Diana Vreeland's "Romantic and Glamorous Hollywood Design" exhibit at the Metropolitan Museum, belying the alleged disinterest in her former career. "I went [because] my periodontist said, 'Oh, it's such a wonderful exhibition of cinema clothes! You are a lot in there,'" she told Sam. "I thought it was absolutely ghastly. They had some horrible rags that they'd gotten together, slaphappy. My clothes, supposedly, weren't my clothes. It was absolutely beastly."

Galleries and fabric shops held greater appeal, and she dropped into many of them over the years, on Fifth and Madison avenues, rarely making a purchase. Those visits were usually pleasant, with an exception or two. In the Rose Cumming showrooms on East Fifty-ninth Street, she asked one day to take home some swatches and was told she had to sign for them. She wrote "G. Garbo," whereupon the maladroit saleswoman exclaimed, "Oh! My mother used to take me to your movies when I was a little kid!" Garbo's comment to Sam Green on the way out was spiced with a rare and funny vulgarism: "Did you hear what that old fuck said?"

The instigator of her infrequent trips to the concert hall was composer David Diamond, whose out-of-sequence Eighth Symphony premiere under Leonard Bernstein and Seventh Symphony premiere under Eugene Ormandy she attended in 1961 and 1962 at Carnegie Hall. Diamond arranged for her to duck in and be seated at the last minute and to depart quickly at the end. What did she say about the pieces and the performances? "Nothing," says Diamond. "I didn't ask her and she didn't tell me."

Garbo's film- and theater-going were likewise sporadic. In the fall of 1962, she saw Vivien Leigh and Jean-Pierre Aumont in *Tovarich* at the Broadway Theatre. Earlier that year, she queued up with the hoi polloi for *The Loneliness of the Long-Distance Runner* at the Baronet Theater. She had also acquired a taste for British actor Terence Stamp, whose performances in *Billy Budd* and *The Collector* she saw and praised.

Producer William Frye, an old California friend, took her to a Saturday matinee of *Funny Girl* in 1964, but she was spotted during the intermission: "It was pandemonium. People swarmed around us, pointing at her. She actually was quite gracious, but it made her so uncomfortable, she said we just had to go. I said, 'G.G., if we try to push our way out of the Winter Garden it'll make things worse.' People eventually calmed down, Garbo too. We had wonderful seats. Streisand was singing, and Garbo loved it."

One show she made certain to avoid, in November 1965, was *The Private Potato Patch of Greta Garbo*, an off-Broadway play by J. Roy Sullivan at Judson Poet's Theater in Washington Square. Its title character, played by Gloria Pages in a Bowery bum's rags, rides the subway with other misfits, convinced that the world is ending and that only she can bring some sort of post-Apocalyptic peace. ("No more wars," she says. "I fixed all that." And to another character: "I see you know God, too. A wonderful man.")

That autumn, the Oscar-winning film composer Dmitri Tiomkin announced plans to direct a movie biography of Tchaikovsky in which he hoped to lure Garbo—for a cool $1 million—to play Madame Von Meck. Leading candidate for the title role was New York Philharmonic conductor Leonard Bernstein, who told David Diamond he was eager to do it with her. Predictably enough, when that Soviet-American joint production was finished in 1970, both Garbo and Bernstein were absent from the cast.

Meanwhile, on the West Coast, Frye discovered that Garbo went where she pleased, and to hell with dress codes. He had booked a dinner reservation at Chasen's, but she was wearing pants. "I called the restaurant and told them I was bringing Miss Garbo to dinner and could she please come in slacks," Frye recalled. "They said no, she could not." Nevertheless, Garbo and Frye dined at Chasen's that night: She simply rolled up her trousers beneath the overcoat she wore to their table.

In 1975, she went to see Deborah Kerr in Edward Albee's *Seascape* and walked backstage afterward to say she admired her performance. "I was so nervous," said Kerr. "It was among the great thrills in my life that she came to see me. But she wouldn't say anything about the play."

Garbo seemed to perk up whenever the subject of playgoing came up. "Are we going to the theater?" she asked Sam Green one day. He said he couldn't get tickets until the following Wednesday. "And here I was thinking, 'Maybe I'll go to the theater,'" she sighed. "It would have been such a revolutionary thing." Her only hesitation about theater trips was the usual one, as she expressed to Sam in 1976 when he asked if she wanted to see Katharine Hepburn in *A Matter of Gravity*.

"I ain't sayin' nothing today," she replied. "How do you get tickets, through an agent? And nobody has to know? That would really be the end of me." Her fears were realized: They went to the play and, at its end, six photographers were lying in wait for her outside. "It's so sad," Garbo said when they finally escaped. "I can never go to the theater again."

New York, she told Ray Daum, "only matters to people who are really participating and who are really New Yorkers. A person like me has no business being in New York. The word 'fun' I don't recognize. . . . If I'm out anywhere, which is very rare, I'm home before seven. There are so many things to do in New York, and if you don't do them, why sit here?" She was becoming more and more solipsistic:

If I hadn't been in the movies and people didn't look you over too carefully, I could go places. I'd go anyplace at the drop of a hat. I've never wanted any kind of attention from anybody, [but] there are these horrible, unbelievable paparazzi. . . . I'm not in the movies many, many years. I'm not worth anything to anybody. Why do they harass me? Pick on people who are au courant. I've always wanted two lives—one for the movies, one for myself.

Once and only once, in Green's experience, was she ever amused by the media's obsession with her:

GG: I got a horrible article sent to me this morning.
SG: What kind of an article?
GG: Well, my latest boyfriend is Van Johnson. . . . You know who that is, don't you?
SG: I think it's an old actor who wears red socks.
GG: Old—don't say that. [Laughs] And don't call him an actor. Absolutely ghastly. They make you into such an idiot, you can't believe it. I wonder what prompts people to sit down and write those sort of things. . . .
SG: Have you ever seen or met Van Johnson?
GG: Met him, yes. He lives down on First Avenue or something. Once in a while, twice a year or so, I meet him in the street. . . .

[She and Sam agree to get together later that day.]

GG: I'll bring Van Johnson, too. Can't live without Van Johnson.

SG: Have you set the date?

GG: For what?

SG: For the wedding. . . .

GG: Oh, no, no, it's not romantic. It's just deep friendship. We just meet every day, whatever it said, [and] go shopping. . . .

SG: What will happen when you go to California and [the reporters] see you there alone? They'll say you're jilting Van Johnson.

GG: He may follow.

The avoidance of photographers was not due to her vanity about aging, Green maintains. It stemmed from her desperation to escape identifiability on the street, which every new photo made easier. Her bewilderment at the captions that accompanied such pictures was poignant. "Can I go in my fisherman's coat?" she once asked Sam before an outing. "It's that horrible thing from Abercrombie and Fitch, [but] I don't want to wear the fur coat. I was photographed in it." She knew of but hadn't seen those photos in the papers and asked Sam what was written beneath them.

"I think it said, 'Greta Garbo Alone' [or] 'Is Finally Alone' or something like that," he replied.

"What did they mean by that? I'm always alone. What do they mean by 'finally'?"

Her ubiquitous sunglasses were as misunderstood as her photophobia, says David Diamond:

The dark glasses were because the light hurt her eyes, which were sensitive, and not just to cover up her face. I recall seeing her on Fifth Avenue with Gayelord Hauser at the corner of Fifty-fifth Street. Some woman walked up and said, "Oh, you're Greta Garbo!" and she looked down and just said, "Yes." She didn't have the elegance of Marlene. I never saw a woman handle a crowd the way Dietrich could—she just hypnotized them. GG couldn't do that, but if somebody got close and said something to her politely, she was nice. She'd say, "I must go, you know, I have to leave," something like that, and then disengage.

Sometimes the adulation got mixed up: In a Third Avenue antique shop one day, Garbo and her MoMA friend Allen Porter were admiring some treasure. "Do you really like it, Miss Dietrich?" the owner asked. As they left, the woman told "Miss Dietrich" she was honored to have her come in. Said Garbo, outside: "She obviously didn't get a look at my legs."

Garbo's antique-store browsings included The Flea Market on Second

Avenue, whose owner, Elmo Avet, reported, "She likes anything with cupids." One of the Third Avenue shops she frequented had an annex where furniture and other antiques were restored. Garbo sometimes sat there in silence for hours watching the craftsmen at work.

Caral Gimbel Lebworth recalled a day when she, Garbo, and Cécile were antiquing and saw something Miss G wanted to buy. The shop owner was asking a lot for it, and one of her companions said to Garbo, "Why don't you tell him who you are? Maybe he'll give you a discount." She went over to him and said, "Do you know who I am?" He looked at her and replied, "No"—and there went the deal. Garbo, says Lebworth, "was absolutely shocked."

For foodstuffs, she patronized a variety of markets in the neighborhood as well as the upscale Wynne & Treanor emporium on Madison Avenue. Her purchases were modest, usually just some smoked salmon or pâté de foie gras, but now and then she splurged on fresh caviar at $32 an ounce, or its humbler cousin, pressed caviar, at $12. On the other end of the spectrum was her beloved fruit stand in the East Fifties, whose white-haired Italian proprietress said, "She always smiles at my little Loretta. She likes to buy persimmons. I try to get her good ones."

She was also fond of takeout food from the nearby Swedish delicatessen, Nyborg & Nelson, at Fiftieth Street and Second Avenue, where cook Bryan Walsh occasionally saw her in a corner, alone or with a companion, drinking a cup of Swedish glögg. She also shopped at the Mid-City Food Market at 932 First Avenue, where, if cashier Lolita Jagdat is to be believed, Garbo picked up a copy of the gossip tabloids *Star* or *Globe* every week.

And, of course, there were many restaurants over the years: In her own East Fifties neighborhood, she was fond of the Viennese Room, where Baron Goldschmidt-Rothschild took her, and of the Brazilian food at Semon's, which was also a favorite of George Schlee's. In later years, Diamond dined with her at Cafe des Artistes on Central Park West, where "she liked to sit at the corner table with her back to the restaurant and listen to the conversation at the table behind her."

But of all that New York had to offer, the simplest things most delighted her—such as the annual St. Patrick's Day Parade, about which she rhapsodized to Sam Green in 1976, with her usual seasoning of ambivalence:

When the bagpipes come, I go completely in a trance. They are so-oo-oo marvelous. Ooh, and the way they walk with the bagpipes, it's worth going there, I'm telling you, I absolutely adore it. I want to take you to the bagpipes, [but] I don't know. I feel brave lying down talking on the phone. Standing up, I'm not as brave. When do the bagpipes come? That's the only important part. Will it say maybe in the *TV Guide*? . . . Life's too complicated. Maybe skip it.

"Unless one is in love, or satisfied, or ambition-driven, or without curiosity, or reconciled," wrote Truman Capote, New York "is like a monumental machine restlessly devised for wasting time, devouring illusions. . . . Where is what you were looking for? And, by the way, what *are* you looking for?"

Garbo was neither in love nor satisfied nor ambitious. But she was curious and restless in the city-machine of New York—always with an eye to getting out of it.

"To run from place to place is not what I'm looking for," she told Ray Daum. "I can't take it. If I was twenty probably I could, but I can't now. You have to show passports, and someone might say, 'Oh, that's the one who used to be in the movies.' [And] I can't go to hotels because I can't stand noise. I have at least forty earplugs."

There were so many reasons why she couldn't travel, and so many travels to contradict them—the cruise to Corsica, for instance, in the summer of 1973, with Cécile, Sam Green, and Caral and Joseph Lebworth on the *Bibo*, a yacht Élie Rothschild had bought with the insurance money he got from losing an eye while playing polo. Garbo fretted beforehand, as always, but once onboard she relaxed among people she trusted and allowed herself to be photographed freely by Green and Lebworth. The *Bibo*'s ultramodern interior design, by Belgian artist Jean-Claude Farhi, included even its furniture and dishes and the unbreakable steel tumblers that not only held liquid but served as sight gags.

Cécile, Green says, was always fun to be with—"nothing standoffish about her at all. If G and I decided to throw peanuts, Cécile would throw one back." At dinner, Garbo never hesitated to point out crumbs on her friend's chin by uttering the code letters "FOF"—"food on face." In New York, Cécile stayed at the Regency, where the unlikely trio often partook of the hotel's fancy Sunday brunch.

"During the meal," says Green, "Garbo always kept her trenchcoat on, making herself conspicuous because everybody else checked their coats. I would sit next to her and slowly fill the pocket of her trenchcoat with silverware. She'd get home, put her hand in her pocket, come up with this stolen silverware, and then call and berate me: 'Mr. Green, don't you know what would happen if they found out?' I said, 'Yes, but they'd never search you and they'd never tell you even if they knew.' The next day, we'd have to meet at Cécile's and sneak the silverware back onto the room-service trays outside of other people's doors."

Garbo with Sam Green, Cécile de Rothschild, and Caral Gimbel, Corsica, 1973

Garbo crowns Cécile on board the Bibo, *with Sam Green at right.*

Why return it after it had been successfully stolen?

"It kept her busy," he says. "Anything to fill up the time with a good drama."

On the Corsica voyage, she was more playful than usual, plopping down next to Cécile at the bow of the boat with a cheerful, "Hi there, boy." She was heavy on the masculine gender during that trip, says Green. "She'd come to the table and say things like, 'Here's a boy who's very hungry after his swim.'"

Once, when Cécile was struggling to read a map in the wind, Garbo put her head on her friend's shoulder and, when Cécile failed to acknowledge her, declared tragically, "Ah, well, there's nothing more heavy than the body of the woman you have ceased to love." With that, she exited. But such lines and such moments, in Green's view, did not confirm the persistent rumor that she and Cécile were lovers:

> I traveled with them rather intimately for fourteen years and saw nothing but a deep, loving friendship. When she called Cécile "boy," it was part of her wordplay. She was delighted if it got a rise out of people. But they were elderly women with high standards, and having sex with each other didn't fit into those standards. They were too dignified. Everyone of both sexes found Garbo attractive, and Cécile was no exception. G was highly aware of it. "Ladies like me," she said. She told me in Paris once that "of course I'll have to see [a lesbian Rothschild relative]. She wants to meet me because that's what I represent to them."

Green found her physically demonstrative but not highly sexual. "Once when we were wandering around Paris and came upon a sex shop," he says, "she said she'd never been in one before and was curious. It was crowded with horny men, but she went in and took a good long look around." Outside, she said, "Ah, the sex thing. I'm glad that part of my life is over."

Garbo had been to Corsica once before and paid homage to Napoleon. He was one of her great heroes, and she was eager to revisit Ajaccio, his birthplace. This time around, she and Sam found the house and were led through it on a group tour during which Garbo paid no attention to the guide, only to odd details that amused her. Of one Napoleon portrait, she remarked, "Ooh, he looks so much like Boyer!"

The trip was a grand success. Joseph Lebworth, observing Garbo's relationship with Cécile during and after that cruise, said they bickered like sisters but depended on each other:

Garbo and Sam Green on the Bibo

These were two women beyond the best years of their lives, each of whom lived off the other in a way. For Garbo, Cécile represented this incredible Rothschild family, which was beyond wealth. It had style, it had everything she loved when she came to Hollywood. But this was real; the other was phony. The houses were real. The pictures were real. The style was real.

For Cécile, Garbo was always a fabulous star. There was more written about Garbo in France than anywhere else. Her family thought Cécile was crazy. "This woman is dull, why spend so much time with her?" But Cécile was a dreamer. She lived, to a large extent, in the glorious past.

For Garbo, it wasn't so much for protection. For protection, she would run to Klosters and Salka. I suspect she was playing one against the other. Cécile was sometimes jealous when she was with Salka. Garbo made the competition active. She had a kind of manipulative mind that tried to get the most out of everyone to satisfy whatever needs she had. She could suddenly become very helpless.

There was affection between them, even though G was always bitch-

*Garbo, next to Napoleon's tomb, at the Museum of
the Army in Paris*

ing about why Cécile didn't do this or that, and Cécile would say, "G
is always late." They were devoted to each other in a peculiar way, but
they used each other. It was a symbiotic relationship that satisfied them
both. It was really the only relationship Garbo could have with anybody.

The following summer, the Lebworths hosted a truly Napoleonic reunion
at their summer home near Mouans-Sartoux in the south of France. "Charles
Boyer had a house there," Lebworth says, "about two hundred meters away
from us. One day, G came in after one of her walks and said, 'I've just seen
Mr. Boyer! . . . He's very old.' I said, 'Well, why don't I ask him to come
over and have a drink?' And I did. They hadn't seen each other since *Madame
Walewska* days." This time, the gag rule on movies was suspended. MGM,
Clarence Brown, and the making of *Conquest* were the topics. "They sat
next to one another and never stopped talking," Caral Lebworth recalls. "It
was a wonderful thing to see."

During a visit to Paris in 1977, Green and Garbo walked to the Left Bank, but she wouldn't go into the shops for fear of "a fuss." At one point, Green left her to look in a window full of Garbo pictures. "Well," she said in response to his enthusiasm when he returned, "I'm supposed to be the 'Queen of Queens.'" In 1979, they went to Versailles on a day when it was closed but got a private tour. Garbo, much taken, shouted *Vive le roi!* as they were leaving. Later, after visiting the Pantheon, Sam and Cécile made a successful dash to the other side of the boulevard while Garbo lost courage and had to wait a long time for another chance. When she finally got across, she mumbled, "Can't they see I'm a former film star and let me cross the street?"

From Paris, it was on to Klosters, where she had broken her wrist a few years earlier while fording a stream. "She showed me the place," says Green, "and I made her cross back and forth three or four times so she wouldn't be afraid, to break the spell." She told Sam that, after her fall, she had gone for help to the nearest house, where a very old woman lived like a hermit all year round. The woman had a phone and a doctor arrived in minutes. Garbo later returned to visit and thank the old lady and heard her life story: "Once she got me in there, she wouldn't let me out. I had to listen to the whole goddamn thing."

Despite her apparent removal from the "real" world, she had a canny awareness of her importance to the local community. "I've done so much for this place," she said. "I've been coming here for years and attracted so many people [and] now people of a certain quality know they can come here and not be bothered. It's good business when the owner of the hotel tells people that a famous ex–movie star is going to eat here. They all come out." But on October 9, 1979, at the Chesa Grischuna, her final night in Klosters that year, she was upset by having been seated at a table instead of a booth. "If the owner were here, this never would have happened," she told Sam. "He always puts me on the platform there in the corner. This new maître d' must not know me."

Later, she apologized. "I'm always nervous just before I have to move," she told Sam, checking her watch every thirty seconds. "While I'm in a hurry, I'm never reasonable. Other times, I'm always reasonable. You want a carrot? I'm too nervous to cut it up any smaller. You can eat it like that. Should I give these eggs to the lady next door? They're good eggs. It's a shame to let them go to waste. Oh, I wish I'd gone out on the mountain with you this morning, but I had to stay and vacuum. . . ." Green thought her possessions "the most pathetic group of belongings ever put into a few boxes": an exercise mat, a favorite sponge, an umbrella, an aluminum deck chair with a mat that had been worn through. "I wonder if it's worth recovering," she said. "They don't make them this wide anymore." Suddenly, she noticed that Sam's shoes weren't shined and told him so. Nobody cares, he said. "Mr. Green, I can afford to go about looking like this," she replied, "but you can't."

After the four-hour drive to Zurich, they arrived at the Baur au Lac Hotel, where they found Cécile in the grill. They had only twenty minutes to eat before meeting Élie Rothschild to fly in his private jet to Paris. Sam had conferred with Cécile beforehand and advised her to order for everyone in advance, but when Garbo's trout arrived, she asked in annoyance how it got there. "Mr. Green, you must stop organizing other people's lives for them. It may be all right for the New York art world but it should cease here." That, says Green, "was my thanks."

But he couldn't stay angry with her for long, especially watching the way she dealt with Cécile's younger brother. Élie had an overbearing manner and a coarse sense of humor. On the way to the airport, he made crass sexual remarks to Garbo and told a joke about an old woman losing her virginity to a gynecologist's exam. On the plane, he was fussy and bullying, but Garbo avoided all bait. "She kept calling him 'the Baron' ceremoniously until eventually he calmed down and took a nap," Sam wrote in his journal. "One can't help but be impressed by her incredible finesse and intelligence. She was sitting opposite me and made eye contact and funny faces the whole time, as a comment about Élie or just to make me laugh. When he was napping, she pretended to do TM and put a Kleenex over her face hung onto her eyeglasses, a very comical sight. She clowned the whole way."

In September 1982, Green, Garbo, and Cécile cruised to the Umbericos family's private island off Poros, where Sam recorded:

> In conversation, I'll say things to fill up the silence if necessary or, if asked, make a good story. But something she deeply dislikes in people is idle talk about other people because she instinctively knows *she* is often the subject of people's small talk and stories.
>
> She drank three whiskeys and was making observations like, "The Russians in the motion picture industry used to be the most extravagant and fun to work with." And, "My first whiskey was when, as a young man, I drank with some people from the motion picture industry and returned home to my cold, dark empty house and paced back and forth like a general, thinking, 'I'm drinking whiskey.'" She was a bit drunk and unguarded tonight.

A week later, they were back in Paris, walking and shopping and visiting Napoleon's tomb for the umpteenth time. "At tea, with little time to prepare for dinner, G decided she must cut her hair," Sam told his journal. "So I wouldn't get into trouble, I let Cécile do it and went to my room. I returned ten minutes later to a disaster. G's hair had been hacked three inches too short on one side, chunks out of the back. I did a pretty good job of repairing it, although it was a mess. But everyone was in a good humor about it. I'd trimmed her in the back where she couldn't reach many times before. G couldn't go to a hairdresser, of course. 'You know what hairdressers do for a living. They talk about whose hair they cut.' Alexander is the only one who doesn't. He would have come to the house to do G but he would have made a 'fuss.' Anyway, it really wasn't so hard—just a matter of snipping across the back."

And this, in the Coiffure Capital of the world.

Sometimes the shortest trips were the most difficult to motivate. Before Green and Garbo met, she once went to see Joseph Lombardo on Fire Island, as reported in the July 28, 1968, "Suzy" column of the *Daily News*: "That weekend visit of Greta Garbo to the Pines at Fire Island had everyone there more a-twitter than usual. . . . Gee-Gee was in hiding most of the weekend but she did come out of seclusion one evening to dine at the Sandpiper and to shop at the Three B's Boutique. . . . Doesn't it sound heaven?" According to legend, she went to the beach and lay for a while, thinking she hadn't been noticed, but when she got up to leave a gay crowd on the periphery chorused, "I vant to be alone!"

One evening during that visit, she and Lombardo were sitting on his veranda and watching the promenade of Fire Islanders along the boardwalk. After a long silence, Garbo ventured a rare pun: "Should be called 'Royal Island.' It's filled with kveens!"

Green had a rustic retreat on a remote part of the island and repeatedly invited her out over the years. He even built a little cottage, detached from his own residence, and dubbed it "The Garbo House," with her and her privacy in mind. She'd enjoy the break from Manhattan, he said—or, on the other hand, maybe she'd hate it.

"I'm sure you can judge whether I will hate it or not," she replied one day on the phone. "You know something? I like to like things, too. Are you surprised at that?" No, he wasn't. "Okay, good. I am not a young man anymore. It's different for young men and other men."

It was New York air-conditioning that finally drove her to accept his invitation to Fire Island for two weeks in the hot summer of 1976. Once there, she enjoyed its beauty, taking walks with and without Sam across the narrow strip of land to the ocean, where she watched the breakers and the half-tame deer roaming the beach. She picked blueberries and helped prepare meals and, of course, hated "The Garbo House," preferring the main house, where she made her bed on a humble Castro Convertible in Sam's rough-hewn sitting room. It afforded a lovely view of the bay and its cormorants and swans.

Green was a compulsive traveler himself. His cousin Henry McIlhenny lived in the fabulous Victorian-folly Glenveagh Castle in County Donegal, Northern Ireland, and Sam thought its 32,000 acres, manicured by forty gardeners, was just the sort of place Garbo might enjoy. After pondering for months, she was inclined to say yes—but not without nailing down the ground rules first, in her usual amusingly direct fashion:

"What do you do when you go there? How long do you stay? You would stay at Mr. Henry's? Is it easy? Does he leave you alone completely? He just expects you for the meal?"

McIlhenny and his staff proved gracious indeed. The table was set for fourteen—a footman behind each chair—and only the most cultivated local gentry were invited. The host let Garbo do just what she wished, which was very little, aside from one trip to an old stone-cottage inn for Irish venison stew. The visit, for which Cécile and Philadelphia Museum of Art curator Joseph Rishel joined them, took place in October 1975. Garbo was pleased about it—until later in New York when, typically, she was thrown into a dither by the follow-up protocol:

GG: I was thinking yesterday in the most awful way about Mr. McIlhenny. I never thanked him. He expected a warm letter and he never got one.

SG: He expected one from me.

GG: No, from me, too. That's only civilized. . . .

SG: I thanked him for you.

GG: That's not the right way to do things. . . . I'm terrible, oh God, I am absolutely the most uncivilized human being—I can't write. It's too late. It's never too late. I'm so whimsical, I don't really know what I'm saying.

This was Sam's cue to help compose and transmit a telegram, with a corollary debate about how to sign the thing. They had this debate periodically. The previous year, in reference to another telegram, she asked Sam: "Shall I just sign it GG? I loathe my first name. I'm so sorry I didn't change it while I was at it. When anyone calls me that, I cringe." In the case at hand, she had drafted a cable to McIlhenny but was wracked with doubt about it:

GG: "Thinking of the enchantment of Glenveagh and the most wonderful host in the world." Is that okay? . . . I don't know if it's tacky or not—"in the world." I don't know many hosts, and of the ones I know, he's most.

SG: He gets the cake.

GG: He gets the cake.

SG: What else are we going to say?

GG: "May heaven bless you."

SG: That's nice.

GG: Well, it's religious. "And grant you the best new year." I can't say, "Happy New Year." It's stupid. Well, the "heaven," maybe, was tacky.

SG: Heaven is nice.

GG: It is nice, I think. . . . So that's okay? So is this wire all right, then? That's all I'm going to say.

SG: We'll just say "GG."

GG: Well, will he know who that is? He may not. If he doesn't, we're out of luck.

SG: Since he called you "Miss G" all the time, it could be "Miss G."

GG: A funny way to sign it, I suppose. . . . I could say "Mr. Green's friend Miss G." He's probably in a state, too, and can't figure out who the hell Miss G is. I could also sign the full name. I never want to sign the full name, but it's more sure that he'll get who it is.

SG: No mistake with "Miss G."

GG: But it would sound terribly funny to other people.

SG: It's not for other people.

GG: Okay, if you think so. If he takes it as fun, that's one thing. If he takes it as that I am always "Miss," then it sounds sort of funny. . . .

SG: You have to consider so many things in this business.

GG: You certainly do.

Visiting England was even more problematic. When she once mentioned London, Sam asked if she wanted to go there. "I want to go somewhere where I can—I don't know . . . ," she trailed off.

"Where you can what?" he pressed.

"Goodbye, Mr. Green," she said, and hung up.

You never knew where the dangerous ground was with her, he thought. Was it the memory of happier days there with Beaton? The greater likelihood of recognition and photographers? No one could plumb the depths of her reluctance, and no one but she could overcome it. But finally she did, and soon after the Irish trip Sam took her to the Albany, a very private apartment complex in Piccadilly, for three weeks.

"We never 'went out' in London," he says. "We brought food into the flat and I cooked every meal. There's nothing easier than cooking for an elderly lady. Sometimes we went off to have fun at the expense of those guards that stamp around and sit on horses. They were the only people she could go up to and look at who couldn't look back and make a scene."

But his best-laid plan produced more comedy than fruit. No one was to know she was there, and no one in the press ever did. Garbo was pleased about the lack of "customers," but Sam thought it might amuse her to meet Queen Elizabeth. He mentioned this to the royal architect, whom he knew, and, soon after, the Albany's doorman stopped them as they were coming in with their bags of string beans from Fortnum & Mason. "Mr. Green, may I speak with you?" he said, as Garbo went on up. There was an embossed invitation: "Thursday, the seventeenth of October, you are requested for tea at Buckingham Palace at 4:30." Written underneath in ballpoint ink was, "You will be alone, ER."

Says Green: "I waited until we had our two whiskeys and our steamed string beans and I said, 'Well, I'm afraid somebody has found out you're here,' and I handed her the invitation. She looked at it and said, 'Aha, aha . . . I can't go, of course. I have nothing to wear. But why don't you go?' Without Garbo, to tea with the Queen? She would have turned the Corgis on me."

Neither of them went to Buckingham Palace. But was it true that Garbo didn't travel with a single dress?

"A *dress?*" Green exclaims. "She hadn't worn a dress in forty years. She traveled with two pairs of pants—one on, one for the laundry. That was it. She had her two cashmere sweaters—one dirty and one on, period." Clothing, in any event, was just the convenient excuse. Green recalls her funny and revealing elaboration later that day: "Once the royal family gets the scent of greasepaint in their nostrils, they'll never let up."

He couldn't get her to the queen's, but Green succeeded in getting Garbo to make a far more difficult visit—to Cecil Beaton. Their last and most serious falling-out was then several years old, caused by the publication of Beaton's diaries—with many intimate Garbo passages—in 1972 and 1973. In her view, publishing the diaries (and their sensational serialization in the London newspapers) was an atomic bomb of betrayal. When Sam asked why he did it, Beaton told him that he had written Garbo to ask permission and, after a year with no reply, phoned her in New York but that she hung up on him. At that point, Beaton said he decided it would be dishonest to eliminate a major part of his life "because of this woman's neurosis." He felt insulted. Naïvely or disingenuously, he thought she would listen to his explanation and was crushed when she would not. Cécile was among many who later confronted him, asking how much money he'd made from Garbo over the years, then adding, "Even Stokowski didn't sell his story to the papers!" Sam Green recalls:

"Diana Cooper wouldn't speak to him again. Diana Vreeland told him he was a horrible person. Truman Capote went on TV and criticized him—the pot calling the kettle black. Everybody attacked. He was humbled and embarrassed and riddled with guilt about it." Even the sweet-tempered Deborah Kerr says, "I cut Beaton off dead when he published that."

Green's loyalty to Beaton—who was partially paralyzed from a 1974 stroke and very depressed—predated his friendship with Garbo by many years, and he was determined to reconcile the irreconcilable. Gently but relentlessly, he worked on her, emphasizing Cecil's pathetic condition and equally pathetic desire to see her one last time:

"In London that trip, I had her on a short leash. She really couldn't move without me. I said, 'You have to finish this up with Cecil. He's very diminished. He's had a stroke. You have to go and see him.' She didn't like the idea at all, but she really didn't have any choice. It was a kind of blackmail, and when she weakened enough to say, 'Well, maybe I should go,' I made the arrangements fast."

Garbo was so nervous that Green thought to the last minute she would back out—and she tried. "What happens if we arrive at the train station in Salisbury and he has photographers hiding in the trees?" she fretted on the train ride. Against all odds, in October 1975, Sam delivered her to Reddish House, Beaton's home near Salisbury in the village of Broadchalke. They arrived just before dark and were led by Eileen Hose, his secretary, upstairs to Beaton's drawing room, where he was seated by the fire in a fawn-colored suit, bright pink cravat, and trademark broad-brimmed hat. On seeing Garbo—her longish gray hair tied back with a shoelace—he began to weep.

"Beatie," she said, "I'm back," leaning over and cupping his face in her hands, then looking straight into his eyes before kissing both checks.

"Greta," he said. "I'm so happy. . . ."

It was the first time Sam had heard him get a name right since the stroke. She sat on his knee and snuggled against him like a child, to his great delight. Sam left them alone but returned just before dinner and helped pull Cecil to his feet. Now for the first time, Garbo saw how incapacitated he truly was. It took twenty minutes to shuffle to the dining room. At dinner, he had to have his food cut and he cried often, pointing to his paralyzed body and apologizing. His dignity was shattered. "Everyone went to bed right after dinner," says Green, "and I'm positive the sandman didn't visit her that night."

The departure next afternoon was no easier. In the middle of his tearful farewell embrace, which seemed to be lasting an eternity, Garbo—over Beaton's shoulder—spotted a guest book by the front door and used it as a polite way to disengage. She had never been so willing or eager to sign her name, says Sam.

Hugo Vickers, Beaton's biographer, called Garbo's visit of forgiveness the most important moment of Beaton's life. Green says it was a brilliant, bittersweet performance and the most generous act of her life. Cecil Beaton died four years later, in January 1980, bequeathing her his painting of a solitary rose.

One day when she was in the midst of enormous angst about papering her walls, Sam Green said, "You just can't break down over some wallpaper."

"Yes, I can," she replied. "I can indeed, and I have."

Garbo's hypersensitivity could be aggravated by anything, including a range of personality types. Among those who really bothered her were "hectic" people. It was "the way they emphasize things that makes me nervous," she told Ray Daum. "It's not necessary to be emphatic always. One can be very quiet with human beings and still talk, but if they constantly say, 'Oh, isn't it great to be out?' or 'Isn't it a *wonderful* day?' then I think the other person is not at ease. And then I get nervous. . . . I'm better off alone." Another time she informed him that "I can't stand people who hum. The moment there's a little pause, they start humming."

She knew herself well enough to steer clear of people, which now, at age seventy-two, meant cutting down on travel. "I am the image of living inertia," she told Green one day. To Daum she said: "I'm sorry for a lot of things, for quitting things. . . . Actually, I've been out of order for years. It takes forever for me . . . to make a move. How can I do anything when I can't even move from my living room to my other room? A friend told me, 'You are like a mollusk,' I didn't know what it meant, so I looked it up—it's an animal that doesn't move, just sits there."

One of Sam's last experiences with her on foreign soil took place in March 1978, at his house in Cartagena, Colombia. As with Fire Island, it had taken years to lure her there, and when she finally acceded and the time grew close her worries mounted. What about the plane tickets? He would take care of them. What would she eat? He sang the praises of Colombian orange juice and coffee. The coffee might make her nervous, she feared.

"You couldn't possibly be nervous there," he assured her.

"You don't know *me*, Mr. Green," she replied.

The Cartagena trip went swimmingly. The trouble came only upon their return. In Green's absence, a reporter asked his assistant about the Garbo-Green "romance." In his eagerness to squelch that notion, the aide revealed lots of details about the Cartagena visit, which greeted her in the March 3, 1978, "Suzy" column the day after she returned. Garbo's anger was chilling in the phone conversation that followed:

GG: That makes me think that I'm forever being used by people, and it's *sickening*. It just makes me so—I get so *tired*, I just want to turn away—everyone using me forever. . . . I don't understand. . . .

SG: *I'm* not using you.

GG: You're a puzzle to me. . . .

SG: Do you really think, after all these years, I'd send a press release and use you to promote Cartagena?

GG: Well, there it is, you see, in the paper—everything we [did there]. I cannot go anywhere where I have to deal with the people in your crowd because I get used for everything. I haven't been in motion pictures for a lifetime, and I'm *sick* of it. . . . I don't know if you're a scoundrel or an idiot. . . .

SG: [It was a friend, not he, who made the leak.]

GG: But imagine having friends who would do that to you!

In the end, she forgave him—this time. But such incidents shook her horribly and took their toll on her shaky faith in people and the world.

It was arguable that Garbo had long been a manic-depressive. "I am very happy one moment, the next there is nothing left for me," she said—and she said it in 1933. To Salka in 1971, she wrote: "I suppose I suffer very deep depression."

As the years wore on, her depressive moments far outnumbered the manic ones. "Poor little people," she said to Ray Daum after one bleak stroll. ". . . I saw a man standing there selling hot dogs and he looked so sad. He looked so awful. He was pudgy and, you know, probably he's twenty and he eats all his life only hot dogs, nothing else. Ah, I felt so sad for him, somebody's son being born and the mamma says he'll probably be President one day."

Another time she told him:

"I wish to God I was religious. I'd like to get a hold of somebody who is and ask them what they think of when they pray. I envy people [with faith]. They seem so unafraid, they have something. Otherwise it's a bloody old mishmash of brushing your teeth and going through the slush and coming home and having a whiskey."

Fewer and fewer things seemed to brighten her spirits, and the Christmas season—which used to—was no longer one of them. On Christmas of 1931, Mercedes de Acosta recalled with rapture, Garbo had closed all the curtains in her Beverly Hills home so they could have candlelight and pretend it was snowing outside. Thirty years later, at Billy Baldwin's house on a sunny Christmas Day in New York, she asked her host to draw the curtains and light candles. It was outrageous, but he complied. The next Christmas, she came again and he had laid in a good supply of candles, but this time it was gloomy outside and she never mentioned curtains or candles. Why not? he asked. "Where I come from," she answered, "there is no sun in winter. . . . I thought how nice it would be to have Christmas just as it was when I was a child." How lovely, he thought—"and how happy it would have made everyone the year before if only she had bothered to explain."

One year in New York, Raymond Daum told Garbo of attending a Christmas Eve party at the apartment of actress Joan Fontaine, who had invited a Salvation Army band that arrived around midnight and passed out songbooks for a caroling session. Garbo was thrilled to hear of it. "Do you mean to tell me that you can get the Salvation Army into your home to celebrate Christmas with you at such close range?" she asked Ray. "Did they play my favorite, 'Roll, Jordan, Roll'? I hope they passed the tambourine, because there could have been some fat wallets there that night, if I know the parties Miss Fontaine arranges."

Sometimes she rose to the Yuletide occasion, saying it made everyone so friendly: "Someone put out their hand to me to help me over a snowdrift. Even *I* helped a lady over a drift." Green remembers her telling him she'd heard car wheels spinning on the ice outside on Fifty-second Street and went down to help push. "I know for a fact she did it more than once," he adds.

One year she told him about a bizarre dream: "I had at least four or five Christmas trees that were in a deplorable state of decay because of dryness, and I didn't know how to get rid of them out of the apartment. I was awfully worried. I thought, 'Well, I have to hack them to bits and that's a mess.' [Laughs] I'm worried in my dream about a stupid thing like that!"*

But as the 1970s drew to a close, the holidays lost their magic.

"If anything ever happened to me over the weekend—my girl doesn't come over the weekend—nobody in the world would know," she told Daum. "I wasn't going to have a Christmas tree this year [but] someone sent me one. I had the lights, so I stuck them on. . . . I won't look at it—it'll stay in there and I'll stay in here. It's about four feet tall, doesn't smell a thing.

---

* "Let us not underestimate dreams!" she wrote Salka Viertel on December 18, 1972. "Someone sent me a magazine which had pages about dreams. Then I dreamed that a cat bit me. I looked it up just for the deviltry of it—it promised troubles and I got them. . . . It's a good thing we don't remember dreams too often. I am not going to look [them up] again."

Trees only smell if you have living candles to heat them up a bit, but then you set the house on fire. You can't win."

Unless she knew the sender, all packages addressed to her went unopened and piled up in a downstairs storage room at 450 East Fifty-second during the Christmas season (and around her birthday) until somebody took them or gave them away.

"I'm a sour little creature," she said. "On New Year's, I go to bed, and if I go to sleep, I go to sleep, and if I don't or if I wake up, I say, 'Happy New Year, Miss Garbo.'"

Green kept trying. Had she ever seen a Fire Island holly tree? He wanted to bring her one.

"No," she said. "I don't want anything. It's just in the way. It's just causing trouble. Holly trees, no. . . . You have to give them water. I don't like anything anymore, anything that you have to bother with." When he tried to cheer her up, she reproached him with, "I'm in no mood to hear about all these nice things, because I'm depressed. Then I envy everybody." Why was she depressed? he asked. No answer.

"Do you think having a cheery drink with me would help?"

"Not much, no. You don't know anything about life."

And that was that.

"I've messed up my life," she said in 1977, "and it's too late to change that. These walks are just an escape. When I walk alone, I think about my life and the past. . . . I am not satisfied with the way I made my life." New York had everything, "but what use is that to me? I might just as well live on a deserted island. I'm restless everywhere. I always have been. . . . If only I knew where to go."

Klosters, too, was losing its appeal. "Fate has chained me [t]here," she said. Salka's health had deteriorated to invalidism. Garbo continued to visit, but now out of obligation. When Green was with her, he drove her down to Lake Lugano on the Italian border, stopping at wonderful restaurants along the way. "Once the idea was presented, she jumped at the chance," he says. "The problem was that nobody pushed her to try anything new." Green recalls his one and only glimpse of Salka:

"We walked about half a mile up the road to a little chalet and, without knocking, went in through a side door. I followed her up to a second-floor balcony where a wizened little lady with flying white hair was sitting wrapped up in a lap robe. She couldn't speak and I don't think she could comprehend, either, but Garbo still made small talk with her, and there was a sense of communication between them."

She had known it was coming, but the death of her dearest friend—in

Salka Viertel in Klosters near the end of her life

1978, in Klosters—hit Garbo hard. Of Salka and a growing number of her friends, she would murmur, "Well, here's another chapter ended."

It was suggested that now might be the time for her to do what she would never let anyone else do for her: write her life's story. A scurrilous biography was then in the works (see Chapter 13, pp. 542–3). Moreover, a rumor that Jacqueline Onassis had persuaded her to write her autobiography for Doubleday was untrue. She told Daum: "If somebody gave me a million dollars I wouldn't write anything about myself. I just couldn't."

She associated memoir writing with betrayal, as Mercedes de Acosta discovered before Cecil Beaton, and just as painfully. Said Mercedes in her 1960 autobiography:

"To write of Greta and things connected with her is the most difficult task I have had in this book. No one knows better than I how much she dislikes being discussed but I cannot write my life and leave her out of it.

[This problem] has caused me untold anguish and anxiety. [But] no one can write an autobiography without bringing back on the stage of her life people who have played major roles in it."

The apologia failed: Garbo never saw or spoke to de Acosta again. Ironically, Cecil Beaton in 1966 tried to play the role Sam Green would later play for him: He attempted to arrange a reunion between Garbo and de Acosta, whose health was failing and who dreaded the thought of being forever unforgiven by the woman she had so loved. But Beaton was unsuccessful.

Mercedes had now been gone for ten years. She died May 9, 1968, in New York. Garbo's brother Sven had passed away in 1967 in New Mexico. Death seemed a constant companion to Garbo in that decade. She was especially pained by the fact that Dag Hammarskjöld—her mysterious compatriot and possible espionage contact from the war—had died in a plane crash on her birthday in 1961. "I remember that," she said, "because I only remember bad things, horrible things."

Such memories did not lend themselves to memoirs. "She's not a woman who enjoys reminiscing," said David Diamond a year before her death. Even the living tended to depress her. "There's hardly no one so good as Pola Negri," Garbo had told a *New York Times* interviewer half a century earlier. "It is always amusing to see her." Now, in their last years, Negri tried numerous times to visit her, but Garbo always declined. "It wasn't because she didn't like Pola," says Diamond. "She did. It was because she has painful memories of those days in Europe when their paths crossed—I don't know exactly what. She's just afraid that seeing Pola would bring those things back."

Gloria Swanson, asked about Garbo in the seventies, replied: "It's a pity that we aren't friends. . . . Maybe the two of us could get together and she could come over and just relax while I paint and putter and do my sculpture. . . . Wouldn't it be a laugh if we two Swedes became good friends? What an item that would make!"

Of course, it would never be.

She was "the gloomiest Scandinavian since Hamlet," said critic Alastair Forbes, and the gloom hardly lessened with age. Nowadays, it was more difficult to get around on her walks. Smoking didn't help, and her constant efforts to stop didn't work. Around 1969, she went to a Zurich hypnotherapist who claimed he could cure anyone of the habit. "I went full of good intentions," she said. "I was not to have a cigarette for four days after treatment. He bet me that if I held out those four days, I would lose all desire to smoke. I really believed him and followed his instructions. On the fifth day I lit up again."

Garbo on the street in New York, c. 1979: "The gloomiest Scandinavian since Hamlet" walked with a stoop these days.

Later, she told Sam Green she had quit briefly but had soon given in. "It's good to stop now and then," he said, encouragingly.

"It is not," she snapped. "I don't see any point to it. It's absolute misery. If it's misery, then what good is it?"

Hostessing of any kind was also becoming harder. She fretted when the hors d'oeuvre tray was emptied but Jane Gunther was almost always there to help out. The simple fare was usually cheese and crackers plus a drink, with Swedish herring or caviar for special occasions. She remained as hopeless and helpless as always at cooking. Even coffee was a challenge. "I could no more stand and wait for a percolator—I'm not made that way," she told Daum. "I throw it in a casserole. . . . Couldn't be simpler. I'm just as much a bachelor as you are. I don't know how to cook. I have the same old dinners I always have—steaks, lamb chops and hamburgers, that's all I do."

Which wasn't the whole truth. She had a few little culinary secrets:

I fry so seldom I don't even bother with non-stick pans. If I ever do fry something, it's potatoes, and I fry them in peanut oil—peanut oil, it's a must. And you don't use a heck of a lot, just a little. . . .

I always buy fresh vegetables. They're everywhere and it doesn't take brains to fix them. They don't taste like anything and they just sit there, [but] I'll tell you a little secret: Buy sour cream. They sell it in buckets. All you do is take a great big heap of sour cream and put it on a vegetable with salt and it's delicious . . . more fun than with margarine. So get your sour cream, and get going. . . .

I adore—probably it's helping make me sick—those Australian apricots, awfully goody. Maison Glacé, also—you can get that at Gristede's. I wonder if they have *spraaten*—fish, like sardines, in cans. Terribly goody . . . I'd adore to eat right now, but I can't. I have a very peculiar stomach department. I haven't got enough things to digest food with . . . if you don't have hydrochloric acid or whatever it is, then the stomach goes on strike. I don't know what the hell is wrong with me, but down we are.

Despite such complaints, she always enjoyed *talking* about food, especially with Sam, informing him of her techniques and results that often resembled those of Lucille Ball:

GG: Two eggs for dinner. I'll boil them. I'll boil the heck out of them. I can't make an omelette. That's a lot of trouble. You have to stand there and watch it and then you slop it over on one side. I've never done one. I've seen somebody do it. I avoid everything which is work except labor work. That I can do. Hard labor I can do. . . . You mess it up first in a bowl, no? . . . It doesn't have to be a very hot pan? Maybe I'll try it. Oh, dear, what ideas you give me. I knew I shouldn't have called you.
SG: If it doesn't work, just throw it away. . . .
GG: I really ought to try to do that. It's terribly boring with boiled eggs. I can poach them also, but that's equally boring. I just throw them in a little potsky with boiling water. . . . Let them run. Whatever is left, I pick up. It works.
SG: And then you put them on toast?
GG: I don't put them on nothin'. On the plate. What's wrong with that? I don't have eggs Benedict, that I can't make. Poached eggs. They slop around there on the plate, very good. I'll make them for you and you'll see.

She loved pasta, though it disagreed with her. In Klosters, she recalled, "if I had spaghetti left over, I used to put [it] out on a piece of newspaper for the birdies. I saw a little birdie [with] a little tiny piece of spaghetti on his beak. He looked so funny. He looked so sweet. They love spaghetti."

The one regular pleasure of her day continued to be those two measured drinks. "I hear people say, 'Oh, I never drink alone,' " she told Daum. "Well, if I didn't drink alone I'd never get a drink. . . . It's necessary to drink, I've discovered. I have it every day, not one day without it. But only a certain amount. I've had this bottle of glögg for years and years—it's Swedish punch, very strong and delicious." She could be quite kittenish about it. "Let's have a martini," she suggested to Ray one day. "I'm going to feel terribly guilty if you have tea."

But she felt more vulnerable than ever, and often the blows came from unexpected sources—such as Ingmar Bergman, whose films had captivated her. Years before in Stockholm, Kerstin Bernadotte had taken her to the Svensk Filmindustri studios to meet Bergman, who wanted her to play a small part in *The Silence*. No chance. But she had enjoyed their meeting and was later devastated to read Bergman's account of it in his autobiography, *The Magic Lantern*:

> Greta Garbo and I were left alone in my modest work room. . . . The room was cramped, a desk, a chair and a sagging sofa. I sat at my desk, the desk lamp switched on. Greta Garbo sat on the sofa. "This was Stiller's room," she declared at once, looking round. . . .
>
> Suddenly she took off her concealing sunglasses and said, "This is what I look like, Mr. Bergman." Her smile was swift and dazzling, teasing. . . .
>
> In the half-light in that cramped room, her beauty was imperishable. If she had been an angel from one of the gospels, I would have said her beauty floated about her. . . . She immediately registered my reaction, was exhilarated and started talking about her work on Selma Lagerlöf's *Gösta Berlings Saga* [and about other Swedish directors].
>
> "Alf Sjöberg wanted us to make a film together. We sat talking in a car out in Djurgården all one summer night. He was so persuasive, he was irresistible. I accepted, but changed my mind the next morning. That was awfully stupid of me. Do you also think that was stupid, Mr. Bergman?"
>
> She leaned over the desk so that the lower half of her face was lit by the desk lamp. Then I saw what I had not seen! Her mouth was ugly, a pale slit surrounded by transverse wrinkles. It was strange and disturbing. All that beauty, and in the middle of the beauty a shrill discord. No plastic surgeon or make-up man could conjure away that mouth and what it told me. She at once read my thoughts and grew silent, bored. A few minutes later we said goodbye.
>
> I have studied her in her last film, when she was thirty-six. Her face is beautiful but tense, her mouth without softness, her gaze largely

unconcentrated and sorrowful despite the comedy. Her audience perhaps had an inkling of what her make-up mirror had already told her.

Bergman's affront, and the other indignities of aging and living, drove
her more and more to cigarettes—"all the time, one after the other," she
told Sam, knowing that "it causes me to pucker up my poor little mouth
all the time, not helping the wrinkles."

"So you'll just have to change your attitude about wrinkles," he suggested.

"And smoke more," she replied.

"Just tell yourself wrinkles are beautiful."

"Well, you can stretch your imagination to the end of the world and it
isn't true," she said. "It just isn't true."

Human faces age in a myriad of ways. Some crinkle around the eyes,
some in a cross-hatching of lines on the cheeks; in some, the skin recedes
into concavities, in others it sags. Dermatology is largely genetic; Garbo's
fine lines—clustered between the perfect nose and lips and at the corners
of the perfect mouth—were inherited from her mother. To Sam one day
she spoke of the whole awful phenomenon with eloquence:

GG: You know, it's so strange how life is. You go along and you accept
whatever is there as fact. You put on your face and your make-up and
everything and you get going. All of a sudden, one day, there's a hand
that comes—in my imagination, every seven or ten years or whatever
—a hand that goes over the face and changes it a bit, puts more weakness
in it. . . . And it's equally revolting each time. The face—the hand has
come to push it about.

SG: You think the hand has visited you recently?

GG: Oh, it has. . . . I don't sit and think about it every minute. But it's
revolting. You wish you could—

SG: Erase it.

GG: Right. That I can do by going to the [surgeon], but that's revolting,
too. . . . Well, it takes me forever to decide on anything, so by the time
I decide, my wrinkles would be so deep you'd have to take off half of
the face. [Laughs] It's revolting. . . . You look like an apple that isn't
young anymore. Have you got any apples? Are they old? That's my
state of affairs.

It was hard enough to bear unmolested. But it was even more insufferable
due to the morbid curiosity of everyone clamoring to watch it. "All they
care about is, 'What does she look like today?'" she said. "And look at me!

I look like the Madwoman of Chaillot." She was like Helen of Troy: To be the fairest woman in the world was a huge responsibility in any age, and at any age. But it got worse as her life drew nearer its end. Garbo felt mocked—as if the world somehow delighted in the crumbling of its own greatest beauty.

New York City, May 1985, on the East Side

CHAPTER 13

GARBO REGAINED
1980–1990

At some point in the half-century search for Garbo, comedy and trag-edy merge. What made this fugitive—and the pursuit of her—as in-triguing in 1990 as in 1930 was largely the elusiveness itself: Had she suddenly stopped and turned on her pursuers, caught them up short, they might have walked away from the chase upon finding the prey more mundane than mythological.

In fact, there was more to Garbo, not less, than met the eye, but it was not the stuff to match The Legend. Chances are she would have hidden even had she been a country schoolteacher instead of a great actress, because her essence was so private. But her privacy became a public game, with Garbo the star player in spite of herself. She was what she played—essentially, a tragedienne. Yet the game still had its comic moments.

A typical round was played during the Thames Live Cinema Festival in March 1987, at Radio City Music Hall, an eleven-day showcase by Kevin Brownlow and David Gill of their restorations of *The Wind*, *The Thief of Baghdad*, *The Big Parade*, and *Flesh and the Devil*. Carl Davis's new scores were rendered by an eighty-piece orchestra whose sonic grandeur matched the quality of the prints, projected on the huge screen. Ageless Lillian Gish was thunderously received at the opening of *The Wind*.

The following night, Radio City was electrified by the "reliable report" that Garbo herself was in the theater for the first full-orchestral revival of *Flesh and the Devil* in fifty years. Even the normally reserved Brownlow was caught up in it. "If the leading lady is out there," he said in his introduction, "we hope you'll know that we respect your privacy and that we will always appreciate your great contribution to the art of film." His remarks were greeted by a roar of approval and the collective twisting of two thousand necks in search of one Face. Every elderly woman wearing a hat or tinted glasses was inspected, and the organizers were subsequently accused of hiring a set of eighty-year-old decoys to heighten the suspense.

Meanwhile, not far away in Manhattan's Upper West Side, a budding dramatist named Merle Fitzroy was occupied with a Pirandellian one-woman play he was writing for Garbo, convinced that once she read it she would rush back to the footlights she had abandoned in Stockholm sixty years before. He never finished it and she would not likely have been tempted if he had, but there was more than a bit of relevance to Garbo in Pirandello. In the Italian playwright's *Henry IV*, the mad king and the sane king-impostor agree on one thing: "We cannot evaluate what we do instinctively." Nor can anyone else evaluate it for us.

"Her instinct, her mastery over the machine, was pure witchcraft," said Bette Davis. "I cannot analyze this woman's acting. I only know that no one else so effectively worked in front of a camera."

Garbo's compulsion for seclusion was as instinctive as her acting, a visceral and not a cerebral property. That she had things to "conceal" strongly reinforced the instinct and made it a necessity for survival. But people in the outside world couldn't understand this, or couldn't let their knowledge of it curtail the need to see and "know" her. The Pointless Pursuit of Garbo continued to the end and grew increasingly absurd. A 1986 wire-service report announced that she was in Barcelona having cataract surgery; in fact, she had no cataracts and never went to Spain in her life. Her niece once read that Garbo was vacationing in Hawaii on the same evening they were dining together in Manhattan. The August 23, 1989, *Hollywood Reporter* said she'd been spotted at a concert in the Hollywood Bowl. That she hadn't been near Los Angeles in years did not affect such reports. The superficiality of the eighties made Garbo an even greater mystery: She was an oddity who "threw it all away" and placed a higher value on something other than money or career.

"I'm convinced she was never bored," says Sam Green. "What she enjoyed most was being alone with her own thoughts and inner dialogues. She had no other great ambition because she'd achieved them all by the time she was thirty-five—she was the most famous, beautiful, and accomplished woman of her time. But she paid the price by losing her privacy, which was the one thing she wanted—just to lead a decent, healthy, honest life out of the public eye. It wasn't *Two-Faced Woman* that made her quit movies. It was about personal development. From the age of seventeen, she'd done nothing but work, and her huge success came before she'd had time to develop an emotional life. In the end, her emotional life was more important. Is that simple or complex?

It was more simple than complex.

"If someone commented on loving her films, she freaked," Green continues. "After one incident in France, she told me, 'I like it when people admire my work, but when they mention it I'm embarrassed. I never know what to say and it makes me terribly uncomfortable.' She thought when she left films, the interest would dissipate. Since she didn't trust anyone, she never understood that basically people *did* leave her alone. Her paranoia was so great, she could never risk having a dinner party for fear it would be in the newspapers. She became a kind of Howard Hughes: She almost literally wouldn't eat unless somebody made or brought in the food, because she felt she couldn't go out without being hassled. She was truly tormented by her fame."

She was the greatest of all stars, and her species was fast becoming extinct. Actors of her magnitude cannot exist today, says historian Alexander Walker, if for no other reason than that "we know far too much about them. No one has the possibility of becoming a star—or staying one—for very long because celebrity has replaced the idea of stardom." For sixty years, writers held an Olympiad of Superlatives to describe her impact on twentieth-century culture, but Garbo never cared what people thought or wrote about her.

Or did she?

Her narcissism was a double-edged sword. In her heyday, after all, despite the professed loathing of publicity, "she was crazy about pictures of herself," said one MGM photo-studio hand. For Clarence Bull alone, she sat for more than four thousand frames without complaint. It was okay for people to adore her from afar. Post-retirement, she engaged a clipping service and read most everything written about her. But unlike Marlene Dietrich, who did the same, Garbo did so out of curiosity, not litigiousness.* "She was like a junkie on a drug he hates but can't give up," says Green. "In her case, it helped fill up the time and was 'more proof of base humanity.'"

The paradox was that she loathed the constant recognition yet, in a way, came to require it. Having dissociated herself from films, she wanted to do the same from film *fans*. Her obsessive hiding was both a joke and the truth: Some of the time and on some levels, Garbo relished the game—including

---

* Her family denies she had a clipping service, but friends say manila envelopes full of articles invariably awaited her in the stack of mail upon her return from trips. A remark she made to Sam Green in the fall of 1975 tends to support the claim: "Somebody photographed me, evidently. . . . I was told that a whole mess of photographs appeared. I see them as a rule. I don't know why I didn't this time."

the 1984 film *Garbo Talks*. Directed by Sidney Lumet and written by Larry Grusin, it was the tale of fatally ill Anne Bancroft, whose dying wish is to meet Garbo. It contained clips from Garbo's greatest films, and many believed it to be a true story.* But a New York *Post* photo purporting to show the real Garbo coming out of the East Side theater in which it was playing was a case of mistaken identity.

"I know she didn't see the movie," says Sam Green, "because I was the one who sent her a telegram saying, 'There's a film called *Garbo Talks* in New York, and they'll be making a fuss. Don't come back until the run is over in two weeks.' And she didn't." But a few years later, she told David Diamond she saw the movie on TV and liked it: "She loved Harvey Fierstein in it—but she wouldn't go to see him in *Torch Song Trilogy*." In any case, it is not true—as many Garbo-philes insist—that she appeared as herself (back to the camera) at the end of *Garbo Talks*. The actress who did so, uncredited, was Betty Comden.

The film was fiction but had some rough equivalents in real life. "She was compassionate about people who were ill to an unusual degree," recalled her friend Jane Gunther. She regularly visited Jessica Dragonette's sister Nadea Loftus at the Mary Manning Walsh Nursing Home on York Avenue. And Sam Green recalls "a decrepit old couple on Fifty-seventh Street she always brought eggnog to and was bored to tears by at Christmastime. She always felt obliged to go cheer them up—'it would break their hearts' if she didn't. This went on year after year."

Gunther most remembers Garbo's "delicious sense of humor"—her sense of the ridiculous and "clownlike, childish delight in all sorts of things" that belied her dour reputation. Indeed, over the years Garbo was mostly good-natured about the endless spoofing of her behavior. She had several amusing run-ins, for example, with pianist Oscar Levant, who—when first introduced to her—said, "Sorry, I didn't catch the name." Levant later recalled dining at Le Pavillon when Garbo came in with a small dinner party. After a while:

> I called the headwaiter over and said, "Please tell Miss Garbo to stop staring at me."
>
> He told her; she laughed and invited me to join her. She was cheer-

---

* "It was completely fictional," says screenwriter Grusin, "a figment of my imagination. It was really germinated by my feeling about Bella Abzug, and then I thought, 'Who is the most difficult person to get to—Abzug, Howard Hughes, Jackie Kennedy?' Of course, it was Garbo. Sidney [Lumet] was concerned there might be a problem about using her name in the title, and he and MGM sent a joint letter through her attorney, saying we weren't trying to invade her privacy and offering to let her read the script. They got a letter back saying, in effect, 'Thank you, but she really couldn't care less.'"

fully drinking a martini with her escort. I explained I was leaving for
Emporia, Kansas, to play a concert.

"Why don't you come with me?" I added.

"What time does the train arrive?" she inquired.

"She's amused by people and things, but doesn't do or say funny things
herself," producer Arthur Hornblow, Jr., once said. The point of American
jokes often eluded her; the more elementary they were, the better she liked
them. British actress Dana Wynter recalled a dinner party with Garbo in a
smart Los Angeles restaurant, at the end of which:

> Stories were being told around the table and it was plainly her turn.
> There was a moment of silence, then she raised her head from the
> peach she was eating, and in her slow, dark, accented voice said:
> "There was a woman walking down the street in Philadelphia, and
> her blouse was open exposing her left breast. A man coming toward
> her [saw she was] unaware of the situation [and] said, 'Excuse me,
> madam, but do you realize that your left breast is revealed?' Startled,
> the woman looked down and exclaimed, 'Oh, my God—I must have
> left the baby on the bus.' "
> With that, she went back to her peach.

Her strength, perhaps, was not joke telling. Nor was she jocular in a
conventional sense—no practical joker, Garbo. But more than one drollery
escaped her lips. One day, S. N. Behrman was waiting for her to show up
for a meeting at MGM. "I went to the men's room," he said, "and there
was Greta. I asked her what she was doing there. She said, 'I'm watching
the view.' "

Many years later, on one of her last California visits, she and Anthony
Palermo's daughter Michelle were sitting in the dark corner of a coffee shop
one evening when a man came over and said, "Aren't you Greta Garbo?"
She looked at him and replied, "What would Greta Garbo be doing in a
place like this?"

Madeline Kahn's immortal chanteuse number in *Blazing Saddles* (1974) is
a parody of Marlene Dietrich, but the sentiment of the lyrics is pure Garbo:
"I'm tired—tired of being admired. . . ."

However odd, Garbo's humor and humanity survived the years and jibed
with her unusual (if not unique) virtue as an actress: In the unanimous
testimony of her co-stars, she was unfailingly "giving" and willing to turn
over a scene to a colleague. If financially frugal, she was artistically generous.
In private life, the obverse of her hesitancy to speak of herself was a deep

interest in the lives of her friends, coupled with a latent maternalism. David Diamond felt it keenly when the topic was his own mother:

> The fact that Mama made me so unhappy, and that I didn't want to be a violinist, I wanted to be a composer, and my teacher had taken me to meet Ravel—this fascinated her. She wanted to know all about Ravel. She was interested in my family and how difficult things were, how Papa was ground into the earth and destroyed by the depression. I found myself one night crying like an idiot about him, and she was very moved. I had a feeling it was because she loved her own father so much, and I might have struck a chord.

In rare moments, she opened up a bit about her own family—brother Sven, for instance. "She spoke about him very fondly," says Diamond, "but for that matter, I don't remember her ever saying a nasty thing about anybody. It was warmth and affection she would always express. I never had a feeling she resented anybody or anything." Cécile once told Sam Green, in Garbo's presence, that after her brother Élie lost his eye Garbo was the only visitor who really touched him. All the others tried to buoy him with romantic talk about a patch—the buccaneer image, the Hathaway man. "You didn't try to cheer him up with pretend?" Sam asked. "Always the truth," she answered quietly.

British playwright Kenneth Jupp recalled the day he met her in a guest bedroom at Zachary Scott's in 1961. She had a gift that was the antonym of speech, he discovered, after he mentioned his new drama, *The Buskers:*

> "What is your play about?" she asked. . . . "It's about gypsies," I told her. She paused, and with that wonderful smile which totally transformed her appearance, she said: "I have always considered myself a gypsy." Whereupon she sat down on the bed, gestured for me to do the same, and asked me to tell her all about it. We sat [there] for almost an hour. . . .
>
> Her true genius was as a listener. I have frequently observed that the opposite of talking is not listening, but waiting. Garbo reversed this. She actually preferred to listen. She had the ability to concentrate totally on what you were saying, as if nothing else in the world mattered. All else vanished, all that existed was you, and what you were telling her. [There] lies the secret of her greatness as a screen actress: the ability to exclude everything but the moment, to exist only for right now, before the camera, or before whoever had captured her interest.

But for a woman who listened so attentively to others and expressed emotion so freely onscreen, self-expression in real life was agonizingly difficult. Obscurity was often taken for profundity. A companion once found her sitting on the floor of her hotel room, wrapped head to foot in blankets, and asked what she was doing. "I am an unborn child," Garbo replied. Another time, chatting with a friend, she fell into a long silence and finally broke it with: "I am a lonely man circling the earth." Asked what she meant, Garbo sipped her vodka and said, "Someday I will tell you," and changed the subject.

Yet her lugubriousness was not unrelieved. She had a silly side that she could indulge with playmates. Green recalls a visit to an art exhibit during which he moved up to within a few inches of one painting to study it. "I sensed someone coming up very close behind me—actually, touching me— and I knew it was Garbo, but I didn't know what she was doing. Then all of a sudden I felt her knees push into mine from behind, and *my* knees buckled and I nearly collapsed on the floor, which was the object. She thought that terribly funny, and it was."

On her many cruises with the Rothschilds, Garbo often joked at the expense of Cécile, whose stolid, mannish, straight-faced exterior made her ripe for it. Cécile was a perfect model for the "designer tumbler" that Garbo placed on her head during the cruise to Corsica; more surprising, a moment later, the great Garbo herself posed willingly in the same headgear, calmly smoking a Marlboro, dignity intact (see back jacket photograph).

By 1983, at seventy-eight, she was walking shorter distances and at a slower pace, but was still as eager to observe human behavior as always. In the Tuilleries one day, she suddenly said to Sam, "Let's go to where the queens are. Someone once took me there—oo-la-la." So they went for a tour of the gay cruising area, where she made comments like, "Ooh, look at that one," or, "Regardez le nègre!" At one point, when two sailors passed, she said, "There's one for each of us."

But her good humor could be erased quickly by some faux pas, which even a Rothschild could commit. The worst offense took place in 1983, when Cécile took her to the family's Château Lafite vineyard. During a tour of the facilities, Garbo paid little attention but was enraptured by the caves, which reminded her of the Roman catacombs. So far so good, but then came trouble, as Green recounts:

> It was the time of the harvest, the wine-selling season, when the growers invite the press and give lavish entertainments at all the châteaux for the buyers and people from *Paris-Match* to come and write about it. Cécile's cousin, Baron Philippe de Rothschild, who was known for his showmanship, invited us to dinner at his vineyard, Château Mouton, saying, "It'll be a tiny little dinner." Garbo was full of trepi-

dation. She didn't want to go, but everything was arranged by Philippe, who made sure we were captives. In the salon, there were hundreds of guests and press. Garbo made a beeline for the corner and sat down. I stood between her and everybody else, and she pretended to be in deep conversation with me. Baron Philippe did not arrive for nearly forty minutes. He was quite old and nearly blind and finally appeared at the top of the stairs of this huge long gallery, wearing an orange brocaded caftan. Everybody hushed and turned around to look because they'd been waiting such a goddamn long time. Then he feebly descended the stairs and, like Moses, made his way through the crowd straight toward Garbo and said, "Is that Greta, my darling? My Greta, the love of my life! It's so good of you to come back to your old friend!" And kissed her dramatically.

He'd only met her once before, briefly, in 1938. He was revealing that he barely knew her because no one who did ever called her by her first name. It was a set-up and an ugly one. The dinner started off with a seafood bisque, which she's allergic to, and went on to pork loin which she wouldn't eat. It was really awful, and there was one toast after another to beautiful Greta. But she behaved perfectly throughout the whole thing, and when dinner was over, she said thank you, embraced, kiss-kiss, down the stairs to the parking lot, and into Cécile's Citroën. On our way back in the car, complete silence. You could see the smoke. Cécile was really in the doghouse. It was a perfect example of why she didn't want to go anywhere.

Back home in New York, it sometimes seemed that her fame was not so universal after all. In 1985, she was attempting to do business with a young clerk at a Second Avenue dry cleaner's shop. "Is that a G or a C?" the teenager asked as she filled out the ticket. "G," said the customer. "G-A-R-B-O," the clerk repeated, and then asked if the first initial was G or C. "G!" she snapped, and left, at which point a customer watching the scene exclaimed, "Do you know who that was?" "Of course," the clerk replied. "It was somebody called 'G. Garbo.'"

On the other hand, she was still playful with Sam. Once she referred to a friend as "a gay man"—speaking of his disposition, not his sexuality—before realizing the ambiguity:

GG: [Laughs] Isn't that funny, one can't use that word anymore. . . . I came into a place once—maybe it's two years ago—and it was very prettily done, lots of colors and things, and I said, "Oh, it's so gay!" And the owner of this place—he laughed. I didn't correct anything, but I realized that that's not what you say. [But] you can't say, "It's such a happy place."

sg: Gay is the right word.

gg: I'll continue to use it. It's so stupid, they're not any more gay than others. . . .

sg: It's got political connotations.

gg: Suppose we say, "Mr. Carter is such a gay man." You say "jolly"?

sg: One would have to say jolly.

gg: Or, "He seems such a happy man." But "happy" is too much, sometimes. "Gay" is, too.

sg: We'll just have to—

gg: Skip the whole thing.

Often in the middle of such a lighthearted exchange, she would turn suddenly serious. One day Sam asked cheerily, "What's for lunch?," to open their phone chat. "Rice," she replied darkly. "You know, I'm getting more and more ill. I can't stand food anymore. I don't know what to eat, and it's a panicky thing. I feel panicky. Goodbye, Mr. Green."

End of conversation.

Before Beaton's death, in the wake of the reconciliation Green had engineered, she often inquired about Cecil's progress from the stroke. ("I keep thinking about Beaton. God, maybe this [faith healer Kathryn] Kuhlman woman is an answer.") Her concern was real, but the subject was always touchy, as Sam discovered one day when she angrily misinterpreted something Beaton had written to Green as a criticism of herself:

gg: It would be so utterly incomprehensible that someone could be that vile [after she had visited him in England]. I mean, if he says one thing to me and then—

sg: No, he wasn't doing that, he was just—

gg: I don't want to believe in ugly things, you see. It's so futile. Everything in life seems so—so double-breasted.

Poor Beaton, in this case, was not being "double-breasted," and Green finally convinced her of it. She forgave Cecil once again. But Sam himself would soon be unforgivable.

In fall of 1985, a writer for the tabloid *Globe* spoke with Green's assistant, who told all he knew of their friendship—and more. "Garbo to Wed at 80," blared the cover of the October 29 issue. "Bridegroom will be art dealer 30 years her junior." Green had been in Colombia and had nothing to do with it, but Garbo saw the piece and was enraged. Upon his return, he called to check in, as usual, and after a long silence, she said, "Mr. Green, you've done a terrible thing"—and hung up. He called back, arguing that he'd never uttered a public word about her in fifteen years and that, were he to do so, it would not be to *Globe*. More silence. "Does this mean we're not speaking anymore?" he asked. "Right," she replied. Was there nothing at all he could do? "Yes," she said, "—hang up."

It was the last time he ever heard her voice.

There was a second reason for her cutoff. Garbo knew he tape-recorded their conversations, and never objected. But at some point in 1985, she was falsely informed that he had played one of the tapes "at a party." Green categorically denies it: "I thought she knew me well enough to know I would never exploit her. God knows I had a thousand opportunities."

He was angry and wounded but, in hindsight, views those incidents as catalysts—an excuse to make a break. By 1985, her health was failing and she didn't want people to see her deteriorating, he believes. "She was very proud. She didn't want to be diminished with her friends." Over the next four years, he learned he wasn't the only one being shut out. Though she spoke to Cécile on the phone, she never saw her again, and even hung up on her, too.

"In the end, did we betray Garbo, or did she betray us?" he wonders. But Green is not a sentimental man. He brightens and suddenly remembers something: One afternoon while he was visiting her, Garbo left the living room to fix drinks and Sam reached for some peanuts, a few of which dropped on the floor. Bending down to retrieve them, he noticed a tiny figure peeking out from under the divan on which he was sitting.

"It was a troll," he says. "You know, those little plastic dwarfs with the ugly, wild, magenta and turquoise Dynel hair? When I bent down further and looked underneath the sofa, there was a whole row of them—at least a dozen, a whole little community of them—in a kind of formation." He said not a word about the discovery, but on subsequent visits, when left alone in her living room, he never failed to check under the couch—and never failed to find the trolls there, always in a different arrangement. Another time in her living room, he noticed a miniature glass candlestick on the floor: "She 'didn't know how it got there' when I pointed it out."

Why the trolls? The look on Sam Green's face says it's a silly question:

"Why not? Children play with dolls. Garbo played with her trolls. They amused her. Alone late at night, when the Sandman wouldn't come—maybe she couldn't get to sleep, maybe she acted out little scenes or games or fantasies with them from some favorite fairy tale—who knows? You tell me."*

---

* Swedish folklore is richly populated with trolls, elves, and house spirits (*tomte*) known as the Hidden People or Underground Folk. Selma Lagerlöf published two volumes of stories

Garbo with Cécile de Rothschild

The eternally young, alluring Garbo was, of course, an illusion. With the curse-blessing of longevity, she became an octogenarian. Once the probings of the icon are exhausted, we are left with the mortal creature whose aging process was not unlike that of a million other single, childless elderly women.

Garbo's lifelong "independence" always hinged on other people doing things for her, even when she was young and healthy. With age and infirmity, she needed people more but trusted them less, and much of her time was spent manipulating to get things done—complicated by the endless series of obstacles she placed (or perceived) in the way of everything. She dreaded every repairman, every appointment, every exigency. Everything was "impossible," or beyond her ability to cope. But for all her negativity, there were no suicidal thoughts.

---

on the subject, *Troll och manniskor* (*Trolls and Humans*), in 1915 and 1921. The *tomte*-trolls are pranksters who bring good or bad luck and are always unpredictable. Even the friendliest of them can be vengeful if offended. They behave like poltergeists, throwing and hiding things, making odd noises, or hitting people invisibly for no apparent reason. They may live in a tree by the front door, in a mound in the meadow, beneath the cowshed—or under the couch. Garbo's belief in them is speculative, but her known superstitiousness—about salt being spilled, hats on beds, open umbrellas indoors—and the presence of the Dynel trolls suggest the possibility.

In one's eighth decade, the mind tends either to seek peace or to give in to turmoil. Garbo's mind, melancholy as it was, seems to have been closer to peace. She had no great "last" project to complete, no discernible personal dilemma to be resolved. Time for Garbo was a different commodity than for the rest of the world. She had never been in a hurry. Her days had always passed slowly, and if she didn't like her own ennui she was at least used to it. Hounded by the world, she was torn between the solitude on which she insisted and the loneliness it sometimes became. She wanted attention and she didn't want attention. She wanted to live, but she also wanted to be done with living—which was something different from wanting to die. She was uncomfortable with the past, the present, and the future in roughly equal measure.

Her "wanting to be alone"—and "let" alone—had always been sincere. Garbo was the *solophile* of all time. Clare Boothe Luce described her nicely in 1932 as "a deer in the body of a woman, living resentfully in the Hollywood zoo," but then went on to declare that Garbo and her life were "incomplete" for her refusal to be paired with a man:

> The only way a woman can gloriously succeed in impressing herself upon her age—the way of love—Garbo has, until now, failed in. . . . History has never reserved a place for a beautiful woman who did not love, or who was not loved by at least one interesting, powerful or brilliant man. . . . When we speak of Helen, we speak in the next breath of Menelaus, of Paris. Pompadour reminds us of Louis Quinze. Salomé would have mattered little but for John the Baptist. . . . Cleopatra had her Caesar, and Mark Antony had Cleopatra. Is the most magnetic woman of her generation, the greatest beauty of her era, to be remembered because her name was 'associated with' John Gilbert's?
>
> Garbo will be forgotten in ten years, and as an actress her memory will be dead when Helen Hayes', Lynn Fontanne's and Katharine Cornell's are beginning to grow greener.

Boothe was no more prescient than enlightened: Garbo never longed for a husband, and the absence of one did not impair either her life or her art. But others were as puzzled as Boothe about her lack of "love interest" and how to categorize her. An Associated Press biographical sketch of her contained an oddly categorical statement: "At times she had an escort, but there was no romance in her life." Odd, but largely true. Even Garbo was a little puzzled. "Isn't it strange?" she once said to Garson Kanin. "I'm no longer young. I've had a long life. And in all my life I have never received a love letter. . . . It's very sad. I think it must be so comforting to have a love letter."

Carolyn Heilbrun notes that many great women artists sought an escape from the "family romance" scenario but that "there were no models of the lives they wanted to live, no exemplars, no stories." Most readers and critics prefer a clear beginning, middle, and end to a series of ambiguities in the story of a life. But Garbo's life defies that tidy formula and disappoints those who require it.

In her early years, she had expressed a desire for children and other domestic instincts of a typical Swede. Once in the seventies, Sam Spiegel took her for a Christmas visit to the wife and children of David O. Selznick in New York. She surprised her hostess with a heartfelt confession, as Irene Mayer Selznick recalled:

> We had a very nice dinner, we opened presents, the whole thing. She said, "Just think, I've known your father, I met your mother when she was a girl." My father was the man who brought her to this country; she worked with David, and they got along well. She saw the complete picture and was so generous and so good with the boys—she made them proud. And then on the way out, she took me aside and said to me, "I envy you more than anybody I know. You have your sons, your children, you have your work, a wonderful life. You have everything. I have nothing."

Throughout her life, Garbo's wistfulness about the family she never had surfaced periodically. Pamela Mason recalled a conversation the day Garbo came to meet her husband, James, for the aborted comeback film in 1949:

> She was very chatty, full of laughter and fun and jokes and surprisingly open. I was a new mother and very excited about it, and she and I were sitting on the floor upstairs talking, playing with the baby who was just learning to walk, and she said, "It's very sad that I shall never have any children." I said, "Why don't you?" She said, "Oh, I'm too old and, in any case, I'm not married." I said, "Well, what difference does that make?" And she said, "Well, it wouldn't be right for me."

She once told Cecil Beaton she could never undertake the terrifying responsibility of having a child. "If she had one she would 'behead' it,' " he quoted her. Her attitude was much like that of Victor Sjöström in Ingmar Bergman's *Wild Strawberries* (1957): "It's absurd to live in this world, but it's even more ridiculous to populate it with new victims, and it's most absurd of all to believe that they will be any better off than we are." She could have become Lady Beaton, Sam Green said, "or married Gayelord Hauser and stayed out there and tended his garden. She could have stayed happily in the country with Cécile, gone to Paris when she wanted, and eventually the 'fuss' would have died down. If she'd become part of a partnership, she would have been a lot happier, because any of those people would have deferred to her eccentricities and indulged her in them. But I think she felt that she couldn't keep the show going for more than a month or so with any one person. Either she couldn't play with the gnomes or be impossibly cranky when she wanted—she felt she couldn't sustain it, being who she was."

She would never marry Hauser, for instance, but she would visit him faithfully to the end. In March 1982, she was staying with him in Coldwater Canyon during the annual Oscar telecast. Even though he knew movies were taboo, "He just had to watch," recalled his friend Nancy de Herrera, who was there. "He said, 'I don't care if she *is* here, I'm not going to miss it.'" Garbo joined in and seemed to enjoy herself, commenting on the winners and losers—until the moment when her own image flashed on the screen in a tribute to stars of the past.

Garbo was a houseguest at Hauser's when he died in December 1984. Shades of George Schlee's death—but this time, she did not take flight. She declined to attend the memorial service at St. Edward's Church in Beverly Hills, but she was among friends and family who gathered later at Hauser's home, and she even took some of the hostessing duties upon herself.

As she would not be a wife, she would not be a widow·for more than a day. There were no children or grandchildren, and so, under the circumstances, Garbo turned to her next closest kin. She had always been on good terms with her niece, but they now began to see each other more frequently. She drew closer to Gray's husband, Dr. Donald R. Reisfield, and to their four children as well.

"The Reisfields were perfect for her," says a close friend. "Of course, they *should* have been, having dealt with her all their lives and knowing *how* to deal with her—not too much, not too little, but always there for her when she needed something. When you 'fold in' at that age, you want to do it with family, and that's exactly what she did."

In the deluge of news stories just before and after her death, reference was often made to Garbo's "bitter old age." It somehow gratified the media to think of her that way—unhappy Garbo, in spite of her millions. But it was another myth.

Melancholia was not bitterness. If anything, Garbo seemed to mellow in her very last years. Her nephew-in-law, Dr. Reisfield, recalled a late conversation in which Garbo was sufficiently serene to say, "You know, I've led a fabulous life." In the fall of 1989, her grandniece Gray Horan came to visit and found Garbo happily sporting a paper party hat and her gold medal from the King of Sweden. On a table in the drawing room, a bottle of champagne had been set out and she made lighthearted reference to the presidential visit that was then tying up traffic in New York City: "Phooey on Bushy and Mama President. We have to brighten up this day."

There were still some sporadic outings. She took in *The Search for Signs of Intelligent Life in the Universe*, Lily Tomlin's one-woman show at the Plymouth Theater, in 1986. In September 1988, David Diamond took her to see *M. Butterfly*, where they were seated, incongruously, next to Tatum O'Neal and John McEnroe. She loved the show and went backstage to meet B. D. Wong, its female impersonator–star. "You are an *artiste*," she told him, then walked away. Wong was flabbergasted. "Why'd you run off so fast?" Diamond asked when he caught up with her. "Because you always talk a long time," she replied. In the late summer of 1989, she slipped into the last row of a West Side movie theater to see her countryman Max von Sydow in the Danish film *Pelle the Conqueror*.

Much of her final year, as in previous years, was spent with the television set, and her tastes were comically unpredictable. To Ray Daum she confessed, "I watch the dreck. *Schmutz*. If a program is advertised as experimental, I never turn it on." She was especially fond of "Matlock" and its star, Andy Griffith, and Sam Green says he learned not to interrupt her 3 p.m. soap opera, "General Hospital." Psychic Kenny Kingston maintains she always watched "Hollywood Squares" and that she "adored Paul Lynde. I think she even wrote him a fan letter." ("It was so boring you didn't have to think at all," says Sam Green, "and it was on at 7:30 and she turned the TV off at 8—a way to wind down waiting for the sandman.")

Claire Koger also remembers Garbo's viewing as largely, but not totally, unremarkable. "She just *looked*," says Claire, who often looked with her at the likes of "Jeopardy" and "Wheel of Fortune." Then the revelation: Garbo, almost surreptitiously, liked to watch movies on television—including her own.

"But *of course* she did," says Claire, contradicting the unanimous testimony of other Garbo intimates. Sometimes "the lady" and her "girl" even watched them together—in which case, during or after, did Garbo ever talk about the film or her performance?

"Not much," she replies, with a look that says she considers the question ridiculous. "It was a *secret*!"

Claire recalls only one memorable utterance from her boss on the subject of movies. It came one day when they were puttering about the living room, half-listening to the tube. During a commercial break, the station was promoting an upcoming made-for-TV film and touting its young star as "the new Greta Garbo." The old one pricked up her ears for a moment and said, in a low, dramatic growl: "There is only one Garbo."

In any case, it was safe to say that Garbo's tastes in entertainment were mainstream and that her life toward the end was largely uneventful—except for an amazing royal interlude.

Swedes love to give and receive medals. In November 1983, Garbo had accepted Sweden's highest civilian decoration and, by order of King Carl XVI Gustaf, was made a Commander of the Swedish Order of the North Star. The Swedish ambassador, Count Wilhelm Wachtmeister, did the honors in a private ceremony in Jane Gunther's East End Avenue apartment. Five years later, as described at the outset of this narrative, the Swedish king and queen themselves—like Anne Bancroft in *Garbo Talks*—were among those who longed to meet her. On their April 1988 state visit to the United States for the 350th anniversary of "New Sweden" (the Swedish colony in Delaware), the royal couple had sought to arrange an audience but the actress could not be budged from her apartment. Since Mohammed would not go to the mountain, King Carl Gustaf and his German-Brazilian Queen Silvia went to Garbo.

Her decline, however, had begun the previous year, in March 1987, when she tripped over an unstowed vacuum cleaner in her living room. "She probably put it there herself and then forgot it," says Sam Green, "because Claire would have been too arthritic to have brought it out." The result was a severely sprained right ankle, and she was more or less housebound thereafter. The worst consequence, physically and psychologically, was that she could no longer take her beloved long walks. For Garbo, the end of walking marked the beginning of the end of living—a mind-set she revealed to her oldest surviving friend, eighty-seven-year-old Mimi Pollack, with whom she had attended the Swedish Royal Dramatic Theater Academy. Their seventy-year correspondence came to a close with a despondent goodbye letter in 1988. "She told me she wouldn't write anymore because she was ill," Pollack recalled.

The specter of death was all around, and perhaps a cynical maxim was true for her, too—that there is nothing so disturbing as to lose an old enemy: On September 14, 1989, the long drama of the Garbo-Valentina feud ended with Valentina's death at age ninety. She was buried four days later, on Garbo's eighty-fourth birthday.

Garbo was not religious, but toward the end of her life she was thinking more about eternity in a philosophical if not theological sense. Like other reflections of the private Garbo, those thoughts would have been lost but for the priceless Sam Green tapes. The subject often came up in connection with the books he gave her and nudged her to read and discuss, despite the fact that she tended to resist spiritual ruminations. Green one day ventured his opinion that "happy people never have a profound thought."

"It's much better that way," she shot back. "They're not getting anywhere anyway because there's no answer, so it's much better if you don't [look for one]. If you sit down and think, 'Why does the sun go up or why does it go down?,' it's not answering anything anyway. I remember once, years and years ago, when I was with a wise, much older man, I asked questions. And he said, 'Don't ask questions, just accept.' "

The wise man can't be known for certain but was probably Mauritz Stiller. In any case, Green was undaunted. Soon after, he gave her Joan Grant's *Far Memory*, a book on reincarnation, and followed up with a phone call to ask what she thought of it:

GG: Well, I only glanced a tiny bit and I don't understand a single word. I probably will eventually. What are you getting out of it?

SG: [Life and death] are fairly important.

GG: I know, but nobody *knows* about it. Do you realize how many billions and billions of human beings are on earth? Do they go somewhere and then gather by the river? Continue on? Where? Without a body? Well, then, what fun do they have?

SG: They go back into other bodies.

GG: All these billions? It's very hard.

SG: We don't have the right concept of what time is.

GG: I don't have any concept. I was just put on this earth and I go by clocks and I don't know anything at all. . . . They go into another form? Are they flowers or earth or stars or horses? . . . That means there would be another world, another level to live on, not this one. [On earth], everybody you see around—idiots, sickly children, all kinds of things—what are these lessons for? You change on this earth so you prepare for the next coming? I wish I would know all about it without having to read any books.

SG: Are you still doing your TM?

GG: Well, I told you the last time, I stand on exactly the same level as when I first started. I'm no further. I'm exactly the way I was when I started in getting any insight. I just sit there quietly and that in itself is helping, but that's as far as I've gotten, [just] sitting there and the same bloody old thoughts are there and I say, "Oh, go away, I haven't got time to go over that now. I want to be quiet for a little while." The same old thoughts.

SG: Don't a few little new ones creep in?

GG: No, no. I just try to push away the same old ones. It helps quiet you a little bit, but that's not getting any further into a bigger scale, not in my case.

SG: Are you fighting it?

GG: I'm not fighting, exactly. I just sort of sit there. . . .

SG: Are you accepting?

GG: No, I'm not doing that either. . . . All I do is get more wrinkles. . . . Do you know that black people do not have wrinkles? I mean, some hundred-year-old person, yes, but they are inclined to have smooth skin. I don't know why.

SG: That tends to be true of the Chinese, too.

GG: Well, if I'd been born in China, I probably wouldn't have any wrinkles. Next time.

Over the years, there were many reports that Garbo was interested in the occult. Kenny Kingston, for one, claims she consulted him often. Garbo's niece dismisses the idea: "I never heard mention of a psychic or an astrologer—you're not dealing with Nancy Reagan, after all." But one extant letter suggests otherwise. It was written by Garbo in 1941 (and sold at auction in 1987 for $6,600) to producer Robert Reud, the friend who had offered to marry her in 1927 (so she could avert deportation) and who was also an amateur astrologer:

"You said I would buy a house. Is that really so? Can you see in the stars if I should buy real estate. . . . Maybe if you looked closely at your planets, they could tell! . . . Do you know if I'm coming to New York. I have sort of vaguely thought of it. But I don't know. . . . If you cannot tell where I am going, I will just have to leave it to the Lord."

When Sam Green once asked her if she believed in astrology, she poohpoohed it, but he thinks she was a secret subscriber and says she knew her zodiacal personality type (Virgo) perfectly. In more serious spiritual terms, however, she never embraced anything except TM—briefly—and a naïve faith in the Catholic patron saint of lost causes.

"I am going to a church were there is a saint called Jude," she once wrote Salka, "and I stand and stare at him and ask him to remember me. There is a guardian there and since I don't cross myself or do anything but stare and ask without words, I am sure he thinks I am some sort of lunatic."

Claire Koger recalls that Garbo always carried a little six-inch statuette of Saint Jude in her purse "because she thought it would keep her safe and lucky." It was so important to her, says Claire, that if by chance she left the apartment without it, Garbo would hurry back to fetch it before sallying forth on her "trot" of the day.

In the late 1970s, she had asked her friend Jessica Dragonette, a very devout Roman Catholic, to "tell me something about the Catholic religion," according to Dragonette's husband, Nicholas Turner. "Jessica would lecture, and this went on for months. I took her to Mass at St. Patrick's off and on for about two years. Jessica was going to turn her over to Bishop Sheen for final conversion. I firmly believe that if Jessica hadn't died when she did [in 1980], GG would've been converted. She had a statue of Saint Jude in her bedroom."

There was a profound yearning in her tone of voice when Sam probed, once again, about her belief in reincarnation:

GG: I wish I knew how to believe in anything. . . .

SG: [People are reincarnated according to their karmic transfer from the previous life and the needs of their spirit in the next.]

GG: I'll tell you one thing, I know a heck of a lot of human beings who wouldn't want to be placed where they're placed. You mean they're placed there because they made mistakes in the former life? They have to come back to something that they don't want? Oh, I must have been a king then in a former life, because I certainly didn't get a square deal in this one!

SG: [Incredulous] O-kaaay. . . . Well, then you'll look around and you'll say, "My, I had so many privileges and I was so unhappy in the last life—maybe this time I'll get it right."

GG: What a bore! Now, who can want to shuffle around human beings that way—what "destiny" or whatever? It's a mighty waste of [time]. It doesn't ring a bell, I'm sorry to say, because it's endless. It seems so—well, I haven't got it. One can't—the human mind cannot picture eternity. Why would any Source want to go on endlessly, endlessly, endlessly, shuffling this thing about?

SG: To try and get it better.

GG: For what? I mean, suppose you do achieve coming to a perfect state, after having gone through millions of existences—then what? What for?

SG: Because that's the way it is.

GG: Goody. It makes one very tired to think of that. I mean, it's wonderful, I suppose, to think there is no end to things—marvelous, *ja*, all is not in vain, but . . . I remember once, when I was under ether, I woke up and I said to this nurse in California—she had a rouged mouth and black hair—I remember her still. And she bent over me and I said to her, "I know about eternity." She looked at me and thought, "Well, she's under, still." But I thought I had discovered eternity. And eternity was not for human beings—so therefore, I didn't discover anything.

The last success in Garbo's lifelong struggle for privacy was keeping the press largely in the dark about her final illnesses—including the fact that she had a mastectomy in 1984. It fell to Sam Green to take her to the hospital for that, but beforehand Cécile had told him that Caral Lebworth had had a similar operation some years earlier and that it might help Garbo to talk with her about it. Sam dutifully arranged the visit.

"I spoke with her both before and after she had the mastectomy," says Caral. "It's absolutely terrifying when you're told that you have cancer. You don't know how to deal with it, and she was nervous and worried about the operation. The fear is terrible and very real. She asked me, 'Could I see your scar?' I said sure, and I undressed for her and let her look at me. . . .

"Afterward, a few weeks or months later, she said, 'Can I come and see you again? I want to talk about it.' She sat right on that sofa—it's such an intimate thing—she was there with one bosom missing and she didn't wear a bra. She said, 'I can't, I've never worn a bra.' What upset her most was that she would have to wear a bra to hold the prosthesis. At her age, she was drooping, like everybody. She was so gorgeous, it didn't matter, but to be asymmetrical, to have a hole there, that really upset her. I said, 'It's not so terrible, wearing a bra.' I don't think she had a radical. It was a partial. A radical takes away the pectoral muscle and leaves a deep cavity. But she didn't have that, and she seemed to get over it well."

Also kept from the public was the fact that she suffered a mild heart attack in Switzerland in August 1988. Dr. Stuart Saal flew there to treat her and, when he arrived, found her and her niece having breakfast in her hotel room. She greeted him with a cheerful, "Hiya, Doc!"

In June 1989, Gray Reisfield engaged a New York limousine service to take her to dialysis treatments at New York Hospital's Rogosin Institute three times a week—Monday, Wednesday, and Friday—for a grueling six hours. There was a serious kidney problem, and other reports said she had a gastrointestinal ailment on the order of diverticulitis in addition to renal failure. Her kidneys and stomach were, in fact, failing fast. Sometimes, for proper care, she left her apartment to stay with Jane Gunther.

Mrs. Gunther's devotion to Garbo was deep, but she was perhaps not—in the final analysis—Garbo's closest friend. That role more rightfully belonged to a woman who would never claim it but who for three decades was almost single-handedly responsible for Garbo's welfare—Claire Koger. Claire herself demurs, when asked. But New York artist Richard Schmidt, Koger's close friend (and legal guardian), declares it unequivocably:

"There is absolutely no doubt about their supreme importance to each other. Those thousands of hours alone in that apartment—the trust and degree of intimacy were unparalleled in either of their lives. Claire, of course, would never say it in so many words. You have to remember that both of them were basically nonverbal, which was why they got on so well together all those years. Once, when I asked Claire directly if they were best friends, she said, 'I suppose so.' She didn't like to talk about it. Another time she told me, 'We were very close—like sisters.' I think that says it all. Their emotional dependence on each other was obvious."

People never saw beyond the superficial employee-employer relationship, says Schmidt, because it was not in the nature of either the employer or the employee ever to indicate otherwise to anyone. No one knew that they took most of their meals together or that Claire had her own room at 450 East Fifty-second Street, where she stayed overnight whenever she chose, which was often. In her last years, Garbo asked Claire to stay more frequently, especially for such holidays as Christmas and Thanksgiving. With callers and visitors, Claire always referred to her as "the lady" or "Madame," but alone together, in private, she called her "GG" and sometimes even "Kata."

Concrete evidence of their closeness came in the form of an extremely rare act of sociability on Garbo's part: "She came to visit once," says Claire, simply. "That was nice."

The occasion was the first trip to America, in 1980, of Claire's Swiss niece and nephew-in-law, Dorly and Heinz Adler, her closest relatives. It was a major event in Claire's solitary life. She had spoken of it to Garbo, who stunned her—on the second morning of the Adlers' visit—by calling and announcing her plan to come to Claire's tiny East Sixty-sixth Street apartment (for the first and only time) to meet them. Claire, who never requested or expected such a thing, recalls being terribly nervous about how her apartment looked. She quickly straightened up, just in time for Garbo's arrival—*sans* hat or sunglasses, and in blue denim slacks and jacket—for a pleasant fifteen minutes of small talk in German.*

Claire Koger, now eighty-eight, lives today in that same walk-up tenement,

---

* Heinz Adler, who escorted Garbo down to the street when she departed, thought Garbo's German rather good. Claire, on the other hand, laughed about it and considered it poor. Alone together, she and Garbo almost always spoke English—reserving German for their rare arguments and moments of anger.

built in the 1880s, and still—with difficulty—negotiates the forty-nine steps
from Sixty-sixth Street to her tiny apartment on the fourth of its six floors.
She has been offered large sums of money to sell her story, both before and
since Garbo's death, from here and abroad. All such offers have been greeted
with a silence as deafening as Garbo's own. But on a stiflingly hot day in
May 1994—in exchange for no money—she reticently agreed to speak of
Garbo for the first time. She is frail, diminutive and now very hard of
hearing. But her straight white hair frames a face with the clear complexion
of a girl, and her eyes signal an undimmed intelligence and sense of humor.
With the help of her friend Richard Schmidt and her home-care provider,
Catherine Grant, she offered her visitor a cup of peppermint tea, proudly
showed off the framed photo of Garbo over her bed, and recalled the woman
whose existence was for so long intertwined with her own:

> She was a very good person, very nice to talk to. . . . Well, she wasn't
> a big talker or joke-maker. She had not the time or the way to joke.
> But oh, yes, she could laugh with me! [Claire laughs.] She would look
> at me and laugh, maybe because of something [I did]—oh, I don't
> remember what we laughed about. But we laughed!

She does remember that Garbo gave her "all sorts of things" over the
years—things she couldn't wear and presents people sent, including jewelry,
clocks, linens, and shoes (they wore the same size), which Claire had repaired
or reworked for herself. Was Garbo a stingy or generous person in general?
"Generous with me," is all she knows. She points proudly to a colorful little
wooden bird Garbo once brought back for her from a trip to Sweden.

They never had "fights," says Claire, though she acknowledges a few
"quarrels." Once when Garbo was quite sick, she yelled at Claire for not
bringing a glass of water quickly enough. Claire's feelings were hurt that
day, she says, with sadness in her voice.* And toward the end, Garbo angrily
resisted Claire's efforts to get her to change clothes. Only then, during the
final illness, did Claire see her cry for the first and last time. But for the
better part of three decades, they got along nicely, she says—and no one
who knew them denies it.

Under the watchful eyes of Claire and Gray Reisfield, Garbo responded
to dialysis rather remarkably for several months. As late as two weeks before
her death, she was seen outdoors, using a cane but mobile. In December,
her nemesis-photographer Ted Leyson, who stalked her almost daily for ten

---

* Desperate as always to help her, Claire at this time created Garbo's new (and last) "favorite"
dish—one of the few she could keep down: a soufflé of boiled noodles baked with eggs,
milk, cheese, and salt, plus grated cheese and dabs of butter on top.

years, caught her on the way to the Rogosin Institute—a windblown mane of gray hair giving her a haunting appearance. She called him "that poor little man who's always lurking" and once told Sam, "I haven't been out for three weeks but he'll be there when I come out. I wonder what he does when I'm not around." To spoil his photographs, she always kept a crumpled tissue in her hand and quickly raised it.

"She meant a lot to me as a photographer," says Leyson. "That's how I express myself—in a strange way—express my regard and admiration for Miss Garbo. It's an overwhelming desire on my part, something I cannot control. It became obsessive. . . . I admire and love her very much. If I caused her any pain, I'm sorry, but I think I did something for her or for posterity. I spent ten years of my life with her—I'm the other 'man who shot Garbo,' after Clarence Bull."

One of her drivers, Sid Howard, saw her for the last time on February 9, 1990, when he took her in his blue Lincoln Mark V for a late-afternoon visit with Helen Hayes and Katharine Hepburn.

Her strength was ebbing, but her dignity was not. On Wednesday, April 11, 1990, she left her apartment for the last time to be admitted to New York Hospital, and lost the final battle of her eleven-year war with Leyson. She was too weak to resist—except with her eyes: In those last pictures, she stares him down with contempt. It seemed, at first, as if there might be hope. Her friends were in frantic touch with Jane Gunther—were the treatments doing anything?

"She's magic, she's just magic," Gunther told them all. "She's so beautiful." Jane thought she looked transcendent, almost beatific. Gray Reisfield was with her constantly. She was in little pain, but when pneumonia set in, there was nothing more to be done.

Each year at winter's end, wrote Selma Lagerlöf, all living creatures are filled with a deep longing for spring. At Easter, in Swedish folklore, the animals gather to watch the great crane dance and to think no more of struggling: "Instead, both the winged and those who had no wings all wanted to raise themselves eternally, lift themselves above the clouds, seek that which was hidden beyond them, leave the oppressive body that dragged them down to earth, and soar away toward the infinite."

Greta Lovisa Gustafson died at 11:30 a.m. on Easter Sunday, April 15, 1990.

Greta Garbo did not.

The memorial service at Frank E. Campbell Funeral Chapel was of course private, attended only by the Reisfields and a very few friends. In compliance with her request, she was cremated and her ashes interred at an undisclosed

location. The final resting place and site of a permanent memorial have yet
to be determined.

The formation of an estate was carried out by the New York law firm
of Debevoise and Plimpton under the supervision of Theodore A. Kurz.
Her March 2, 1984, will bequeathed everything she owned to Gray Reisfield
and her family. She left no money to charity or to anyone else. Faithful
Claire Koger was dismissed with a modest $3,500 in severance pay. There
was a new round of grumbling about her tightness: Her annual twenty-five-
dollar Christmas gift to the doormen had never been adjusted upward, from
1953 to 1990, either for inflation or for fidelity.

Anthony Palermo was especially outraged, having handled her financial
affairs and, he claimed, having been the one who convinced her to have
dialysis. He expressed his disappointment candidly: "I worked for her for
fourteen years for nothing because I was promised to be in the will."

Garbo's estate was first estimated at $55 million, but that figure was much
inflated. The reports that she owned many fine investment properties, including a large portion of Rodeo Drive and other real estate in Beverly Hills,
were not true. Her few commercial buildings in California had all been sold
long before her death—one parcel to an Arab whose wife wanted to open
a dress shop. Arabs, it seems, often made proposals to Garbo; one offered
her $50 million to attend a single dinner party! (She declined.) American
Express had repeatedly approached her with a standing $10 million offer to
do one of its "Do you know me?" advertisements—without success.

Garbo's primary assets were in art, the bulk of which was sold in November
1990, at Sotheby's for a total of $19 million. From the purchase prices, her
art had appreciated roughly 2,000 percent. "She probably paid less than
$100,000 for nearly $20 million worth of art," says Green. Two Renoirs alone
brought $11.6 million on an investment of about $35,000—not that she lived
to realize or spend it.

Most of the rest of her fortune was in stocks and bonds. Her major holdings
consisted of $3 million in Federal Farm Credit Bank notes, $469,000 in
Anheiser-Busch, $587,000 in Eastman Kodak, $211,000 in General Electric,
$101,000 in General Motors, $1,656,000 in General Re Corp., $431,000 in
IBM, $303,000 in Newmont Mining, $365,000 in Ralston Purina, $267,000
in Schering-Plough, $318,000 in Time Warner, and $233,000 in Texaco.
Total stocks and bonds at the time of her death: $9.861 million.

Her Chase Manhattan checking and money-market accounts contained a
combined balance of $640,000. She was getting annual annuities totaling
$36,500 from two insurance policies. Her personal clothing was valued at a
mere $5,800. Her only other significant asset was her apartment at 450 East

Fifty-second Street, now appraised at $850,000. Including her art, the total value of Garbo's estate, as filed in New York County Surrogate's Court on February 21, 1991, was $32,042,429. And two cents.*

The designation of her brother Sven's daughter as sole heir went unchallenged for four months after Garbo's death. A man claiming to be Sven's second illegitimate son, Sven Fredriksson, when contacted in the small Swedish town of Oxelösund, said he never expected anything from his famous aunt and had no plans to pursue the matter. But in August 1990, Fredriksson changed his mind and filed a suit to break the will, charging that Garbo was an alcoholic, of unsound body and mind, and unduly influenced by Gray Reisfield in writing her will.

"I laughed when I read about the half-nephew claiming Gray pressured her on the will," says one close friend. "Anybody who knew GG knew *nobody* influenced her will, and anybody who knew Gray knew the thought would never have crossed her mind."

The case was dismissed by Manhattan Surrogate Court Judge Eve Preminger in July 1991.

It was assumed that Garbo left behind a priceless cache of papers and memorabilia from her Hollywood days. The most famous people in the world sought her out, including Adolf Hitler, who had written her fan letters. But Garbo was not a saver, and there were no Hitler letters, or much else of historical interest, in her trunks in the basement of the Campanile. "She pruned extensively," says her niece. "She didn't want people going through her things after she was gone."

Among the many things Garbo did not leave behind was a wish to memorialize herself. Whatever her narcissism in life, she had no postmortem ego—no desire to perpetuate her name any further. She hardly needed to, of course. She had overdosed early on fame and acclaim and their fallout. The human obsession with accomplishment and recognition—the past and the future—comes usually at the expense of the present, and in her own odd way, Garbo had a realization of that. In the phenomenon of her life, she was able to discern what *didn't* matter but could never quite figure out what *did*. It wasn't immortality, but what were the alternative raisons d'être? Money? Adulation? High Art? What if, by the age of twenty-one, you had enough of all three?

---

* These totals do not include trust funds, set up during Garbo's lifetime, that were excluded from probate and from the resulting tax documents on file. The Estate declines to reveal any information concerning the beneficiaries or the amounts of those trusts, which are believed to be considerable.

How tiring was the human condition, and even more tiring the thought of an eternity of it.

The posthumous exploitation of Garbo began instantly. Of the inevitable new deluge of articles and books, the most cynical by far was Antoni Gronowicz's *Garbo: Her Story*, published by Simon and Schuster just forty-five days after she died. Its genesis was some two decades earlier, in 1971, when Dodd, Mead and Company published Gronowicz's novel, *An Orange Full of Dreams*, containing a foreword allegedly written by Garbo herself:

> From early childhood I was dreaming about oranges. . . . In my mouth, there was a most sweet liquid given to me by angels.
>
> When I was dreaming about oranges as a teen-age girl, I was grabbing them with both my hands. I was tearing at the skin with long sharp nails as I would try to tear open a curtain. The lights of the proscenium were blinding me, and on each quarter of the orange I saw the faces of great actresses of the nineteenth century: Sarah Bernhardt, Eleonora Duse, Fanny Davenport. . . . All of them were smiling at me and waving to me to come in. . . . I was dreaming to become a great theatrical actress, and in my mind and in my soul I was quarreling with God. . . .
>
> Today, I would give anything for the right to see myself, even only once, in an orange full of dreams.

It seemed a fortuitous coincidence for Gronowicz that the most famous woman in the world shared his precise fantasy and, in articulating it, employed the very title of his book. In fact, it was Gronowicz and not Garbo who had an obsession with oranges.

"It's inconceivable that she would have written this," says Gray Reisfield. "She never wrote or spoke this way, and the whole business of 'a most sweet liquid given to me by angels' is impossible. Oranges in Sweden came from Israel and were very sour—most people hated them. She was advised by her attorney not to go further on it because of publicity—and was later very sorry she didn't."

Silly novels, products that infringed her name—those kinds of things she overlooked, since the costs and publicity of legal action were more trouble than they were worth. But Gronowicz's announcement of his impending biography of her was too much.

On the recommendation of Sam Green and Cécile Rothschild, Garbo engaged New York attorney Lillian Poses, through whom, on February 7, 1978, she issued a short affidavit—the first and only public legal statement of her lifetime—denying any friendship with Gronowicz or approval of his project. Simon and Schuster temporarily backed down, announcing it would not publish the book "in her lifetime." The Gronowicz book, when published in 1990, was disavowed by every living person mentioned in it, but the dead could not be reached for comment, and the common reader did not much care. Garbo dead, no less than Garbo alive, was worth plenty to a new set of entrepreneurs for whom the truth was immaterial.*

"Who is Garbo?" was a question asked for so many years by so many millions in so much print in so many countries that Garbo had to have asked it of herself at least now and then. The answers, no matter how profound or ridiculous, always increased the myth. The prevailing notion remains that she was like Churchill's famous description of Russia: "a riddle wrapped in a mystery inside an enigma." Kenneth Tynan reinforced the idea: "Except physically, we know little more about Garbo than we know about Shakespeare." The testimony of her friends and the twenty-seven motion pictures that reveal more than just her physique belie Tynan's hyperbole, but his poetic point is made.

Was there an epic struggle or a perfect meshing between Garbo the person and Garbo the artist? In the harshest view, she was, finally, "a vulgar peasant whose pride prevailed over her art." Truman Capote was gentler: "For artists without an art, it is always tension without release, irritation with no resulting pearl." And what of her mind? George Cukor said she had "a great native intelligence." Howard Dietz, on the other hand, said, "She had no intellectual depth, but she had a depth that was perhaps greater."

Alexander Walker sidesteps the issue of how smart or dumb, vulgar or soignée, she was: "By not leading the conventional life expected of a Hollywood star, she unwittingly ensured that real life would never wear away the mystery that the public insisted existed." Ask not why she quit, he says, but why she wanted to become a star in the first place. The answer relates to escaping poverty and living out a set of fantasies. But dreams-come-true can be nightmares, and Garbo's was a doozy: Her mega-celebrity and "ful-

---

* See Appendix A, "Garbo and Oranges: The Fantasies of Antoni Gronowicz," p. 555, for a full listing of the factual mistakes, fabrications, and anachronisms contained in *Garbo: Her Story* and details of the other Gronowicz hoaxes. A sample of other profiteering: In 1979, a signed Garbo photo sold for $675. Shortly before her death, her autograph alone was selling for about $800. In 1987, a signed letter was auctioned for $6,000. After her death, the value of her signature skyrocketed to $3,000 and often more: A signed photograph sold for $25,000 in Boynton Beach, Florida, in August 1991. There are now restaurants bearing her name in Stockholm, Tokyo ("Cafe Garbo"), Milwaukee, Pittsburgh, Westbury, Long Island, and many other cities—none of them paying royalties.

fillment" in terms of money and glamour were as frightening as her former deprivation. In the end, her brooding soul was always unsatisfied and unsatisfiable; there was never any simple motivation for what she did or why.

But if there is no key to the private soul, there may be one to the creative artist. Salka Viertel had touched on it back in 1932: "I do not think she has reached the artistic heights of which she is capable, nor am I sure that films are her milieu. Perhaps, ultimately, the stage will be." David Diamond declares it categorically: "What interested her was not film but theater. She wanted to be a great stage actress." His own friendship with Garbo was launched, at their first meeting, when he told her his mother had been a costumer to Bertha Kalish (1874–1939), the great Romanian-born tragedienne who performed in New York Yiddish theater productions of *A Doll's House* and *Madame Sans-Gêne*—both of which plays were dear to Garbo.

"She knew all about Bertha Kalish," says Diamond. "She was very interested in the old theatrical actresses—she regretted that she'd never seen Duse. Theater always intrigued her more than film." During quiet evenings at home, he says, she sometimes charmed her intimates with impromptu readings from the great nineteenth-century Russian novels or from *Hamlet* or *King Lear*. On the occasion of *Lear*, Diamond recalls, he took Cordelia and Garbo chided him with, "You always want to play the *good* sister!"

"She didn't do it too often," he says, "only sometimes when we had a little too much vodka and I'd say, 'Let's do a scene' from this or that. She would sit at one end of the love seat and I'd sit at the other. She was very funny. It was mock acting, not the real McCoy—sort of going through the motions without really trying to convince anybody. But it was lovely."

Garbo told Diamond she would have liked to return to Sweden and to have done stage work but that she simply "couldn't." Max Reinhardt had often tried to interest her in theatrical projects. Inexplicably, she never took a serious step toward returning to the stage—or maybe not so inexplicably.

In 1970, when Katharine Hepburn starred on Broadway in *Coco*, the Chanel musical designed by Cecil Beaton, Garbo took in a matinee with Cécile. "I applauded like mad," she told Ray Daum. "She can't sing—my God, she sounds like Rose Kennedy—but she's full of energy. . . . How does she do it? The mere thought slays me. It's enough to kill an ox in a week." She marveled that Gloria Swanson, at sixty-seven, wanted to follow Hepburn in the role.

For that matter, her attitude toward films was similar. One summer in Klosters, Deborah Kerr was home from making a film in London but suddenly was called back to resume shooting. Jack Larson recalled: "Amidst the excitement and affectionate farewells I heard Garbo muttering, 'How does she do it?' and as she embraced Deborah, 'Heavens, how do you do it?' The Viertels sped away and left us standing there. Salka turned to Garbo and asked, 'What are you doing today?' Garbo replied sadly, 'I don't know. I walk. That's what I'm doing. I walk.' I felt there was some envy in Garbo's 'How does she do it?' and that she might have liked to be rushing off to work in some movie herself."

For such a painfully shy person, the difficulty of dealing with a single film director paled by comparison with the nightly torment of relating to an audience of strangers from a stage. Her niece says theater was never a serious option for a simpler, no-nonsense "Swedish" reason: "She was not a person who stayed up late at night, and if you're in theater you have to do that." Nor does she view indecision as the reason for her aunt's non-return to the stage: "I always saw her as decisive. Once she made up her mind, that was it. She never canceled a plane reservation. If she'd seen a script she liked, she'd have done it, but things just didn't break right." Circumstances always seemed to work mysteriously against Garbo's return to film, as well as her transfer to the stage.

Lina Basquette, Garbo's contemporary in silent-sound films, thinks it just as well—that the Garbo magic would not have worked in the theater: "The thing about great film stars such as Garbo and Gilbert is that they were *individuals*, they were *unique*. They couldn't necessarily act their way out of a paper bag in a three-act play on stage. But turn a camera on them, and they came across. On a fifty-foot screen, the charisma or the sex or whatever the hell they had was so *magnified*—that's what made the impact. Without that, they were nothing."

In 1931, Garbo told a member of the cast of *Inspiration*, "I should like to go on the stage." But what would she do about rehearsals? "I wouldn't do them," she said. "I'd have the whole cast rehearse and have another woman do my part. Then, when it was ready, I'd come in and play the role."

Once, and only once, she is said to have agreed seriously to return to the stage, but only on one tragicomic condition: that the first dozen rows of seats be removed.

Garbo's Hamlet-like self-absorption annoyed her friends to distraction. Among the things in which she never took much interest was the United States of America: She made a few forays to the Sierra Nevada and New Mexico but never expressed a desire to experience New England, Yellowstone, the South, or anywhere else. It was all too "outside" her, or she was too fearful of whom and what she might encounter along the way.

Cecil Beaton groused bitterly to his diary that if she hadn't been "Garbo," nobody would've wanted to be around her for ten minutes. But since she *was* Garbo, the only choice was to accept her for what she was—"a woman with a child's charming innocence," with a childlike indifference to all desires but her own. Mercedes de Acosta, too, called her "often superficially childlike. [She] can more thoroughly evoke an emotion of pity and defense than anyone I have ever known. . . . Though there may be nothing particular to defend her against, I want to defend her, to protect her [because] there is a strange sadness in her, underlying everything she does. [It] makes me continually conscious of the eternal sufferings of all creatures. It awakens in me a readiness to forgive her any shortcoming—a desire to take upon my own shoulders her slightest pain or sorrow. . . . This is the hold, I believe, she has had on the public."

Marie Dressler saw it when they were making *Anna Christie* together: "Garbo is lonely. She always has been and she always will be. She lives in the core of a vast aching aloneness." Mercedes elaborated: "She is a lone wolf. No matter how much she may love a person and try to hold on to that person's life and be part of it, in the end she has to let go and pursue her own lonely course. . . . Her standards of friendship áre so high that few people can meet them. In her self-imposed isolation, she cannot understand a friend who has a need to go about socially and partake of the innocent frivolities of life."

Beaton took it personally. "She is incapable of love," he fumed. "She is not interested in anything or anybody in particular, and she has become quite as difficult as an invalid and as selfish, quite unprepared to put herself out for anyone; she [is] continuously sighing and full of tragic regrets; she is superstitious and suspicious . . . and does not know the meaning of friendship. She would make a secret out of whether she had an egg for breakfast."

Beaton had made his serious charge against Garbo in rage, years earlier. If he still felt that way at the end, it was perhaps because he was a textbook case of someone who had failed to live up to Garbo's impossibly high standards. Sam Green notes, for example: "She knew people thought she was rude when she turned down their requests for autographs, but she said the reason she wouldn't do it was because those people were demeaning themselves, putting themselves in a subservient position of, in fact, begging, and she couldn't stand it or encourage it."

Garbo's conflicted approach to trust and friendship troubled not only her intimates but herself. Late in life, she told Jane Gunther, then her closest friend, "I don't know you at all." If true, it was because she could not allow Jane—or anyone else—to know *her*. Gilbert Adrian expressed it from the viewpoint of wounded male vanity: "Many of [her friends and would-be lovers] were men of talent and have contributed much to her. She has never hesitated to take, but she has taken with the selfishness of a spoiled child and turned away petulantly. . . . After years of jumping through her hoops, her friends either get bored [or] accept her eccentricities because they cannot forget the enchantment of her screen performances or her beauty."

A woman who knew Garbo for years in both Hollywood and New York said, "Greta is like the Mona Lisa—one of the great things in life. And as unattached to you as that." But that was not always true. She was frantically concerned about Sam Green in 1976 when she learned that he had collapsed and been rushed to the hospital and a pacemaker implanted in his heart. When he reached her later, she said, "Oh, thank God! I can't tell you what a relief it is that you called. . . . God bless you . . . I bless you, bless you, bless you! I'm so glad. I didn't know whether you were alive or not."

The fact that she never entertained more than a friend or two at a time, and then only modestly (perhaps for tea, never dinner), seemed proof of an unwillingness to put herself out for anybody—or was it proof that she just didn't know *how?* A psychiatrist acquaintance said she was tortured "by a feeling that whenever she makes a choice or a decision it is probably wrong. Even her mildest expressions of opinion begin with 'I don't know anything about this,' or 'I know this sounds silly but . . .' She has solved the problem by deciding to say little and do nothing." Garbo herself confirmed it. "You will never find me saying anything without a reason," she told Sam one day. Earlier she had declared: "Being in the newspapers is awfully silly to me. It is all right for important people who have something to contribute to talk. I have nothing to contribute."

Modesty or false modesty? Privately, she seemed to have a very keen sense of her importance. She meant, simply, that she had nothing to contribute to *social* issues; that her status in film did not qualify her to make political or philosophical pronouncements. The truth and the irony of that had struck her long before, in 1926, at the beginning of her life in America: "Important sardines, important Garbo. . . ." Both the truth and the irony remained with her to the end.

Garbo's niece sees her as "one of the early feminists—when you think of someone coming over at nineteen and taking on the studio, and not getting into drugs or alcohol." Though not actively sympathetic to the later feminist movement, "she fought for equal pay for equal work" in her day at MGM, and she won. Had she not crossed the Atlantic—had her remarkable beauty and talent never been discovered—she might have remained behind a ladies'-hat counter, and been no more or less melancholy. But as things turned out, "Garbo" was a concept beyond Greta Gustafson's understanding. "The greater Garbo became," says Walker, "the more strain was put on Gustafson till in the end she resolved the dilemma by denying us Garbo."

She said she wanted two lives—one for the movies and one for herself.

But Greta Gustafson, formerly of Stockholm and finally of New York, had invented the role of Garbo and was stuck with the life that went with it.

The stated goal of this search was not to knock Garbo off her pedestal, but simply to climb up for a closer look. Yet when we get there—she is gone. Indeed, she "dethroned" herself. Like all queens—movie and imperial—she had a gambit in reserve: abdication. The most obvious analogy was Queen Christina, whose words upon giving up her throne were more akin to Garbo than any of her dialogue in the film: "I am not keen on applause. I know that the part I have played cannot be governed by ordinary stage rules. . . . Others know nothing of my motives and little or nothing of my character and way of life, for I let no one look inside me."

But perhaps the more striking parallel was the 1936 abdication—just five years before Garbo's—of King Edward VIII of England. Both he and Garbo gave up their thrones for The Woman They Loved. In Edward's case, it was Wallis Simpson. In Garbo's, it was herself.

If there was less to her than met the eye, it was because so much met the eye—and because no one, least of all Greta Gustafson, could live up to a woman whose mystery lay in the erotic consciousness of her beholders. As Kenneth Tynan marveled: "Nothing intrudes between her and the observer except the observer's neuroses: She gives to each onlooker what he needs." Since film is the only art that provides its performers with a fountain of youth, the Garbo spell was cast year after year, decade after decade, with no additional expenditure of effort on her part. The Ineffable Movies: Each time they're screened, they disappear but never die. Because Garbo left the screen at age thirty-six, no movie camera would ever record her aging process. She achieved in life what Marilyn Monroe and James Dean got only in death: perpetual youth and regeneration.

Garbo's impact on her own and subsequent generations is as difficult to apprehend as the impact of the Mona Lisa or of Beethoven's Ninth—of all great works of art—but made more complex by the greater sexual charge of film and of the actor's physical self. Leonardo the man can be removed from how we experience the Mona Lisa, and Beethoven from his Ninth Symphony, but one cannot separate the flesh and blood of Garbo from *Camille*. The scope of its distribution makes film a vastly more powerful canvas, and Garbo's image affected and inspired people everywhere. Artists have celebrated her in countless books, plays, musical compositions—in all media for half a century. Of the hundreds of screenplays written for her, only twenty-seven turned into motion pictures, and only half a dozen of those were superior. But hers was a triumph of ability over material. People were bowled over by the credibility of her passion, and whether Garbo liked it or not their response was the final ingredient of her art.

"She gave you the impression," says Alistair Cooke, "that if your imagination had to sin, it could at least congratulate itself on its impeccable taste." But even as they worshiped her, Garbo's fans were frustrated: She was never explained to them because she was never explained to herself. After retiring into her private world, even further out of reach, the result was a mass form of unrequited love.

Film historian Lawrence Quirk calls her "almost an idiot savant." Genius, wrote Robert Herring, "does not make the exponent cease to be ordinary. It merely makes them something else as well." Truman Capote said it didn't matter one way or the other: "Surely it is enough that such a face could even exist, though Garbo herself must have come to regret the rather tragic responsibility of owning it."

In a rare expansive moment, Garbo once said, "We gradually find our true aim in life and try to fulfill its mission, [and] our work tells this best in its own language." She meant it very literally. Her own art flowered in a few shadow plays, uttering sentences that, in Tynan's words, "were plainly designed to speed the end of literature." But her beauty represented "the furthest stage to which the human face could progress, the nth degree of cultured refinement, complexity, mystery and strength"—and her motion pictures were transcended thereby.

Offscreen, Garbo was guided by the same saturnine qualities that infused her film characters. She spent most of her career trying vainly to shake off the side effects of success but ended up shaking off her career instead. The public's euphoria was her dysphoria, and in order to escape, she cut off her nose to spite her audience's face, or so it seemed to the adoring millions.

"It is foolish to lament that her fabulous success did not give her greater confidence in herself," says Walker. Foolish but unavoidable. How we would have loved those fifty years of stage and screen performances she didn't give; to have seen her do Shakespeare or Faulkner or Tennessee Williams or Albee. To have had her on film—just once—with Brando or Clift or Hepburn or Davis. One critic called her retirement "unforgivable if only because it means that now we shall never see her as Masha in *Three Sisters*, a part Chekhov might have written for her."

S. N. Behrman said, "The failure of her talent to bolster her ego is tragic and strange and is the essence of her."

Her own opinion was brutal: "I never liked my work," she told Jean Negulesco. "I'm not a versatile actress." Mercedes de Acosta had the bottom line: "I believe today, in her mature years, Greta could give the most moving and inspired performance of her life. But why should she unless things are perfect for her? She has already contributed enough of herself to art in our era."

As for the comeback, she would have been forced to fight her own myth. "Who would want a second term as President?" she once said to Ray Daum. "I've always lived my own peculiar way, willy-nilly. I'm sort of a free-going spirit, otherwise I can't exist."

Her *Conquest* co-star, Leif Erickson, called her "the hippie of the world." Billy Wilder said she was "as incongruous in Hollywood as Sibelius would have been if he had come to write incidental music for Warner Brothers." Tynan concluded that we'll never know for sure whether or not she was a great actress:

"Do I not find the death-scene of *Camille* or the bedroom-stroking scene of *Queen Christina* commensurate with the demands of great acting? On balance, no. The great actress . . . must show her greatness in the highest reaches of her art; and it must strictly be counted against Garbo that she never attempted Hedda, or Masha, or St. Joan, or Medea. . . . The final accolade must, if we are honest, be withheld."

It is an arguable verdict, though it neglects to consider that in her fifteen sound films, counting the German version of *Anna Christie*, Garbo had to speak a language that was not her own—a major detriment to attempting great tragic roles. There is no denying that due to MGM's conservatism and her own complacency, she made fewer good films than any other major star. But because she never did a horror movie or a coffee commercial or a road-show version of *Mame*, it is easier to retain the vision of Garbo the great actress. "Indeed," as Richard Corliss observes, "we have no other vision to retain."

In the end, Garbo's brilliance is a matter of taste and debate. But, with the possible exception of Lillian Gish, she is the first great actress of whom there is a reliable record. The art of all her stage predecessors disappeared at their deaths. Garbo may not be adored by posterity, but at least she can be seen by it.

Her nobility, in any event, is undisputed, and so is the fact that she practiced both her art and her life with pure, creative indifference to public opinion and all prevailing norms. "Anybody who is truthful and consistent and lives up to his word is a freak," said MGM publicist Howard Dietz. One of her friends put it more specifically: "She is brave, poor Garbo. She has the bravery to be herself."

One looks in vain for an insight that applies equally to the woman and the artist. David Diamond puts Garbo in the diverse company of George Sand

and James Dean as examples of "unique people lost in their environments." Like Sand, whom she always wanted to portray, Garbo was a child of simple birth who became one of the greatest ornaments of her age. She was perhaps the only star who could satisfy both the idealism of her own time and the realism of ours.

To reprise the initial question: Was her allure merely a function of elusiveness? Did her talent conceal substance or just the vacuum of a two-faced woman?

"The truth," George Bernard Shaw once said, "is hardly any of us have ethical energy enough for more than one really inflexible point of honor. An actor, a painter, a composer, an author, may be as selfish as he likes without reproach from the public if only his art is superb; and he cannot fulfil this condition without sufficient effort and sacrifice to make him feel noble and martyred in spite of his selfishness."

The artist-recluse is not unique to Garbo. Many creative people have found it necessary to distance themselves from the crowd, from the world, from their own society and friends, in order to hear the music within themselves. Garbo's inner music was a kind of lugubrious sarabande, but listening to it was indeed an inflexible point of honor with her. Louise Brooks put it with flippant wisdom:

"Alfred Lunt said Garbo couldn't sustain a long scene. But she has probably sustained the longest scene in theatrical history, ever since 1925—her private life."

When the mysteries of Garbo's art are resolved and those of her heart left unresolved, we are left with a woman who tried to keep the two in balance and her dignity intact. To no avail, she reproached her adopted culture for needing royalty and divinity and finding it in movie stars. Her reaction was as "American" and democratic as the phenomenon around her was not: Why do they make such a fuss? she wanted to know, and her life was a tortured testament to the common sense of that question.

"She was a very quiet girl who happened to photograph terrifically," said pioneer director-producer Hal Roach. "She could not reconcile herself to the importance she had attained. She hated the idea that she was a star, but she didn't know what she could do about it."

Garbo, the sex fantasy of the century, was the creation of Mauritz Stiller, MGM, and the collective imagination of millions inside dark movie theatres, not of Garbo herself. It was a great, unintentional joke on the public: For sixty-five years, people forced her to play The Game—and she won.

The Game has gone on for decades with no sign of diminishing, despite the star player's departure. Among the countless turns at it was a 1933 article, "Solving the Garbo Mystery," that, like all the rest, didn't quite live up to

its title. It would be unnoteworthy but for a quotation attributed to "George
F. Babbitt," who was in fact Sinclair Lewis. The writer of the piece, a friend,
talked Lewis into speaking anonymously about Garbo, by whom he was
smitten:

"I'll say there's no mystery at all [about her], except how a woman could
be in fillums so long without 'going Hollywood.' I meet a lot of actors and
actresses in my business. Rent and sell houses to some of 'em, have to foreclose
mortgages on others. She's the only normal one in the lot. The rest of 'em
do their best acting in the swell eating places, and down at the beach, and
walking on Hollywood Boulevard and going to church. Garbo's the only
movie star I know who does all her acting on the screen."

There can never be another Garbo, or such mystery as she embodied,
because there are no more Garbos who truly want to protect their privacy
—or have a privacy worth protecting. On and off the screen, she was an
original. Upon seeing *Camille*, Otis Ferguson—America's greatest film
critic—called her "the dramatic phenomenon of our time," unspoiled by
adulation and wealth and able to project not only the moods of a character
but the complete image of her own person: "Seeing her here, one realizes
that this is more than there are words for, that it is simply the most absolutely
beautiful thing of a generation."

For the denizens of the first half of the twentieth century, when such
images still counted, Garbo *was* the moviegoing experience—theory and
practice alike. Some quirk of Nature and Art created a face, a personality,
and an erotic presence unprecedented in history. In a way, she could hardly
be held accountable for the person she became. Garbo was an anomaly, not a
mystery. She was something to be experienced rather than adored, but people
did both. And as that experience and adoration continue, so does the restless
resistance of her spirit.

The king and queen of silence: Covarrubias's caricature of Garbo with Calvin Coolidge, for Vanity Fair

GARBO AND ORANGES:
THE FANTASIES OF ANTONI GRONOWICZ

A full listing of errata in the Antoni Gronowicz book *Garbo: Her Story* is found below, but certain facts should come first.

Garbo: Her Story was published by Simon and Schuster in a massive edition of 150,000 just 45 days after Garbo died. The book's genesis, however, was nearly two decades earlier, in 1971, when Dodd, Mead and Company published Gronowicz's novel, *An Orange Full of Dreams*, with a foreword allegedly written by Garbo herself.

"She wouldn't have written a foreword for this man's novel," said Gaylord Hauser around that time. "Why, she wouldn't write a foreword to any of *my* books, and she is my best friend!"

Gronowicz had transferred his own lifelong obsession with oranges to Garbo. His new obsession was Garbo herself, in a variety of literary forms. On November 27, 1971, for example, he wrote Gloria Swanson, asking her to "please let me know when I could see you [to] discuss my new play, *Greta.*"

Garbo never responded to anything published "by" or about her. That policy was normally wise, but her failure to disavow the *Orange* foreword encouraged Gronowicz to proceed with a sensational Garbo book that was ready for publication in 1976. Garbo learned of it through friends who saw the manuscript when it was circulated at the Frankfurt Book Fair. The cost of legal action and its attendant publicity had always been beyond what she was willing to pay, but this time she was moved to action.

On the recommendation of Sam Green and Cécile Rothschild, Garbo engaged New York attorney Lillian Poses to challenge the Gronowicz book. When Gronowicz failed to provide documentation that he knew Garbo, his publisher, Dodd, Mead, dropped the book. But Simon and Schuster quickly snapped it up (for $150,000) and announced its own intention to publish. Through Poses on February 7, 1978, Garbo issued her first-ever affidavit to debunk the book.

"I have never at any time entertained any type of human relationship whether of friendship, acquaintance or otherwise with Antoni Gronowicz. To the best of my knowledge I have never even met him at any time in my life.

"I have never at any time collaborated in any manner whatsoever with Mr. Gronowicz or anybody else on any memoirs, autobiography or biography of my life, nor have I ever authorised [sic] or approved any such work, or been involved in any way with any literary or journalistic work."

Three months later, on May 2, she issued a second sworn statement through Poses, belatedly addressing the foreword: "Regarding Mr. Gronowicz' "An Orange Full of Dreams," I deny, without reservation, writing an introduction to such book, and deny that I had anything whatever to do with it."

To Jane Gunther and others, she said, categorically, "I never met him."

A "Shop Talk" item in *Publishers Weekly*, September 29, 1951, noting that Garbo was seen in Manhattan's Little Bookshop with "author-friend Anton Gronowicz," is the sole indication they knew each other personally. But such blurbs were routinely phoned or sent in and not always double-checked. Gronowicz most likely "leaked" it himself—and others to follow.

A 1956 report said three Broadway producers were in a bidding war for stage rights to a vehicle that Garbo was *paying* Gronowicz to write for her. A June 29, 1960, *Variety* notice claimed Garbo herself had bid $100,000 for *Modjeska*, her "old friend" Gronowicz's biography of the great Polish actress, which would first be seen as a play "next season on Broadway with Katharine Hepburn." Garbo was said to "recognize in Izio Neufeld, the Polish artist who committed suicide over Modjeska, an analogy to Mauritz Stiller" and to be planning a film version at Paramount. But there is no evidence that the project existed anywhere except in Gronowicz' mind.

Gronowicz was capable of far larger fabrications. His 1943 biography *Paderewski: Pianist and Patriot* was purportedly based on many meetings with the Polish hero at his Swiss chalet. It was there, Gronowicz claimed, that he first met Garbo when she visited Paderewski in 1938. But according to Mrs. Anne Strakacz Appleton, the daughter of Paderewski's personal secretary, who kept meticulous appointment records, Paderewski never met either Gronowicz or Garbo, and neither Garbo nor Gronowicz was at the chalet in 1938. Gronowicz waited until Paderewski died to bring out his biography, which was "pure trash" but not particularly harmful, said Appleton, so her father did not bother to refute it. "My aunt was never in Poland," maintains Garbo's niece. "All the Polish socialist-political statements attributed to her throughout that book are totally uncharacteristic of her."

In 1984, *God's Broker*, Gronowicz's book on Pope John Paul II, was shredded at the last minute by its publisher, Richardson & Snyder, with the approval of the U.S. Supreme Court, after the Vatican provided evidence that the author's alleged papal interviews never took place. A grand jury was investigating Gronowicz for fraud when he died a year later.

When Garbo's 1978 affidavit was made public, Simon and Schuster temporarily backed down, announcing it would not publish the book "in her lifetime." But between the book's shelving then and Gronowicz's death in 1985, the biography metamorphosed into an "autobiography" largely in Garbo's first-person voice. Gronowicz's credibility had been shredded along with his book on the Pope, but Simon and Schuster played a waiting game. After her death, the Garbo book was denounced as a phony, but the publisher replied that it "seems irrefutable" (indeed, its subject was dead) and claimed that certain hotel registrations proved Garbo and Gronowicz had spent time with each other.

Garbo's estate sued to stop publication on May 18, 1990, but the parties entered into a surprise, confidential settlement just days later. "The libel laws dry up when the subject dies, but you have federal and state laws that require a publisher to sell a book honestly," explained one of the lawyers at the time the suit was filed. Simon and Schuster subsequently incorporated the following disclaimer into its advertising:

> This book uses the first-person literary device to emulate the voice of Greta Garbo. The words are those of Antoni Gronowicz, not Miss Garbo, who publicly denied having any involvement with Gronowicz or making any contribution to this book. Neither Miss Garbo nor her Estate authorized or consented to the publication of this book.

To lend the book some credence, Simon and Schuster hired *Time* magazine critic Richard Schickel to write an afterword in which he finessed the issues of authenticity and accuracy. In fact, the Gronowicz book contains at least ninety major factual errors, not counting hundreds of thoughts manufactured in Garbo's "voice" and the sadomasochistic portrayal of her parents, which has no basis in fact. In his most astonishing passage, Gronowicz puts himself in bed with Garbo—on page seven—and never again refers to their alleged relationship.

The end result was an unscrupulous hoax. Some eighty thousand copies were sold, with the careless complicity of *The New York Times*, whose long critique of the book included many Garbo "quotes" with a perfunctory "Is it or isn't it legitimate?" sidebar. For the sake of film history and future Garbo scholars, the following list of errata in the Gronowicz book has been compiled, with the assistance of Gray Reisfield, Lew Ayres, Irene Mayer Selznick, Raymond Daum, David Diamond, and Scott Eyman, inter alia:

p. 1, ff. through the book: Gronowicz—like most Garbo writers over the decades—misspells the family surname. In her official, December 21, 1923, name-change application, both Garbo and her mother sign their names "Gustafson," not "Gustafsson." Her brother and her niece consistently spelled their names Sven Gustafson and Gray Gustafson Reisfield.

p. 14: Stiller's "suicide" is contradicted by every other source, of which the most authoritative is Stiller biographer Gösta Werner in Stockholm, who told the author on August 17, 1991, that Stiller's death certificate lists "water in the lungs" as the cause of death.

p. 15: The alleged Garbo-Gronowicz meeting at Paderewski's Chalet Riond-Bosson on Lake Geneva in 1938 never took place (see above). Gronowicz's statement, "[Paderewski] asked me here to arrange his papers," is likewise false.

p. 21: Leopold Stokowski's alleged impotence is belied by the fact that he had two sons, Chris and Stan, and three daughters, Lyuba, Sadja, and Sonya.

p. 30: The claim that Garbo's father, Karl Gustafson, was a "janitor" is contradicted by all other sources indicating he was an outdoor laborer who worked for the city of Stockholm as a gardener-landscaper.

p. 31: Karl and Anna Gustafson were not married in 1896, but in 1898. Their daughter Alva was not born in 1904, but 1902.

p. 31 and p. 39: "For no good reason [Garbo] became known at once as Keta." This error was probably copied from Bainbridge. In fact, Garbo's family called her "Kata," as that was how she pronounced her own name as a toddler.

p. 32: Garbo's mother beating her father with a rolling pin and sexually taunting him by dancing nude in front of the children: see entry re: page 41, below.

p. 34: Garbo's sister Alva did not die of tuberculosis but of cancer.

p. 35: The "element" joke (concerning the Swedish liqueur *brännvin*) does not work in English. Further, Gray Reisfield notes that Garbo had the same teacher throughout grade school, a woman named Miss Rösenqvist, and not a man, as Gronowicz claims.

p. 39–40: "As far back as I can reach with my memory, I dreamed about oranges. . . . Oranges became more and more a part of my secret life." No other Garbo source mentions her interest in oranges, including Gayelord Hauser, who certainly would have observed it. (See Gray Reisfield's rebuttal, Chapter 13, p. 542.)

p. 41: Garbo's mother's cruelty to her father and beatings of her children. "This characterization is total fantasy," says Gray Reisfield. "She was a *tiny* woman, maybe five-feet-three or five-feet-four, and my grandfather was well over six feet tall."

p. 44: "At 14, Garbo was already 5 feet 6 inches tall." In fact, she had attained that height at the age of twelve.

p. 51, ff.: That GG hated her mother and that her mother and father had violent fights is denied by all family sources and Garbo friends, e.g., David Diamond, who says, "I remember her talking only with the greatest warmth about her mother."

p. 52: Concerning Pastor Ahlfeldt. Gray Reisfield says, "It is totally false and irresponsible to suggest that he took my grandmother home as a mistress." (See entry re: page 61, below.) It was not Pastor Ahlfeldt but Garbo's sister, Alva, who secured her employment at PUB.

p. 53: "David Fisher, manager of the [PUB] department store, thought if he was the first to find her, all the girls and Greta would remember him as the one who had transmitted her first offer to act." This first of many anachronistic hindsights implies the manager somehow knew his salesgirl would become a great star.

p. 58: The existence of Aga Andersson and her jealous rivalry with Garbo is nowhere else to be found or confirmed. This is the first of many examples of Gronowicz's quotation not only of GG's precise words but of her thoughts, as well.

p. 61: "[Garbo's] mother began her sexual career; I noticed she only worked for the rich." That Anna Gustafson would carry on an affair with a local parish priest is "a complete miserable fabrication," says Garbo's niece, and is unsubstantiated by any other source or account.

pp. 62–3: The claim that Garbo's sexual initiation came through her sister: Incest with Alva, and the notion that Garbo would have discussed such a thing with anyone, are both "absurd," according to her niece.

pp. 69–70: The alleged GG shoplifting incident is belied by the fact that the store detective never asked about the package being wrapped up. There is no mention of such an occurrence in her PUB employment records, which were well detailed and preserved.

p. 83: Gronowicz claims Stiller may have been born in Lvov, Poland. In fact, he was born in Helsinki, Finland. His mother was born in Poland.

p. 95: Contrary to Gronowicz's claim and Stiller's alleged instructions, Garbo never had any teeth removed—least of all, her front teeth—according to her dentist, Dr. Joseph Fertig.

p. 97: The claim that Stiller "teaches" Garbo to smoke in 1924 during *Gösta Berling* is false. In fact, as she often told people, she was smoking from 1917 at the age of twelve.

p. 108: "[*Gösta Berling*] was the first European film produced in two segments." Michael Curtiz's two-part *Sodom und Gomorra* (1922), among others, preceded it.

p. 113: "When I discovered that L. B. Mayer was in Berlin, I used every conceivable connection I had to get in touch with him." Garbo had no such connections and never attempted to contact Mayer on her own. Stiller did all the "connecting."

p. 115: The bizarre claim that Stiller engaged a prostitute to give G. W. Pabst a venereal disease in Berlin is unsubstantiated by any other account.

p. 117: Stiller allegedly "placed an article" in a Berlin newspaper saying that "L. B. Mayer was thinking of engaging Mauritz Stiller and GG for a new film." There is no such Berlin newspaper clipping to substantiate this, and Mayer's daughter Irene Selznick declared there was "no such thing."

pp. 117–18: According to Gronowicz, Mayer and his daughter Irene were staying at the Hotel Esplanade in Berlin. According to Irene, it was "definitely the Adlon."

p. 119: In Berlin, Stiller and Mayer allegedly talked at length in Yiddish: Irene Mayer Selznick maintained, "I never heard my father conduct a business conversation in Yiddish ever."

p. 119: The "farewell reception" held by Stiller at the Esplanade on the occasion of Stiller's and Garbo's departure from Berlin never took place, according to Irene Mayer Selznick. Or, if it did, "My father never attended such a thing."

p. 120: Stiller claims Sam Goldwyn is a distant relative. There is no evidence of such.

p. 144: The claim that Mayer was forced to sign Garbo in order to get Stiller is a myth (see Chapter 4). So is the theory that MGM Vice President Edward Bowes took it upon himself to keep Stiller and Garbo in New York in order to "put them in their place." The studio simply hadn't yet decided what to do with them.

pp. 148–51: Gronowicz's account of Garbo's trip to Coney Island is fabricated. She went to the amusement park with MGM publicist Hubert Voight, not with Stiller—and certainly not with fashion photographer Arnold Genthe, whose detailed Garbo account never mentions Coney Island. Moreover, there could not have been "hundreds of thousands" of people there in the 1920s, and there were never signs advertising "wienies." Americans called them "hot dogs," and Swedes called them "korv."

p. 158: The unlikelihood of Bogart asking Garbo for a date in 1925 is exceeded only by his alleged remark about Sinclair Lewis, "If he doesn't write detective stories, I'm not going to read him." Bogart did not make a detective film or show any interest in the genre until 1941.

p. 163: Stiller says he, through Chaplin, could introduce Garbo to George Cukor. But in 1925, Cukor was still directing plays in Rochester and just beginning to embark on a Broadway career. He didn't go to Hollywood until four years later and Stiller could not have heard of him in 1925. Nor is there any evidence that Stiller and Chaplin knew each other.

p. 165: The 1920 incident in which Chaplin hit L. B. Mayer in the face was not the result of Mayer's attempted seduction of Chaplin's wife, Mildred Harris, but because Chaplin resented Mayer's rushing Harris into a new contract soon after her marriage to Chaplin and against his wishes.

p. 165–6: The Garbo-Chaplin impromptu pantomime parody of *Camille* is a fantasy. It was allegedly performed at a large New York party in front of many prominent guests—not one of whom ever mentioned it. Moreover, Garbo did not meet Chaplin in New York but much later in Hollywood.

p. 169: For their departure to Hollywood, Garbo and Stiller are allegedly accompanied to Grand Central Station by "a group of photographers." But not a single photo of that event has ever been seen or published.

p. 171: In this most bizarre explanation of the origin of Garbo's name, Stiller allegedly tells her it comes from the Polish word *wygarbować*, meaning the process of tanning leather. Stiller knew Russian and Finnish but, despite Gronowicz's wishful thinking, there is no evidence he knew Polish or that he ever made such a far-fetched semantic connection.

pp. 173–5: Gronowicz's account of Garbo's transcontinental train trip includes stops in cities that were not, in fact, on the Atchison, Topeka & Santa Fe route—including Santa Fe itself.

p. 186: MGM director Monta Bell was never for a moment "under the supervision of Stiller" during the making of Garbo's first film, *Torrent*. Stiller, in fact, was banned from that set.

p. 189–90: Neither Dorothy Farnum nor Antonio Moreno, in dozens of interviews, ever mentioned the Stiller "suicide attempt" which they allegedly helped to thwart.

p. 191: In 1926, Mayer allegedly shows Garbo the famous "Swedish Sphinx" photo of her head superimposed on the Egyptian sphinx. But that trick picture did not exist until five years later, fashioned by Clarence Sinclair Bull in 1931.

p. 192–3: There is no evidence, in or out of the MGM files, that Garbo threatened to return to Sweden unless Mayer promised to let Stiller be in charge of *The Temptress*. The claim that Mayer agreed to triple their salaries is verifiably false.

p. 195: Gronowicz says Chaplin was working "from the beginning of 1925" on *The Circus* and had agreed to appear in *The Temptress* if Stiller would insert a circus scene in it (to help Chaplin defray the costs of his own circus film). But production on *The Circus* did not begin until November 1925, and Chaplin in his whole career after 1915 never agreed to appear in anyone else's film.

p. 202: "Niblo had decided to scrap all the work that Moje had done [on *The Temptress*] and begin again." MGM would have permitted no such thing. Stiller's extravagant opening masked-ball scenes were retained and are in the film.

p. 209: "I asked [Stiller] who this mysterious Pola was." The European Garbo was well aware of Pola Negri, who had made a dozen films in Poland and Germany between 1916 and 1923, and ten more in the United States between 1923 and 1926.

p. 209: Garbo's alleged disappointment that Stiller chose Negri to star in his *Hotel Imperial* is specious. As an MGM player, Garbo could never have appeared in a Paramount film at that point in her career even if she had wanted to.

pp. 210–11: The glib prose attributed to Garbo reaches its apotheosis here: "Speaking of a complicated love affair, it was [at Charles Chaplin's home] that I met for the first time John Gilbert." The first Garbo-Gilbert meeting was, in fact, on the MGM lot during preparations for *Flesh and the Devil*.

p. 214: Similarly, Garbo was not introduced to Gilbert's manager, Harry Edington, at a Chaplin party, but much later at a private meeting arranged by Gilbert.

p. 217: John Gilbert and Dorothy Parker were never lovers. They met and spent a few evenings together—chaparoned by other members of the Algonquin Round Table—during one of Gilbert's visits to New York.

p. 220: L. B. Mayer would not have attended the premiere of Stiller's *Hotel Imperial* (1927), made by the rival Paramount studio. Nor would Clark Gable, a stage actor with just two bit parts in film to his credit then, have been invited.

p. 228: The third of many newspaper review quotes throughout the book (which Garbo allegedly says "I still remember by heart") is, like the others, taken from John Bainbridge's *Garbo* (1955), complete with the same ellipses. A close friend of Garbo's observes, "It's absurd that she memorized reviews of her films. She barely glanced at them."

p. 230: After *Flesh and the Devil*, Garbo demanded—and eventually got—a salary increase to $5,000 a week (not $10,000, which Gilbert was getting).

p. 234: Stiller's *Street of Sin* (1928) was not finished by his friend Ludwig Berger, but by Josef von Sternberg.

p. 238: Richard Watts, Jr.,'s *Herald Tribune* comparison of Garbo with Dempster, Talmadge, Pitts, and Swanson appeared in a review of *Torrent*, not of *Love*.

pp. 250–1: There is no other source to support the claim that Gustav von Seiffertitz and Conrad Nagel had a brawl in her living room over Garbo during the making of *Mysterious Lady*, or, indeed, that either man ever visited her home.

p. 257: "I never grasped . . . the reasons I was cast in films like *A Woman of Affairs*." Michael Arlen's *The Green Hat*, the basis for *A Woman of Affairs*, was the most popular novel of its time. Garbo had seen Katharine Cornell in the 1925 Broadway version and actively sought to play the screen role.

p. 258: In *A Woman of Affairs*, "I played the role of a brother, and I played the role of a sister, two inseparable souls, lost forever together." This baffling statement is inexplicable. In *A Woman of Affairs*, Garbo played the single role of Diana Merrick.

p. 258: Garbo did not "always refuse" L. B. Mayer's invitations. His daughter Irene recalled occasions on which she appeared at social gatherings in the Mayer home.

p. 259: No other source confirms Gronowicz's claim that L. B. Mayer personally came on the set of *Wild Orchids* in September 1928 to deliver the telegram announcing Stiller's death. Nor was it sent by Mimi Pollack, but, rather, by Victor Sjöström.

p. 275: Garbo's alleged intention to put flowers on Stiller's grave is not credible. She was sophisticated enough to know that that was not the Jewish tradition, which is summed up in a nineteenth-century verse that appears in many Jewish cemeteries:

> Lay no flowers on monuments over men's bones.
> Life gave them no laurels, only stones.
> Upon their monuments, lay stones.

p. 276: During her transatlantic crossing, Garbo allegedly "notices" a report in a New York paper concerning her departure. How the newspaper magically reached the ship in midocean is unexplained.

p. 279: In her discussion with Stiller's ghost, Garbo tells him she has "recently developed" a craving for alcohol, tobacco, and sleeping pills. As noted above, she had been smoking heavily for ten years; she never in her life took sleeping pills.

p. 286: Garbo's copy of *Anna Christie* was given to her not by Wilhelm Sörensen during her ocean voyage but by MGM publicist Hubert Voight some months earlier.

p. 295: Garbo's alleged love of animals was "shared with my friend Paderewski, whose house in Switzerland was full of animals that he adored." In fact, Garbo was never there and never met Paderewski. Her niece observes that, "While I knew my aunt in New York City, she never had a pet—be it bird, cat, or dog. She left nothing to any animal societies in her will. I don't know if she had animals in California, but if she ever taught a parrot to talk, the words would definitely have been in Swedish."

p. 297: (1) "[Lew Ayres] developed the impression that I was in love with him." According to Lew Ayres in a May 31, 1990, interview with the author in Los Angeles, "This is absolutely untrue. That was the *movie!* I was in love with her in the *movie*. It shows what an ass [Gronowicz] is."

(2) "Lew was a pacifist . . . and I would suggest that he go into politics and organize people to work against war and social injustice." Responds Ayres, "She never suggested any such thing. At that time, I was twenty and hadn't even made *All Quiet on the Western Front* yet."

p. 298: (1) "I took [Lew Ayres] with me everywhere I went, including Jacques Feyder's house." Responds Ayres, "I wish she had. I'd have gone."

(2) "Soon after the premiere of *The Kiss*, I ran into Lew on a Hollywood street and asked him to my house. During dinner, all he could talk about was my supposed jinx on actors." Responds Ayres, "Never. Not true at all. He just dreamed it all up."

(3) "During the Second World War, Lew was blacklisted because he refused to serve in the army." Ayres was a conscientious objector who served with great distinction in the medical corps, saw much battle action in the Pacific, and was decorated for his performance in the line of duty.

p. 301: This fifth of a dozen references to Garbo's "jinx" on her male co-stars—and her alleged concern about it—is lifted from a fan magazine article of July 29, 1934, "Thirteen Males All Trailed by Bad Luck" (subtitled, "Gilbert, Asther, Bickford, Cortez, Moreno, Hansen, Nagel, Gordon and Others Hit Slump After Playing Opposite GG"). The claim that it "led me to astrology, occultism and magic" is unsubstantiated by anything except a passing interest in her zodiacal sign and chart years later.

p. 302: There is no evidence that photographer William Daniels also "believed in mysticism." Nor is there anything to indicate that Daniels was partial to Italian dramatist Luigi Pirandello and his "mystical" philosophy and transferred that interest to Garbo, who "systematically" studied Pirandello thereafter.

p. 303: "The critics were devastating" about her performances in *Susan Lenox* and *Mata Hari*: In fact, most of the reviews were highly favorable, and both films made large profits—*Mata Hari* the second largest ($879,000) of all Garbo films.

p. 311: Garbo's relationship with Marie Dressler: "I will never forget her warm body. . . . She taught me not to be ashamed of this kind of love." They allegedly spent many nights together, after which, "To pay her back in a small way, I persuaded MGM to engage her to play Marthy in *Anna Christie*." But Garbo and Dressler barely met before *Anna Christie*. It was screenwriter Frances Marion, not Garbo, who lobbied MGM to give Dressler the Marthy role (see Chapter 8).

p. 311: Similarly "deep" if not sexual relationships are suggested between Garbo and actresses Barbara Kent, Paulette Duval, and Florence Lake. The sole surviving one, Barbara Kent Edington Monroe, denies she and Garbo were really even friends, let alone lovers. (Barbara Kent to author, March 11, 1991.)

p. 320: Queen Christina "carried on an extensive sexual life with men and women." In fact, Christina led a largely celibate life with the likelihood of one female affair and no male ones (see Chapter 9 and Sven Stolpe's *Christina of Sweden*).

pp. 335–6: Barbara Barondess: "The Gronowicz book is a lot of *merde*. He [has Garbo call] me Barbara MacLean, but I never dreamed I would marry Douglas MacLean in 1933. He says she 'let' me on the set. She didn't *let* me on the set. I was in the movie and *had* to be on the set. I was being paid for it. He intimates that this was a lesbian relationship, while everybody knows that I never was or could be interested in women." (Barbara Barondess MacLean to author, January 29, 1991.)

pp. 339–42: Hazel Washington. Says Garbo's niece: "If my aunt had a maid named Hazel Washington, I never heard of her. That name was never mentioned. Picking up someone on the side of the road and taking her home in her chauffeured limo would have been highly improbable for my aunt, to say the least."

p. 348: According to Garbo's family, she never had a home or apartment at 10 Artillerigatan or anywhere else in Stockholm after 1925. "It wasn't characteristic of her to maintain two residences. She wasn't in Sweden often enough, and it simply wasn't practical."

p. 368: Gronowicz claims that a few days after Germany invaded Poland in September 1939, Mayer called Garbo into his office and said he wanted her to play "a glamorous, fun-loving American girl." That reference to *Two-Faced Woman* is impossible since the story wasn't unearthed and decided upon until 1941.

p. 369: "I sent a radiogram insisting that my mother and my brother Sven and his wife drop everything and join me in Hollywood [when the war began in September 1939]. I immediately rented a house in Inglewood for [them]." According to Garbo's niece, the cablegram arrived in July, and there was no Inglewood rental house. "We stayed with my aunt, of course." (Gray Reisfield to author, New York City, July 15, 1991.)

p. 370: The accounts of battles between Garbo and her mother in California are fabricated. "It was a gigantic house with plenty of room to avoid any friction. Besides that, you never fought with my aunt in my family." (Gray Reisfield to author, New York City, July 15, 1991.)

p. 371: The account of her mother's death is a fabrication. Anna Gustafson did not die in California, but in Westchester, New York, attended not by Garbo but by her daughter-in-law, Marguerite Batzer Gustafson.

p. 372: More flowers on Stiller's grave (see above, re: page 275).

p. 405: Valentina Nikolayevna Sanina [Schlee] was born in Russia, not "eastern Europe."

p. 409: Anthony Beauchamp's photos of Garbo were not taken until almost a decade later, in the early 1950s.

p. 410: Gayelord Hauser's manager was Frey, not "Fred," Brown.

p. 419: "Sometimes I was even sure that [Schlee] had talked to various motion-picture entrepreneurs about my films." In concocting a sexual relationship between Schlee and Garbo, Gronowicz overlooked their real business relationship—Schlee was actively involved in Garbo's *Duchesse de Langeais* film project, with her full knowledge and approval, as the Walter Wanger files at the University of Wisconsin prove.

p. 420: Garbo did not discover Schlee dead in his room "the next day." He was out walking when he had the heart attack, not at the Hotel Crillon, and he died at American Hospital in Paris.

The last word on *Garbo: Her Story* belongs to Scott Eyman in his Cox News Service review of June 1990:

"An educated guess might be that Antoni Gronowicz was on good terms with people who knew Garbo well and thus acquired a secondhand sense of her character. Or he might actually have observed her at close range for some brief time and extrapolated [her] psychology. . . . This book must be considered a fraud by any rational, knowledgeable reader. As such, it's the saddest movie book by a major publishing house since Irving Schulman's *Harlow*."

APPENDIX B

DOCUMENTED GARBO INTERVIEWS
1924–1990

Hundreds of Garbo articles and books employ quotations taken from purportedly authentic interviews with her, but only the following dozen or so pass a reasonable test of scrutiny and documentation:

1. Inga Gaate, interview conducted in Stockholm in 1924 during the filming of *The Saga of Gösta Berling*.

2. Ruth Biery, *Photoplay*, April–June 1928. Interview conducted on New Year's Eve 1927 in a tearoom in Santa Monica. "Harry Edington secured me the interviews for the life story," said Biery later. "The studio did not even know that I had written it."

3. Mordaunt Hall, *New York Times*, March 24, 1929, section 10, page 7. Interview conducted the previous day at the Hotel Marguery in New York.

4. Åke Sundborg, "That Gustafsson Girl," *Photoplay*, April and May 1930. Interviews conducted in late 1929 or early 1930 during Garbo's visit to Sweden.

5. Val Lewton, "Glorious Greta: The Life Story of the Garbo," *Moving Picture Stories*, October 13, 1931. Interviews conducted by MGM publicist Lewton at various times and places in 1925 and 1926.

6. Rilla Page Palmborg, *The Private Life of Greta Garbo* (New York: Doubleday & Co., 1931). Interviews conducted July to October 1927 on MGM sets.

7. Garbo with Lars Saxon, "My Life as an Artist," *Lektyr*, 1930. Based on conversations and letters written in late 1929 or early 1930 by Garbo to her friend Saxon, who was editor of the Swedish magazine.

8. Shipboard press conference, *Gripsholm*, New York, 1932.

9. Shipboard press conference, *Gripsholm*, New York, June 1936. "The scribes, to their surprise, were ushered into the ship's smoking room, where Garbo agreed to meet them and answer questions for ten minutes."

10. Kay Proctor, "At Last Garbo Really Talks," *Screen Guide*, July 1936. Also Jim Mason, "Garbo Talks At Last," *Photoplay*, July 1936. Both brief interviews conducted onboard train.

11. Garbo-Stokowski "emergency" press conference in Ravello, Italy, March 17, 1938.

12. *Kungsholm* shipboard press conference, October 7, 1938.

Aside from an occasional comment pried or bullied out of her on the run, Garbo never willingly spoke to the press after 1938. There were certain borderline cases, such as Cecil Beaton and Kenneth Tynan, who she knew were likely to quote her in print. But even those "qualified" interviews—extended conversations with friends, not really intended for publication—can be reduced in the final analysis to just four of significance:

13. In August 1977, the West German magazine *Bunte Illustrierte* heralded its coup of obtaining the first interview with Garbo in thirty years, given to a writer who met her at Salka Viertel's home in Klosters. This was Frederick Sands, whose long talks and walks with her (secretly photographed) formed the basis of his book *The Divine Garbo* (New York: Grosset & Dunlap, 1979).

14. Raymond Daum, *Walking with Garbo* (1991), based on conversations, some tape-recorded, between 1964 and her death.

15. Sven Broman, *Garbo on Garbo* (1991), based on conversations, some tape-recorded, between 1979 and her death.

16. The tape-recorded conversations with Sam Green, 1972–1985.

Included below—for the first time in any Garbo filmography—in addition to the standard cast and credits I have listed the producers, the number of production days, the production costs, the domestic and foreign earnings, and the profit or loss on all MGM Garbo films. The apparent discrepancy between cost and profit figures is due to the omission of distribution and advertising expenses in MGM's method of accounting for its production costs.

1. *How Not to Dress* (1921), advertising film for Paul U. Bergstrom department store (PUB) in Stockholm. Produced by Hasse W. Tullbergs. Directed by Captain Ragnar Ring. Running time: c. 5 min.

2. *Our Daily Bread* (1922), advertising film for bakery products of the Consumer's Cooperative Association of Stockholm. Produced by Fribergs Filmbrya. Directed by Captain Ragnar Ring. Running time: c. 8 min.

3. *Luffar-Petter* (*Peter the Tramp*) (1922). Produced, directed and written by Erik A. Petschler. Photography by Oscar Norberg. Released in Stockholm, December 26, 1922. Slapstick comedy of a soldier and his romantic highjinks. Cast: Erik A. Petschler (Fire Lieutenant Erik Silverjalm and Max August Petterson), Greta Gustafson (Greta), Helmer Larsson (artillery captain), Fredrik Olsson (police officer), Tyra Ryman (Tyra), Gucken Cederborg (mayor's wife). Running time: c. 37 min.

4. *The Saga of Gösta Berling* (1924). Produced by Svensk Filmindustri. Directed by Mauritz Stiller. Screenplay by Mauritz Stiller and Ragnar Hyltén-Cavallius from the novel by Selma Lagerlöf. Photography by Julius Jaenzon. Released in Stockholm, March 10 (Part I) and March 17 (Part II), 1924. A defrocked minister sins long and hard before falling in love with, and being redeemed by, a pure young countess. Cast: Lars Hanson (Gösta Berling), Gerda Lundeqvist (Majorskan Samzelius), Otto Elg-Lundberg (Major Samzelius), Sixten Malmerfeldt

(Melchior Sinclair), Karin Swanström (Gustafva Sinclair), Jenny Hasselqvist (Marianne Sinclair), Ellen Cederström (Countess Martha Dohna), Mona Mårtenson (Countess Ebba Dohna), Torsten Hammarén (Count Henrik Dohna), Greta Garbo (Countess Elisabeth Dohna). Running time: 91 min. (U.S. condensed version); other prints exist ranging in length from 105 to 165 min.

5. *Die Freudlose Gasse* (*The Joyless Street*) (1925). Produced by Sofar-Film. Directed by G. W. Pabst. Screenplay by Pabst and Willy Haas from the novel by Hugo Bettauer. Photography by Guido Seeber. Released in Berlin, May 18, 1925. In corrupt, chaotic postwar Vienna, a young woman on the verge of prostitution is saved by a Yankee lieutenant. Cast: Jaro Fürth (Councillor Franz Rumfort), Werner Krauss (butcher of Melchior Street), Asta Nielsen (Maria Lechner), Greta Garbo (Greta Rumfort), Valeska Gert (Frau Greifer), Einar Hanson (Lieutenant Davy), Agnes Esterhazy (Regina Rosenow), Loni Nest (Rosa Rumfort), Egon Stirner (Henry Stuart). Running time: 96 min.

All of Garbo's subsequent films were produced for Metro-Goldwyn-Mayer.

6. *Torrent* (1926). Produced by Irving Thalberg. Directed by Monta Bell. Screenplay by Dorothy Farnum from the novel *Entre Naranjos* by Vicente Blasco Ibáñez. Titles by Katherine Hilliker and H. H. Caldwell. Edited by Frank Sullivan. Photography by William Daniels. Released February 21, 1926. In a Spanish village, a mother-dominated young politician and a budding diva, of different classes, are continually separated and bitterly reunited. Cast: Greta Garbo (Leonora), Ricardo Cortez (Don Rafael Brull), Gertrude Olmstead (Remedios), Edward Connelly (Pedro Moreno), Lucien Littlefield (Cupido), Martha Mattox (Doña Bernarda Brull), Lucy Beaumont (Doña Pepa), Tully Marshall (Don Andreas). Running time: 68 min. (6,679 feet). Production days: 23. Cost: $250,000. Earnings: domestic $460,000; foreign $208,000; total $668,000. Profit: $126,000.

7. *The Temptress* (1926). Produced by Irving Thalberg. Directed initially by Mauritz Stiller, who was replaced by Fred Niblo. Screenplay by Dorothy Farnum from the novel *La Tierra de Todos* by Vicente Blasco Ibáñez. Titles by Marion Ainslee. Photography by Tony Gaudio. Edited by Lloyd Nosler. Released October 10, 1926. A married woman follows her lover, an engineer, to the wilds of Argentina with resultant tragedy and ruin. Cast: Greto Garbo (Elena), Antonio Moreno (Robledo), Roy D'Arcy (Manos Duros), Marc McDermott (M. Fontenoy), Lionel Barrymore (Canterac), Virginia Browne Faire (Celinda), Armand Kaliz (Torre Blanca), Alys Murrell (Josephine). Running time: 95 min. (8,862 feet). Production days: 83. Cost: $669,000. Earnings: domestic $587,000; foreign $378,000; total $965,000. Loss: $43,000.

8. *Flesh and the Devil* (1927). Produced by Irving Thalberg. Directed by Clarence Brown. Screenplay by Benjamin Glazer from the novel *The Undying Past* by Hermann Sudermann. Titles by Marion Ainslee. Photography by William Daniels. Edited by Lloyd Nosler. Released January 9, 1927. An unfaithful wife vamps two soldier buddies and meets a violent end after luring one of them into resuming their affair. Cast: Greta Garbo (Felicitas), John Gilbert (Leo Von Sellinthin), Lars Hanson (Ulrich Van Kletzingk), Barbara Kent (Hertha Prochvitz), William Orlamond (Uncle Kutowski), George Fawcett (Pastor Breckenburg), Eugenie Besserer (Leo's mother), Marc McDermott (Count Von Rhaden). Running time: 95 min. (8,759

feet). Production days: 43. Cost: $373,000. Earnings: domestic $603,000; foreign $658,000; total $1,261,000. Profit: $466,000.

9. *Love* (1927). Produced by Irving Thalberg. Directed by Edmund Goulding. Screenplay by Francis Marion from the novel *Anna Karenina* by Leo Tolstoy. Titles by Marion Ainslee and Ruth Cummings. Photography by William Daniels. Edited by Hugh Wynn. Released November 29, 1927. A woman leaves her husband and child for her lover, then realizes she is losing him as well. Cast: Greta Garbo (Anna Karenina), John Gilbert (Vronsky), George Fawcett (Grand Duke), Emily Fitzroy (Grand Duchess), Brandon Hurst (Karenin), Philippe de Lacy (Seryosha). Running time: 84 min. (7,351 feet). Production days: 48. Cost $488,000. Earnings: domestic $946,000; foreign $731,000; total $1,677,000. Profit: $571,000.

10. *The Divine Woman* (1928). Produced by Irving Thalberg. Directed by Victor Seastrom. Screenplay by Dorothy Farnum from the play *Starlight* by Gladys Unger. Titles by John Colton. Photography by Oliver Marsh. Edited by Conrad A. Nervig. Released January 14, 1928. A great stage star—loosely based on Sarah Bernhardt—finds true love with a soldier. Cast: Greta Garbo (Marianne), Lars Hanson (Lucien), Lowell Sherman (M. Legrande), Polly Moran (Mme. Pigonier), Dorothy Cumming (Mme. Zizi Rouck), John Mack Brown (Jean Lery), Cesare Gravina (Gigi), Paulette Duval (Paulette). Running time 80 min. (7,135 feet). Production days: 35. Cost: $267,000. Earnings: domestic $541,000; foreign $390,000; total $931,000. Profit: $354,000. This is the only Garbo film that has not survived.

11. *The Mysterious Lady* (1928). Produced by Harry Rapf. Directed by Fred Niblo. Screenplay by Bess Meredyth from the novel *War in the Dark* by Ludwig Wolff. Titles by Marion Ainslee and Ruth Cummings. Photography by William Daniels. Edited by Margaret Booth. Released August 4, 1928. A Russian spy double-crosses her chief in favor of her Austrian lover. Cast: Greta Garbo (Tania), Conrad Nagel (Karl), Gustav von Seyffertitz (General Alexandroff), Edward Connelly (Colonel Von Raden), Albert Pollett (Max), Richard Alexander (General's Aide). Running time: 96 min. (7,757 feet). Production days: 31. Cost: $337,000. Earnings: domestic $543,000; foreign $551,000; total $1,084,000. Profit: $369,000.

12. *A Woman of Affairs* (1928). Produced by Irving Thalberg. Directed by Clarence Brown. Screenplay by Bess Meredyth from the novel *The Green Hat* by Michael Arlen. Photography by William Daniels. Edited by Hugh Wynn. Released January 19, 1929. Star-crossed English lovers, thwarted by their families and by scandal, go separate ways to self-sacrifice. Cast: Greta Garbo (Diana), John Gilbert (Neville), Lewis Stone (Hugh), John Mack Brown (David), Douglas Fairbanks, Jr. (Geoffrey), Hobart Bosworth (Sir Montague), Dorothy Sebastian (Constance). Running time: 108 min. (8,716 feet). Production days: 39. Cost: $383,000. Earnings: domestic $850,000; foreign $520,000; total $1,370,000. Profit: $417,000.

13. *Wild Orchids* (1929). Produced by Irving Thalberg. Directed by Sidney Franklin. Screenplay by Hans Kraly, Richard Schayer, and Willis Goldbeck from an original story, "Heat," by John Colton. Photography by William Daniels. Titles by Marion Ainslee. Edited by Conrad Nervig. Released March 30, 1929. A bored but faithful wife has a near-affair with a Javanese prince before finally reconciling with her husband. Cast: Greta Garbo (Lillie Sterling), Lewis Stone (John Sterling), Nils Asther (Prince De Gace). Running time: 102 min. (9,558 feet).

Production days: 36. Cost: $322,000. Earnings: domestic $622,000; foreign, $543,000; total $1,165,000. Profit: $380,000.

14. *The Single Standard* (1929). Produced by Hunt Stromberg. Directed by John S. Robertson. Screenplay by Josephine Lovett from the novel by Adela Rogers St. John. Photography by Oliver Marsh. Titles by Marion Ainslee. Edited by Blanche Sewell. Released July 27, 1929. A San Francisco debutante and "free soul" has a seagoing love affair but finally decides her husband and child are more important. Cast: Greta Garbo (Arden Stuart), Nils Asther (Packy Cannon), John Mack Brown (Tommy Hewlett), Dorothy Sebastian (Mercedes), Lane Chandler (Ding Stuart), Robert Castle (Anthony Kendall), Mahlon Hamilton (Mr. Glendenning), Kathlyn Williams (Mrs. Glendenning). Running time: 73 min. (6,559 feet). Production days: 45. Cost: $336,000. Earnings: domestic $659,000; foreign $389,000; total $1,048,000. Profit: $333,000.

15. *A Man's Man* (1929). Produced by MGM. Directed by James Cruz. Screenplay by Forrest Halsey from the 1925 play by Patrick Kearney. Romance between a soda-fountain boy and a Hollywood actress. Cast: William Haines, Josephine Dunn, May Busch, Sam Hardy. In brief documentary footage, Garbo, John Gilbert, and director Fred Niblo make cameo appearances as themselves at a movie premiere.

16. *The Kiss* (1929). Produced by Albert Lewin. Directed by Jacques Feyder. Screenplay by Hans Kraly from a story by George M. Saville. Photography by William Daniels. Edited by Ben Lewis. Released November 15, 1929. A jealous husband, discovering his wife in a clinch with a young man, is murdered and the wife is defended in court by her former lover. Cast: Greta Garbo (Mme. Irene Guarry), Conrad Nagel (André), Anders Randolf (M. Guarry), Holmes Herbert (Lassalle), Lew Ayres (Pierre), George Davis (Durant). Running time: 89 min. (5,749 feet). Production days: 40. Cost: $257,000. Earnings: domestic $518,000; foreign $387,000; total $905,000. Profit: $448,000.

17. *Anna Christie* (1930). Produced by Irving Thalberg. Directed by Clarence Brown. Screenplay by Frances Marion from the play by Eugene O'Neill. Photography by William Daniels. Edited by Hugh Wynn. A fallen woman saves a sailor from drowning and they fall in problematic love. Released March 14, 1930. Cast: Greta Garbo (Anna), Charles Bickford (Matt Burke), Marie Dressler (Marthy), George F. Marion (Chris), James T. Mack (Johnny the Priest), Lee Phelps (Larry). Running time: 74 min. (8,263 feet). Production days: 30. Cost: $376,000. Earnings: domestic $1,013,000; foreign $486,000; total $1,499,000. Profit: $576,000.

18. *Anna Christie* (1930), German version. Produced by MGM. Directed by Jacques Feyder. (Other production credits same as above.) Cast: Greta Garbo (Anna), Hans Junkermann (Matt Burke), Salka Steuermann [Viertel] (Marthy), Theo Shall (Chris), Hermann Bing (Johnny). Running time: 82 min. Production days: 20. Cost and earnings figures combined with the English version, above.

19. *Romance* (1930). Produced by Paul Bern. Directed by Clarence Brown. Screenplay by Bess Meredyth and Edwin Justus Mayer from the play *Signora Cavallini* by Edward Sheldon. Photography by William Daniels. Edited by Hugh Wynn and Leslie F. Wilder. Released

August 22, 1930. A bishop tells his grandson the story of his heartbreaking affair with an opera star. Cast: Greta Garbo (Rita Cavallini), Lewis Stone (Cornelius Van Tuyl), Gavin Gordon (Tom Armstrong), Elliott Nugent (Harry), Florence Lake (Susan Van Tuyl), Clara Blandick (Miss Armstrong), Henry Armetta (Beppo). Running time: 76 min. (7,081 feet). Production days: 30. Cost: $496,000. Earnings: domestic $733,000; foreign $523,000; total $1,256,000. Profit: $287,000.

20. *Inspiration* (1931). Produced by Irving Thalberg. Directed by Clarence Brown. Story and screenplay by Gene Markey, loosely derived from Alphonse Daudet's *Sappho*. Photography by William Daniels. Edited by Conrad A. Nervig. Released February 6, 1931. An artist's model loves a stuffy young diplomat but leaves him for the sake of his career. Cast: Greta Garbo (Yvonne), Robert Montgomery (André), Lewis Stone (Delval), Marjorie Rambeau (Lulu), Judith Vosselli (Odette), Beryl Mercer (Marthe), John Miljan (Coutant), Edwin Maxwell (Julian Montell). Running time: 74 min. (7,159 feet). Production days: 32. Cost: $438,000. Earnings: domestic $725,000; foreign $402,000; total $1,127,000. Profit: $286,000.

21. *Susan Lenox: Her Fall and Rise* (1931). Produced by Paul Bern. Directed by Robert Z. Leonard. Screenplay by Wanda Tuchock from the novel by David Graham Phillips. Dialogue by Zelda Sears, Edith Fitzgerald, and Leon Gordon. Photography by William Daniels. Edited by Margaret Booth. Released October 16, 1931. To escape her rape-minded "fiancé," a farm girl runs away, joins a carnival, and eventually finds love with a feisty engineer. Cast: Greta Garbo (Susan Lenox), Clark Gable (Rodney), Jean Hersholt (Ohlin), John Miljan (Burlingham), Alan Hale (Mondstrum), Hale Hamilton (Mike Kelly), Hilda Vaughn (Astrid), Russell Simpson (Doctor). Running time: 76 min. (7,143 feet). Production days: 49. Cost: $580,000. Earnings: domestic $806,000; foreign $700,000; total $1,506,000. Profit: $364,000.

22. *Mata Hari* (1931). Produced by MGM. Directed by George Fitzmaurice. Original story and screenplay by Benjamin Glazer and Leo Birinski. Dialogue by Doris Anderson and Gilbert Emery. Photography by William Daniels. Edited by Frank Sullivan. Released December 31, 1931. The legendary Dutch spy poses as a dancer in Paris, makes good headway with two Russian officers, but keeps her date with the firing squad. Cast: Greta Garbo (Mata Hari), Ramon Navarro (Lt. Alexis Rosanoff), Lionel Barrymore (General Shubin), Lewis Stone (Adriani), C. Henry Gordon (Dubois), Karen Morley (Carlotta), Alec B. Francis (Caros), Blanche Frederici (Sister Angelica). Running time: 90 min. (8,740 feet). Production days: 43. Cost: $558,000. Earnings: domestic $931,000. foreign $1,296,000; total $2,227,000. Profit: $879,000. Domestic reissue of 1940 and 1941: $81,000 earnings, $27,000 profit.

23. *Grand Hotel* (1932). Produced by Paul Bern. Directed by Edmund Goulding. Screenplay by William Drake from the play by Vicki Baum. Photography by William Daniels. Edited by Blanche Sewell. Released April 12, 1932. The intertwining stories of troubled, all-star guests at Berlin's Grand Hotel. Cast: Greta Garbo (Grushinskaya), John Barrymore (Baron von Gaigern), Joan Crawford (Flaemmchen), Wallace Beery (Preysing), Lionel Barrymore (Otto Kringelein), Jean Hersholt (Senf), Robert McWade (Meierheim), Purnell B. Pratt (Zinnowitz), Lewis Stone (Dr. Otternschlag), Tully Marshall (Gerstenkorn). Running time: 113 min. (10,545 feet). Production days: 49. Cost: $700,000. Earnings: domestic $1,235,000; foreign $1,359,000; total $2,594,000. Profit: $947,000.

24. *As You Desire Me* (1932). Produced by Paul Bern. Directed by George Fitzmaurice. Screenplay and dialogue by Gene Markey from the play by Luigi Pirandello. Photography by William Daniels. Edited by George Hively. Released June 2, 1932. A cabaret artist from Budapest has amnesia and is torn between her sadistic "protector" and the man who claims to be her true husband. Cast: Greta Garbo (Maria/Zara), Melvyn Douglas (Count Bruno Varelli), Erich von Stroheim (Carol Salter), Owen Moore (Tony Boffie), Hedda Hopper (Mme. Mantari), Rafaela Ottiano (Lena), Warburton Gamble (Baron), Albert Conti (Captain). Running time: 71 min. (6,533 feet). Production days: 42. Cost: $469,000. Earnings: domestic $705,000; foreign $658,000; total $1,362,000. Profit: $449,000.

25. *Queen Christina* (1933). Produced by Walter Wanger. Directed by Rouben Mamoulian. Screenplay by H. M. Harwood and Salka Viertel from a story by Salka Viertel and Margaret F. Levino. Dialogue by S. N. Behrman. Photography by William Daniels. Music by Herbert Stothart. Edited by Blanche Sewell. Released December 26, 1933. The Swedish queen falls in love with a Spanish ambassador and abdicates her throne. Cast: Greta Garbo (Queen Christina), John Gilbert (Don Antonio de la Prada), Ian Keith (Magnus), Lewis Stone (Chancellor Oxenstierna), Elizabeth Young (Ebba), C. Aubrey Smith (Aage), Reginald Owen (Prince Charles Gustavus), George Renevent (French ambassador). Running time: 97 min. (9,298 feet). Production days: 68. Cost: $1,144,000. Earnings: domestic $767,000; foreign $1,843,000; total $2,610,000. Profit: $632,000.

26. *The Painted Veil* (1934). Produced by Hunt Stromberg. Directed by Richard Boleslawski. Screenplay by John Meehan, Salka Viertel, and Edith Fitzgerland from the novel by W. Somerset Maugham. Photography by William Daniels. Edited by Hugh Wynn. Music by Herbert Stothart. Released December 7, 1934. In China, a doctor's wife has an affair with a diplomat but finds salvation by helping her husband and his cholera victims. Cast: Greta Garbo (Katrin), Herbert Marshall (Walter Fane), George Brent (Jack Townsend), Warner Oland (General Yu), Jean Hersholt (Herr Koerber), Beulah Bondi (Frau Koerber), Katherine Alexander (Mrs. Townsend), Cecilia Parker (Olga), Soo Yong (Amah). Running time: 83 min. (7,785 feet). Production days: 59. Cost: $947,000 Earnings: domestic $538,000; foreign $1,120,000; total $1,658,000. Profit: $138,000.

27. *Anna Karenina* (1935). Produced by David O. Selznick. Directed by Clarence Brown. Screenplay by Clemence Dane, Salka Viertel, and S. N. Behrman from the novel by Leo Tolstoy. Photography by William Daniels. Edited by Robert J. Kern. Music by Herbert Stothart. Released August 30, 1935. A woman leaves her husband and child for her lover, then loses him, too. Cast: Greta Garbo (Anna Karenina), Frederic March (Vronsky), Freddie Batholomew (Sergei), Maureen O'Sullivan (Kitty), May Robson (Countess Vronsky), Basil Rathbone (Karenin), Reginald Owen (Stiva), Reginald Denny (Yashvin). Running time: 95 min. (8,545 feet). Production days: 46. Cost $1,152,000. Earnings: domestic $865,000; foreign $1,439,000; total $2,304,000. Profit: $320,000.

28. *Camille* (1936). Produced by Irving Thalberg. Directed by George Cukor. Screenplay by Zoe Akins, Francis Marion, and James Hilton from the novel and play *La Dame aux Camellias* by Alexander Dumas *fils*. Photography by William Daniels. Edited by Margaret Booth. Music by Herbert Stothart. Released January 22, 1937. A beautiful courtesan forsakes her beloved

so as not to ruin his life and career. Cast: Greta Garbo (Marguerite), Robert Taylor (Armand), Henry Daniell (Baron de Varville), Lenore Ulric (Olympe), Laura Hope Crews (Prudence), Lionel Barrymore (Monsieur Duval), Rex O'Malley (Gaston), Elizabeth Allan (Nichette), Jessie Ralph (Nanine). Running time: 108 min. (9,929 feet). Production days: 75. Cost: $1,486,000. Earnings: domestic $1,154,000; foreign $1,688,000; total $2,842,000. Profit: $388,000. Domestic reissue of 1954 and 1955: $300,000 earnings, $134,000 profit.

29. *Conquest* (European title: *Marie Walewska*) (1937). Produced by Bernard H. Hyman. Directed by Clarence Brown. Screenplay by Samuel Hoffenstein, Salka Viertel, and S. N. Behrman from the novel *Pani Walewska* by Waclaw Gasiorowski and a play by Helen Jerome. Photography by Karl Freund. Edited by Tom Held. Music by Herbert Stothart. Released November 4, 1937. The love affair between Napoleon and the Polish countess-patriot Marie Walewska. Cast: Greta Garbo (Marie Walewska), Charles Boyer (Napoleon), Reginald Owen (Talleyrand), Alan Marshal (Captain d'Ornano), Henry Stephenson (Count Walewski), Leif Erickson (Paul Lachinski), Dame May Whitty (Laetitia Bonaparte), C. Henry Gordon (Prince Poniatowski), Maria Ouspenskaya (Countess Pelagia). Running time: 112 min. (10,183 feet). Production days: 127. Cost: $2,732,000. Earnings: domestic $730,000; foreign $1,411,000; total $2,141,000. Loss: $1,397,000.

30. *Ninotchka* (1939). Produced and directed by Ernst Lubitsch. Screenplay by Charles Brackett, Billy Wilder, and Walter Reisch from a story by Melchior Lengyel. Photography by William Daniels. Edited by Gene Ruggiero. Music by Werner R. Heymann. Released November 9, 1939. A Soviet woman commissar comes to Paris, strictly on business, but falls in love with a decadent French playboy in spite of herself. Cast: Greta Garbo (Ninotchka), Melvyn Douglas (Count Leon d'Algout), Ina Claire (Duchess Swana), Sig Rumann (Iranoff), Felix Bressart (Buljanoff), Alexander Granach (Kopalski), Bela Lugosi (Commissar Razinin), Gregory Gaye (Count Rakonin). Running time: 110 min. (10,068 feet). Production days: 57. Cost: $1,365,000. Earnings: domestic $1,187,000; foreign $1,092,000; total $2,279,000. Profit: $138,000. Reissue of 1952 and 1953: Earnings $63,000 domestic; $506,000 foreign; $569,000 total. Profit: $416,000.

31. *Two-Faced Woman* (1941). Produced by Gottfried Reinhardt. Directed by George Cukor. Screenplay by S. N. Behrman, Salka Viertel, and George Oppenheimer from the play by Ludwig Fulda. Photography by Joseph Ruttenberg. Edited by George Boemler. Music by Bronislau Kaper. Released December 31, 1941. A ski instructress impersonates her own twin in order to compete with a glamorous rival and win back her own husband. Cast: Greta Garbo (Karin), Melvyn Douglas (Larry Blake), Constance Bennett (Griselda Vaughn), Roland Young (O. O. Miller), Robert Sterling (Dick Williams), Ruth Gordon (Miss Ellis), Frances Carson (Miss Dunbar), Bob Alton (dancer). Running time: 94 min. (8,236 feet). Production days: 60. Cost: $1,247,000. Earnings: domestic $875,000; foreign $925,000; total $1,800,000. Loss: $62,000.

CHAPTER 1:
GRETA GUSTAFSSON 1905–1922

p. 3 "I was born": GG to Rilla Page Palmborg, *The Private Life of Greta Garbo* (New York: Doubleday, 1931), 1.

4 "There is so": Selma Lagerlöf, *The Saga of Gösta Berling* (Karlstad, Sweden: Press' Förlagstryckeri, 1982), 300.

5 "Some people were": Quoted in John Bainbridge, *Garbo* (New York: Doubleday, 1955), 22.

Birth of brother Sven: Sven Broman, *Garbo on Garbo* (London: Bloomsbury, 1991), 12–15.

7 Adoption offer: Frederick Sands and Sven Broman, *The Divine Garbo* (New York: Grosset & Dunlap, 1979), 13.

Farm life: Raymond Daum, "Greta Garbo: Memories of a Swedish Christmas," *Scandinavian Review* (Winter 1990), 66–70.

"and came home": Kaj Gynt as told to Adela Rogers St. John, *Liberty* (August 25, 1934).

8 "Local custom was": Sands and Broman, *The Divine Garbo*, 13–14.

"She was a": Gray Reisfield to BP (New York, May 7, 1991).

"I was always": Åke Sundborg, "That Gustafsson Girl" (Part I), *Photoplay* (April 1930), 41.

9 "My sister! My": Ibid., 42; variant in Lars Saxon "Greta Garbo Ungomsminnen," *Lektyr* (1931), Stockholm.

Söder and Göta: Fritiof Billquist, *Garbo* (New York: Putnam, 1960), 9.

10 "I'm going to": Sands and Broman, 14–15; similar Uncle David account in Billquist, 19–20.

10 "When I was a little": Sundborg (Part I), 42–43.

11 "Felt that shyness": Selma Lagerlöf, *Nils Holgersson's Wonderful Journey* (London: Puffin Books, 1990), 111.

12 "I lived in": Broman, 20, quoting *Lektyr* (1931), probably taken from Sundborg. "I went to": Ibid., 43.

13 "When I was seven": Sundborg (Part I), 42–43.

14 "No-oo! A sheik": Billquist, 16.

"When we were": Elizabeth Malcolm, *Movie Mirror* (August 1935), 26.

16 GG running away: Billquist, 13.

"Everywhere people seemed": Sundborg (Part I), 127.

Drunk-on-pavement story: Malcolm, 68; and Billquist, 13–14. This incident was, indeed, often misreported later as involving her own father.

GG running away: Sands and Broman, 16–17.

17 "Our lives were": Ibid., 20–21, quoting GG in *Lektyr*.

Sven's child: Ibid., 17; rebuttal by Gray Reisfield to BP (New York, May 7, 1991).

18 "Roll, Jordan, Roll": Daum, 66–70.

"She found that": Quoted by S. N. Behrman to David Davidson (October 2, 1962).

"From that time": GG in *Lektyr*, quoted in Sands and Broman, 20–21.

19 "I never remember": Reisfield to BP.

"Well, so you": GG to Eva Blomgren (August 7, 1920), quoted in Billquist, 22–24.

21 "Like most Söder": Billquist, 15.

"Very free": Einar Lauritzen to BP (Stockholm, August 17, 1991).

"We were all": Bainbridge, 28.

22 Brisson singles GG out: Carl Brisson, *London Sunday Express* (June 1, 1930).

"Never! I never": Sundborg (Part I), 129 and 128.

23 GG's movie idols: Billquist, 15; Malcolm, 68.

Attic Theater: Malcolm, 68.

Josef Fischer encounter: Billquist, 17–18.

GG at PUB: Bainbridge, 30; and Sundborg, 127. A less likely version has it that she got the job through Kristian Bergström, the PUB owner's son, who had been one of her customers at the Ekengren barbershop in Söder—in which case, he must have been slumming that day.

"I have got": GG to Eva Blomgren, quoted in Billquist, 24.

24 "I was really": Sundborg (Part I), 128.

"As beautiful as": Max Gumpel, *Tales and Reality*, quoted in Bainbridge, 200.

25 "None of us could excel": Rogers St. John, *Liberty* (August 25, 1934).

"They all look": Billquist, 24.

"Eva child, . . . To": Ibid., 27.

26 "That was not": Sundborg (Part I), 128.

"Miss Gustafsson should": Sands and Broman, 24–25.

29 GG wants Eva to seduce Sven: Billquist, 29.

"I felt that": Sundborg (Part I), 129.

"I am the": *Lektyr*, probably taken from Sundborg quote about preferring to play alone as a child.

31 GG's formative elements: Carolyn G. Heilbrun, *Writing a Woman's Life* (New York: Ballantine, 1989), 52–53.

CHAPTER 2:
BEAUTY AND THE BEAST 1922–1924

33 Petschler's account of spotting Garbo: Fritzlof Billquist, *Garbo* (New York: Putnam's, 1960), 32–33.

34 "To this day": Åke Sundborg, "That Gustafsson Girl" (Part I), *Photoplay* (April 1930), 48 and 130.

"I don't care . . . what is best for you": Sundborg, 130.

"Greta was quite shy": Billquist, 34.

"I particularly remember": Ibid., 35.

36 "Miss Gustafsson had": Ibid., 36.

Swedish theaters: John Bainbridge, *Garbo* (New York: Doubleday, 1955), 29.

37 "as young people": Sundborg (Part I), 130.

"May I just wait": Billquist, 39.

"my handwriting is": Ibid., 40.

38 "I'm haunted by": Henrik Ibsen, *The Lady from the Sea* (London: Penguin, 1965), 265; Billquist says the third audition piece was from Selma Lagerlöf's *Wedding at Ulvasa*.

"I approached the": Sundborg (Part I), 130.

Royal Danish Theatre Academy competition: Billquist, 40.

"There were about": Combined quotations from Val Lewton, "Moving Picture Stories" (October 13, 1931), 31; and Sundborg (Part I), 131.

"Oh, God, I": Sundborg (Part I), 131.

39 "When she did": Bainbridge, 41–42.

Poverty in school: Ibid., 46.

"We never knew": Possibly Mimi Pollack, quoted in *Garbo*, by Brad Steiger and Chaw Mank (Chicago: Camerarts, 1965), 21.

"It was a necessary": Sundborg (Part I), 131.

Garbo among friends: Billquist, 45–50.

"I was a": Lewton, 31.

41 "Any forward movement": Garbo's drama school notebook, courtesy of Swedish Film Institute. Translation by Ann Sitrick.

"What a wonderful": Sundborg (Part I), 131.

"always shy": Benchley, "This is Garbo," *Collier's* (March 1, 1952), 13.

Karlsbad performance: Billquist, 46–47.

"Who was Maria": Ibid., 47.

"I should like": Ibid., 49.

42 "In the winter": Ibid.

Hermione in *Winter's Tale*: Sundborg (Part I), 131.

Garbo roles in school: Billquist, 50–51.

Stiller during political upheaval in Helsinki: Ibid., 58.

43 Nature: Aleksander Kwiatkowski, *Swedish Film Classics: A Pictorial Survey of 25 Films from 1913 to 1957* (New York: Dover, 1983), vi–vii.

"You may film": Billquist, 59.

Bard of Sweden: Bosley Crowther, *The Great Films* (New York: Putnam's, 1967), 32.

Sjöström-Stiller comparison: Bardéche and Brasillach, quoted in Kwiatkowski, vi.

44 Stiller ahead of Sjöström: Bengt Forslund, *Victor Sjöström, His Life and His Work*
     (New York: Zoëtrope, 1988), 96.

45 *The Phantom Carriage*: Kwiatkowski, 102ff.
     Stiller and Sjöström relationship: Forslund, 96–99.
     "What we talked": "Oskrivna memoarer," *Dagens Nyheter* (May 7, 1933).

46 Esbenson's suicide: Forslund, 98.
     "the Stanislavski of ": David Robinson, *Hollywood in the Twenties* (New York: Barnes,
     1968), 70.
     Stiller public and private life: Alexander Walker, *Sex in the Movies* (Middlesex, U.K.:
     Penguin, 1968), 107.

47 "I was over-awed": Sundborg (Part I), 132.

48 "If you want": Billquist, 53.
     "Look, isn't she": Bainbridge, 52.
     "It was hard": Sundborg (Part I), 132.

49 "That's because she's": Billquist, 55.
     "I was deliriously happy": Sundborg (Part I), 132.
     Name derived from Polish word: Antoni Gronowicz, *Garbo, Her Story* (New York:
     Simon & Schuster, 1990), 170–71.
     Garbo named as derivation of Gabor: See Walker, 108, note 48. A similar account
     from Bengt Idestam-Almquist is found in Bainbridge, 50.

50 "a mysterious being": Frederick L. Collins, "Why Garbo is Making her Last Picture,"
     Liberty (May 30, 1936), 4; and Billquist, 48. Gray Reisfield to BP (New York, May 7,
     1991) and Norwegian actress Liv Ullmann to BP (Boston, May 18, 1992) are among
     the Scandinavians who debunk the "wood sprite" definition. The claim and the
     confusion stem from the archaic Norwegian word *gardbo*, a type of "farm-guardian
     spirit" akin to the Swedish *nisse* or *tomte* elves. But there is no way Stiller would have
     known this. Source: *Scandinavian Folk Tales*, ed. and trans. Jacqueline Simpson (Lon-
     don: Penguin, 1988), 173.
     Mimi Pollack claim concerning Garbo name: Billquist, 48.
     Female pseudonym: Carolyn G. Heilbrun, *Writing a Woman's Life* (New York: Bal-
     lantine, 1989), 33, 110, and 116.

51 Stiller intuitive sense: Bainbridge, 53–54.
     Stiller's belief in Garbo: Walker, 107.
     Lagerlöf approves screenplay: Kwiatkowski, 29.
     Production details: Bainbridge, 54–55.

52 "You move your": Billquist, 60.

53 "I'm doing as" and "Damn it, Stiller!" and "No, but Garbo": Ibid.
     "On the first": Sundborg (Part I), 133.
     "She cried a": Bainbridge, 55, quoting "a man closely associated with the production."

54 Asked for champagne: Billquist, 62.
     "She's afraid of ": S. N. Behrman to David Davidson (October 2, 1962).
     "Stiller has [cast]" and "I venture the paradox": Sundborg, 133.

56 "I didn't think": Billquist, 63.
     "To us, she": Bainbridge, 55.

57 "You must not": Ibid., 56.
     Stiller molds her personality: Ibid., 56–57.

58 "She is like": Ibid., 57.

"When he was very displeased": Carl Brisson, *London Sunday Express* (June 1, 1930).

Garbo adopting Stiller characteristics and phobias: Walker, 108.

59 "She was always sorry": Valeska Gert to David Diamond, circa 1950.

"I had never": Åke Sundborg, "That Gustafsson Girl" (Part II), *Photoplay* (May 1930), 40.

"Put your feet": Billquist, 66.

"Berlin received us": Sundborg (Part II), 40–41.

"Don't you try": Billquist, 67.

60 Trianon letter to Stiller ("Not to worry"): David Schratter letter to Mauritz Stiller (September 10, 1924), translated by Jan-Christopher Horak of Eastman House; document courtesy of Swedish Film Institute.

61 Constantinople trip and residence: Bainbridge, 65–67; and Billquist, 69.

63 Swedish legation party: Billquist, 69.

Financial arrangements: Marc Sorkin, "Six Talks on G. W. Pabst," *Cinemages* 3 (May 1955), 27.

"I didn't receive": Ruth Phillips, *New York Mirror* (March 11, 1938); Bainbridge, 67.

"Don't worry": Bainbridge, 67.

CHAPTER 3:
PABST AND BERLIN 1925

65 SFI correspondence: Stiller's secret negotiations with MGM and UFA: MGM telegrams to Stiller (November 8 and 13, 1924); L. B. Mayer letter to Stiller (November 27, 1924); miscellaneous correspondence to and from Stiller, courtesy Swedish Film Institute.

Trio at Esplanade Hotel: John Bainbridge, *Garbo* (New York: Doubleday, 1955), 68. Fritzlof Billquist, *Garbo* (New York: Putnam, 1960), 71 and 74, says they were in "a luxurious pensione at the Tiergarten" and moved to the Esplanade only after MS secured GG's fat contract with Pabst.

66 *Gösta Berling* still playing: Salka Viertel, *The Kindness of Strangers* (New York: Holt, Rhinehart and Winston, 1969), 110–11.

"We saw Garbo": Marc Sorkin, quoted in Gideon Bachmann, ed., "Six Talks on G. W. Pabst," *Cinemages* 3 (May 1955), 26–30.

Ibid., 28. Billquist, 71, says that Garbo became doubtful about Stiller's ability to negotiate the Pabst deal, took matters into her own hands, and went to see the great Danish star Asta Nielsen, who said she would ask Pabst to give her a part and did so.

67 The New Objectivity: Siegfried Kracauer, *From Caligari to Hitler: A Psychological History of the German Film* (Princeton: Princeton University Press, 1947), 165–66.

Pillars and nuances: Harry Potamkin, "Pabst and the Social Film," *Hound & Horn*, vol. 6, no. 2 (January–March 1933), 294.

68 "In order to": Louise Brooks, *Lulu in Hollywood* (New York: Knopf, 1982), 100–101.

"Pabst never demonstrated": Sorkin, 37.

"The only effective": Lotte Eisner, *The Haunted Screen* (Berkeley and Los Angeles: University of California Press, 1969), 43.

"As I have": David Robinson, *Chaplin: His Life and Art* (New York: McGraw-Hill, 1985), 321.

69 "Everybody, down to": Sorkin, 38 and 40.

"If you find": Ibid., 37.

"that movies were": Sorkin, 42.

70 "Stiller then gave": Sorkin, 29.

Kodak vs. Agfa film: Ibid., 30.

"as if I'd": Bainbridge, 70.

Garbo's nervous twitch: Alexander Walker, *Sex in the Movies* (Middlesex, U.K.: Penguin, 1968), 109.

"Such a face": Billquist, 72–73.

73 "This was a time": Sorkin, 30.

74 American medicine man: Morton Cooper, "Garbo," *Diner's Club Magazine* (December 1964), 63–64.

"The film [shows] how": Patrice Petro, "Film Censorship and the Female Spectator," in Eric Rentschler, ed., *The Films of G. W. Pabst: An Extraterritorial Cinema* (New Brunswick, N.J.: Rutgers University Press, 1990), 38.

"The Germanic visions": Eisner, 251.

"wavering between images": Kracauer, 168.

76 "No film or novel": Paul Rotha, *The Film Till Now* (Middlesex, U.K.: Hamlyn House, 1967), 264.

Pabst's influence on Garbo's style of acting: George Pratt's notes on *Joyless Street* (February 5, 1953).

"No director can": Louise Brooks letter to George Pratt (September 22, 1969).

"When I met": Brooks to Ricky Leacock, Lulu in Berlin film documentary transcript (March 1974), 28.

Garbo wants to stay in Berlin: Rilla Page Palmborg, *The Private Life of Greta Garbo* (New York: Doubleday, 1931), 33–34.

77 "Stay with me": Bainbridge, 72.

"everyone was screaming": Brooks to Pauline Kael (May 26, 1962).

CHAPTER 4:
THE GREAT TRANSITION 1925–1926

79 "My father was": Irene Mayer Selznick to BP (New York City, September 8, 1990).

80 Screening of *Gösta Berling*: Kevin Brownlow, *The Parade's Gone By . . .* (New York: Knopf, 1968), 465. According to some accounts, it was Wrangell who both organized the Berlin trip and told Mayer he must see *Gösta Berling*.

Mayer's first viewing of *Gösta Berling:* Leatrice Gilbert Fountain, *Dark Star* (New York: St. Martin's, 1985), 103.

"The first look": Selznick to BP.

82 "He was such": All but last sentence Selznick to BP. Final sentence from Selznick, *A Private View* (New York: Knopf, 1983), 60.

"Not much was": Åke Sundborg, "That Gustafsson Girl" (Part II), *Photoplay* (May 1930), 42.

Von Sternberg's claim: Josef von Sternberg, *Fun in a Chinese Laundry* (New York: Collier Books, 1965), 209.

83 "Both Mother and": Sundborg (Part II), 42.

84 "The sea is": Ibid.

"I hate that": Larry Englemann, "I Was the Man Who Made the Starshine," *Los Angeles* (November 1983), 264–71, 316–23.

GG arrived in U.S.: Frederick L. Collins, "Why Garbo is Making her Last Picture," *Liberty* (May 30, 1936), 4.

85 "It would not": *Motion Picture Magazine* (November 1925), quoted in George Pratt *Joyless Street* notes (February 5, 1953).

Voight and Garbo in New York: Hubert Voight, "I Loved Garbo," *New Movie Magazine* (February 1934).

86 Kaj Gynt, as told to Adela Rogers St. John, *Liberty* (August 25, 1934), Kevin Brownlow Collection.

"I tried to": Sundborg (Part II), 42.

Garbo-Genthe photo session: John Bainbridge, *Garbo* (New York: Doubleday, 1955), 80.

87 Garbo's photogenic essence: Fountain, 115.

"What an awkward": Larry Englemann, "Little Garbo," *American Way* (October 15, 1988), 74–79, 132–34.

88 Olaf Rolf: Alexander Walker, *Garbo: A Portrait* (New York: Macmillan, 1980), 35.

"The most beautiful": Leslie Halliwell, *The Filmgoer's Book of Quotes* (New York: Signet, 1975), 96–100.

89 Garbo at Miramar Hotel: Richard Alleman, *The Movie Lover's Guide to Hollywood* (Harper Colophon, 1985), 254–55.

Stiller and Garbo: Ruth Phillips, *New York Mirror* (March 11, 1938).

"They were a": Jay Brien Chapman, "Solving the Garbo Mystery," unidentified clipping (circa 1933), Billy Rose Collection.

90 "She spoke very": Fountain, 116.

"During the shooting": Selznick, 61; "Movies aren't made": Halliwell, 180.

92 "I felt that": David Robinson, *Hollywood in the Twenties* (New York: Barnes, 1968), 71–75.

Development of Sjöström: Bengt Forslund, *Victor Sjöström, His Life and His Work* (New York: Zoëtrope, 1988), 203.

Garbo learns from Gish: Fountain, 120.

93 "If you let them": Quoted in *Hollywood Legends: The Life and Films of Humphrey Bogart and Greta Garbo*, vol. 1, no. 1, ed. Robert Osborne (Corvina, Calif.: Marvin Miller, 1968), 66.

"Garbo's temperament reflected": Lillian Gish, *The Movies, Mr. Griffith and Me* (Englewood Cliffs, N.J.: Prentice-Hall, 1969), 293. "They were humiliating": Forslund, 208.

"No more pictures": Norman Zierold, *Garbo* (New York: Stein & Day, 1969), 44.

"I had the reputation": Kevin Brownlow interview with Hendrik Sartov (1964).

96 "He was rude": Lina Basquette to BP (Wheeling, W.Va., September 28, 1990).

"No one had": Ricardo Cortez interview with Brownlow (October 28, 1965).

98 "I used to ask": Val Lewton, "Moving Picture Stories" (October 13, 1931).

Garbo and the fig tree: Larry Carr, *Four Fabulous Faces* (New York: Galahad, 1970), 4.

Richard Koszarski, *Hollywood Directors: 1914–1940* (New York: Oxford, 1976), 194–95.

"Get that big": Robinson, 115.

"My job was": *The Brooklyn Eagle* (March 1, 1942).

101 "He gave Garbo": Aileen Pringle to BP (New York, October 15, 1986).

"Tony Moreno was": Basquette to BP.

103 "They get me": Rilla Page Palmborg, *The Private Life of Greta Garbo* (New York: Doubleday, 1931), 47.

"I was frantic": Ibid., 49–50. "I was heartbroken": Sundborg (Part II), 156.

106 "I used to make": Lewton.

"made a little": Ibid.

"Oh, Hoobert!": Hubert Voight, "I Loved Garbo," *New Movie Magazine* (February 1934).

Alva's death: Gray Reisfield to BP (New York, July 15, 1991).

"Tears came to": Lillian Gish, *The Movies, Mr. Griffith and Me* (Englewood Cliffs, N.J.: Prentice-Hall, 1969), 293.

107 "My poor little": Sundborg (Part II), 156.

"I could hardly": Åke Sundborg, "That Gustafsson Girl" (Part I), *Photoplay* (April 1930), 42.

108 Death of Stiller's dog: Cable to Stiller (January 1, 1926), Swedish Film Institute.

"He wasn't going": Selznick to BP.

CHAPTER 5:
THE ICON IN SILENCE 1926–1929

111 "If you knew": Quoted in Brian O'Dowd, "Why Garbo Quit Movies," *Hollywood Studio Magazine* (November 1987), 14. Date of quote unknown, probably said to Lars Saxon.

112 "Success acted on": Alexander Walker, *Sex in the Movies* (Middlesex, U.K.: Penguin, 1968), 103.

Flappers: Sumiko Higashi, *Virgins, Vamps and Flappers: The American Silent Movie Heroine* (St. Albans, Vt.: Eden, 1978), 102.

"an acceptance based": Louise Brooks, *Lulu in Hollywood* (New York: Knopf, 1982), 87.

113 "From the moment": Ibid., 89.

Garbo's anemia: Åke Sundborg, "That Gustafsson Girl" (Part I), *Photoplay* (April 1930), 128. Walker: "[She had] a metabolism in which her blood pressure is low and her heartbeat slower than the norm, which is evidence of a physical character which is frequently listless."

Mysterious being: Walker, 110 and 114.

"I did not": Sundborg (Part II), 156.

114 "If you are": Quoted in Leslie Halliwell, *The Filmgoer's Book of Quotes* (New York: Signet, 1975), 84.

"We met at": Ben Hecht, *A Child of the Century* (New York: Simon & Schuster, 1954), 497–98.

Mayer-Gilbert altercation: Leatrice Gilbert Fountain, *Dark Star* (New York: St. Martin's, 1985), 122.

"Everyone was very": Irene Mayer Selznick to BP (New York, September 8, 1990).

116 "I told him": Sundborg (Part II), 156.

"You are hereby": MGM letter to GG (August 4, 1926), signature page lost, Kevin Brownlow Collection.

"He was a good executive": Selznick to BP.

117 Sudermann as Teutonic Blasco Ibáñez: Richard Corliss, *Garbo* (New York: Pyramid Books, 1974), 50.

"cupping her hands": Kenneth Tynan, "Garbo," *Sight & Sound*, vol. 23, no. 4 (April–June 1954), 189.

"You can actually": Leatrice Gilbert Fountain, introductory remarks (Radio City Music Hall, March 6, 1987).

"It was the": Fountain, *Dark Star*, 125.

119 "That's how we": Quoted in Brownlow, *The Parade's Gone By . . .* (New York: Knopf, 1968), 170.

"I synchronized the": Ibid.

"another variation of": *National Board of Review Magazine*, vol. 2, no. 2 (February 1927), 11–13, quoted in George C. Pratt, *Spellbound in Darkness* (Greenwich, Conn.: New York Graphic Society, 1973), 451–52.

121 Gilbert deferred to Garbo: Fountain, 126.

"I don't know": Sundborg (Part II), 156.

"He had the": Hedda Hopper, "The House that Jack Built," AMPAS clipping (April 30, 1940).

"When Mr. Gilbert": *Los Angeles Times* (January 4, 1987).

122 Gilbert's pine grove for Garbo: Fountain, 128.

"a bulwark of": Raymond Daum, *Walking With Garbo* (New York: HarperCollins, 1991), 149.

"You don't understand one word": Richard Merryman, *Mank* (New York: William Morrow, 1973).

"Gilbert's was her": Eleanor Boardman to BP (Montecito, Calif., September 2, 1990).

Premiere of *Bardeleys the Magnificent:* Gavin Lambert, *Norma Shearer* (New York: Knopf, 1990), 65; and Ruth Phillips, *New York Mirror* (March 14, 1938).

124 "She was very": Boardman to BP.

Gilbert-Stiller conflict: Fountain, 128–29.

"very impetuous and": Scott Eyman, "Clarence Brown: Garbo and Beyond," *Velvet Light Trap* (Spring 1978), 20–21.

Garbo-Gilbert "wedding story": Fountain, 130–31.

125 "What's the matter": Ibid., 131.

"You're finished, Gilbert": Ibid.

"Oh, sure—expected": Boardman to BP.

"Off again, on": Fountain, 132.

126 "It is a friendship": Rilla Page Palmborg, *The Private Life of Greta Garbo* (New York: Doubleday, 1931), 71.

"He took one": Fountain, 134–35.

"My direct need": Sundborg (Part II), 156.

Harry Edington: Barbara Kent Edington Monroe to BP (March 11, 1991).

"Most of my": Sundborg (Part II), 156.

127 "Now he's even": Irene Mayer Selznick, in Fountain, 135.

"Always the vamp": Walker, 114.

"This upset": Sundborg (Part II), 156.

"Yesterday you were": Letter from Louis B. Mayer to GG (November 5, 1936), Kevin Brownlow Collection.

128 "her refusal to": AMPAS clipping (March 18, 1927).

129 GG fan mail: Fountain, 135.

"I don't understand": Garbo in 1979, quoted by Sam Green to BP (April 8, 1991).

"The studio had not": Louise Brooks, *Lulu in Hollywood* (New York: Knopf, 1982), 92.

130 "We were on": Ricardo Cortez interview with Brownlow (October 28, 1965).

"a mess of": Louise Brooks letter to Brownlow (January 28, 1966).

"We go around": Gilbert, undated Los Angeles newspaper clipping (circa June–July, 1927).

132 "No one present": Fountain, 142.

de Lacy bathed by Garbo: Film historian James Card.

"*Love* is certainly": *Time*, vol. 10, no. 24 (December 12, 1927), 43–44, quoted in George C. Pratt, *Spellbound in Darkness* (Greenwich, Conn.: New York Graphic Society, 1973), 464.

135 "My father was": Selznick to BP.

"I watched [Charlie]": Brooks letter to "Frank" [surname lost] (November 27, 1964).

"I could tell": Lambert, 108.

"The flicka and": Fountain, 137–38.

136 "Garbo was at": Salka Viertel to George Oppenheimer, quoted in Fountain, 126.

Garbo imitating Hollywood stars: Norman Zierold, *Garbo* (New York: Stein & Day, 1969), 101–2.

"More of a": Boardman to BP.

"He was still": Joan Crawford to Fountain, 139; and Crawford to Gregory Mank, in "The Divine Garbo," *Films in Review*, vol. 30, no. 9 (November 1979), 519.

137 "After a while": Colleen Moore to Fountain, 136–37.

138 "It's amazing, isn't it?": AMPAS clipping (April 19, 1927).

"I mean to": AMPAS clipping (April 18, 1927).

139 "I find I'm": Cecil Beaton, *Self-Portrait with Friends: The Selected Diaries of Cecil Beaton, 1926–1974* (New York: Times Books, 1979), 206.

140 "Louis B. Mayer": Margit Siwertz and Lars Hanson quoted in Bengt Forslund, *Victor Sjöström, His Life and His Work* (New York: Zoëtrope, 1988), 222.

"It is tempting": Forslund, 216.

Garbo-Sjöström friendship: Forslund, 224.

142 "less of a": Paul Rotha, *The Film Till Now* (Middlesex, U.K.: Hamlyn, 1967), 187.

"This picture is a huge": Quoted in Michael Conway et al., *The Films of Greta Garbo*, (New York: Bonanza Books, 1963), 63.

"You mustn't do": Forslund, 224.

143 "They were good": Walker, 102–3.

Garbo and the elements: Walker, 115–16.

"With Garbo, you": David Robinson, *Hollywood in the Twenties* (New York: Barnes, 1968), 164–65.

Excuse for her visual presence: Charles Affron, *Star Acting: Gish, Garbo, Davis* (New York: Dutton, 1977), 98.

144 Steichen photo shoot: Quoted in Daum, 124.

"On a very": Marion Davies, *The Times We Had: Life with William Randolph Hearst* (Indianapolis: Bobbs-Merrill, 1975), 84–86.

145 "The heroine was": Mercedes de Acosta, *Here Lies the Heart* (New York: Reynal, 1960), 128.

146 "Everyone trembled when": Paul Hawkins, "A New Slant on Garbo," *Screenland* (June 1931), 112.

147 "When Garbo dropped": Ibid.

148 "They would have": Interview, *Face-to-Face With Connie Chung*: "The Last Days of Garbo," CBS documentary (September 3, 1990).

"Gilbert's part was": Fountain, 160, quoting unidentified New York newspaper interview with Clarence Brown.

150 "Knowing his temper": Robinson, 74.

Garbo wants to go to Paramount: David Davidson interview with Howard Dietz (October 11, 1962), Kevin Brownlow Collection.

"You doubtlessly know": Mauritz Stiller letter to Louis B. Mayer (December 18, 1926), Swedish Film Institute.

Stiller's composite set and "flying camera" in *Hotel Imperial*: L'Estrange Fawcett, quoted in Rotha, 184.

152 "I would give": Pola Negri, *Memoirs of a Star* (Garden City, N.Y.: Doubleday, 1970), 292.

"Camera angles, lap": R. E. Sherwood, *Life*, vol. 89, no. 2308 (January 27, 1927), 24.

"This kindly man": Negri, 286.

"Stiller was getting": Sundborg (Part II), 156.

Hanson's death: Ruth Phillips, *New York Mirror* (March 14, 1938).

The Street of Sin: Josef von Sternberg, *Fun in a Chinese Laundry* (New York: Collier Books, 1965), 134.

153 "His return was just": Hubert Voight, quoted in Larry Englemann, "I Was the Man Who Made the Starshine," *Los Angeles* (November 1983), 320.

155 Thalberg liked Franklin: Brooks letter to Brownlow (November 21, 1968).

"I thought he wanted": Victor Sjöström, "As I remember . . . ," in *Classics of the Swedish Cinema* (Stockholm: The Swedish Institute/Svensk Filmindustri, 1951), 7.

Stiller cause of death: Stiller biographer Werner to BP (Stockholm, August 17, 1991).

156 "What I knew about Java": Sidney A. Franklin, *We Laughed, We Cried* (Unpublished AFI oral history, 1970).

Garbo hatred of Mayer: S. N. Behrman to David Davidson (October 2, 1962), Kevin Brownlow Collection.

"What shall we": Selma Lagerlöf, *The Saga of Gösta Berling* (Karlstad, Sweden: Press' Förlagstryckeri, 1982), 264.

"He has meant": Frederick L. Collins, "Why Garbo is Making her Last Picture," *Liberty* (May 30, 1936), 6.

"Why can't she": *Hollywood Legends: The Life and Films of Humphrey Bogart and Greta Garbo*, vol. 1, no. 1, ed. Robert Osborne (Corvina, Calif: Marvin Miller, 1968), 78.

157 Garbo's reunion with her mother: Sundborg (Part II), 41.

Resurrection in Stockholm: "M.H." in *The New York Times* (March 24, 1929), quoted in Pratt, 476.

158 "After supper, we walked": Carl Brisson, *London Sunday Express* (June 1, 1930).

160 "I'm going to": Frederick Sands and Sven Broman, *The Divine Garbo* (New York: Grosset & Dunlap, 1979), 14–15.

Garbo return to U.S.: Hubert Voight, "I Loved Garbo," *New Movie Magazine* (February 1934).

"I am so": Ibid.

"Joan of Arc": "M.H." in *New York Times* (March 24, 1929), quoted in Pratt, 474.

161 "When I said": Fountain, 168–69.

"You are a": Ibid., 169.

162 Garbo-Edington phone call to stop Gilbert-Claire marriage: Leonore Coffee, *Storyline*. Confirmed by Edington's wife, Barbara Kent Edington Monroe, to BP (March 11, 1991).

"in the course": Noël Coward, *Present Indicative* (New York: Doubleday, 1937), 305.

163 "an unkind, empty": Laurence Olivier, *Confessions of an Actor* (New York: Simon & Schuster, 1982), 95.

"Jack built this house": AMPAS clipping (November 20, 1681929).

165 "Johnny was a": Lina Basquette to BP (Wheeling, W.Va., September 28, 1990).

166 "Like Garbo": Quoted in *Picture Show* (October 1935), reprinted in Peter Haining, *The Legend of Garbo* (London: W. H. Allen, 1990), 23–25.

168 "I had an": Asther, quoted in Nathaniel Benchley, "This is Garbo," *Collier's* (March 1, 1952), 14.

"no show, except": *Variety*, July 30, 1929.

169 "Garbo is exactitude": Raymond Durgnat and John Kobal, *Greta Garbo* (New York: Dutton, 1965), 45, 59.

"What do you mean": Quoted in Paul Hawkins, *Screenland* (June 1931), 21.

"because he didn't carouse": Basquette to BP.

"She always quits" Hawkins, 21.

"she threw the scene": Ibid., 112.

"I was a little greenhorn": Lew Ayres to BP (Los Angeles, November 13, 1989).

170 "I was in my car": Ibid.

172 "Charles Farrell in": *Variety* (October 31, 1929), quoted in Walker, 171.

"the latent sadism": Walker, 75–76.

"It really began": Brooks letter to Brownlow (July 29, 1977).

"In *Flesh and the Devil*": Fountain, 151–52.

173 Gilbert million-dollar deal: Unidentified AMPAS clipping (December 13, 1928).

174 Love scenes spoken on screen: Walker, 169–70.

"Gilbert had a well-trained . . . certainly did": Brooks to Brownlow, *The Parade's Gone By . . .* (New York: Knopf, 1968), 665.

175 "I know what": Fountain, 184.

"After His Glorious Night": Colleen Moore, *Silent Star* (Garden City, N.Y.: Doubleday, 1968), 207.

CHAPTER 6:
SALKA'S SALON 1930–1931

177 "Garbo was not enchanted": Howard Dietz, *Dancing in the Dark* (New York: Quadrangle, 1975), 152.

178 "she was a disappointed ham": Louise Brooks letter to Kevin Brownlow (April 29, 1969).

"In 1926, Garbo learned": Brooks letter to Herman Weinberg (November 9, 1977).

"Excavate the Spanish torture": Katherine Albert, "Exploding the Garbo Myth," *Photoplay* (April 1931), 70 and 98.

179 "She was sincere": David Davidson interview with Howard Dietz (October 11, 1962), Kevin Brownlow Collection.

"burned up about her" and "The MGM publicity department": Brownlow letter to Brooks (February 12, 1972).

"turned out to be": Dietz, 152.

"I envy Garbo": *Hollywood Legends: The Life and Films of Humphrey Bogart and Greta Garbo*, vol. 1, no. 1, ed. Robert Osborne (Corvina, Calif.: Marvin Miller, 1968), 105.

180 "There were many beggars": Salka Viertel, *The Kindness of Strangers* (New York: Holt, Rinehart and Winston, 1969), 13.

"A favorite pastime": Ibid., 43.

181 "because of its extravagance": Ibid., 55.

182 "For a stage director": Ibid., 129.

"We heard a cacophony": Ibid., 131.

"Throughout the evening": Ibid., 132–33.

183 Berthold Viertel's personality: John Russell Taylor, *Strangers in Paradise: The Hollywood Émigrés, 1933–1950* (New York: Holt, Rinehart and Winston, 1983), 26.

"He was gentle and sympathetic": Mercedes de Acosta, *Here Lies the Heart* (New York: Reynal, 1960), 213.

Boyer in *The Magnificent Lie:* Larry Swindell, *Charles Boyer, The Reluctant Lover* (New York: Doubleday, 1983), 43–44.

"Tosca. With Garbo": Christopher Isherwood, *Prater Violet* (New York: Farrar, Straus and Giroux, 1987), 20–21.

184 "The film is an infernal machine": Ibid., 30–31, 60, 58, 36–37.

"She posed willingly": Jean Negulesco, *Things I did . . . and Things I Think I Did* (New York: Simon & Schuster, 1984), 208.

"Contrary to predictions": Viertel, 139.

Viertel house: Taylor, 27.

Arrival of new emigres: Ibid., 59.

185 "Salka was a very close friend": Stella Adler to BP (Beverly Hills, Calif., October 15, 1992). This was the last interview with Adler, who died on December 21, 1992.

186 "The movie kings housed": Paul Rotha, *The Film Till Now* (Middlesex, U.K.: Hamlyn, 1967), 135.

"She was a busybody": Irene Mayer Selznick to BP (New York, September 8, 1990).

"the experience did not make": Viertel, 140.

"She told me . . . inadequate German and English": Ibid., 142.

187 "If they want me to talk": "M.H." in *New York Times* (March 24, 1929), 7, quoted in George C. Pratt, *Spellbound in Darkness* (Greenwich, Conn.: New York Graphic Society, 1973), 476.

Experimental sound sequence: Alexander Walker, *The Shattered Silents: How the Talkies Came to Stay* (New York: Morrow, 1979), 44.

"Taste, perhaps, or Smell": Isherwood, 65.

"Garbo's present contract": M. E. Greenwood to Thalberg and/or Mayer (October 14, 1929). Kevin Brownlow Collection.

188 *Anna Christie* chosen: Gavin Lambert, *Norma Shearer* (New York: Knopf, 1990), 151.

189 "Phlegmatic. . . . She always seemed": Paul Hawkins, *Screenland* (June 1931), 20.

190 "There is no doubt": Marie Dressler, *My Own Story* (Boston: Little, Brown, 1934), 248.

Marie Dressler's career: Marjorie Rosen, *Popcorn Venus* (New York: Avon, 1974), 96.

"Of course this was": Dressler, 249, 251–52.

Charles Bickford: Lina Basquette to BP (Wheeling, W.Va., September 28, 1990).

Reviews of Garbo's voice: Watts and Lusk quoted in Conway, et al., *The Films of Greta Garbo* (New York: Bonanza Books, 1964), 89.

"complained about the Lesbian lowness": Brooks letter to Brownlow (January 18, 1966).

"Some of the strange": Unidentified Rochester (N.Y.) clipping, David Diamond Collection.

192 "Her judgment on matters": Paul Hawkins, *Screenland* (June 1931), 19–20.

193 "She worked hard . . . from different angles": Viertel, 151.

194 *Anna Christie* earnings: Eddie Mannix, MGM profit-and-loss register, AMPAS.

"I was very sad": Quoted in Elza Schallert, "Do You Know About the New Garbo?" *Movie Classic* (undated, circa 1933), 54.

"All that fame": Viertel, 143.

196 Garbo wanted Sjöström to direct *Anna Christie*: "Oskrivna memoarer," *Dagens Nyheter* (May 21, 1933), quoted in Bengt Forslund, *Victor Sjöström, His Life and His Work* (New York: Zoëtrope, 1988), 228.

"I was on my father's side": Viertel, 12.

198 "Stone was very much": Basquette to BP.

"If they know" and "Please do not": Quoted in Adela Rogers St. Johns, "The Heart of Garbo," *New Movie Magazine* (July 1930), 83–84.

199 "She is original": Hawkins, 21.

201 "Garbo did not like": Katherine Albert, "Did Brown and Garbo Fight?," *Photoplay* (March 1931), 33, 130–31.

"It is the secret": Hawkins, 112.

202 "I'm not interested": Quoted in Norman Zierold, *Garbo* (New York: Stein & Day, 1969), 101.

"Naturally, I shall attempt": Jack Grant, "Does Garbo Tank She Go Home Now?" *Motion Picture Classic* (June 25, 1931).

"She must think": David Shipman, *Movie Talk* (New York: St. Martin's, 1989), 79.

"Hollywood is betting": Leatrice Gilbert Fountain, *Dark Star* (New York: St. Martin's, 1985), 203.

Susan Lenox: Paul Rotha, *The Film Till Now* (Middlesex, U.K.: Hamlyn, 1967), 437.

203 Clark Gable's career: Ephraim Katz, *The Film Encyclopedia* (New York: Crowell, 1979), 460.

205 "Neither hero nor heroine": Quoted in Raymond Durgnat and John Kobal, *Greta Garbo* (New York: Dutton, 1965), 131.

206 "Aren't you happy?": de Acosta, 214.

"I made several": Myrna Loy, *Being & Becoming* (New York: Knopf, 1990), 121.

"In the early days": Zierold, 96.

Garbo house hunting: Nathaniel Benchley, "This is Garbo," *Collier's* (March 1, 1952), 15.

207 Sven Gustafson's career: Svenska Filminstitutet, Svensk filmografi, vol. 2 (1920–29); also *Svenskt filmskådespelarlexikon*, Sven G. Winquist & Torsten Jungstedt, Stockholm: Forum (SFI), 1973.

208 "The happiest times": Gray Reisfield to BP (New York, July 15, 1991).

"Thank you for everything": GG telegram to Salka Viertel (July 28, 1932).

Salka meets King Camp Gillette: Viertel, 143.

209 "Never refuse": Taylor, 29.

"Eisenstein and his friends": Viertel, 145.

Salka and Eisenstein: Peter Viertel to BP (Málaga, Spain, March 24, 1992).

Eisenstein-Salka relationship and *Que Viva Mexico!:* Salka Viertel, 145 and 154–59.

210 "I was neither beautiful": Ibid., 151–52.

CHAPTER 7:
THE ICON IN SOUND 1931–1932

213 "I'm a woman who's": Quoted in Leslie Halliwell, *The Filmgoer's Book of Quotes* (New York: Signet, 1975), 84.

Pola Negri planning *Mata Hari*: Pola Negri, *Memoirs of a Star* (Garden City, N.Y.: Doubleday, 1970), 355.

"Greta Garbo is my ideal": Quoted in Rosina Cannon, "The Most Eligible Couple Will Never Marry," *New Movie Magazine* (May 1932), courtesy Bill Donati.

215 "The moment she began": Quoted in *Hollywood Legends: The Life and Films of Humphrey Bogart and Greta Garbo*, vol. 1, no. 1, ed. Robert Osborne (Corvina, Calif.: Marvin Miller, 1968), 89.

"I even carry out . . . when it is wrong": George Fitzmaurice, "The Art of Directing," *New York Dramatic Mirror* (March 11, 1916), quoted in Richard Koszarski, *Hollywood Directors, 1914–1940* (New York: Oxford, 1976), 34–35.

217 "She [took] me to": Mercedes de Acosta, *Here Lies the Heart* (New York: Reynal, 1960), 230.

Paul Bern: Gavin Lambert, *Norma Shearer* (New York: Knopf, 1990), 151 and 181.

218 "There goes my ambition": Quoted in Osborne, 90.

"I am glad we": Jerry Asher, "Giving Garbo Away," *Silver Screen* (May 1936), 66.

"You have no idea": Gregory Mank, "The Divine Garbo," *Films in Review*, vol. 30, no. 9 (November 1979), 523.

219 "If you stay in": Quoted in Halliwell, 16–17.

"Who's holding onto whom?": Condensed from Rachel Gallagher, *The Girl Who Loved Garbo* (New York: Donald I. Fine, 1990).

"She takes us out": Quoted in Richard Corliss, *Garbo* (New York: Pyramid Books, 1974), 106.

"stylized sexuality": Charles Affron, "Uncensored Garbo," in Mast and Cohen, *Film Theory and Criticism*, 737.

"Mr. Louie B. Mayer": Will Rogers, column (May 15, 1932); third paragraph and last sentence from rough-draft notes on Western Union telegraph paper, courtesy Ben Yagoda.

221 Garbo's best-known, least-visible film: Corliss, 102.

222 Garbo-Cornell story: de Acosta, 238–39.

Garbo's visit backstage: Katharine Cornell, *I Wanted to Be an Actress* (New York: Random House, 1938), 105–7.

"Next to Miss Bankhead": Tallulah Bankhead, *Tallulah* (New York: Harper, 1952), 199.

223 "Socially, I don't . . . more than a year!": Paul Hawkins, "A New Slant on Garbo," *Screenland* (June 1931), 19. "We had a homey . . . love to work with her:" Quoted in Nathaniel Benchley, "This Is Garbo," *Collier's* (March 1, 1952), 15. "She is perfect to . . . what she pleases": Hawkins, 19.

"had something . . . ever had been": Scott Eyman, "Clarence Brown: Garbo and Beyond," *Velvet Light Trap* (Spring 1978), 21.

"I would take a scene . . . come in and do the scene": Kevin Brownlow, *The Parade's Gone By . . .* (New York: Knopf, 1968), 167–69. "In silent days . . . put her off balance": Benchley, 15. "She didn't act for . . . sits in the corner": Eyman, 22. "We could never get her . . . she wouldn't watch it": Brownlow, 169.

224 "In his repressed way . . . wife, Alice Joyce": Louise Brooks letters to Kevin Brownlow (June 10 and October 19, 1968).

"He perfected the Garbo face": Brooks letter to Brownlow (April 2, 1968).

"Whenever we saw . . . on the face": Brownlow, 161 and 164.

"Why does no one": Brooks letter to Brownlow (August 31, 1968).

225 Garbo shyness: Alexander Walker, *Sex in Movies* (Middlesex, U.K.: Penguin, 1968), 110.

"In the studios she is": *Picturegoer* (March 1928), quoted in Walker, 110.

"A comprehensive knowledge of": George Fitzmaurice, "The Art of Directing," *New York Dramatic Mirror* (March 11, 1916), quoted in Richard Koszarski, *Hollywood Directors, 1914–1940* (New York: Oxford, 1976), 34–35.

William Daniels: Walker, 117.

226 "Like a trump": Quoted in Halliwell, 208.

"I don't think": William Stull, "Garbo's Cameraman," *Hollywood* (October 1935), Kevin Brownlow Collection.

"Often, she will grow": Ibid.

"We always made": Brownlow, 488.

"He would tell": Ibid.

227 "She worked with": David Robinson, *Hollywood in the Twenties* (New York: Barnes, 1968), 164–65.

"At five o'clock": de Acosta, 232.

"Great actresses like Garbo": "Louise Brooks par elle-même," *Objectif* (February–March 1964), 12.

"The sensual side . . . glamour symbol": Kenneth Tynan, "Garbo," *Sight & Sound*, vol. 23, no. 4 (April–June 1954), 189.

228 "I was so big": Quoted in Val Lewton, *Moving Picture Stories* (October 13, 1931), 31.

"In repose, Garbo was": Walker, 102.

"Everything is built": Quoted in Brownlow, 407.

"She walked obliquely": Tynan, 189.

Ferragamo: Unidentified AMPAS clipping (September 1, 1949).

"Garbo's feet were": Quoted in Raymond R. Sarlot and Fred E. Basten, *Life at the Marmont* (Santa Monica, Calif.: Roundtable, 1987), 154.

"She usually wore flats": Gray Reisfield to BP (New York, July 15, 1991).

229 "I went in to her": Stella Adler to BP (Beverly Hills, Calif., October 15, 1992).

"the perfection of her": Brooks letter to Brownlow (April 2, 1968).

Observer and participator: Thomas Wiseman, quoted in Raymond Durgnat and John Kobal, *Greta Garbo* (New York: Dutton, 1965), 97–98.

Garbo influence on women's appearance: de Acosta, 315.

"I found her more": *The Film Criticism of Otis Ferguson*, ed. Robert Wilson (Philadelphia: Temple University Press, 1971), 275.

230 "uniformly languorous and inscrutable": John Bainbridge, *Garbo* (New York: Doubleday, 1955), 9.

231 Garbo's teeth: Dr. Joseph Fertig, one of the last dentists to see her in the late 1980s, maintains Garbo's teeth were never radically altered by pulling, capping, or bracing.

"With a single gesture": Quoted in unidentified clipping, Kevin Brownlow Collection.

232 "One day she came": Jerry Asher, "Giving Garbo Away," *Silver Screen* (May 1936), 66–67.

"I have never been": Review of *The Single Standard*, quoted in Michael Conway et al., *The Films of Greta Garbo* (New York: Bonanza Books, 1963), 81.

"What matter if the": Norbert Lusk, *Picture Play* (n.d., circa September 1930).

"Don't act, think!": Quoted in Leslie Halliwell, *The Filmgoer's Book of Quotes* (New York: Signet, 1975), 134.

233 "enigmatic incarnations . . . changed her mind": Marjorie Rosen, *Popcorn Venus* (New York: Avon, 1974), 169–71.

"When Garbo made love": Ibid., 172.

"With perhaps too much care": Alistair Cooke, *Garbo and the Night Watchmen* (New York: McGraw Hill, 1971), 123.

234 "How cleverly the": Rosen, 173.

"It is the nature": Josef von Sternberg, *Fun in a Chinese Laundry* (New York: Collier Books, 1965), 120.

"The displaced person": Tynan, 189.

"melancholy, sexually enigmatic": Walker, 117–18.

"What she did was": Eleanor Boardman to BP (Montecito, Calif., September 2, 1990).

"the plot and the": Charles Affron, "Uncensored Garbo," in Mast and Cohen, 739.

235 "whose most cherished": Ibid., 740.

"What, when drunk": Tynan, 187.

"From pin-ups to strip-tease": Laura Mulvey, "Visual Pleasure and Narrative Cinema" (1975), in *Feminism and Film Theory*, ed. Constance Penley (New York: Routledge, 1988), 62.

"I know I'm not alone": Meyer Levin in *Garbo and the Night Watchmen*, ed. Alistair Cooke (New York: McGraw-Hill, 1971), 108–10.

236 Garbo relationship between hypnosis and film viewing: John Barba to BP (Washington, D.C., June 25, 1991).

CHAPTER 8:
SEX AND PSYCHOLOGY 1932

239 Wayne Morris labeled bathroom faucets: *New York Daily News* (October 25, 1938).

"Gilbert managed to lure": Ruth Phillips, *New York Mirror* (March 14, 1938).

"Garbo and Gilbert slipped": Bengt Forslund, *Victor Sjöström, His Life and Work* (New York: Zoëtrope, 1988), 25.

"It was a love affair": Fritiof Billquist, *Garbo* (New York: Putnam, 1960), 7.

240 "I was in love with him": Quoted in Michael Gross, "Garbo's Last Days," *New York* (May 21, 1990), 42.

"You are aware": Brian O'Dowd, "Why Garbo Quit Movies," *Hollywood Studio Magazine* (November 1987), 14.

"I cannot bear to fight": Jay Brien Chapman, "Solving the Garbo Mystery" (unidentified magazine clipping, circa 1933).

"If I see an accident": Val Lewton, *Moving Picture Stories* (October 13, 1931), 31.

"She was flattered": Larry Engelmann, "I Was the Man Who Made the Starshine," *Los Angeles* (November 1983), 264–71, 316–23.

"Almost all men disliked Gilbert": Louise Brooks letters to Kevin Brownlow (October 19, 1968, and December 5, 1966).

241 "She did the right thing": Eleanor Boardman to BP (Montecito, Calif., September 2, 1990).

"Definitely overrated . . . discussing a brother" and "He crossed one of": Quoted in Boze Hadleigh, *Conversations with My Elders* (New York: St. Martin's, 1986), 67–69.

"They were poor lovers": Alexander Walker, *Sex in the Movies* (Middlesex, U.K.: Penguin, 1968), 65.

"Love? It is the": Åke Sundborg, "That Gustafsson Girl" (Part II), *Photoplay* (May 1930), 157.

242 Any success, and no failings, of this effort are due to the analyses of Shelley von Strunckel (New York, June 9, 1991), Cathy Henkel (Wichita, Kans., November 30, 1991), John Barba (Washington, D.C., October 14, 1991), Dr. Laurie L. Lankin (Pittsburgh, Pa., October 26, 1989), and Maria Ciaccia (New York, September 23, 1989).

"Who are all these people": Chapman.

243 "She spent many hours": Ruth Biery, "Hollywood's Cruelty to Greta Garbo," *Photoplay* (January 1932), 28.

"Citizenship Urged for Garbo and Chevalier," unidentified AMPAS clipping (February 24, 1932).

"Damn!": Biery, 102.

"I never said": AP biographical service (1976). Other accounts say, "I want to be let alone," grammatically wrong but equally possible.

244 "People make me nervous": Quoted in Raymond Daum, "Garbo Talks (A Little)," *Life* (Spring 1989), 100.

"Her Nordic blood may": Cecil Beaton, "Garbo," *Theatre* (September 1961), 9.

"No one could ever": Adrian, 38–43.

"Garbo is of a": Elza Schallert, "Do You Know About the New Garbo?" *Movie Classic* (circa 1933), 54.

245 "To trudge about": Quoted in *Liberty* (October 22, 1932).

"Garbo is lonely": Marie Dressler, *My Own Story* (Boston: Little, Brown, 1934), 251–52.

"is harboring a powerful": Charles Affron, *Star Acting: Gish, Garbo, Davis* (New York: Dutton, 1977), 18.

246 "I think often of": Edgar Sirmont letter to Mauritz Stiller (January 12, 1927), Swedish Film Institute.

247 "the adoration of a student": Quoted in Raymond Daum, *People* (April 30, 1990).

Murnau in the South Seas: Lotte Eisner, *The Haunted Screen* (Berkeley and Los Angeles: University of California Press, 1973), 98.

Murnau death: Salka Viertel, *The Kindness of Strangers* (New York: Holt, Rinehart and Winston, 1969), 147. Kenneth Anger, *Hollywood Babylon* (city: publisher, date), 172.

248 "I am in despair": Honoré Balzac, *La Duchesse de Langeais* (Philadelphia: Avil Publishing, 1901), vol. 35 (The Thirteen), 212.

249 "A couple of them": S. N. Behrman interview with David Davidson (October 2, 1962). Garbo allegedly had *eight* abortions, according to Charles Higham, *Merchant of Dreams: Louise B. Mayer, MGM and the Secret Hollywood* (New York: Donald I. Fine, 1993), 110.

250 Garbo relationship with Mona Mårtenson: David Diamond to BP (Rochester, N.Y., March 4, 1990).

"After finally freeing herself": Brooks letter to Herman Weinberg (November 9, 1977).

251 "Lilyan wasn't a great": Lina Basquette to BP (Louisville, Ky., March 16, 1990).

"Garbo never wore them": Hedda Hopper, *Los Angeles Times* (April 10, 1938).

"She really has": Rilla Page Palmborg, *The Private Life of Greta Garbo* (New York: Doubleday, 1931), 79.

253 "Greta Garbo and Fifi D'Orsay": Untitled Los Angeles newspaper clipping (February 16, 1930). AMPAS.

254 "I nevair played tennees": Quoted in *Los Angeles Record* (June 13, 1930).

"She liked Fifi D'Orsay": Ruth Biery, "Hollywood's Cruelty to Greta Garbo," *Photoplay* (January 1932), 102.

"I suppose she is": *Screenland* (June 1931), 7.

255 "When Lilyan had": Irene Mayer Selznick to BP (New York, September 8, 1990).

"I had violent attacks": Mercedes de Acosta, *Here Lies the Heart* (New York: Reynal, 1960), 38.

"desperately unhappy and unadjusted": Ibid., 61–62.

256 "Friends were kind": Ibid., 206.

"In my own experience": Ibid., 39.

257 "to make you regret": Ibid., 162.

"She was dressed in": Ibid., 213.

258 "Only a few hours": Ibid., 217.

259 "Then, finally, as the moon": Ibid., 219–20.

"George Cukor used to": Ibid., 214.

260 "How to describe the": Ibid., 221–26.

262 Garbo horse-riding expertise: Quoted in unidentified AMPAS clipping, "Reveal Secrets of Hollywood Horsewomen" (February 17, 1932).

263 "Sewing Circle": David King Dunaway, *Huxley in Hollywood* (New York: Doubleday, 1990), 70.

"Salka was AC/DC": Selznick to BP.

"When would she": Peter Viertel to BP (Marbella, Spain, March 25, 1992).

Women's afternoon activities: Dunaway, 70–71.

264 "fascinating, bizarre, a little": Selznick to BP.

"A mouse in a topcoat": Brendan Gill, *Tallulah* (New York: Harper & Row, 1972), 52.

"Mercedes was so *persistent*": Viertel to BP.

"Here lies the heart": Jack Larson to BP (Brentwood, Calif., July 26, 1991).

"You can't dispose of": Alice B. Toklas letter to Anita Loos (May 8, 1960).

Garbo and Mercedes were not lovers: Nicholas Turner to BP (New York, June 17, 1992).

"To know Greta": de Acosta, 319.

"I consider her a": Paul Hawkins, "A New Slant on Garbo," *Screenland* (June 1931), 20.

265 "From the age of": Brooks letters to Brownlow (October 19, 1968 and August 23, 1966).

266 "She made a pass at me": John Kobal, *People Will Talk* (New York: Knopf, 1985), 79.

"Garbo was a completely": Brooks letter to Brownlow (October 19, 1968).

"I have been smoking": Gross, 45. "He's got to be in bed": John Bainbridge, "Garbo is 65," *Look* (September 8, 1970), 57.

"I am a lonely . . . I will tell you": Ibid., 56.

"Give an oold man": Gross, 45.

"the era when": de Acosta, 162.

"When I had known": Ibid., 227.

267 Garbo as Hamlet at costume party: Jerry Asher, "Giving Garbo Away," *Silver Screen* (May 1936).

"Well, look who's": Ibid.

Garbo attendance as retaliation: Laurence Olivier, *Confessions of an Actor* (New York: Penguin, 1982), 95.

"I care nothing about": Åke Sundborg, "That Gustafsson Girl" (Part II), *Photoplay* (May 1930), 156. "I like to live simply": Roland Wild, *Greta Garbo* (London: Rich & Cowan, 1933), 50.

Garbo's wardrobe: Parker Tyler, "The Garbo Image," introduction to *The Films of Greta Garbo*, ed. Michael Conway, Dion McGregor, and Mark Ricci (New York: Bonanza Books, 1963), 16.

268 "She simply liked . . . wanted to": Gray Reisfield to BP (New York, April 5, 1991).

Male-female difference in transvestism: Camille Paglia, *Sexual Personae* (New Haven: Yale University Press, 1990), 416.

Gender assignments and dress: Carolyn G. Heilbrun, *Writing a Woman's Life* (New York: Ballantine, 1989), 96–97. "I had legs as strong": George Sand, *My Life*, quoted in Heilbrun, 34.

269 "You must be . . . the story is out": de Acosta, 231–33.

270 "He became so excited": Ibid., 258.

"What stupidity": Quoted in Riva, 169.

"For some time after": Ibid., 259–60.

271 von Stroheim employable as actor: Don Whittemore and Philip Alan Cecchettini, *Passport to Hollywood: Film Immigrants Anthology* (New York: McGraw-Hill, 1976), 98–99.

Garbo wanted von Stroheim for film: Thomas Quinn Curtiss, *Von Stroheim* (New York: Farrar, Straus and Giroux, 1971), 283–84.

272 von Stroheim frequent absences: Ibid., 287.

"clearly Garbo's playful": Richard Corliss, *Garbo* (New York: Pyramid Books, 1974), 108.

273 "It took me three": Hedda Hopper, *Los Angeles Times* (April 9, 1938).

"It is rare for": de Acosta, 239.

"Her acting made you": Quoted in *Empire* (June 1990).

"she absorbs dialogue": Quoted in Alexander Walker, *Sex in the Movies* (Middlesex, U.K.: Penguin, 1968), 110, from Markey interview in the *Daily Telegraph* (April 17, 1932).

"I don't think they're as ugly": Nathaniel Benchley, "This is Garbo," *Collier's* (March 1, 1952), 56.

274 Similarities between Garbo and Queen Elizabeth I: Walker, *Sex in the Movies*, 106. And Alexander Walker, *The Celluloid Sacrifice* (New York: Hawthorne, 1966), 99. Sexual theorist Cathy Henkel of Seattle, Wash., noting other striking similarities between Elizabeth and Garbo, speculates that the actress, no less than the queen, might well have remained a virgin for life.

"he talks to newspapers": Cecil Beaton, *Self-Portrait with Friends: The Selected Diaries of Cecil Beaton, 1926–1974*, ed. Richard Buckle (New York: Times Books, 1979), 34.

"If a unicorn had": Ibid., 34–35.

Garbo-Beaton conversation: Ibid., 36.

276 "Once in a while": Quoted by Karl Freund to Norman Zierold in *Garbo* (New York: Stein & Day, 1969), 89.

Feminine friendship: Heilbrun, 98–99ff.

"She was in need": Corliss, 28–30.

"crazy about pictures": Frederick L. Collins, "Why Garbo is Making her Last Picture," *Liberty* (May 30, 1936), 4.

277 "The great Garbo": Terrence Pepper and John Kobal, *The Man Who Shot Garbo: The Hollywood Photographs of Clarence Sinclair Bull* (New York: Simon & Schuster, 1989), 21.

"He would be getting": John Kobal, *The Art of the Great Hollywood Portrait Photographers, 1925–1940* (New York: Knopf, 1980), 237.

"When the pose": Pepper and Kobal, 25.

"Her face was": Kobal, 237.

Ruth Harriet Louise: Raymond Daum, *Walking with Garbo*, ed. Vance Muse (New York: HarperCollins, 1991), 58.

279 "autoerotic intimacy, a": Marjorie Rosen, *Popcorn Venus* (New York: Avon, 1974), 172.

"the primordial wish": Laura Mulvey, "Visual Pleasure and Narrative Cinema," in *Feminism and Film Theory*, ed. Constance Penley (New York: Routledge, 1988), 60.

"her passive orality": Charles Affron, "Uncensored Garbo," Mast and Cohen, *Film Theory and Criticism* (city: pub, date), 733.

280 "Probably not a": Shelley von Strunckel to BP (New York, June 9, 1991).

"Something in Garbo wanted": Parker Tyler, "The Garbo Image," introduction to Michael Conway et al., eds., *The Films of Greta Garbo* (New York: Bonanza Books, 1963), 18.

"She associated sex with": Gross, 44.

"Miss Marie thought": Selma Lagerlöf, *The Saga of Gösta Berling* (Karlstad, Sweden: Press' Förlagstryckeri, 1982), 161.

"To any man she": Dr. Louis E. Bisch, "Why Garbo is the World's Love Ideal," unidentified journal (circa 1929).

281 "broad yoke of . . . spirituality of her looks": Walker, *Sex in the Movies*, 102–3.

"Her independence of": Tynan, 188.

"an intense form": Walker, quoted in *New York Daily News* (November 3, 1980), 10.

CHAPTER 9:
GARBONOMICS 1933–1937

284 "the triumph of the apathetic": Alexander Walker, quoted in *New York Daily News* (November 3, 1980), 10.

"Other studios made fantastic": Salka Viertel, *The Kindness of Strangers* (New York: Holt, Rinehart and Winston, 1969), 152.

285 "When I had finished": Cecil Beaton, *Self-Portrait with Friends: The Selected Diaries of Cecil Beaton, 1926–1974,* ed. Richard Buckle (New York: Times Books, 1979), 201.

"Miss Garbo had not": Harry Edington quoted in "Garbo Off for Europe," unidentified AMPAS clipping (July 21, 1932).

286 "Hollywood is all excited": Will Rogers collected columns, 146.

Garbo and Mercedes see Gerhard in Stockholm's Comedy Theatre: Unidentified newspaper clipping (September 19, 1932), Billy Rose Collection.

"she continues her Hollywood-style": Unidentified clipping (September 19, 1932), Billy Rose Collection.

Never-to-be Garbo stage productions: Unidentified AMPAS clippings, Prince Lennart's play (October 23, 1932) and Ekman's Grand Hotel (October 28, 1932).

287 Garbo's relationship with Max Gumpel: John Bainbridge, *Garbo* (New York: Doubleday, 1955), 200.

"I couldn't face that": Beaton, 181.

Garbo disguised in Paris to elude press: Unidentified newspaper clippings from Paris (November 17, 1932), Kevin Brownlow Collection.

"one of the most lurid": Ibid. (November 19, 1932), Kevin Brownlow Collection.

288 "tired and frustrated. I've": GG letter no. 4 to Salka Viertel (Stockholm; undated, circa 1932; from the German, translated by Jan-Christopher Horak and Michael Horton).

"I am going to": GG letter no. 5 to Viertel (Stockholm; December 31, 1932).

"I sailed on a freighter": Raymond Daum, "Garbo Talks (A Little)," *Life* (Spring 1989), 98.

Garbo's audition speech for Royal Dramatic Academy: Henrik Ibsen, *The Lady from the Sea* (London: Penguin, 1965), 280.

"Do you want to": GG letter no. 6 to Viertel (Canal Zone; April 17, 1933; translated from the German by Jan-Christopher Horak and Michael Horton).

289 "I have never known": Marie Dressler quoted by Paul Hawkins, *Screenland* (June 1931), 20.

"It would be a wonderful": Viertel, 152.

"but as things often": Mercedes de Acosta, *Here Lies the Heart* (New York: Reynal, 1960), 251.

290 "Salka, I know that": GG letter no. 4 to Viertel.

294 "Abruptly, he asked if": Viertel, 175.

"Relations with Edington Strained": *Photoplay* (January 1933), 37. "have now parted": Unidentified clipping (June 9, 1933), Kevin Brownlow Collection.

295 Olivier as Garbo's leading man in *Queen Christina*: Alexander Walker, *Garbo: A Portrait* (New York: Macmillan, 1980), 134.

"I was thinking of": Rouben Mamoulian to Kevin Brownlow, 1970, 12.

"I realized in the first": Laurence Olivier, *Confessions of an Actor* (New York: Simon & Schuster, 1982), 93.

296 "What am I going": S. N. Behrman, "People in a Diary" (Part II), *New Yorker* (May 20, 1972), 76–79.

"Sir Laurence and I": Charles Higham and Joel Greenberg, eds., *The Celluloid Muse: Hollywood Directors Speak* (New York: Signet, 1969), 154.

297 "I told Mr. Mayer": Rouben Mamoulian to Kevin Brownlow, (1970), 12.

Gilbert's screen test for *Queen Christina*: Walter Wanger quoted in Leatrice Gilbert Fountain, *Dark Star* (New York: St. Martin's, 1985), 233–34.

"Gilbert, who a few": Unidentified AMPAS clipping (August 11, 1933).

298 "This is the first": Quoted in Raymond Durgnat and John Kobal, *Greta Garbo* (New York: Dutton, 1965), 141.

299 "In part of that": Barbara Barondess MacLean to BP (New York, January 29, 1991).

300 "She said, 'I can't'": Mamoulian to Brownlow (1970), 12.

"the morning after" inn scene in *Queen Christina:* Alexander Walker, *Sex in the Movies* (Middlesex, U.K.: Penguin, 1968), 111–12.

301 "I remember vividly how": Stiller's lawyer quoted in John Bainbridge, *Garbo* (New York: Doubleday, 1955), 129.

"Garbo works intuitively . . . sonnet in action": Higham and Greenberg, 154. "I explained to . . . it to music": Tom Milne to Rouben Mamoulian, 74, quoted in Charles Affron, *Star Acting: Gish, Garbo, Davis* (New York: Dutton, 1977).

"emotional illumination, like Braille": Walker, *Sex in the Movies,* 114.

"no reason to censor": Walter Ramsey, *Modern Screen* review, quoted in Michael Conway et al., *The Films of Greta Garbo* (New York: Bonanza Books, 1963), 122.

"An actress is no": Raymond Daum, *Walking with Garbo* (New York: HarperCollins, 1991), 86.

302 "She was magnificent to": Fountain, 235.

"Backward, turn backward, O": Ibid.

"It was a rhetorical": Behrman, 78.

305 "I said, 'Mr. Mayer' ": Mamoulian interview with Brownlow (1970).

306 "she could legitimately be": Robert Payne, *The Great Garbo* (New York: Praeger, 1976), 207.

"In the end, it": Otis Ferguson (January 31, 1934), in *The Film Criticism of Otis Ferguson,* ed. Robert Wilson (Philadelphia: Temple University Press, 1971), 29.

307 "I was feeling on": Fountain, 236.

Garbo-Gilbert team "lost its drawing power": Ibid., 237–38.

309 John Gilbert's full-page ad concerning MGM contract: *Hollywood Reporter* (March 20, 1934).

Garbo-Mamoulian trip to Arizona: Unidentified newspaper clipping (January 13, 1934), Kevin Brownlow Collection.

310 Garbo-Mamoulian trip to Arizona: Unidentified clippings (January 13, 14, 16, 18, 1934), AMPAS and Kevin Brownlow Collections.

311 Garbo and de Acosta lost in Yosemite forest: de Acosta, 254–56.

Hollywood outgrows fascination with Maugham's work: Marjorie Rosen, *Popcorn Venus* (New York: Avon, 1974), 178.

312 "Marshall [is] intractably British": Graham Greene, in Alistair Cooke, ed., *Garbo and the Night Watchman* (New York: McGraw-Hill, 1971), 175.

313 "Miss Garbo displayed . . . anxious about it": "What It's Like to Work with Garbo," Herbert Marshall interview, *Photoplay* (November 1934), 80.

315 "I'm free and I'm": Quoted in Jim Mason, "Garbo Talks at Last," *Photoplay* (July 1936), 113.

Brent is "the male edition of Garbo": Sidney Skolsky, *Hollywood Citizen-News* (April 16, 1940).

"I'd rather have a": Ibid.

316 Selznick preferring Garbo do *Dark Victory: Memo from David O. Selznick,* ed. Rudy Behlmer (New York: Viking, 1972), 76–78.

317 "she was having trouble": Behrman interview with David Davidson (October 2, 1962).

"My aunt Cissy": Quoted in *MGM: When the Lion Roars,* Turner Pictures documentary (1991).

"An actress is usually": Cooke, 121–23.

319 "Nothing mattered to Garbo": Irene Mayer Selznick to BP (New York, September 8, 1990).

"When working with her": David Shipman, *Movie Talk* (New York: St. Martin's, 1989), 80.

"Do you mean you watched": Quoted in Brian O'Dowd, "Why Garbo Quit Movies," *Hollywood Studio Magazine* (November 1987), 14.

"co-starring with Garbo hardly": Quoted in Leslie Halliwell, *The Filmgoer's Book of Quotes* (New York: Signet, 1975), 84.

320 "The things which have": Quoted by AP biography service (1976).

"the Hollywood compromise between": Unidentified newspaper clipping (Stockholm, July 6, 1935).

Studios "spying" on Garbo to keep her out of trouble: Alexander Walker to BP (London, January 23, 1992).

"It's a public profession": Quoted in Hollis Alpert, "The Saga of Greta Lovisa Gustafsson," *New York Times Magazine* (September 5, 1965), 56. GG-Coward "engagement": Graham Payn and Sheridan Morley, eds., *The Noël Coward Diaries* (Boston: Little, Brown, 1982), 23 (December 30, 1943, entry).

"Believe me, Noël, I": Cole Lesley, *The Life of Noël Coward* (London: Jonathan Cape, 1976), 176.

"my little bridegroom": Lesley, 177.

321 "Noël Coward was very": GG letter no. 9 to Viertel (undated, circa December 1935).

"The evening was a": de Acosta, 268.

"I am in bed": GG letter no. 8 to Viertel (November 22, 1935).

322 Quoted in Walker, *Garbo: A Portrait*, 148.

"Agreed. Thank you. Feeling": Ibid.

Gilbert's acute myocarditis: *Hollywood Reporter* (January 10, 1936). Reported the cause of death as "heart failure": *Variety* (January 15, 1936). New "closest friend": Hedda Hopper.

"There's never been a": Quoted in Adela Rogers St. Johns, "Love, Laughter and Tears," *The American Weekly* (January 21, 1951).

Garbo's response to Gilbert's death: Quoted in Kay Proctor, "Scoop! At Last Garbo Really Talks," *Screen Guide* (July 1936), 35.

"I do not know": Quoted in Mason, 48.

323 "Always when I come": Proctor, 35.

"of my poor little": Ibid.

324 "It is not that": Ibid.

"like a homing pigeon": Mason, 112.

325 Amorphous character of intellectual ghetto-in-exile: Gottfried Reinhardt, *The Genius: A Memoir of Max Reinhardt* (New York: Knopf, 1979), 301.

"It *was* a salon": Reinhardt, 303–4.

326 "The conversation would cease": Peter Viertel to BP (Marbella, Spain, March 25, 1992).

"personal trouble gave way": Christopher Isherwood (New York: Farrar, Straus and Giroux, 1987), 98, 100.

"Political discussions, verging on": John Russell Taylor, *Strangers in Paradise: The*

Hollywood Émigrés, 1933–1950 (New York: Holt, Rinehart and Winston, 1983), 117–18.

327 Upton Sinclair's radical utopia in California: Taylor, 111.

"I encourage personal extravagance": Reinhardt, 292.

The Reinhardts dining with Garbo at Cafe Trocadero: Unidentified newspaper clippings (January 26 and 27, 1935), Billy Rose Collection.

328 "The Europeans would rather": Reinhardt, 304–5.

Reinhardt's *Midsummer Night's Dream* "dream cast": Ibid., 297.

"The first conference, however": Donald Ogden Stewart, *By a Stroke of Luck!* (London: Paddington Press, 1975), 227–28.

329 "I do not understand": GG letter no. 8 to Salka Viertel (November 22, 1935).

"She would prefer to": Frederick L. Collins, "Why Garbo is Making her Last Picture," *Liberty* (May 30, 1936), 4.

330 Garbo getting Jeannette MacDonald's house: de Acosta, 273.

"She is such a tragic": Proctor, 35.

"Don't you understand?": Payne, 246.

332 "I liked her sense": Quoted in Norman Zierold, *Garbo* (New York: Stein & Day, 1969), 92.

"whose lips have been": Corliss, 128.

"I am terribly worried": Payne, 248.

334 "she could barely stand": de Acosta, 274.

"I have some idea": Payne, 252.

"had she seen herself": de Acosta, 232.

Robert Taylor's "deeply hygienic" *Camille* performance: Cecelia Ager quoted in Cooke, 250.

"Armand is historically a": Higham and Greenberg, 61.

335 The sexual levels of *Camille*: Charles Affron, "Uncensored Garbo," in Mast and Cohen, *Film Theory and Criticism* (New York: Oxford University Press, 1979), 738–39.

336 "She walked over to": Katharine Hepburn, *Me* (New York: Knopf, 1991), 187.

Garbo unable to accept compliment: Bainbridge, *Garbo* (New York: Doubleday, 1955), 18.

337 "She described the unpleasantness": Jack Larson, *The Washington Post* (April 20, 1990).

Choice of Boyer to play Napoleon: Larry Swindell, *Charles Boyer, The Reluctant Lover* (New York: Doubleday, 1983), 97–98.

"I would have been": Ibid., 99.

339 "his own intelligence and": Ibid.

340 "I was thinking about": GG letter no. 7 to Viertel (Stockholm, July 10, 1935).

"Can it help in": GG letter no. 12 to Viertel (undated, circa 1936–37).

341 "You could read on": Swindell, 101–2.

"and I enjoyed every": Scott Eyman, "Clarence Brown: Garbo and Beyond," *Velvet Light Trap* (Spring 1978), 21–22.

"Madame Garbo's elegant anemia": John Mosher, *The New Yorker* (November 6, 1937), 9.

343 "She had a fanatical": Quoted in Kevin Brownlow, *The Parade's Gone By . . .* (New York: Knopf, 1968), 169.

"She has saved enough": Quoted in Jack Grant, "Does Garbo Tank She Go Home Now?" *Motion Picture Classic* (June 25, 1931).

344 Word "Garbo" in connection with a refuse container: Walker, 130.

Stocks and trust funds: Nicholas Turner in Michael Gross, "Garbo's Last Days," *New York* (May 21, 1990), 41. The trust-fund income: Gaylord Hauser told Dorothy Kilgallen in 1948 that Garbo had $500,000 in the bank and a $3,500 annuity to begin in 1955 when she turned fifty.

"She was very stingy": Eleanor Boardman to BP (Montecito, Calif., September 2, 1990).

"When he refused to": Rilla Page Palmborg, *The Private Life of Greta Garbo* (New York: Doubleday, 1931), 231–32.

345 Garbo unsure how to tip hotel attendants: Hubert Voight, "I Loved Garbo," *New Movie Magazine* (February 1934).

"She was terribly tight": Barbara Barondess MacLean to BP (New York, January 29, 1991).

"If you want to": Kerstin Bernadotte, "Greta Garbo," *Ladies' Home Journal* (April 1976), 93 and 150.

"She truly never considered": Sam Green to BP (New York, June 5, 1991).

"Garbo is very considerate": Jim Heimann, *Out With the Stars* (New York: Abbeville, 1985), 125–26.

Garbo's financial integrity: David Davidson interview with Howard Dietz (October 11, 1962), Kevin Brownlow Collection.

346 Garbo's discretion in accepting money for engagements: *Screenland* (February 1934).

"My God! Doesn't she": John Bainbridge, "Garbo is 65," *Look* (September 8, 1970), 54.

"When it became known": Behlmer, 95.

"Reports that Metro is": *New York Daily News* (May 15, 1942).

CHAPTER 10:
HEALTH, EDUCATION, AND WARFARE 1938–1945

349 "Stokowski had it in": Anita Loos (September 11, 1978), quoted in Oliver Daniel, *Stokowski: A Counterpoint of View* (New York: Dodd, Mead, 1982), 357–58.

350 "Stoky didn't waste much": John Bainbridge, *Garbo* (New York: Doubleday, 1955), 226; Galahad edition, 190.

"Garbo knelt before Stokowski": Gottfried Reinhardt, *The Genius: A Memoir of Max Reinhardt* (New York: Knopf, 1979), 303.

351 "No, no—I will": quoted in Jim Simmons, "I Won't Marry Stokowski—Says Greta Garbo," *Photoplay* (January 1938), 16.

352 "On these days she": Hettie Grimstead, "With Garbo at Home," *Screenland* (April 1938), 80.

353 "I do not believe": GG letter no. 11 to Salka Viertel (circa mid-February 1938).

"[Garbo's] luggage consisted of": E. W. Selsey, *The New Yorker* (April 23, 1938), 77.

354 "His role was that": David Diamond to BP (Rochester, N.Y., November 3, 1991).

355 "I haven't many friends": Quoted in Bainbridge, Galahad edition, 234–35.

Beaton on Stokowski: Sam Green to BP, quoting Beaton (April 8, 1991). Lubitsch on Stokowski: Quoted in Garson Kanin, *Hollywood* (New York: Viking, 1967), 87–88.

356 "If you have my": GG letter no. 10 to Viertel (October 19, 1938).

357 "You just accumulate culture": GG–Sam Green tape (November 14–December 9, 1975).

"I must have seen": Ibid. (January 26, 1977).

"Oscar Levant was there": Peter Viertel to BP (Marbella, Spain, March 25, 1992).

"and they were always": David Diamond to BP (Rochester, N.Y., November 3, 1991).

358 "She has no set": Quoted in Nathaniel Benchley, "This is Garbo," *Collier's* (March 1, 1952), 56.

Garbo and Erich Maria Remarque: Paulette Goddard to Sam Green (Zurich, Switzerland, 1982).

"Gatsby is short, but": Quoted in Raymond Daum, *Walking with Garbo* (New York: HarperCollins, 1991), 186.

"Tell Madame Garbo that": Daum, *Walking*, 188.

Aldous and Maria Huxley: Mercedes de Acosta, *Here Lies the Heart* (New York: Reynal, 1960), 322.

359 Huxley meets Salka, does Marie Curie script: John Russell Taylor, *Strangers in Paradise: The Hollywood Émigrés, 1933–1950* (New York: Holt, Rinehart and Winston, 1983), 109.

Huxley's Marie Curie script: David King Dunaway, *Huxley in Hollywood* (New York: Harper & Row, 1989), 87.

Curie as protofeminist; Huxley waits for response to his script: Ibid., 102–3.

"It was instantly forgotten": Salka Viertel, *The Kindness of Strangers* (New York: Holt, Rinehart and Winston, 1969), 222–23.

"I would have been": Hettie Grimstead, *Screenland* (April 1938), 28.

360 "He was a small": de Acosta, 239–40.

"Garbo arrived, said she": Walter Reisch, quoted in Norman Zierold, *Garbo* (New York: Stein & Day, 1969), 98–99.

361 Original idea for *Ninotchka*: Maurice Zolotow, *Billy Wilder in Hollywood* (New York: Putnam's, 1977), 79.

"When I arrived, Miss": Quoted in *Hollywood Legends: The Life and Films of Humphrey Bogart and Greta Garbo*, vol. 1, no. 1, ed. Robert Osborne (Corvina, Calif.: Marvin Miller, 1968), 100.

"That idea of rigid": Billy Wilder to BP (Los Angeles, October 16, 1992).

362 *Ninotchka* breaking film taboo of day: Zolotow, 80.

"Because she was funny": Garson Kanin, *Hollywood* (New York: Viking, 1967), 87–88.

363 "Having worked with . . . all the extras": Undated "Cinegram Preview" by Ernst Lubitsch, Kevin Brownlow Collection. Also Raymond Daum, *Walking*, 134.

Garbo offended by posterior jokes: Zolotow, 83.

"Never since I had": de Acosta, 306.

365 "I am here to": Zierold, 65–66.

Ina Claire tap-danced for Garbo: Fritiof Billquist, *Garbo* (New York: Putnam's, 1960), 222.

366 "MGM employed her . . . sad roles": de Acosta, 225.

"Garbo's *Ninotchka* is one": Frank Nugent, *New York Times* (November 10, 1939).

"neither heavy with Thought": November 1, 1939, in *The Film Criticism of Otis Ferguson*, ed. by Robert Wilson (Philadelphia: Temple University Press, 1971), 275.

"I would never impose": Quoted in Kevin Brownlow, *The Parade's Gone By . . .* (New York: Knopf, 1968), 173.

367 "We have gardens" to "Ah, there you are": Kanin, 82–85.

368 "You never fought": Gray Reisfield to BP (New York, July 15, 1991).

"She eats intelligently": Gayelord Hauser, *W* (July 26, 1974), 5.

369 Garbo "ferocious" about punctuality and content of meals: Dana Wynter, *London Guardian* (May 10, 1990).

370 "That skinny Swedish actress": Daum, *People*.

Garbo disguised to look at house: Nathaniel Benchley, "This is Garbo," *Collier's* (March 1, 1952), 56.

"To dine on pineapple": Quoted in Daum, *Walking*, 157.

"They were obviously": Pamela Mason to BP (Beverly Hills, Calif., September 20, 1990).

371 "she credited him": Sam Green to BP (Fire Island, N.Y., June 29, 1991).

Garbo-Hauser properties: Camilla Snyder, "Gayelord Hauser: On the Move at 80," *New York Times* (March 24, 1974).

372 Jessica Dragonette's apartment as mini-salon: Zierold, 150. And Nicholas Turner to BP (New York, June 17, 1992).

"Will you vote": Jessica Dragonette, *Faith is a Song* (Paterson, N.J.: St. Anthony Guild Press, 1967), 254.

"I spoke to Salka Viertel": S. N. Behrman, "People in a Diary" (Part II), *New Yorker* (May 20, 1972), 79–80.

Behrman thought Salka was resentful of being cut out of *Ninotchka*: Louise Brooks letter to Kevin Brownlow (June 1, 1972).

373 "A pity that we": Gottfried Reinhardt, *The Genius: A Memoir of Max Reinhardt* (New York: Knopf, 1979), 100.

"Contrary to all the": Viertel, 152.

"She was the only one": Irene Mayer Selznick to BP (New York, September 8, 1990).

Script of *Two-Faced Woman*: Viertel, 247.

374 "At the time when": Ibid., 248.

"In those days, cinematized": Reinhardt, 104–5.

375 Constance Bennett's costume suggestions for Garbo: Quoted by George Oppenheimer, *New York Post* (July 24, 1990).

"Go away, Rhumba!": Hollis Alpert, "Saga of Greta Lovisa Gustafsson," *New York Times Magazine* (September 5, 1965), 56.

378 "Two days before": Quoted in Scott Eyman, *Five American Cinematographers* (Scarecrow Press, 1987), 43.

Garbo declines to autograph photo: Quoted in Benchley, 14–15.

"They are trying to": de Acosta, 314.

379 "Every last one of us": Reinhardt, 104–5.

380 "a challenge to every": Quoted in Charles Affron, "Uncensored Garbo," in Mast and Cohen, *Film Theory and Criticism* (New York: Oxford University Press, 1979), 731.

"simple-minded idea": Louise Brooks letter to Kevin Brownlow (April 19, 1972).

"We really had no": Quoted in Charles Higham and Joel Greenberg, eds., *The Celluloid Muse* (New York: New American Library, 1969), 66.

"was a shitty decision": Quoted in Boze Hadleigh, *Conversations with My Elders* (New York: St. Martin's, 1986), 135–36.

381 "Serious people naturally want": December 15, 1941, in Wilson, 400–2.

"Greta was humiliated by": de Acosta, 315.

"I'm very sorry that": Quoted by Irene Mayer Selznick to BP, New York, September 8, 1990.

382 Garbo agrees to charity engagements: Cholly Knickerbocker, *New York Journal-American* (February 22, 1942).

The Girl from Leningrad: Alexander Walker, *Garbo: A Portrait* (New York: Macmillan, 1980), 165.

383 "Garbo did the greatest thing": Quoted in Brownlow, 169–70.

"it was a Hollywood weariness": Jan Wahl, *Movie & Film Collector's World*, no. 166 (August 5, 1983).

"People often say glibly": Quoted in Higham and Greenberg, 66.

"Because the movie was so terrible": S. N. Behrman interview with David Davidson (October 2, 1962).

Grable-Garbo comparison: George Perry, *London Sunday Times* (April 22, 1990), E4.

384 "I don't think many people": Walter Reisch, quoted in Zierold, 97–98.

"Otto, I have wonderful news!": Otto Preminger, *Preminger* (New York: Doubleday, 1977), 84–86.

385 Heinrich Mann's birthday party: John Russell Taylor, *Strangers in Paradise: The Hollywood Émigrés, 1933–1950* (New York: Holt, Rinehart and Winston, 1983), 150.

386 "I had seen Garbo": Christopher Isherwood diaries, excerpted in *Buzz* (October 1991), 17–18.

"I said perhaps, someday": David Diamond to BP (Rochester, N.Y., March 4, 1990).

387 "All those wonderful people": David Diamond to BP.

"I walked in the": Quoted in Michael Shnayerson, *Irwin Shaw* (New York: Putnams's, 1989), 117.

"There was always a": Ibid. (June 10, 1990).

388 "I'm so happy here": Behrman interview with Davidson.

Cornell destroyed his box of Garbo: Cornell biographer Deborah Solomon to BP (New York, December 5, 1992).

389 "When she heard it": Barbara Barondess MacLean to BP (New York, January 29, 1991).

"She looked at pictures": David Davidson interview with Howard Dietz (October 11, 1962).

"I never played with": Edward G. Robinson, with Leonard Spiegelgass, *All My Yesterdays* (New York: Hawthorn, 1973), 219–21.

391 "Salka was horribly shattered": Diamond to BP (New York City, May 15, 1991).

Home burglarized: Unidentified clipping (July 8, 1944), Billy Rose Collection.

"Swedish film interests": Unidentified clipping (November 1, 1944), Billy Rose Collection.

"We used to signal": de Acosta, 324.

392 "At that time, I": Marcia Davenport to BP (Pebble Beach, Calif., April 17, 1990).

"if not—": Quoted in Dorothy Kilgallen, "Affairs of an Odd 'Old Maid'," *Saturday Home Magazine* (1948).

"Once she said": Sam Green to BP (Fire Island, N.Y., April 8, 1991).

393 "I might shorten the": Sven Broman, *Garbo on Garbo* (London: Bloomsbury, 1991), 20, quoting Lars Saxon article in *Lektyr* (1931).

Mercedes laments loss of gardener: de Acosta, 322.

MGM in World War II: Otto Friedrich, *City of Nets: A Portrait of Hollywood in the 1940s* (New York: Harper & Row, 1986), 49–51.

"He answered the door": Hugo Vickers, *Cecil Beaton* (Boston: Little, Brown, 1985), 326.

Garbo identification of Nazi collaborators: William Stevenson, *A Man Called Intrepid: The Secret War* (New York: Harcourt Brace Jovanovich, 1976), 54.

Garbo involved with British secret service: *New York Post* (February 13, 1980), 3.

394 "There were some things": Daum, *Walking*, 172 and 175.

Contribution to Swedish Relief Fund: Gray Reisfield to BP (July 15, 1991), and Daum, *Walking*, 174.

"If anyone has made": Quoted in Daum, *Walking*, 173–74.

CHAPTER 11:
MADEMOISELLE HAMLET 1946–1959

397 "I do not know": *Los Angeles Examiner* (February 20, 1947).

398 "She drinks champagne": *Newsweek* (August 25 and October 8, 1947).

"Her eyes were still": Cecil Beaton, *Self-Portrait With Friends: The Selected Diaries of Cecil Beaton, 1926–1974* (New York: Times Books, 1979), 176–77.

399 "a rather wacky": Ibid., 178.

"To be part of nature": Ibid., 180.

"Why don't you marry me?": Ibid., 179.

400 "Is that my beloved?" Ibid., 180–81.

"It would have been": Ibid., 181.

402 "Oo-la-la, no": "Sweden Welcomes Its Greta Garbo," unidentified newspaper clipping (July 17, 1946), Kevin Brownlow Collection.

"if more than one": Beaton, 182–83.

"Number one, he thought": Sam Green to BP (New York, September 29, 1991).

"This is no good": Beaton, 183–84.

404 "You're being a dope": Ibid., 198.

"Can I come around": Ibid., 199.

"I don't give": Ibid., 200.

"I was completely surprised": Hugo Vickers, *Cecil Beaton* (Boston: Little, Brown, 1985), 318.

405 "She said firmly that": Ibid., quoting Beaton diary entry (December 1, 1947), 319.

"The homosexual life": Ibid. (January 3, 1948), 325.

"That's just like her": Ibid. (December 11, 1947), 321.

"Here I was with": Ibid. (January 3, 1948), 325.

"I feel that the": Beaton, 201.

406 "It is really terrible": Beaton letter to GG (September 29, 1947), in Vickers, 315.

"I am so unexpectedly": Vickers, quoting Beaton diary entry (January ", 1948), 327.

"To make my winter's": Vickers, 329.

407 "when we do go": Beaton, 204.

"We suddenly looked": Vickers, 329.

"Curiously enough, Cecil": Vickers to BP (London, January 28, 1992).

"She was the only one": Boze Hadleigh, *Conversations with My Elders* (New York: St. Martin's, 1986), 68.

"the one thing": Beaton, 208.

408 "She was in high": Ibid., 206.

"and she was ecstatically": Ibid., diary entry (March 4, 1948).

"What a waste of": Beaton, 207.

Dinner party at Clemence Dane's: Ibid., 208–10.

409 Screening of *Anna Karenina:* Ibid., 210.

"With arms linked": Ibid., diary entry (March 14, 1948), 212.

"I'm an honest clear-cut": Ibid., 202.

410 GG and Tennessee Williams: Dotson Rader, *Tennessee: Cry of the Heart* (New York: Doubleday, 1985), 200–4.

"I got a big": Tennessee Williams letter to Donald Windham, quoted in Raymond Daum, *Walking with Garbo*, ed. by Vance Muse (New York: HarperCollins, 1991), 184–85.

"Garbo arrived all bundled": Rader, 200–4.

411 "Mink is for football": Quoted in Daum, 127.

"I can't give you": Valentina Schlee to Hugo Vickers (August 17, 1983), in Vickers, 313.

412 "had terrible nerves": Irene Mayer Selznick to BP (New York, September 8, 1990).

413 Schlee as the Stiller of GG's middle age: Daum, 211.

"She whistled and sighed": Beaton, 180.

"On every day that": David G. Townsend letter to BP (October 18, 1989).

414 "Mademoiselle Hamlet": Quoted in John Bainbridge, *Garbo* (New York: Doubleday, 1955), 228.

"I'm annoyed, I want": Green to BP.

"I thought, 'What's the'": Daum, 215–16.

415 "a woman of every": Quoted in Jhan Robbins, "The Secret Life of Greta Garbo," *This Week* (October 4, 1959), 17.

Garbo, Schlee, and Valentina: John Bainbridge, *Garbo*, 229–30; Marcia Davenport to BP (Pebble Beach, Calif., April 17, 1990).

"I love [Garbo]": Dorothy Kilgallen, "Affairs of an Odd 'Old Maid'," *Saturday Home Magazine* (1948).

"Drinks with Valentina": *The Noël Coward Diaries*, ed. Graham Payn and Sheridan Morley (Boston: Little, Brown, 1982), 91 (September 9, 1947), 265 (April 15, 1955), 289 (October 30, 1955).

416 "a connoisseur of the": Bainbridge, *Look*.

"That Russian sturgeon": Beaton letter to GG (September 29, 1947), in Vickers, 315.

"she possesses a new": Unidentified newspaper clipping (1949), Kevin Brownlow Collection.

"Garbo moved in and": Quoted in Michael Gross, "Garbo's Last Days," *New York* (May 21, 1990), 42.

"He had absolute control": Quoted in Bainbridge, *Look*.

417 "She will not fight": Paraphrased by Nathaniel Benchley, "This is Garbo," *Collier's* (March 1, 1952), 56.

"I came into the": Quoted in Brian O'Dowd, "Why Garbo Quit Movies," *Hollywood Studio Magazine* (November 1987), 14.

"She reminds me of": Quoted in Bainbridge, *Garbo*, 229.

"I have no plans": Quoted by Croswell Bowen, *New York Herald Tribune* (September 6, 1946).

"I was quite anxious": Katharine Hepburn, *Me* (New York: Knopf, 1991), 224.

418 "she could be": *Memo from David O. Selznick*, ed. Rudy Behlmer (New York: Viking, 1972), 360, 370.

Hitchcock claims concerning Garbo dropping *Paradine Case:* Quoted in Charles Higham and Joel Greenberg, eds., *The Celluloid Muse: Hollywood Directors Speak* (New York: Signet, 1969), 105.

419 "I spoke to Hayward": GG letter no. 15 to Salka Viertel (undated, circa 1947).

"She said, 'Yes' ": Billy Wilder to BP (Los Angeles, October 16, 1992).

"Billy started with the": Walter Reisch, quoted in Norman Zierold, *Garbo* (New York: Stein & Day, 1969), 99–100.

420 Phèdre: Unidentified clipping, probably from *Variety* (October 15, 1949), Billy Rose Collection.

421 "I'm meeting with Miss G": Walter Wanger Collection, University of Wisconsin.

"Greta will have a": Salka Viertel letter to George Cukor (June 16, 1948), AMPAS.

"I could see Greta": Beaton, 208.

422 "Greta was deeply moved": Viertel letter to Cukor (September 28, 1948), AMPAS.

Pabst and *Odyssey:* Herman G. Weinberg, *New York Times* (March 19, 1950); and [Los Angeles?] *Citizen News* (February 1, 1950).

"Salka became another mother": Patricia Bosworth, *Montgomery Clift: A Biography* (New York: Harcourt Brace Jovanovich, 1976), 142.

"Every studio wants him": Viertel letter to Cukor (September 28, 1948).

423 Eugene Frenke telegram to Walter Wanger (September 25, 1948), Walter Wanger Collection, University of Wisconsin.

"Garbo anxious to": Wanger telegram to Frenke (October 1, 1948). Walter Wanger Collection, University of Wisconsin.

"When can I look": Ibid. (October 19, 1948).

"We do it right": Beaton, 202.

"I'll do it": Ibid., 202–3.

"It seems the Almighty": Ibid., diary entry (March 9, 1948), 208.

424 "yet she harks back": Ibid. (March 10, 1948).

"a woman whose instincts": Honoré de Balzac, *La Duchesse de Langeais* (Philadelphia: Avil Publishing, 1901), vol. 35 (*The Thirteen*), 165.

"Nations, like women": Ibid., 155.

425 "I drove there": Joshua Logan, *Josh: My Up and Down, In and Out Life* (New York: Delacorte Press, 1976), 131.

James Wong Howe, quoted in *Empire* (June 1990).

427 "She was like a": Howe, paraphrased by Benchley, 15.

428 "She was very outgoing": Pamela Mason to BP (Beverly Hills, Calif., 1991).
"James wasn't much": Ibid.

429 "asked for her usual": Dana Wynter, *London Guardian* (May 10, 1990).

430 "according to how well": Quoted in *Photoplay* (November 1927).
"I haven't mentioned her": S. N. Behrman interview with David Davidson (October 2, 1962).
"She came over": Quoted in *Face-to-Face with Connie Chung:* "The Last Days of Garbo," CBS documentary (September 3, 1990).

431 "I was informed that": Quoted in Scott Eyman, "Clarence Brown: Garbo and Beyond," *Velvet Light Trap* (Spring 1978), 22.

433 "I'm sorry, I": Quoted in O'Dowd, 14.
"two crazy monsters": Quoted in Richard Corliss, *Garbo* (New York: Pyramid Books, 1974), 142.

434 "I think she would": Quoted in Bainbridge, *Look*.
"She just throws": Jessica Dragonette, *Faith is a Song* (Paterson, N.J.: St. Anthony Guild Press, 1967), 257.
"It's amazing when you": Roddy McDowall to BP (Los Angeles, September 1, 1991).
"It is nice here": *Letters of E. B. White*, ed. by Dorothy Lobrano Guth (New York: Harper & Row, 1976), 392.
Removal of sign: Daum, 129.

435 "She seems to be": Paraphrased by Benchley, 14.
"I saw her quite": Davenport to BP.
Gunther arrangements for Garbo: Robbins.
"She has a poetic": Quoted in Hollis Alpert, "Saga of Greta Lovisa Gustafsson," *New York Times Magazine* (September 5, 1965), 57.
Clift and Garbo: Bosworth, 280.
"the first naked": David Niven, *The Moon's a Balloon* (New York: Putnam's, 1972), 311.

436 "The Swedish members": Ibid., 322.
"I usually go somewhere": GG letter no. 17 to Salka Viertel (May 6, 1954).
"The high spot": Payn, 359.
"Oh, Greta just": Raymond R. Sarlot and Fred E. Basten, *Life at the Marmont* (Santa Monica: Roundtable, 1987), 155, courtesy William Donati.
"She hadn't picked up": Ibid., 156.
Garbo and Chevalier: Ibid., 156–57.

437 "I have disappeared": GG letter no. 14 to Viertel (postmarked Santa Fe, New Mexico, circa 1954).
Two kinds of men in Garbo's life: Alexander Walker, quoted in *New York Daily News* (November 3, 1980), 10.
"Beaton and every other": Green to BP.

438 "She has the most": letter (December 2, 1951), quoted in Vickers, 354.
Huxley's opinion of Garbo: Quoted in Philip Hoare, *Serious Pleasures: The Life of Stephen Tennant* (London: Hamish Hamilton, 1990), 313.
"There's nothing left now": Beaton, 238.
"The way he has managed": Vickers quoting Beaton diary (October 2, 1949), 343.

439 "Try and mention": Ibid. (June 27, 1949).

"how vulgar my": Ibid. (December 1950), 348.

"I do love you": Beaton, 303–4.

440 "Fame, by insulating her": Kenneth Tynan, *Sight & Sound*, vol. 23, no. 4 (April–June 1954), 187.

"Thank you, but": Jean Negulesco, *Things I Did . . . and Things I Think I Did* (New York: Simon & Schuster, 1984), 211.

"Look, now she's": Benchley, 56.

GG left *Romance* in middle: David Diamond to BP (Rochester, N.Y., March 4, 1990).

441 "Maybe people don't want": Benchley.

Menotti attempts to interest Garbo in *The Medium:* Oliver Daniel, *Stokowski: A Counterpoint of View* (New York: Dodd, Mead, 1982), 357–58.

"She wanted so much": John Springer (circa 1961).

Anna Karenina and *Camille* on Italian TV: Bainbridge, *Look.*

442 Sellout Garbo festival: Ibid.

CHAPTER 12:
GARBO LOST 1960–1979

445 "I don't have to live": Raymond Daum, *Walking with Garbo* (New York: HarperCollins, 1991), 197.

No royalties: Theodore Kurz to BP (New York, May 7, 1991).

"I'm lucky to be": Daum, 207.

446 "I was thinking maybe": Ibid., 213.

447 "There's no point in": William Baldwin, *Billy Baldwin Remembers* (New York: Harcourt Brace Jovanovich, 1974), 174.

"like a ballet dancer": Ibid., 171.

"I have never worn": Ibid., 173.

"We put her into": Mary Martin, *My Heart Belongs* (New York: Warner, 1977), 221–22.

"We lived in the": Nin Ryan to Maria Ciaccia (New York, March 8, 1993).

448 "Sometimes I put on": Nathaniel Benchley, "This is Garbo," *Collier's* (March 1, 1952), 56.

"Cécile just bullied her": Sam Green to BP (Fire Island, N.Y., June 29, 1991).

"[The Rothschilds] don't have": GG to Sam Green, tape (New York, December 15–January 10, 1976). This and all subsequent Garbo-Green tapes are dated and indicated in these notes with the general (and sometimes incomplete) labels affixed to the original cassettes.

449 "If you had something": Quoted in Michael Gross, "Garbo's Last Days," *New York* (April 20, 1990), 42.

"People have always tried": Quoted in Hugo Vickers, *Cecil Beaton* (Boston: Little, Brown, 1985), 499. Cécile de Rothschild to Cecil Beaton quoted in Beaton diary entry of August 1965.

"There was a camaraderie": Green to BP.

451 "Do you mind if a": Jean Negulesco, *Things I Did . . . and Things I Think I Did* (New York: Simon & Schuster, 1984), 206–7.

"A simple, delicious" to "more specific suggestion": Quoted in Jhan Robbins, "The Secret Life of Greta Garbo," *This Week* (October 4, 1959), 17.

"a warm and scented night": Kerstin Bernadotte, "Greta Garbo," *Ladies' Home Journal* (April 1976), photographs by Carl Johan Bernadotte, 93 and 150–52.

"She couldn't compete with": Green to BP.

452 "I have to leave you": Daum, 211.

"My little friend G.S.": GG letter no. 22 to Salka Viertel (undated, circa 1961).

"I am leaving for": GG letter no. 20 to Viertel (undated, circa 1961).

453 "I have had it": Quoted by Diana Vreeland to Hugo Vickers (November 15, 1981).

"The exorcising was": John Bainbridge, "Garbo is 65," *Look* (September 8, 1970), 52.

454 Schlee put Garbo possessions in his name; and Beaton quotes: Green to BP.

"Madame V. [is] forever praying": Daum, 211.

"You would never know": GG letter no. 21 to Viertel (July 10, 1962).

"It has been so": GG letter no. 28 to Viertel (undated, circa 1966).

455 "Will arrive in Zurich": GG letter no. 36 to Viertel (July 1, 1967).

"I shall wire when": GG letter no. 41 to Viertel (July 13, 1968).

"She used to pay": Peter Viertel to BP (Marbella, Spain, March 24, 1992).

Garbo's habits in Klosters: Bainbridge, 52.

456 "For Garbo, Salka is": Ibid.

"We'd all go to": Quoted in Michael Shnayerson, *Irwin Shaw: A Biography* (New York: Putnam, 1989), 224.

"Brian, Eleonore and Greta": *The Noël Coward Diaries*, ed. Graham Payn and Sheridan Morley (Boston: Little, Brown, 1982), 568.

457 "GG complained about the": Negulesco, 212–13.

"I am here with my": GG letter no. 54 to Salka Viertel (December 20, 1971).

"I am living in my": GG letter no. 65 to Viertel (undated, circa 1972).

458 "Many times I went": Frederick Sands and Sven Broman, *The Divine Garbo* (New York: Grosset & Dunlap, 1979), 225.

"I spend three months": Daum, 206.

"It's so boring year": GG to Green, quoted to BP.

459 "Once in the late": Deborah Kerr to BP (Marbella, Spain, March 27, 1992).

"She couldn't have been": Jack Larson, *Washington Post* (April 20, 1990).

"Salka was a very": Gray Reisfield to BP (New York, July 15, 1991).

Garbo at Bernadotte villa: Bernadotte, 93 and 150–52.

460 "I am very pleased": Daum, 194.

"She knew when to": Quoted in David Shipman, *Movie Talk* (New York: St. Martin's, 1989), 80.

461 "Entering it from the": Truman Capote, *Local Color* (New York: Random House, 1950), 13–15.

462 "The story of my": Daum, 199.

"Garbo appeared fascinated by": Alan Levy, "Garbo Walks," *Show* (June 1963), 93.

"What are we doing": Ibid., 196 and 199.

463 "I did most of the cooking": Claire Koger to BP, New York City, May 10, 1994. Also, Claire Koger to Richard Schmidt, May 19, 1994.

"My girl is coming": GG to Green (undated, circa 1976).

"I just listen to": Daum, 210.

464 "It's all so": Quoted by Ray Daum to BP, November 13, 1992.

"It can be terribly": Pamela Mason to BP (Beverly Hills, Calif., September 20, 1990).

465 "Everyone who knows Garbo": Jessica Dragonette, *Faith is a Song* (Paterson, N.J.: St. Anthony Guild Press, 1967), 255–57.

"She was interested in": Kitty Carlisle Hart to Maria Ciaccia (New York, April 6, 1993).

466 "I saw [Garbo] last": Truman Capote, "La Côte Basque 1965," *Esquire* (November 1972), 119.

"The overall impression is": Daum, *Walking*, 209.

"a dreadful hotchpotch": Vickers quoting Beaton, diary entry (January 1954), 375.

"Truman Capote isn't first": Ibid. (December 1948), 342.

"[Garbo] will never be": Vickers, 359.

"I'll be right over": Vickers quoting Beaton, diary entry (Spring 1959), 429.

Beaton upset over marriage of Anthony Armstrong-Jones to Princess Margaret: Ibid. (Spring 1960), 436.

467 Beaton visits to Valentina Schlee: Vickers, 552.

"He liked to give": GG to Green (March 2, 1975).

468 "She kept us all": Quoted in Gross, 40.

Garbo attends Galitzine show: New York *Herald Tribune* (October 23, 1963).

"Well, there was a": GG to Green (January 26, 1977).

"I think she was": Bainbridge, 56.

"longer than I have": Bernadotte, 152.

469 "Lem was sure": David Michaelis, *The Best of Friends: Profiles of Extraordinary Friendships* (New York: Morrow, 1983), 177–78.

470 "after his death she": Daum, *People*.

Garbo attending séances: Kenny Kingston to BP (Los Angeles, July 16, 1992).

471 "She ate that": Green to BP.

Scandinavian Folk Tales, ed. Jacqueline Simpson (London: Penguin, 1988), 158.

"We developed a little": Green to BP. This interview is also the source of the quotations contained in the following nine paragraphs.

473 "That I cannot do": Peter Hanson to BP (New York, April 20, 1988).

"You can tell all": Radie Harris, *Radie's World* (New York: Putnam, 1975), 50–51.

"It has nothing to do": GG to Green (November 3–12, 1975).

"That's not the way": Ibid. (November 14–December 9, 1975).

474 "What do I buy?": Ibid. (March 10–16, 1976?).

475 "because I don't get": Ibid. (March 1, 1976).

"You may-tain": Ibid. (February 1975).

476 "She had to do *something*": Claire Koger to BP, New York City, May 10, 1994.

"No. I should": GG to Green (December 15–January 10, 1976).

"No. Never be anything": Ibid. (November 3–12, 1975).

"Did you get up": Ibid. (January 24–March 2, 1975).

477 "It was dark by": Green to BP (New York, May 8, 1991).

478 "Sometimes somebody will call": GG to Green (February 17, 1975).

"I have no idea": Ibid. (February 17, 1975).

"Is there anything I": Ibid. (January 30, 1976).

480 Garbo visit to Halston: Green to BP (New York, May 8, 1991).

"You send it on": GG to Green (November 14–December 9, 1975, and January–March 1976).

481 "I've got a wart": Ibid. (June 23, 1977).

"That shattered the whole": Green to BP (New York, May 8, 1991).

"I'm frightened. I don't": GG to Green (January 24–28, 1975 or 1976?).

"You went to": Ibid. (December 15, 1975–January 10, 1976).

482 "I am the mystery": Gross, 41.

"I have tax that": GG to Green (November 14–December 9, 1975).

"I don't know about": Ibid. (December 15, 1975–January 28, 1976).

483 "I don't want to": Ibid. (December 15, 1975–January 10, 1976).

"I can't do that": Ibid. (March 10–16, 1976).

"I wish my good": Ibid. (June 23, 1977).

484 "She changed into a": Ava Gardner, *Ava: My Story* (New York: Bantam, 1990), 169–70.

"Don't you think it's": Daum, *Walking*, 167.

"I got there first": Ibid., 165.

"George's way of choreographing": Roddy McDowall to BP (Beverly Hills, Calif., July 16, 1992).

"Thank you. I would": GG telegram to Ingrid Bergman, July 9, 1939. Courtesy of Jeanine Basinger and Leith Johnson, Cinema Archives of Wesleyan University.

485 "I was there for three": Ingrid Bergman, *My Story* (New York: Delacorte, 1980), 95.

Garbo-Bergman meeting: Ibid., 96–97.

486 "I wanted to express": Liv Ullmann to BP (Boston, May 18, 1992).

"She must think I": Green to BP (New York, May 8, 1991).

"As he watched her": Dotson Rader, *Tennessee: Cry of the Heart* (Garden City, N.Y.: Doubleday, 1985), 202.

487 John Lennon signed name "Greta Hughes": Green to BP (September 29, 1991).

"I've only experienced love": Steven Naifeh and Gregory White Smith, *Jackson Pollock: An American Saga* (New York: Clarkson Potter, 1989), 769.

"She lights on your": Bainbridge, 235.

"People don't understand that": GG to Green (November 3–12, 1975).

"I was in a trance": Daum, *Walking*, 210.

Garbo at the Peppermint Lounge: Bernadotte, 150.

488 "The best thing is": Daum, *Life*, 98.

"What I saw was": Michael J. W. Green, "The Day I Saw Garbo," *7 Days* (May 6, 1990), 53.

"I went [because] my periodontist": GG to Green (January 24–28, 1975?).

489 "Nothing. I didn't ask": David Diamond to BP (Rochester, N.Y., November 3, 1991).

"It was pandemonium": Daum, *Walking*, 25.

Garbo at Chasen's: Ibid., 120.

"I was so nervous": Kerr to BP (Marbella, Spain, March 27, 1992).

490 "Are we going to": GG to Green (January–March 1976).

"I ain't sayin' nothin' ": Ibid. (Fall 1975).

"only matters to people": Daum, *Walking*, 23.

"If I hadn't been": Ibid., 137.

"I got a horrible": GG to Green (1975).

491 "Can I go in my": Ibid. (March 10–16, 1976?).

"The dark glasses were": Diamond to BP.

"Do you really like it": Norman Zierold, *Garbo* (New York: Stein & Day, 1969), 148.

492 Garbo watching craftsmen: John Bainbridge, *Garbo* (New York: Doubleday, 1955), 234–35.

Garbo purchased tabloids: Quoted on *Face-to-Face with Connie Chung:* "The Last Days of Garbo," CBS documentary (September 3, 1990).

"she liked to sit": Diamond to BP (March 4, 1990).

"When the bagpipes come": GG to Green (March 10–16, 1976?).

493 "Unless one is in": Truman Capote, *Local Color*, 13–15.

"To run from place": Daum, *Life*, 98; and *People*.

495 "I traveled with them": Green to BP (Fire Island, N.Y., September 29, 1991).

"Oooh, he looks so much": Ibid.

496 "These were two women": Joseph Lebworth to BP (New York, February 22, 1992).

497 "They sat next to": Caral Gimbel Lebworth to BP (New York, February 22, 1992).

498 "Can't they see I'm": This and quoted material in the subsequent four paragraphs, Green to BP (September 29, 1991), quoting from his journal entries of the time.

499 "In conversation, I'll say": Green journal entries (September 3 and 9, 1982).

500 "That weekend visit": "Suzy Says" (July 28, 1968), quoted in Daum, *Walking*, 206.

"I'm sure you can": GG to Green (November 14–December 9, 1975).

501 "What do you do": Ibid. (December 15, 1975–January 10, 1976).

"I was thinking yesterday": Ibid. (November 3–12, 1975).

"Thinking of the enchantment": Ibid.

503 "Once the royal family": Green to BP (Fire Island, N.Y., September 28, 1991).

504 "Even Stokowski didn't sell": Vickers, 563, quoting Beaton diary (May 21, 1972).

"I cut Beaton off": Kerr to BP (Marbella, Spain, March 27, 1992).

"In London that trip": This and quoted material in the subsequent five paragraphs, Green to BP (Fire Island, N.Y., September 28, 1991).

505 "Yes, I can": GG to Green (March 2, 1975).

"the way they emphasize": Daum, *Walking*, 97.

"I can't stand people": Daum, *Life*, 100.

"I am the image": Daum, *Walking*, 180.

506 "That makes me think": GG to Green (March 3, 1978).

"I am very happy": Jay Brien Chapman, "Solving the Garbo Mystery" (unidentified magazine article, circa 1933).

"I suppose I suffer": GG letter no. 52 to Salka Viertel (February 6, 1971).

"Poor little people": Daum, *Life*, 98.

"I wish to God . . . when they pray": Daum, *People*. "I envy people . . . having a whiskey": Daum, *Life*, 100.

507 "and how happy it": Baldwin, 171–72.

"Do you mean to": Daum, "Greta Garbo: Memories of a Swedish Christmas," *Scandinavian Review* (Winter 1990), 66–70.

"Someone put out their": Daum, *Walking*, 218.

"I had at least": GG to Green (February 1, 1976).

508 "I'm a sour little": Daum, *Life*, 100.

"Not much, no": GG to Green (December 15, 1975).

"I've messed up my": Sands and Broman, 234.

509 "Well, here's another chapter": Daum, *People*.

"If somebody gave me": Daum, *Life*, 100.

"To write of Greta": Mercedes de Acosta, *Here Lies the Heart* (New York: Reynal, 1960), 226.

510 "I remember that, because": Daum, *Walking*, 172.

"There's hardly no one": Quoted by Mordaunt Hall, *New York Times* (March 24, 1929), section 10, 7.

"I went full of": Sands and Broman, 226.

511 "It is not": GG to Green (January–March 1976).

"I could no more": Daum, *Life*, 98.

"I fry so seldom": Daum, *Walking*, 142–43, 156.

512 "Two eggs for dinner": GG to Green (February 1975).

"if I had spaghetti": GG to Green (March 2, 1975).

513 "I hear people say": Daum, *Walking*, 158.

"Greta Garbo and I were": Ingmar Bergman, *The Magic Lantern* (New York: Penguin, 1988), 239–41.

514 "all the time, one": GG to Green (January 24–28, 1975?).

"You know, it's so": Ibid.

"All they care about": Daum, *People*.

CHAPTER 13:
GARBO REGAINED 1980–1990

518 "Her instinct, her mastery": Quoted in *Hollywood Legends, The Life and Films of Humphrey Bogart and Greta Garbo*, vol. 1, no. 1, ed. Robert Osborne (Corvina, Calif.: Marvin Miller, 1968), 105.

"I'm convinced she was": Sam Green to BP (Fire Island, N.Y., June 29, 1991).

519 "If someone commented on": Ibid.

"we know far too": Quoted in *New York Daily News* (November 3, 1980), 10.

520 "She was compassionate about": Jane Gunther, tribute to Garbo in Sotheby's "The Greta Garbo Collection" (1990), 9.

"I called the headwaiter": Oscar Levant, *The Unimportance of Being Oscar* (New York: Putnam's, 1968), 125–26.

521 "She's amused by people": Nathaniel Benchley, "This is Garbo," *Collier's* (March 1, 1952), 15.

"Stories were being told": Quoted in Dana Wynter, "Why Garbo Retired at 36," *London Guardian* (May 10, 1990).

"I went to the": Quoted in S. N. Behrman interview with David Davidson (October 2, 1962).

"Aren't you Greta Garbo?": Quoted by Michelle Palermo, interviewed on *Face-to-Face with Connie Chung:* "The Last Days of Garbo" CBS documentary (September 3, 1990).

522 "The fact that Mama": David Diamond to BP (New York, March 4, 1990).

"What is your play": Kenneth Jupp, "One Hour Alone with Garbo," *Independent on Sunday* (April 22, 1990), 8.

523 "I am a lonely": Bainbridge, "Garbo is 65," *Look*, 56.

"I sensed someone coming": Green to BP.

"It was the time": Ibid.

524 "Do you know who": Quoted in David W. Dunlap and Sara Rimer, "New York Day by Day," *New York Times* (April 3, 1985).

"Isn't that funny, one": GG to Green (November 14–December 9, 1975).

525 "Rice. You know, I'm": Ibid. (January 28, 1976).

"I keep thinking": Ibid. (November 14–December 9, 1975).

"It would be so": Ibid. (December 15, 1975).

"Garbo To Wed At 80": *Globe*, vol. 32, no. 44 (October 29, 1985), 17.

526 "Why not? Children play": Green to BP.

Tomte-trolls: *Scandinavian Folktales*, ed. and trans. Jacqueline Simpson (London: Penguin, 1988), 165–68.

528 "The only way a woman": Clare Boothe Brokaw [Luce], "The Great Garbo," *Vanity Fair* (February 1932), 63, 87.

"Isn't it strange?": Garson Kanin, *Hollywood* (New York: Viking, 1967), 86.

529 "there were no models": Carolyn G. Heilbrun, *Writing a Woman's Life* (New York: Ballantine, 1989), 111, 31, 50.

"We had a very nice": Irene Mayer Selznick to BP (New York, September 8, 1990).

"She was very chatty": Pamela Mason to BP (Beverly Hills, Calif., September 20, 1990).

"If she had one she": Quoted in *New York Times* (May 26, 1972).

"or married Gayelord Hauser": Green to BP.

530 "He just had to": Quoted in Ray Daum, *Walking with Garbo* (New York: HarperCollins, 1991), 167.

531 "Phooey on Bushy and": GG to Gray Horan, quoted in "Garbo's Refuge," *New York Times Magazine* (September 2, 1990), 33.

"I watch the dreck": Quoted in *People*, April 30, 1990, p. 95; also Green to BP (New York, May 8, 1991).

"She just *looked*," "It was a secret," and "There is only one Garbo": Claire Koger to BP, New York City, May 10, 1994. Also, Claire Koger to Richard Schmidt, May 19, 1994.

Garbo made a Commander of the Swedish Order of the North Star: *New York Times* (November 3, 1983).

533 "It's much better that": GG to Green (November 1975).

"Well, I only glanced a": Ibid. (January 24–28, 1975?).

534 "You said I would": GG letter to Robert Reud (1941), quoted in *New York Post* (September 6, 1987).

"I am going to a": GG letter no. 22 to Salka Viertel (undated, circa early 1960s).

"because she thought it": Claire Koger to Richard Schmidt, New York City, May 19, 1994.

535 "Jessica would lecture, and": Nicholas Turner to BP (New York, June 17, 1992).

"I wish I knew": GG to Green (February 1, 1976).

536 "I spoke with her": Caral Gimbel Lebworth to BP (New York, February 22, 1992).

"Hiya, Doc!" Quoted in *New York Post* (September 5, 1990).

537 "There is absolutely no": Richard Schmidt to BP, New York City, May 10, 1994.

"She came to visit once": Claire Koger to BP, New York City, May 10, 1994. Also, Claire Koger to Richard Schmidt, May 19, 1994.

538 "She was a very good person": Claire Koger to BP, New York City, May 10, 1994. They got along nicely: Claire Koger to BP, New York City, May 10, 1994. Also, Claire Koger to Richard Schmidt, May 19, 1994.

539 "She meant a lot to me . . . became obsessive": Ted Leyson, interview, *Face-to-Face with Connie Chung:* "The Last Days of Garbo." "I admire and love . . . after Clarence Bull": Leyson to BP (New York, February 27, 1992).

"Instead, both the winged": Selma Lagerlöf, *The Wonderful Adventures of Nils* (London: Puffin, 1990), 256.

540 "I worked for her": Quoted in Gross, 41.

541 "She pruned extensively": Gray Reisfield to BP (New York, July 15, 1991).

542 "From early childhood": Original Gronowicz typescript for *An Orange Full of Dreams*. The published version differs slightly.

"It's inconceivable that she": Ibid. (May 7, 1991).

"Except physically, we know": Tynan, 188.

543 "a vulgar peasant whose": Louise Brooks letter to Kevin Brownlow (October 18, 1968).

"For artists without an": Truman Capote, *Local Color* (New York: Random House, 1950), 15.

"a great native intelligence": Quoted in Boze Hadleigh, *Conversations with My Elders* (New York: St. Martin's, 1986), 135–36.

"She had no intellectual": David Davidson interview with Howard Dietz (October 11, 1962), Kevin Brownlow Collection.

"By not leading the": Alexander Walker, *Sex in the Movies* (Middlesex, U.K.: Penguin, 1968), 101.

544 "I applauded like mad": Daum, 194.

"Amidst the excitement and affectionate": Jack Larson, *Washington Post* (April 20, 1990).

545 "She was not a person": Gray Reisfield to BP (July 15, 1991).

"The thing about great": Lina Basquette to BP (Wheeling, W.Va., April 19, 1992).

"I should like to": Katherine Albert, "Did Brown and Garbo Fight?" *Photoplay* (March 1931), 130.

546 "often superficially childlike": de Acosta, 318–19.

"Garbo is lonely": Marie Dressler, *My Own Story* (Boston: Little, Brown, 1934), 251–52.

"She is a lone wolf": de Acosta, 318–19.

"She is incapable of": Quoted in Bainbridge, *Garbo*, 224.

"She knew people thought": Green to BP.

"Many of [her friends]": Gilbert Adrian, *Ladies, Lions, and Life* (unpublished manuscript, 195?), 42.

547 "Oh, thank God!" GG to Green ("Garbo, Rothschilds, McIlhenny," 1976).

Garbo never entertained more than a friend or two at a time: Bainbridge, *Garbo*, 237.

"by a feeling that": Quoted in Jhan Robbins, *This Week* (October 4, 1959), 17.

"You will never find": GG to Green (January–March 1976).

"One of the early": Reisfield to BP (July 15, 1991).

"The greater Garbo became": Walker, 120.

548 "I am not keen": Quoted in Sven Stolpe, *Christina of Sweden* (New York: Macmillan, 1966), 146.

"Nothing intrudes between": Tynan, 187.

549 "She gave you the": Bainbridge, *Garbo*, 218.

"does not make the": Robert Herring in *Garbo and the Night Watchmen*, ed. Alistair Cooke (New York: McGraw-Hill, 1971), 258.

"Surely it is enough": Truman Capote, *Local Color*, 14.

"We gradually find out": Åke Sundborg, "That Gustafsson Girl" (Part I), *Photoplay* (April 1930), 40.

"were plainly designed to": Kenneth Tynan, "Garbo," *Sight and Sound*, vol. 23, no. 4 (April–June 1954), 188.

"The furthest stage to which": Isabel Quigley, quoted in Raymond Durgnat and John Kobal, *Greta Garbo* (New York: Dutton, 1965), 70.

"unforgivable if only because": Quoted in Bainbridge, *Garbo*, 219.

"The failure of her": Behrman interview with Davidson.

"I never liked my": Quoted in Jean Negulesco, *Things I Did . . . and Things I Think I Did* (New York: Simon & Schuster, 1984), 214.

"I'm not a versatile": Quoted in Leslie Halliwell, *The Filmgoer's Book of Quotes* (New York: Signet, 1975), 83.

"I believe today, in": de Acosta, 316.

550 Garbo comeback: Walker, 119.

"Who would want a second": Daum, 180.

"Do I not find": Tynan, 220.

"Indeed, we have no": Richard Corliss, *Garbo* (New York: Pyramid Books, 1974), 145.

"Anybody who is truthful": Davidson interview with Dietz.

"She is brave, poor": Bainbridge, *Garbo*, 238.

551 GG as ornament of her age: Ibid., 11.

GG's idealism and realism: Durgnat and Kobal, 13.

"Alfred Lunt said Garbo": Brooks letter to Brownlow.

"She was a very quiet": Quoted in Bernard Rosenberg and Harry Silverstein, *The Real Tinsel* (London: Macmillan Co., 1970), 27.

552 "Seeing her here, one": *The Film Criticism of Otis Ferguson*, ed. Robert Wilson (Philadelphia: Temple University Press, 1971), 171.

BIBLIOGRAPHY

BOOKS

Acosta, Mercedes de. *Here Lies the Heart*. New York: Reynal, 1960.

Adrian, Gilbert. *Ladies, Lions, and Life*. Unpublished manuscript, circa 195?.

Affron, Charles. *Star Acting: Gish, Garbo, Davis*. New York: E. P. Dutton, 1977.

Agee, James. *Agee on Film*, Vol. 1, "Essays and Reviews." New York: Perigee Books, 1983.

Alleman, Richard. *The Movie Lover's Guide to Hollywood*. New York: Harper Colophon Books, 1985.

Bainbridge, John. *Garbo*. New York: Doubleday & Co., 1955.

Baldwin, William. *Billy Baldwin Remembers*. New York: Harcourt Brace Jovanovich, 1974.

Balzac, Honoré de. *La Duchesse de Langeais*. Philadelphia: Avil Publishing Co., 1901. Vol. 35 (*The Thirteen*).

Bankhead, Tallulah. *Tallulah*. New York: Harper & Brothers, 1952.

Barthes, Roland. *Mythologies*. 1957 Editions du Seuil (Paris) translated from the French by Jonathan Cape, 1972, reprinted by permission of Hill and Wang in Mast and Cohen, *Film Theory and Criticism*, "The Face of Garbo," 720–21.

Beaton, Cecil. *Self-Portrait With Friends: The Selected Diaries of Cecil Beaton, 1926–1974*. Edited by Richard Buckle. New York: Times Books, 1979; London: Weidenfeld & Nicholson, 1979.

Bergman, Ingmar. *The Magic Lantern*. Translated by Joan Tate. New York: Penguin Books, 1988.

Bergman, Ingrid, and Alan Burgess. *Ingrid Bergman: My Story*. New York: Delacorte Press, 1980.

Billquist, Fritiof. *Garbo*. Translated by Maurice Michael and Arthur Barker. New York: G. P. Putnam's Sons, 1960.

Blei, Franz. *Die Gottliche Garbo*. Giessen, Germany: Kindt und Bucher, 1930.

Broman, Sven. *Garbo on Garbo*. London: Bloomsbury Publishing, 1992.

Brooks, Louise. *Lulu in Hollywood*. New York: Alfred A. Knopf, 1982.

Brownlow, Kevin. *The Parade's Gone By . . .* New York: Alfred A. Knopf, 1968.

Capote, Truman. *Local Color*. New York: Random House, 1950.

Carr, Larry. *Four Fabulous Faces*. New York: Galahad Books, 1970.

Conway, Michael, Dion McGregor, and Mark Ricci, eds. *The Films of Greta Garbo*. With an introductory essay by Parker Tyler, "The Garbo Image." New York: Bonanza Books, 1963.

Cooke, Alistair, ed. *Garbo and the Night Watchmen*. New York: McGraw-Hill Book Co., 1971. Originally published in 1937.

Corliss, Richard. *Garbo*. New York: Pyramid Books, 1974.

Cornell, Katharine, as told to Ruth Woodbury Sedgwick. *I Wanted to Be an Actress*. New York: Random House, 1938.

Coward, Noël. *Present Indicative*. New York: Doubleday Doran & Co., 1937.

Crowther, Bosley. *Hollywood Rajah*. New York: Holt, Rinehart and Winston, 1960.

————. *The Great Films*. New York: G. P. Putnam's Sons, 1967.

————. *Reruns: Fifty Memorable Films*. New York: G. P. Putnam's Sons, 1978.

Curtiss, Thomas Quinn. *Von Stroheim*. New York: Farrar, Straus and Giroux, 1971.

Daniel, Oliver. *Stokowski: A Counterpoint of View*. New York: Dodd, Mead & Co., 1982.

Daum, Raymond. *Walking with Garbo*. Edited and annotated by Vance Muse. New York: HarperCollins Publishers, 1991.

Davies, Marion. *The Times We Had: Life with William Randolph Hearst*. Indianapolis: Bobbs-Merrill, 1975.

Dietz, Howard. *Dancing in the Dark*. New York: Quadrangle/The New York Times Book Co., 1974.

Dragonette, Jessica. *Faith is a Song*. Paterson, N.J.: St. Anthony Guild Press, 1967.

Dressler, Marie, as told to Mildred Harrington. *My Own Story*. Boston: Little, Brown and Co., 1934.

Dunaway, David King. *Huxley in Hollywood*. New York: Harper & Row, 1989; Anchor-Doubleday, 1989.

Durgnat, Raymond, and John Kobal. *Greta Garbo*. New York: E. P. Dutton & Co., 1965.

Eames, John Douglas. *The MGM Story*. New York: Crown Publishers, 1987.

Eisner, Lotte. *L'Ecran dèmoniaque* [*The Haunted Screen: Expressionism in the German Cinema and the Influence of Max Reinhardt*], 1952. Paris: Terrain Vague, 1965. English editions, London: Secker & Warburg, 1968; Berkeley and Los Angeles: University of California Press, 1969.

Everson, William K. *American Silent Film*. New York: Oxford University Press, 1978.

Eyman, Scott. *Five American Cinematographers*. Metuchen, N.J.: Scarecrow Press, 1987.

Foltin, Lore B., ed. *Franz Werfel 1890–1945*. Pittsburgh: University of Pittsburgh Press, 1961.

Forslund, Bengt. *Victor Sjöström, His Life and His Work*. New York: Zoëtrope, 1988.

Fountain, Leatrice Gilbert, with John R. Maxim. *Dark Star*. New York: St. Martin's Press, 1985. The life of John Gilbert.

Friedrich, Otto. *City of Nets: A Portrait of Hollywood in the 1940s*. New York: Harper & Row, 1986.

Gallagher, Rachel. *The Girl Who Loved Garbo*. New York: Donald I. Fine, 1990.

Gardner, Ava. *Ava: My Story*. New York: Bantam Books, 1990.

Gill, Brendan. *Tallulah*. New York: Harper & Row, 1972.

Gish, Lillian. *The Movies, Mr. Griffith and Me*. Englewood Cliffs, N.J.: Prentice-Hall, 1969.

Gronowicz, Antoni. *Garbo: Her Story*. New York: Simon & Schuster, 1990.

Hadleigh, Boze. *Conversations with My Elders*. New York: St. Martin's Press, 1986.

Haining, Peter. *The Legend of Garbo*. London: W. H. Allen & Co., 1990.

Halliwell, Leslie. *The Filmgoer's Book of Quotes*. New York: Signet, 1975.

Harris, Radie. *Radie's World*. New York: G. P. Putnam's Sons, 1975.

Hart, Kitty Carlisle. *Kitty: An Autobiography*. New York: Doubleday & Co., 1988.

Haskell, Molly. *From Rape to Reverence: The Treatment of Women in the Movies*. New York: Holt, Rinehart and Winston, 1973.

Hay, Peter. *MGM: When the Lion Roars*. Atlanta: Turner Publishing, Inc., 1991.

Hecht, Ben. *A Child of the Century*. New York: Simon & Schuster, 1954.

Heilbrun, Carolyn G. *Writing a Woman's Life*. New York: Ballantine Books, 1989; W. W. Norton & Co., 1988.

Hepburn, Katharine. *Me*. New York: Alfred A. Knopf, 1991.

Higham, Charles. *Merchant of Dreams: Louis B. Mayer, MGM and the Secret Hollywood*. New York: Donald I. Fine, 1993.

———, and Joel Greenberg, eds. *The Celluloid Muse: Hollywood Directors Speak*. New York: Signet/New American Library, 1969.

Ibsen, Henrik. *The Lady from the Sea* (1888). Translated by Peter Watts. London: Penguin Books, 1965.

Isherwood, Christopher. *Prater Violet* (1945). New York: Farrar, Straus and Giroux, 1987.

Kanin, Garson. *Hollywood*. New York: The Viking Press, 1967.

Katz, Ephraim. *The Film Encyclopedia*. New York: Thomas Y. Crowell, Publishers, 1979.

Kobal, John. *The Art of the Great Hollywood Portrait Photographers, 1925–1940*. New York: Alfred A. Knopf, 1980.

———. *People Will Talk*. New York: Alfred A. Knopf, 1985.

Koszarski, Richard. *Hollywood Directors, 1914–1940*. New York: Oxford University Press, 1976.

Kracauer, Siegfried. *From Caligari to Hitler: A Psychological History of the German Film*. Princeton, N.J.: Princeton University Press, 1947.

Kwiatkowski, Aleksander. *Swedish Film Classics: A Pictorial Survey of 25 Films from 1913 to 1957*. New York: Dover Publications, in association with Svenska Filminstitutet, Stockholm, 1983.

Lagerlöf, Selma. *The Saga of Gösta Berling* (1891). Translated by Robert Bly. Karlstad, Sweden: Press' Förlagstryckeri, 1982.

———. *The Wonderful Adventures of Nils* (1906). Translated by Velma Swanston Howard. London: Puffin Books, 1990.

Laing, E. E. *Greta Garbo: The Story of a Specialist*. London: John Gifford, 1946.

Lambert, Gavin. *Norma Shearer*. New York: Alfred A. Knopf, 1990.

———. *On Cukor*. New York: G. P. Putnam's Sons, 1972.

Lesley, Cole. *The Life of Noël Coward*. London: Jonathan Cape, 1976.

Levant, Oscar. *The Memoirs of an Amnesiac*. New York: G. P. Putnam's Sons, 1965.

———. *The Unimportance of Being Oscar*. New York: G. P. Putnam's Sons, 1968.

Loy, Myrna, with James Kotsilibas-Davis. *Myrna Loy: On Being & Becoming*. New York: Alfred A. Knopf, 1987.

Maltin, Leonard. *TV Movies*. New York: Signet, 1992.

Merryman, Richard. *Mank* [biography of Herman Mankiewicz]. New York: William Morrow & Co., 1978.

Michaelis, David. *The Best of Friends: Profiles of Extraordinary Friendships*. New York: William Morrow & Co., 1983.

Moore, Colleen. *Silent Star*. Garden City, N.Y.: Doubleday & Co., 1968.

Negri, Pola. *Memoirs of a Star*. Garden City, N.Y.: Doubleday & Co., 1970.

Negulesco, Jean. *Things I Did . . . and Things I Think I Did*. New York: Simon & Schuster/ Linden Press, 1984.

Niven, David. *The Moon's a Balloon*. New York: G. P. Putnam's Sons, 1972.

Olivier, Laurence. *Confessions of an Actor*. New York: Simon & Schuster, 1982; Penguin Books, 1982.

Palmborg, Rilla Page. *The Private Life of Greta Garbo*. New York: Doubleday & Co., 1931.

Paris, Barry. *Louise Brooks*. New York: Alfred A. Knopf, 1989.

Payn, Graham, and Sheridan Morley, eds. *The Noël Coward Diaries*. Boston: Little, Brown and Co., 1982.

Payne, Robert. *The Great Garbo*. New York: Praeger Publishers, 1976.

Penley, Constance, ed. *Feminism and Film Theory*. New York: Routledge, 1988.

Pensel, Hans. *Seastrom and Stiller in Hollywood*. New York: Vantage Press, 1969.

Pepper, Terrence, and John Kobal. *The Man Who Shot Garbo: The Hollywood Photographs of Clarence Sinclair Bull*. New York: Simon & Schuster, 1989.

Pratt, George C. *Spellbound in Darkness*. Greenwich, Conn.: New York Graphic Society, 1973.

Preminger, Otto. *Preminger*. New York: Doubleday & Co., 1977.

Quirk, Lawrence J. *The Great Romantic Films*. New York: Citadel.

Rader, Dotson. *Tennessee: Cry of the Heart*. Garden City, N.Y.: Doubleday & Co., 1985.

Ragan, David. *Who's Who in Hollywood, 1900–1976*. New Rochelle, N.Y.: Arlington House Publishers, 1977.

Reinhardt, Gottfried. *The Genius: A Memoir of Max Reinhardt*. New York: Alfred A. Knopf, 1979.

Riva, Maria. *Marlene Dietrich*. New York: Alfred A. Knopf, 1993.

Robinson, David. *Chaplin: His Life and Art*. New York: McGraw-Hill Books Co., 1985.

———. *Hollywood in the Twenties*. New York: Barnes, 1968; London: A. Zweimmer Ltd., 1968.

Rosen, Marjorie. *Popcorn Venus*. New York: Avon Books, 1974.

Rosenberg, Bernard, and Harry Silverstein. *The Real Tinsel*. New York: Macmillan, 1970.

Rotha, Paul. *The Film Till Now*. Middlesex, U.K.: Hamlyn House/Spring Books, 1967; originally published in 1930 by Jonathan Cape.

Russo, Vito. *The Celluloid Closet: Homosexuality in the Movies*. New York: Harper & Row, 1981.

Sands, Frederick, and Sven Broman. *The Divine Garbo*. New York: Grosset & Dunlap, 1979.

Sarlot, Raymond R., and Fred E. Basten. *Life at the Marmont*. Santa Monica, Calif.: Roundtable Publishing, 1987.

Selznick, David. *Memo from David O. Selznick*. Edited by Rudy Behlmer. New York: The Viking Press, 1972.

Selznick, Irene Mayer. *A Private View*. New York: Alfred A. Knopf, 1983.

Sembach, Klaus-Jürgen. *Greta Garbo Portraits: 1920–1951*. New York: Rizzoli, 1985.

Shipman, David. *The Story of Cinema*. New York: St. Martin's Press, 1982.

Shnayerson, Michael. *Irwin Shaw: A Biography*. New York: G. P. Putnam's Sons, 1989.

Simpson, Jacqueline, ed. and trans. *Scandinavian Folktales*. London: Penguin Books, 1988.

Sjolander, Ture. *Garbo*. New York: Harper & Row, 1971.

Steiger, Brad, and Chaw Mank. *Garbo*. Chicago: Merit Books/Camerarts Publishing Co., 1965.

Sternberg, Josef von. *Fun in a Chinese Laundry*. New York: Collier Books, 1965.

Stevenson, William. *A Man Called Intrepid: The Secret War*. New York: Harcourt Brace Jovanovich, 1976.

Stewart, Donald Ogden. *By a Stroke of Luck!* London: Paddington Press, 1975.

Stolpe, Sven. *Christina of Sweden*. New York: Macmillan Publishing Co., 1966.

Swindell, Larry. *Charles Boyer, The Reluctant Lover*. New York: Doubleday & Co., 1983.

Taylor, John Russell. *Strangers in Paradise: The Hollywood Émigrés, 1933–1950*. New York: Holt, Rinehart and Winston, 1983.

Tyler, Parker. *The Hollywood Hallucination*. 1944.

Tynan, Kenneth, and Cecil Beaton. *Persona Grata*. London: Wingate Publishers, 1953; New York: G. P. Putnam's Sons, 1954.

Vickers, Hugo. *Cecil Beaton*. Boston: Little, Brown and Co., 1985.

Vidor, King. *A Tree Is a Tree*. Hollywood, Calif.: Samuel French, 1989.

Viertel, Salka. *The Kindness of Strangers*. New York: Holt, Rinehart and Winston, 1969.

Walker, Alexander. *Garbo: A Portrait*. New York: Macmillan Publishing Co., 1980.

———. *Sex in the Movies*. Middlesex, U.K.: Penguin Books, Harmondsworth, 1968. Retitled paperback version of *The Celluloid Sacrifice (Aspects of Sex in the Movies)*. New York: Hawthorn Books, 1966.

———. *The Shattered Silents: How the Talkies Came to Stay*. New York: William Morrow, 1979.

Weaver, John T. *Twenty Years of Silents: 1908–1928*. Metuchen, N.J.: Scarecrow Press, 1971.

White, E. B. *Letters of E. B. White*. Edited by Dorothy Lobrano Guth. New York: Harper & Row, 1976.

Whittemore, Don, and Philip Alan Cecchettini. *Passport to Hollywood: Film Immigrants Anthology*. New York: McGraw-Hill Book Co., 1976.

Wild, Roland. *Greta Garbo*. Popular Lives Series. London: Rich & Cowan, 1933.

Wilson, Robert, ed. *The Film Criticism of Otis Ferguson*. Philadelphia: Temple University Press, 1971.

Winquist, Sven G., and Torsten Jungstedt, eds. *Svenskt filmskådespelarlexikon*. Stockholm: Forum (SFI), 1973.

Zierold, Norman. *Garbo*. New York: Stein & Day, 1969.

Zolotow, Maurice. *Billy Wilder in Hollywood*. New York: G. P. Putnam's Sons, 1977.

MAJOR ARTICLES

Affron, Charles. "Uncensored Garbo." In Gerald Mast and Marshall Cohen, eds. *Film Theory and Criticism*. New York: Oxford University Press, 1979, 730–40.

Alpert, Hollis. "Saga of Greta Lovisa Gustafsson." *The New York Times Magazine*, September 5, 1965, 27, 56–58.

Asher, Jerry. "Giving Garbo Away." *Silver Screen*, May 1936.

Bachmann, Gideon, ed. "Six Talks on G. W. Pabst," *Cinemages*, May 1955.

Bainbridge, John. "Garbo is 65." *Look*, September 8, 1970, 48–57.

Beaton, Cecil. "Garbo." *Theatre*, September 1961, 9–11, 30.

Benchley, Nathaniel. "This is Garbo." *Collier's*, March 1, 1952, 13–15, 56.

Bernadotte, Kerstin. "Greta Garbo." *Ladies Home Journal*, April 1976, 93, 150–52.

Biery, Ruth. "The Story of Greta Garbo." *Photoplay*, April 1928, 30–31, 78, 102; May 1928, 36–37, 127–28; June 1928, 65, 144–47.

Brooks, Louise. "Gish and Garbo." *Sight and Sound*, Winter 1958–1959. Reprinted in Brooks's *Lulu in Hollywood*. New York: Alfred A. Knopf, 1982.

Capote, Truman. "La Côte Basque 1965." *Esquire*, November 1972, 110–20, 158.

Collins, Frederick L. "Why Garbo is Making her Last Picture." *Liberty*, May 30, 1936, 4–6.

Cooper, Morton. "Garbo." *Diner's Club Magazine*, December 1964, 63–64.

Daum, Raymond. "Greta Garbo: Memories of a Swedish Christmas." *Scandinavian Review*, Winter 1990, 66–70.

———. "Garbo Talks (A Little)," *Life*, Spring, 1989.

Delblanc, Sven. "Selma Lagerlöf." Swedish Institute, 1986. Pamphlet.

Engelmann, Larry. "I Was the Man Who Made the Starshine" [Hubert Voight], *Los Angeles*, November 1983, 264–71, 316–23.

———. "Little Garbo" [Eva von Berne], *American Way*, October 15, 1988, 74–79, 132–34.

Eyman, Scott. "Clarence Brown: Garbo and Beyond." *Velvet Light Trap*, Spring 1978 (University of Wisconsin), 19–23.

Gaines, Jane. "The Queen Christina Tie-Ups: Convergence of Show Window and Screen," *Quarterly Review of Film & Video*, vol. 2, no. 1 (Harwood Academic Publishers, 1989), 35–60.

Gomery, Douglas. "Researching Film History." In Robert C. Allen and Douglas Gomery, *Film History: Theory and Practice*. New York: Alfred A. Knopf, 1985.

Grimstead, Hettie. "With Garbo at Home." *Screenland*, April 1938, 28–29, 80–82.

Gross, Michael. "Garbo's Last Days." *New York*, May 21, 1990, 38–46.

Hawkins, Paul. "A New Slant on Garbo." *Screenland*, June 1931, 19–21, 112.

Horan, Gray. "Garbo's Refuge." *The New York Times Magazine*, September 2, 1990, 30–33.

Lewton, Val. "Glorious Greta," *Moving Picture Stories*, October 13, 1931, 3, 31, 102.

Mank, Gregory. "The Divine Garbo," *Films in Review*, vol. 30, no. 9, November 1979, 513–37.

Miller, Marvin, publisher. *Hollywood Legends: The Life and Films of Humphrey Bogart and Greta Garbo*, vol. 1, no. 1. Covina, Calif.: Marvin Miller Publications, 1968.

O'Dowd, Brian. "Why Garbo Quit Movies," *Hollywood Studio Magazine*, November 1987, 12–16.

Petro, Patrice. "Film Censorship and the Female Spectator: *The Joyless Street* (1925)." In Eric Rentschler, ed. *The Films of G. W. Pabst: An Extraterritorial Cinema*. New Brunswick, N.J.: Rutgers University Press, 1990.

Robbins, Jhan. "The Secret Life of Greta Garbo." *This Week*, October 4, 1959, 14–17.

Saxon, Lars. "Greta Garbos ungdomsminnen." *Lektyr*, 1931.

Sundborg, Åke. "That Gustafsson Girl," Parts I and II. *Photoplay*, April 1930, 40–43, 127–33, and May 1930, 40–42, 156–59.

Tynan, Kenneth. "Garbo." *Sight and Sound*, vol. 23, no. 4, April–June 1954, 187–90, 220.

Voight, Hubert. "I Loved Garbo," *New Movie Magazine*, February 1934.

ACKNOWLEDGMENTS

Thanking everyone who made this book possible is nearly as monumental as the research. The cliché is the truth: I couldn't have done it without them—and the facts, favors, and insights they provided over the course of five years. I have always advocated the establishment of a Tomb of the Unknown Archivist. I salute them all, professionals and amateurs alike. In this case, the names of those on whom I relied most heavily are to be found in the Preface. The others are so numerous that the only way to acknowledge them is geo-alphabetically, since the Garbo research took place in many cities, states, and countries. I could write a page in homage to each but, as Richard Nixon says, "It would be wrong." So instead, I must record them—and my gratitude—collectively. A biography is a mosaic, and the random pieces arrive in no logical order; some never arrive at all. But each of the individuals and institutions listed below gave me a piece of the Garbo mosaic, or the advice and support needed to shape those pieces into a coherent whole. With deep appreciation, this book is of, by, and for the following:

NEW YORK

New York City: *Art and Antiques* (ex-editors Jeffrey Schaire, my wonderful friend, and Rob Kenner; and Lorraine Glennon); Richard Barrios; Patricia Bosworth; Charles Busch; John Clynes; Tom Dallow; The James Danziger Gallery; William K. and Karen Everson; Ruth Ford; The Greta Garbo Estate (Gray Reisfield, Dr. Donald Reisfield, Scott and Derek Reisfield, Gray

Horan, and Theodore A. Kurz); Tamara Glenny (*Travel-Holiday*); Gotham Book Mart (Flip Ahrens and Andreas Brown); Bob Gottlieb (and Maria Tucci and Nicky, for his inimitable telephone manner); Samuel Adams Green; Jane Gunther; Kitty Carlisle Hart; Dr. Rose Hayden (for bio-shrinking and the Hayden Hilton); Roger Jones; Frida Itor-Kahn; Martha Kaplan (for her profound unflappability); my editor, Victoria A. Wilson and her ace assistant, Bill Spruill; Kobal Collection (Bob Cosenza); Claire Koger; Kenneth L. Koyen; Benjamin Laba; Joseph and Caral Gimbel Lebworth; Wayne Lawson of *Vanity Fair*; Ted Leyson; Viveca Lindfors; Barbara Barondess MacLean; The Pierpoint Morgan Library (Fredric Woodbridge Wilson and Herbert Cahoon); William Morris Agency (my fabulous agent, Dan Strone; his fabulous assistant, Sarah Winer; and their fabulous boss, Owen Laster); Lillian Morrison; The Museum of Modern Art (Rona Roob and Charles Silver, film archives; Eric Myers; Mary Corliss and Virginia Dotier, film stills; and Allen Porter friends Joanne Stern, Elizabeth Shaw, and Inga Heckel); Babette New; *The New Yorker* (Martin Barron and Jocelyn Simpson, fact checkers extraordinaire); New York Public Library's Billy Rose Theatre Collection; Russell Perrault (Doubleday); Photofest (Howard and Ron Mandelbaum); Gregory Rabassa (for the Columbia inspiration of a lifetime); Richard Schmidt; The Searchers (Maria Ciaccia, Howard Cutler, Ellen Martin); Cornelius Seon of the Electric Railroaders Assn.; the late Irene Mayer Selznick; Anne Sitrick; Deborah Solomon; John Springer; David Stenn, greatest of the biographer-sleuths; Shelley von Strunckel; the one and only (and only one-named) magician Teller; Nicholas Meredith Turner; Bryan Walsh; Shelley Wanger and the memory of her parents; Patricia Wilks-Battle of the *New York Post*; and Ron Wisniski—actor, director, and designer of book pyramids.

Rochester: James Card, legendary founding curator of the George Eastman House film collection, and his long-suffering Jeanne; Jan-Christopher Horak, current curator of Eastman House, and his better two-thirds, Martha Horak and Janet Schirn; the Grande Dame of GEH, Kaye MacRae; composer David Diamond; faithful Alex Jeshke; and the Louise Brooks Estate (Daniel R. Brooks and Benjamin Phelosof, co-executors).

Dancer Jane Sherman and composer Ned Lehac of New Paltz; film collector Tom Scalzo of Niagara Falls; and screenwriter Sarah Kernochan of South Salem, wherever that is.

CALIFORNIA

Los Angeles area: I owe much to the Margaret Herrick Collection of the Academy of Motion Picture Arts and Sciences (Sam Gill, long may he reign); the late Stella Adler; Joyce Aimee; Rudy Behlmer; the late Jim Bridges; Joe Cohn; William Donati; Nikki Finke; John Gaby; Irene Gilbert; Larry Grusin; Randy Haberkamp of the Hollywood Studio Museum; Charles Higham; Kenny Kingston; Judd Klinger; Gavin Lambert; Jack Larson; Frederika Maas; Leonard and Alice Maltin; Pamela (Mrs. James) Mason; Roddy McDowall; Barbara Kent Edington Monroe; Gottfried Reinhardt; the incomparable Bernard Schwartz (known to a few as Tony Curtis); David Shepherd; Joseph R. Spano of the Miramar-Sheraton Hotel; Marc Taslitt and Patricia Sheridan; Kevin Thomas of the *Los Angeles Times*; and the incomparable Billy Wilder.

Thanks also to Dan Aikman of Palm Springs, Marcia Davenport of Pebble Beach, Larry Engelmann of San Jose, my beloved Rick and Deborah Geary of San Diego, Joe Hix of Long Beach, Michael Horton of Laguna Beach, Charles and Deirdre Jackson of San Francisco, Richard Lamparski of Montecito, Guy Roop of Santa Barbara, and the world's greatest indexer, Alan Schroeder of Alameda.

PITTSBURGH

Myrna Paris heads the list for literary, secretarial, and psychiatric services far beyond the call of conjugal or even artistic duty, while her offspring, Merica Claire and Wyoming Benjamin Paris III, provided valuable eleventh-hour computer-transcription help. The other "family" members who supplied me with ideas and helped preserve my sanity were Albert French (for his definition of rewriting), Doris Bauer Kalina, James and Queen Christina O'Toole, Bill Bollendorf and Dr. Madalyn Simasek.

Additional supportive Pittsburghers include David Bandler, Steven Baum, Ken and Betty Behrend, Judi Cannava and Dr. Tom Allen, Dan Cook, Jim Cunningham, Ron and Lynn Curry, Jay Dantry, Donnis DeCamp, Sarah D. Eldridge, Barbara and Daniel Ernsberger, Janet Fanale, Frederick A. Hetzel, Charlie Humphrey, Peter Kountz, Michael McGough, Sally Meckling, E. K. and Gertrude Myers, Fred and Joanne Rogers (who like me just the way I am), John Ezra Schulman, Mark Selvaggio, Andrew Sheehan, Ceci Sommers (for opening up the world of ironing centers to me), Mike Staropoli, Tina Thoburn, Marylynne Uricchio, Mike Vargo, Amy Villarejo, and Tim Ziaukas. Nor can I forget the always excellent culinary skills of John Pappas and Rebecca Willis.

WASHINGTON, D.C.

My master researcher in Washington, as ever, was John Barba, with the indulgence of Margie Yep-Barba. Ken and Denise Cummins and Richard and Elvira Crocker cheered me on, as did Jackie Pessaud (buttons R her) of Arlington, Va. My thanks, also, to James Lee Auchincloss; to the world's greatest reference librarian, Katharine Loughney, formerly of the Library of Congress's Motion Picture Broadcasting and Recorded Sound Division; to its chief, Paul Spehr; and to Stephen M. Weissman, fellow Knopf biographer (of Chaplin), who gave me a Garbo-Brooks connection that was right under my nose but that I otherwise would have missed.

KANSAS

My faithful Wichitans: Wyoming B. and Claire Gill Paris, and E. Reid and Genevieve Fletcher—first and foremost—followed by Pamela and David Loyle. Todd Loyle was a most dependable pal (and Ben-entertainer). Thanks, too, to Randy Brown, Jack Fishback, Kent and Janet Fletcher, Larry and Karen Guggisberg, Marilynn Gump, Howard Inglish, Fran Kentling, Diane Lewis, Heather and Paris Loyle, Trever Patton, Harry and Margaret Saums, and the decidedly dangerous Daniel R. Rouser. Victoria Page and Earl Levine were inspirational—next time you're in Abilene, stay at the Spruce House and ask for the Jean Harlow Room.

ELSEWHERE IN THE UNITED STATES

The Divine Miss Lina Basquette—former prima ballerina of the Ziegfield Follies, now of Wheeling, W. Va.—is the woman whose Hollywood memories and personal friendship I most cherish. For help and advice, I also thank James and Frances Benner of Morgantown, W. Va.; Donald F. Collins of Longmeadow, Mass.; Kendra Crossen of Somerville, Mass.; Raymond Daum of Austin, Tex.; Emmett Davis of Ashville, N.C.; Rev. Robert J. DeRouen, S.J., of Denver; Nathan Dodell of Rockville, Md.; Scott Eyman of Palm Beach, Fla.; Leatrice Gilbert Fountain of Riverside, Conn.; Arthur and Gracelyn Greenwald of Arlington, Mass.; Cathy Henkel of Seattle; Gregory Hesselberg of Rockport, Mass.; Chris Hodenfield of Norwalk, Conn.; Sid Howard of Englewood, N.J.; Dr. Laurie L. Lankin of Macon, Ga.; M. J. Miller of Easton, Pa.; Dave McClelland of Langley, Wash.; Mimi Muray of Alta, Utah; Stuart Oderman of East Orange, N.J.; Nancy and Wyoming B. Paris II of Bel Air, Md.; Maestro Gerard Schwarz of Seattle; David G. Townsend of Falls Village, Conn.; Richard Tussey of Langley, Wash.; Liv Ullmann of Boston; The David O. Selznick Collection of the University of Texas (Charles Bell, curator), Austin; The Wesleyan University Cinema Archives (Jeanine Basinger and Leith Johnson), Middletown, Conn.; Wisconsin Center for Film Research (Maxine Fleckner, curator), Madison; and Will Rogers biographer Ben Yagoda of Philadelphia.

SWEDEN

The most important foreign research took place in Sweden, and Annika Goldfarb—formerly of the Swedish Tourist Board, now of Hanslin Travel Service in New York City—made it possible, along with Viveca Nordström and Christer Thunell of the Swedish Tourist Board. Sincere thanks also to lovely Sylvie Kjellin and to Christina Guggenberger and Mathias Fock of the Stockholm Information Service; Solveig Linka of the Swedish Information Service (New York); Robert Nygardhs of the Swedish Tourist Board (Stockholm); Catharina Mannheimer of The Swedish Institute (Stockholm); and Nils Flo of SAS Scandinavian Airlines.

No film archives in the world is more author-friendly than the Swedish Film Institute (Svenska Filminstitutet), and this book owes a great debt to the screenings, files, photos, and unfailing aid of SFI's Margareta Nordström and Elisabet Helge. Among other Stockholmers, I thank Mimi Pollack and Lars Lundell; Sven Broman; Matts Ehrenpreis of the Grand Hotel; Bengt Forslund, Sjöström biographer and managing director of the Nordisk Film and Television Fund; Gösta Werner, Stiller biographer; film historian Einar Lauritzen; and Ebbe Carlsson, managing director of the great (and my own) Swedish publishing house, Bonnier.

ENGLAND

To Kevin Brownlow, the human film encyclopedia, I extend deepest thanks (and to Virginia for letting me invade and occupy her home at excessive length). The two fine previous Garbo biographers, John Bainbridge and Alexander Walker, were very generous in responding to the queries of their successor. Hugo Vickers, Cecil Beaton's superb biographer and literary executor, provided invaluable assistance. My patient British editor, Susan Hill, and her assistant, Susan Malvern, of Sidgwick & Jackson Ltd. gave me just what I needed—unwavering support and no reproaches for lateness—as did Lavinia Trevor of the William Morris Agency in London. Thanks also to Meredith Etherington-Smith for her delicious Garbo-Dali story, Rhoda Koenig for tea and critical encouragement, and John Russell Taylor for writing *Strangers in Paradise*, by far the best book on Hollywood's emigré set.

Of many other wonderful Brits who helped me, the most important and beloved are Peter and Catherine Green of Hessett, Reginald and Constance Green and Mary Tunbridge of Stowmarket, and Geoffrey, Edward, and Bryan, too.

ELSEWHERE GLOBALLY

The single most enjoyable experience of the Garbo research was my extended meeting in Marbella, Spain, with Peter Viertel and Deborah Kerr—delightful hosts and generous providers of Garbo information, correspondence, and reminiscences. Their trust and cooperation was essential and will never be forgotten.

Fellow film writer-biographer Steven Bach (*Final Cut*, *Marlene Dietrich*) was a devoted friend and supporter throughout the process, especially in Munich, where he alerted (and escorted) me to a rare screening of the German *Anna Christie* at the Münchner Stadtmuseum and to the existence of marvelous Eva Kačurova of the Czechoslovak Film Archives in Prague.

Ricky Leacock, that lovable rogue and tsar of the film-documentary world, was with me, in spirit and voice, from Paris.

So, in spirit and in person, was Gwendolyn Grant Mellon, who had a different biographical agenda but watched *Queen Christina* and *Camille* with me, and had fresh insights into both, on two enchanted evenings at her home in Deschapelles, Haiti—with a faint, magical rhythm of voodoo drums in the background.

Italicized page numbers indicate photographs.

PERMISSIONS ACKNOWLEDGMENTS

Grateful acknowledgment is made to the following for permission to reprint previously published and unpublished material:

Rupert Crew Ltd.: Excerpts from *Self-Portrait with Friends* by Cecil Beaton, edited by Richard Buckle (Times Books, 1979), copyright © 1979 by Cecil Beaton, Introduction and compilation copyright © 1979 by Richard Buckle. Reprinted by permission of Rupert Crew Limited, London, on behalf of the Literary Executors of the late Sir Cecil Beaton; Hugo Vickers, Literary Trustee.

HarperCollins Publishers, Inc.: Excerpts from *Walking with Garbo* by Raymond Daum and Vance Muse, copyright © 1991 by Raymond Daum and Vance Muse; excerpts from Christopher Isherwood's diaries, copyright © 1991 by Don Bachardy. Reprinted by permission of HarperCollins Publishers, Inc.

Henry Holt and Company, Inc.: Excerpts from *Kindness of Strangers* by Salka Viertel (Holt, Rinehart & Winston, 1969), copyright © 1969 by Salka Viertel. Reprinted by permission of Henry Holt and Company, Inc.

Alfred A. Knopf, Inc.: Excerpts from *Lulu in Hollywood* by Louise Brooks, copyright © 1974, 1982 by Louise Brooks. Reprinted by permission of Alfred A. Knopf, Inc.

Random House, Inc.: Excerpt from *Local Color* by Truman Capote, copyright © 1963 by Random House, Inc. Reprinted by permission of Random House, Inc.

Peter Viertel: Excerpts from unpublished material of Salka Viertel. Reprinted by permission of Peter Viertel.

PHOTOGRAPHIC CREDITS

Courtesy of Cecil Beaton Archive, Sotheby's London (Lydia Cresswell-Jones): photographs on pp. 252 (top), 401 (top and bottom) and 403.

Courtesy of the James Card Collection: photographs on pp. 118, 197, portfolio photographs #3, #4 and #7.

Courtesy of the Walt Disney Company: caricature on p. 574.

Courtesy of George Eastman House (Jan-Christopher Horak and Kay MacRae), Rochester, New York: photographs on pp. 147 and 188.

Courtesy of Joseph Lebworth: photographs on pp. 494 (top and bottom) and 496.

Courtesy of Ted Leyson: photographs on pp. 511, 516, and 552.

Courtesy of MGM and the Kobal Collection (Bob Cosenza), New York and London: photographs on pp. 35 (bottom), 73, 78, 89, 91, 94 (top and bottom), 110, 120 (top), 123 (top), 133 (bottom), 134, 141, 148, 149, 164, 165, 166, 167, 171, 189, 195 (top and bottom), 200, 214, 303 (bottom), 305, 307, 314 (top and bottom), 318 (top), 324, 331 (bottom), 342 (top), 350, 364 (bottom), 369, 376 (top and bottom), portfolio photograph #5.

Courtesy of the Museum of Modern Art: photograph on p. 75.

The Barry Paris Collection: photographs on pp. 71, 72, 97, 100, 105, 115, 118, 123 (bottom), 133 (top), 154 (bottom), 162, 191, (top), 204 (top and bottom), 216 (top and bottom), 220 (top and bottom), 252 (bottom), 253, 272, 282, 291 (bottom), 303 (top), 318 (bottom), 333 (top and bottom), 364 (top), 377, 426, 427, portfolio photograph #2.

Courtesy of Photofest (Howard and Ron Mandelbaum), New York: photographs on pp. 336, 342 (bottom), 374.

Courtesy of the Edward Steichen Estate: portfolio photograph #6.

Courtesy of the Swedish Film Institute (Margareta Nordström and Elisabet Helge), Stockholm: photographs on pp. 2, 6 (top and bottom), 10, 20, 27, 28, 30 (top and bottom), 32, 35 (top), 40, 44, 48, 52, 53, 55, 60, 61, 62, 99 (top and bottom), 107, 151 (top and bottom), 158, 159 (top and bottom), 193, 207 and portfolio photograph #1.

Courtesy of *Vanity Fair*: reproductions on pp. 230 and 554.

Barry Paris is an award-winning biographer, writer, and film and music critic. He is the author of several books, including *Louise Brooks: A Biography* (Minnesota, 2000).